Heroin Addiction: Theory, Research and Treatment *by Jerome J*

Children's Rights and the Mental Health Profession *edited by Ger.*

The Role of the Father in Child Development *edited by Michael E. Lamb*

Handbook of Behavioral Assessment *edited by Anthony R. Ciminero, Karen S. Calhoun, and Henry E. Adams*

Counseling and Psychotherapy: A Behavioral Approach *by E. Lakin Phillips*

Dimensions of Personality *edited by Harvey London and John E. Exner, Jr.*

The Mental Health Industry: A Cultural Phenomenon *by Peter A. Magaro, Robert Gripp, David McDowell, and Ivan W. Miller III*

Nonverbal Communication: The State of the Art *by Robert G. Harper, Arthur N. Wiens, and Joseph D. Matarazzo*

Alcoholism and Treatment *by David J. Armor, J. Michael Polich, and Harriet B. Stambul*

A Biodevelopmental Approach to Clinical Child Psychology: Cognitive Controls and Cognitive Control Theory *by Sebastiano Santostefano*

Handbook of Infant Development *edited by Joy D. Osofsky*

Understanding the Rape Victim: A Synthesis of Research Findings *by Sedelle Katz and Mary Ann Mazur*

Childhood Pathology and Later Adjustment: The Question of Prediction *by Loretta K. Cass and Carolyn B. Thomas*

Intelligent Testing with the WISC-R *by Alan S. Kaufman*

Adaptation in Schizophrenia: The Theory of Segmental Set *by David Shakow*

Psychotherapy: An Eclectic Approach *by Sol L. Garfield*

Handbook of Minimal Brain Dysfunctions *edited by Herbert E. Rie and Ellen D. Rie*

Handbook of Behavioral Interventions: A Clinical Guide *edited by Alan Goldstein and Edna B. Foa*

Art Psychotherapy *by Harriet Wadeson*

Handbook of Adolescent Psychology *edited by Joseph Adelson*

Psychotherapy Supervision: Theory, Research and Practice *edited by Allen K. Hess*

Psychology and Psychiatry in Courts and Corrections: Controversy and Change *by Ellsworth A. Fersch, Jr.*

Restricted Environmental Stimulation: Research and Clinical Applications *by Peter Suedfeld*

Personal Construct Psychology: Psychotherapy and Personality *edited by Alvin W. Landfield and Larry M. Leitner*

Mothers, Grandmothers, and Daughters: Personality and Child Care in Three-Generation Families *by Bertram J. Cohler and Henry U. Grunebaum*

Further Explorations in Personality *edited by A.I. Rabin, Joel Aronoff, Andrew M. Barclay, and Robert A. Zucker*

Hypnosis and Relaxation: Modern Verification of an Old Equation *by William E. Edmonston, Jr.*

Handbook of Clinical Behavior Therapy *edited by Samuel M. Turner, Karen S. Calhoun, and Henry E. Adams*

Handbook of Clinical Neuropsychology *edited by Susan B. Filskov and Thomas J. Boll*

The Course of Alcoholism: Four Years After Treatment *by J. Michael Polich, David J. Armor, and Harriet B. Braiker*

Handbook of Innovative Psychotherapies *edited by Raymond J. Corsini*

The Role of the Father in Child Development (Second Edition) *edited by Michael E. Lamb*

Behavioral Medicine: Clinical Applications *by Susan S. Pinkerton, Howard Hughes, and W.W. Wenrich*

(*continued on back*)

THE FATHER'S ROLE
APPLIED PERSPECTIVES

The Father's Role
Applied Perspectives

Edited by

Michael E. Lamb
University of Utah

A WILEY-INTERSCIENCE PUBLICATION

JOHN WILEY & SONS

New York · Chichester · Brisbane · Toronto · Singapore

Library of Congress Cataloging in Publication Data:

Main entry under title:

The father's role.

    (Wiley series on personality processes)
    "A Wiley-Interscience publication."
    1. Father and child. 2. Fathers—Psychology.
3. Family psychotherapy. 4. Parent and child (Law)
I. Lamb, Michael E., 1953–   II. Series.

BF723.F35F374 1986   306.8'742   85-29497
ISBN 0-471-82046-6

Printed in the United States of America

10 9 8 7 6 5 4 3 2 1

For Damon

Contributors

RICHARD N. ATKINS, Division of Child and Adolescent Psychiatry, New York Medical College, Valhalla, New York

ASHLEY BEITEL, Department of Psychology, University of Illinois, Champaign, Illinois

FRANK G. BOLTON, JR., Coordinator of Psychological Services, Arizona Department of Economic Security, Phoenix, Arizona

JOHANNA DETMERING, School of Behavioural Sciences, Macquarie University, North Ryde, New South Wales, Australia

ARTHUR B. ELSTER, Department of Pediatrics, University of Utah Medical Center, Salt Lake City, Utah

GORDON FARLEY, Department of Psychiatry, University of Colorado School of Medicine, Denver, Colorado

MARGARET STANLEY HAGAN, Department of Psychology, University of Virginia, Charlottesville, Virginia

E. MAVIS HETHERINGTON, Department of Psychology, University of Virginia, Charlottesville, Virginia

BERNDT HEUBECK, School of Behavioural Sciences, Macquarie University, North Ryde, New South Wales, Australia

DEBRA G. KLINMAN, Bank Street College of Education, New York City, New York

MICHAEL E. LAMB, Departments of Psychology, Psychiatry, and Pediatrics, University of Utah, Salt Lake City, Utah

MELVIN R. LANSKY, Neuropsychiatric Institute, University of California at Los Angeles, Los Angeles, California

VONNIE C. McLOYD, Department of Psychology, University of Michigan, Ann Arbor, Michigan

DONALD J. MEYER, Program for Fathers, Siblings, and Grandparents of Children With Special Needs, Child Development and Mental Retardation Center, University of Washington, Seattle, Washington

ROSS D. PARKE, Department of Psychology, University of Illinois, Champaign, Illinois

JOSEPH H. PLECK, Center for Research on Women, Wellesley College, Wellesley, Massachusetts

SHIRLEY AISHA RAY, Department of Psychology, University of Michigan, Ann Arbor, Michigan

GRAEME RUSSELL, School of Behavioural Sciences, Macquarie University, North Ryde, New South Wales, Australia

JOHN W. SANTROCK, Department of Psychology, University of Texas at Dallas, Richardson, Texas

ROSS A. THOMPSON, Department of Psychology, University of Nebraska, Lincoln, Nebraska

ANN H. TYLER, Family Support Center, Salt Lake City, Utah

RICHARD A. WARSHAK, Department of Psychology, University of Texas at Dallas, Dallas, Texas

SIDNEY WERKMAN, Department of Psychiatry, University of Colorado School of Medicine, Denver, Colorado

Series Preface

This series of books is addressed to behavioral scientists interested in the nature of human personality. Its scope should prove pertinent to personality theorists and researchers as well as to clinicians concerned with applying an understanding of personality processes to the amelioration of emotional difficulties in living. To this end, the series provides a scholarly integration of theoretical formulations, empirical data, and practical recommendations.

Six major aspects of studying and learning about human personality can be designated: personality theory, personality structure and dynamics, personality development, personality assessment, personality change, and personality adjustment. In exploring these aspects of personality, the books in the series discuss a number of distinct but related subject areas: the nature and implications of various theories of personality; personality characteristics that account for consistencies and variations in human behavior; the emergence of personality processes in children and adolescents; the use of interviewing and testing procedures to evaluate individual differences in personality; efforts to modify personality styles through psychotherapy, counseling, behavior therapy, and other methods of influence; and patterns of abnormal personality functioning that impair individual competence.

IRVING B. WEINER

University of Denver
Denver, Colorado

Preface

In 1975 I published a paper in which I described fathers as the "forgotten contributors to child development." Today, little more than a decade later, that description is clearly inappropriate. In the interim, fathers have been discovered by social scientists and social services professionals, and the literature—popular and professional—on fathers has burgeoned accordingly. Unfortunately, the professional literature has been narrowly directed to researchers and academics, with relatively little attention being paid to the needs of social services providers. This book was written to meet their needs.

From the outset, social services providers, especially clinical psychologists, social workers, and psychiatrists, expressed the keenest interest in the literature on fatherhood. Their interest reflected not casual curiosity but an awareness that problematic father-child relationships characterized many of their clients. In an increasing number of cases fathers were absent—many following divorce. Others had hostile or indifferent relationships with their children. To social services providers and mental health practitioners, it has become increasingly important to understand what the implications of such events are, and how the adverse effects might be ameliorated or muted.

In this book we provide comprehensive and practically oriented summaries of the literature on fatherhood. Chapters focus on such topics as increased paternal involvement, custody adjudication and the effects of divorce, family and marital therapy, poverty and unemployment, and several more specialized topics, including adolescent parenthood and child maltreatment. All of the chapters have been written by scholars with clinical orientations and/or experience, and all have been written with the needs and questions of practitioners as well as researchers in mind. The book should be of value to social workers, custody mediators, child psychiatrists, clinical psychologists, policymakers, developmental psychologists, and all those interested in the mental health of young children.

MICHAEL E. LAMB

Salt Lake City, Utah
February 1986

Contents

PART 1   INTRODUCTION

1. The Changing Roles of Fathers.   *Michael E. Lamb*   3

2. Primary Caretaking and Role Sharing Fathers.
   Graeme Russell   29

PART 2   LEGAL ISSUES

3. Fathers and the Child's "Best Interests": Judicial Decision-Making in Custody Disputes.   *Ross A. Thompson*   61

4. Divorced Fathers: Stress, Coping, and Adjustment.
   E. Mavis Hetherington and *Margaret Stanley Hagan*   103

5. Development of Father Custody, Relationships, and Legal/Clinical Considerations in Father-Custody Families.   *John W. Santrock* and *Richard A. Warshak*   135

PART 3   CLINICAL ISSUES

6. The Father in Family Therapy: Psychoanalytic Perspectives.   *Richard N. Atkins* and *Melvin R. Lansky*   167

7. Father Involvement and Responsibility in Family Therapy.
   Berndt Heubeck, Johanna Detmering, and *Graeme Russell*   191

8. Fathers of Children with Mental Handicaps.
   Donald J. Meyer   227

9. The Abusing Father.   *Ann H. Tyler*   255

10. Overseas Fathers: Vulnerabilities and Treatment Strategies.
Gordon Farley and *Sidney Werkman*   277

11. Hospital-Based Intervention for Fathers.   *Ross D. Parke* and
Ashley Beitel   293

12. Adolescent Fathers from a Clinical Perspective.
Arthur B. Elster   325

PART 4   PROGRAMS AND POLICIES

13. Fathers in Hard Times: The Impact of Unemployment and
Poverty on Paternal and Marital Relations.   *Shirley Aisha
Ray* and *Vonnie C. McLoyd*   339

14. Employment and Fatherhood: Issues and Innovative Policies.
Joseph H. Pleck   385

15. Fathers and the Educational System.   *Debra G.
Klinman*   413

16. Today's Father and the Social Services Delivery System:
A False Promise.   *Frank G. Bolton Jr.*   429

Author Index   443

Subject Index   455

THE FATHER'S ROLE
APPLIED PERSPECTIVES

ONE
Introduction

CHAPTER 1

The Changing Roles
of Fathers

MICHAEL E. LAMB
University of Utah

In the last decade and a half, professional and public interest in the roles played by fathers in their children's development has increased enormously. Early in this era of paternal rediscovery, psychologists believed that fathers might have an important role to play in child rearing, even if their involvement (relative to that of mothers) was severely limited. Specifically, psychologists questioned the implicit assumptions (1) that there is a direct correlation between extent of involvement and extent of influence, and (2) that if mothers are more influential than fathers, they must be exclusively influential (e.g., Lamb 1976, 1981c; Lynn 1974). Interest in fathers was subsequently accentuated by the popular and professional discovery of "the new fatherhood." The new father, immortalized for many by Dustin Hoffman's performance in *Kramer vs. Kramer,* was an active, involved, nurturant participant in all aspects of child care and child rearing. Not surprisingly, belief in the existence and proliferation of such fathers led to further speculation about the importance of paternal influences on child development. As a result, rhetorical exchanges concerning the new father abounded; unfortunately, rhetoric continues to outpace serious analysis. This chapter attempts to redress that imbalance by providing a brief integrative overview of research and theorizing concerning the role (or multiple roles) that fathers play.

The thesis advanced here is that we are currently witnessing the fourth of a series of changes in popular conceptualizations of the father's roles and responsibilities. Today's fathers are expected to be more actively involved in child care than in the past, and to a modest extent the average contemporary father is indeed more involved than was his predecessor. However, to assume that this increased involvement is necessarily beneficial in all family

3

circumstances may be a mistake (Lamb, Pleck, & Levine, 1985). Rather, individual circumstances have to be considered to understand how children are affected by variations in paternal involvement.

In the recent debate about the changing roles of fathers, much of the discussion has focused on their increasing role in the direct care and rearing of their children. This new focus highlights a shift from a concern with fathers as persons primarily involved in the economic support of the family and perhaps in the discipline and control of older children (e.g., Benson, 1968; Bowlby, 1951) to a view that places increasing stress on the role that fathers play in the direct care of children of all ages. To fully appreciate this shift, and to explain better the ways in which contemporary fathers are influential, it is helpful to examine historical changes in the conceptualization of paternal roles and responsibilities. Consequently, this chapter begins with a brief historical review designed to place contemporary paternal roles into perspective. In the second section, evidence concerning the nature and extent of paternal involvement today is discussed, as well as data concerning the extent to which father involvement has changed over the last several years. Paternal effects on child development are then considered, and the findings generated by research of three different genres conducted over the last four decades is summarized. Finally, the factors that influence the degree and type of involvement that fathers have in their children's lives are described. Because the chapter surveys a broad range of topics and issues, its coverage is necessarily selective. For those readers moved to obtain further detail or documentation concerning the conclusions presented here, references to key empirical studies and major integrative reviews of the literature are included.

FATHERS IN AMERICAN HISTORY

To understand the contemporary concern with and confusion about fatherhood, it may be helpful to step back historically and examine the changes in the conceptualization of paternal roles that have taken place. The available data are obviously limited, but social historians argue that much can be learned by examining letters (admittedly, few wrote letters and even fewer thought to preserve them for posterity) and literature written or popular during particular eras. According to Pleck (1984a), one can actually discern four phases or periods over the last two centuries of American social history. In each of these, a different dominant motif came into focus, making other aspects of a complex, multifaceted role seem much less important by comparison.

The Moral Teacher

The earliest phase was one that extended from Puritan times through the Colonial period into early Republican times. During this lengthy period, the father's role was perceived as being dominated by responsibility for moral oversight and moral teaching. By popular consensus, fathers were primarily responsible for ensuring that their children grew up with an appropriate sense of values, acquired primarily from the study of religious materials like the Bible. To the extent that a broader role was defined, fathers assumed responsibility for the education of children—not because education and literacy were valued in their own right, but because children had to be literate to read the Scriptures. Thus the father's responsibility for education was secondary; helping children become literate served to advance the father's role as moral guardian by ensuring that children were academically equipped to adopt and maintain Christian ways. In their reviews, Demos (1982) and Pleck (1984a) pointed out that, during this era, good fathers were defined as men who provided a model of good Christian living and versed their children well in the Scriptures.

The Breadwinner

Around the time of centralized industrialization, a shift occurred in the dominant conceptualization of the father's role (Pleck, 1984a). Instead of being defined in terms of moral teaching, his role came to be defined largely in terms of breadwinning, and this conceptualization of the father endured from the mid nineteenth century through the Great Depression (Pleck, 1976). An analysis of the then-popular literature and of letters written between fathers and children during that period confirms the dominant conceptualization of fatherhood in terms of breadwinning. This is not to say that other aspects of the father's role, such as the presumed responsibility for moral guardianship, had disappeared. Rather, breadwinning came into focus as the most important and defining characteristic offatherhood and as the criterion by which "good fathers" could be appraised.

The Sex-Role Model

Perhaps as a result of the Great Depression, the New Deal, and the disruption and dislocation brought about by the Second World War, the end of this war brought a new conceptualization of fatherhood. Although breadwinning and moral guardianship remained important, focus now shifted to the father's function as a sex-role model, especially for his sons. Many books and articles in the professional literature focused on the need for strong sex-role models, and many professionals concluded that fathers were clearly not doing a good job in this regard (e.g., Levy, 1943; Strecker, 1946). Their inadequacies were underscored in dramatic works, such as *Rebel Without a Cause,* and were ridiculed in comedies and cartoons, for example, *Blondie* and *All in the Family* (Ehrenreich & English, 1979).

The New Nurturant Father

Around the mid 1970s, finally, a fourth stage was reached. For the first time there was widespread identification of fathers as active, nurturant, caretaking parents. Active parenting was defined as the central component of fatherhood and as the yardstick by which "good fathers" might be assessed. This redefining of the most noteworthy and laudable aspect of fatherhood occurred first in the popular media, where it was promulgated in works like *Kramer vs. Kramer* and *The World According to Garp.* Professional interest in the new fatherhood soon followed.

It is important to acknowledge the changing conceptualization of fathering, because all four of the images or functions just outlined remain important today, although the extent of their importance varies across groups. In a pluralistic society like ours, various conceptions of the father's role coexist, and it is important to bear in mind that while journalists and filmmakers here have been lauding active and nurturant fatherhood for the last 10 years, many citizens have a very different conception of fathering. In addition, one must recognize that fathers fill many roles, that the relative importance of each varies from one context to another, and that active fathering—the key focus here—must be viewed in the context of the various other things that fathers do for their children (for example, breadwinning, sex-role modeling, moral guidance, emotional support of mothers).

Modes of Paternal Influence Today

If one thinks about fatherhood simply in terms of the ways in which fathers are likely to influence their children, one can discern at least four ways in which fathers can have a substantial impact on their children and their children's development. Clearly, breadwinning remains a key component of the father's role in most segments of society today (Benson, 1968; Cazenave, 1979; Pleck, 1983). Even in the vast majority of families in which there are two wage earners, the father is still seen as the primary breadwinner, if only because of continuing disparities between the salaries of male and female workers. Economic support of the family constitutes an indirect but important way in which fathers contribute to the rearing and emotional health of their children.

A second important but indirect source of influence stems from the father's role as a source of emotional support to the other people, principally the mother, involved in the direct care of children (Parke, Power, & Gottman, 1979). The father's functioning as a source of emotional support for the mother and others in the family tends to enhance the quality of the mother-child relationship and thus facilitates positive adjustment by the children; by contrast, when fathers are unsupportive, children may suffer (Rutter, 1973, 1979). Fathers can also affect the quality of family dynamics by being involved in child-related housework, thus easing the mother's workload (Pleck, 1983, 1984b). (Paternal involvement in housework may also provide a good model for children.)

Fathers also influence their children by interacting with the children directly, and much of this chapter is concerned with paternal influences deriving from the caretaking, teaching, play, and one-on-one interaction with particular children (Lamb, 1981b). Most of the research on paternal influences is concerned with such direct influence patterns, even though the father's role has multiple aspects and fathers can affect their children's development in many ways other than direct interaction.

QUANTIFYING THE NEW FATHERHOOD

Much attention has recently been paid to the changing roles of fathers, with particular focus on "the new father," who is, by definition, deeply involved in the day-to-day care and rearing of his children. Unfortunately, much of the evidence concerning the new fatherhood is journalistic in nature, and we do not know how representative the men featured in such accounts really are. Before pursuing our topic further, therefore, we need to ask: What does the average American father do, and how has that changed over the last several years?

Components of Father Involvement

A large number of studies have been designed to determine both how much time fathers spend with their children and what sorts of activities occupy that time (Lamb, Pleck, Charnov, & Levine, 1985, in press; Pleck,

1983). Many of these studies involve small and often unrepresentative samples—a perennial problem in developmental research. Fortunately, this area of research can boast of several studies involving nationally representative samples of individuals (both mothers and fathers) who are asked what fathers do and how much they do.

Given the availability of these data, it would seem easy to determine what contemporary fathers really do. Sadly, the task is not as easy as it sounds because the results of different surveys vary dramatically. One problem is that different researchers have invoked very different implicit definitions as parental involvement, using different activities as aspects of paternal involvement. Thus a comparison of results becomes very difficult. To make sense of the data, therefore, it is first necessary to group the studies in terms of their similarities in the implicit definitions of paternal involvement (Lamb, Pleck, Charnov, & Levine, in press).

For purposes of analysis, one can distinguish three components of parental involvement. The first and most restrictive type is time spent in actual one-on-one interaction with the child (whether feeding her, helping him with homework, or playing catch in the garden). This time, which Lamb and coworkers (in press) labeled time of *engagement* or *interaction,* does not include time spent in child-related housework, or time spent sitting in one room while the child plays in the next room. Lamb and colleagues included these times in a second category comprised of activities involving less intense degrees of interaction. These activities imply parental *accessibility* to the child, rather than direct interaction. Cooking in the kitchen while the child plays in the next room, or even cooking in the kitchen while the child plays at the parent's feet, are examples.

The final type of involvement is the hardest to define but is perhaps the most important of all. It is the extent to which the parent takes ultimate *responsibility* for the child's welfare and care. It can be illustrated by the difference between being responsible for child care and being able and willing to "help out" when it is convenient. Responsibility involves knowing when the child needs to go to the pediatrician, making the appointment, and making sure that the child gets to it. Responsibility involves making child-care and babysitting arrangements, ensuring that the child has clothes to wear, and making arrangements for supervision when the child is sick. Much of the time involved in being a responsible parent is not spent in direct interaction with the child. Consequently, survey researchers can easily overlook this type of involvement. It is hard to quantify the time involved, particularly because the anxiety, worry, and contingency planning that comprise parental responsibility often occur when the parent is ostensibly doing something else.

When the different components or types of parental involvement covered in various studies are differentiated, greater consistency is found from study to study than was apparent earlier, but a considerable degree of inconsistency remains. In part, this is because the recent distinction between the three types of involvement has been applied retrospectively to the results of independent investigations conducted years earlier, and thus there are still differences across studies in specific definitions of engagement, accessibility, and responsibility. For example, in one of the major national surveys, "watching TV together" was grouped with activities of the interaction type, whereas in another study, it was included as a component of accessibility.

To integrate and compare the findings of different studies, each researcher's idiosyncratic definition of involvement must be allowed to stand, but *relative* rather than *absolute* measures of paternal involvement must be used to compare results. Instead of comparing those figures purporting to measure the amount of time that fathers spend "interacting with" their children, proportional figures must first be computed (i.e., compared with the amount of time that mothers devote to interaction, how much time do fathers devote to it?) and these proportional figures be compared. The picture then becomes much clearer. Surprisingly similar results are obtained in the various studies, despite major differences in the methods used to assess time use (diary versus estimate), the size and regional representation of the samples employed, and the date when the studies were conducted.

Extent of Paternal Involvement

Consider, first, figures concerning the degree of involvement by fathers in two-parent families in which the mother is unemployed (Lamb et al., in press; Pleck, 1983). In such families the data suggest that the father spends about 20 to 25 percent as much time as the mother does in direct interaction or engagement with their children, and about a third as much time being accessible to their children. The largest discrepancy between paternal and maternal involvement is in the area of responsibility. Many studies show that fathers assume essentially no responsibility (as previously defined) for their children's care or rearing.

In two-parent families with an employed mother, the levels of paternal compared with maternal engagement and accessibility are both substantially higher than in families with an unemployed mother (Lamb et al., in press; Pleck, 1983). The figures for direct interaction and accessibility average 33 percent and 65 percent, respectively. As far as responsibility is concerned, however, there is no evidence that maternal employment has any effect on the level of paternal involvement. Even when both mother and father are employed 30 or more hours per week, the amount of responsibility assumed by fathers appears as negligible as when mothers are unemployed.

In light of the controversies that have arisen on this score, it is worth noting that fathers do not spend more time interacting with their children when mothers are employed, but rather the proportions just cited go up only because mothers are doing less. Thus, fathers are proportionately more involved when mothers are employed, even though the depth of their involvement, in absolute terms, does not change to any meaningful extent. The unfortunate controversies in this area appear attributable to a confusion between proportional figures and absolute figures.

Child and Family Characteristics Affecting Paternal Involvement

Researchers have also explored changes in paternal involvement related to the age of the child (Pleck, 1983). Interestingly, the changes that take place are the same for mothers and fathers. Both parents spend more time in child care when the children are younger—a trend that, although understandable, contradicts the popular assumption that fathers become more involved as the children get older. Fathers may know more about older children than about younger children, they may feel more comfortable and competent, and they may appear more interested, but they apparently do not spend more time with their older children. In part, this may be because older children no longer want to interact with parents as much; they prefer to interact with peers and/or siblings.

Popular presumptions are correct, however, so far as the effects of the child's gender are concerned (Lamb, 1981b). Fathers are indeed more interested in and more involved with their sons than their daughters. They tend to spend more time with boys than with girls, regardless of the children's ages. Beyond these variations associated with age and gender, however, there are no consistent regional, ethnic, or religious variations in the amount of time that parents—mothers or fathers—spend with their children (Pleck, 1983).

Changes Over Time

The term "new fatherhood" implies that today's fathers differ from fathers of the past. Unfortunately, few data are available concerning changes over time in levels of paternal involvement.

The best data available come from a recent report by Juster (in press) who compared figures from a 1975 national survey with figures obtained in a follow-up survey undertaken six years later. In 1981, the average father spent much more time (26 percent more) in the most intensive type of child care (direct interaction) than in 1975. The percentage increase for mothers was substantially smaller (7 percent), at least in part because the changes for mothers took place relative to higher baseline levels. In any event, the discrepancy between the levels of maternal and paternal involvement remained substantial: Mothers in 1981 still engaged in substantially more interaction with their children than did fathers, despite the larger increase in paternal involvement. In both 1976 and 1981, paternal involvement was about a third that of mothers, rising from 29 percent in 1976 to 34 percent in 1981.

Behavioral Styles of Mothers and Fathers

Thus far we have considered only how much time parents spend with their children, ignoring the fact that there may be variations in terms of the content of their interactions. Both observational and survey data suggest that mothers and fathers engage in rather different types of interaction with their children (Goldman & Goldman, 1983; Lamb, 1981a, b). Mothers' interactions with their children are dominated by caretaking, whereas fathers are behaviorally defined as playmates. Mothers actually play with their children much more than fathers do, but as a proportion of the total amount of child-parent interaction, play is a much more prominent component of father-child interaction and caretaking is more salient with mothers.

Although mothers are associated with caretaking and fathers with play, we cannot assume that fathers are less capable of child care. A number of researchers have attempted to investigate the relative competencies of mothers and fathers with respect to caretaking and parenting functions, and the results of these studies are fairly clear (Lamb, 1981a). First, they show that, in the newborn period, there are no differences in competence between mothers and fathers—both parents can do equally well (or equally poorly). Contrary to the notion of a maternal instinct, parenting skills are usually acquired "on the job" by both mothers and fathers. Mothers are "on the job" more than fathers are, however; not surprisingly, mothers become more sensitive to their children, more in tune with them, and more aware of each child's characteristics and needs. By virtue of their lack of experience, fathers become correspondingly less sensitive and come to feel less confidence in their parenting abilities. Fathers thus continue to defer to and cede responsibility to mothers, whereas mothers increasingly assume responsibility, not only because they see it as their role, but also because their partners do not seem to be especially competent care providers. As a result, the differences between mothers and fathers become more marked over time. These differences are not irreversible, however. When circumstances thrust fathers into the primary caretaking role, or when fathers choose to redefine their parental roles and their parent-child relationships, they are perfectly capable of acquiring the necessary skills (Hipgrave, 1982; Levine, 1976; Russell, 1983). In reality, of course, most fathers never get as involved in child care as their partner, and so the differences between mothers and fathers tend to increase.

Summary

There have been increases over time in average degrees of paternal involvement, so the notion of a "new emergent nurturant father" is not entirely mythical. Mothers continue to spend more time in and to take responsibility for most of the day-to-day care of their children. The discrepancy between mothers and fathers is especially great in the area of what we have called responsibility; in this regard, few data are available concerning secular changes in paternal behavior. In other areas the changes, although significant, are still quite modest. In addition, the characteristics of mothers' and fathers' interactions with their children have for the most part remained remarkably consistent over time. Mothers are identified with caretaking, fathers with play.

PATERNAL INFLUENCES ON CHILD DEVELOPMENT

The focus of this chapter now switches from fathers' actions to fathers' influences on their children's development. Over the decades of research on this topic, three bodies of literature have emerged: (1) correlational studies, (2) studies concerned with the effects of father absence, and (3) studies concerned with the impact of high father involvement. All are important to an understanding of paternal influences on child development. The three approaches are described and their results summarized separately in this section. The summaries, however, are by no means exhaustive: Indeed, in the first two subsections discussion is limited to illustrative research involving fathers and sons. More detailed and comprehensive reviews are provided elsewhere (Adams, Milner, & Schrepf, 1984; Lamb, 1981c; Lamb, Pleck, & Levine, 1985). The goal here is to illustrate the key features of empirical research that have prompted major changes in our conceptualization of paternal influence patterns.

The Correlational Approach

Let us first consider studies concerned with the search for correlations between paternal and filial characteristics. In such studies, researchers might try to measure the warmth, closeness, or hostility (for reviews see Biller, 1971; Lamb, 1976, 1981c) of father-child relationships, or the masculinity or authoritarianism of fathers, and then correlate measures of these paternal or relational constructs with measures of some theoretically related characteristics in the children. This strategy was adopted in many of the earliest studies of paternal influences, the vast majority of which focused on sex-role development, especially in sons. This is understandable, since many of these studies were done from the 1940s to the early 1960s when the father's role as a sex-role model was considered most important. The design of these early studies was quite simple: The researchers assessed masculinity in fathers and in sons, and then determined how strongly the two sets of scores were correlated. To the researchers' great surprise, there was no consistent correlation between the two, a puzzling finding because it seemed to violate a guiding assumption about the crucial function served by fathers. If fathers did not make their boys into men, what role did they really serve?

It took a while for psychologists to realize that the guiding assumption might have been inappropriate. Researchers failed to ask: Why should boys *want to be like* their father? Presumably they should only want to resemble a father whom they like and respect, and with whom their relationship is warm or positive. In fact, the quality of father-son relationships was found to be an important mediating variable: When the relationship between masculine fathers and their sons was good, the boys were indeed more masculine. Subsequent research suggested that the quality of the relationship was actually the crucial variable so far as the development of filial masculinity was concerned (Mussen & Rutherford, 1963; Payne & Mussen, 1956; Sears, Maccoby, & Levin, 1957). By contrast, the masculinity of the father was rather unimportant. In other words, boys seemed to conform to the sex-role standards of their culture when their relationships with their fathers were warm, regardless of how "masculine" the fathers were. Because of this we might expect that the effects of close father-son relationships have changed over the last 15 years, during which cultural preferences for and expectations of male behavior have changed also. Today, for example, we might expect warm fathers who have close relationships with their children to have more androgynous sons than other fathers (since androgyny seems to be the contemporary goal), just as similarly close relationships formerly potentiated the development of masculine sons (Baruch & Barnett, 1983; Radin, 1978; Radin & Sagi, 1982).

As far as paternal influences on sex-role development are concerned, then, the key finding is that characteristics of the father (such as masculinity) are much less important formatively than the father's warmth and the closeness and nature of his relationship with his son. This is an interesting and important finding, because warmth and closeness have traditionally been seen as feminine characteristics. Thus "feminine" characteristics of the father—his warmth and nurturance—seem to be associated with better adjustment in sons, at least to the extent that adjustment is defined in terms of sex role.[*]

Similar findings have been obtained in studies concerned with paternal influences on achievement (Radin, 1981). Initially, the assumption was that fathers would influence achievement motivation positively, because they were the family members who exemplified achievement in "the real world" and their sons would surely want to emulate them in this regard. Once more, it soon became clear that the father's warmth, closeness, and involvement were most important; fathers with these characteristics tended to have competent and achievement-oriented sons (Radin, 1978, 1981, 1982). The same characteristics are important with regard to a mothers' influence on her child's achievement, again implying that fathers influence children not by virtue of "male" characteristics (like masculinity) but by virtue of nurturant personal and social characteristics.

A similar conclusion is suggested by research on psychosocial adjustment: Paternal warmth or closeness is advantageous, whereas paternal masculinity is irrelevant (Biller, 1971; Lamb, 1981b). Thus across these three areas of development—sex-role development, achievement, and psychosocial adjustment—children seem better off when their relationship with their father is close and warm. In general, the same is true in the case of mothers, and children who have close relationships with both parents benefit greatly. As far as influence on children is concerned, very little about the gender of the parent seems to be distinctly important. The characteristics of the father as a parent rather than the characteristics of the father as a man appear to influence child development.

Father Absence Research

While the whole body of research that is here termed "correlational" was burgeoning in the 1950s, another body of literature was developing. This involved investigations in which researchers tried to understand the

---

[*] This is a questionable assumption, particularly given the ways in which sex roles are usually operationalized in the research literature. Readers are referred to Pleck (1981) and Lamb et al. (1985) for further discussion of these issues, which are not critical to the argument being developed here.

father's role by studying families without fathers. The assumption was that by comparing the behavior and personalities of children raised with and without fathers, one could—essentially by a process of subtraction—estimate what sort of influence fathers typically had. The chief father-absence and correlational studies were conducted in roughly the same era; not surprisingly, the outcomes studied were very similar and the results were in many ways similar. In the case of father-absence studies, the results also appeared consistent with popular assumptions. Unfortunately, the literature on father absence is voluminous and controversial; readers are referred elsewhere for more detailed discussions (Adams, Milner, & Schrepf, 1984; Biller, 1974; Lamb, 1981; Herzog & Sudia, 1973). In the present context, suffice it to say that boys growing up without fathers seemed to have "problems" in the areas of sex-role and gender-identity development, school performance, psychosocial adjustment, and perhaps in the control of aggression.

Two related issues arising from father-absence research must be addressed, however. First, even if one agrees that there are differences between children raised in families with the father present and those raised in families with the father absent, one must ask *why* those differences exist and how to interpret them. Second, it is important to remember that although there may be *group differences* between, say, 100 boys growing up without fathers and 100 boys growing up with fathers, this does not mean that every child growing up without a father has problems in some if not all of the areas just mentioned, or that all boys whose fathers live at home develop normatively. One cannot make inferences about individuals from data concerning groups simply because there is great within-group heterogeneity. This forces us to ask why such heterogeneity exists. Why do some boys appear to suffer deleterious consequences as a result of father absence, while others do not? More broadly, the question is: What is it about the father-absence context that makes for group differences between children in father-absent and father-present contexts, and what accounts for the impressive within-group variance?

Researchers and theorists first sought to explain the effects of father absence in terms of the absence of a male sex-role model. In the absence of a masculine parental model, it was assumed that boys could not acquire strong masculine identities or sex roles and would not have a model of achievement with which to identify (Biller, 1974). The problem with this interpretation is that many boys without fathers seem to develop quite normally so far as sex-role development and achievement are concerned. Clearly, an explanation that emphasizes the absence of a male sex-role model cannot be complete or inclusive. It has thus become increasingly clear that some other factors may be at least as important as (if not much more important than) the availability of a sex-role model in mediating the effects of father absence on child development.

First, there is the absence of a coparent—someone to help out with child care, to be there when one parent needs a break, to supplement one parent's resources in relation to the demands of the child (Maccoby, 1977). Second, there is the economic stress that goes along with single parenthood, especially single motherhood. The median and mean incomes for single women heads of household are significantly lower than the average income in any other group, and the disparity is even larger when one considers per capita income rather than income per household (Glick & Norton, 1979). Third, the tremendous economic stress experienced by single mothers is accompanied by emotional stress occasioned by a degree of social isolation and the largely disapproving attitudes that society continues to hold with respect to single or divorced mothers and children (Hetherington, Cox, & Cox, 1982). Lastly, there is the predivorce (and postdivorce) marital conflict, an important issue because, of all the findings in the area of socialization, the best validated is the fact that children suffer when there is hostility or conflict in the family (Rutter, 1973, 1979; Lamb, 1981b). Since most single-parent families are produced by divorce, and since divorce is often preceded by periods of overt and covert spousal hostility, predivorce conflict may play a major role in explaining the problems of fatherless children. By contrast, fatherless children who have good relationships with both parents before and after the divorce tend to be better adjusted than those who do not (Hess & Camara, 1979).

In sum, the evidence suggests that father absence may be harmful not necessarily because a sex-role model is absent, but because many aspects of the father's role—economic, social, emotional—go unfilled or inappropriately filled. Recognition of the father's multiple roles as breadwinner, parent, and emotional support for partner is essential in understanding how fathers influence children's development.

Studies of Increased Paternal Involvement

Finally we must consider more recent studies concerned with the effects on children of increased father involvement, as exemplified by fathers who either share in or take primary responsibility for child care (Lamb et al., 1985; Russell, 1983; Russell & Radin, 1983; Chapter 2). This question has been addressed in three or four studies, and results have been remarkably consistent with respect to preschool-aged children whose fathers are responsible for at least 40 percent to 45 percent of the within-family child care. Children with highly involved fathers are characterized by increased cognitive competence, increased empathy, less sex-stereotyped beliefs, and a more internal locus of control (Pruett, 1983; Radin, 1982; Radin & Sagi, 1982; Sagi, 1982). Again the question that has to be asked is, "*Why* do these sorts of differences occur?"

Three factors are probably important in this regard (Lamb et al., 1985). First, when parents assume less sex-stereotyped roles, their children have less sex-stereotyped attitudes themselves about male and female roles. Second, particularly in the area of cognitive competence, these children may benefit from having two highly involved parents rather than just one. This assures them the diversity of stimulation that comes from interacting with people who have different behavioral styles. A third important issue has to do with the family context in which these children are raised. In every study reported thus far, a high degree of paternal involvement made it possible for both parents to do what was subjectively important to them. It allowed fathers to satisfy a desire to become close to their children and mothers to have adequately close relationships with their children while also pursuing career goals. In other words, increased paternal involvement may have made both parents feel much more fulfilled. As a result, the relationships were probably much warmer and richer than might otherwise have been the case. One can speculate that the positive outcome obtained by children with a highly involved father is largely attributable to the fact that the father's involvement created a family context in which the parents felt good about their marriage and the arrangements they had been able to work out.

In all of these studies, fathers were involved because both they and their partners desired this. The results might be very different in cases with fathers forced to become involved, perhaps because of a layoff from work, while their partner could get and hold a job. In such circumstances the wife might resent the fact that her husband could not hold a job and support his family while the husband might resent having to do "woman's work" with the children when he really wanted to be "out there" earning a living and supporting his family (see Russell, 1983). This constellation of factors might well have adverse effects on children, just as the same degree of involvement has positive effects when the circumstances are more benign. The key point is that the extent of paternal involvement may be much less significant (so far as the effects on children are concerned) than are the reasons for his involvement and his and his partner's evaluation of that involvement.

In sum, the effects may in many cases have more to do with the context of father involvement than with father involvement per se. What matters is not so much who is at home, but how that person feels about being at home, for the person's feelings will color the way he or she behaves with the children. Behavior is also influenced by the other partner's feelings about the arrangement: Both parents' emotional states affect the family dynamics.

Summary

The three genres of research on paternal influences together paint a remarkably consistent picture. First, by and large fathers and mothers seem to influence their children in similar rather than dissimilar ways. The important dimensions of parental influence are those that have to do with parental characteristics rather than gender-related characteristics. Second, the nature of the effect may vary substantially, depending on individual and cultural values. A classic example of this can be found in the literature on sex-role development. As a result of cultural changes, the assumed sex-role goals for boys and girls have changed, and this has produced changes in the effect of father involvement on children. In the 1950s sex-appropriate masculinity or femininity was the desired goal; today androgyny or sex-role flexibility is desired. And whereas father involvement in the 1950s seemed to be associated with greater masculinity in boys, it is associated today with less sex-stereotyped sex-role standards in both sons and daughters. Third, influence patterns vary substantially, depending on social factors that define the meaning of father involvement for children in particular families in particular social milieus. Finally, the amount of time that fathers and children spend together is probably much less important than what they do with that time and how fathers, mothers, children, and other important people in their lives perceive and evaluate the father-child relationship.

All of this means that high paternal involvement may have positive effects in some circumstances and negative effects in others. The same is true of low paternal involvement. We must not lose sight, however, of recent historical changes in average levels of paternal involvement (Juster, in press). If the trend continues, the number of families in which greater father involvement would be beneficial will increase.

THE DETERMINANTS OF FATHER INVOLVEMENT

Motivation

Four factors are crucial to understanding variations in the degree of paternal involvement (Lamb et al., in press). First, there is motivation—the extent to which the father wants to be involved. Survey data suggest that 40 percent of fathers would like to have more time to spend with their children than they currently have (Quinn & Staines, 1979). This implies that a substantial number of men are motivated to be more involved. On the other hand, the same data suggest that more than half of the fathers in the

Figure 1.1. Cover of a brochure on parental leave published by the Swedish government.

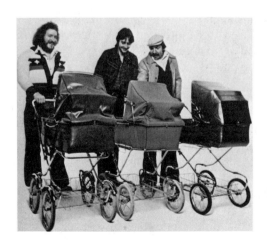

Figure 1.2. Another brochure illustration published by the Swedish government; all of the men are masculine sporty figures.

country do not want to spend more time with their children than they currently do. Clearly there is no unanimity about the desirability of increased paternal involvement, an important point when one considers the need to evaluate parental motivations when attempting to understand parental influences (see previous section).

Changes in the level of paternal motivation have recently taken place, however, and can be attributed primarily to the women's movement and the questions it raises about traditional male and female roles. In addition, media hype about the "new father" has also affected motivation levels. The most impressive official program yet undertaken was initiated by the Swedish government in the early 1970s in an attempt to encourage men to become more involved in child care (Lamb & Levine, 1983). Figures 1.1 and 1.2 depict images from the brochures and posters published by the Swedish government. The man shown in Figure 1.1 is not an ordinary man but a very large muscular man holding a tiny baby. This picture implicitly addresses one of the key attitudinal barriers to male involvement: the notion that it is effeminate for men to be involved in child care. The illustration in Figure 1.2 likewise conveys the message that "real men" can be actively involved in child care. The message is important, because many men continue to feel that active parenting and masculinity are incompatible. Continuing fears of this sort help explain why some motivational shifts have been so slow, and particularly why the number of fathers who take a major role in child care has not increased very much (nationally or internationally) despite tremendous changes in female employment patterns.

Skills and Self-Confidence

Motivation alone cannot ensure increased involvement: Skills and self-confidence are also necessary. Ostensibly motivated men often complain that a lack of skills (exemplified by ignorance or clumsiness) prevents increased involvement. These complaints can constitute excuses, but they can also reflect a very real fear.

When men are motivated and the absence of skills poses a major barrier, formal skill-development programs may be critically important. However, the best way for men to start getting involved with their children may be for them to do things with the children that they can enjoy doing together. The goal should be for them to develop a sense of self-confidence, so that they come to enjoy being with their children and to feel increasingly self-confident. Once fathers realize that their children really are fun, adore them, and do not generate an endless succession of embarrassing crises, they should be willing to expand the range of activities and contexts in which they and their children successfully function together. The key thing is development of confidence—skills can be acquired later. Many fathers do not realize that most first-time mothers are just as incompetent and terrified as they are. The difference is that women are expected to know how to parent and cannot just withdraw from the challenges involved. They have to pretend that they know what they are doing, and thus must learn the necessary skills as soon as they can.

In addition to self-confidence, sensitivity is also crucial (Lamb, 1980). Sensitivity involves being able to read the child's signals, know what he or she wants, know how to respond appropriately, know what expectations are realistic, and so on. Both sensitivity and self-confidence are abstract characteristics, but both are probably much more important than specific skills. Specific skills may provide useful vehicles for the development of sensitivity and self-confidence, however.

Support

The third factor influencing paternal involvement is support, especially support within the family from the mother. The same surveys that show a majority of men wanting to be more involved show that somewhere between 80 percent and 60 percent of women do *not* want their husbands to be more involved than they currently are (Pleck, 1982; Quinn & Staines, 1979). This suggests that, although many mothers would like their husbands to do more, a substantial majority are quite satisfied with the status quo.

There may be many reasons for this attitude. Some mothers may feel that their husbands are incompetent and that their involvement may create more work than it saves. More importantly, increased paternal involvement may threaten to upset fundamental power dynamics within the family (Polatnick, 1973–1974). The roles of mother and manager of the household are the two roles in which women's authority has not been questioned; together they constitute the one area in which women have real power and control. Increased paternal involvement may threaten this power and preeminence. The tradeoff is of dubious value, because although women in increasing numbers have entered the work force in the last two decades, they are usually restricted to low-paying, low-prestige, low-advancement occupations. In essence, women are being asked to give up power in the one area where power and authority are unquestioned in exchange for the possibility of power in another area. Many women prefer to maintain authority in the child-care arena, even if that means physical and mental exhaustion.

Women's attitudes toward paternal involvement have changed very little over the last 15 years or so (Pleck, 1982; Polatnick, 1973–1974). Their resistance is likely to endure until fundamental changes within society at large change the basic distribution of power. Even those women who say they would welcome increased paternal involvement may be more ambivalent than survey results indicate.

The differences in women's attitudes regarding paternal involvement raise important issues about father involvement and the likely effects on young children. As mentioned earlier, the effects of involvement on family dynamics may be critical. Thus, when deciding whether father involvement should be encouraged in particular families, one must take into account the preferences and attitudes of *both* parents. To do so involves articulating individual assumptions and values and then negotiating in an attempt to achieve some satisfactory consensus.

Because women's attitudes and assumptions appear to be changing faster than men's, conflict between partners may become increasingly common. In this regard, it may be significant that in the two longitudinal studies of intensive father involvement (Russell, 1983; Radin & Goldsmith, in press), a remarkably high rate of family dissolution was evident when families were later relocated. Thus despite good dynamics early on (at least in Radin's subject families), substantial and fundamental problems concerning roles and responsibilities may arise later, particularly in this era of ambivalence and confusion. It is important to remember this "dark side" of paternal involvement, even though, on the whole, father involvement is important and desirable for an increasing number of families.

Institutional Practices

The last of the factors influencing paternal involvement is institutional practices. The needs of the family for economic support and the barriers imposed by the work place rank among the most important reasons given by fathers to explain low levels of paternal involvement (e.g., Yankelovich, 1974). Clearly this is an important issue for many men, and it will remain important as long as men take on and are expected to assume the primary breadwinning role. It is also true, however, that men do not trade work time for family time in a one-to-one fashion. Survey data show that women translate each extra hour of nonwork time into an extra 40 to 45 minutes of family work, whereas for men, each hour not spent in paid work translates into less than 20 minutes of family work (Pleck, 1983). Thus while the pressures of work do have a significant effect on parental involvement, the effects for men and women are somewhat different. Being at work does reduce the amount of time that fathers can spend with their children, but even when they have time they spend only a small portion of it with their children.*

Paternity leave is the most frequently discussed means of enhancing paternal involvement. This near-exclusive focus is really misdirected, because paternity leave is unlikely to provide *the* answer to increased paternal involvement. One has to remember that less than one third of the working women in this country have any type of *paid* maternity leave; if maternity leave is not allowed, paternity leave must rank as an unrealistic goal. In addition, paternity leave facilitates involvement only during a very short period of time at the beginning of the child's life, and appears to have a limited effect on later paternal involvement or behavior (Hwang et al., 1985). Practices that allow men to be involved over the long haul would be more helpful than paternity leave. Flexible time scheduling would certainly be of greatest value to many involved but employed fathers (and mothers), as Pleck suggests in Chapter 14 of this book.

Summary

One can conceive of the four factors—motivation, skills and self-confidence, support, and institutional practices—as a hierarchy of factors influencing fathers' involvement with their children. Favorable conditions must exist at each level if increased paternal involvement is to be possible and beneficial. Successful interventions will be those that can address people at each of these levels, focusing on areas in which the inhibiting factors are most prominent. Later in this book, Parke and Beitel (Chapter 11), Elster (Chapter 12), Ray and McLoyd (Chapter 13), Pleck (Chapter 14), Klinman (Chapter 15), and Bolton (Chapter 16) discuss the ways in which major agencies and institutions in our society might allow fathers to consider increased involvement as a viable option. Institutional barriers are much harder to change than any of the other. Nevertheless, institutions create much more flexibility than most people admit; while they pose major barriers, they could also allow many men to be more involved than they actually are.

SUMMARY

A number of issues pertaining to paternal involvement in child care have been addressed, albeit briefly, in this chapter. As mentioned earlier, the

*In addition to the constraints imposed by actual work time, the whole identification of fatherhood with breadwinning serves to limit male involvement in child care.

current high degree of interest in paternal roles and functions on the part of scholars and researchers reflects the latest in a series of shifts in the way in which American society conceptualizes and idealizes fatherhood. Consistent with the notion of a "new fatherhood," the average level of paternal involvement has increased in the last several years, although the increase has been modest. Mothers still spend much more time than do fathers in interaction with or accessibility to their children, and this remains true even when both parents are employed. Furthermore, ultimate responsibility for child care and child rearing remains the near-exclusive province of mothers, while fathers "help out when they can (or when it is convenient)." A number of factors, including motivation, skills and self-confidence, support, and institutional factors, appear to affect levels of paternal involvement, but many of these reflect manifestations of an underlying assumption: Men are first and foremost workers and breadwinners, women are primarily nurturers.

Whatever the extent of their involvement, fathers do appear to influence their children's development, both directly by means of interaction and indirectly by virtue of their impact (positive and negative) on the family's social and emotional climate. Attitudes concerning appropriate levels of paternal involvement vary widely. Thus paternal involvement, whether of a high or low level, can be beneficial or harmful to child development, depending on the attitudes and values of the parents concerned. It is thus critically important to recognize intercultural and intracultural diversity when exploring paternal influences on child development.

REFERENCES

Adams, P.L., Milner, J. R., & Schrepf, N. A. (1984). *Fatherless children.* New York: Wiley.

Baruch, G. K., & Barnett, R. C. (1979). Fathers' participation in the care of their preschool children. Unpublished manuscript, Wellesley College, Wellesley, MA.

Baruch, G. K., & Barnett, R. C. (1983). Correlates of fathers' participation in family work: A technical report. Wellesley, MA: Wellesley College Center for Research on Women, working paper #106.

Benson, L. (1968). *Fatherhood: A sociological perspective.* New York: Random House.

Biller, H. B. (1971). *Father, child, and sex role.* Lexington, MA: Heath.

Biller, H. B. (1974). *Paternal deprivation: Family, school, sexuality and society.* Lexington, MA: Heath.

Bowlby, J. (1951). *Maternal care and mental health.* Geneva: WHO.

Cazenave, N. A. (1979). Middle-income black fathers: An analysis of the provider role. *Family Coordinator, 27*, 583–593.

Demos, J. (1982). The changing faces of fatherhood: A new exploration in American family history. In S. H. Cath, A. R. Gurwitt, & J. M. Ross (Eds.), *Father and child: Developmental and clinical perspectives.* Boston: Little, Brown.

Ehrenreich, B., & English D. (1979). *For her own good.* New York: Anchor Books.

Glick, P. C., & Norton, A. J. (1979). Marrying, divorcing, and living together in the US today. *Population Bulletin, 32*(5, whole issue).

Goldman, J. D. G., & Goldman, R. J. (1983). Children's perceptions of parents and their roles: A cross-national study in Australia, England, North America, and Sweden. *Sex Roles, 9,* 791–812.

Herzog, R., & Sudia, C. E. (1973). Children in fatherless families. In B. M. Caldwell & H. N. Ricciuti (Eds.), *Review of child development research* (Vol. 3). Chicago: University of Chicago Press.

Hess, R. D., & Camara, K. A. (1979). Post-divorce family relationships as mediating factors in the consequences of divorce for children. *Journal of Social Issues, 35,* 79–96.

Hetherington, E. M., Cox, M., & Cox, R. (1982). Effects of divorce on parents and children. In M. E. Lamb (Ed.), *Nontraditional families.* Hillsdale, NJ: Erlbaum.

Hipgrave, T. (1982). Childrearing by lone fathers. In R. Chester, P. Diggory, & M. Sutherland (Eds.), *Changing patterns of child bearing and child rearing.* London: Academic.

Hwang, C.-P., Lamb, M. E., Broberg, A., Frodi, M., & Hulth, G. (1985, April). *Effects of early father participation on later paternal involvement and responsibility.* Paper presented to Society for Research in Child Development, Toronto.

Juster, F. T. (in press). A note on recent changes in time use. In F. T. Juster & F. Stafford (Eds.), *Studies in the measurement of time allocation.* Ann Arbor, MI: Institute for Social Research.

Lamb, M. E. (1980). What can "research experts" tell parents about effective socialization? In M. D. Fantini & R. Cardenas (Eds.), *Parenting in a multicultural society.* New York: Longman.

Lamb, M. E. (1981a). The development of father-infant relationships. In M. E. Lamb (Ed.), *The role of the father in child development.* New York: Wiley.

Lamb, M. E. (1981b). Fathers and child development: An integrative overview. In M. E. Lamb (Ed.), *The role of the father in child development.* New York: Wiley.

Lamb, M. E. (1981c). *The role of the father in child development.* Rev. ed. New York: Wiley.

Lamb, M. E., and Levine, J. A. (1983). The Swedish parental insurance policy: An experiment in social engineering. In M. E. Lamb & A. Sagi (Eds.), *Fatherhood and family policy.* Hillsdale, NJ: Erlbaum.

Lamb, M. E., Pleck, J. H., Charnov, E. L., & Levine, J. A. (1985). Paternal behavior in humans. *American Zoologist, 25,* 883–894.

Lamb, M. E., Pleck, J. H., Charnov, E. L., & Levine, J. A. (in press). A biosocial perspective on paternal behavior and involvement. In J. B. Lancaster, J. Altmann, A. Rossi, & L. R. Sherrod (Eds.), *Parenting across the life span: Biosocial perspectives.* Chicago: Aldine.

Lamb, M. E., Pleck, J. H., & Levine, J. A. (1985). The role of the father in child development: The effects of increased paternal involvement. In B. S. Lahey & A. E. Kazdin (Eds.), *Advances in clinical child psychology* (Vol. 8). New York: Plenum.

Levine, J. A. (1976). *And who will raise the children? New options for fathers (and mothers).* Philadelphia: Lippincott.

Levy, D. M. (1943). *Maternal overprotection.* New York: Columbia University Press.

Lynn, D. (1974). *The father: His role in development.* Monterey, CA: Brooks/Cole.

Maccoby, E. E. (1977, September). *Current changes in the family and their impact upon the socialization of children.* Paper presented to American Sociological Association, Chicago.

Mussen, P. H., & Rutherford, E. (1963). Parent-child relations and parental personality in relation to young children's sex-role preferences. *Child Development, 34,* 589–607.

Parke, R. D., Power, T. G., & Gottman, J. (1979). Conceptualizing and quantifying influence patterns in the family triad. In M. E. Lamb, S. J. Suomi, & G. R. Stephenson (Eds.), *Social interaction analysis: Methodological issues.* Madison: University of Wisconsin Press.

Payne, D. E., & Mussen, P. H. (1956). Parent-child relations and father identification among adolescent boys. *Journal of Abnormal and Social Psychology, 52,* 358–362.

Pleck, E. (1976). Two worlds in one: Work and family. *Journal of Social History, 10,* 178–195.

Pleck, J. H. (1981). *The myth of masculinity.* Cambridge, MA: MIT Press.

Pleck, J. H. (1982). Husbands' and wives' paid work, family work, and adjustment. Wellesley, MA: Wellesley College Center for Research on Women.

Pleck, J. H. (1983). Husbands' paid work and family roles: Current research issues. In H. Lopata & J. H. Pleck (Eds.), *Research in the interweave of social roles* (Vol. 3), *Families and jobs.* Greenwich, CT: JAI Press.

Pleck, J. H. (1984a). Changing fatherhood. Unpublished manuscript, Wellesley, MA: Wellesley College Center for Research on Women.

Pleck, J. H. (1984b). *Working wives and family well-being.* Beverly Hills, CA: Sage.

Polatnick, M. (1973–1974). Why men don't rear children: A power analysis. *Berkeley Journal of Sociology, 18,* 44–86.

Pruett, K. D. (1983, April). *Two year followup of infants of primary nurturing fathers in intact families.* Paper presented to Second World Congress on Infant Psychiatry, Cannes, France.

Quinn, R. P., & Staines, G. L. (1979). *The 1977 Quality of Employment survey.* Ann Arbor, MI: Survey Research Center.

Radin, N. (1978, September). *Childrearing fathers in intact families with preschoolers.* Paper presented to American Psychological Association, Toronto.

Radin, N. (1981). The role of the father in cognitive, academic, and intellectual development. In M. E. Lamb (Ed.), *The role of the father in child development.* New York: Wiley.

Radin, N. (1982). Primary caregiving and role-sharing fathers. In M. E. Lamb (Ed.), *Nontraditional families: Parenting and child development.* Hillsdale, NJ: Erlbaum.

Radin, N., & Goldsmith, R. (in press). Caregiving fathers of preschoolers: Four years later. *Merrill-Palmer Quarterly.*

Radin, N., & Russell, G. (1983). Increased father participation and child development outcomes. In M. E. Lamb & A. Sagi (Eds.), *Fatherhood and family policy.* Hillsdale, NJ: Erlbaum.

Radin, N., & Sagi, A. (1982). Childrearing fathers in intact families in Israel and the U.S.A. *Merrill-Palmer Quarterly, 28,* 111–136.

Russell, G. (1982). Shared-caregiving families: An Australian study. In M. E. Lamb (Ed.), *Nontraditional families: Parenting and child development.* Hillsdale, NJ: Erlbaum.

Russell, G. (1983). *The changing role of fathers?* St. Lucia, Queensland: University of Queensland Press.

Rutter, M. (1973). Why are London children so disturbed? *Proceedings of the Royal Society of Medicine, 66,* 1221–1225.

Rutter, M. (1979). Maternal deprivation, 1972–1978: New findings, new concepts, new approaches. *Child Development, 50,* 283–305.

Sagi, A. (1982). Antecedents and consequences of various degrees of paternal involvement in child rearing: The Israeli project. In M. E. Lamb (Ed.), *Nontraditional families: Parenting and child development.* Hillsdale, NJ: Erlbaum.

Sears, R. R., Maccoby, E. E., & Levin, H. (1957). *Patterns of child rearing.* Evanston, IL: Peterson.

Strecker, E. (1946). *Their mothers' sons.* Philadelphia: Lippincott.

Yankelovich, D. (1974). The meaning of work. In J. Rosow (Ed.), *The worker and the job.* Englewood Cliffs, NJ: Prentice-Hall.

CHAPTER 2

Primary Caretaking and Role-Sharing Fathers

GRAEME RUSSELL

Macquarie University

With the recent heightened interest in the "new fatherhood" (see Chapter 1), families that adopt nontraditional caregiving patterns in which the father has the major responsibility for day-to-day child care or shares this with his spouse—families commonly referred to as reversed or shared-role—have received considerable attention from media and social commentators. Many have advocated this particular family pattern as the ideal or as the panacea for family and gender-related problems, despite the relative absence of research findings to support this position. A critical assessment of families of this type is important, however, as they form the basis of our knowledge about possibilities for change in the balance of work and family commitments for men and women. They also provide the best examples yet of the practice of shared parenting and the difficulties likely to be encountered in attempts to implement such an option, both at the personal and the policy level.

The few studies that have been conducted indicate that there are a small but significant number of these nontraditional families and that some have chosen to adopt this pattern while others have been forced to do so primarily for economic reasons. It also seems clear that others would like to have the option of a nontraditional pattern, and that still others would choose it if there were a greater understanding of the consequences of it for children and parents, if it was a more feasible option, and if it became more common or socially acceptable.

Despite their obvious social and theoretical importance, little attempt has been made either to describe or define the characteristics of families that adopt nontraditional caregiving patterns, or to examine systematically their possible antecedents or consequences. These issues are addressed in the present chapter. There are four general aims: (1) to examine the nature of the division of labor in nontraditional families and the extent to which these families differ from traditional patterns, (2) to examine the reasons why people adopt the nontraditional pattern, emphasizing both the possible antecedents and the social and personal factors that tend to facilitate the change, (3) to review findings about the impact that a nontraditional pattern has on children, fathers, and mothers, and (4) to examine the implications of research findings for expanding the options for shared parenting and for the development of family policies and practices. A common theme throughout the chapter is that our knowledge is limited because few research studies have been done on primary caretaking and role-sharing fathers, and that most studies have methodological limitations.

THE NATURE OF THE FAMILY PATTERN

Several recent publications have reported on families defined as nontraditional on the basis of the fact that the father was highly participant in child care—that he was either the primary caregiver or shared this job with his spouse. This family pattern has been noted in Norway (Grønseth, 1978), Sweden (Lamb et al., 1982), Australia (Harper, 1980; Russell, 1983a), the United States (De Frain, 1979; Field, 1978; Levine, 1976; Radin, 1981, 1982), and Israel (Sagi, 1982). Little emphasis was placed in this research, however, on providing basic descriptive details about family life-styles, and therefore the specific nature of the families studied is unknown. Nevertheless, we can be certain about two features of the families studied:

1.   Two distinct types of families can be defined by parental employment patterns: those in which only the mother is employed and the father is at home full-time as the primary daytime caregiver, and those in which both parents are employed and they share child care but in which the father usually has more responsibility for caregiving during the day. Studies have not been consistent, however, in providing details of either maternal or paternal employment characteristics (e.g., the nature of jobs, hours of employment, work schedules).

2.   In comparison with modal patterns of participation (Russell & Radin, 1983), the fathers described in these studies are indeed highly participant. In Radin's (1982) U.S. study, the group defined as father prime performed 57 percent of child-care tasks, whereas De Frain (1979) reported a figure of 46 percent. In another study of nontraditional Australian families (Russell, 1983a), fathers spent an average of 26 hours

per week taking sole responsibility for their children during the day when the children were awake (compared with 16 hours per week for mothers and one hour for traditional fathers), and they performed 43 percent of child-care tasks (compared with 11 percent for traditional fathers), spending an average of eight hours per week doing these tasks.

Few studies have provided comprehensive details of the nature of paternal participation. Commonly, researchers have simply stated that fathers were highly participant (e.g., that they were the primary caretakers) or were the primary caretakers for a specified time period, or have reported fathers' participation relative to mothers' participation or to other fathers' participation. This approach to the definition of high father participation is consistent with the general tendency of researchers to define families in terms of one dimension only (e.g., whether a mother is employed). Definitions are also likely to emphasize measures of general involvement, and the frequency of or amount of time spent on performance of basic child-care tasks (see Chapter 1 as well).

It has become clear, however, that high father involvement in day-to-day child care combined with maternal employment does not necessarily lead to the sharing of other aspects of parenting (Russell, 1983a). In particular, in some families the mother still retains the greater responsibility for child management and socialization and performs more child-care tasks than does the father when they are both at home. She is also more likely to have the responsibility for planning, monitoring, and anticipating the needs of the children. As one mother said: "I am still the executive director of children." These findings are consistent with those of Radin (1982), who has reported a relatively low correlation between "decision making about childcare" and other dimensions of father involvement. Equally, however, research also shows that in some nontraditional families, fathers are still seen as having more responsibility for family financial management and breadwinning, with the mother's employment being considered a short-term option (Russell, 1983a).

A more complete analysis of nontraditional child-care patterns, therefore, would involve considerations of divisions of labor for employment, the provision of day-to-day child care, the performance of child-care and domestic tasks, and the acceptance and implementation of shared responsibilities and commitment for family management and child socialization. Unfortunately, very few studies of high father participation have provided such a comprehensive analysis, and therefore this review of necessity places more emphasis on traditional definitions of shared parenting associated with employment and child care. The issue of responsibility is, however, emphasized toward the end of the chapter, when implications are discussed.

POSSIBLE ANTECEDENTS OF FATHER PARTICIPATION

Given the obvious importance of understanding *why* families adopt the particular patterns they do, especially for interpreting possible effects, it is surprising how few research studies have systematically examined this issue. Although there has been a noticeable shift recently toward the study of the antecedents of father participation (see Barnett & Baruch, 1984; Feldman, Nash, & Aschenbrenner, 1983; McHale & Huston, 1984), overall, research into fatherhood is still characterized by a lack of emphasis on the critical factors associated with whether and how a father will interact with his children (Russell, 1978).

The antecedents of nontraditional patterns would be expected to differ somewhat from those associated with whether a father in a traditional family becomes involved during evenings or on weekends when he is home from work. Families in which the father is unemployed and is the primary day-to-day caregiver, or in which he is employed and shares child care more or less equally with the mother but in which the mother too is employed, represent radical departures from accepted cultural beliefs and norms for family lifestyles. That this type of family pattern is adopted in the first place or is continued in the face of constant implicit or explicit social criticism (explored later), suggests that the underlying determinants must be very strong indeed. Although a few studies have considered the question of antecedents, clearcut statements of cause and effect can still not be made. Furthermore, the samples studied have rarely been selected in a random fashion, and research has tended to focus on the professional middle-class population. Antecedents might be very different in other populations.

What Do Parents Themselves Say?

In earlier research (Russell, 1983a), parental explanations for their nontraditional pattern were of four types, and these have since been given support by other research studies (e.g., Kimball, 1984; Radin, 1985): (1) the inability of the father to gain employment, (2) a desire to increase the family income (either by having both parents employed or having the mother employed when she has a greater earning capacity), (3) career factors, mainly associated with the strong desire of the mother to pursue a career, but also with the father having less interest in his job or career, and (4) egalitarian beliefs about child-care responsibilities and sex roles. Those who gave either of the first two types of explanation usually argued that the change was an economic necessity, whereas the others usually saw the change as being a matter of choice. As was noted, however (Russell, 1983a), all but 10 of the 71 families were better off financially after they changed to a nontraditional lifestyle. Families who saw the change in their employment and child-care patterns as a matter of choice were also more likely to be identified with the professional middle-class.

Russell (1983a) reported three other aspects of parental explanations. Many of the parents in dual-employment families said that they had opted for the father as the caregiver, rather than employing others to do this, because they believed very strongly that child care was the responsibility of individual families. Further, many said that they chose jobs and work hours that suited shared child care so that they could retain the major influence over their children's development. Second, mothers were perceived as being more influential over the decision to change lifestyles than were fathers. Mothers, however, were found to be more influential when the parents had been forced to change lifestyles, whereas fathers tended to be more influential when the change was seen as a matter of choice (Russell, 1983a).

Finally, the actual experience of a nontraditional lifestyle had the effect of changing the views of some, so that the reason they continued the lifestyle was seen as being different from the reason they adopted the lifestyle initially. Two reactions stood out as having the most impact: For mothers, it was the satisfaction they derived from their job; for fathers, it was the enjoyment they derived from having improved relationships with their children.

Although the family financial or employment situation is clearly prominent in parental explanations of a nontraditional lifestyle, and therefore needs to be given high priority in any discussion of possible antecedents, it is obvious that this factor cannot explain everything. There are several possibilities for family change, given economic and career demands. If a family is in financial difficulty, possible alternatives might be for the father to take a second job or for both parents to work and the children to be cared for by someone else. These alternatives, or course, are the most commonly chosen ones. Why is it, then, that in some families this problem is solved by having the father share in child care? And why is it that some of the families who have egalitarian beliefs choose this pattern and others do not? Are there any family or personal characteristics that make it more likely for a family to make this choice? Recent research indicates that there are, and it is these factors that will now be discussed.

Family Characteristics

Comparisons with traditional families show that nontraditional families are more likely to have fewer and older children. In the sample of 71 families studied by Russell (1983a), 52 percent had only one child, and only 10 had a child under 6 months of age (although all had a preschool-aged child). Two of the possible reasons for this are: Fathers will take on or continue in this lifestyle only if child-care demands are low (Radin, 1985), or fathers who care for fewer and older children conflict less with cultural beliefs about child care, such as the desirability of breastfeeding, the importance of mother-infant bonding, or the very strong belief that young babies need their mothers (see Lamb, Frodi, Hwang, & Frodi, 1982).

Potential for and Type of Employment

Findings from several studies show that this nontraditional family pattern is associated with mothers having higher status and potentially more rewarding jobs than their spouse (Kimball, 1984; Radin, 1985; Russell, 1983a). Associations with paternal employment characteristics have not been consistently reported, except that there is a trend toward fathers being less career oriented. Shared child care has also been found to be associated with flexibility in or reduced hours of employment (De Frain, 1979; Kimball, 1984; Radin, 1985; Russell, 1983a). Nevertheless, Russell (1983a) reported that in 29 percent of his sample, people had either changed their job, selected work hours to enable them to change caregiving patterns, or reduced their commitments to their job. This accommodation of work to family was more common for fathers than for mothers. Employment factors, therefore, might need to be considered in conjunction with other factors.

That the adoption of shared caregiving may be dependent on interaction between having job flexibility and other factors is supported by recent findings about participation patterns in the parental leave scheme in Sweden. Commenting on the consistent finding that flexibility in work hours and leave provisions does not result in a marked increase in fathers' family involvement, Lamb and colleagues (1984) argued that changes in institutional practices might be critical only for fathers who are highly motivated and feel they have the necessary skills.

Socialization Factors

One of the most obvious places to look for antecedents of paternal participation is in the father's own family experiences. Two hypotheses have been put forward (Radin, 1981; Sagi, 1982), and both have received support from studies in which fathers have been asked for retrospective accounts of their own fathers' involvement. Support for the hypothesis that fathers become highly participant as a reaction to their own fathers' lack of involvement comes both from research into nontraditional families (De Frain, 1979; Eiduson & Alexander, 1978; Kimball, 1984; Radin, 1985) and from studies of more traditional families (Barnett & Baruch, 1984; Russell, 1985). Support for the hypothesis that fathers model their own highly involved father comes from the study of Sagi (1982), who found high correlations between the two generations on six specific measures of involvement.

Equally, however, it may be that mothers' socialization experiences have an important bearing on the adoption of a nontraditional lifestyle, as this pattern involves a radical departure from cultural norms for them as well (being employed and not being the primary caregiver). As was reported previously, mothers were perceived to be more influential in the decision to change. A mother having had a nurturant relationship with her father as a child has been found to be associated with the adoption and continuation of a nontraditional family pattern (Radin, 1982, 1985) and with high father participation in traditional families (Feldman, Nash, & Aschenbrenner, 1983). A high degree of father involvement has also been associated with mothers whose own mother had been employed (Radin, 1982, 1985). Additional data presented here lend further support to the hypothesis that the mother plays an important role in both the adoption and maintenance of a nontraditional life-style.

Skills and Knowledge

Although research evidence now convincingly shows that fathers can be just as competent as mothers in child care, preparation for parenthood is still directed primarily at mothers, fathers being given only limited opportunities to learn basic child-care skills (Russell, 1983a, b). It is possible, therefore, that only fathers who have the necessary child-care skills become involved. In support of this hypothesis, nontraditional fathers, in comparison with traditional fathers, have been found to be more likely to have attended childbirth classes and the actual birth and to have read books on child rearing (Russell, 1983a). These factors may not be causally linked with father participation, as perhaps only committed and competent fathers seek out information to begin with. Nevertheless, they are consistent with two recent studies of traditional families. Parke and coworkers (1979) have shown that new fathers who were provided with information about child development in the hospital were more involved in child care three months later than were fathers not given such information. McHale and Huston

(1984) reported strong correlations between fathers' perceived skill at child-care tasks prior to their child's birth and involvement when their child was 3 to 15 months of age.

In contrast to these arguments, findings presented here show quite clearly that many fathers (like many mothers!) become caregivers without being particularly skillful or knowledgeable in the child-care or domestic areas. Other findings show, however, that the opportunity to acquire these skills "on the job" might be critical for the long-term satisfaction of fathers and therefore for whether the family continues in this pattern.

Personal Characteristics

Given both that there is an absence of role models for caregiving fathers and that this activity contradicts accepted cultural beliefs, it may be that only people who have high self-esteem and independence contemplate, adopt, or feel comfortable in going against the tide in this way. Little research has been conducted to investigate this hypothesis, although two findings give some support to it. Coysh (1983), in a study of traditional families, found that fathers with high self-esteem before the child arrived were more likely to become involved in child care. Russell (1983a) reported that nontraditional parents were more likely than traditional parents to value their children being "independent in thought and action" and less likely to value them "conforming to social norms," values that were consistent with their behavior and perhaps with their own personalities.

We might also expect nontraditional fathers to be more androgynous, that is, to endorse both traditional masculine characteristics (e.g., independence, self-confidence, assertiveness) and traditional feminine characteristics (e.g., interpersonal sensitivity, expressiveness), than traditional fathers. Findings do not support this hypothesis consistently, however. Studies by Russell (1983a) and Kimball (1984) provide positive evidence, whereas those by De Frain (1979), Lamb and colleagues (1982), and Radin (1982) with nontraditional families and McHale and Huston (1984) with traditional families provide contrary evidence.

Arguments about relationships among personality variables, sex-role orientation, and family lifestyles, of course, also present problems with regard to conclusions about cause and effect. We cannot be certain about what causes what—whether the lifestyle is a consequence of personality factors or whether the personality factors are a consequence of the lifestyle (see Abrahams, Feldman, & Nash, 1978). Further, it may yet be that while personality factors are not critical for adoption of the nontraditional lifestyle, they may be critical for the process of adjustment, especially if the parents perceive themselves as having been forced to change.

Sex-Role Ideology and Beliefs about Parenting

Pleck (1983), in a major review of findings across a range of family types, concluded that while these findings generally show a relationship between sex-role attitudes and male involvement in family work, the relationship is small in absolute terms. Nevertheless, sex-role ideology may be critical in the adoption of nontraditional patterns. It was seen previously that a group of parents explained their participation in nontraditional family patterns in terms of their egalitarian beliefs about sex roles, and this is consistent with findings reported by De Frain (1979) and with the arguments presented by Kimball (1984).

Beliefs about parenting competence might also be important. A common objection to proposals that fathers could share more in the responsibility for child care is that fathers are not competent (Russell, 1983b). In a survey of traditional families (Russell, 1983a), 78 percent of fathers and 66 percent of mothers agreed that a maternal instinct enabled mothers to be more competent caregivers, and 51 percent of fathers and 35 percent of mothers thought that fathers did not have the ability to care for children. In contrast, while nearly 50 percent of parents in nontraditional families agreed that mothers had a head start because of biology, 88 percent thought that fathers could be competent caregivers. We cannot know, of course, whether the experience of this family pattern has changed these parents' beliefs, but the hypothesis is reasonable that the beliefs people hold about parenting powerfully influence the type of child-care arrangement they adopt (especially when they perceive consequences for their children's development).

Beliefs about breadwinning and commitments to work and career could also be important contributors to the adoption of nontraditional patterns. There is a cultural expectation that fathers should be the primary breadwinners, and research studies show that fathers commonly define their family responsibilities in terms of breadwinning (Russell, 1983a). The evidence presented previously indicates that fathers in nontraditional families are less career and work oriented, and therefore are less likely to be constrained by cultural views about breadwinning responsibilities. Again, however, we cannot be certain whether this belief is an antecedent or a consequence of being in a nontraditional family. The findings of Radin (1985) suggest, however, that the belief might be critical for the maintenance of this family pattern.

Couple Support

A final antecedent of high paternal participation, which has been noted in studies of both nontraditional and traditional families, is the degree of support given by parents to each other (Cowan & Cowan, 1984). As was noted earlier, mothers have been found to be more influential in the decision to change to a nontraditional lifestyle. In their study of dual- and single-employment families, Barnett and Baruch (1984) reported that the mother's attitude to the male role is critical; as was reported earlier, McHale and Huston (1984) found that fathers are more involved when mothers have more egalitarian attitudes toward parenting. Further, Coysh (reported in Cowan & Cowan, 1984) found that the amount of father involvement is correlated with the spouse's rating of the father's competence in child care. Finally, in her follow-up study, Radin (1985) reported that the continuation of a nontraditional family pattern is associated with a father being supportive of his spouse in her career.

Longer-Term Considerations

Three research studies have followed primary caretaking and role-sharing fathers and their families over a period of time, and all point to the relative instability of this pattern. Lamb and colleagues (1982), who studied Swedish families in which fathers had taken paternity leave, found difficulty in retaining a sample of families in which the father was at home, despite the father's having planned before the birth to be at home. Unfortunately, little data are available concerning the reasons why these families reverted to more traditional patterns so quickly.

Russell (1983a) reinterviewed 27 of his sample of 71 families two years later. Only 10 of the 27 were in the same nontraditional family pattern, whereas 11 had reverted to the traditional family pattern, the mother being at home and the father employed. In four of the other six families the children were of school age and both parents were employed, but the mother took more responsibility for child care. Finally, in two families the parents had separated, with one family opting for a shared-custody arrangement. Two factors were identified in this study as being the most important for a reversion to traditional divisions of labor:

1.   The first factor was the extent to which the nontraditional pattern differed from cultural norms and expectations. Reversion was more likely when the children were very young and when the father was at home full-time. A situation in which a father is not employed and is caring for a 6-month-old, it can be argued, will generate more social disapproval than one in which a father is employed part-time and cares for a 4-year-old. Fathers, especially, reported that with time the absence of genuine social support made it more difficult to cope with the day-to-day demands of being in a nontraditional family.

2.   The second factor was economic in nature. Of the 11 families, 9 were better off financially after changing back. Indeed, two families who said that they reverted for financial reasons were among the most strongly committed to egalitarian values in the initial interview.

There did seem to be some lasting effects of shared child care, however. Mothers and fathers agreed that the improved father-child relationship continued, and that fathers were more involved and more willing to take responsibility for child care than they had been prior to having the child-care experience. These fathers were also found to be more highly partici-pant than a comparable group of traditional fathers.

In a third study, Radin (1985) recontacted the 20 fathers from her original sample who had been primary caregivers and found that only four were in exactly the same pattern four years later. Among the factors found to be critical for longer-term stability were residing in a community that was supportive of a nontraditional pattern, the mother having a high salary and a strong investment in her career (and being supported in this by her family), the father having flexibility in work hours and finding caring for children gratifying, and low demands of child care (in terms of numbers and characteristics of children).

Conclusions

It seems that there are many paths to the adoption of a family pattern in which the father is either the primary day-to-day caregiver or shares this with his spouse, and in which the mother is employed. No simple expla-nation has emerged as yet, and perhaps a simple explanation is not possible, given the diversity of the samples studied. It may be that in some families, financial factors provide the necessary and sufficient con-ditions, at least for the initial decision to change; for others, financial considerations might represent necessary preconditions for change, but the change may be mediated by sex-role self-concepts and beliefs; and for still others, fathers having the necessary skills and confidence and moth-ers having egalitarian beliefs about parental roles, combined with em-ployment flexibility, might provide the necessary and sufficient condi-tions (even to the extent of being critical in the decision to have only one or two children). The evidence reviewed here also suggests that these variables might combine in complex ways within families. Future re-search, therefore, will need to place more emphasis on investigation of the complex interaction between these variables if we are to improve our understanding of this type of family pattern and the effects that it might have on family members.

CONSEQUENCES OF HIGH FATHER INVOLVEMENT

Whenever there is talk about fathers being caregivers, one of the first questions asked is: "What about the children, what effect will it have on them?" Some have advocated shared parenting, with the argument that this is likely to have a positive effect on children (Baumrind, 1980). In contrast, an issue that has been given much less attention is the impact that this family pattern might have on fathers and mothers. Given the interactive nature of the family system, an emphasis on the consequences and effects for all family members seems especially important. This is the approach taken here.

Before reviewing the literature, it is necessary to draw attention to some of the methodological limitations of studies conducted to date. Most of the few studies that have focused on the effects of nontraditional lifestyles have relied either on comparisons between nontraditional and traditional families or on correlations between paternal involvement and child-development measures. No comprehensive study has been conducted in which large samples of randomly selected families were examined before and after the adoption of a nontraditional lifestyle. Few studies have provided complete details of child care and employment patterns for both fathers and mothers, information that is critical for the interpretation of effects. Neither have studies systematically reported the antecedents of the adoption of a nontraditional lifestyle. Further, the consequences of this action are likely to be very different depending on whether it was chosen or not and on whether or not both parents are satisfied with it, irrespective of why they adopted the pattern in the first place. As has been noted elsewhere (Russell, 1982, 1983a), parents in this type of family may differ from other parents on a whole range of variables (e.g., commitment and sensitivity to children, personality), and any effects may be associated with these rather than with specific differences in father involvement.

Effects on Children

As mentioned previously, the possible effects on children of caregiving by the father have been emphasized in popular discussions. People tend to polarize into two groups: those who want to be shown how such caregiving can have a positive effect, and those who want to be convinced that it will not have a detrimental effect. Many express fears about "damaging" effects such as children not being well adjusted because fathers do not have the ability to form the necessary attachment relationships with them; fathers lacking the sensitivity that mothers have and thus becoming frustrated more easily and abusing their children; fathers not being able to handle the intimacy of child-care and incest being a possible outcome; and children becoming confused by the change in roles, with male children being more likely than those in other families to develop a homosexual orientation (Russell, 1983a, 1983b).

Although the proposition that high father involvement will result in quite significant changes in child development is an attractive one, the effects might not necessarily be very great at all. For one thing, the family represents just one of a wide range of possible influences over the children; others include the media, peers, etc. Furthermore, the quantity and content of parent-child interactions are but two of a multitude of possible contributors to parental child-rearing practices and parental influences over children. Other potential contributors include the quality of interaction (e.g., the sensitivity and warmth of parents' responses to children), parental values and beliefs, and the characteristics of the children themselves. The findings presented in the following are generally consistent with this argument that the effects on children may not be very dramatic.

Father-Child Relationships.   Caregiving fathers have been found to differ from traditional fathers in time spent with their children and the frequency and content of interactions (Russell, 1983a). Differences therefore might be expected in the quality of father-child relationships, and findings from the father's perspective presented later strongly support this hypothesis. Results of the study by Lamb and colleagues (1982) comparing nontraditional (defined as fathers who have been primary caregivers for at least a month—the average was 2.8 months) and traditional Swedish families, however do not. Observational data were collected at 3 months, 8 months, 12 months, and 16 months after the birth; the 12-month data collection also involving an assessment of security of attachment. Overall, the findings indicated few differences in father-child relationships between the two family types. However, this study has several methodological limitations which make its results questionable with regard to the effects of high father involvement. Further, Lamb and coworkers (1983) have argued that the most critical variables for the quality of father-child relationships might not be those involved only with time spent at home with children but rather those associated with play. In comparison with relatively uninvolved U. S. fathers, nontraditional Swedish fathers are not renowned for their playfulness.

Sex-Role Development.   The possible impact of nontraditional child-care patterns on children's sex-role development has been investigated by Radin (1982) in the United States and by Sagi (1982) in Israel. Both defined father involvement in the same way, focused on preschool-aged children, and used the same outcome measure (the It Scale), although, as was noted by Radin and Russell (1983), there were other significant methodologic differences. In neither study was high father involvement found to be associated with boys' sex-role development. Sagi, however, found that it was associated with girls scoring higher on masculinity traits. Differences in the types of sample used (e.g., in Sagi's sample 55 percent of the mothers were not employed) and the fact that the studies were conducted in different countries are likely to explain these differences in findings. Given the methodological problems of both studies, however, it is difficult to accept either one as having provided an adequate test of the effects of high father involvement.

Cognitive Development.   Radin (1982) has reported positive correlations between the degree of father involvement and verbal intelligence scores for both boys and girls. Highly involved fathers also spent more time in efforts to stimulate their children's cognitive growth; this difference between nontraditional and traditional fathers was more pronounced for sons than for daughters. Although the latter finding suggests that the "effect" on cognitive test performance is associated with increased stimulation from two involved parents (in most families there is usually only one, the mother), it may yet be that it is associated with fathers being more achievement oriented (see Lamb, Pleck, & Levine, 1985).

Social Competence.   Both Radin (1982) and Sagi (1982) examined relationships between father participation and children's level of empathy and locus of control, both using the same tests. Sagi (but not Radin) reported that children of highly involved fathers were more empathetic, suggesting a direct association of this trait with these fathers being more supportive, nurturant, sensitive, and warm. Both studies agreed that high father participation is associated with increased levels of internality. This latter finding is as we might expect: Parents may need to be focused on internality in order to engage in a nontraditional lifestyle.

Conclusions.   It is difficult at this very early stage of research to be confident about drawing any conclusions. The findings discussed here are derived from very few studies, all of which have one or more major methodologic inadequacies. Because of the absence of details about the exact nature of father involvement, we cannot be certain whether an adequate test of the effects of high father participation has been made. Further, most of the research to date has focused on the impact of a nontraditional life-style on very young children. Studies are needed that focus on the possible longer-term effects for sex-role development, adolescent and adult attitudes and interests, and the types of parental roles adopted.

It appears obvious from these studies, however, that caregiving fathers have neither a dramatic negative nor a dramatic positive effect on their children. The studies offer little support for those who express fears about possible negative consequences or for those who want to demonstrate positive effects. Rather, the most remarkable aspect of the findings is just how little effect the change appears to have. This conclusion is consistent with the assessments by parents reported by Russell (1983a). In this study, 76 percent of fathers and 64 percent of mothers in nontraditional families said that their children had not experienced difficulties with the father being the caregiver, and many were surprised that this hadn't had a major impact. No fathers reported continuing major problems and only 6 percent of mothers. None talked in terms of sex-role development or improved cognitive performance. In contrast, parents were much more likely to report consequences for themselves and for their marital relationship. These findings are discussed next.

Effects on Fathers

A common reaction from parents participating in a nontraditional lifestyle is that the person who gains most is the father (Russell, 1983a). While findings generally agree with this, it is not all plain sailing, and many fathers report experiencing major difficulties, especially if they feel that they have been forced to change. Consequences for fathers are evident in their relationships with their children and in their personal development.

Father-Child Relationship. In contrast to earlier reported findings from observational studies, mothers and fathers in nontraditional families report major changes in the father-child relationship in three dimensions: Closeness, sensitivity, and tension and conflict. Both Grønseth (1978) and Russell (1983a) reported that fathers become closer to their children. Parents in Russell's (1983a) study were asked what the major advantage of a nontraditional lifestyle was for fathers. Approximately two thirds of both mothers and fathers said that it was the improved relationship between father and child, and the same number reported that this was because fathers were physically closer to their children. Several other studies have reported a similar finding for highly participant fathers in traditional families (see Russell and Radin, 1983, for a review).

Grønseth (1978) and Russell (1983a) also reported that a nontraditional child-care pattern results in fathers understanding their children better and being more sensitive to them. Fathers in Russell's (1983a) study also reported that it was not just the increased time they spent with their children that affected their understanding, but the way in which the time was spent. Specifically, fathers argued that the most important factor was spending time alone with their children and taking sole responsibility for them on a continuing day-to-day basis. Fathers also reported that this increased understanding and sensitivity had produced a change in their views about their roles as parents; they felt more self-confident and effective.

Increased tension and conflict in father-child relationships has been noted as another outcome of the frustrations and demands of being a full-time caregiver (Russell, 1983a; see also Russell and Radin, 1983). However, this has not been viewed as an entirely negative consequence. Many mothers welcomed the better balance in parent-child relationships and what they saw as a more realistic father-child relationship. Some fathers also looked on it as a personal development experience, seeing their reactions to the increased tension and conflict as providing them with insights into themselves.

Additional issues have been raised in groups conducted for fathers that have not yet been included in published studies. Perhaps these issues have not emerged in studies to date because of the relatively young age groups being examined. An experience of nontraditional fathers who have older children is that they sometimes find themselves in conflict with their teenagers who expect greater conformity to social norms. One father reported that he was in constant conflict with his son because he was perceived as not being a "normal" father—unlike the son's friends' fathers, he did not spend his hours helping his son with his car or taking him to football matches. Another father had conflicts with his teenage daughter because she did not want him to participate in her school, helping out in the canteen, supervising classes, and so on.

It should be noted here that the studies discussed, and others to be reviewed subsequently, also suffer from methodological limitations, and findings should be treated with caution. All are self-report studies; none includes data collected before and after the adoption of a nontraditional pattern.

Personal Development.   Few fathers were able to anticipate the difficulties they encountered staying at home caring for children (Russell, 1983a). Although many looked on their new job with enthusiasm and had expectations about what they would be able to achieve while at home (e.g., renovating the house), commonly these expectations had to be completely revised because of the demanding nature of child care, especially in the first few months. Similar to most "new" mothers, 45 percent of the fathers in Russell's (1983a) sample reported that they had difficulty in the initial stages of child-care in *adjusting to the demands* associated with child care and housework (the constancy, boredom, physical work, and lack of adult company). Further, changing back to a traditional lifestyle was often associated with the father having had difficulty adjusting to being the full-time caregiver/homemaker. Fathers reported that the process of adjustment was more difficult because of the lack of support from male friends and neighbors. Only 27 percent of fathers in this sample said that their male peers were generally supportive of their heavy commitment to child care.

Several recent studies have found that fathers who are more highly participant in child-care report *enhanced self-esteem, self-confidence,* or *satisfaction* with their parental role (Grønseth, 1978; Lamb et al., 1982; Lein, 1979; Russell, 1983a; Sagi, 1982). Russell (1983a) suggests that increased self-esteem and satisfaction are associated with the fathers having taken on a job that men are not normally expected to be capable of performing, being subject to a good deal of criticism from others and experiencing difficulties in adjusting, but after all that, considering themselves and being considered by others as having been successful.

Russell (1983a) reports that a common response from fathers and mothers in nontraditional families is that the father's experiences produced a major *shift in his attitudes* toward children (e.g., he placed more value on child welfare), child-care (e.g., he was more sensitive to the needs for family support systems), and the role of women (e.g., he had more egalitarian views about male/female roles). Changed attitudes in these areas were rated as a major *advantage* of the change in roles by 24 percent of fathers, and (probably of greater importance) by 26 percent of mothers.

One of the most obvious possible consequences for fathers is that they may not feel comfortable in the child-care role and will see it as a threat to their identity and status as a male. Cultural stereotypes of masculinity do not include nurturant or caregiving behavior, and males are expected to fulfill an instrumental role in the paid work force—to be the breadwinner. Indeed, this is an integral part of male socialization in most Western societies. Yet only 1 of 16 fathers in Grønseth's (1978) study, and 5 of 71 in Russell's (1983a) study, reported any major difficulty with their identity as males. However, 28 percent rated the loss of status and the reduction in self-esteem associated with paid employment as major disadvantages of their lifestyle. Russell (1983a) has suggested two possible reasons for the small numbers who were concerned about these issues: (1) More may have been concerned about them but found it difficult to admit this during an interview, and (2) it may be that only those fathers who do not identify strongly with cultural stereotypes of masculinity and are not as career or work oriented become involved in this type of family pattern in the first place. The findings discussed previously tend to support the latter hypothesis.

A small number of fathers reported feeling relieved about not having to carry all the responsibility for family income and career success. In families where both parents were employed, some fathers reported that they no longer felt the need to push so hard in their careers (Russell, 1983a).

Effects on Mothers

As with fathers, we cannot be certain at this stage of research about what impact the nontraditional caregiving pattern has on mothers. In addition, researchers have tended to place more emphasis on the fathers and the children. As has already been mentioned, any effects on mothers will also be mediated by the reasons why families adopt the nontraditional pattern in the first place, and especially by whether the pattern has been chosen or has been forced on the family. Effects on mothers are likely to resemble those already noted in the maternal employment literature, although many differences are likely as well because of the nature of the child-care pattern. Possible effects for mothers noted here are for the mother-child relationship and the impact of paid employment.

Mother-Child Relationship.   Two research studies are relevant in this context: the Swedish observational study of Lamb and colleagues (1982) and the Australian interview study of Russell (1983a). Lamb and coworkers (1982) reported that the quality of the mother-child relationship in nontraditional Swedish families does not differ significantly from that in traditional families, indicating the absence of an overall detrimental effect of the family's lifestyle. This finding is consistent with Russell's (1983a) interview study, in which 67 percent of mothers and 59 percent of fathers reported that the mother-child relationship had not changed in any significant way. Nevertheless, other data suggested that the mothers were concerned about having less contact with their children and had feelings of guilt about leaving their children. Thirty-three percent of mothers reported that they disliked having reduced contact with their children, and worried that they were missing and losing influence over their children. In the follow-up study of families who returned to a traditional lifestyle, this reduced contact with children was rated by mothers (and especially those who felt they had been forced to change) as a major disadvantage of shared caregiving.

Employment: A Mixed Reaction.   High on the list of positive consequences for mothers were increased satisfaction, self-esteem, and independence associated with employment (Radin, 1985; Russell, 1983a). Such a finding is consistent with the bias in the samples toward more highly educated and career-oriented women. Similar to findings from studies of employed mothers, mothers in nontraditional families reported that having dual roles meant that they constantly felt physically and emotionally exhausted. This was also mentioned by mothers who reverted to the traditional lifestyle as a major disadvantage of their previous lifestyle. But as has been suggested by Russell (1983a), it may be that in families where mothers experienced role overload most acutely, fathers were not highly participant in housework. Systematic data are not available on the degree to which fathers at home share in all aspects of family work, although anecdotal reports (Russell, 1983a) tend to suggest that mothers still retain more responsibility for housework.

Consequences for Couple Relationships

High value is usually placed on marital stability in Western societies, and the divorce rate is often used by various groups as an indicator of social or moral decay. Despite this, little research has been conducted on the marital relationship in nontraditional families. Only one study provides any systematic data on the marital relationship (Russell, 1983a), and this one suffers yet again from methodologic limitations and therefore must be regarded with caution when discussing cause and effect. It does have the strength, however, of having data collected in two ways: with use of the Spanier Dyadic Adjustment Scale (Spanier, 1976) and comparison of scores from nontraditional and traditional families; and from an in-depth interview that probed perceptions of changes in the marital relationship. Summary data are presented here for these two aspects of the study, and a final section focuses more specifically on the nature of conflicts between mothers and fathers.

Marital Quality.   Comparisons between traditional and nontraditional families on the Spanier Dyadic Adjustment Scale revealed that the latter group scored lower overall, indicating marital relationships of a poorer quality. A closer inspection of the findings, however, revealed that this difference was primarily attributable to differences in responses on one subscale, *dyadic satisfaction.* Nontraditional parents were more likely to have recently considered ending their relationship, to have had recent quarrels, and to have been irritated by one another. These findings can be interpreted in several ways. The nontraditional families might have had poor relationships before they changed their lifestyle. A nontraditional lifestyle may very well have the effect of increasing tension in these areas of the marital relationship, especially given the problems that might be associated with negotiating new family patterns and new divisions of labor. Or it may be that because of their experiences, nontraditional parents are more sensitive to these issues and are more open about reporting these intimate aspects of their relationships in an interview. Additional data presented by Russell (1983a) suggest that fathers in these families rate their marital relationships higher when they are more influential in the decision to change and when they have chosen this lifestyle, and mothers rate their relationships higher when fathers are more highly participant in family work. The number of hours spent by either mothers or fathers in paid work was of little consequence by itself.

Perceptions of Changes.   Parents in Russell's (1983a) study were asked whether a nontraditional lifestyle had changed their marital relationship. Approximately 45 percent reported positive consequences, including increased sensitivity, understanding, and equality. About 40 percent reported negative consequences, including greater conflict and dissatisfaction and problems associated with the rushed lifestyle (e.g., tiredness, irritability, and less time spent together). Further, the majority of families reported that these difficulties were more acute during the first few months of changing their family pattern. During this period there was more uncertainty about child-care and housework responsibilities, and both had to cope with the physical and emotional demands of new jobs.

An increase in conflict in the first few months of such a radical change in lifestyle is to be expected. It is probably all the more likely if people are genuinely trying to share equally the responsibilities for child care and housework. The attempt to do this in a serious way might sensitize people to the problems and thus produce more conflicts. Whether this is necessarily a negative thing is an open question. The distinct impression from the interviews presented by Russell (1983a) is that those couples who "stuck at it" and attempted to communicate their problems and doubts to one another viewed it as a positive experience.

Tensions and Conflicts.   Russell (1983a) presented extensive data on the tensions and conflicts that emerged as part of the process of renegotiating family tasks and responsibilities, but especially in renegotiating a new balance in the nature of the male/female relationship. These issues are particularly relevant to those who are involved in counseling or education of parents. Understandably, mothers and fathers saw these tensions and conflicts from slightly different perspectives.

One of the tensions experienced by fathers concerned the reluctance of their partner to let them make decisions about the children or housework. Some fathers resented their partners considering them to be the secondary parent or simply "the helper." One father felt that he was not given the same independence to develop at home that his partner was given to develop outside the home; another was angry because he felt that his partner considered the child to be hers and he was just looking after it.

These findings confirm the arguments of others (e.g., Hoffman, 1983): Some mothers may be reluctant to give up their power and status within the domestic domain. This is consistent with findings that mothers may not be as keen to have fathers more involved in child care as we might expect. A national survey conducted in the United States has found that only 23 percent of employed and 31 percent of nonemployed "wives" would like "more help with the children" from their husband (Pleck, 1982). At the same time, however, the findings from nontraditional families question the suggestions by some (e.g., Bryson, 1983) that this reluctance is simply associated with the lack of power and status that women have in the public domain. Clearly there is something more involved, as the majority of these women were in relatively high-status jobs.

Tension reportedly has also resulted from an apparent lack of genuine support given by mothers to their partners (Russell, 1983a). Although it might reasonably be expected that mothers would be very supportive of the fathers in their nontraditional job (see Harper, 1980), this was not always found to be the case, and some fathers became resentful. Although the majority of spouses accepted the father as being a competent caregiver, and many even displayed pride in the fact that their spouse was the primary caregiver, many found it difficult to accept their husbands in "the domestic role," or the fact that their husbands sometimes became frustrated and depressed and were not always able to keep the house up to standard. Failure of the spouse to fully acknowledge the problems and doubts of the father in the caregiving role was also reported (Russell, 1983a). It was suggested by some fathers that their spouses had stereotyped assumptions of men and did not expect them to have problems, and so were not sensitive to the clues that they gave when they felt a need to talk about their problems.

Mothers, especially, had difficulty in accepting a change in the balance of affective relationships between parents and children (Russell, 1983a). Many resented the fact that the children became more closely attached to the father and went to him when they needed comfort and support. Mothers also became irritated because their spouses' standards of housework and child care were not as high as they wanted them to be. Fathers, too, were frequently seen as being too soft with the children and inclined to allow them to have the run of the house. A final area of resentment from mothers concerned the status and credit that other people (especially other women) often gave their spouse because of his involvement in child care. The comment that irritated most was, "Oh, isn't he marvelous." As these mothers pointed out, they had been the caregiver before, and no one had referred to them as being marvelous because of it.

Tensions in Male/Female Relationships.   Russell (1983a) also reported tensions between fathers and women with whom they came in contact in the community. Although women were generally more supportive of this lifestyle than were men, some fathers, especially those very committed to the child-care job, sometimes doubted the genuineness of the support from other women. Much is said about how men feel threatened by women changing roles, but very little is said about how women might feel threatened by men wanting to share more in child care. Fathers who shared in child care sometimes found themselves described by women as just good babysitters; not trusted by other mothers to care for their children (because of the fear of child abuse); not accepted by women as one of the group in the neighborhood or at school functions; and not given genuine support during some of the tough times that occurred while caring for the children. Some fathers also discussed the problems involved in developing a close supportive network with women in the neighborhood, because many saw this as a threat to marital relationships. What all this might mean in the longer term is that fathers at home become even more socially isolated than women at home. This issue obviously requires more attention by researchers and practitioners.

Fathers who stuck at the task of shared child care often became extremely sensitive to how others reacted to them. Simple statements like, "Gee, Joan must feel lucky to have you helping so much with the children," became big issues for some fathers. Would it ever be said that "John was lucky to have Joan helping so much with the children"? This issue about fathers being given equal status and presuming equal parenting opportunities is discussed in the summary.

SUMMARY AND CONCLUSIONS

Given both the paucity of research into two-parent families in which the father is either the primary caregiver or shares this task more or less equally with the mother, and the major problems of methodology noted throughout this chapter, conclusions are necessarily limited. Research studies conducted to date indicate that a multitude of factors possibly antecede or facilitate the adoption of this type of nontraditional family pattern, and that these factors interact in complex ways within individual families. Two major groups of families have been identified: those who have adopted this pattern essentially out of economic necessity and those who have chosen this lifestyle because of considerations of career aspirations for mothers or commitments to egalitarian male/female roles. Other factors that have been found to be important are the presence of fewer and older children; mothers being highly educated and having a high-status job; mothers and fathers being employed in jobs that permit some flexibility in career structure and work times; the socialization experiences of fathers and mothers; fathers who have had prior experience in child care; the personality characteristics of mothers and fathers; nontraditional beliefs about parental competence; and support and encouragement from the mother for the father to adopt a nontraditional pattern.

Another factor to emerge was that people were changed by their experiences in a nontraditional lifestyle. Some fathers became very positive about their relationships with their children; with time, they emphasized this rather than economic factors as the reason why they continued. Equally true, however, was the fact that despite having said they chose to be caregivers because of their strong commitment to egalitarianism, some fathers found the demands too great and quickly reverted to a more traditional pattern. It would be a mistake, therefore, to consider the issues associated with this lifestyle simply in terms of the initial reasons for adopting the pattern, and to expect that those who have chosen it rather than it choosing them will necessarily experience less difficulty.

As has been detailed, problems of method preclude definitive statements about the effects of this lifestyle. In general, however, findings do not indicate that having the father as the primary caregiver has a dramatically negative effect on families. As far as the children are concerned, findings are more remarkable for the absence of reported effects! Fathers and mothers both perceived the major benefits of this lifestyle to be the improved father-child relationship and the increased sensitivity and understanding that fathers had of their children and of child-care issues as a result of their experiences. An experience that was seen as especially critical was that of having responsibility for the day-to-day care of their children. For mothers the major benefits were the increased satisfaction, self-esteem, and independence they gained from being in paid employment.

The research reviewed here, however, does reveal that adjustment problems are common for both mothers and fathers. Findings especially highlighted the difficulties that fathers had in adjusting to the demands of child care and domestic life, to the loss of status from not being employed, and to the lack of support from their male peers and women at the neighborhood level; the difficulties that mothers had in coping with feelings of guilt about leaving their children, adjusting to the reduced contact and influence that they felt they had over their children, adjusting to having dual roles, and feeling tired and rushed; poorer marital relationships during the early period of change (especially in families where the change was seen as being necessary); and continuing tensions between mothers and fathers about power and influence in the child-care and domestic domains and in their relationships with their children.

Given the assumption that the nontraditional family pattern described here is likely to become more common in the future and it will continue to include two major groups—those who have been forced into the pattern for economic reasons, and those who choose to adopt it for a range of personal characteristics and opportunities provided by their own employment—it seems important that more attention be given to this pattern by researchers, family practitioners, and family educators. Attention is also warranted because of the increasing emphasis being given to the problems many see as resulting from a lack of shared parenting (Russell, 1984). Encouraging more equality in parenting has been seen as relevant for increasing the employment options for women, reducing the psychological difficulties women experience in carrying the major burden of child care, and reducing the problems that children experience when mothers have the sole responsibility for them (see Chapter 7). Further consideration of issues associated with shared parenting, requires that more attention be given to two issues in particular—responsibility for child management and socialization and equality of parenting opportunities.

Responsibility for Child Management and Socialization

Little attention has been given by researchers to issues of responsibility for child management and socialization. As has been pointed out here and in Chapter 1, there need not be a high correlation between time available, task performance, and the degree of responsibility taken. While it has become more common for researchers and policymakers to broaden their concepts of family tasks and to talk in terms of responsibilities (e.g., Baruch & Barnett, 1984; Lamb, Pleck, Charnov, & Levine, 1986; Russell, 1983a; Russell & Radin, 1983), there has been little attempt to define or evaluate critically the concept of responsibility. A definition of responsibility would include tasks such as decision making, planning, monitoring and anticipating children's needs, feelings, and behaviors. The degree to which responsibilities are shared could be highly critical for the adoption and continuation of the nontraditional family pattern, for general parental satisfaction, and for child-development outcomes.

Research indicates that there is less likelihood for sharing of responsibilities for child management and socialization if there is no continuing day-to-day involvement in child care and family work. Studies of traditional families indicate that very few fathers take responsibility for child management. In my own research (Russell, 1983a), parents were asked who had the overall responsibility for children. Shared responsibility was reported by one percent of parents in traditional families, five percent of those in which mothers were employed part-time, and 18 percent of those in which mothers were employed full-time. Kotelchuck (1976), again focusing on global aspects of responsibility, reported that in only 7.5 percent of his families did fathers share child-care responsibilities equally. Finally, in a recent study by Baruch and Barnett (1984), responsibility defined as "remembering, planning and scheduling" was assessed for 11 child-care tasks. Of the 160 fathers, 113 were not responsible for any tasks, 35 were responsible for one, and 12 were responsible for two or three.

In contrast to these findings, shared responsibility was reported in 47 percent of nontraditional families in Russell's (1983a) study. Indeed, a common argument from fathers who shared the day-to-day child care was that it was only through taking the sole and extended responsibility for the care of their children that they gained the knowledge and experience necessary for them to share more specific responsibilities for child management and socialization and to develop close relationships with their children. Given this finding, it may be that those interested in encouraging shared responsibilities for parenting might place more emphasis on fathers spending time as caregivers.

Equality of Parenting Opportunities

Despite the recent emphasis on fathers, especially on the "new breed" of highly involved ones, both in research and in the media, little evidence indicates that such emphasis has produced a fundamental shift in presumptions about parenting. It is still common for fathers to be seen as secondary parents in research or to appear to be tacked on as necessary "afterthoughts" in parent education material (Russell, 1983b, 1984). Further, the presumption that the mother is the primary parent is implicit in many of the policy initiatives associated with increasing employment options for women (e.g., maternity leave, arguments about funding for child care, permanent part-time work).

Support for this presumption also comes from findings discussed in this chapter concerning highly committed fathers who became very sensitive to the lack of genuine support from women and to the apparent reluctance of others to give them full status as parents. Many felt that they were considered secondary parents and that little social equality existed in the parenting domain. They also became sensitive to the basic sexist approach of many institutions, policies, and advertisements that simply assume that only mothers have any responsibility for children.

If shared parenting and fathers having a major commitment to parenting responsibilities are to become *real* options, and if fathers and families are to receive genuine support in these patterns, a fundamental shift to a *presumption* of equality of parenting opportunities may be needed, a presumption similar to the one most Western societies currently have about equal employment opportunities for women. The argument with employment is that policies and practices *should* be adopted that presume equality of opportunities and choices.

In the same way, policies and practices could be adopted which acknowledge that both mothers and fathers have parenting responsibilities, and which aim to facilitate equality of parenting opportunities and choices. Changes which might facilitate this process include (1) the development of policies that acknowledge the interaction between male involvement in child care and women's employment opportunities; (2) a greater recognition and acceptance by employers of work/family conflicts for both mothers and fathers; (3) the development of alternatives to work-related skills/personal development courses for women, including programs and services that might both expand men's options to participate more extensively in their family and help employees cope with the difficulties of balancing work and family commitments; (4) implementation of parenting courses for boys (in school) and for fathers (e.g., in hospitals or places of employment), to give them greater opportunities to learn child-care skills; (5) special initiatives to develop support and information groups for men and fathers (see Klinman, Kohl, & The Fatherhood Project, 1984); development of couple parent-education and support programs (especially during the antenatal and postnatal periods) that emphasize the difficulties that fathers and mothers both have in sharing child care (see Cowan & Cowan, 1984; Jackson, 1984); and routine involvement of fathers when family services are provided.

These arguments for equality of parenting opportunities, are not meant to imply that the nontraditional family pattern described in this chapter is ideal and should be the preferred pattern. Rather, they are based on acceptance of the fact that current employment structure, social policies, social institutions, attitudes, and beliefs reduce the real options families have to adopt shared parenting. The presumption of equality of parenting opportunities, therefore, is seen as the basis for establishing more realistic choices for families and for facilitating the adjustment process of families in which the father is the caregiver either by choice or by necessity.

REFERENCES

Abrahams, B., Feldman, S. S., & Nash, S. C. (1978). Sex-role self-concept and sex-role attitudes: Enduring personality characteristics, or adaptations to changing life situations. *Developmental Psychology, 14,* 393–400.

Barnett, R. C. & Baruch, G. K. (1984). Determinants of fathers' participation in family work. Wellesley, MA: Wellesley College Center for Research on Women.

Baumrind, D. (1980). New directions in socialization research. *American Psychologist, 35,* 639–652.

Bryson, L. (1983). Thirty years of research on the division of labour in Australian families. *Australian Journal of Sex, Marriage and Family, 4,* 125–132.

Cowan, C. P. & Cowan, P. A. (1984). Becoming a father: Individual and marital aspects of father involvement. In P. Berman & F. Pedersen (Eds.), *Father transitions to parenthood.* Bethesda, MD.

Coysh, W. S. (1983). Predictive and concurrent factors related to fathers' involvement in childrearing. Paper presented to American Psychological Association, Anaheim, CA.

De Frain, J. (1979). Androgynous parents tell who they are and what they need. *The Family Coordinator, 28,* 237–243.

Eiduson, B. T. & Alexander, J. W. (1978). The role of children in alternative family styles. *Social Issues, 34,* 149–167.

Feldman, S. S., Nash, S. C., & Aschenbrenner, B. G. (1983). Antecedents of fathering. *Child Development, 54,* 1628–1636.

Field, T. (1978). Interaction behaviors of primary versus secondary caretaker fathers. *Developmental Psychology, 49,* 183–184.

Gronseth, E. (1978). Work sharing: A Norwegian example. In R. Rapoport & R. N. Rapoport (Eds.), *Working couples.* St. Lucia, Queensland: University of Queensland Press.

Harper, J. (1980). *Fathers at home.* Melbourne: Penguin.

Hoffman, L. W. (1983). Increased fathering: Effects on the mother. In M. E. Lamb & A. Sagi (Eds.), *Fatherhood and family policy.* Hillsdale, NJ: Erlbaum.

Jackson, B. (1984). *Fatherhood.* London: George Allen & Unwin.

Kimball, G. (1984). Why do couples role share? Unpublished paper, University of California, Chico, CA.

Klinman, D. G., Kohl, R., & The Fatherhood Project (1984). *Fatherhood U.S.A.* New York: Garland.

Kotelchuck, M. (1976). The infant's relationship to the father: Experimental evidence. In M. E. Lamb (Ed.), *The role of the father in child development.* New York: Wiley.

Lamb, M. E. (Ed.) (1981). *The role of the father in child development.* (Rev. ed.) New York: Wiley.

Lamb, M. E., Frodi, M., Hwang, C.-P., & Frodi, A. M. (1983). Effects of paternal involvement on infant preferences for mothers and fathers. *Child Development, 54,* 450–458.

Lamb, M. E., Frodi, A. M., Hwang, C.-P., Frodi, M., & Steinberg, J. (1982). Mother- and father-infant interaction involving play and holding in traditional and nontraditional Swedish families. *Developmental Psychology, 18,* 215–221.

Lamb, M. E., Pleck, J. H., Charnov, E. L., & Levine, J. A. (1986). A biosocial perspective on paternal behavior and involvement. In J. B. Lancaster, J. Altmann, A. Rossi, & L. Sherrod (Eds.), *Parenting across the lifespan: Biosocial perspectives.* Chicago: Aldine.

Lamb, M. E., Pleck, J. H., & Levine, J. A. (1985). The role of the father in child development: The effects of increased paternal involvement. In B. B. Lahey & A. E. Kazdin (Eds.), *Advances in clinical child psychology* (Vol. 8). New York: Plenum.

Lein, L. (1979). Male participation in home life: Impact of social supports and breadwinner responsibility on the allocation of tasks. *The Family Coordinator, 29,* 489–496.

Levine, J. (1976). *Who will raise the children? New options for fathers (and mothers).* New York: Bantam.

McHale, S. M., & Huston, T. L. (1984). Men and women as parents: Sex role orientations, employment, and parental roles with infants. *Child Development, 55,* 1349–1361.

Parke, R. D., Hymel, S., Power, T. G., & Tinsley, B. R. (1979). Fathers and risk: A hospital based model of intervention. In D. B. Sawin, R. C. Hawkins, L. O. Walker, & J. H. Penticuff (Eds.), *Psychosocial risks in infant-environment transactions.* New York: Brunner/Mazel.

Pleck, J. H. (1982). Husbands' and wives' paid work, family work, and adjustment. Wellesley MA: Wellesley College Center for Research on Women.

Pleck, J. H. (1983). Husbands' paid work and family roles: Current research issues. In H. Z. Lopata & J. H. Pleck (Eds.), *Research on the interweave of social roles (Vol. 3): Families and Jobs.* Greenwich, CT: JAI Press.

Radin, N. (1981). Childrearing fathers in intact families: An exploration of some antecedents and consequences. *Merrill-Palmer Quarterly, 27,* 489–514.

Radin, N. (1982). Primary caregiving and role-sharing fathers of pre-schoolers. In M. E. Lamb (Ed.), *Nontraditional families: Parenting and child development.* Hillsdale, NJ: Erlbaum.

Radin, N. (1985, February). Antecedents of stability in high father involvement. Paper presented at Conference on Equal Parenting: Families of the future, University of California, Chico, CA.

Radin, N., & Russell, G. (1983). Increased father participation and child development outcomes. In M. E. Lamb & A. Sagi (Eds.), *Fatherhood and family policy.* Hillsdale, NJ: Erlbaum.

Russell, G. (1978). The father role and its relation to masculinity, femininity and androgyny. *Child Development, 49,* 1174–1181.

Russell, G. (1982). Shared-caregiving families: An Australian study. In M. E. Lamb (Ed.), *Nontraditional families: Parenting and child development.* Hillsdale, NJ: Erlbaum.

Russell, G. (1983a). *The changing role of fathers?* St. Lucia, Queensland: University of Queensland Press.

Russell, G. (1983b). *A practical guide for fathers*. Melbourne, Australia: Thomas Nelson.

Russell, G. (1984). Changing patterns of divisions of labor for paid work and child care. Paper presented to ISA–CFR International Seminar on Social Change and Family Policies, Melbourne, Australia.

Russell, G. (1985). Grandfathers: Making up for lost opportunities? In R. A. Lewis & R. E. Salt (Eds.), *Men in families*. Beverly Hills: Sage.

Russell, G., & Radin, N. (1983). Paternal involvement: Fathers' perspectives. In M. E. Lamb & A. Sagi (Eds.), *Fatherhood and family policy*. Hillsdale, NJ: Erlbaum.

Sagi, A. (1982). Antecedents and consequences of various degrees of parental involvement in childrearing: The Israeli project. In M. E. Lamb (Ed.), *Nontraditional families: Parenting and child development*. Hillsdale, NJ: Erlbaum.

Spanier, G. B. (1976). Measuring dyadic adjustment: New scales for assessing the quality of marriage and similar dyads. *Journal of Marriage and Family, 38*, 15–30.

TWO

Legal Issues

CHAPTER 3

Fathers and the Child's "Best Interests": Judicial Decision Making in Custody Disputes

ROSS A. THOMPSON
University of Nebraska

When social norms and values change, the result often is revised legal policy, either in the form of new legislative statutes, modified judicial precedent, or case law. Not surprisingly, therefore, many issues in family law have recently been reexamined within the legal community in view of changing gender and parenting roles, the growth of dual-career families and extra-familial care, the increasing incidence of divorce with consequent single-parent and stepparenting families, and the growth of various other forms of nontraditional family arrangements. As these trends suggest, the reformulation of guidelines for the adjudication of child custody disputes can be among the most difficult tasks encountered by legal scholars, since many of these social changes pertain directly to the issues encountered in custody adjudication.

The guideline currently used in the United States for custody disputes between natural parents is the "best interests of the child." This gender-neutral standard permits mothers and fathers to compete on an equal footing for the custody of their offspring, justifying their case in terms of the child's overall future well-being. It thus offers a number of advantages over earlier gender-based custody standards, especially in the recognition that fathers may now be assuming significant caregiving responsibilities more often than was traditionally the case. Yet what *are* a child's "best interests" as they apply to a custody dispute between parents? Which of the child's many interests should be most pertinent to determining a custody award, and how may the potential contributions of the mother and father to these interests be properly assessed and compared? In general, how should the court address the complex and difficult predictive judgments that are entailed in deciding whether the child should live with mother or father, or should experience some form of joint-custody arrangement?

This chapter reviews current research findings relevant to the father's case in child custody disputes with the goal of suggesting ways in which the child's "best interests" can be viewed. Obviously, a complex network of factors specific to the particular family must be considered in any custody dispute, including the nature of the temporary custody arrangement, considerations pertaining to siblings remaining together, and the child's wishes. The role of research knowledge is to provide a framework for understanding parent-child relationships, parenting roles, and other factors by means of which these specific considerations may be put into perspective. In addition, research on single-mother and single-father homes, children's experience in stepparenting families, and joint-custody arrangements can assist in making the predictive judgments that form the basis for a custody award. Thus the research findings reviewed in this chapter may provide a limited but important contribution to the adjudication of child custody disputes in the future.

We turn first, however, to the "best interests" standard and some of the problems entailed in applying this guideline to custody adjudication. Following this, we consider research pertaining to paternal involvement with children in both traditional and nontraditional family structures, which may assist in the application of this standard to specific custody disputes.

THE BEST INTERESTS STANDARD

Viewed historically, the best interests standard for resolving custody disputes is the least explicit in English and American legal tradition and is thus the most difficult to apply. Interestingly, English common law long asserted a paternal preference in custody decisions, owing to the father's absolute control over his legitimate children and his legal obligation to support, protect, and educate them (Derdeyn, 1976, 1978). Thus it was reasonable for courts to assign custody regularly to the father at a time when offspring were regarded as heirs to privilege and wealth, and to protect the father's economic interest in his children. It was not until the mid-nineteenth century that both statute and case law began to formally acknowledge the child's interests in the custody decision, and this was accompanied by a growing maternal preference, especially when minor children were concerned (Roth, 1977).

The gradual shift in legal policy from a paternal to a maternal preference can be attributed to several sociocultural changes. Among these were the dislocation of the family unit from the traditional rural community to the urbanized environment brought about by the Industrial Revolution, and the growing reliance on relational ties within the family unit (Shorter, 1975). Accompanying these were changes in social philosophy brought about by writers like Rousseau and Dickens, who emphasized the young child's need for protection from social vices and for nurturance at home. These changes helped to enact legislation concerning child labor, abuse and neglect, and minimum education. Since the same changes in social philosophy (especially those that occurred in the Victorian era) characterized maternal care as being especially important, particularly during the child's "tender years" (generally speaking, under 7 years of age), courts increasingly awarded custody of young children to their mothers. Later, after the turn of the century, this belief in the importance of "mother love" was supported by psychoanalytic theory, which stressed the unique role of maternal care to early psychological development (see Freud, 1940). Accompanying this was an increasing emphasis on the availability of child support from the noncustodial father, which reduced the economic disincentives of awarding custody to the mother (Derdeyn, 1976).

Thus by the end of the nineteenth century, both English and American law enabled the mother to compete for custody of offspring on an equal footing with the father. However, a strong tradition was developing within case law which favored the award of children (especially minors) to their mothers for the reasons just noted. In addition, since custody decisions were based on an evaluation of parental fitness, wives were in a better position to argue against their husbands, since they were the usual initiators of divorce action (Mnookin, 1975). Thus an implicit maternal preference had become consolidated in custody adjudication by the turn of the century.

Although an early interest in a broader "best interests of the child" standard for custody disputes can be observed early in the current century (Derdeyn, 1976, 1978; Whobrey, Sales, & Lou, in press), this standard has become widely used only relatively recently. There are at least two reasons for this growing interest in the best interests standard. First, and primarily, it appropriately refocuses judicial attention from parent-centered considerations (e.g., parental "fitness") to child-centered considerations. That is, it emphasizes how the *child* is likely to be affected by a custody decision, with due attention to parental characteristics only as they are likely to affect the child outcome. Second, it is a gender-neutral guideline that enables the mother and father to compete on a more equal basis for custody of offspring. In this respect it is a more flexible and egalitarian guideline, which takes into account changing gender and caregiving roles and does not presume a perpetuation of traditional roles or their institutionalization in legal statute.

The best interests standard is, in one form or another, currently used throughout all 50 states as the determinative standard for custody disputes between natural parents (Whobrey, Sales, & Lou, in press). Most states have, in statutory law, included more specific factors by which the child's interests may be appraised. In many cases these factors are identical with those specified in Section 402 of the Uniform Marriage and Divorce Act, which includes consideration of the wishes of the child; the nature of parent-child interaction; the child's adjustment to home, school, and community; and the mental and physical health of all the individuals involved. Other statutes include alternative or additional factors for consideration, including the child's moral and "spiritual" well-being, the stability and "wholesomeness" of the child's living conditions, and the parents' lifestyle, income, marital status, and conduct (Whobrey, Sales, & Lou, in press).

As these factors suggest, however, most statutory guidelines provide few *explicit* standards by which a child's best interests may be determined, perhaps due in some cases to an absence of legislative agreement. Moreover, few of these guidelines take into consideration the changing developmental needs and abilities of the child, implicitly assuming that a very young child's interests are similar to those of an older child. In addition, the guidelines that are included often entail value judgments of the child's current and expected living conditions as well as of each parent's personal characteristics and qualities as a caregiver. Because of the breadth with which the child's best interests are defined, therefore, a great deal of discretionary authority is in the hands of the judges who determine custody awards as well as of those who advise them, such as social workers and forensic psychologists.

Problems with the Best Interests Standard

There are several reasons why legal scholars are uncomfortable with this current state of custody adjudication (Chambers, 1984; Mnookin, 1975). First and primarily, in the absence of clearly prevailing social consensus concerning optimal child-rearing goals and the parental practices that foster these goals, broadly defined decisional guidelines for custody awards are likely to be interpreted in different ways by judges who have different values. Thus an identical set of family conditions may result in much different custody determinations by different judges. This is an important concern since, in our pluralistic society, the courts have traditionally hesitated to infringe on the parents' freedom to raise their children as they prefer. Instead, parents are accorded a wide latitude of decision-making autonomy in areas such as religious training, moral instruction, education, and medical care within the broad parameters of the behaviors our society defines as manifestly abusive or neglectful (see Melton & Thompson, 1985, Thompson, 1985). It is thus inconsistent with this long-standing tradition of substantive parental autonomy to base custody determinations on value judgments of a parent's child-rearing style or expressions of affection, even though this may be statutorily permitted. Moreover, in implementing such vague guidelines, judges may be guilty not only of personal bias involving moral or religious attitudes, but also of cultural, ethnic, or sexist bias, and thus be acting in a discriminatory fashion. In interpreting the best interests standard, therefore, judges may apply (often unintentionally) intuitive, usually unarticulated value judgments that are relative to their values and beliefs and thus entail a more parochial basis for decision making than is appropriate for adjudication. For example, is living with the parent who earns a comfortable income more or less important than residential stability? Is one parent's warm but permissive child-rearing approach preferable to the other's less affectionate limit setting?

The risks inherent in subjective decision making are not limited to judges. Indeed, expert testimony from various sources, including forensic specialists and social workers, has also been criticized as being unreliable for a number of reasons (Chambers, 1984; Ennis & Litwack, 1974; Mnookin, 1975; Okpaku, 1976). First, since the marital breakup and process of divorce is highly stressful for all participants, forensic specialists encounter a family in emotional turmoil whose patterns of interaction may resemble neither their condition prior to divorce nor their relational harmony following this upheaval. Second, in view of the limited resources of the court and in the absence of sufficient financial resources from the family, it is unlikely that any kind of forensic assessment would entail more than one or two brief observations of parent-child interaction. This is unlikely to provide a reliable basis for a judgment of parent-child relationships. Third, even when the court does have available staff members who can perform assessments and offer custody recommendations, court workers are likely to have little training in child development or family sociology. In short, *any* assessment of a family under stress is likely to result in speculative and unreliable judgments, especially in view of the breadth and ambiguity of the best interests standard.

A second reason why legal scholars are uncomfortable with the current status of custody adjudication using the best interests standard is that it complicates the kinds of negotiation in which marital partners typically engage prior to the divorce (Mnookin & Kornhauser, 1979). Legal guidelines such as those pertaining to child custody usually provide negotiating parameters by which both parents can assess their relative chances of success in adjudication and can modify their demands and expectations accordingly. The absence of clear, explicit, and easily applied legal standards for resolving custody disputes may encourage parents to contend for custody as a negotiating strategy without a firm perception that doing so is for the child's well-being. This condition is not only likely to result in inappropriate custody disputes (and, on occasion, unwise custody awards), but also threatens to tax an overburdened judicial system by adding a substantial number of new cases.

Finally, legal scholars have voiced concern about the current status of custody adjudication under the best interests guideline because judgments require the kind of abstract decision making that most judges are poorly trained and ill equipped to address (Mnookin, 1975). Most legal disputes focus on the documentation of facts relevant to a case; custody decisions entail more ambiguous judgments of relational harmony and parental care. Furthermore, custody disputes cannot easily be resolved with recourse to judicial precedent, but must rather be addressed on a case-by-case basis, taking into consideration the unique history and circumstances of the family in question. Custody disputes are person oriented rather than act oriented, and they require complex predictive judgments rather than the determination of past actions. Finally, but most notably, unlike most legal contests, child custody disputes do not have all parties represented, and thus the needs and rights of the child must be indirectly advocated. For all these reasons, most judges report that child custody disputes are among the most difficult cases to resolve (Mnookin, 1975; Whobrey, Sales, & Lou, in press).

Given the inherent ambiguity of the best interests standard and its statutory definition, and the excruciatingly difficult decision making required in custody disputes, it is not surprising to find that many judges rely on simple, informal decision rules that are easier to apply. For example, many judges simply adhere to a maternal presumption despite the changed legislative mandate (Roth, 1977; Weitzman & Dixon, 1979). Clearly, the overall intent of the best interests standard may be significantly undermined by the difficulty of adequately defining these interests and in applying the standard on a case-by-case basis.

In addressing this problem, legal scholars have been divided. While some have defended the ambiguity inherent in the current standard as essential to judicial flexibility to make appropriate case-by-case decisions (even though decision making is difficult), others have suggested a return to more specific, all-encompassing statutory decision rules (e.g., custody awarded to the mother if the child is age 5 or younger; custody awarded to the same-sex parent with older children) (e.g., Watson, 1969). This would limit judicial discretion, even though a sizable proportion of cases might be resolved unfairly.

Another proposal is for greater emphasis on predivorce mediation to encourage parents to find their own solution to the custody dispute short of a court battle. Other scholars have argued that currently, custody adjudication under the best interests standard is *inherently* indeterminate—that is, there is frequently no reliable, objective, and legally satisfactory way of awarding custody to a parent on the basis of the child's best interests (Mnookin, 1975; Okpaku, 1976). In this view, a procedure akin to a judicial coin flip would enable courts to make the custody decision expected of them without presuming to have the requisite expertise, and thus contending parties are spared the anguish of having been deemed less suitable for a custody award owing to their qualities as a caregiver.

While the last argument seems persuasive in view of the foregoing considerations, it gives up too quickly. Since a custody decision is inherently a probabilistic, predictive judgment (i.e., it is *inherently* uncertain), the fundamental question is whether the court has access to reliable information that can meaningfully reduce the likelihood of its making an incorrect decision in predicting the child's eventual well-being in different child-care settings. A number of legal scholars (e.g., Chambers, 1984; Whobrey, Sales, & Lou, in press) have argued that recent research from the social sciences can have a limited but important role in custody adjudication by providing this kind of information. In particular, research knowledge may be especially helpful in providing an overall interpretive framework within which the range of specific factors pertinent to the family in question can be considered and evaluated. Within this framework, specific considerations may be weighed in light of research findings, further questions can be raised, and alternative predictive judgments can be better evaluated. Furthermore, such research can also be useful by informing legal scholars and judges of the impact that recent social changes (e.g., dual-career families, shared-caregiving families, stepparenting families, etc.) should have in the calculus of factors that enter into a specific custody decision.

While the inclusion of research knowledge into the matrix of considerations relevant to a custody dispute may not completely curb judicial discretion, it may reduce the tendency toward idiosyncratic and value-laden decision making by establishing a broader empirical frame of reference within which decisions are justified. Furthermore, such knowledge may also assist judicial considerations, since it is oriented toward the kinds of relational, person-oriented, predictive judgments that jurists are poorly trained to address. Obviously, such information is not determinative, since it must be integrated with the range of factors that are specific to the case at hand. Indeed, the complaints of some critics (e.g., Mnookin, 1975; Okpaku, 1976) that research findings are insufficiently determinative to be of use to specific custody disputes are incongruous in view of the fact that *no one* can predict with certainty how a specific child will fare in a particular set of caregiving circumstances. Thus given the inherently probabilistic nature of such predictive judgments, it would appear that *any* contribution to judicial decision making that can meaningfully reduce the likelihood of incorrect judgments merits consideration (Litwack, Gerber, and Fenster, 1980).

Research knowledge may provide one such contribution to custody adjudication, especially that which concerns the role of fathers as caregivers. In the following pages, research concerning the role of fathers in traditional and nontraditional families is surveyed, and its implications for the father's case in child custody disputes are assessed. These implications are summarized in the concluding section of this chapter.

FATHERS IN TRADITIONAL FAMILIES

Although a few custody disputes may be resolved by identifying and awarding custody to the child's "psychological parent" (see Goldstein, Freud, & Solnit, 1973), that is, the parent to whom the child has developed a strong emotional bond, it is likely that in most disputes *both* parents are "psychological parents" to the child. Except for cases in which one parent has been markedly uninvolved, a child typically forms attachments to both mother and father, and this is what makes custody disputes so difficult to resolve. How can a judge assess the relative strength of the child's tie to each parent?

Even though both parents assume important roles in the child's life, it is likely that the *kind* of relationship the child shares with each parent differs. Thus, one important perspective on a child's "best interests" is in terms of the role and significance of each parent in the child's life experience. This is likely to vary with the child's development, and perhaps also with the child's gender, as well as with other factors related to family structure (e.g., the distribution of parental care responsibilities). It is in providing a framework for understanding the nature of mother-child and father-child relationships that research from the social sciences may be helpful in determining how a child is likely to be affected by different custody awards.

In the following section, research pertaining to fathers in traditional (i.e., single wage-earner) families is reviewed and evaluated. Although the research that follows concerns children of various ages, special attention is devoted to studies with infants and toddlers, since these are the ages for which there is greatest concern about the adequacy of fathers as caregivers. We consider first the general question of paternal sensitivity and responsiveness to young children, to determine whether there is evidence that fathers lack certain qualities of caregiving which mothers, by virtue of their special early role in the child's life, may uniquely possess. Next we consider the quality of paternal care of infants and toddlers, to understand the role of fathers in early development. Third, the research concerning paternal influences with older children is summarized, in order to compare the nature of paternal involvement with younger and older children. Finally, these findings are summarized with special attention to their implications for custody decision making.

Paternal Sensitivity and Responsiveness to Young Children

Women have traditionally been assumed to have unique capabilities pertaining to the nurturance and care of infants and young children. This assumption, usually based on the maternal childbearing role and the mother's physiological capacity to nurse the child, can be found in early psychoanalytic theory (Freud, 1940); in more recent perspectives within ego psychology (e.g., Erikson, 1963), attachment theory (Bowlby, 1969), and modern sociobiology (e.g., Babchuk, Hames, & Thompson, 1985; Rossi, 1977, 1984); and in other contemporary viewpoints (see Lamb, 1981 for a review). Taken together, these views suggest that women have certain special propensities as caregivers owing to the psychological consequences of their unique status in early child care.

Whatever the merits of these arguments, the derivative research on sex differences in behavior related to nurturance and caregiving does not provide a clear portrayal of female prepotency (see Berman, 1980; Maccoby & Jacklin, 1974, for reviews). Typically, researchers find substantial overlap in the distributions of scores for men and women on measures of nurturance, sensitivity, and responsiveness to the young, even when there are significant sex differences on these measures. Quite often, research studies reveal sex differences on some measures of responsiveness but not on others. Moreover, the *kind* of responsiveness measure that is used in research studies is important. Berman (1980) found, for example, that studies using self-report measures yielded the clearest and most consistent evidence for greater female responsiveness to the young, while those employing psychophysiological measures (e.g., heart rate, blood pressure) provided the least support. Berman noted that self-report measures are more likely to be influenced by gender-related role prescriptions, which affect the self-presentation of men and women, but may not provide as reliable information about actual sex differences in sensitivity to infants and young children.

Another significant influence identified by Berman (1980) is the adult's family role: Responsiveness fluctuates according to whether the adult's role entails caregiving involvement or not (see also Gutmann, 1975). For example, in a series of cross-sectional investigations, Feldman and Nash (1978, 1979a; Feldman, Nash, & Cutrona, 1977; Nash & Feldman, 1980; see Nash & Feldman, 1981 for a review) compared the responsiveness of adults of various ages toward an unfamiliar infant in a contrived waiting-room situation, and found that sex differences were strongest and most consistent among adults whose current roles entailed accentuated gender differences in caregiving involvement, such as young parents.[*] In one study (Feldman & Nash, 1978), for example, adults of comparable age who were either unmarried cohabitants, married but childless, expectant parents, or the parents of infants were compared, and only the last group exhibited strong and consistent sex differences in responsiveness to the baby. These findings suggest that sex differences in responsiveness to the young may be, in part, a function of the extent of an adult's involvement in child care, with sex differences being most apparent when men and women assume much different caregiving roles. In a reversal of the typical assumption, then, heightened maternal responsiveness to infants and young children may be partly a derivative of a mother's enhanced involvement with offspring rather than just a determinant of it.

For men also, responsiveness may vary with their current involvement in child care rather than reflect an enduring, gender-related characteristic. This perspective is supported by research concerning maternal and paternal responsiveness to the firstborn child before the parents have had substantial experience with differential responsibilities for child care at home (Parke, 1979; Parke & O'Leary, 1976; Parke & Sawin, 1976; Parke & Tinsley, 1981; Sawin & Parke, 1979). Parke and colleagues found that first-time fathers held, rocked, kissed, looked at, explored, and vocalized to the neonate as much as or more than mothers did, and fathers were comparably sensitive and responsive to the baby's cues. This portrayal of early paternal caregiving competence is ironic in view of the fact that subsequently most fathers are largely uninvolved in routine caregiving tasks, even when the mother also works (Ban & Lewis, 1974; Kotelchuck, 1976; Pedersen & Robson, 1969; Pleck, 1979; Pleck & Lang, 1978; Pleck &

---

[*]Interestingly, in a short-term longitudinal study, Nash and Feldman (1981) studied a sample of 31 nontraditional couples who were observed in the waiting-room situation both prenatally and six months after the baby's birth. This group was deemed "nontraditional" owing to the father's extensive involvement in child-care. Nash and Feldman found that *both* men and women exhibited a significant and highly comparable increase in their interest in the unfamiliar baby after the advent of their own caregiving involvement, in contrast to the differential interest shown by women (but not men) in the more traditional families they studied.

Rustad, 1980; Robinson, 1977; Szalai, Converse, Feldheim, Scheuch, & Stone, 1972; Walker & Woods, 1976). Kotelchuck (1976) found, for example, that only 25 percent of his 144 middle-class Boston fathers had any regular daily caregiving responsibilities, while Ban and Lewis (1974) noted that fathers reported an average of only 15 to 20 minutes of daily contact with their infants. In short, fathers do not spend a great deal of time involved in the care of their infants and young children, even though they are competent to do so from the baby's birth.

Taken together, the research reviewed by Berman (1980) and the studies of Parke, and Feldman and Nash, suggest that these early emerging differences between paternal and maternal involvement in child care may arise not because of fundamental differences in the parents' sensitivity or competence but partly because of gender-related role prescriptions concerning child care in our society. Because men as well as women remain convinced of the importance of maternal care to the young (in accord with most psychological theories), mothers assume the majority of caregiving responsibilities whether or not they also work outside the home. Once parents have begun to assume these kinds of traditional caregiving roles, many factors contribute to perpetuation of the roles, including differences in perceived competence between men and women. These factors notwithstanding, it seems apparent from these studies that the caregiving role is a better predictor of competence in child care than is gender alone, and that it is important to distinguish between caregiving competence and caregiving performance. That is, *both* men and women can be effective caregivers of infants and young children; what distinguishes them in the traditional family are the roles they assume in relation to young children, not characteristics associated with gender per se.

The Quality of Early Paternal Involvement

Given the relatively minimal involvement of fathers in routine caregiving tasks, what *do* fathers do with their infants and toddlers? Consistently, researchers have found that fathers devote proportionately more time to playing with their infant sons and daughters than do mothers (Belsky, 1979; Clarke-Stewart, 1978; Kotelchuck, 1976; Lamb, 1976a, 1977a). Furthermore, when they play with their babies, mothers and fathers play in qualitatively different ways. Several investigators (Belsky, 1979; Clarke-Stewart, 1978, 1980; Lamb, 1976a, b; Power & Parke, 1982; Yogman, 1977; Yogman et al., 1976) have reported that fathers play more physically active rough-and-tumble games with their infants at home, while mothers use more low-key conventional games (e.g., peek-a-boo, pat-a-cake) and toy-mediated games. Play is thus not only a more significant interactive context for infants with their fathers, but different kinds of play activity also distinguish each parent.

There is evidence that different social expectations for each parent take shape from an early age on the basis of these interactions, since before the end of the first year infants react differently to their mothers and fathers (Lamb, 1977a). Differential responsiveness to mothers and fathers is even more clearly evident in the second year. For example, Belsky (1979) found that 15-month-olds were more likely to vocalize to, move toward, and show things to their fathers than to their mothers, while Clarke-Stewart (1978) noted that 30-month-olds were rated as more involved, interested, and cooperative with their fathers than with their mothers during a set of specific play initiatives. These researchers have argued that the infant's affiliative preference for the father may be largely a derivative of the father's more active, vigorous, stimulating play style. In other words, because play is such a salient feature of father-infant interaction and because fathers regularly play in more exciting ways than do mothers, infants and toddlers respond with greater excitement and with a range of sociable initiatives when father is near, and they also respond more positively to his play initiatives.

Most of these observations of father-infant and mother-infant interaction took place in the comfortable home environment. In more stressful situations, such as during unfamiliar laboratory procedures, different kinds of parental preferences are apparent. For example, Lamb (1976b) observed 20 12-month-olds during a one-half-hour laboratory procedure, and found that by the end of the period—when the infants were fatigued and were encountering an unfamiliar adult—the infants displayed a clear preference for mother in their attachment behavior, and there was no longer a paternal preference in the display of affiliative behavior. Other researchers have reported similar results. For example, Cohen and Campos (1974), using a six-minute laboratory procedure that entailed frequent disruptions of the infant's behavior and recurrent encounters with strangers, found that on nearly all of their measures of proximity seeking, 10- to 16-month-olds were oriented toward the mother (see also Kotelchuck, 1976). Thus when infants and toddlers are stressed and both parents are present, mothers are preferred as sources of help and soothing. This is perhaps unsurprising in view of the caregiving role assumed by mothers in most traditional families, which includes providing comfort when upsetting events occur. Thus infants have learned that mothers are sources of soothing during stress.

Taken together, these studies of early parent-child interactions indicate that in the early years of life, children are remarkably attuned to the different caregiving roles assumed by the mother and father and develop different kinds of social expectations for each parent as a result. With fathers, play is a more significant and salient interactive context than with mothers, and thus infants learn to expect exciting, arousing play with their fathers and respond to them sociably as preferred play partners. Mothers, on the other hand, are encountered more frequently in the context of routine caregiving activities, and thus mother is known by the baby through her association with these activities, including her role as a comforter when stressful events occur. Therefore, while there are significant differences in the overall *quantity* of parental involvement with young offspring, this difference seems to be less important than the *quality* of parental care. While infants and toddlers develop strong emotional attachments to both parents, their relationships with mother and father differ because of the different situations in which parents are encountered and the different kinds of social expectations these encounters engender in the baby.

Paternal Influences at Later Ages

As children grow older and fathers become more intimately involved in the child's life, the paternal role becomes more complex and multifaceted. Researchers who are interested in the role of the father in child development have identified several areas of sociopersonality and cognitive functioning to which paternal influences make important contributions in older children.

One area is gender socialization. A large number of studies indicate that fathers treat their sons and daughters much differently from an early age, and this contributes to the development of gender-typed behavior by children (see Biller, 1981 for a review). Virtually from birth, fathers are more interested and involved with their sons than their daughters (Parke & O'Leary, 1976), and this differential attention continues throughout the early years (see Belsky, 1979; Kotelchuck, 1976). It is thus not surprising to find that boys and girls soon begin responding differently to their parents. For example, Lamb (1977c) found that at the end of the second year, all but one of the boys in his sample showed greater responsiveness to the father, while nearly all of the toddlers preferring the mother were female (see also Lynn & Cross, 1974). With older children, fathers provide more consistent reinforcement for appropriate sex-typed behavior than do mothers (Langlois & Downs, 1980), they praise independent behavior more (Cantor, Wood, & Gelfand, 1977), they differentiate more between sons and daughters in their encouragement of active play (Tauber, 1981), and they use different teaching styles with their sons compared with their daughters (Block, Block, & Harrington, 1974, 1975; described in Block, 1983). In the last study, fathers set higher standards for their sons, focused attention on the cognitive aspects of the task, and stressed task performance; with their daughters they concentrated more on the interpersonal aspects of the learning situation and tried to make it fun. Taken together, this differential treatment of sons and daughters means that paternal influence is an important contributor to the gender socialization of boys and girls.

Another area in which paternal influence is important is in academic achievement and intellectual development. This influence also appears to begin early in life (Clarke-Stewart, 1978), and in view of the father's differential treatment of sons and daughters, it is not surprising that research with older children reveals significant sex differences in paternal influence on intellectual development (see Radin, 1981 for a review). With sons, fathers actively encourage intellectual and instrumental competence, and paternal involvement and nurturance foster the cognitive development of boys. With daughters, in contrast, fathers tend to deemphasize intellectual accomplishments, and the effects of paternal involvement are more ambiguous. When fathers have high expectations for their daughters' academic accomplishments and actively encourage them, however, girls' cognitive competencies are more likely to improve (Lamb, Owen, & Chase-Lansdale, 1979; Radin, 1981; Radin & Russell, 1983). Thus the paternal contribution to the intellectual performance of offspring may apply to *both* sons and daughters, but, especially for the latter, may depend on the paternal commitment to fostering academic achievement in children of both genders.

Finally, there is some evidence that father involvement contributes to the development of social competence and social responsibility in offspring, especially in boys. With respect to moral internalization, for example, Hoffman (1981) has noted that although mothers typically assume the major role in discipline and moral socialization (especially during the early years), fathers may serve as identification figures for sons and assist in their acquisition of moral values. With respect to social competence, a number of studies have found that paternal warmth is associated with indices of self-esteem, sociability, and personality adjustment, especially in boys (see Lamb, 1981 for a review).

Taken together, it is clear that the father's role in the postinfancy period is considerably more complex and multifaceted than it is in the infant and toddler years, and studies reveal that paternal influences vary according to at least two factors. One is the child's sex: Fathers are more intimately involved with their sons than with their daughters from a very early age, and accordingly have a more profound influence on their sons' development. Although fathers shape the experience of offspring of both sexes, they are clearly more salient to sons. The second mediating factor is the extent of the father's involvement: When he is physically and psychologically accessible to the child, his influence is greater, and this is true for both sons and daughters. More generally, it is apparent that for both sons and daughters, the father assumes a more significant role in the child's development as his involvement with the child increases with age.

Summary and Conclusions

In considering the father's role in traditional (i.e., single wage-earner) families, the research reviewed in this section provides a coherent, albeit complex, picture of paternal influences. At the outset, it appears that sex differences in caregiving sensitivity and competence are due in large measure to caregiving role rather than to gender per se. From this perspective, differential interest and sensitivity to young children by women and men may be largely a function of gender-related role prescriptions rather than of enduring gender-based competencies. Thus fathers *can* be competent and sensitive in their handling of infants and toddlers even though they tend to be little involved in early care. For this reason, it is probably more useful, in examining parenting within the family, to distinguish between the kinds of caregiving roles assumed by each parent than to distinguish on the basis of parental gender alone. That is, rather than considering whether mothers are more important to young children than are fathers, it is more valuable to distinguish between parents in their roles and responsibilities vis-a-vis the child. Such an approach not only provides a more versatile way of appraising the nature of parenting in traditional as well as nontraditional families but also takes into account the *capacity* of each parent to assume any caregiving role.

Within traditional families, of course, mothers and fathers typically assume much different roles in the care of infants and young children. As the child's primary caregiver, the mother typically assumes responsibility for basic caregiving tasks and is with the child for most of the child's waking hours. As secondary caregiver, the father typically spends less time with the child, but a greater proportion of the time is devoted to play. And it is clear that, quite early, infants begin to respond differently to each parent on the basis of the expectations engendered by these different interactive contexts. From their father they expect a good time in rousing play, while they turn to their mother for comfort and soothing in stressful circumstances.

When considering a custody decision pertaining to very young children, there is reason to favor the parent who is the child's primary caregiver, whether this role is assumed by mother or father. A preference for the parent who assumes the range of basic caregiving ministrations derives primarily from the importance of these activities to the infant and toddler. Major theories of early development are in agreement concerning the intimate connections that exist between the adequacy and consistency with which the child's needs are satisfied and the development of fundamental psychological processes such as a nascent self-concept, feelings of predictability and agency, and confidence in the social surround. The child's cognitive egocentrism probably contributes to a strong association between these primary caregiving experiences and the person who provides them. Thus, in contrast to the experience of older children, with younger children there may be broader ramifications deriving from the loss of the primary caregiver in terms of the children's perceptions of themselves and their surroundings, especially if the caregiver is known by the children primarily in terms of these ministrations.

Such a view realistically reflects the dependence of the infant and young child on the social surroundings and the special importance of the adult who provides for these basic needs in the early years. Thus, placement of the child with the parent who has been the primary caregiver is likely to result in a less difficult transition for the child than if another person assumes these responsibilities, however adequately. Furthermore, a custody award that results in the primary caregiver becoming a visiting noncustodial parent may be especially stressful for very young children, who are likely to have difficulty renegotiating relational expectations for this parent. In view of their strong attachment to the parent, their identification of the parent with basic caregiving roles, and their limited understanding of temporal durations, the children may experience renewed stress and feelings of loss with each visit from this parent. These considerations are especially important in view of the fact that younger children generally experience much greater difficulty in the period following a divorce than do older children (Wallerstein & Kelly, 1980a). Maintenance of consistency in caregiving may help to buffer the impact of this stressful transition for very young children.[*]

These considerations apply primarily to custody decisions for infants, toddlers, and young preschoolers (i.e., to age 3 or 4), for whom caregiving responsibilities are most salient and differential caregiving roles can be most easily distinguished in traditional families. With older children—especially school age and older—it is not at all clear that similar considerations apply. As indicated in the preceding review, the diversity and multidimensionality of parenting influences in traditional families make it very difficult to assign "primary" or "secondary" caregiving roles to either

---

[*]It is worth mentioning that several legal scholars have also advocated a preference for the young child's primary caregiver in custody disputes from the standpoint of the adult's interests (see, for example, Chambers 1984).

parent. In other words, *both* parents are primary caregivers in view of the increasingly diverse needs of older children and the capability and willingness of both parents to meet these needs. Although paternal influence on the child's development does vary with the degree of the father's involvement, it is apparent that even minimally involved fathers have important and unique effects on child development, especially that of boys. Owing to a broader range of shared experiences between parents and older offspring (e.g., trips together, conversing about experiences, instruction, discipline, etc.), the concept of primary versus secondary caregiving roles becomes more problematic when applied to older children.

In addition, the child has become a cognitively and behaviorally more complex individual, and this contributes, in part, to the changed parenting roles and responsibilities. As a result, older children can better cope with the changed family conditions resulting from divorce (Wallerstein & Kelly, 1980a), tolerating better the renegotiation of relational expectations that is entailed in the establishment of a visiting relationship with the noncustodial parent, and appreciating better the circumstances leading to the divorce. Their increasingly sophisticated understanding of self and others means that while for older children the experience of divorce is likely to be stressful, it is unlikely to have the kinds of broader psychological ramifications it may have for the infant or toddler. Finally, older children have access to social networks outside the family in which certain individuals (e.g., teachers, peers) may help to buffer the impact of divorce. Thus, while a preference for the primary caretaker (likely the mother) in traditional families can be justified for infants and young children, such a consideration is not useful with respect to older children, and other factors should be given greater weight.

FATHERS IN NONTRADITIONAL FAMILIES

What are the effects of nontraditional family systems on child development and on the nature of parent-child interaction? Partly because so much theory and research in developmental psychology presumes a traditional family structure, which is becoming increasingly uncommon in our society, students of child development have recently devoted increasing attention to the nature of nontraditional family arrangements and their effects on children (see, for example, the 1982 anthology edited by Lamb). Findings from such studies can assist in the determination of custody disputes under the best interests standard in at least three ways. First, they can provide some understanding of the nature of parenting and of parent-child relationships in nontraditional families, so that the relationship shared by the child with each parent may be appreciated. Thus the costs and benefits of alternative custody decisions can better be assessed for these families. Second, and more generally, they can provide a useful perspective on the flexibility of fathers when faced with family structures and caregiving demands different from those encountered in a traditional family. For example, how effectively do fathers function in a single-parent family, such as would be encountered in a custody award favoring the father? Third, they can help us to appreciate the child's experience in a home in which the father assumes primary or exclusive caregiving responsibilities.

We turn first to a discussion of the very limited research concerning maternal and paternal roles in dual-career families, and then consider a larger body of studies about shared-caregiving families. Fathers as single parents occupy our consideration in the third part of this review, followed by a brief discussion of the effects of the father's remarriage on children.

Fathers in Dual-Career Families

In dual-career families, the maternal assumption of caregiving responsibilities inevitably competes with work-related concerns, forcing the delegation of some child-care tasks to the spouse. As noted earlier, however, time-use studies have indicated that there is little change in fathers' involvement in child-care activities in dual-career compared with single-wage-earner families (Pleck, 1979; Pleck & Lang, 1978; Robinson, 1977; Szalai et al., 1972; Walker & Woods, 1976). In other words, the traditional division of child-care responsibilities seems to remain in most dual-career families.

Why does this happen? Some perspective on this question may be derived from the findings of an important study by Pedersen, Cain, Zaslow and Anderson (1982), who observed single- and dual-wage-earner couples at home interacting with their firstborn 5-month-old infants. These investigators found that employed mothers assumed a highly active role during their interactions with the child: They talked to their infants much more than did other parents and (in contrast to the reverse pattern found in traditional families) played with their babies much more than did their spouses. Indeed, Pedersen and colleagues noticed that in most behaviors, employed mothers were more highly interactive with their infants than were other parents, while their husbands were least interactive. In view of the early evening period during which these observations were conducted, these researchers suggested that the working mothers were using this time to reestablish contact with their babies after having been away for the day. In traditional families, of course, this is the father's accustomed period for focused parent-child interaction. Instead, in dual-career families, the fathers were "crowded out" (Pedersen et al., 1980) by the mothers, and they gave precedence to their wives at this time.

The dual-wage-earner families in this study were thus characterized by a *greater* division of interactive involvement with the baby, in marked contrast to an expectation that such families would evince a more equal sharing of involvement with the baby at the end of the day. However, several cautions are necessary before we draw strong conclusions from this single study. For example, we do not know whether similar differences in parent-infant interaction would be apparent with toddlers or preschoolers, who can take greater interactive initiative on their own. In addition, the employed mothers in this study had returned to work shortly before these observations took place, and thus they were probably still negotiating the transition from full-time to part-time caregiver. It is possible that their level of interactive involvement diminished once home and work activities became more routine. As a result of questions like these, it is clear that further research is required into the nature of parent-infant and parent-child interaction in dual-career families, and the findings of Pedersen and colleagues must be viewed as suggestive at present.

Fathers in Shared-Caregiving Families

When mothers elect to work, fathers can choose to assume major caregiving responsibilities on their own, sometimes by reducing their own work-related commitments or, at times, by reason of unemployment. Such families are likely to differ from the dual-career families observed by Pedersen and colleagues by virtue of the enhanced paternal commitment to a caregiving role and the reduction or elimination of competing job responsibilities. What is the experience of children growing up in families in which fathers adopt a shared-caregiving role?

Several major investigations have been conducted recently to examine this question. Russell (1982a, 1982b, 1983), for example, compared 145 traditional families with 71 shared-caregiving families in Australia, "shared-caregiving" being defined as child-care responsibilities being shared between mother and father *and* father assuming exclusive responsibility for offspring more than 15 hours weekly (the average was 26 hours weekly). Both mothers and fathers in shared-caregiving families viewed a closer father-child relationship as the primary advantage of this caregiving arrangement, and they perceived (often to their surprise) that children experienced no major difficulties with this lifestyle (Russell, 1982a). Unfortunately, since there were no direct observations of the children or of parent-child interactions, the reliability of this parental report is difficult to assess.

In a study with American families, Radin (1982; Radin & Sagi, 1982) interviewed 59 middle-class couples in which both parents assumed major responsibilities for the care of their preschool child. In addition, the children were assessed on a battery of standardized measures of cognitive and sociopersonality functioning. Only a few significant effects on the child from increased paternal participation in child care were discerned (e.g., children with more highly involved fathers scored higher on a measure of internal locus of control), and there were no differences by father involvement on most measures, such as those assessing the child's sex-role orientation, empathy, or intelligence. In a study of very similar design conducted in Israel by Sagi (1982; Radin & Sagi, 1982), increased paternal involvement had more pervasive effects on child behavior, perhaps because of cultural differences in the mother's role in these two societies (see Radin & Russell, 1983; Radin & Sagi, 1982).

Only three studies exist in which father-child interactions were directly observed. In the first, Field (1978) observed three parent groups—12 primary caregiver mothers, 12 primary caregiver fathers, and 12 secondary caregiver fathers—as they interacted with their 4-month-old during three three-minute episodes. Field reported that fathers differed from mothers in some parenting behaviors regardless of their caregiving status, while primary caregiver fathers more closely resembled primary caregiver mothers in other behaviors, displaying more smiling, imitative facial expressions, and high-pitched imitative vocalizations than did secondary caregiver fathers. In short, primary caregiver fathers resembled traditional fathers in certain ways and traditional mothers in other ways.

In another study, Pruett (1983) studied 17 families in which the father had assumed a primary caregiving role with his 2- to 24-month-old infant. Interviews with the fathers and home observations of father-infant interactions revealed that fathers behaved nurturantly toward the infants and developed strong attachments to them. The infants, in turn, performed well on standard developmental assessments.

Somewhat different results were obtained in another cross-cultural study of nontraditional parenting roles in Sweden conducted by Lamb, Frodi, Hwang, Frodi, and Steinberg (1982a, 1982b; Lamb, Frodi, Frodi, & Hwang, 1982; Lamb, Frodi, Hwang, & Frodi, 1982). These researchers contacted couples prenatally through childbirth preparation classes and later observed them interacting with their 8-month-old infants. The sample was divided into two groups on the basis of the extent of the father's caregiving involvement during the preceding three months. Fourteen fathers had been the baby's primary caregiver for one or more months (the average was about three months), while the remaining 34 fathers had never assumed exclusive responsibility for child care. Parent-infant interactions were observed during the early evening hours when both parents were present.

To their surprise, Lamb and colleagues found that parental gender was a more significant determinant of interactive behavior than was the extent of caregiving involvement. Regardless of their caregiving role, mothers vocalized, smiled, tended, held, and displayed more affection toward their infants than did fathers. They were also more likely to hold their babies for soothing or discipline (e.g., removing the infant from a forbidden activity). These differences between maternal and paternal behaviors are, of course, very similar to those described earlier for traditional American families. In contrast, the only differences attributable to family structure concerned play behavior: Traditional parents played *more* with their babies than did nontraditional parents! When the infants were 16 months old these families were observed again and similar findings were obtained (Lamb, Frodi, Frodi, & Hwang, 1982).

To be sure, it is unclear whether the nontraditional Swedish fathers had, in fact, made a serious commitment to caregiving involvement. Lamb, Frodi, Hwang, & Frodi (1982) noted, for example, that there were no differences between traditional and nontraditional fathers in the amount of time they had spent as primary caregivers by the time the infants were 5 months old, and thus their differential involvement occurred later in the child's life and was an avowedly temporary commitment. Since the nontraditional fathers had experienced a sustained period during which caregiving roles were traditional in nature, knew that they were home full-time for a limited period, and expected to return to work soon afterward, it is perhaps not surprising that gender differences in caregiving behavior were unaltered and family structure did not have a stronger effect.

Taken together, the results of studies concerned with the effects of enhanced paternal caregiving involvement in shared-caregiving families suggest that fathers can adapt well to this kind of family structure and competently assume major roles in child-care without adversely affecting the children. Indeed, several studies provide suggestive evidence that certain benefits may accrue to the child as a result of increased paternal involvement, perhaps owing to the father's increased salience in the life of his offspring. At the very least, there is no evidence that child development is hindered in any way as a result of the child's growing up in a shared-caregiving family. Based on more direct observations of parent-child interaction in nontraditional families, there is some evidence that as primary caregivers, fathers seem to develop a synthesis of characteristically paternal interactive behavior with the gentler verbal and affectionate activities more commonly noted with mothers. The extent to which this occurs may depend, however, on the degree of paternal commitment to a shared-caregiving role. Whether or not this synthesis of "maternal" and "paternal" interactive behavior occurs, however, children thrive. Further research is required to elaborate and clarify the scanty array of findings reported thus far.

Fathers as Single Parents

The adjudication of child custody disputes entails not only an understanding of parent-child relationships in the intact family but also predictive judgments concerning the child's experience in a mother-headed or father-headed single-parent home. In custody adjudication, special concern is sometimes voiced concerning the competence of fathers as single parents, and in this section we survey research specifically concerned with single-father families.

Unfortunately, the research studies we have to draw on in this area are limited in several important ways (see Bartz & Witcher, 1978; Chang & Deinard, 1982; Ferri, 1973; Gasser & Taylor, 1976; George & Wilding, 1972; Greif, 1979; Hipgrave, 1978; Katz, 1979; Keshet & Rosenthal, 1978a, 1978b; Luepnitz, 1982; Mendes, 1976a, 1976b; Orthner, Brown, & Ferguson 1976; Rosenthal & Keshet 1981; Schlesinger, 1979; Schlesinger & Todres, 1976; Smith & Smith, 1981; Todres, 1975). First, nearly all of them relied on interviews with single fathers without direct observation of father-child interaction, and thus they are likely to yield a subjective and probably optimistic portrayal of the child's adjustment to a single-father family. Second, the fathers who were interviewed included widowed and abandoned fathers as well as those who were divorced, although the large majority were in the last category. Moreover, among the divorced group most fathers obtained custody by mutual consent of both spouses, which may limit the generalizability of these findings, since different results may obtain for fathers who fought for custody. Third, nearly all of these studies reported on single fathers who were interviewed long after completing the adjustment to the role of single parent, and since their reports of the stresses involved in negotiating this transition were retrospective rather than concurrent, they may also be unrealistically optimistic. Finally, in many studies the sample of single fathers was obtained in a manner that may have yielded a select, highly motivated and committed group which may not be representative of most single fathers.

These cautions are necessary in view of the rather consistent portrayal of single fathers in these studies as competent, concerned, and involved parents. To be sure, their transition to single parenting—especially after a divorce—entailed many of the same stresses and difficulties as those commonly experienced by divorced mothers (compare with Hetherington,

Cox, & Cox 1978, 1982; Wallerstein & Kelly 1980a). These interview studies of single fathers characterized the first year of the transition as being especially stressful, with fathers required to negotiate personal problems (e.g., loneliness, depression) as well as the reorganization of the household. Keshet and Rosenthal (1978a), for example, described this period as "a series of trial-and-error adjustments" in home management and child-care arrangements, and fathers in this study and in others reported feeling inadequate, overtaxed, and even somewhat frightened. Juggling work and child-care responsibilities was especially difficult for many owing to their longstanding job commitments. While some managed to modify their working hours and responsibilities, others suffered financial difficulties from reducing their work hours or, in a few cases, quitting work altogether to become full-time caregivers.

Following this initial period, however, these studies almost uniformly reported that fathers felt increasingly competent and successful in their new domestic responsibilities. Very few fathers employed housekeepers or babysitters; most assumed cooking, cleaning, and caregiving demands by themselves, and most reported enjoying, to some extent, these new obligations. There was none of the disarray at home and neglect of children's needs which some might expect in families with single fathers. And, according to the fathers' reports, the children also fared well. To be sure, some fathers voiced concern over their ability to provide for the child's "emotional needs" (e.g., nurturance), and the fathers of daughters were concerned with the child's sexuality and the lack of an appropriate female role model at home, especially as girls reached puberty. Some enlisted the help of a trusted female friend (e.g., a relative or family friend) to help remedy some of these difficulties. On the whole, however, fathers reported substantial satisfaction with their children's adjustment to single fathering.

Three studies that involved direct assessments of the children of single fathers provide some support for these paternal reports. Hipgrave (1978) found no behavior problems and generally good adjustment among the 33 preschool offspring of the 16 single fathers he studied. Luepnitz (1982) found no differences among children in maternal-, paternal-, and joint-custody homes on a standardized measure of children's self-concept. Nor were there family differences on a measure of the emotional atmosphere within the home. Lowenstein and Koopman (1978) found no differences in self-esteem in boys (ages 9 to 14) living in single-mother or single-father divorced homes, nor was self-esteem related to the amount of time the boys had lived in a single-parent home. While very limited in scope, these studies suggest that the fathers' reports concerning the overall adjustment of their children may not have been unduly optimistic.

Taken together, these interview studies of single fathers characterize these parents as competent and resourceful in their sole caregiving role, despite the fact that, by and large, they had had little preparation for assuming domestic and child-care responsibilities. Thus, on the basis of these studies, there is little reason to doubt the competence or commitment of fathers as single parents. The major qualification to this conclusion was noted earlier: Since they are based on paternal interviews and selected samples, and the interviews were obtained long after the immediate postdivorce adjustment phase, these studies are likely to offer an optimistic portrayal of family life in single-father homes. In order to draw more definitive conclusions, direct observations of parent-child interaction comparing single-father, single-mother, and intact two-parent families are essential.

Only one study has accomplished this, conducted by Santrock and colleagues (Santrock & Warshak, 1979; Santrock, Warshak, & Elliott, 1982; Warshak & Santrock, 1980, 1983). In their Texas Custody Research Project, a sample of 64 white, predominantly middle-class families were administered a battery of personality and self-report measures, interviewed, and observed both at home and in the laboratory. Approximately one third of the families were single-father families, one third were single-mother families, and the remaining third were intact two-parent families. The children ranged in age from 6 to 11 years (average age $8\frac{1}{2}$) at the time of the assessment, at which time parents in divorced families had been separated an average of three years. Thus the portrayal of family functioning offered by this study reflects the adjustment of both children and parents following the immediate postdivorce period.

The findings are striking. On many of the measures of parent-child interaction, as well as in interviews with the children themselves, a child's adjustment was importantly predicted by whether he or she was living with a same-sex parent. For example, on measures of maturity, sociability, and independence in parent-child interaction, boys in father-custody homes uniformly showed greater social competence than did father-custody girls. In fact, the sons of single fathers were rated higher on these measures than were boys from intact families, while daughters of single fathers were rated as less mature, warm, and sociable and more demanding than girls from intact families. In contrast, in mother-custody homes, girls were rated as more socially competent than boys (Santrock & Warshak, 1979). Similar findings were obtained from ratings derived from the child interviews (Santrock, Warshak, & Elliott, 1982; Warshak & Santrock, 1980), although these results were somewhat less reliable. Taken together, however, these findings indicate that children exhibited better adjustment with the same-sex custodial parent.

As Santrock and colleagues noted, these provocative findings invite caution before they are directly applied to issues of custody adjudication. The sample was small and was not randomly selected. More important, in none of the father-custody families had there been a fight over custody, suggesting that the greater difficulty experienced by daughters in single-father homes may have been due to preexisting problems in the mother-daughter relationship and/or feelings of having been deserted by a mother who did not want the single-parent role. Thus the difficulties encountered by daughters of single fathers in Santrock and Warshak's study may have been due to conflicts in the mother-daughter relationship rather than to the father's particular disadvantages as a caregiver of daughters.

Even so, the finding that sons show better adjustment in father-custody homes is consistent with research reviewed earlier concerning the father's greater involvement and influence in the development of sons in intact families. In addition, it is consistent with evidence of greater mother-son conflict and adjustment difficulties of sons in mother-custody homes reported both by Hetherington, Cox, and Cox (1979a, b, 1982) and Wallerstein and Kelly (1980a). Apart from the concerns expressed in interview studies by single fathers about their daughters' adjustment, however, there is less convergent evidence for father-daughter conflict, inviting further interpretational caution. There are several reasons to expect more positive interactions of children with the same-sex parent, however. Children may benefit from the availability of a same-sex adult role model at home, especially while negotiating the difficult transition to the postdivorce family, and parents in turn may be able to offer greater understanding and sympathy to a child of the same sex. On the other hand, greater difficulty may characterize the relationship between a child and an opposite-sex custodial parent because of the child's resemblance to the divorced spouse. On the basis of these considerations, it seems reasonable to expect that parental and filial gender may be predictive of the quality of the child's experience in the postdivorce family.

Taken together, these studies of single fathers indicate that fathers can be competent in an exclusive caregiving role following a period of adjustment to new demands and responsibilities. The initial difficulties they encounter in juggling domestic, employment, child-care, and personal needs are not significantly different from those experienced by single mothers during the first year of postdivorce adjustment; like mothers, fathers eventually manage these new demands. Most important, single fathers—like mothers—exhibit an appropriate concern for the needs of their children, and their offspring (especially sons) seem to fare well.

Remarriage.   It is not unusual for the father's future marital plans to enter into a custody dispute, especially if the expectation of remarriage can be used to argue that a "mother's touch" will soon be evident in the paternal home. While it is clearly unnecessary, in view of the research described here, for fathers to seek to support their custody argument with the expectation of remarriage, the fact that this occurs raises important questions concerning the child's experience in a family with a step-mother.

In a recent review of research on the effects of remarriage on children, Ganong and Coleman (1984) concluded that children neither benefit nor are hurt by remarriage. In their summary of 38 studies in this area, these reviewers found no reliable evidence that children in stepfamilies differ significantly from children in other family structures in intellectual and cognitive achievement, personality and social behavior, adjustment, and family relationships. To be sure, most of the studies they reviewed are flawed, showing a disconcertingly limited appreciation of the complexity of stepparent families; relying on small and nonrepresentative samples, retrospective interviews, and reports from a single family member; using measures of limited reliability; and failing to control for the reason the intact family separated, type of stepparenting relationship (i.e., stepmother or stepfather), and family size, as well as other variables. Very few studies have entailed direct observation of parent-child interactions, and very few involved young children. The conclusion of this review is thus limited by the quality of the research, but suggests that remarriage has no significant positive or negative effects on children.

It is noteworthy, however, that most of the research reviewed by Ganong and Coleman (1984) examined the effects of stepparenting long after the children had made the adjustment to this kind of family structure, and thus may underestimate the difficulties children encounter in making the *transition* to a stepparent family. In this regard, several investigators (e.g., Fast & Cain, 1966; Kompara, 1980; Messinger, 1976; Thies, 1977; Visher & Visher, 1978, 1979) have commented on the problems experienced by parents and children in the reconstitution of a stepparenting or "blended" family, especially if it follows soon after a divorce. On the one hand, stepparents themselves experience significant role ambiguity and uncertainty in how to treat their stepchildren (Fast & Cain, 1966; Kompara, 1980). On the other hand, children may experience intense feelings of rejection, abandonment, and divided loyalties when coping with a divorce followed by remarriage. These include concerns about losing the affection of the custodial parent (in competition with the new spouse and possibly also with stepsiblings), and about diminished contact with the noncustodial parent. In addition, a new set of family relationships have to be negotiated in the context of continuing loyalty to members of the original family (especially the noncustodial parent). Remarriage also undermines any remaining hopes of the child for reconciliation of the parents. Partly for these reasons, therefore, it is not surprising that several researchers have noted children's active efforts to undermine the remarriage of a parent, and that they often respond to the stepparent with hostility in the initial transition to a blended family (e.g., Visher & Visher, 1979). In addition, as Wallerstein and Kelly (1980a) noted in their study, the age of the child at remarriage may also be an important predictor of the child's adjustment, with younger children adapting more easily and harmoniously to the blended family than older children and adolescents.

It appears, therefore, that the short-term and long-term ramifications of remarriage for children may vary significantly. A parent's immediate remarriage may add significantly more stressful demands to the child's post-divorce adjustment, complicating the transition to a new family structure by adding another set of relationships to negotiate. Thus contrary to the view that children will benefit when their custodial fathers remarry through the addition of a maternal influence in the home, it appears that remarriage may importantly exacerbate the child's adjustment difficulties in the short term. Over the long term, however, existing research evidence suggests that once adjustments are made, children neither benefit nor are harmed by life in a stepparenting family. Rather, their experience within this reconstituted family does not seem to have significant effects on their intellectual, personality, and social functioning, suggesting that family structure per se may not be as important as relational harmony in determining a child's family experience.

Summary and Conclusions

In accord with the formulations of Nash and Feldman (1981), studies of the role of fathers in nontraditional families conclude rather consistently that fathers can assume enhanced caregiving responsibilities competently and effectively, following a period of adjustment to the new role. That is, rather than encountering the enduring difficulties that might be predicted by a gender-based approach to caregiving competence, most of the men in these studies evinced the kind of nurturance and child-centered concern that are typically noted in women in traditional child-care roles. More important, these studies almost uniformly report that the children in a father's care fare well: There is no consistent evidence of any kind of intellectual, psychosocial, emotional, or relational difficulties experienced by children in dual-career, shared-caregiving, single-father, or stepparenting families. Indeed, there is suggestive evidence that some children (especially sons) may benefit from certain kinds of nontraditional family structures in which the father has an enhanced role.

These conclusions have several implications for custody adjudication. First, they add validity to one of the conclusions drawn from the preceding section: That it is more valuable to examine parenting within the family in terms of parenting role rather than gender in view of the capacity of either parent to assume a primary caregiving role. Furthermore, they suggest that the decision rule proposed earlier—awarding custody of children up to the age of 3 or 4 to the primary caregiver—applies equally well when fathers are the primary caregiver. Although definitive evidence is in short supply, there seems to be no reason to doubt the ability of men to assume responsibility for children this young on the basis of their gender alone.

Second, there is suggestive evidence in the studies reviewed here that the gender of the child (especially an older child) might be an important factor in predicting the child's adjustment to mother-custody or father-custody families. There are intriguing indications that sons fare worse in mother-custody homes and better in father-custody families, which is consistent with research reviewed earlier concerning the father's early salient influence in the life of his son. With respect to daughters, the picture is much less clear, but suggests better adjustment of the child in a mother-custody family. Historically, there has been much judicial abuse of sex of parent-sex of child guidelines concerning custody disputes (Derdeyn, 1976, 1978), partly because they can be so indiscriminantly applied. For this reason one is hesitant to recommend the child's gender as an important factor in custody decision making, especially when there are countervailing factors in the relational harmony shared by the child with each parent. Even so, the weight of the evidence, drawn from studies of fathers in traditional as well as nontraditional families, must certainly be taken seriously in judicial considerations.

Third and finally, in view of these considerations there seems to be little reason in custody disputes to favor fathers who can anticipate remarriage. Indeed, not only is it unnecessary for fathers to buttress their custody claim with the expectation of providing the child with "a mother's touch," but research indicates that children have little to gain (or lose) by living in a stepmother family. Indeed, there is reason to believe that remarriage soon after a divorce exacerbates rather than diminishes a child's postdivorce adjustment difficulties.

The strength of these conclusions is tempered by the nature of the research on which they are based. The interpretational cautions that are inherent in studies relying on select samples, parent interviews, and retrospective accounts have been discussed, but they introduce an important caveat to the application of these findings to custody disputes. Since there is little good research concerning fathering in nontraditional families and fathers' effects on children, further studies are essential. For the present, however, conclusions drawn from existing research, while reasonably consistent across multiple studies, must be viewed with appropriate caution.

WHEN IS JOINT CUSTODY A VIABLE OPTION?

When custody is awarded to one parent, the quantity and quality of the child's interactions with the noncustodial parent inevitably change. It is also clear that variations in the quality and quantity of the visiting relationship have a significant effect on the child's postdivorce experience and adjustment. Hess and Camara (1979) studied the adjustment of 16 children (ages 9 to 11) from mother-custody homes on the basis of teacher ratings and parent checklists two to three years after the parents had separated. They found that children who had maintained relatively positive relationships with both parents received lower ratings on stress and aggression and higher ratings on social relations and "work effectiveness" at school, compared with children who had positive relationships with only one parent or with neither parent. The harmony of parent-child relationships was a more significant predictor of child adjustment than was even the nature of the relationship between the two parents (see also Jacobson, 1978).

In view of these considerations, the growing popularity of joint custody as a way of resolving custody disputes seems warranted. In a joint custody arrangement, the child can maintain ongoing and positive relationships with each parent and does not "lose" one parent relationally while residing with the other. There is reason to expect children to cope better with the divorce when they can maintain regular contact with both parents. There are other perceived advantages to joint custody. For mothers (especially those with longstanding career commitments), it relieves some of the burden of single parenthood, while it gives fathers more consistent and "natural" opportunities for maintaining a parent-child relationship than does a visiting noncustodial relationship. Judges find that a joint custody alternative relieves them of many of the intrinsically difficult decisions entailed in determining sole custody under the best interests standard, since it reduces the need for judgments of parental caregiving competence or for making complex predictive judgments concerning the child's experience with either parent. Finally, there is evidence that the joint custody alternative offers benefits to the legal system, since one study has found that relitigation is markedly less frequent in joint custody compared with single-custody arrangements (Ilfeld, Ilfeld, & Alexander, 1982). Perhaps for many of these reasons, the majority of states have enacted joint custody statutes, with a handful adopting a statutory preference for joint custody in adjudication (Derdeyn & Scott, 1984).

To be sure, the term "joint custody" summarizes a range of different custody agreements (Cox & Cease, 1978). Most commonly, it entails joint *legal* custody in which parents share decision making concerning the child's education, health care, and related issues, even though the child permanently resides with one parent. Indeed, except for its legal basis, this form of joint custody may not differ significantly from many single-custody arrangements in which a former spouse enjoys a liberal visiting agreement and shares decision making concerning the child. Less frequent are joint *physical* custody arrangements, in which the child resides with each parent on a regular alternating basis or, very rarely, the child remains in one home while parents alternate in residence. What all these forms of joint custody share in common is the increased opportunity provided for the child to maintain an ongoing relationship with each parent, and the increased requirement that the parents cooperate in child-related concerns, compared with most single-custody arrangements.

Because of the wide variations in the nature of joint custody arrangements and their likely effects on the child, this custody alternative has received a great deal of attention from legal scholars and social scientists alike. Some have offered it as "a viable and ideal alternative" (Grote & Weinstein, 1977; see also Roman & Haddad, 1978), while others have expressed concern about its potentially negative effects on children (Goldstein, Freud, & Solnit, 1973). Unfortunately, research to date is insufficiently clear to permit any strong conclusions about the child's experience in joint custody arrangements (Abarbanel, 1979; Ahrons, 1980; Galper, 1978; Greif, 1979; Keshet & Rosenthal, 1978a; Luepnitz, 1982; Morgenbesser & Nehls, 1981; Roman & Haddad, 1978; Steinman, 1981). Like the studies of single fathers, most of these studies rely exclusively on parental interviews to assess child outcomes and, since the samples themselves were selected in such a manner as to yield a group of conscientious and highly motivated families, they may exaggerate the positive effects of joint custody on children. We have no studies of families while they are negotiating the transition to this form of shared caregiving; instead, the families were interviewed long after this arrangement became consolidated. The three studies that involved any direct examination of children (i.e., Abarbanel, 1979; Luepnitz, 1982; Steinman, 1981) relied primarily on interviews, so we have no direct observation of parent-child interactions in joint custody families. No study has used appropriate comparison groups, the samples are generally rather small, and information is lacking concerning the experience of children most likely to suffer from joint custody caregiving: those younger than 4 years of age. All of these factors are likely to contribute to an optimistic portrayal of the effects of joint custody on children.

Not surprisingly, these studies fail to confirm the concerns of some about the potentially detrimental effects of joint custody arrangements. While parents (especially fathers) report satisfaction with the maintenance of close ties with their offspring, the children themselves seem to adapt well to this form of shared caregiving and value their ongoing relationships with each parent (Luepnitz, 1982). While none of this research effectively distinguishes joint legal custody from joint physical custody arrangements, the tenor of the findings suggests no general harm to children from these caregiving conditions. Yet embedded within these reports are some cautionary comments. Luepnitz (1982), for example, noted that children's adjustment and self-esteem were lower in families with parental conflict, and this was true of both joint custody and single-custody homes. Similarly, Abarbanel (1979) reported that the child's adjustment to living in two homes was fostered when parents cooperated and shared important information about the child. Steinman (1981) also noted that although loyalty conflicts were not prevalent, the children devoted significant effort to maintaining an equal share of their time with each parent. While this "hyper-loyalty" (Steinman's phrase) was motivated by an effort to be fair to each parent, it sometimes imposed a burden on the children. Moreover, a quarter of Steinman's sample (many of them the youngest children) experienced considerable confusion and anxiety about switching homes.

These findings rather consistently indicate that the most important contributors to a beneficial joint custody arrangement for children are in the supportive and cooperative attitudes and behavior of the parents. Thus joint custody is clearly not a viable option for *all* divorcing parents (contrary to the claims of its strongest supporters), but it does offer the child significant benefits *if* parents can ally in this manner for the child's interests (contrary to the fears of its strongest critics). The problem in interpreting these findings is that the same factors that foster a successful joint custody arrangement—interparental cooperation and mutual respect—are also predictive of the child's successful adjustment to a single-parent home (e.g., Hess & Camara, 1979). Given these conditions, it seems that joint custody offers advantages over sole custody by fostering the child's ongoing relationship with each parent. In the absence of parental cooperation, however, it is not clear that joint custody offers any benefits over a single-parent family.

Other factors also help to predict the quality of the child's experience in joint custody, including how the child's regular shifts in residence are negotiated and the similarity of the alternating home environments (Clingempeel & Reppucci 1982). An important variable that is strangely neglected in the research on the effects of joint custody is the age of the child (Kelly & Wallerstein, 1976; Wallerstein & Kelly, 1974, 1975, 1976).

Since preschool children have difficulty understanding causes of divorce, they are often subject to intense fears of abandonment, together with self-blame and unrealistic hopes for a parental reconciliation. Such children also may have difficulty sustaining an attachment to a parent across recurrent separations of several days or weeks. Further, the regular alternation of living environments involved in joint physical custody may be perceived as unpredictable and somewhat frightening by the young child, a disadvantage that may outweigh the benefits of such an arrangement. In contrast, the school-age child and adolescent can better understand the interpersonal dynamics underlying the divorce and are cognitively more competent to cope with the practical considerations involved in sharing two home environments. For these children, joint custody may be more advantageous.

Clearly, when conditions surrounding the divorce are supportive, joint custody can offer a number of benefits to children, which are consistent with their best interests, especially if the children are school age or older. Conversely, it may be disadvantageous for very young children, or if parents remain conflictual. Thus, joint custody is not an ideal alternative in all cases. One important implication of these conclusions is that a joint custody arrangement should not be judicially imposed on parents who do not desire it, which is currently possible in several jurisdictions. On the other hand, barring extremely unusual circumstances, there is no reason for courts to deny joint custody to parents who are agreeable and cooperative with this arrangement.

CONCLUSION

The clear conclusion emerging from the research reviewed in this chapter is that there is no basis for concern over awarding custody to fathers because of gender. The research on gender differences in responsiveness to the young, and studies of fathers in shared-caregiving and single-parent families, all point to the fact that fathers are capable of sensitively and capably caring for children of various ages. Rather than being a function of gender, variations in caregiving interest and ability in both traditional and nontraditional families seem to be largely a function of the nature of the caregiving roles that parents assume in the home. Many studies suggest that following a period of transition, fathers who had previously assumed little responsibility for child care adapt well to a shift in caregiving responsibility brought about by changed family conditions (e.g., from a two-parent to a single-parent family), which indicates considerable flexibility in their caregiving competence in response to different role requirements. Thus substantial experience as a secondary caregiver may not, in fact, predict that a father will have serious difficulty in assuming a primary caregiving role, even of very young children.

With respect to child outcomes, the research reviewed here is equally sanguine concerning the child's experience in a father-as-primary-caregiver family structure. Although direct observational evidence is scanty, the weight of the evidence is that children fare well in families in which fathers are highly involved in caregiving. Part of the reason for this, of course, is that children develop strong emotional ties to both parents, each of whom assumes salient and important roles in the child's life regardless of the caregiving role. While research occasionally suggests that some children (especially sons) benefit from living in a single-father home (and that daughters may have some difficulty), there seem to be no general advantages or disadvantages accruing to children living in a family with enhanced paternal involvement. It seems safe to conclude, therefore, that fathers should be considered seriously as potential caregivers in custody disputes, even if they had not assumed major responsibility for child-care in the intact family.

Several considerations have emerged from this research review that are relevant to a child's best interests in a custody dispute. Concerning infants and very young children, there seems to be some basis for preference being given to the child's primary caregiver (whether this is the mother or the father) in view of the significance of basic caregiving ministrations to certain aspects of early psychological development and the importance of these kinds of relational expectations for each parent to the child's perceptions of predictability in the surround. There is no reason to maintain this preference for the primary caregiver for children beyond the ages of 3 and 4, however, since by this time the child is a cognitively more sophisticated individual, and the multidimensionality of paternal and maternal involvement makes a distinction between primary and secondary caregivers increasingly problematic. With older children, however, there may be some basis for considering the interaction of parental gender and child gender in predicting the child's postdivorce adjustment, although further study of this issue is essential. Moreover, there seems to be reason for serious consideration of the option of joint custody *provided that* parents are supportive of this alternative and are likely to cooperate in its implementation. In the absence of parental support, there is no basis for assuming that joint custody offers any advantages to the child over a single-parent custody arrangement.

It should be noted that these considerations apply in terms of a ceteris paribus assumption, that is, all other things being equal. In custody disputes, of course, all other things are certainly *not* equal, since a host of factors specific to the family merit great weight in a custody dispute. These include the nature of the temporary custody arrangements following the parents' separation, considerations pertaining to keeping siblings together, the child's wishes (even when the child is young), and other factors. Indeed, these family-specific considerations are likely to be weightier in the determination of a custody award than are the broader considerations drawn from the research described in this chapter, and this reflects the inherently idiosyncratic nature of any custody award. The broader decision rules outlined in this review are also relevant, however, to the difficult predictive judgments entailed in each custody award. Their contributions may help to curb judicial discretion in custody adjudication by providing an overall framework within which custody awards may be justified.

This research review has also highlighted a variety of areas requiring substantial new research initiatives. We have disconcertingly little direct observational information, for example, about the experience of children in joint custody homes or in a family with enhanced paternal caregiving involvement. Similarly, our knowledge of the child's experience in a single-father home is based almost entirely on paternal reports, which have the interpretational limitations earlier described. We know almost nothing about children's experience in a dual-career intact home, a home becoming increasingly normative in our society. These are important deficiencies in our research knowledge.

In the end, however, it is unlikely that even the generation of new research findings will significantly reduce the inherently difficult decisions faced by judges in determining a custody award. The growing emphasis on predivorce counseling and mediation offers hope that parents can be strongly encouraged to agree among themselves concerning custody arrangements and other aspects of a divorce settlement without judicial intervention. When parents turn to the courts, however, the dispute they present is inherently difficult. It is to be hoped that judicial wisdom can be fostered by the contributions of behavioral scientists and others who are concerned with children.

REFERENCES

Abarbanel, A. (1979). Shared parenting after separation and divorce: A study of joint custody. *American Journal of Orthopsychiatry, 49,* 320–328.

Ahrons, C. R. (1980). Joint custody arrangements in the postdivorce family. *Journal of Divorce, 3,* 189–205.

Babchuk, W. A., Hames, R. B., & Thompson, R. A. (1985). Sex differences in the recognition of infant facial expressions of emotion: The primary caretaker hypothesis. *Ethology and Sociobiology, 6,* 5–17.

Ban, P. L., & Lewis, M. (1974). Mothers and fathers, girls and boys: Attachment behavior in the one-year-old. *Merrill-Palmer Quarterly, 20,* 195–204.

Bartz, K. W., & Witcher, W. C. (1978). When father gets custody. *Children Today, 7,* 2–35.

Belsky, J. (1979). Mother-father-infant interaction: A naturalistic observational study. *Developmental Psychology, 15,* 601–607.

Berman, P. W. (1980). Are women more responsive than men to the young? A review of developmental and situational variables. *Psychological Bulletin, 88,* 668–695.

Biller, H. B. (1981). The father and sex role development. In M. E. Lamb (Ed.), *The role of the father in child development.* Rev. ed. New York: Wiley.

Block, J. H. (1983). Differential premises arising from differential socialization of the sexes: Some conjectures. *Child Development, 54,* 1335–1354.

Block, J. H., Block, J., & Harrington, D. M. (1974, April). The relationship of parental teaching strategies to ego-resiliency in preschool children. Paper presented to meeting of Western Psychological Association, San Francisco.

Block, J. H., Block, J., & Harrington, D. M. (1975, April). Sex role typing and instrumental behavior: A developmental study. Paper presented to meeting of Society for Research in Child Development, Denver.

Bowlby, J. (1969). *Attachment and loss.* Vol. 1. *Attachment.* New York: Basic.

Cantor, N. L., Wood, D. D., & Gelfand, D. M. (1977). Effects of responsiveness and sex of children on adult males' behavior. *Child Development, 48,* 1426–1430.

Chambers, D. L. (1984). Rethinking the substantive rules for custody disputes in divorce. *Michigan Law Review, 83,* 477–569.

Chang, P.-N., & Deinard, A. S. (1982). Single-father caretakers: Demographic characteristics and adjustment processes. *American Journal of Orthopsychiatry, 52,* 236–243.

Clarke-Stewart, K. A. (1978). And daddy makes three: The father's impact on mother and young child. *Child Development, 49,* 466–478.

Clarke-Stewart, K. A. (1980). The father's contribution to children's cognitive and social development in early childhood. In F. A. Pedersen (Ed.), *The father-infant relationship: Observational studies in the family setting.* New York: Praeger.

Clingempeel, W. G., & Reppucci, N. D. (1982). Joint custody after divorce: Major issues and goals for research. *Psychological Bulletin, 91,* 102–127.

Cohen, L. J., & Campos, J. J. (1974). Father, mother, and stranger as elicitors of attachment behaviors in infancy. *Developmental Psychology, 10,* 146–154.

Cox, M. J., & Cease, L. (1978). Joint custody: What does it mean? How does it work? *Family Advocate, 1,* 10–13.

Derdeyn, A. P. (1976). Child custody contests in historical perspective. *American Journal of Psychiatry, 133,* 1369–1376.

Derdeyn, A. P. (1978). Child custody: A reflection of cultural change. *Journal of Clinical Child Psychology, 7,* 169–173.

Derdeyn, A. P., & Scott, E. (1984). Joint custody: A critical analysis and appraisal. *American Journal of Orthopsychiatry, 54,* 199–209.

Ennis, D., & Litwack, T. R. (1974). Psychology and the presumption of expertise: Flipping coins in the courtroom. *California Law Review, 62,* 693–752.

Erikson, E. H. (1963). *Childhood and society.* 2nd ed. New York: Norton.

Fast, I., & Cain, A. C. (1966). The stepparent role: Potential for disturbances in family functioning. *American Journal of Orthopsychiatry, 36,* 485–491.

Feldman, S. S., & Nash, S. C. (1978). Interest in babies during young adulthood. *Child Development, 49,* 617–622.

Feldman, S. S., & Nash, S. C. (1979a). Changes in responsiveness to babies during adolescence. *Child Development, 50,* 942–949.

Feldman, S. S., & Nash, S. C. (1979b). Sex differences in responsiveness to babies among mature adults. *Developmental Psychology, 15,* 430–436.

Feldman, S. S., Nash, S. C., & Cutrona, C. (1977). The influence of age and sex on responsiveness to babies. *Developmental Psychology, 13,* 675–676.

Ferri, E. (1978). Characteristics of motherless families. *British Journal of Social Work, 3,* 91–100.

Field, T. (1978). Interaction behaviors of primary versus secondary caretaker fathers. *Developmental Psychology, 14,* 183–184.

Freud, S. (1940). *An outline of psychoanalysis.* New York: Norton.

Galper, M. (1978). *Co-parenting.* Philadelphia: Running Press.

Ganong, L. H., & Coleman, M. (1984). The effects of remarriage on children: A review of the empirical literature. *Family Relations, 33,* 389–406.

Gasser, R. D., & Taylor, C. M. (1976). Role adjustment of single parent fathers with dependent children. *The Family Coordinator, 25,* 397–401.

George, V., & Wilding, P. (1972). *Motherless families.* London: Routledge and Kegan Paul.

Goldstein, J., Freud, A., & Solnit, A. J. (1973). *Beyond the best interests of the child.* New York: Free Press.

Greif, J. B. (1979). Fathers, children, and joint custody. *American Journal of Orthopsychiatry, 49,* 311–319.

Grote, D. F., & Weinstein, J. R. (1977). Joint custody: A viable and ideal alternative. *Journal of Divorce, 1,* 43–53.

Gutmann, D. (1975). Parenthood: A key to the comparative study of the life cycle. In N. Datan & L. H. Ginsburg (Eds.), *Life-span developmental psychology: Normative life crises.* New York: Academic.

Hess, R. K., & Camara, K. A. (1979). Post-divorce family relationships as mediating factors in the consequences of divorce for children. *Journal of Social Issues, 35,* 79–96.

Hetherington, E. M., Cox, M., & Cox, R. (1976). Divorced fathers. *Family Coordinator, 25,* 417–428.

Hetherington, E. M., Cox, M., & Cox, R. (1978). The aftermath of divorce. In J. H. Stevens and M. Matthews (Eds.), *Mother/child father/child relationships.* Washington, DC: National Association for the Education of Young Children.

Hetherington, E. M., Cox, M., & Cox, R. (1979a). Family interaction and the social, emotional, and cognitive development of children following divorce. In V. Vaughn & T. B. Brazelton (Eds.), *The family: Setting priorities.* New York: Science and Medicine.

Hetherington, E. M., Cox, M., & Cox, R. (1979b). Play and social interaction in children following divorce. *Journal of Social Issues, 35,* 26–49.

Hetherington, E. M., Cox, M., & Cox, R. (1982). Effects of divorce on parents and children. In M. E. Lamb (Ed.), *Nontraditional families.* Hillsdale, NJ: Erlbaum.

Hipgrave, T. J. (1978). *When the mother is gone: Profile studies of 16 lone fathers with preschool children.* Unpublished master's thesis, Nottingham University, Child Development Research Unit, Nottingham, England.

Hoffman, M. L. (1981). The role of the father in moral internalization. In M. E. Lamb (Ed.), *The role of the father in child development.* Rev. ed. New York: Wiley.

Ilfeld, F., Ilfeld, H., & Alexander, J. (1982). Does joint custody work? A first look at outcome data of relitigation. *American Journal of Psychiatry, 139,* 62–66.

Jacobson, D. S. (1978). The impact of marital separation/divorce on children: I. Parent-child separation and child adjustment. *Journal of Divorce, 1,* 341–360.

Katz, A. J. (1979). Lone fathers: Perspectives and implications for family policy. *The Family Coordinator, 28,* 521–528.

Kelly, J., & Wallerstein, J. (1976). The effects of parental divorce: Experiences of the child in early latency. *American Journal of Orthopsychiatry, 46,* 20–32.

Kelly, J. B., & Wallerstein, J. S. (1977). Part-time parent, part-time child: Visiting after divorce. *Journal of Clinical Child Psychology, 6,* 51–54.

Keshet, H. F., & Rosenthal, K. M. (1978a). Fathering after marital separation. *Social Work, 23,* 11–18.

Keshet, H. F., & Rosenthal, K. M. (1978b). Single parent fathers: A new study. *Children Today, 7,* 13–17.

Kompara, D. R. (1980). Difficulties in the socialization process of stepparenting. *Family Relations, 29,* 69–73.

Kotelchuck, M. (1976). The infant's relationship to the father: Experimental evidence. In M. E. Lamb (Ed.), *The role of the father in child development.* New York: Wiley.

Lamb, M. E. (1976a). Interactions between 8-month-old children and their fathers and mothers. In M. E. Lamb (Ed.), *The role of the father in child development.* New York: Wiley.

Lamb, M. E. (1976b). Twelve-month-olds and their parents: Interaction in a laboratory playroom. *Developmental Psychology, 12,* 237–244.

Lamb, M. E. (1976c). Effects of stress and cohort on mother- and father-infant interaction. *Developmental Psychology, 12,* 435–443.

Lamb, M. E. (1976d). Interactions between two-year-olds and their mothers and fathers. *Psychological Reports, 38,* 447–450.

Lamb, M. E. (1977a). Father-infant and mother-infant interaction in the first year of life. *Child Development, 48,* 167–181.

Lamb, M. E. (1977b). The development of mother-infant and father-infant attachments in the second year of life. *Developmental Psychology, 13,* 637–648.

Lamb, M. E. (1977c). The development of parental preferences in the first two years of life. *Sex Roles, 3,* 495–497.

Lamb, M. E. (1981). Fathers and child development: An integrative overview. In M. E. Lamb (Ed.), *The role of the father in child development.* Rev. ed. New York: Wiley.

Lamb, M. E. (Ed.) (1982). *Nontraditional families.* Hillsdale, NJ: Erlbaum.

Lamb, M. E., Frodi, A. M., Frodi, M., & Hwang, C.-P. (1982). Characteristics of maternal and paternal behavior in traditional and nontraditional Swedish families. *International Journal of Behavioral Development, 5,* 131–141.

Lamb, M. E., Frodi, A. M., Hwang, C.-P., & Frodi, M. (1982). Varying degrees of paternal involvement in infant care: Attitudinal and behavioral correlates. In M. E. Lamb (Ed.), *Nontraditional families.* Hillsdale, NJ: Erlbaum.

Lamb, M. E., Frodi, A. M., Hwang, C.-P., Frodi, M., & Steinberg, J. (1982a). Effects of gender and caretaking role on parent-infant interaction. In R. Emde & R. Harmon (Eds.), *The development of attachment and affiliative systems.* New York: Plenum.

Lamb, M. E., Frodi, A. M., Hwang, C.-P., Frodi, M., & Steinberg, J. (1982b). Mother- and father-infant interaction involving play and holding in traditional and nontraditional Swedish families. *Developmental Psychology, 18,* 215–221.

Lamb, M. E., Owen, M. T., & Chase-Lansdale, L. (1979). The father-daughter relationship: Past, present and future. In C. B. Kopp & M. Kirkpatrick (Eds.), *Becoming female: Perspectives on development.* New York: Plenum.

Langlois, J. H., & Downs, A. C. (1980). Mothers, fathers and peers as socialization agents of sex-typed play behaviors in young children. *Child Development, 51,* 1237–1247.

Litwack, T. R., Gerber, G. L., & Fenster, C. A. (1980). The proper role of psychology in child custody disputes. *Journal of Family Law, 18,* 269–300.

Lowenstein, J. S., & Koopman, E. J. (1978). A comparison of the self-esteem between boys living with single-parent mothers and single-parent fathers. *Journal of Divorce, 2,* 195–208.

Luepnitz, D. A. (1982). *Child custody: A study of families after divorce.* Lexington, MA: Lexington.

Lynn, D. R., & Cross, A. D. (1974). Parent preferences of preschool children. *Journal of Marriage and the Family, 36,* 555–559.

Maccoby, E. E., & Jacklin, C. N. (1974). *The psychology of sex differences.* Stanford, CA: Stanford University Press.

Melton, G. B., & Thompson, R. A. (1985). Legislative approaches to psychological maltreatment: A social policy analysis. In M. Brassard, R. Germain, & S. N. Hart (Eds.), *The psychological maltreatment of children and youth.* New York: Pergamon.

Mendes, H. A. (1976a). Single fatherhood. *Social Work, 21,* 308–312.

Mendes, H. A. (1976b). Single fathers. *The Family Coordinator, 25,* 439–444.

Messinger, L. (1976). Remarriage between divorced people with children from previous marriages: A proposal for preparation for remarriage. *Journal of Marriage and Family Counseling, 2,* 193–200.

Mnookin, R. H. (1975). Child-custody adjudication: Judicial functions in the face of indeterminacy. *Law and Contemporary Problems, 39,* 226–293.

Mnookin, R. H., & Kornhauser, L. (1979). Bargaining in the shadow of the law: The case of divorce. *Yale Law Journal, 88,* 950–997.

Morgenbesser, M., & Nehls, N. (1981). *Joint custody.* Chicago: Nelson-Hall.

Nash, S. C., & Feldman, S. S. (1980). Responsiveness to babies: Life-situation specific sex differences in adulthood. *Sex Roles, 6,* 751–758.

Nash, S. C., & Feldman, S. S. (1981). Sex role and sex-related attributions: Constancy and change across the family life cycle. In M. E. Lamb & A. Brown (Eds.), *Advances in developmental psychology* (Vol. I). Hillsdale, NJ: Erlbaum.

Okpaku, S. R. (1976). Psychology: Impediment or aid in child custody cases? *Rutgers Law Review, 29,* 1117–1153.

Orthner, D. K., Brown, T., & Ferguson, D. (1976). Single-parent fatherhood: An emerging life style. *The Family Coordinator, 25,* 429–437.

Parke, R. D. (1979). Perspectives on father-infant interaction. In J. D. Osofsky (Ed.), *Handbook of infant development.* New York: Wiley.

Parke, R. D., & O'Leary, S. E. (1976). Family interaction in the newborn period: Some findings, some observations, and some unresolved issues. In K. Riegel & J. Meacham (Eds.), *The developing individual in a changing world* (Vol. 2). The Hague: Mouton.

Parke, R. D., & Sawin, D. B. (1976). The father's role in infancy: A re-evaluation. *The Family Coordinator, 25,* 365–371.

Parke, R. D., & Tinsley, B. R. (1981). The father's role in infancy: Determinants of involvement in caregiving and play. In M. E. Lamb (Ed.), *The role of the father in child development.* Rev. ed. New York: Wiley.

Pedersen, F. A., Anderson, B. J., & Cain, R. L. (1980). Parent–infant and husband–wife interactions observed at age 5 months. In F. A. Pedersen (Ed.), *The father–infant relationship: Observational studies in the family setting.* New York: Praeger.

Pedersen, F. A., Cain, R. L., Zaslow, M. J., & Anderson, B. J. (1982). Variation in infant experience associated with alternative family roles. In L. Laosa & I. Sigel (Eds.), *Families as learning environments for children.* New York: Plenum.

Pedersen, F. A., & Robson, K. S. (1969). Father participation in infancy. *American Journal of Orthopsychiatry, 39,* 466–472.

Pleck, J. H. (1979). Men's family work: Three perspectives and some new data. *The Family Coordinator, 28,* 481–488.

Pleck, J. H., & Lang, L. (1978). *Men's family role: Its nature and consequences.* Wellesley, MA: Wellesley College Center for Research on Women, Working Paper #10.

Pleck, J. H., & Rustad, M. (1980). *Husbands' and wives' time in family work and paid work in the 1975–76 study of time use.* Wellesley, MA: Wellesley College Center for Research on Women, Working Paper #63.

Power, T. G., & Parke, R. D. (1982). Play as a context for early learning: Lab and home analyses. In I. Sigel & L. M. Laosa (Eds.), *The family as a learning environment.* New York: Plenum.

Pruett, K. D. (1983). Infants of primary nurturing fathers. *Psychoanalytic study of the child, 38,* 257–277.

Radin, N. (1981). The role of the father in cognitive, academic, and intellectual development. In M. E. Lamb (Ed.), *The role of the father in child development.* Rev. ed. New York: Wiley.

Radin, N. (1982). Primary caregiving and role-sharing fathers. In M. E. Lamb (Ed.), *Nontraditional families: Parenting and child development.* Hillsdale, NJ: Erlbaum.

Radin, N., & Russell, G. (1983). Increased father participation and child development outcomes. In M. E. Lamb & A. Sagi (Eds.), *Fatherhood and family policy.* Hillsdale, NJ: Erlbaum.

Radin, N., & Sagi, A. (1982). Childrearing fathers in Israel and the USA. *Merrill-Palmer Quarterly, 1,* 111–136.

Robinson, J. P. (1977). *How Americans use time.* New York: Praeger.

Roman, M., & Haddad, W. (1978). *The disposable parent: The case for joint custody.* New York: Holt, Rinehart and Winston.

Rosenthal, K. M., & Keshet, H. F. (1981). *Fathers without partners.* Totowa, NJ: Rowman and Littlefield.

Rossi, A. S. (1977). A biosocial perspective on parenting. *Daedalus, 106,* 1–30.

Rossi, A. S. (1984). Gender and parenthood. *American Sociological Review, 49,* 1–19.

Roth, A. (1977). The tender years presumption in child custody disputes. *Journal of Family Law, 15,* 423–462.

Russell, G. (1982a). Shared-caregiving families: An Australian study. In M. E. Lamb (Ed.), *Nontraditional families: Parenting and child development.* Hillsdale, NJ: Erlbaum.

Russell, G. (1982b). Highly participant Australian fathers: Some preliminary findings. *Merrill-Palmer Quarterly, 28,* 137–156.

Russell, G. (1983). *The changing role of fathers?* St. Lucia, Queensland: University of Queensland Press.

Sagi, A. Antecedents and consequences of various degrees of paternal involvement in child rearing: The Israeli project. In M. E. Lamb (Ed.), *Nontraditional families: Parenting and child development.* Hillsdale, NJ: Erlbaum.

Santrock, J. W., & Warshak, R. A. (1979). Father custody and social development in boys and girls. *Journal of Social Issues, 35,* 112–125.

Santrock, J. W., Warshak, R. A., & Elliott, G. L. (1982). Social development and parent-child interaction in father-custody and stepmother families. In M. E. Lamb (Ed.), *Nontraditional families: Parenting and child development.* Hillsdale, NJ: Erlbaum.

Santrock, J. W., Warshak, R. A., Sitterle, K. A., Dozier, C., & Stephens, M. (1985, April). The social behavior of children and parents in stepmother, stepfather, and intact families. Paper presented to meeting of Society for Research in Child Development, Toronto.

Sawin, D. B., & Parke, R. D. (1979). Fathers' affectionate stimulation and caregiving behaviors with newborn infants. *The Family Coordinator, 28,* 509–513.

Schlesinger, B. (1979). Single parent fathers: A research review. *Children Today, 7,* 12–39.

Schlesinger, B., & Todres, R. (1976). Motherless families: An increasing societal pattern. *Child Welfare, 55,* 553–558.

Shorter, E. (1975). *The making of the modern family.* New York: Basic.

Smith, R. M., & Smith, C. W. (1981). Child rearing and single-parent fathers. *Family Relations, 30,* 411–417.

Steinman, S. (1981). The experience of children in a joint-custody arrangement. *American Journal of Orthopsychiatry, 51,* 403–414.

Szalai, A., Converse, P. E., Feldheim, P., Scheuch, E. K., & Stone, P. J. (1972). *The use of time.* The Hague: Mouton.

Tauber, M. A. (1981). Sex differences in parent-child interaction styles during a free-play session. *Child Development, 50,* 981–988.

Thies, J. M. (1977). Beyond divorce: The impact of remarriage on children. *Journal of Clinical Child Psychology, 6,* 59–61.

Thompson, R. A. (1985, August). Defining and assessing the "psychological maltreatment" of children. In G. B. Melton (Chair), *Recent developments in the law affecting children, youth, and families.* Symposium conducted at meeting of American Psychological Association, Los Angeles.

Todres, R. (1975). Motherless families. *Canadian Welfare, 51,* 11–13.

Visher, E. B., & Visher, J. S. (1978). Common problems of stepparents and their spouses. *American Journal of Orthopsychiatry, 48,* 252–262.

Visher, E. B., & Visher, J. S. (1979). *Stepfamilies: A guide to working with stepparents and stepchildren.* New York: Brunner/Mazel.

Walker, K., & Woods, M. (1976). *Time use.* Washington, DC: American Home Economics Association.

Wallerstein, J., & Kelly, J. (1974). The effects of parental divorce: The adolescent experience. In E. J. Anthony & C. Koupernik (Eds.), *The child in his family: Children at psychiatric risk.* New York: Wiley.

Wallerstein, J., & Kelly, J. (1975). The effects of parental divorce: The experiences of the preschool child. *Journal of the American Academy of Child Psychiatry, 14,* 600–616.

Wallerstein, J., & Kelly, J. (1976). The effects of parental divorce: Experiences of the child in later latency. *American Journal of Orthopsychiatry, 46,* 259–269.

Wallerstein, J., & Kelly, J. (1980a). *Surviving the breakup: How children and parents cope with divorce.* New York: Basic Books.

Wallerstein, J. S., & Kelly, J. B. (1980b). Effects of divorce on the visiting father-child relationship. *American Journal of Psychiatry, 137,* 1534–1539.

Warshak, R. A., & Santrock, J. W. (1980). Children of divorce: Impact of custody disposition on social development. In E. J. Callahan & K. A. McCluskey (Eds.), *Life-span developmental psychology: Non-normative life events.* New York: Academic.

Warshak, R. A., & Santrock, J. W. (1983). The impact of divorce in father-custody and mother-custody homes: The child's perspective. In L. A. Kurdek (Ed.), *Children and divorce* (New Directions in Child Development #19, W. Damon, general editor). San Francisco: Jossey-Bass.

Watson, A. S. (1969). The children of Armageddon: Problems of custody following divorce. *Syracuse Law Review, 21,* 55–86.

Weitzman, L. J., & Dixon, R. B. (1979). Child custody awards: Legal standards and empirical patterns for child custody, support and visitation after divorce. *University of California Davis Law Review, 12,* 472–521.

Whobrey, L., Sales, B. & Lou, M. (in press). Determining the best interests of the child in custody disputes. In L. Weithorn (Ed.), *Psychology and child custody determinations: Roles, knowledge, and expertise.* Lincoln, NE: University of Nebraska Press.

Yogman, M. W. (1977, March). The goals and structure of face-to-face interaction between infants and fathers. Paper presented at biennial meeting of Society for Research in Child Development, New Orleans.

Yogman, M. W., Dixon, S., Tronick, E., Adamson, L., Als, H., & Brazelton, T. B. (1976, April). Development of infant social interaction with fathers. Paper presented at meeting of Eastern Psychological Association, New York

CHAPTER 4

Divorced Fathers: Stress, Coping, and Adjustment

E. MAVIS HETHERINGTON AND MARGARET STANLEY HAGAN
University of Virginia

In 1982, for the first time in 20 years, the American divorce rate declined, although it remains by far the highest divorce rate in the world (National Center for Health Statistics, 1985). It still is estimated that almost half of the marriages occurring in the 1970s and 1980s will end in divorce, and that before reaching the age of 18 one third of American children will experience their parents' divorce (Cherlin, 1981; Norton, 1983). There are now approximately 1.2 million divorces per year in the United States, and they involve over 1 million children. Further, the interval between first marriage and divorce has decreased; thus the modal age of divorcing parents has dropped and the children involved are younger. Couples who are young or expecting a child when first married, are of low socioeconomic status or black, or in which the husband has an unstable income are most likely to divorce (Kitson & Raschke, 1981).

For many divorced parents and their children, divorce is just one in a series of family transitions and family reorganizations. After a period of time in a one-parent household, 75 percent of women and 80 percent of men remarry, and 55 percent of these divorce for a second time. Four of 10 marriages now involve at least one spouse who has previously been married. A divorced man is more likely than a divorced woman to remarry within three years of the divorce and to select a new spouse who is younger and/or who has never before been married (Cherlin & McCarthy, 1983). Moreover, one sixth of American children, a total of 9.6 million children, live in stepfamily households (Select Committee on Children, Youth, and Families, 1983).

What might contribute to these changing patterns of conjugal succession? They have been attributed variously to the women's movement, the

103

increase in the number of women in the work place and their consequent greater economic independence, the growth of welfare, changing social attitudes, the easing of legal requirements for divorce, and the contemporary emphasis on self-satisfaction in American culture. Although accepting that all of these factors may contribute to the high divorce rate, Furstenberg and Spanier (1984) have argued that marriage is no longer the core in the standard sequence of status transitions involving courtship, marriage, rapid childbearing, and commitment of the father to working and the mother to homemaking that formerly served as the key in the passage to adulthood. They proposed that the acceptance of premarital relations and cohabitation by both men and women, the preference of many couples for childless marriages or delayed parenthood, the increase in the number of children born out of wedlock, and the relatively greater financial self-sufficiency of women have contributed to disrupting a common and predictable trajectory in young adulthood triggered by marriage. Marriage has become a more optional, less permanent relationship. These changes, in combination with contemporary encouragement of personal fulfillment, have led couples to have higher expectations for marital relationships. They are less constrained to remain in an unsatisfactory conjugal arrangement and more prone to use divorce and successive marriages as a chance to upgrade their marital situation. This position might be called "bootstrapping your way to marital happiness." It is reflected in the only partly facetious comment of a young man, marrying for the third time, who said "I'm going to keep on trying until I get it right."

This chapter examines primarily the experiences of noncustodial fathers, the problems they encounter, and changes in their lives as they go through divorce and its aftermath. The experiences of sole- and joint-custody fathers are briefly addressed. The experiences of custodial fathers are presented in greater detail in this volume in Chapter 5. Problems and life changes differ at different points in the divorce cycle. Fathers, mothers, and children usually find separation and divorce as stressful. However, unless divorce is compounded by other continuing stressors such as family conflict, poverty, multiple environmental changes, inept parenting, and mental or physical health problems in parents, most family members are able to adjust to divorce within a two- or three-year period.

ACCOUNTS OF THE DECISION TO SEPARATE OR DIVORCE

Most studies of separation and divorce use reports, usually retrospective ones by the divorcing spouses, of the status of the preseparation marriage and the factors that contributed to divorce. Since divorce often is a period of intense emotion and acrimony, these accounts are likely to be distorted and altered, and reconstructed over time. The divorcing couple's perceptions of what went on during marital dissolution, however, may be as or more important than what actually occurred in predicting the outcomes of divorce (Hetherington, Cox, & Cox, 1985). Marital accounts vary with race, age, social class, rural or urban residence, and length of marriage (Kitson & Sussman, 1982). Moreover, sex differences in accounts are so marked that conjugal relationships have been described as "his and her" marriages (Bernard, 1972) and "his and her" divorces (Hetherington, 1981). In one report, when identifying material such as names of family members, places, and occupations were removed from wive's and husbands' descriptions of marriage, divorce clinicians were able to pair the reports accurately in only about one third of the couples (Hetherington, Cox, & Cox, 1985). It has been suggested that some of the alterations in perceptions, interpretations, and affect in accounts associated with divorce may be based on the family member's attempt to make the experience seem more rational, understandable, and manageable (Gehrhardt, 1979; Taylor, 1983; Venters, 1979). However, discrepancies in family accounts and perceptions are related to distress, conflict, unhappiness, and dissatisfaction in relationships between married and divorced couples (Hetherington, Cox, & Cox, 1985; Gottman, 1979; Pasley, Ihinger-Tallman, & Coleman, 1984). Moreover, sustained or increased discrepancies in accounts of the marriage and the divorce reported during the six years following divorce have been found to be associated with continued acrimony and dissatisfaction with the postdivorce relationship (Hetherington, Cox, & Cox, 1985).

The final separation before a divorce has been preceded by other separations in about half of divorcing couples, and most divorcing spouses report that this period is associated with disagreement and/or disengagement from the family or emotional withdrawal (Spanier & Thompson, 1984). The two main complaints of marital conflict and lack of involvement have been prevalent in studies of separation and divorce for the past 30 years (Goode, 1956; Kitson & Sussman, 1982; Spanier & Thompson, 1984). Recently, however, divorcing couples have placed more emphasis on dissatisfaction with affectional and sexual involvement rather than just with involvement in household and family tasks and responsibilities (Kitson & Sussman, 1982). Although both divorcing men and women are disappointed in their spouses as companions and sources of emotional support, both married and divorced women are more likely than their husbands to express dissatisfaction with the marital relationship (Albrecht, Bahr, & Goodman, 1983; Campbell, Converse, & Rodgers, 1976; Glenn & Weaver, 1978; Kitson & Sussman, 1982; Spanier & Thompson,

1984). Divorced women more frequently than men complain of lack of tenderness, poor communication, and lack of shared activities or involvement with children as being important factors contributing to the divorce. Men more often cite in-law problems or sexual incompatibility as precipitating factors. It should be noted, however, that in describing sexual relationships, husbands are more likely to complain about the low frequency of sexual intercourse, whereas wives complain about the quality of sexual relations (Spanier and Thompson, 1984). Joint and personal conflicts over gender roles are increasingly common, although they are more frequent for women (Kitson & Sussman, 1982; Spanier & Thompson, 1984). Women's dissatisfaction is greatest with their husbands' help in tasks traditionally viewed as part of the female role, such as grocery shopping, washing dishes, and cleaning. The frequency with which these complaints are made suggests that contemporary couples, but especially wives, are struggling to resolve the need for personal growth and the allocation of roles within the family. When husbands' and wives' expectations and preferences cannot be reconciled, pervasive dissension occurs in the marital relationship.

Almost twice as many men as women report still loving their partner at the time of final separation (Spanier & Thompson, 1984), and many more husbands say that they are unsure about what caused the breakup (Kitson & Sussman, 1982). Moreover, more men than women blame themselves and are blamed by their spouse for the breakup (Kitson & Sussman, 1982). These findings suggest that there may be more ambivalence, guilt, and confusion in the responses of husbands than of wives to marital dissolution. Certainly, divorced women are more likely to describe their marriages with only mild affection, affection tempered with considerable dissatisfaction and aggravation, or even with hate, and after the divorce hostility and anger are more likely to be sustained in women than in men (Hetherington, Cox, & Cox, 1982).

Finally, the attitudes and responses of people other than the divorcing couple influence the decision to divorce. The presence of children, particularly of sons, makes parents more reluctant to separate and divorce (Glick, 1979; Hetherington, 1981). Moreover the encouragement or approval of family and friends facilitates the decision to divorce (Furstenberg & Spanier, 1984; Kitson & Sussman, 1982). In addition, in a substantial number of divorcing couples, extramarital relationships contribute to the divorce (Albrecht, Bahr, & Goodman, 1983; Furstenberg & Spanier, 1984; Hetherington, 1981; Hetherington, Cox, & Cox, 1982). Only a small group (6 percent) see their own extramarital affairs as a cause of marital problems, whereas 52 percent of men and 46 percent of women view their spouse's extramarital relationships as creating significant difficulties (Spanier and Thompson, 1984). Although men have more frequent extramarital affairs, women are more likely to report being emotionally involved with their extramarital sexual partners (Furstenberg & Spanier, 1984). A supportive extramarital relationship often helps divorcing individuals go through the difficult decision to leave the marriage without the fear of being alone that is so pervasive in marital separation. Relationships with "transition partners" usually are temporary and seldom lead to marriage, since emotional supportive needs change as the decision to divorce is made and adaptation to a new single status proceeds (Hetherington, 1981).

THE LEGAL DIVORCE

For most divorcing couples, involvement with the legal system is burdensome and accelerates their conflicts (Spanier & Anderson, 1979). Only 10 percent of divorces involve formal court hearings (Bodenheimer, 1977); lawyer negotiated divorce settlements are most common for divorcing couples (Mnookin & Kornhauser, 1979). Subsequent litigation ensues, however, in over one third of divorces involving children (Bodenheimer, 1977). The prominent issues in divorce settlements and litigation involve custody, visitation, and financial support.

Approximately 90 percent of children live with their mother following divorce, a proportion that has stayed the same for the past 20 years. Thus, although attitudes toward custody awards and the competence of fathers to care for children may be changing, custody outcomes do not reflect the change. Moreover, in spite of the fact that the "best interests of the child" doctrine suggests that both parents legally are to receive equal consideration, this view in practice has been translated to mean mother custody (Emery, Hetherington, & DiLalla, 1984). It should be noted, however, that only 17 percent of divorcing fathers seek custody; 65 percent of these fathers are awarded custody with most decisions being settled out of court (Rosenthal & Keshet, 1981). This low rate of custody-seeking by fathers has been attributed to the fathers' beliefs that their wives are more competent to raise children, concerns that they would be unable to juggle employment and child-care demands, discouragement by lawyers and friends of attempts to gain custody, apprehension about social disapproval, and perceptions that the court system is biased against them. When fathers do gain custody of the children, it is often because the mothers are viewed as incompetent by the courts or because the mothers do not wish to have custody because of desired changes in their lifestyles. Although about 10 percent of all children reside with their father after divorce, only 4 percent live with a father who has custody of all the children. Split custody, in which some of the children reside with the father and some with the mother, is more likely to be the case when fathers have custody. Fathers are more likely to have custody of sons than of daughters and of older rather than younger children (Spanier & Glick, 1981). To mitigate some of the problems with sole custody and split custody, there recently has been a push toward joint custody. This was dealt with somewhat in Chapter 3, and will be discussed in some detail in the last section of this chapter.

Although in most cases noncustodial parents are assigned visitation rights, contact between children and noncustodial parents may actually increase immediately following divorce, but will rapidly diminish over time (Furstenberg et al., 1983; Furstenberg & Spanier, 1984; Hetherington, Cox, & Cox, 1981). In a recent study, one half of the children from maritally disrupted families had not seen their father in the previous five years and only one in six saw their noncustodial father on the average of once a week (Furstenberg et al., 1983). Nonresidential mothers are more likely than nonresidential fathers to maintain an active role in child rearing and to sustain contact with their children with regular visits, overnights, phone calls, and letters (Furstenberg & Nord, 1982; Furstenberg & Spanier, 1984). Moreover, as will be discussed later, the quality as well as the frequency of contact between the noncustodial parent and child changes following divorce. The noncustodial parent assumes a social rather than an instrumental role with the children.

Finally, financial support is a central area of conflict during and following divorce. Although gender-neutral laws propose that the spouse with the greatest financial resources should provide support to his or her partner, it usually is the father who is ordered to pay child support. Awards most often are based on schedules involving the father's and mother's income and the number of children. Although the level of the award is supposed to be adequate to provide for the child's needs, court-ordered support payments are less than half the level required to raise a child in a low-income family (Weitzman, 1981; Weitzman & Dixon, 1979). Moreover, most fathers do not pay the full amount of allotted child support. About 47 percent of women receive the scheduled amount, 25 percent receive partial or occasional payments, and 28 percent receive nothing. The average annual support provided by fathers who do make payments is $2000 (Select Committee on Children, Youth, and Families, 1983). It is not surprising, then, that divorced mothers experience a sharp decline in income and are overrepresented on welfare roles following divorce, whereas fathers experience little or no economic duress.

NONCUSTODIAL FATHERS

The vast majority of studies of divorce investigate mother-custody families and in only a small number of these studies has attention been focused on the responses of fathers to divorce. The greater concern with mothers and children following divorce has to some extent been based on the fallacious beliefs that mothers are more often victims and fathers the perpetrators in divorce, that fathers are less emotionally distressed by divorce, and that fathers are less important in the development of children than are mothers. The major problems associated with separation and divorce with which divorced fathers must cope can be identified as: (1) pragmatic problems related to domestic tasks, finances, and employment; (2) emotional and psychological problems; and (3) problems in relations with the exspouse, in social relations, and in parent-child relations.

Pragmatic Problems

As already noted, long-term negative economic consequences of divorce are more marked for women than for men. Although costs directly associated with the legal divorce, such as lawyers' fees, court costs, and early contributions to maintaining two households, may cause financial duress for most fathers, this is short lived. Support payments usually are modest and often are rapidly terminated. Some fathers report an inability to work effectively as a concomitant of the emotional distress experienced during separation and in the early stages of divorce. Others report an attempt to increase their income by assuming greater work responsibilities shortly after divorce (Hetherington, Cox, & Cox, 1981). Little research is available, however, on the impact of divorce on father's work.

Considerable household reorganization, which requires that both parents adopt cross-gender skills, occurs after separation and divorce (Luepnitz, 1982). Divorced husbands and wives who maintained nontraditional sex roles during marriage and who are relatively independent, self-sufficient individuals are better able to cope with this transition. While both mothers and fathers experience difficulty in restructuring their home life immediately following divorce, many noncustodial fathers continue to experience erratic schedules, household disorganization, and residential instability for several years after divorce or until they remarry (Hetherington, Cox, & Cox,

1981). The noncustodial father is likely to eat out often, to have erratic sleep patterns, and to have difficulty with routine chores such as housecleaning, shopping, and laundry (Hetherington, Cox, & Cox, 1981). However, the divorced noncustodial father is more likely than his exwife to receive help with housekeeping chores from female friends and relatives or to employ a housekeeper (Brandwein, Brown, & Fox, 1974; Hetherington, Cox, & Cox, 1981).

Living conditions and patterns of child care and visitation by noncustodial fathers appear to be related. The father who does not change his traditional approach to his children and who has only infrequent contact with them is more likely than the father who pursues frequent contact to live alone, to move frequently, and to exclude others from father-child outings. The noncustodial father who sets up his own home and arranges his life to accommodate frequent contact, home visits, and overnights with his children is better able to develop close relationships with his children (Russell, 1983). The noncustodial father's sense of confidence and accomplishment increases (Keshet & Rosenthal, 1978) and his own and his children's lives gain in structure (Dominic & Schlesinger, 1980). Such structured home conditions reduce many of the tensions associated with where to go and what to do during visitation. It facilitates more relaxed interchanges, activities that normally are shared by parents and children, and the pursuit of independent interests in a familiar stable setting. Some of the stressful intensity and datelike quality of visits are eliminated and fathers are able to assume a more relaxed parental role and avoid being what has been called "tour guide" fathers or "Sunday Santas."

Emotional and Psychologic Adjustment

No matter how unsatisfying the relationship was prior to separation, most members of separated or divorcing families experience considerable trepidation and distress associated with marital dissolution. A minority of divorcing spouses from conflict-ridden or disengaged families report relief at separation; however, even this relief is often tempered by considerable ambivalence and periods of anxiety or depression (Cheriboga & Culture, 1977; Hetherington, Cox, & Cox, 1981; Kitson & Sussman, 1982; Kraus, 1979; Spanier & Thompson, 1984). Although the person who considered divorce the longest and who initiated the divorce is initially least disturbed, this difference soon disappears (Hetherington, Cox, & Cox, 1981; Thompson, 1983). Anger, guilt, fear, bitterness, regret, anxiety, grief, depression, loneliness, continued attachment to the spouse, low self-esteem, low life satisfaction, and feelings of personal failure are frequent responses to separation and divorce (Albrecht, 1980; Cheriboga, Roberts, & Stein, 1978; Furstenberg & Spanier, 1984; Hetherington, Cox, & Cox, 1981;

Kitson & Sussman, 1982; Spanier & Thompson, 1984; Wallerstein & Kelly, 1980; Weiss, 1975, 1976; Yoder & Nichols, 1980).

A predominant characteristic in the period following divorce is emotional liability, with soaring emotional highs associated with freedom and prospects for personal development, a new more gratifying life-style, and the possibility of new fulfilling intimate relationships, alternating with crashing depressions and anxiety associated with loneliness, loss, and the uncertainty of the future (Hetherington, Cox, & Cox, 1981; Weiss, 1975). Feelings of incompetence, low self-esteem, and changes in self-concept frequently are reported by separated and divorced adults. Feelings of incompetence appear as a result of perceived failure as a spouse and parent, and lead to doubts about current social competence and future adjustment to remarriage. Moreover, this self-doubt is reflected in disruptions in sexual functioning and impotence in some divorced men (Hetherington, Cox, & Cox, 1981).

Women experience less initial change in their self-esteem than do men, a fact attributed to the greater likelihood of keeping the marital home and custody of the children and thus having continuity. The man who loses home, spouse, and children experiences greater initial change in self-esteem and often engages in an increased round of social and self-improvement activities in an attempt to reestablish an identity, roots, relationships, and a life structure. During separation and the early phase of divorce, divorced men and women complain of feelings of depersonalization and of not knowing who they are as roles and relationships shift. Divorced men talk about "not me" experiences, and they say such things as "I can't believe I crouched in the bushes and peered through the window at what she was doing with that guy in her room," or "I would never have believed that I could hit a woman," or "I wondered who this wimp was with the tears in his eyes, sniveling there taking all this crap from a bitchy broad, and it turned out to be me." Men who have been extremely dependent on their wives for emotional and social support have the most difficulty in their postdivorce emotional adjustment (Hetherington, Cox, & Cox, 1981; White & Asher, 1976).

Most divorcing spouses adjust to their new single status within a few years. For some, however, there are more long-term consequences for mental and physical health. Bloom and associates (Bloom, 1975; Bloom, Asher, & White, 1978) determined that both divorced men and women are overrepresented in suicides, homicides, deaths due to illness, and automobile accidents. Moreover, divorced men and women are more often found in psychiatric institutions than are their married counterparts. Divorced women are three times more likely than their counterparts in intact families to be admitted to psychiatric hospitals, but for divorced men the rate is nine times higher (Bloom, Asher, & White, 1978).

Reports of the relationship of marital status and sex to psychological well-being do not present consistent findings. Several explanations have been offered. First, the manifestations of disturbance may differ for men and women, men being more likely to manifest acting out, angry, aggressive behavior and women being more likely to be depressed (Kitson & Raschke, 1981). Second, the time in the cycle of separation and divorce at which husbands and wives are most distressed may vary (Bloom & Caldwell, 1981). Women may experience more stress prior to separation but may feel a temporary sense of relief at the time of separation and divorce, a time when men may just be recognizing the great losses and rearrangements in their lives that divorce entails (Berman & Turk, 1981; Cheriboga, Roberts, & Stein, 1978; Hetherington, Cox, & Cox, 1981). Men are less able than women to tolerate rejection (Rubin, Peplau, & Hill, 1979) and have a greater need to control their feelings and their lives (Gilligan, 1982), and divorce may be particularly troublesome in these respects. However, as women confront greater economic, social, and parental problems in their single life situation, their psychological distress may increase (Spanier & Casto, 1979; Wallerstein & Kelly, 1980).

Social Relations and Support Systems

For men, divorce usually involves the loss of a spouse, separation from children, rearrangements in friendship and kin networks, and a search for new intimate relationships. Marked changes in social relationships and available support systems occur with divorce. In fact, it has been suggested that the greatest impact of divorce is the disruption of social roles and systems of interpersonal attachment that are basic to self-identity (Putney, 1981). Although the common image is that family and friends rally around in times of duress, divorce may polarize friendships and split loyalties, and support may be short lived (Hetherington, Cox, & Cox, 1981; Spanier & Thompson, 1984; Weiss, 1975).

Loneliness is a common complaint of both divorced men and women. Weiss (1975) has distinguished between social isolation and emotional isolation. Social isolation is related to the loss of friendship networks and results in boredom and feelings of rejection. Emotional isolation is related to lack of intimate relations and is associated with feelings of emptiness, depression, anxiety, and tension. Although socializing and friendship and kin networks may reduce social isolation, a meaningful, intimate relationship is the best solution to emotional isolation for both men and women (Brown, Felton, Whiteman, & Manuda, 1980; Hetherington, Cox, & Cox, 1981; Wallerstein & Kelly, 1980; Weiss, 1979).

A common complaint of divorced men and women is that American society is a couple-oriented society. Following divorce, relationships with married couples who were friends prior to the divorce decline (Hetherington, Cox, & Cox, 1981; Spanier & Thompson, 1984). Men are more likely to maintain contact with previously known couples, since many of these friendships were based on his occupational network. In addition, divorced fathers use other married couples with children as resources on visitation days. Men, however, are less likely than women to make frequent use of social supports and are less likely to confide in relatives or a close friend about their problems (Brown & Felton, 1978; Cheriboga, Coho, Steen, & Roberts, 1979; Hetherington, Cox, & Cox, 1985).

Immediately after divorce, many divorced mothers and fathers have restricted social lives. Divorced women with custody of children complain of being isolated and trapped in a child's world; divorced fathers complain of suffering from the loss of their children and home, of feeling shut out and rootless, and of having to engage in social activities even if these often are not pleasurable. During the first year after separation, the patterns of social and sexual activities engaged in by men and women differ significantly. Men tend to report a satisfying increase in sexual activity with a variety of partners over the first postdivorce year (Gasser & Taylor, 1976; Hetherington, Cox, & Cox, 1976; Orthner, Brown, & Ferguson, 1976; Spanier & Thompson, 1984). However, Hetherington and associates (1975) found that by one year after divorce, both exspouses are seeking closeness and greater permanency in relationships.

Although at one year after divorce many men are engaging in a frenzy of social activity, by two years after divorce the intensity of the men's search for social activity lessens and parallels the activity level of divorced women (Hetherington, Cox, & Cox, 1981). The frantic search may be counterproductive for the man seeking to reestablish confidence and high self-esteem and to dispel loneliness. The existence of meaningful intimate relationships rather than numerous casual sexual encounters and social activities is the most salient factor related to the reestablishment of happiness and psychological well-being. This is reflected in the rapid and high rate of remarriage.

Kin are often turned to as sources of financial, moral, and service-providing support by custodial mothers, but are used less frequently as sources of support by fathers (Furstenberg & Spanier, 1984; Spanier & Thompson, 1984). Family disapproval of divorce makes it less likely that families will provide support and may be associated with poorer adjustment to the divorce (Goode, 1956; Kitson, Moir, & Mason, 1982). In general, ties with own kin remain stable or (for women) may increase following divorce, whereas contact with the divorced spouse's relatives declines following divorce (Albrecht, 1980; Spanier & Thompson, 1984; Spicer & Hampe, 1975).

The Relationship Between Divorced Spouses

Although divorce may signal the legal termination of marriage, continued emotional bonds and the shared responsibility for child rearing and finances may cause divorced parents to maintain a relationship, albeit a greatly altered relationship. For many divorced men and women, attachment lingers or sometimes increases following divorce, although such attachment gradually fades and is usually tempered by considerable hostility, anger, or ambivalence. Continued attachment interferes with the development of autonomy and the role redefinitions needed in adjusting to divorce (Brown, Felton, Whiteman, & Manuda, 1980; Hetherington, Cox, & Cox, 1981; Hynes, 1979; Kitson & Sussman, 1982).

For divorced parents, the most common reason for continued contact lies in the shared parenting function. However, expartners with children seem less willing to discuss personal matters about their past marriage than divorced childless couples (Spanier & Thompson, 1984). Although most divorced men and women prefer to keep their contacts to a minimum, for divorced parents visitation and parenting roles necessitate some contact, and unfortunately shortly after divorce these contacts often involve high rates of conflict (Fulton, 1979; Hetherington, Cox, & Cox, 1981; Wallerstein & Kelly, 1980; Westman, Cline, Swift, & Kramer, 1970). The prime areas of conflict parallel those reported by many nondivorced couples: child-rearing responsibility and practices, and finances. One study reported that 72 percent of wives and 55 percent of husbands were critical of their divorced spouse's child-rearing practices (Fulton, 1979), and that noncustodial parents perceived their children as being more distressed by the divorce and their current living situation than did custodial parents.

Research is consistent in showing that conflict can have extremely adverse effects on parents and children in both nondivorced and divorced families (Emery, 1982). A nonacrimonious relationship between divorced parents is related not only to enhanced well-being of children but also to more positive interactions between the custodial mother and child (Hetherington, Cox, & Cox, 1981; Jacobs, 1982; Wallerstein & Kelly, 1980). A competent, stable, involved noncustodial father can be a major support for both the divorced mother and the child if the parents are able to resolve their conflicts and moderate their animosity.

Relationships Between Noncustodial Fathers and Their Children

An examination of father-child relations in divorce must be considered against the framework of the divorced father's experience. As we have noted, divorced fathers go through a period of emotional turmoil, loss, conflict, changes in self-concept, and reorganization of family and social roles. In this period of psychological distress and life changes, fathers not only may see increasingly less of their children but also the quality of the relationship may change. Although there is some continuity in the pre-divorce and postdivorce quality of maternal parenting behavior, there is little predictability from predivorce father-child relations as to either the amount or quality of paternal contact after the divorce. Some previously intensely attached fathers become disengaged and gradually fade out of their children's lives. Other previously uninvolved fathers become extremely active with their children.

Involvement of noncustodial fathers with their children not only is an effective support system for the custodial mother and child but also benefits the divorced father. Even when fathers continue to experience conflict with their exwife, those fathers who maintain regular contact with children and who stay involved in child-rearing decisions are themselves better adjusted to their divorce (Greif, 1979; Hetherington, Cox, & Cox, 1979; Jacobs, 1982). Parental conflicts over child support and the father's parenting abilities not only interfere with the child's postdivorce adjustment but accentuate the loss felt by the father. Noncustodial fathers separated from their children experience a profound sense of loss of their children, a feeling that retards their own adjustment as they work through what closely resembles grief (Dominic & Schlesinger, 1980; Greif, 1979; Hetherington, Cox, & Cox, 1976, 1981; Jacobs, 1982; Seagull & Seagull, 1977; Tepp, 1983). The grief reported by fathers is compounded by the move from the marital home and by repeated postvisitation separations (Hetherington, Cox, & Cox, 1976; Seagull & Seagull, 1977).

Fathers' responses to their grief appear to change over time. During the first few months following divorce, noncustodial fathers maintain the same or greater involvement with their children than before the separation. However, fathers may continue to interact with their children for different reasons. A father may wish to maximize visitation rights because of guilt, a sense of duty, a strong attachment to his child, a lingering attachment to his wife, or a desire to maintain some continuity or structure in his life (Dominic & Schlesinger, 1980; Hetherington, Cox, & Cox, 1981; Wallerstein & Kelly, 1980; Weiss, 1975). Some of the motives for a continued relationship may, however, be more defensive or less admirable. Some fathers maintain contact to dispel their children's fears of desertion, to prevent the wife from turning the children against him, or as a way of annoying or retaliating against his exspouse.

As previously discussed, over time the amount of contact between the noncustodial father and his children declines. This decline has been attributed to several factors. Mothers may discourage the relationship between the noncustodial father and child and actively make visitation uncomfortable or difficult. In addition, the pain of repeated separations may lead some fathers to extend the time between visits and eventually to eliminate visits. Moreover, visitation is often stressful in other ways. Scheduling shared times and finding mutually interesting things to do during visits may become increasingly difficult as children grow older, move into the peer group, and become more self-sufficient. Many fathers complain of the abnormality of the intense entertainment-oriented contact during visitation and of the difficulty in having time alone with any one child in multiple-child families. Mothers view this relationship somewhat differently and see fathers as having the opportunity to enjoy the pleasures of parenting without assuming the day-to-day responsibilities of child rearing (Fulton, 1979; Furstenberg & Spanier, 1984; Kitson & Sussman, 1982; Spanier & Thompson, 1984). Eventually both fathers and children develop other interests and relationships, particularly those involved in remarriage, which may lessen the motivation and opportunities for contact (Furstenberg & Spanier, 1984; Hetherington, Cox, & Cox, 1981; Hingst, 1981; Palmer, 1969; Seagull & Seagull, 1977; Spanier & Thompson, 1984).

A substantial group of divorced parents report that the removal of marital conflict following divorce leads to an improvement in relationships with their children, and such noncustodial parents increase contact with their children (Furstenberg & Spanier, 1984; Kitson & Sussman, 1982; Spanier & Thompson, 1984). Continued parental involvement also occurs when fathers are older, more conservative, have strong traditional images of family life, or have the desire to remarry and gain custody of their children (Rosenthal & Keshet, 1981). When custody is settled in court rather than out of court, fathers continue to hope that either the court decision will be reversed or that the children will request to live with them. Fathers are more likely to acquiesce to their noncustodial role when the decision is made out of court (Dominic & Schlesinger, 1980). Out-of-court settlements, however, usually involve more lenient visitation rights, and ease of visitation is an important factor in continued involvement of the noncustodial father (Tepp, 1983).

Noncustodial fathers are more likely to maintain contact with sons than with daughters, to have longer visits with sons than daughters, and to have sons make a later shift in residence to the father's home from the custodial mother's home (Hess & Camara, 1979; Hetherington, Cox, & Cox, 1981; Tepp, 1983). This may be attributed to greater shared interests and emotional involvement of fathers with sons, to a belief that fathers are more essential for the development of sons than daughters, or to the fact that divorced mothers have more problems raising sons than daughters, and that boys in mother-custody families show more deviant behavior in the home and in the school than do girls (Guidubaldi, Cleminshaw, Perry, & McLoughlin, 1983; Guidubaldi, Cleminshaw, Perry, Nastasi, & Adams, 1984; Hetherington, Cox, & Cox, 1981, 1985; Peterson & Zill, 1983; Santrock & Warshak, 1979).

The quality of both mothers' and fathers' parenting skills diminishes around the time of separation and divorce but improves later (Fulton, 1979; Hetherington, Cox, & Cox, 1981; Wallerstein & Kelly, 1980). Whereas mothers tend to become more erratically and ineffectively authoritarian, fathers become more disengaged, permissive, and indulgent, and communicate less effectively with their children. In spite of this indulgence, divorced fathers encounter less noncompliance and are less likely to become involved in coercive cycles with their children than are divorced mothers. It should be remembered that around the time of separation and divorce, both parents and children are likely to be distressed and to show disruptions in behavior. The whining, nagging, dependent, angry, resistant behavior of children interacts with the anxiety, guilt, depression, and self-doubts of the parents and contributes to their inept parenting.

Although divorced fathers who remain involved with their children play an important role in shaping the adjustment of their children, particularly sons, in most divorced families the behavior of the custodial mother becomes increasingly salient. When the father is not available, both the constructive and destructive behavior of the divorced mother are funneled more directly to the child. A good relationship with a noncustodial father cannot buffer the adverse effects of a destructive relationship between the mother and child in the same way that occurs with a residential father who is regularly available (Hetherington, Cox, & Cox, 1981).

Problems in children's adjustment following divorce are least likely to occur if both parents assume a role in helping the children cope successfully. Low conflict, an absence of denigration between parents, high parental agreement and support in child rearing, and availability of the noncustodial father, if the father is not extremely deviant or destructive, are associated with positive adjustment in children. In addition, a rapid recovery from the divorce by children is related to a stable environment, to the happiness and adjustment of the parents, and to parental discipline that is authoritative, consistent, and warm with open communication, respect, and trust between parents and children (Hess & Camara, 1979; Hetherington, Cox, & Cox, 1981; Jacobson, 1978; Nelson, 1981; Wallerstein & Kelly, 1980).

Although divorce may signal the end of the marital relationship, it does not terminate the parental roles. The constructive reorganization and continuation of parental responsibilities and cooperation between divorced parents aimed at enhancing the well-being of their children is one of the most difficult challenges confronting divorcing couples.

CUSTODIAL FATHERS

When fathers gain custody of children, the arrangement is likely to follow an atypical marriage and a divorce in which the mother did not want custody for a variety of reasons or was unable to care for the children (Orthner, Brown, & Ferguson, 1976). Thus the majority of custodial fathers have not been awarded custody after a court-settled dispute. When confronted with caring for their children on a day-to-day basis, some fathers are resentful, confused, or apprehensive, while others value the increased opportunity to nurture and become more intimate with their children. Most fathers experience some combination of these feelings.

Although the research literature on custodial fathers is meager and the studies suffer from methodologic shortcomings, the conditions under which fathers attain custody have been found to influence their response to the new household situation. Mendes (1976a, 1976b) identified two types of non-custodial fathers which she labeled "seekers" and "assenters." Seekers are fathers who sought custody and appear to be content with child-rearing responsibilities as well as better adjusted to their divorces. Assenters are fathers who did not want custody but were awarded it owing to a variety of circumstances. These fathers experience severe problems in their parenting roles.

Mendes' emphasis on the importance of volition in obtaining custody of children is supported by Gasser and Taylor (1976) in their investigation of the role adjustment and family management of a group of divorced and a group of widowed custodial fathers. The divorced fathers who had sought custody were far more likely than the widowers to report that they were adjusting well, were in control of their children and their life situations, and were managing their homes and child care duties satisfactorily.

Compared with noncustodial fathers and "assenters," fathers who actively seek custody may very well be an atypical group. They are likely to be older and more conservative (Gersick, 1979), to be of a higher socioeconomic status (Gersick, 1979; Orthner, Brown, & Ferguson, 1976), to have had some college experience, and to hold a professional or managerial position (Chang & Deinard, 1982). In addition, they are likely to be middle or last-born children with both brothers and sisters (Gersick, 1979) and are usually awarded custody of school-age children rather than infants (Glick & Norton, 1978). Care should be taken to not generalize findings from fathers who actively seek custody to all divorced fathers.

Both custodial mothers and fathers complain of task overload. One-parent households are understaffed households because the single parent has professional, housekeeping, and child-care responsibilities. Like custodial mothers, custodial fathers express difficulty in finding strategies for dealing with these problems while still maintaining an adequate social life. Custodial fathers are more isolated and have fewer community contacts than do nondivorced or noncustodial fathers (Murch, 1973; Schlesinger, 1977; Spanier & Thompson, 1984; Tedder, Libbee, & Scherman, 1981).

Luepnitz (1982) found that single-custody fathers do more housework than they did when married but have had to learn fewer new household skills than have single-custody mothers. Luepnitz attributed these differences to the fact that tasks normally performed by women in a two-parent home are made easier by washers, dryers, permanent press, disposable diapers, and so on and are easy to perform, while those tasks normally performed by men involve nonmechanized tools and more danger.

In spite of the task overload, Luepnitz reported that custodial fathers repeatedly express a casual attitude toward domestic demands. However, children in father-custody homes usually have more household duties assigned to them, and noncustodial fathers frequently rely on help from extended family, professionals, community support services, and particularly day-care facilities (Gasser & Taylor, 1976; Gersick, 1979; Hetherington, Cox, & Cox, 1976; Levinger & Moles, 1979; Spanier & Thompson, 1984). One study found that custodial fathers engage outside help for 24 hours per week on the average, compared with 11 hours per week for custodial mothers (Gasser & Taylor, 1976).

There are other practical and financial differences between custodial and noncustodial fathers and their children. Unlike their noncustodial counterparts, custodial fathers tend to remain residentially stable (Rosenthal & Keshet, 1981). Also unlike mother-custody households, which experience a marked drop in real family income, father-custody households seldom experience financial duress and often have an increase in real family income (Duncan & Morgan, 1976; Espenshade, 1979).

Father-Child Relationships

Society has expectations of ineptness by custodial fathers in both the performance of household tasks and parenting. In line with these expectations, the custodial fathers studied reported feeling isolated or ostracized in the community because of their unique caretaking status. They often felt that few people could offer them understanding and helpful advice, and they initially voiced concern over a lack of knowledge about child development. However, custodial fathers do far better than expected. It should be recalled that both mothers and fathers recognize that their ability to parent effectively decreases around the time of the divorce and for some time after (Fulton, 1979; Hetherington, Cox, & Cox, 1978; Wallerstein & Kelly, 1980). While parenting skills improve for both parents over time, by two years after the final separation custodial fathers report better family adjustment and fewer problems with their children than do custodial mothers (Ambert, 1982; Mendes, 1976a, 1976b; Santrock & Warshak, 1979). This may be because of the fewer economic resources and alternatives available to custodial mothers. In addition, it is important to remember that fathers who actively seek custody tend to be more involved in child rearing and report closer relationships and fewer problems with their children than do fathers who do not seek but are given custody (Gasser & Taylor, 1976; Mendes, 1976a, 1976b; Orthner, Brown, & Ferguson, 1976).

There is mounting evidence that children may develop better in the custody of a same-sexed parent. Boys in father-custody families are more mature, social and independent, are less demanding, and have higher self-esteem than do girls, while the reverse is true in mother-custody homes (Hetherington, Cox, & Cox, 1976, 1978; Santrock & Warshak, 1979). However, sons are less communicative and less overtly affectionate in father-custody than mother-custody homes, perhaps as a result of less exposure to female expressiveness (Ambert, 1982; Mendes, 1976). Custodial fathers themselves report more problems with daughters, particularly with the sex education of adolescent daughters, than do custodial mothers (Amber, 1982; Santrock & Warshak, 1979). It has been proposed that parents may find it easier to identify with same-sex children and that an opposite-sex child may remind the parent of the exspouse and thus become a target of displaced aggression or withdrawal of affection (Hetherington, Cox, & Cox, 1978; Santrock & Warshak, 1979). In addition, although both parents make major contributions to the development of their children, the presence of a same-sex parent may be particularly important to the children in acquiring social skills and roles.

From the little research available on father-custody families, it can be concluded that these families may function as well as or better than mother-custody families, but that these differences are shaped by whether the father has sought custody, the sex and age of the child, and the economic and social circumstances of the family. For greater detail, see the discussion of custodial fathers in Chapter 5.

JOINT CUSTODY

A recent interest in joint custody has developed on the basis of the belief that when parents share custody, many problems experienced by both children and parents in single-parent custody arrangements are alleviated. Under joint custody, parents are given equal legal rights and responsibilities for their children. However, there are many variations of joint custody. The most common arrangements are alternation of child care between parents on a weekly or biweekly basis, or a division of the week with either split or alternative weekends (Rosenthal and Keshet 1981). In some cases, however, arrangements are very similar to single-custody homes, with the child residing in one home and having visitation with the nonresidential parent. In other more unusual situations, the child may remain in one household and the parents may move in and out.

Researchers supporting joint custody as a viable option claim that while the child in the joint-custody situation still mourns the loss of the intact family, neither the child nor the noncustodial parent experiences the intense feelings of loss common in sole-custody situations (Nehls & Morgenbesser, 1980; Rothberg, 1983). Neither parent is relegated to the position of visitor, and the child is not placed in a situation in which he or she feels neglected by a nonresidential parent. Moreover, joint custody is purported to relieve the parents of some of the task overload and lack of support in child rearing found in sole-custody families. Finally, proponents of joint custody argue that it facilitates continued involvement of both parents with the children and that such involvement has been demonstrated to have positive effects on children's adjustment (Clingempeel & Reppucci, 1982).

Problems with Joint Custody

It should be noted that arguments for joint custody assume a reasonable cooperative relationship between the parents, in spite of research findings indicating that acrimony often persists or even increases after divorce (Hetherington, Cox, & Cox, 1981; Wallerstein & Kelly, 1980). Furthermore, joint custody may result in undesired or undesirable shifts between neighborhoods, friends, schools, and residences for children. Such multiple changes may be difficult for children to cope with (Hetherington, Cox, & Cox, 1985; Hodges, Wechsler, & Ballentine, 1979; Stolberg & Anker, 1983).

Even parents who agree to joint custody often experience considerable ambivalence about their situation. Luepnitz (1982) found that joint-custody mothers often feel resentful about "giving up" their children. Some mothers talked of having a right to their children because they had raised them. Other women were concerned about the social disapproval they would encounter if they did not receive full custody. Interestingly, rather than finding societal support for their interest in their children, the joint-custody fathers reported being the recipients of negative comments from peers and business associates. Thus the fathers received negative feedback at a time when they themselves were dealing with ambivalent feelings about the loss of free time and the career sacrifices they were making to maintain custody. Further evidence of maternal ambivalence is found in a recent study by Rothberg (1983). While 43 percent of the mothers in Rothberg's sample said that both parents wanted to try the joint-custody arrangement, 57 percent of the mothers agreed to the option because of the father's desire for it.

In addition to the parental ambivalence, both mothers and fathers report concern for the problems their children have in making the transitions from home to home. Frequently, joint-custody families are forced to make several schedule changes before arriving at the one that works best in relation to both the children's and parents' school, business, and social schedules. Critical to the ease of transition is geographic proximity. The child is better adjusted when parents live close enough to allow the child to remain in the same school and to play with the same circle of friends. While close proximity benefits the child, it frequently creates problems for the father. It appears that a high proportion of both mothers and fathers agreeing to joint custody are building professional careers. However, while fathers are more likely to report that they have forfeited career advances that would necessitate longer work hours or a geographic move, mothers report that the time they have gained, free from child-care responsibilities, is a professional asset (Rothberg, 1983). In addition, fathers are likely to report that child custody interferes in the establishment of new interpersonal relationships, a report not made by joint-custody mothers (Rothberg, 1983).

Conflicts in joint-custody families also arise over issues of parenting practices and such specifics as who gets the children on which holidays. However, parents are motivated to resolve such conflicts in order to maintain joint parenting. Another major problem area in joint-custody families is the necessary continuing interaction between exspouses. As noted earlier, many men and women find it difficult to end their interdependence, and continued attachment interferes with adjustment to their new single role. The interaction necessitated by the joint-custody arrangement can impede the divorced couples' attempts at adjustment. In an attempt to minimize contact, many parents with joint custody arrange for children to be picked up at school or the daycare center, or to come to the home from school on their own.

The problems of the father are compounded by the fact that many men are aware of the critical importance of the goodwill of the exwife in the continuation of shared parenting (Luepnitz, 1982). Social mores point to the mother as the "real" parent, and it is the father who must prove himself to be a competent, responsible parent.

Benefits of Joint Custody

In spite of the fact that joint custody does not guarantee freedom from postdivorce problems, benefits of this custodial arrangement are far more easily cited than are benefits of single-parent custody. Indeed, 67 percent of Rothberg's (1983) respondents reported generally positive feelings about the custody situation, as opposed to 20 percent who reported ambivalent feelings and 13 percent with negative feelings. The benefits cited by parents with joint custody closely parallel the reasons given by proponents of this custodial option. Foremost is the opportunity for the children to benefit from the continued availability and involvement of two parents who both want to remain a part of their lives (Luepnitz, 1982; Rosenthal & Keshet, 1983; Rothberg, 1983). In addition, the children are allowed continued contact with both sets of extended families.

Furthermore, parents are awarded time free from child-care responsibilities. This is not to say that intermittent full-time responsibility is not difficult for the parents, but that regularly scheduled "time off" may lessen feelings of being trapped. In her comparison of joint- with sole-custody parents, Luepnitz (1982) found that, although half of her single-custody respondents reported feeling overwhelmed by their parenting responsibilities, none of the joint-custody parents reported such feelings.

Moreover, mothers and fathers in joint-custody homes report that both parents share in disciplining the children and that they share this function more than they did when the family was intact. Fathers in joint-custody homes become increasingly confident of their domestic and parenting skills, and both parents tend to view the other as a reasonably competent parent (Luepnitz, 1982). Unlike the changing postdivorce disciplinary strictness recorded for single-custody parents (Hetherington, Cox, & Cox, 1978), no such change has been found for joint-custody parents. While there are different rules in the two houses, reports that children play one parent against the other are infrequent (Luepnitz, 1982).

After the initial postdivorce crisis, joint-custody parents experience no more conflict than do single-custody parents, and most couples report less conflict. There is frequent child-related contact between exspouses, but on a personal level the exhusbands describe their relationship with their exwife as distant but friendly (Rosenthal & Keshet, 1981). A more practical benefit of the joint-custody arrangement is less conflict concerning financial settlements and support payments. Unlike the mother-custody situation, in which fathers frequently fail to pay court-awarded child support, joint-custody parents rarely renege on their financial responsibilities. Thus a potential source of conflict is eliminated (Luepnitz, 1982; Rosenthal & Keshet, 1981). It should be noted, however, that 37 percent of the men and women in Rothberg's sample were not satisfied with the financial settlement. The women tended to feel that their exhusband made more and should share more. The men felt they were paying too much in support considering that they too maintained a home for their children.

The joint situation does not eliminate all postdivorce problems. Like their single-custody parent counterparts, both joint-custody mothers and fathers report high stress related to feelings of loneliness. Fathers rank loneliness first on their list of stressors, and mothers rank it second. There is a difference, however, between single- and joint-custody parents in their attributions about loneliness. Sole-custody parents report that the commitment of full responsibility for child care is the primary source of their loneliness, while joint-custody parents attribute it to a lack of an intimate relationship (Luepnitz, 1982).

In summary, joint custody may be a reasonable and a salutary option in cases in which interparental conflict is low, parents are willing to make compromises for the well-being of their children, neither parent insists on sole custody, and living arrangements will not be disruptive in the children's lives. When these conditions are not met, joint custody may be unsuccessful or damaging (Folberg & Graham, 1979). In addition, the results of studies of parents who have opted for joint custody may have little relevance for mandatory joint custody, since these parents may already be less acrimonious and more child oriented than other divorcing parents. Mandatory joint custody could actually exacerbate parental conflict through requiring joint decision making and shared responsibilities and by increasing the amount of contact between parents (Derdeyn, 1984; Emery, Hetherington, & DiLalla, 1984). Moreover, to date studies of joint custody have relied on parental reports, have not examined the effects on children of different ages, and have not investigated long-term outcomes (Thompson, 1983). Since 1975, 29 states have passed laws allowing for or requiring consideration of joint-custody decisions (Derdeyn, 1984). Most of the remaining states have such legislation under consideration. Before joint custody becomes the mandated common arrangement, more research is needed on the factors that make it and alternative custodial arrangements successful or destructive for different kinds of parents and children.

IMPLICATIONS, APPLICATIONS, AND PRECAUTIONARY NOTES

Although most recommendations about intervention programs or changes in social policy related to divorce need to be substantiated by further research, evidence has accumulated that permits some generalizations.

The main disruptions in family functioning and child development related to divorce are associated with separation and loss; family conflict; deterioration in the quality of parenting; multiple negative life changes such as diminished finances; shifts in housing, neighborhoods and schools; and lack of support and resources. These problem areas should be the focus of social policy changes and interventions. The legal system, in dealing with issues of custody, visitation, and economic support, confronts these issues. However, the legal process in divorce often exacerbates the adversarial aspects of the family breakdown. The use of impartial divorce mediators as a means of resolving disputes, a promising alternative to litigation, should be encouraged. Furthermore, attorneys should be permitted to place their obligations to serve the best interests of their client second to a systemic obligation to serve the best interests of children and families.

Intervention should begin early, before stressors and their negative outcomes have begun to accumulate and escalate. It could be argued that the most advantageous strategy would be to begin focusing on distressed families and troubled marriages before separation or divorce occurs, since many adverse processes such as conflict and poor parenting practices arise in distressed families long before the separation or the legal divorce.

There are also wide individual variations in the way different families and family members respond to marital dissolution, based on history, needs, personal attributes, and available resources. A satisfactory solution for one family member may be deleterious for the well-being of another. Currently "the best interests of the child" doctrine serves as the foundation for divorce decisions, but consideration of how "best interests" are to be determined remains ambiguous and wide judicial discretion is permitted. Although reduction in indeterminancy of child-custody laws is desirable, social science has been able to provide no firm guidelines to the legal system in this regard.

As criteria for the best interests of the child, custody decisions have been based on parental status as primary caretaker, the psychological and economic well being of the parent, and the age and sex of the child. It is difficult to establish which functions and roles in the parent-child relationship with children of different ages should be viewed as primary. Unfortunately, primary is often translated to mean the amount of time spent with the child, and such a definition often penalizes fathers, especially fathers of young children. Following divorce, most children are likely to find themselves in some form of alternative child care, since the majority of both divorced men and women are employed. Therefore, quantity rather than quality of care and resources is an inappropriate main ground on which to base a custody decision. However, since there is little continuity between predivorce and postdivorce father-child relations, prediction of the quality of future relations is difficult. Differentiation between short- and long-term outcomes of custody relationships is important. In the long run, the child is likely to benefit from being with the parent who can provide him or her with the most stable and emotionally supportive environment.

Fathers have been demonstrated to play an important role in the development of children and to be competent caregivers even of infants. Moreover, fathers may play a particularly important role in the social and cognitive development of sons. As we have noted, recent research findings indicate that a school-aged child may benefit from placement with the same-sex parent. Thus although in general gender of the parent should not be the major determinant in custodial arrangements, if other factors are equal placement of children with the same-sex parent should be considered. A precautionary note, however, is in order here. Such placement often involves split custody and the separation of siblings. We know nothing about the problems that may arise from sibling separation, and whether such problems might add to the child's sense of family disruption and loss.

Most children wish to maintain contact with both parents, and custodial and visitation arrangements that facilitate such contact are desirable if they do not escalate conflict or expose the child to pathogenic parental influences. If divorced parents can agree on child-rearing goals, are supportive of the child, and can control their acrimony, and if the noncustodial parent is a reasonably stable, responsible parent, continued involvement of the noncustodial parent can be beneficial for the child and for both parents.

Findings of research based on reports of parents who have voluntarily opted for joint custody may have little relevance to outcomes where courts mandate or strongly promote this arrangement. Joint custody should be considered an option, not a panacea for postdivorce adjustment. As noted in this chapter, research on this arrangement indicates that a positive outcome is likely in low-conflict families and in situations where both mothers and fathers are atypical with respect to age, educational and professional background, and predivorce child involvement. In families where joint custody is legally mandated but is not chosen by the divorcing couple, the outcome is not as positive and may be deleterious if continued contact and shared responsibilities escalate conflict. Children seem better adjusted in sole-custody arrangements when there is high parental conflict. The living arrangements of children in joint custody vary, and little is known about the long-term outcomes of the various forms of joint custody on children of different ages. Although parents need to be informed and have the opportunity to consider all possible custody options including joint custody, the contemporary movement to encourage all parents to elect joint custody is misguided.

The financial settlement is an important component of the legal divorce and one of the major causes of recurrent returns to court. Establishing the economic stability of the custodial household is essential. Adequate child support should be assigned and enforced. Self-starting systems involving wage assignment and stringent automatic penalties for nonpayment of child support increase compliance. Since such systems are automatic, they may create less family conflict, resentment, and stress than would litigation initiated by the custodial parent. Moreover, since self-starting systems reduce public costs, such programs should be promoted. In addition, property and short-term alimony awards that facilitate education and job training of the custodial parent leading to eventual self-sufficiency should be encouraged. Although many divorced custodial mothers will continue to need public assistance, any divorce settlement and retraining program that promotes long-term economic independence and employment of the custodial parent will be beneficial.

Mental health and community support systems frequently fail to adjust their services to the particular needs of divorcing families. However, early intervention by trained mental health professionals sensitive to the unique emotional, social, legal, and economic problems of divorcing families is useful. Services need to be responsive to the transitional problems in personal identity, problems in establishing new roles and relationships, economic needs, and difficulties in parent-child relations encountered by these families. Efforts should be made to involve some community organizations such as schools and churches, which have been underutilized as resources in systematically providing support services for divorcing families. Finally, self-help groups such as Parents Without Partners, Rights for Fathers, and child-care networks formed by divorced parents have been found to be effective support groups for divorced families, and their use and development should be encouraged. Such groups provide opportunities to initiate new social relationships, to build support networks, to share experiences, and to learn possible solutions to practical problems.

Intervention programs for divorced families require a new perspective on family relations that recognizes that although cohabitation has ended, the family continues in a reorganized form spread across multiple households. A focus on family rather than individual intervention strategies should be the preferred approach to assisting most divorced families. In addition, it should be recognized that separation and divorce are likely to initiate a series of transitions involving multiple reorganizations in the family, each with its own special stresses, needs, and resources. Social policy and intervention programs should be made more flexible and responsive to the varied needs of diverse family forms undergoing a variety of family transitions. A more detailed discussion of this topic is covered in Emery, Hetherington, and DiLalla (1984).

CONCLUSION

The response to divorce varies widely for different parents and children. Long- and short-term outcomes of divorce are shaped by characteristics of the family members, previous experiences, resources for coping with this difficult life transition, and continued or new stresses and available support systems. An impediment to the adjustment of fathers and their continued involvement in child rearing following divorce is the acceptance of traditional views of the family and of family roles held by society, the legal system, other social institutions, and the family members themselves. Only recently has it been recognized that the attainment of women's rights must involve changes in men's roles. Both in married and in divorced families, participation of the father is often desirable or may be essential. In spite of research evidence to the contrary, fathers are often viewed as the less competent, salient, and essential parent. This perspective is reflected in divorce, in which most fathers are forced or elect to accept separation from their children and to become less actively engaged in child rearing.

There are few institutionalized supports available for divorced fathers, although these fathers have great needs for emotional and social support and encouragement in their parental role. It has been proposed that critical to the adjustment of the divorced father is his ability to participate in both "father" and "mother" roles and to see himself as a sensitive, nurturant, and competent parent. Not all fathers desire or are able to assume such a role, however. Conditions that facilitate contact between fathers and their children promote changes in fathers' views of their responsibilities and competence as parents after divorce (Greif, 1979). This can become self-reinforcing. Fathers who have little opportunity for contact with their children or who view themselves as unimportant or inept in relations with their children have little motivation to maintain their parenting role. In contrast, fathers who perceive themselves as important are more likely to maintain this role.

As gender-role stereotypes change, as men's perceptions of themselves change, and as custody awards change, fathers may remain more involved in their children's lives following divorce to the mutual gratification of the fathers and the children.

REFERENCES

Albrecht, S. L. (1980). Reactions and adjustments to divorce: Differences in the experience of males and females. *Family Relations, 29,* 59–68.

Albrecht, S. L., Bahr, H. M., & Goodman, R. L. (1983). *Divorce and remarriage.* Westport, CT: Greenwood.

Ambert, A. M. (1982). Differences in children's behavior toward custodial mothers and custodial fathers. *Journal of Marriage and the Family, 44,* 73–86.

Anthony, E. J. (1974). Children at risk from divorce: A review. In E. J. Anthony & C. Koupernik (Eds.), *The child in his family: Children at psychiatric risk* (Vol. 3). New York: Wiley, pp. 461–478.

Berman, W. H., & Turk, D. C. (1981). Adaptation to divorce: Problems and coping strategies. *Journal of Marriage and the Family, 43,* 179–189.

Bernard, J. (1972). *The future of marriage.* New York: Bantam.

Bloom, B. J. (1975). *Changing patterns of psychiatric care.* New York: Human Sciences.

Bloom, B. L., Asher, S. J., & White, S. W. (1978). Marital disruption as a stressor: A review and analysis. *Psychological Bulletin, 85,* 867–894.

Bloom, B. L., & Caldwell, R. A. (1981). Sex differences in adjustment during the process of marital separation. *Journal of Marriage and the Family, 43,* 693–701.

Bodenheimer, B. M. (1977). Progress under the uniform child jurisdiction act and remaining problems: Punitive decrees, joint custody and excessive modifications. *California Law Review, 65,* 978–1014.

Bodenheimer, B. M. (1979). New approaches to psychiatry: Implications for divorce reform. *Utah Law Review, 1970,* 191–220.

Brandwein, R. A., Brown, C. A., & Fox, E. M. (1974). Women and children last: The social situation of divorced mothers and their families. *Journal of Marriage and the Family, 36,* 498–514.

Brown, P., & Felton, B. J. (1978, March). Coping with marital disruption in later life: Use of social supports by men and women. Paper presented at the meeting of American Orthopsychiatric Association, San Francisco.

Brown, P., Felton, B. J., Whiteman, V., & Manuda, R. (1980). Attachment and distress following marital separation. *Journal of Divorce, 3,* 303–317.

Campbell, A., Converse, P. E., & Rodgers, W. L. (1976). *The quality of American life.* New York: Russell Sage Foundation.

Chang, P., & Deinard, A. S. (1982). Single-father caretakers: Demographic characteristics and adjustment processes. *American Journal of Orthopsychiatry, 52*(2), 236–243.

Cherlin, A. (1981). *Marriage, divorce, remarriage: Changing patterns in the postwar United States.* Cambridge, MA: Harvard University Press.

Cherlin, A., & McCarthy, J. (1983). Remarried couples households. Paper presented at annual meeting of Population Association of America.

Cheriboga, D. A., Coho, A., Stein, J. A., & Roberts, J. (1979). Divorce, stress and social supports: A study in helpseeking behavior, *Journal of Divorce, 3,* 121–135.

Cheriboga, D. A., & Cutler, L. (1977). Stress responses among divorcing men and women. *Journal of Divorce, 1,* 95–105.

Cheriboga, D. A., Roberts, J., & Stein, J. A. (1978). Psychological well-being during marital separation. *Journal of Divorce, 2,* 21–36.

Clingempeel, W. G., & Reppucci, N. D. (1982). Joint custody after divorce: Major issues and goals of research. *Psychological Bulletin, 91,* 102–127.

Derdeyn, A. P. (1984). The family and divorce: Issues of parental anger. *Journal of the American Academy of Child Psychiatry, 22*(4), 385–391.

Dominic, K. T., & Schlesinger, B. (1980). Weekend fathers: Family shadows. *Journal of Divorce, 3*, 241–247.

Duncan, G. J., & Morgan, J. N. (1976). Young children and "other" family members. In G. J. Duncan and J. N. Morgan (Eds.), *Five thousand American families—Patterns of economic progress* (Vol. 4). Ann Arbor: University of Michigan Press.

Every, R. E. (1982). Interparental conflict and the children of discord and divorce. *Psychological Bulletin, 92,* 310–330.

Emery, R. E., Hetherington, E. M., & DiLalla, L. (1984). Divorce, children and social policy. In H. W. Stevenson and A. E. Siegel (Eds.), *Child development research and social policy.* Chicago: University of Chicago Press.

Espenshade, T. J. (1979). The economic consequences of divorce. *Journal of Marriage and the Family, 41,* 615–625.

Folberg, H. J., & Graham, M. (1979). Joint custody of children following divorce. *University of California at Davis Law Review, 12,* 523–581.

Fulton, J. A. (1979). Parental reports of children's post-divorce adjustment. *Journal of Social Issues, 35*, 126–139.

Furstenberg, F. F., & Nord, C. W. (1982). Parenting apart: Patterns of childrearing after divorce. Paper presented at annual meeting of American Sociological Association, San Francisco.

Furstenberg, F. F., Nord, C. W., Peterson, J. L., & Zill, N. (1983). The life course of children of divorce: Marital disruption and parental contact. *American Sociological Review, 48,* 656–668.

Furstenberg, F. F, & Spanier, G. B. (1984). *Recycling the family: Remarriage after divorce.* Beverly Hills, CA: Sage.

Gasser, R. D., & Taylor, C. M. (1976). Role adjustment of single-parent fathers with dependent children. *The Family Coordinator, 25*, 397–401.

Gerhardt, V. (1979). Coping and social action: Theoretical reconstruction of the life event approach. *Sociology of Health and Illness, 1,* 195–225.

Gersick, K. E. (1979). Fathers by choice: Divorced men who receive custody of their children. In G. Levinger & O. C. Moles (Eds.), *Divorce and separation: Context, causes, and consequences.* New York: Basic.

Gilligan, D. (1982). *In a different voice: Psychological theory and women's development.* Cambridge, MA: Harvard University Press.

Glenn, N. D., & Weaver, C. N. (1978). A multivariate study of marital happiness. *Journal of Marriage and the Family, 40,* 269–282.

Glick, P. C. (1979). Children of divorced parents in demographic perspective. *Journal of Social Issues, 35,* 112–125.

Glick, P. C., & Norton, A. J. (1978). Marrying divorcing, and living together in the U. S. today. *Population Bulletin, 32,* 3–38.

Goode, W. J. (1956). *After divorce.* New York: Free Press.

Gottman, J. M. (1979). *Marital interaction: Experimental investigations.* New York: Academic.

Greif, J. B. (1979). Fathers, children and joint custody. *American Journal of Orthopsychiatry, 49,* 311–319.

Guidubaldi, J., Cleminshaw, H. K., Perry, J. D., & McCloughlin, C. S. (1983, March). The impact of parental divorce on children: Report of the nationwide NASP study. Paper presented at annual convention of National Association for School Psychologists, Detroit.

Guidubaldi, J., Cleminshaw, H. K., Perry, J. D., Nastasi, B. K., & Adams, B. (1984, August). Longitudinal effects of divorce on children. Paper presented at annual convention of American Psychological Association, Toronto.

Hess, R. D., & Camara, L. A. (1979). Post-divorce family relationships as mediating factors in the consequences of divorce for children. *Journal of Social Issues, 35,* 79–97.

Hetherington, E. M. (1981). Children and Divorce. In R. Henderson (Ed.), *Parent-child interaction: Theory, research and prospects.* New York: Academic.

Hetherington, E. M., Cox, M., & Cox, R. (1976). Divorced fathers. *Family Coordinator, 25,* 417–428.

Hetherington, E. M., Cox, M., & Cox, R. (1978). The aftermath of divorce. In J. H. Stevens Jr. & M. Matthews (Eds.), *Mother-child, father-child relations.* Washington, DC: National Association for the Education of Young Children.

Hetherington, E. M., Cox, M., & Cox, R. (1979). Family interaction and the social, emotional and cognitive development of children following divorce. In V. Vaughn & T. B. Brazelton (Eds.), *The family: Setting priorities.* New York: Science and Medicine Publishing.

Hetherington, E. M., Cox, M., & Cox, R. (1981). The effects of divorce on parents and children. In M. Lamb (Ed.), *Nontraditional families.* Hillsdale, NJ: Erlbaum.

Hetherington, E. M., Cox, M. & Cox, R. (in press). Long term effects of divorce and remarriage on the adjustment of children. *Journal of the American Academy of Child Psychiatry.*

Hetherington, E. M., Cox, M., & Cox, R. (in preparation). Six years after divorce.

Hingst, A. (1981, Fall). Children and divorce: The child's view. *Journal of Clinical Child Psychology,* 161–164.

Hodges, W. F., Wechsler, R. C., & Ballentine, C. (1979). Divorce and the preschool child: Cumulative stress. *Journal of Divorce, 3,* 55–68.

Hynes, W. J. (1979). Single parent mothers and distress. Unpublished doctoral dissertation, Catholic University of America, Washington, DC.

Jacobs, J. W. (1982). The effect of divorce on fathers: An overview of the literature. *American Journal of Psychiatry, 139*(10), 1235–1241.

Jacobson, D. (1978). The impact of marital separation-divorce on children: Inter-parent hostility and child adjustment. *Journal of Divorce, 2,* 3–17.

Keshet, H. F., & Rosenthal, K. M. (1978, January). Fathering after marital separa-tion. *Social Work, 23* (January), 11–18.

Kitson, G. C., Moir, R. N., & Mason, P. R. (1982). Family social support in crises: The special case of divorce. *American Journal of Orthopsychiatry, 52,* 161–165.

Kitson, G. C., & Raschke, H. J. (1981). Divorce research: What we know; what we need to know. *Journal of Divorce, 4,* 1–37.

Kitson, G. C., & Sussman, M. B. (1982). Marital complaints, demographic charac-teristics and symptoms of mental distress in divorce. *Journal of Marriage and the Family, 44,* 87–102.

Kraus, S. (1979). The crisis of divorce: Growth promoting or pathogenic? *Journal of Divorce, 3,* 107–119.

Levinger, G., & Moles, O. C. (Eds.) (1979). *Divorce and separation: Context, causes and consequences.* New York: Basic Books.

Luepnitz, D. A. (1982). *Child custody.* Lexington, MA: Lexington Books.

Mendes, H. A. (1976a). Single-fatherhood. *Social Work, 21,* 308–312.

Mendes, H. A. (1976b). Single fathers. *Family Coordinator, 25,* 439–444.

Mnookin, R. H., & Kornhauser, L. (1979). Bargaining in the shadow of the law: The case of divorce. *Yale Law Journal, 88,* 950–957.

Murch, M. (1973). Motherless families project. *British Journal of Social Work, 3,* 365–376.

National Center for Health Statistics (1985). Monthly Vital Statistics Reports. Washington, DC: U. S. Government Printing Office.

Nehlo, N. & Morgenbesser, M. (1980). Joint custody: An exploration of the issues. *Family Process, 19,* 117–125.

Nelson, G. (1981). Moderators of women's and children's adjustment following parental divorce. *Journal of Divorce, 4,* 71–83.

Norton, A. J. (1983). Family life cycle: 1980. *Journal of Marriage and the Family, 45,* 267–275.

Orthner, D. K., Brown, T., & Ferguson, D. (1976). Single-parent fatherhood: An emerging family life style. *Family Coordinator, 25,* 429–437.

Palmer, S. (1969). *Parents and children in divorce.* Ottawa National Health and Welfare.

Pasley, K., Ihinger-Tallman, M., & Coleman, C. (1984). Consensus styles among happy and unhappy remarried couples. *Family Relations, 33,* 451–457.

Peterson, J. L., & Zill, N. (1983, April). Marital disruption, parent/child relation-ships and behavioral problems in children. Paper presented at annual meeting of Society for Research in Child Development, Detroit.

Putney, R. S. (1981). Impact of marital loss on support systems. *The Personnel and Guidance Journal, 59,* 351–354.

Rosenthal, K. M., & Keshet, H. F. (1981). *Fathers without partners: A study of fathers and the family after marital separation.* NJ: Rowman and Littlefield.

Rothberg, B. (1983). Joint custody: Parental problems and satisfactions. *Family Process, 22,* 43–52.

Rubin, Z., Peplau, L., & Hill, C. T. (1979). Loving and leaving: Sex differences in romantic attachments. Unpublished manuscript.

Russell, G. (1983). *Changing roles of fathers.* Milton Keynes, England: Open University Press.

Santrock, J. W., & Warshak, R. A. (1979). Father custody and social development in boys and girls. *Journal of Social Issues, 35,* 112–125.

Schlesinger, B. (1977). Husband-wife relationships in reconstituted families. *Social Science, 52,* 152–157.

Seagull, A. A., & Seagull, A. W. (1977). The non-custodial father's relationship to his child: Conflicts and solutions. *Journal of Clinical Child Psychology, Summer,* 11–15.

Select Committee on Children, Youth, and Families (SCCYF) of the United States House of Representatives (1983). *U. S. Children and their families: Current conditions and recent trends.* Washington, DC: U. S. Government Printing Office.

Spanier, G. B., & Anderson, E. A. (1979). The impact of the legal system on adjustment to marital separation. *Journal of Marriage and the Family, 41,* 605–613.

Spanier, G. B., & Casto, R. F. (1979). Adjustment to separation and divorce: A qualitative analysis. In G. Levinger & O. C. Moles (Eds.), *Divorce and separation: Context, causes, and consequences.* New York: Basic Books.

Spanier, G. B., & Glick, P. C. (1981). Marital instability in the United States: Some correlates and recent changes. *Family Relations, 30,* 329–338.

Spanier, G. B., & Thompson, L. (1984). *Parting: The aftermath of separation of divorce.* Beverly Hills, CA: Sage.

Spicer, J. W., & Hampe, G. D. (1975). Kinship interaction after divorce. *Journal of Marriage and the Family, 37,* 113–119.

Stolberg, A. L., & Anker, J. (1983). Cognitive and behavioral changes in children resulting from parenting divorce and consequent environmental changes. *Journal of Divorce, 7,* 23–41.

Taylor, S. E. (1983). Adjustment to threatening events: A theory of cognitive adaptation. *American Psychologist, 38,* 1161–1173.

Tedder, S. L., Libbee, K. M., & Scherman, A. (1981). A community support group for single fathers. *Personnel and Guidance Journal, 60,* 115–119.

Tepp, A. V. (1983). Divorced fathers: Predictors of continued paternal involvement. *American Journal of Psychiatry, 140,* 1465–1469.

Thompson, R. A. (1983). The father's case in child custody disputes: The contributions of psychological research. In M. Lamb & A. Sagi (Eds.), *Fatherhood and family policy.* Hillsdale, NJ: Erlbaum.

Venters, M. (1979). Chronic childhood illness, disability and familial coping: The case of cystic fibrosis. Unpublished doctoral dissertation, University of Minnesota, Minneapolis.

Wallerstein, J. S., & Kelly, J. B. (1980). *Surviving the breakup: How children and parents cope with divorce.* New York: Basic Books.

Weiss, R. S. (1975). *Marital Separation.* New York: Basic Books.

Weiss, R. S. (1976). The emotional impact of marital separation. *Journal of Social Issues, 32,* 135–145.

Weitzman, L. J. (1981). The economics of divorce: Social and economic consequences of property, alimony and child support awards. *University of California at Los Angeles Law Review, 28,* 1181–1268.

Weitzman, L. J., & Dixon, R. B. (1979). Child custody awards: Legal standards and empirical patterns for child custody, support, and visitation after divorce. *University of California at Davis Law Review, 12,* 473–521.

Westman, J. C., Cline, D. W., & Kramer, D. A. (1970). Role of child psychiatry in divorce. *Archives of General Psychiatry, 23,* 416–420.

White, S. W., & Asher, S. J. (1976). Separations and divorce: A study of the male perspective. Unpublished manuscript. Cited in B. L. Bloom, S. J. Asher, & S. W. White (1978). Marital disruption as a stressor: A review and analysis. *Psychological Bulletin, 85,* 867–894.

Yoder, J. D., & Nichols, R. C. (1980). A life perspective comparison of married and divorced persons. *Journal of Marriage and the Family, 42,* 413–419.

CHAPTER 5

Development, Relationships, and Legal/Clinical Considerations in Father-Custody Families

JOHN W. SANTROCK

University of Texas at Dallas

and

RICHARD A. WARSHAK

University of Texas Health Science Center at Dallas

This chapter looks at some of the complex puzzles involving children in father-custody families. Many of the pieces of the puzzle are still missing, although within the last decade increased interest in custodial matters has produced research with implications for children. We live in a rapidly changing society, one in which the roles of men and women are being reassessed in terms of parenting, work obligations, and interests. It is a time of evaluation of the judicial practice of awarding custody to mothers rather than to fathers unless there are extenuating circumstances. This chapter initially focuses on the history of father custody. Then important themes in the study and consideration of father-custody families are outlined. Finally, legal and clinical implications of custody research conclude the chapter.

HISTORY OF FATHER CUSTODY

The Father's Role and Father Custody

Social scientists have historically labeled the father's role in child rearing as much weaker than the mother's (LeMasters, 1970). It has been argued that (1) the mother-child relationship has a biological basis, but the father-child relationship does not, (2) the father is poorly prepared for his parental role because as a boy he was not taught the duties and responsibilities of a father outside his economic role as provider, and (3) success of the father as a parent depends on his success in the pair bond with his wife.

Despite these sociological role prescriptions that emphasize the prominence of the mother's role over the father's, during much of the twentieth century psychoanalytic theorists have promoted the Freudian belief that the father serves an important function in the boy's development but only during the first five years of his life. However, even in psychoanalytic theory, the mother's love has continually been the central ingredient believed to be responsible for the development of a psychologically healthy child (Freud, 1938).

During much of the twentieth century, mothers have been viewed as the primary caregivers for children and have been the parents most involved in the everyday monitoring of the child's needs and development. Twentieth-century fathers for the most part have been much less involved with their children on a daily basis than was the frontier father, who was the sole provider for the family, performed virtually all of the decision making, and commanded a high degree of respect from his children. In many instances, sons worked in an apprentice relationship with the father, learning a vocation by spending long hours under the father's tutelage.

In addition to interest in the father's role in the child's development, there has been a long history of interest in custody decisions. For instance, in 1817 the well-known poet Percy Shelley was denied custody of his children because of his "vicious and immoral" atheistic beliefs. This was unusual in Shelley's era, since early English law gave fathers near-absolute right to custody of their children. At the beginning of the twentieth century, the tradition of awarding custody of children to mothers was created, a tradition with roots in the assumption that mothers, by nature, are uniquely suited to caring for children. The child will suffer irreversible damage, according to this argument, if separated from the mother during the formative "tender years."

Contemporary Social and Legal Climates

The role of the father in the child's development has become a prominent issue in contemporary American society, because the role of the female and the rights of women have become central concerns. No longer content to remain in a homemaker role, millions of American women have developed a strong career orientation. As the percentage of women entering the work force has increased, role demands on these women have increased.

No longer is the dominant family portrait one of a child being cared for during the day by a traditional homemaker mother. Rather the characteristic family portrait is now one of a woman working long hours, coming home and taking care of her children, and having to meet the needs of her husband, or one of children being reared in a mother-custody divorced home in which the mother faces the same career and parenting demands. Social scientists have described the contemporary circumstances of the mother as one of role overload in the sense that there often do not seem to be enough hours in the day for the career mother to meet all of the demands placed on her.

As the mother has increasingly provided economic support for the family, the question of the father's contribution to parenting and caregiving has logically been raised. If mothers are to share in the economic support of the family, should not the father be involved to a greater degree in the parenting process?

While interest in fathering seems to have increased on the part of some American men, evidence suggests that the majority of fathers spend little time in parenting. In one investigation (Szalai, 1975), American fathers spent an average of 12 minutes a day with their children! Other investigations of time use by parents also suggest that the majority of fathers are involved very little in the routine caregiving and parenting of everyday life (Pleck & Rustad, 1980; Walker & Woods, 1976). Thus despite consciousness-raising efforts to make society aware of the role overload of career mothers, in daily family activities fathers remain more of an indirect support system for the mother, operating in the background, than an active, frequent participant in the parenting process. Even when mothers work outside the home, fathers reportedly spend less than two thirds the amount of time that the mothers do in child rearing (Pleck, 1979).

It is not only in intact families that fathers spend little time with their children. There is reason to believe that in divorced mother-custody families, while fathers often show an increased interest in the children during the year following separation and divorce, by two years after the divorce his involvement has diminished considerably. For example, Furstenberg and colleagues (1983) found that children's contact with their father was frequent (defined as an average of at least once a week for a year) in only 17 percent of the mother-custody families regardless of their race. More about the noncustodial parent's importance appears later in this chapter. In sum, the majority of children in intact and divorced families do not have a high level of social interaction and involvement with their father. This was true in 1960 and seems to continue to be true in 1986.

As the roles of men and women have changed, so has the divorce rate. The figures are staggering. From 1970 to 1980, the ratio of all divorced persons per 1000 husbands and wives in intact families rose by 113 percent, from 47 per 1000 to 100 per 1000 (U. S. Census Bureau 1981). Cherlin (1981) has estimated that if current rates of divorce continue for the next several decades, approximately one half of the marriages started in the mid 1970s will end in divorce. Approximately 1.2 million children experience the divorce or separation of parents each year. The majority of children from divorced families live with their mother. Ninety-three percent of all children living in single-parent families reside with their mother, and less than 10 percent of divorce decrees give custody of the child to the father. In many instances in which the father does receive custody, it is when the mother is not motivated to assume custody rather than the judge deliberating that the father is best suited to be the custodial parent.

The "tender years" doctrine has emerged as the legal guideline supporting the mother's preferential claim to custody. Until recently, fathers were awarded custody only if the mother was proven grossly unfit. While courts have paid lip service to a "best interests of the child" doctrine, in practice most courts continue to award custody to the mother except in extreme circumstances. Exceptions have appeared in the 1980s. In custody disputes in California, the judicial system has recognized the important continuing influence of both parents on the child's development by recommending joint custody as the first alternative. Later in the chapter we will consider the importance of both parents in child development as well as the belief that joint custody is not a panacea for children from divorced homes.

FATHER-CUSTODY RESEARCH

Although much is known about the influence of divorce on children living with their mother, relatively few studies have been done of children reared in father-custody families. In most early studies, fathers with custody were interviewed or administered a questionnaire regarding their motivations for gaining custody, their general life style, their psychological characteristics and functioning, their parental role adjustment, their use of social support systems, and the children's adjustment (Gasser & Taylor, 1976; George & Wilding, 1972; Gersick, 1979; Mendes, 1976; Orthner, Brown & Ferguson, 1976; Schlesinger & Todres, 1976). This research provided a good beginning inquiry into father-custody homes. However, the lack of appropriate control groups and reliance on parental report are methodologic limitations that dictate caution in interpreting the results of these studies.

While parental report has long been criticized as an inadequate index of child development, this may be particularly true in divorce and custody studies. Wallerstein and Kelly (1980) commented on how parents' own needs biased their perceptions of their children's reactions to divorce: Parents who opposed the divorce tended to emphasize the distress of the child, and the parent who was eager to dissolve the marriage minimized the adverse impact on the child.

Investigations of father-custody families that intend to provide more valid and useful information should include direct study of the children, observations of parent-child interactions, and other indices of child development beyond parental impressions. Also appropriate comparison groups of children living in mother-custody and intact homes should be included. Five studies that have directly assessed children in father-custody families are those of Camara (1985), Luepnitz (1982), Rholes, Clark, and Morgan (1982), Rosen (1977, 1979), and the Texas Custody Research Project (Santrock & Warshak, 1979; Santrock, Warshak, & Elliot, 1982; Warshak & Santrock, 1983a, 1983b).

Camara (1985) studied 82 9- to 12-year-old children living in divorced and nondivorced families, 10 of whom were in the custody of their father. Although her sample was small, Camara employed a sophisticated research design with multiple measures, and thus we consider her father-custody data worthy of consideration.

Luepnitz (1982) studied 91 children, ages 2 through 17, in mother-custody, father-custody, and joint-custody families. Family functioning and child adjustment were assessed with use of self-report scales, parent interviews, and structured family interactions.

Rholes, Clark, and Morgan (1982) studied 117 college students who were reared in a single-father, single-mother, or two-parent household. Sex-role development, self-esteem, anxiety, and social maturity were assessed with standardized self-report scales.

Rosen (1977, 1979) administered interviews and sentence-completion tests to 92 South Africans ranging in age from 9 to 28 years, 6 to 10 years after their parents' divorce. There were 41 father-custody children and 51 mother-custody children. Judges rated the children on various personality attributes; the rater, however, was not kept naive about the family status of the children and there was no assessment of the reliability of the ratings.

In the Texas Custody Research Project, we have studied 64 6- to 11-year-old boys and girls from a mother-custody, father-custody, or parentally intact family (Santrock & Warshak, 1979; Santrock, Warshak, & Elliot, 1982; Warshak, 1979; Warshak & Santrock, 1983a, 1983b). A multimethod approach to studying personality was followed. Parents and children were videotaped interacting in a laboratory situation; structured interviews and self-report scales were given to parents and children; projective tasks were responded to by parents and children; and teachers reported their perceptions of the children on rating forms. Procedures for ensuring high reliability were used for all ratings. Where possible, raters were kept naive about the family structure of the children.

Motivation for Custody

Many judges and lawyers are concerned that men who seek custody are not as interested in the welfare of their children as they are in avoiding child-support payments or in inflicting pain on their wives. This was not the case according to the three studies that explored this issue (Gersick, 1979; Mendes, 1976; Orthner, Brown, & Ferguson, 1976). As a group, the men who actively sought custody highly valued their relationship with their children. There was no support for the notion that they were using custody as a weapon to harrass their exwives. Certainly there are some parents who seek custody for that reason. But there is ample evidence that many fathers desire custody because of a deep commitment to their children and a genuine interest in assuming primary responsibility for their care. Regardless of motives, the issue remains: Is this a responsibility that men are capable of managing?

Competence of the Father as Custodial Parent

One problem in assessing parental competence is that it is often difficult to determine the direction of effects in parent-child relations. For example, if a divorced mother has problems enforcing discipline, does this indicate a maternal deficiency or is it an index of the child's behavioral adjustment, or both? The focus here is limited to a discussion of parental attitudes and behaviors. Subsequent sections of this chapter detail children's adjustment in father-custody homes; this adjustment is assumed to reflect, in part, the level of parental competence.

All of the early interview studies addressed the issue of competence and arrived at the same conclusion: Men who gained custody generally felt that they were handling their child-care responsibilities effectively and that their children were coping successfully with the altered family structure. Furthermore, the fathers seemed highly involved with their children and did not overuse mother substitutes, as some have suggested they might (Weiss, 1975).

Several factors emerged as correlates of single-father competence (Orthner & Lewis, 1979). Initial adjustment to the single-parent role was facilitated by a predivorce history of regular involvement in nurturance, support, and discipline of their children. Also the men who had reallocated their time in favor of their children felt more competent in their parental role. High levels of confidence in parenting abilities, in turn, were associated with easier adjustment to single fatherhood. Income level and child's sex were not considered major factors affecting a father's competence. Many fathers were rearing daughters and appeared to be doing so capably, although some expressed anxiety about dealing with sexual issues in relation to daughters (Mendes, 1976).

The consistency of these findings across different samples cannot be easily dismissed. Nevertheless, it must be recalled that these studies are based solely on the report of the fathers.

Direct observations of parents interacting with their children have revealed that custodial fathers are less permissive and less likely to allow the child to control them than are custodial mothers (Santrock, Warshak, & Elliot, 1982). Naturally, in assessing fathers' competence as custodial parents, it is important to look at how their children are developing under their care. We now turn our attention to this topic.

CHILD DEVELOPMENT IN FATHER-CUSTODY HOMES

In this section we rely strongly on our own research as we look at father-custody children's reactions to the marital breakup; their perspectives on the divorce; their social, emotional, and personality development; and their relationships with their parents.

Reactions to the Separation

The initial event of their parents' separation is distressing to children regardless of whether it is father or mother who leaves the home. All of the fathers in the Texas study recalled some adverse reactions by their youngsters in the weeks and months immediately following the breakup (Warshak & Santrock, 1983a). In fact, these reactions were very similar to those occurring in mother-custody homes (Hetherington, Cox, & Cox, 1982; Wallerstein & Kelly, 1980; Warshak & Santrock, 1983a). The most frequently reported changes were increases in demands for parental attention, fears of abandonment and separation, and generalized anxiety.

Some reactions of father-custody children differed from those of children in mother-custody families. Mothers with custody reported a deteriorating relationship between father and child; in contrast, half the custodial fathers who detected changes in their child's relationship with the mother viewed these changes as positive (Warshak & Santrock, 1983a). Some confirmation of this pattern was evident in a sample of 14 young adolescents interviewed within a year after their parents' separation. Of the 11 children living with their mother, four declined to visit their father, whereas none of the three father-custody children declined to visit their mother (Springer & Wallerstein, 1983).

Another difference between the two custodial arrangements is that, in one study, custodial mothers were much more likely than custodial fathers to report increases in discipline problems in the period immediately following the marital breakup (Luepnitz, 1982). Such problems in child rearing were documented by Hetherington, Cox, and Cox (1982) and by Wallerstein and Kelly (1980) in their studies of mother-custody families.

Perspectives on the Divorce

Father-custody and mother-custody children hold common attitudes about their parents' divorce. In the Texas investigation (Warshak & Santrock, 1983b), when children were asked to tell the good and bad things about their parents being divorced, it was striking how they zeroed in on two variables that divorce researchers have identified as major factors influencing the outcome of divorce (Hess & Camara, 1979; Hetherington, Cox, & Cox, 1982; Wallerstein & Kelly, 1980). Most children pointed to the reduction in parental conflict as the benefit of divorce and the reduced availability of the noncustodial parent as the major drawback.

Most children did not expect their parents to marry each other again, but 84 percent of the children we interviewed expressed continuing wishes for reconciliation, most of these intense longings. An outstanding 98 percent of children attributed reconciliation wishes to the child in their projective story. Also just over two thirds of these children indicated that they would like things to be the way they had been before the divorce. Custodial status made no difference in these attitudes. The predominantly negative attitudes we found parallel the conclusions drawn by Wallerstein and Kelly (1980) in their work with mother-custody children.

Social, Emotional, and Personality Development

Children's initial reactions to the separation can be distinguished from their long-range psychological development. All five studies that compared children in father-custody homes with those living in mother-custody homes shared a common finding. There were no main effects attributable to custodial status alone, that is, in no instance was custody type, independent of other factors, linked with better or poorer functioning of children. A wide range of features of social, emotional, and personality development were studied. These outcome variables included self-esteem (Luepnitz, 1982; Rholes, Clark, & Morgan, 1982; Rosen, 1979; Santrock & Warshak, 1979;

Santrock, Warshak, & Elliot, 1982; Warshak & Santrock, 1983a); social competence (Camara, 1985; Rosen, 1979; Santrock & Warshak, 1979; Santrock, Warshak, & Elliot, 1982; Warshak & Santrock, 1983a); independence, warmth, and mood (Rosen 1979, Santrock and Warshak 1979); anxiety and sex-role typing (Rholes, Clark, & Morgan, 1982; Santrock & Warshak, 1979; Santrock, Warshak, & Elliot, 1982; Warshak & Santrock, 1983a,b); psychosomatic and behavior problems (Luepnitz, 1982); peer relations (Camara, 1985); and maturity (Rholes, Clark, & Morgan, 1982; Santrock & Warshak, 1979).

These findings of no difference in longer-term adjustment between children in father-custody and mother-custody homes are noteworthy. They do not support the current sociolegal preference for mother-custody arrangements. However, as we shall see later, when the child's sex is added to the equation, important differences between adjustment in mother-custody and father-custody homes do emerge.

Child-Parent Relations

The most obvious change in family life after a divorce is the fact that one parent has left the home. Restructuring the noncustodial parent-child relationship to accommodate new parameters of place and time is more problematic than many mental health professionals have appreciated. Both the quantity of contact and the quality of the relationship are apt to change.

In most mother-custody homes, the father becomes progressively less available to his children over time (Furstenberg, Nord, Peterson, & Zill, 1983; Hetherington, Cox, & Cox, 1982; Wallerstein & Kelly, 1980). There are no comparable data on changes over time in noncustodial mothers' involvement with their children. However, comparisons have been made between noncustodial mothers and fathers in the current amount of contact they maintained with their children. The findings have been discrepant. In two samples, noncustodial mothers had more contact with children (Luepnitz, 1982; Warshak & Santrock, 1983a); in another sample they had less contact (Fischer & Cardea, 1981); and in two samples there were no differences between noncustodial mothers and fathers in the amount of time they spent with their children (Constantatos, 1984; Defrain & Eirick, 1981).

The quality of children's relationships with their noncustodial parent has been investigated through interviews with custodial and noncustodial parents and children. Custodial mothers of school-age children report a deterioration in father-child relationships over time, whereas custodial fathers report an improvement in mother-child relations following divorce (Constantatos, 1984; Warshak & Santrock, 1983a). On the basis of interview responses, judges rated mothers with custody and mothers who had voluntarily relinquished custody as having equally positive relationships with their children, and the mothers' own ratings agreed with this (Constantatos, 1984). Nevertheless, certain benefits in the mother-child relationship appear to be gained from relinquishing custody. Noncustodial mothers, compared with custodial mothers, reported the least conflict and the most enjoyment in their relationship with their children (Constantatos, 1984).

Children in both father-custody and mother-custody homes enjoy their time with the noncustodial parent, and most want more frequent contact (Rosen, 1977; Wallerstein & Kelly, 1980; Warshak & Santrock, 1983b). There are no differences in these attitudes that can be attributed to custodial status alone, but when we consider boys and girls separately later in this chapter, some differences do emerge.

To summarize the information on noncustodial parent-child relations based on self-report data, it appears that school-age children in father-custody homes enjoy positive relations with their mothers; these relationships are described by parents, but not by children, as being better than noncustodial father-child relationships. There is an obvious need for direct observations of noncustodial parent-child interactions to supplement our understanding of these relationships.

Children's relationships with their custodial parent also undergo changes following a divorce. It has been observed that children in mother-custody homes may experience maternal as well as paternal deprivation because of the multiple demands placed on the single mother (Brandwein, Brown, & Fox, 1974; Hetherington, Cox, & Cox, 1978; Luepnitz, 1982; Weitzman, 1981). This situation has been linked to the substantial drop in income suffered by divorced women. Many custodial mothers must enter the work force or take on more career responsibilities to make ends meet, just at the time that their children need a great deal of parental support and attention to help them through the postdivorce adjustment period. Many mothers must place their young children in day-care or preschool programs, the quality of which is often suspect, particularly when the divorced mother must make her decision on the basis of the cost of such care. Thus there is a clear downward economic spiral for most mother-custody families, and this is a great source of stress that has harmful repercussions on the custodial mother-child relationship.

In comparison, for men divorce is usually not followed by a drop in income (Cherlin, 1981; Espenshade, 1979; Warshak & Santrock, 1983a). Custodial fathers cite the cost of child care as a disadvantage but not as a major problem, as do custodial mothers (Luepnitz, 1982). Without the economic constraints present in mother-custody families, the custodial father-child relationship is able to flourish, in most cases becoming more rewarding than it was before the divorce.

In one study, 87 percent of custodial fathers reported spending more time with their children after the divorce, whereas 50 percent of custodial mothers reported spending less time (Luepnitz, 1982). A typical comment of a father with custody was: "I have more contact with them now. I used to go to every meeting I could think of to be away from the house. I enjoy being with the kids now" (Luepnitz, 1982, p. 117).

The perceptions of the children in the Texas study followed the same pattern. Twenty-one percent reported spending less time with their custodial parent since the divorce, and there was a strong trend for mother-custody children to predominate over father-custody children in this attitude (Warshak & Santrock, 1983b). The father-custody children, although feeling that they, compared with peers, spent less time with their mother, did not report feelings of paternal deprivation, as did children in mother-custody and intact homes. Unfortunately no precise data are available on the exact amount of time custodial fathers spend with their children.

The quality of the custodial parent-child relationship has been assessed through direct observations of family interaction and interviews with parents and children. In structured laboratory tasks, children were rated on such dimensions as warmth and sociability while interacting with their custodial parents (Santrock & Warshak, 1979). In structured interaction tasks at home, the degree of supportive collaboration among the custodial parent and the children was studied (Luepnitz, 1982). In neither of these investigations were there differences between father-custody and mother-custody families that could be attributed to custodial status alone.

The absence of a main effect for custodial status holds true with respect to the interview data. In the Texas study, though a majority of parents viewed their youngsters as more demanding, aggressive, and angry since the divorce, 72 percent felt their relationship with their child improved after the divorce (Warshak & Santrock, 1983a), and 50 percent of the children rated their custodial parent as nicer to be with since the divorce (Warshak & Santrock, 1983b). Luepnitz's (1982) findings paralleled these, with custodial fathers and mothers feeling as close or closer to their children following the divorce.

This phenomenon has several explanations. First, the feeling of closeness is engendered by the experience of struggling through a trauma together. Second, after successfully sustaining the crisis of the ruptured family, many custodial parents are happier themselves and therefore better able to enjoy their children (Kelly, 1982). A third reason is that, with the other parent out of the home, custodial parents and children are more dependent on each other for a variety of needs (Weiss, 1979).

It should be noted that increased closeness between custodial parents and their children may be a mixed blessing. Indeed, single parents often express the wish to have time away from the children. In addition, custodial parents often lean on their children and turn to them for emotional and social support (Wallerstein, 1985). This results in role reversals and expectations that may leave children feeling overburdened, overwhelmed, and emotionally enmeshed (Hetherington & Camara, 1984; Warshak & Santrock, 1983a). We will return to this issue in the next section as we explore sex differences in children's adjustment in father-custody and mother-custody homes.

FACTORS INFLUENCING CHILD DEVELOPMENT IN FATHER-CUSTODY HOMES

In the preceding section, global comparisons were made between father-custody and mother-custody families. On the basis of those comparisons, the general conclusion is that one cannot predict the quality of a child's postdivorce functioning by custodial status alone. This section explores some factors that contribute to variability in children's responses to divorce.

Sex Differences

The previous discussion alluded to differences between boys and girls in their adjustment to a father-custody home. The most salient findings in the Texas study all involved an interaction between custodial status and the sex of the children. The pattern of results converging from six different (relatively independent) data sources has consistently revealed more socially competent behavior in children living with the same-sex parent (father-custody boys and mother-custody girls) than in children living with the opposite-sex parent (father-custody girls and mother-custody boys) (Santrock & Warshak, 1979; Santrock, Warshak, & Elliot, 1982; Warshak & Santrock, 1983a, 1983b). This same pattern of results has received support from three additional investigations (Camara, 1982, 1985; Gregory, 1965; Rholes, Clark, & Morgan, 1982). Because of the potential importance of this finding for developmental theory and legal and clinical practice, the specific results will be discussed here.

In laboratory interactions with their custodial parent, father-custody boys and mother-custody girls were rated less demanding and more mature, sociable, and independent than were mother-custody boys and father-custody girls (Santrock & Warshak, 1979). In a videotaped interview, children living with the same-sex parent showed more social competence, higher self-esteem, and less anxiety than children living with the opposite-sex parent (Santrock, Warshak, & Elliot, 1982). Interviewers found the children who lived with the same-sex parent easier to establish rapport with, more cooperative, more honest, and overall more appealing than children living with the opposite-sex parent (Warshak & Santrock, 1983a).

Girls in father-custody families were more likely than girls in mother-custody families to express separation anxiety, but there were no differences between boys from the two custody types on this variable (Warshak & Santrock, 1983b). In their projective stories, children were much more likely to indicate a preference for the same-sex parent-child custodial arrangement than for the opposite-sex arrangement. Also in the interview, more children living with the opposite-sex parent expressed a wish for increased contact with the noncustodial parent than did children living with the same-sex parent (Warshak & Santrock, 1983b). All of these results are from the Texas study; no results from this study showed more competent behavior in mother-custody boys or father-custody girls.

Three studies support the conclusion of the Texas study. Using self-report personality scales, Rholes, Clark, and Morgan (1982) found higher levels of anxiety in females who were reared from a relatively young age in a single-father home than those reared in a single-mother home. Males reared in a single-father home resembled males from single-mother and two-parent homes.

On many variables Camara (1985) found no differences between boys and girls in their adjustment to father-custody and mother-custody arrangements. However, where interactions between family structure and sex of child did occur, the data always fit the pattern found in the Texas study. Mother-custody boys, compared with boys in father-custody and two-parent homes, were more likely to play with girls, and father-custody girls, compared with the other girls in the study, were more likely to play with boys. Also in noncustodial parents' ratings of children's social competence, father-custody boys were seen as most competent. Camara (1982) also found that a positive relationship with the same-sex parent was associated with children's social competence with same-sex peers. We must caution that the sample in Camara's study was very small, and the study must be replicated before great weight is put on the findings.

The third study to support the conclusion of more competent behavior in children reared by same-sex parents was one by Gregory (1965) of 11,329 Minnesota high-school students. He found that the rate of delinquency among boys who were living in a single-father home was close to average and was lower than that of boys living in a single-mother home, regardless of whether parental absence was caused by death, divorce, or separation. The opposite was true for girls: A higher rate of delinquency was associated with living in a single-father home than in a single-mother home, although both were higher than average. It should be noted, however, that there were no controls for the age of onset or duration of parental absence.

The only study comparing children reared in the two custody arrangements that did not find an interaction between family structure and sex of child was that of Rosen (1977, 1979). In her work, boys and girls adjusted equally well in father-custody and mother-custody homes. It is difficult to assess the significance of this finding because of the numerous methodologic limitations of Rosen's study. Finally, Luepnitz (1982) failed to investigate the potential effects of the sex of the child in her comparison of children in different custody situations.

Further evidence for the validity of the finding of more problematic adjustment of children in the custody of the opposite-sex parent is provided by the consensus of research with mother-custody families. A number of investigators have reported that more intense, dramatic, and enduring difficulties in response to divorce are found among preschool and elementary school-age boys than girls (Guidubaldi, Perry, & Cleminshaw, 1983; Hess & Camara, 1979; Hetherington, Cox, & Cox, 1982; McDermott, 1968; Wallerstein & Kelly, 1980; Zill, 1984). Difficulty in self-control and increase in aggression appear to be the most common problems, along with academic deficits (Guidubaldi, Perry, & Cleminshaw, 1983; Zill, 1984) and disruptions in traditional sex-role typing (Biller, 1976; Biller & Bahm, 1971; Hetherington, Cox, & Cox, 1982; Santrock, 1972). Later in the chapter we discuss alternative explanations for the differences in adjustment between boys and girls in father-custody and mother-custody homes.

Coparental Relationships

A highly conflictual and tumultuous relationship between parents is associated with negative outcomes in children from mother-custody homes (Chess & Thomas, 1984; Emery & O'Leary, 1982; Hess & Camara, 1979; Hetherington, Cox, & Cox, 1982; Jacobson, 1978; Raschke & Raschke, 1979; Rutter, 1979; Wallerstein & Kelly, 1980). Two studies have extended this finding to father-custody homes; that is, regardless of custodial status, children's adjustment suffers in families with high postdivorce conflict (Luepnitz, 1982; Rosen, 1979).

There is evidence from two investigations that in families in which the mother voluntarily relinquishes custody, there is less conflict between the exspouses than in mother-custody families. In a recent study, Constantatos (1984) found that noncustodial mothers, relative to custodial mothers, reported less conflict and more sharing, cooperation, and satisfaction with their relationship with their exspouse. Also noncustodial mothers were more likely than custodial mothers to increase their respect for their exspouse's abilities as a parent after the divorce. In the Texas study, custodial fathers rated their relationship with their exwife as improved since the divorce, whereas custodial mothers more often indicated a deterioration in their relationship with their exhusband (Warshak & Santrock, 1983a).

Thus some father-custody children may have the advantage of being exposed to less parental discord and turmoil. When a father gains custody through a legal battle, however, the children are apt to have a more difficult experience with higher levels of parental acrimony (Luepnitz, 1982).

Parenting Style

Adjustment problems of children in mother-custody homes are minimized when parenting is authoritative and there is warm, communicative support for the children (Hetherington, Cox, & Cox, 1982; Wallerstein & Kelly, 1980). In the Texas study authoritative parenting was linked with healthier adjustment of children in both father-custody and mother-custody homes (Santrock & Warshak, 1979; Santrock, Warshak, & Elliot, 1982).

Support Systems

A high-quality relationship with the nonresidential parent is a major support to children who have experienced the breakup of their family. Such a relationship can reduce the child's fear of abandonment and loss of love and confirm the fact that interparental discord does not involve him or her. The continuing availability of the noncustodial father has been identified as a significant factor associated with children's, particularly boy's, positive adjustment in mother-custody homes (Hess & Camara, 1979; Hetherington, Cox, & Cox, 1982; Wallerstein & Kelly, 1980). This relationship apparently holds for availability of the mother for children in father-custody families as well.

In interviews with children reared in father-custody and mother-custody homes, Rosen (1977) found that the extent to which their parents' divorce was perceived by the children as untraumatic was related to the children's easy access to both parents. It should be recalled that the children in the Texas study most frequently cited reduced availability of the noncustodial parent as the worst aspect of the divorce. Also 62 percent of these children expressed a wish for more frequent visits with their noncustodial parent, although this was more prevalent among children living with the opposite-sex parent (Warshak & Santrock, 1983b). Unfortunately, we still await direct analyses of the relationship between extent of contact with the noncustodial mother and psychological adjustment in children. Thus it is a reasonable, but as yet untested, speculation that the quality of adjustment of children in father-custody homes will be associated with access to their mother.

Other support systems available to divorced parents include day-care centers, babysitters, relatives, and friends. In one sample, custodial fathers and custodial mothers used approximately the same amount of substitute daytime care (Luepnitz, 1982), and in another sample custodial fathers relied on more substitute child care than did custodial mothers (Santrock & Warshak, 1979; Warshak, 1979). In the latter case it is not known whether fathers sought support systems more frequently or whether relatives, friends, and others felt that fathers needed more help than mothers in rearing children (Meredith, 1985). It is known that in both types of custody dispositions, contact with additional adult caretakers was positively associated with the child's behavior toward the custodial parent (Santrock & Warshak, 1979).

Other Mediating Variables

In addition to the factors just discussed, there are several important variables that have not yet been investigated but that can be expected to mediate children's adjustment in father-custody homes. Father-custody families are not a homogeneous group.

How and why a father attains custody may have significant impact on the family's ability to cope. For example, some fathers attain custody after both spouses mutually agree that this would best serve their children's needs. Other fathers are forced to assume custody when a mother unilaterally decides to relinquish her role as the primary caretaker. And some fathers gain custody through an actual, or threatened, court battle. One would expect that each of these routes to custody would be associated with a different outcome for the children, and it is hoped that future research will address this issue.

In describing the development of children in father-custody homes, it is important to identify whether the children lived with the father from the time of the divorce or whether they were initially in the custody of their mother and then transferred to their father at a later time. The latter circumstance describes nearly half of Luepnitz's (1982) sample, whereas the former arrangement describes the Texas sample (Warshak, 1979). If this variable is not taken into account in sample selection or data analyses, the observed effects of father custody could be confounded with the impact of custody modification. This will limit the utility and generalizability of any findings.

With samples in which there has been a change of custody, it is important to consider the reasons for the change. For example, some mothers transfer custody when they run into major problems with their children (Luepnitz, 1982). If these children are then studied as part of a father-custody sample, their problems should not be attributed to the custodial situation.

Other variables that can be expected to influence adjustment in father-custody homes are the ages of the child at the time of the marital breakup and at the time of being studied, duration since the separation, sociocultural background, sibling status, and whether custody of siblings was split between the parents. A relevant set of variables that has not been adequately investigated in father-custody homes pertains to the personality of custodial parents and their experiences in their family of origin. Important intergenerational relationships to explore include parents' relationships to their own parents as well as their perceptions and memories of their parents' marital relationship. There is an obvious need for more systematic investigations of father-custody families.

PROCESS UNDERLYING SEX-OF-CHILD EFFECTS IN FATHER-CUSTODY FAMILIES

The differences between boys and girls in their adjustment to father-custody and mother-custody homes are evident in the results of four father-custody studies and in the consensus of mother-custody research. Evidence seems to be compelling favoring a match between the sex of the child and of the custodial parent. Several explanations could account for this.

Psychoanalytic theory has emphasized the importance of the child's identification with the same-sex parent. Social learning theory has continued this emphasis, but has attached more importance to the behavioral aspects of modeling and imitation. These types of identification with the parent may be more difficult to sustain when the parent is less available. Also a custodial parent's negative attitude toward the exspouse can introduce a disruptive element of ambivalence in the child's attachment to, and identification with, the noncustodial parent. A counteridentification process may also be operative: Parents may know how to interact more effectively and feel more comfortable with a child of the same sex.

Another factor that may contribute to the poorer adjustment of some children living with the opposite-sex parent is what may be termed a "reverse oedipal" situation. In this, the custodial parent seeks from the children emotional gratifications that are more appropriately provided by a spouse. Feeling lonely, emotionally deprived, or stressed, the parent turns to the children, most often a child of the opposite sex, for such needs as comfort and nurturance (Weiss, 1975). Most children, however, are not capable of meeting a parent's emotional needs. Thus the parent is frustrated and disappointed and the children feel inadequate at not being able to meet the parent's expectations. This feeling may lead to the immature behaviors noted in research findings. The long-range risk is that as these children grow older, they will feel (and thus be) less competent than others in dealing with persons of the opposite sex.

Parental wishes for nurturance are not the only feelings that are inappropriately directed toward children. At times a custodial parent's anger at the exspouse gets displaced onto a child. The child is most likely to be of the opposite sex. It is not uncommon to hear of a divorced mother overreacting to her son's behavior while exclaiming in a derisive tone, "You're acting just like your father."

Other explanations for sex differences in children's response to divorce have been advanced. It has been argued that disruptions in self-control in boys from mother-custody homes may be traced to the fact that boys are less compliant than girls; to be controlled, boys need the stronger authority image our culture ascribes to the father (Hetherington, 1979). This does not explain, however, why girls in father-custody homes seem less well adjusted than girls in mother-custody homes. Despite this finding, father custody should not be assumed to be a poor choice for girls. It is important not to infer a causal relationship from an association between two variables. Girls whose mother relinquished custody may have been disturbed to begin with. The giving of custody of a son to the father rather than the mother may be seen as more socially acceptable because there is a popular notion that "a boy needs his father." However, mothers who gave up custody of a girl may have done so, in part, because there was some impairment in the mother-daughter relationship. This needs to be explored further.

LEGAL AND CLINICAL IMPLICATIONS OF RESEARCH

The question can be asked whether results of psychological research can be applied to individual custody decisions. Further, it is important to evaluate the current state of our knowledge about the custodial circumstance and what it does and does not mean.

Relevance of Psychological Research to Legal Decisions about Custody

Thompson (1983) has pointed out an important discrepancy in the interest of judges, lawyers, expert witnesses, and social scientists. Judges, lawyers, and expert witnesses take an idiographic approach to the custodial circumstance, whereas social scientists adopt a nomothetic approach. That is, the judicial system focuses on the unique circumstances of a single case. The social scientist seeks to discover threads of similarity among many cases, ultimately hoping to draw some general conclusions.

As pointed out by Thompson in Chapter 3, the actors in the judicial drama are involved in a very subjective judgmental process. We are not even close to the point where we can predict the outcome of a custody case in terms of its positive or negative effects on the child. However, as was seen in our review of the mother- and father-custody research literature, some themes have begun to characterize the results of different studies. While such information can serve only as a small part of a large body of information to be considered in making a very complex judgment, it nonetheless may increase the likelihood of a more accurate decision being made about the future life of a child. Further, such information may serve as a guide for expert witnesses who are called to testify in custody disputes, by bringing their attention to important aspects of the custody circumstances. Mental health professionals are often requested by courts to evaluate families and render recommendations regarding custody and visitation. Expert witnesses who do not adequately appreciate the father's role in child development usually operate under the assumption that, unless the mother is severely disturbed, the children would be better off in her custody. Being familiar with the findings reviewed here, expert witnesses can conduct custody evaluations without this bias and, it is hoped, render a more objective recommendation. Thus we believe the results of psychological research have a role in custodial decision making, although we still are at an early state of knowledge in our research inquiry about father custody.

Implications of Research for Legal Decisions about Custody

What do we know from psychological research that can be used in judicial decision making about custody? First, we know that an ongoing positive relationship with both parents seems to have a positive effect on children in the custody of the mother. Thus in mother-custody situations, every effort should be made by the judicial system to encourage such relationships. There is every reason to believe that a similar circumstance occurs with father custody, although no research data bear on this important question. The traditional pattern of 12 days with one parent and 2 days with the other clearly has not met the best interests of most children.

The question arises whether joint custody might be the panacea for the children in a divorce. While the literature on mother custody implies that an increased amount of involvement by the father should help the child's adjustment, we cannot generalize this information to joint-custody circumstances. There clearly is a strong need for empirical research on the effects of joint custody on children's development (Clingempeel & Reppucci, 1982). Some have argued that joint custody is confusing to children, interfering with their security and stability. Others say failure to allow joint custody inadvertently may promote anger and a profound sense of loss (Kelly, 1980). Before joint custody is prescribed it is important to resolve such questions as: In the face of the aftermath of divorce, can both parents work cooperatively in the best interests of the child when placed in a joint-custody circumstance? Does the alternation of the child from one parent to the other disrupt the development of a secure attachment to either parent? Clearly it does not seem appropriate to recommend joint custody unless both parents are motivated to pursue this avenue. Many therapists view with suspicion a divorcing couple's wish to share custody. This desire is often interpreted as disguising a wish to avoid the full emotional reality of divorce. While this may be one motive, another just as likely is that the spouses are acknowledging the reality that the end of the marriage does not undo the permanence of their dual parental roles. Indeed, the wish to relinquish custody or to deprive the exspouse of custody may represent an attempt to deny the full reality of the parental relationship.

In addition to psychological research implying the importance of a positive ongoing relationship with both parents in the child's adjustment, evidence has accumulated to suggest that the system of always awarding custody to the mother unless there are extenuating circumstances should be eliminated. The research information reviewed here has revealed that fathers indeed can be competent caregivers and that some children seem to show better adjustment in father custody than in mother custody. There also is a growing body of research on the father's role in the infant's development, suggesting that fathers can be competent in rearing very young children when motivated to do so (Lamb, 1981; Parke & Sawin, 1976).

However, as seen earlier in this chapter, the vast majority of fathers in the United States apparently are not motivated to be highly active participants in the lives of their children, whether in intact or divorced family circumstances. At this point in American culture, about 90 percent of children in divorced families live with their mother. On the basis of evidence involving the father's motivation to participate in caregiving, this decision for the most part appears to be a wise one. However, in a certain percentage of cases the best interests of the child are probably not being served. In this minority of cases, rigid, stereotyped decisions rather than informed, flexible judgments are likely to have long-term negative consequences for the children involved.

Our research has made its way into a number of custodial disputes. It has not been unusual over the last five years to receive calls from three or four professionals daily regarding research information about children's custodial arrangements. In many instances, these professionals are lawyers or expert witnesses wishing to obtain custody of a boy for a father or a girl for a mother. Does our research support the belief that a custodial decision should favor the father in the case of a son and the mother in the case of a daughter? All things being equal, it does; however, all things are never equal, and the complexity of the custodial decision must be emphasized. This complexity entails sex of the child but a great deal more as well, including such crucial matters as parenting competence, willingness to continue being involved on a regular basis with the child even as a noncustodial parent, the degree of support systems available to each parent, and willingness to facilitate the child's relationship with the noncustodial parent. The issue also is raised as to the extent that the information about father-custody and mother-custody families in Dallas, Texas, generalizes to other children in other sociocultural circumstances. For example, the children in our investigation were from middle-class white family backgrounds and were of elementary school age. Generalizations to other sociocultural millieus, lower social class circumstances, and other age children may not be warranted. Nonetheless, the fact that a thorough investigation of the lives of father-custody children showed sex of child to be an important adjustment factor suggests that sex of child should indeed be one of the many factors a judge considers in making a custodial decision.

Other qualifications also must be made. The findings of studies such as the Texas Custody Research Project should not necessarily be used to infer the desirability of splitting custody of siblings between parents along sex-related lines. Although in certain selected cases this may serve the best interests of the children, we need more research on the contribution of the sibling system to children's postdivorce adjustment (Springer & Wallerstein, 1983). The subjects in the Texas study all were living in families in which custody of siblings was not split.

In addition, the results of these studies may not always apply when modification of custody is being considered. In these cases, the advantages of continuity and consistency of caretaking arrangements may override other concerns.

It should be pointed out that knowledge is very limited regarding the benefits or pitfalls of mother custody, father custody, and joint custody. No long-term investigations have simultaneously investigated these different arrangements, so even the mention here of sex of child as one of many variables to consider in a custody decision is based on cross-sectional rather than longitudinal data. The 1980s represent intriguing years, however, despite research limitations. Today there is true interest in discovering the best living circumstances for children and in determining what the future impact of these circumstances will be on children. This interest still escapes many people, but it rarely existed at all several decades earlier.

In view of the fact that prevailing legal practices do not always reflect current understanding of divorce and its aftermath, an important strategy in the application of research findings is to publicize them. Parents, mental health professionals, lawyers, and judges need to be educated about the impact of various postdivorce arrangements. This education should always include an emphasis on the father's healthy involvement in the child's development. In some circumstances this emphasis might encourage fathers to pursue custody of their children; in others it might motivate joint custody.

Clinical Implications of Research

Empirical findings on the consequences of various custody arrangements have implications in the clinical sphere. To begin with, the availability of results from methodologically sound studies enables professionals conversant with the literature to act as authoritative consultants to divorcing families. This, in fact was an important aspect of the California Children of Divorce Project (Kelly & Wallerstein, 1977; Wallerstein & Kelly, 1977), in which preventive counseling was offered. Parents want help in facilitating their children's coping with divorce. Findings from empirical research aid in educating parents about the factors that aid or compromise their children's postdivorce adjustment.

Application of research findings can occur in several different contexts. In consulting with parents of emotionally or behaviorally disturbed children, many clinicians have accepted rather than questioned the visiting arrangements of the children. This has led to treatment aimed at helping the child adjust to paternal deprivation, rather than to efforts that facilitate a more adequate relationship between father and child. When the importance of this relationship is appreciated, clinicians can focus more energy on helping it than is now typical. For example, during the initial clinical contact it is not unusual for mothers from both intact and divorced homes to indicate that the child's father is not involved with the child and is not interested in participating in an evaluation or treatment. Rather than accept this at face value, the clinician should make every attempt to secure the father's involvement in the consultation.

In a surprising number of instances, such efforts pay off. If the father resembles many of those studied by Wallerstein and Kelly, he may have reduced the frequency of his visits for one or more of the following reasons: He may have become frustrated or depressed in his attempts to forge a relationship given the real constraints of time and place and dependence on his exwife's cooperation, or he may have an inadequate understanding of the importance of his role in his children's lives. With brief, primarily educational interventions and support, these fathers are willing, often eager, to become more involved and to cement better relationships with their children.

In response to the popularization of the idea that divorce can have a harmful impact on children, many parents who would not seek, and may not need, psychotherapeutic "treatment" are willing to meet with clinicians acting in the role of "divorce consultant." Thus clinicians may be in a position to help families who might not otherwise seek the services of a mental health professional.

SUMMARY AND CONCLUSIONS

This chapter has explored the social, psychological, legal, and clinical worlds of children in father-custody families. Information was presented about the historical and cultural background of the father's role in his children's development and of father custody. The changing social roles of women and men were described with particular attention on career and parenting demands and modifications. The conclusion was that a large majority of fathers spend very little time with their children, but that fathers can be competent caregivers to children. The tradition of awarding custody to mothers, referred to as the "tender years" doctrine, began in the twentieth century. Recently this tradition has been questioned, current thinking being focused on the "best interests" of the child.

Research on the effects of divorce on children suggests that divorce is a highly stressful experience for all family members. The first year after the separation and divorce is often the most stressful, with more stability occurring, particularly for girls in mother-custody circumstances, two years after separation. Most divorces involve high degrees of conflict. Conflict is stressful in intact families but may be even more stressful in divorced families because of the absence of protective buffering by another parent. Parents make the decision to divorce, not children. A large majority of children show strong wishes that their parents will get back together—the separation and sense of loss when one parent leaves the home is an emotionally draining experience for a child. Adjustment problems of children are diminished when parenting in divorced families is authoritative and there is warm, communicative support by parents as well as a positive, harmonious relationship between the custodial parent and the exspouse.

Finances often are a major problem following the divorce for mothers with custody. Support systems to the family are an important ingredient for the child's adjustment in both mother-custody and father-custody families. Relationships are carried forward in time. Adolescents whose parents were divorced when they were in early childhood and young adults whose parents were divorced when they were in adolescence usually attempt to reconstruct their past and fit the pieces of the attachment puzzle together. In both sets of circumstances, the adolescents and young adults reminisce about how their lives may have been better if they had grown up in an intact family. The young adults are more conscious of the surroundings of the divorce in adolescence than the adolescents are aware of such matters that occurred in early childhood.

Research focused specifically on father custody has not been as extensive, or in most instances as empirically based, as mother-custody research. Basically many of the same factors that seem to predict competent adjustment of children in mother-custody families do likewise in father-custody families—authoritative parenting and the availability and use of support systems, for example. As yet we do not have much research information about the continuing ongoing relationships of children in father-custody circumstances with their mothers, but we would expect that these, as well as a continuing harmonious relationship between the custodial parent and the exspouse, would be salient in promoting healthy psychological adjustment of the child.

One difference in father-custody and mother-custody adjustment appears to be related to the sex of the child: Sons seem to show better adjustment in father-custody circumstances, while daughters are more socially competent in mother-custody arrangements.

There has been a discrepancy in the interests of the judicial system and social science, the judicial system emphasizing idiographic information about the child and social scientists focusing on nomothetic matters. As currently practiced, the judicial process surrounding custodial decision making is often highly biased and subjective. Bias and subjectivity are not limited to judges and lawyers but extend to mental health practitioners who serve as expert witnesses as well. In too many instances, such witnesses are unfamiliar with the divorce literature and call on information from sources that were not designed for the purpose of determining custodial suitability.

While we are at a very early state in the ability to predict the outcome of custodial decisions in terms of the child's long-term mental health, the body of knowledge we do have provides a more objective data source than what has been traditionally relied on in custody matters. While every custodial case must be decided on its own merits, the research literature can serve as a guide to inform judges and expert witnesses about which variables and constructs to place more weight on in custodial decisions. In particular, a positive ongoing relationship with both parents following the divorce is important in the child's postdivorce adjustment, at least in mother-custody arrangements. It likely is very important in father-custody arrangements as well, particularly for girls. As yet we can only speculate about the pluses and minuses of joint custody, and we cannot generalize from research on single-parent divorce studies to joint custody in terms of equal participation of parenting. Clearly, however, evidence currently suggests that the "tender years" doctrine should be removed as the standard custodial benchmark. Nonetheless, while a "best interests" doctrine is the best strategy, it is likely, at least in the near future, that a large majority of single-parent families will remain of the mother-custody variety, given data showing how little time most fathers spend with their children. We believe one of the most important tasks ahead is to publicize this low degree of involvement and popularize in the culture how the father's involvement in intact, mother-custody, father-custody, and joint-custody families is a salient factor in the child's healthy psychological development. Our own research has been used by expert witnesses primarily to argue for a same-sex custodial parent-child judicial decision. It is important to remember that although sex of child is one of the factors that should be considered in a custodial decision, it is only one of many factors in the equation for predicting the future psychological development of the child. Just as it is inappropriate to not weigh it at all in the custodial decision-making process, we should not overweigh it by ignoring other crucial factors such as the quality of parenting, availability of support systems, and parent-child relationships.

The availability of results from competent empirical studies of divorce can benefit clinicians who work with families of divorced children. One area that deserves particular attention is encouragement of the father's participation in the child's development in divorced families.

REFERENCES

Baumrind, D. (1971). Current patterns of parental authority. *Developmental Psychology Monographs, 4*(1, Part 2), 1–103.

Biller, H. (1976). The father and personality development: Paternal deprivation and sex-role development. In M. Lamb (Ed.), *The role of the father in child development.* New York: Wiley.

Biller, H., & Bahm, R. (1971). Father absence, perceived maternal behavior and masculinity of self-concept among junior high school boys. *Developmental Psychology, 4,* 178–181.

Brandwein, R. A., Brown, C. A., & Fox, E. M., (1974). Women and children last: The social situation of divorced mothers and their families. *Journal of Marriage and the Family, 36,* 498–514.

Camara, K. A. (1982, July). *Social interaction of children in divorced and intact households.* Paper presented at 10th International Congress of Psychiatry and Allied Professions, Dublin, Ireland.

Camara, K. A. (1985, April). *Social knowledge and behavior of children in single-parent and two-parent households.* Paper presented at 62nd annual meeting of American Orthopsychiatric Association, New York.

Cherlin, A. J. (1981). *Marriage, divorce, and remarriage.* Cambridge, MA: Harvard University Press.

Chess, S., & Thomas, A. (1984). *Origins and evaluation of behavior disorders.* New York: Brunner/Mazel.

Clingempell, W. G., & Reppucci, N. D. (1982). Joint custody after divorce: Major issues and goals of research. *Psychological Bulletin, 91,* 102–127.

Constantatos, M. (1984). *Non-custodial versus custodial divorced mothers: Antecedents and consequences of custody choice.* Unpublished doctoral dissertation, University of Texas Health Science Center at Dallas.

Defrain, J., & Eirick, R. (1981). Coping as divorced single parents: A comparative study of fathers and mothers. *Family Relations, 30,* 265–274.

Emery, R. E., & O'Leary, K. D. (1982). Children's perceptions of marital discord and behavior problems of girls and boys. *Journal of Abnormal Child Psychology, 10,* 11–24.

Espenshade, T. J. (1979). The economic consequences of divorce. *Journal of Marriage and the Family, 41,* 615–625.

Fischer, J. L., & Cardea, J. M. (1981). Mothers living apart from their children: A study in stress and coping. *Alternative Lifestyles, 4*(2), 218–227.

Freud, S. (1938). *An outline of psychoanalysis.* London: Hogarth.

Furstenberg, F. F., Nord, C. W., Peterson, J. S., & Zill, N. (1983). The life course of children of divorce: Marital disruption and parental contact. *American Sociological Review, 48,* 656–668.

Gasser, R., & Taylor, C. (1976). Role-adjustment of single-parent fathers. *The Family Coordinator, 25,* 397–401.

George, V., & Wilding, P. (1972). *Motherless families.* London: Routledge and Kegan Paul.

Gersick, K. (1979). Fathers by choice: Divorced men who receive custody of their children. In G. Levinger & O. Moles (Eds.), *Divorce and separation.* New York: Basic.

Gregory, I. (1965). Anterospective data following childhood loss of a parent: I. Delinquency and high school dropout. *Archives of General Psychiatry, 13,* 99–109.

Guidubaldi, J., Perry, J. D., & Cleminshaw, H. K. (1983). The legacy of parental divorce: A nationwide study of family status and selected mediating variables on children's academic and social competencies. *School Psychology Review, 2,* 148.

Hess, R., & Camara, K. (1979). Post-divorce family relationships as mediating factors in the consequences of divorce for children. *Journal of Social Issues, 35,* 79–96.

Hetherington, E. M. (1979). Divorce: A child's perspective. *American Psychologist, 34,* 851–858.

Hetherington, E. M., & Camara, K. A. (1984). Families in transition: The processes of dissolution and reconstitution. In R. Parke (Ed.), *Review of child development research* (Vol. 7). Chicago: University of Chicago Press.

Hetherington, E. M., Cox, M., & Cox, R. (1978). The aftermath of divorce. In J. H. Stevens and M. Mathews (Eds.), *Mother-child/father-child relations.* Washington, DC: National Association for the Education of Young Children.

Hetherington, E. M., Cox, M., & Cox, R. (1982). Effects of divorce on parents and children. In M. E. Lamb (Ed.) *Nontraditional families.* Hillsdale, NJ: Erlbaum.

Jacobson, D. S. (1978). The impact of marital separation and divorce on children: II. Interparent hostility and child adjustment. *Journal of Divorce, 3,* 3–19.

Kelly, J. (1980). Recent divorce research: Implications for visitation decisions. In R. Warshak (Chair), *Recent divorce research: implications for clinical services.* Panel presented at annual meeting of American Association of Psychiatric Services to Children, New Orleans.

Kelly, J. B. (1982). Divorce: The adult perspective. In B. B. Wolman, G. Stricker, S. J. Ellman, P. Keith-Spiegel, & D. S. Palermo (Eds.), *Handbook of developmental psychology.* Engelwood Cliffs, NJ: Prentice-Hall.

Kelly, J. B., & Wallerstein, J. S. (1977). Brief interventions with children in divorcing families. *American Journal of Orthopsychiatry, 47,* 23–39.

Lamb, M. E. (1981). *The role of the father in the child's development.* 2nd ed. New York: Wiley.

LeMasters, E. E. (1970). Parents in modern America. Homewood, IL: Dorsey.

Lowery, C. R. (1981). Child custody decisions in divorce proceedings: A survey of judges. *Professional Psychology, 12,* 492–498.

Luepnitz, D. A. (1982). *Child custody.* Lexington, MA: Heath.

Maccoby, E. E., & Martin, J. A. (1983). Socialization in the context of the family: Parent child interaction. In P. E. Mussen (Ed.), *Handbook of child psychology* Vol. 4, 4th ed. New York: Wiley.

McDermott, J. (1968). Parental divorce in early childhood. *American Journal of Psychiatry, 124,* 118–126.

Mendes, H. (1976). Single fathers. *The Family Coordinator, 25,* 439–444.

Meredith, D. (1985, June). Dad and the kids. *Psychology Today,* 62–67.

Orthner, D., Brown, T., & Ferguson, D. (1976). Single-parent fatherhood: An emerging lifestyle. *The Family Coordinator, 25,* 429–437.

Orthner, D., & Lewis, K. (1979). Evidence of single-father competence in child-rearing. *Family Law Quarterly, 13,* 37–47.

Parke, R. D., & Sawin, D. B. (1976). The father's role in infancy: A re-evaluation. *The Family Coordinator, 25,* 365–371.

Pleck, J. H. (1979). Men's family work: Three perspectives and some new data. *Family Coordinator, 25,* 481–488.

Pleck, J. H., & Rustad, M. (1980). *Husbands' and wives' time in family work and paid work in the 1975–76 study of time use.* Wellesley, MA: Wellesley College Center for Research on Working Women (unpublished).

Porter, B., & O'Leary, K. D. (1980). Marital discord and childhood behavior problems. *Journal of Abnormal Child Psychology, 8,* 287–295.

Raschke, H., & Raschke, V. (1979). Family conflict and children's self-concepts: A comparison of intact and single-parent families. *Journal of Marriage and the Family, 41,* 367–374.

Rholes, W. S., Clark, T. L., & Morgan, R. (1982). *The effects of single father families on personality development.* Unpublished manuscript, Texas A&M University, Department of Psychology, College Station, TX.

Rosen, R. (1977). Children of divorce: What they feel about access and other aspects of the divorce experience. *Journal of Clinical Child Psychology, 6,* 24–27.

Rosen, R. (1979). Children of divorce: An evaluation of two common assumptions. *Canadian Journal of Family Law, 2,* 403–415.

Rutter, M. (1979). Maternal deprivation, 1972–1978. New findings, new concepts, new approaches. *Child Development, 50,* 283–305.

Santrock, J. W. (1972). The relation of onset and type of father absence to cognitive development. *Child Development, 43,* 455–469.

Santrock, J. W., & Warshak, R. A. (1979). Father custody and social development in boys and girls. *Journal of Social Issues, 35,* 112–135.

Santrock, J. W., Warshak, R. A., & Elliot, G. L. (1982). Social development and parent-child interaction in father-custody and stepmother families. In M. E. Lamb (Ed.), *Nontraditional families.* Hillsdale, NJ: Erlbaum.

Schlesinger, B., & Todres, R. (1976). Motherless families: An increasing societal pattern. *Child Welfare, 55,* 553–558.

Springer, C., & Wallerstein, J. S. (1983). Young adolescents' responses to their parents' divorces. In L. A. Kurdek (Ed.), *Children and divorce.* San Francisco: Jossey-Bass.

Szalai, A. (1975). *The use of time: Daily activities of urban and suburban populations in twelve countries.* The Hague: Mouton.

Thompson, R. A. (1983). The father's case in child custody disputes: The contributions of psychological research. In M. E. Lamb & A. Sagi (Eds.), *Fatherhood and family policy.* Hillsdale, NJ: Erlbaum.

Walker, K., & Woods, M. (1976). *Time use.* Washington, DC: American Home Economics Association.

Wallerstein, J. S. (1985). Children of divorce: Preliminary report of a ten-year follow-up of older children and adolescents. *Journal of the American Academy of Child Psychiatry, 24,* 545–553.

Wallerstein, J. S., & Kelly, J. B. (1977). Divorce counseling: A community service for families in the midst of divorce. *American Journal of Orthopsychiatry, 47,* 4–22.

Wallerstein, J. W., & Kelly, J. B. (1980). *Surviving the break-up: How children and parents cope with divorce.* New York: Basic.

Warshak, R. A. (1979). The effects of father-custody and mother-custody on children's personality development. *Dissertation Abstracts International, 40,* 940B (University Microfilms No. 7918709).

Warshak, R. A., & Santrock, J. W. (1983a). Children of divorce: Impact of custody disposition on social development. In E. J. Callahan & K. A. McCluskey (Eds.), *Life-span developmental psychology.* New York: Academic.

Warshak, R. A., & Santrock, J. W. (1983b). The impact of divorce in father-custody and mother-custody homes: The child's perspective. In L. A. Kurdek (Ed.), *Children and divorce.* San Francisco: Jossey-Bass.

Weiss, R. (1975). *Marital separation.* New York: Basic.

Weiss, R. S. (1979). Growing up a little faster. *Journal of Social Issues, 35,* 97–111.

Weitzman, L. J. (1981). The economics of divorce: Social and economic consequences of property, alimony and child custody awards. *University of California at Los Angeles Law Review, 28,* 1181–1268.

Zill, N. (1984). *Happy, healthy, and insecure.* New York: Doubleday.

THREE

Clinical Issues

CHAPTER 6

The Father in Family Therapy: Psychoanalytic Perspectives

RICHARD N. ATKINS
New York Medical College

and

MELVIN R. LANSKY
University of California, Los Angeles

Family therapists have long debated the advantages, the problems, and the pitfalls of involving fathers in treatment. There seems to be a clinical rule of thumb, supported by some research literature, that family treatment is more likely to be successful when the father is an active participant. Our clinical experience suggests that not only father unavailability but also varieties of pernicious father "involvement" in the family and in the therapy need to be understood and worked through. This chapter discusses ways to understand the father's participation or lack thereof in the assessment of dysfunctional families, in family-based treatments, and in everyday life. In particular, it concentrates on the psychoanalytic concepts of transference, resistance, countertransference, and counterresistance to explain dynamically some of the personality issues (in individual family members and in the therapist) and systems issues (in the family as a whole and in the therapeutic community) that arise.

CLINICAL PERSPECTIVE

Less than a generation ago many psychoanalytically oriented developmentalists began systematic studies to review the role of fathers in the life cycle (Abelin, 1971, 1975; Atkins, 1981, 1982, 1984; Cath, Gurwitt, & Ross, 1982; Ross, 1975, 1977, 1979). These investigations shifted the focus from a singular concern with the mother as the mediator of a child's early psychological experience to a more naturalistic interest in the family as a whole. Building on that burgeoning body of knowledge, some of us are now turning our attention to the clinical implications that derive from inquiries into the role of the father (Lansky, 1984) in child development.

This chapter explores the father's role in family therapies where his child is the identified patient. In the few investigations in the clinical literature that look at the father's role in such family treatments, researchers have often correlated poor clinical outcome with the lack of father involvement in the therapeutic process. We believe, however, that it is not the simple presence or absence of the father that predicts treatment outcome. Rather we think that unsuccessful treatment often results from the therapist's failure to make use of any difficulties surrounding the father's involvement in family therapy in a clinically meaningful way. Those difficulties can be appreciated (and minimized) only if the psychodynamic factors from which they arise are understood. Particularly important are two sets of clinical variables: the father's and other family members' reactions to the therapist and to the therapy (most of which include significant transferential components) and the therapist's and the therapeutic community's responses to family members and to the father. (Many of these, especially in failed cases, are tinged with countertransference.) We will demonstrate, in several clinical examples, that the therapist's capacity to identify, assimilate, and creatively and therapeutically utilize these dynamic variables can influence treatment successes and failures in the family therapy setting.

To amplify our clinical position, let us turn to a brief review of the literature. It largely supports the value of a father's involvement in family therapy. Repeatedly (Shapiro & Budman, 1973; Slipp, Ellis, & Kressel, 1974; Berg & Rosenblum, 1977), father appears to be a pivotal family figure, one who either terminates treatment (if it ends prematurely) or is responsible for the continuation of therapy. In Berg and Rosenblum's (1977) survey of 60 family therapists, father was judged to be the family member most resistant to the treatment process (e.g., in no-show rate and in the termination of treatment). While these authors identified some therapist behaviors that contributed to their label of paternal "resistance," we understand their "resistance" to be the opposite of "compliance." Hence, as these authors used the word it is devoid of rich psychoanalytic meaning, that is, illuminating the self-sabotaging forces generating such behaviors in ways that allow resistance to be increasingly clarified and possibly overcome. Moreover, it is unclear whether "resistance" resulted from what we would identify as countertransference difficulties imposed by the therapist. Such countertransferences may have left these fathers feeling misunderstood or rejected. Furthermore, little attention was paid to the understanding of paternal resistance as a manifestation of paternal transference in the dysfunctional treatments. It might have been, for example, that in those families that remained in treatment, the therapist was better able to utilize aspects of the father's transference that favored therapeutic alliance and to calm those anxieties that might otherwise have resulted in manifest refusal to continue with treatment.

Blotcky, Titler, Friedman, and DeCarlo (1980) suggested, in a study of 16 families each with a child as the identified patient, that the relationship most likely to "change" in the therapeutic process is that between child and father. The measured changes were limited in their dimension, as the investigators looked only at a particular dysfunctional communication (the so-called "double binding" process) and at a global rating of interpersonal distance. The processes effecting the changes in behavior and attitude were not outlined. Shifts in father-child and child-father (and other intrafamilial) distortions, based on transferences, that were likely to herald improved relatedness when they were removed were also not examined.

While Blotcky and coworkers looked only at intact families, Wylder (1982) has made a similar claim for the families of divorced coparents.

Not every investigator, however, believes that the father's role is pivotally associated with therapeutic outcome. Martin (1977), for example, randomly assigned 43 families, each with a child as the identified patient, to a father-included treatment group, a father-not-included treatment group, or a wait control group. Treatment groups had more favorable outcomes than did the control group. But Martin noted no statistical differences in outcomes between the two treatment groups.

Clinically we agree that it is important to include father in family-based treatments whenever feasible. Furthermore, it is important to consider father's absence from treatment or his treatment avoidance as an ongoing feature in a therapy that may otherwise appear to be going well. Even so, it is too simple to conclude that father's presence is a sine qua non for successful treatment or that his absence forbodes disaster. In the absence of an understanding of both individual and family dynamics, such a rule is not reliable. In fact, father's presence in the therapy can cause major difficulties, as the following example illustrates:

EXAMPLE 1:

A family of five, with parents in their late 40s and children ranging in age from 16 to 5, were referred for a family evaluation. Raul, the second child, was the identified patient. An anxious, giggly, and apparently immature young man, he was not achieving in school at his expected academic level. He was seen initially with his father, Ramon, a successful real estate developer.

One year previously, Anna, the mother, had experienced a brief, tumultuous, psychoticlike reaction to the death of her father. She had now taken a lover.

In subsequent sessions, the children seen together were bratty, unruly, and challenging. They jumped on the furniture. They were rude to the therapist. They teased the therapist: "I'm not crazy. I can do anything at the crazy doctor's." The therapist consistently interpreted the anxiety behind these provocations. But interpretation rarely assuaged the children's anxieties or eliminated the aggressive acts.

Anna was also teased, disobeyed, taunted, and debunked in the family sessions. There was openly hostile talk of her boyfriend. The therapist noted that the boyfriend was the easiest to hate and to blame for the family breaking up. The children agreed, but the anxiety and the attacks on the mother did not subside.

Ramon appeared to exercise a linchpinlike control over the children's misbehavior. As the children provoked and disorganized Anna, he maintained silent composure, as if to encourage their nastiness toward mother and her allies. Anna flew into rages, yelling at Ramon for help in stabilizing the unruly mob. While Ramon would begrudgingly comply, the help that he offered was seasoned with wounding insinuations and humiliations. Ramon talked to Anna in the same way that an auditor might accost an employee over accounting errors—frozen and meticulous.

Ramon said that he wanted Anna to move out of the house and to leave all of the children with him. She wanted a divorce and joint child custody, emphasizing her wish for cooperative work. Ramon said that he would never babysit while she went out with her lover. After several sessions during which he remained intransigent, Anna moved out of the house with the youngest child and refused, despite the therapist's support of her position, to appear for subsequent sessions.

In the family meetings that followed, Ramon came alone with the children. The therapist noted both Anna's absence and her ongoing discomfort. The older children and Ramon seemed to be relatively oblivious of mother's disappearance. During the sessions, Ramon's overindulgence of the children was noted; he provided them with an abundance of material possessions and he refused to punish them. Ramon's singular preoccupations were his business and his children. He maintained a cohesiveness between himself and the children by fostering an embedded self-serving loyalty.

At one session the youngest child, Sarah, called the boyfriend a "horrid man," and she explained to father that she refused to kiss the man. Everybody laughed, and all gave further testimony to his allegedly dreadful qualities. The therapist pointed out how these comments located the blame for the impending divorce on the boyfriend and indicated that Sarah might be palliating and appeasing father rather than articulating her true feelings, either about Anna or her lover. Sarah said she felt that it was expected that she would talk against the boyfriend.

In the next session, Ramon had become very troubled by Sarah's revelation. He wondered if his child had become a "prisoner of war." At that point the eldest daughter requested individual sessions. She said that she wanted her mother, and couldn't fight against her any more. Raul, the identified patient, had consistently cut short his visits to mother by deliberate provocations and fights. With the provocative participation of all the children, the structure of equitable visitation began to collapse under the weight of the loyalty conflict. As the anxiety in the eldest child became more evident, Ramon became disturbed. He canceled a session on short notice, saying that he wanted individual therapy for each of the children because their problems were not improving.

Ramon's brittle self-esteem maintained its cohesion only through the children's loyalty. They protected him from the anxiety that might have overwhelmed him after his wife left. As the loyalty issues became more apparent in the treatment process, Ramon could not continue participating. He sacrificed the therapy—much as he had sacrificed the marriage— so that he could maintain a view of himself as competent, powerful, and good.

Loyalty issues may also undermine therapy in cases where the father makes every attempt to be cooperative. In the following illustration, the father was a willing and accommodating participant in family therapy, until the situation became untenable:

EXAMPLE 2:

The therapist was contacted by the internist of a psychosomatically ill mother in her 40s. Carrie said that she wanted Stephen, the exhusband whom she had divorced several years previously, to become involved with their two sons, ages 12 and 15. She appeared alone at the first visit, spoke angrily of Stephen, and was vehement that she was not going to be in therapy on her own account. She only wanted this "irresponsible man to become involved with his children!" She became enraged at any suggestion, however tentatively voiced, that she might have difficulties of her own.

Stephen voiced no opposition to his participation, but before the first family session could take place, Carrie was hospitalized with a serious gastrointestinal complaint, probably emotionally triggered. Stephen agreed to remain available to the therapy whenever Carrie's health improved. Several weeks later, when Carrie had recuperated, they had a conjoint session and agreed to focus the family work on his relationship with the children.

Stephen said that Carrie constantly criticized him: his attributes, particularly his honesty; and his possessions, his car, and the new woman in his life. He claimed that the boys sided with Carrie; they sniped at him constantly during every visitation. In general, the children created such an unpleasant atmosphere for him that he often opted to stay away. Carrie berated him for his irresponsible avoidance of his sons, for his incessant tardiness in picking the children up, for the lack of safety features in his car, for alleged financial mismanagement, and for carrying on with a hussy. These unpleasant allegations were interrupted by the therapist who asked Carrie about her expectations of her exhusband. Did she want to deal with past injustices in the marriage and put them to rest? She vehemently insisted that she did not. She wanted to "correct his relationship with the children." The therapist asked her to be specific regarding expectations: What were Stephen's responsibilities regarding visitations and the children's safety and as a corollary, what were the children's responsibilities regarding their father? Carrie claimed that this approach was superficial, and she resumed her criticism. Ultimately, however, it was agreed that the treatment would continue only if a focus were kept on such very specific expectations. Within several sessions, it became clear that Stephen had lived up to all of the identified obligations.

The boys' florid disrespect of their father then became a core part of the treatment. Both parents agreed that such effrontery could not continue. Through the manifest agreement of both parents, the boys were facilitated into more than a modicum of civilized comportment. In the ensuing several months, Stephen's participation with the children expanded to include additional evenings and weekends. As the boys became more involved with their father, Carrier's unhappiness was exacerbated. She said that there were issues of dishonesty that were not being addressed and that the therapist was being duped into not seeing how dishonest Stephen had always been. The therapist countered by saying that it was entirely legitimate to open up unresolved issues in the marriage, if that is what Carrie wanted to do. Carrie said that she did not, but she continued to insist that the therapist was being duped, never addressing or, perhaps, recognizing Stephen's fundamental dishonesty. Despite the protest, Stephen continued to see the children for increasing amounts of time, and, by everyone's admission, including Carrie's, was fulfilling every obligation that he had made.

As the months progressed, Carrie became more and more angry. On one occasion, she was ill and forced to stay at home during a Little League baseball game that Stephen was able to attend with the boys. She became furious that Stephen did not phone. Asked what she meant, Carrie admitted that her anger was directed more toward the boys on account of what sounded like their newly found loyalty to their father. Stephen, according to Carrie, should also have fostered the boys' interest in her and not "leave me at home to die there, sick."

Several weeks later, father announced that he was going to marry the woman who had now been in his life for several years. Soon after he did so. At that time, Carrie had another serious gastrointestinal malady, and she was hospitalized. She called the therapist, hurling her fury at him for the inadequately managed treatment, now well over a year in its duration. Carrie refused to attend further sessions. In the face of mother's illness, the boys guiltily returned to her side. Accused by Carrie of making her sick, the boys viciously renewed their epithets at their father. Stephen returned for one additional session, again despairing that he could not remain in the picture with his children in the face of the aspersions that the boys, in agreement with their mother, persisted in casting at him.

These examples make it clear that a successful outcome in family therapy is contingent on many factors emanating from both individual and family dynamics. Such dynamics encompass considerably more than an axiom stipulating that fathers should be involved in any treatment. Moreover, the complexities in most treatment situations demand a comprehensive, fluid, and dynamic theoretical perspective. Such a comprehensive view is often missing in clinical formulations in the family therapy literature. When a clinical family theory that is primarily descriptive and operational holds sway, therapists may see a father's dysfunction in the family system too simplistically—as reflective of either *enmeshment* or *disengagement* (Minuchin, 1974). Fathers in enmeshed family systems are said to be in need of "strengthening their paternal authority." Fathers in disengaged family systems are said to be in need of relaxing their (authoritarian, work-oriented, obsessional, etc.) role rigidity. But a clinical theory that confines itself exclusively to the family system ignores the personalities of its component members. Such a theory tacitly assumes that the individuals comprising the system are interchangeable with other individuals in similar circumstances. This kind of theory, by ignoring the unique contributions of the personalities that make up the family system, flies in the face of all that we know about individual character and experience.

A psychoanalytic perspective that ignores the transpersonal, or familial, aspects of conflict and defense—and of transference and resistance—is equally inadequate. The intrafamilial and intergenerational contexts must be seen as impacting strongly on the identified patient, and these contexts must be understood as greater than the sum of their component dyadic relationships. An exclusive focus on the individual or on the dyad has been an acute limitation of contemporary psychoanalytic thinking.

Because the concepts of transference (and countertransference) and resistance (and counterresistance) are central to our clinical approach, we should clarify their use in an arena outside that of individual psychoanalytic treatment. We understand that *transference* is the replay of archaic conflicts in the present with persons that are in some way representative of important individuals in the patient's past. We differentiate between transference, which is a ubiquitous phenomenon and a useful concept in all types of treatment, and the transference neurosis, which is more strictly confined to psychoanalysis. Thus in family treatments, the vehicle of the therapy is *not* the elaboration and working through of a transference neurosis that the family makes to the therapist. Rather most of the relevant transferences are those individual family members make to each other. These transferences are always to be found in the marital dyad. When that unit seems to be taking a malignant course in relation to what is required by the therapy, it is usually important to understand the transferences that the spouses or exspouses have to each other. Inevitably, the replay of archaic conflicts becomes an agenda for any marriage, or for its dissolution. These ancient issues especially affect any child's emotional well-being. The therapist as well will experience inevitable transferences, which should be worked with as they post obstacles to the treatment process.

Another term that can be expanded from its restricted psychoanalytic sense is *resistance:* an unconscious opposition to the awareness of unconscious conflict. The term can be transplanted to the family therapy modality if one understands it to mean an unexplained sabotage of the treatment effort, or a self-sabotage, the deeper roots of which are unknown to the patient. We see resistance as a dynamic force (or forces) which opposes the stated aim of treatment: cooperation and collaboration in the understanding of and minimizing of conflicts in the family system.

Transferences (as defined here) are also important in the family therapy setting because they affect collaboration with the treatment. As such, transferences can constitute a form of resistance. That is, a replay of any of the family member's archaic conflicts is critical because it serves as an obstruction to a therapy aimed at the amelioration of the patient's dysfunctional situated in the here and now.

Countertransference and counterresistance refer to those corollary dynamic forces emanating from the therapist or from the mental health profession which impede the desired course of treatment.

SPHERES OF FATHER INVOLVEMENT

The therapist must be aware that three spheres of father involvement will impact on the course of work with families. First, fathers may be involved in the initial assessment of a child's (or family's) dysfunction. During this assessment the therapist may see the whole family or its individual members, in order to arrive at a comprehensive understanding of the patient's difficulties. Second, the father will be involved in treatment, as the modality is decided on and implemented. Finally, the father will be involved in his child's life, apart from the assessment process or the therapeutic context. We cannot emphasize too strongly that father may be involved in any combination of these three spheres and not necessarily in all of them. The clinician's failure to distinguish among these three spheres can be a source of confusion in conceptualizing the clinical material.

The Assessment Sphere

Cohen (1979), as a spokesperson for modern American child psychiatry, has recommended that all initial assessments of children take place with only one parent, preferably the mother, providing developmental and historical information. A sole informant, Cohen argues, mitigates against the inevitable parental acrimony which would cloud, in his opinion, the picture of a child's emotional health. Such a parochial position has sparked a lively debate between Cohen on the one hand and Gurwitt and Ferholt (1984), as national spokespeople for the father, on the other. This debate may seem on the surface to lack any substantive value to those like ourselves who have studied the role of the father in child development. But points of view such as Cohen's are nonetheless part of the mainstream of child mental health and are derivative of an institutional historical bias that has mitigated against the inclusion of the father in the critical pretreatment process.

We recommend that the assessment be formulated in terms that are mindful of the entire family system, no matter which of its members are actually in attendance. Father involvement is almost always an asset in the evaluation process. Essential input can also be derived from the circumstance in which the father refuses to come for the evaluation or the mother refuses to have him present. If father does not attend treatment assessment and planning meetings, it is wise for the therapist to explicitly comment on the father's lack of participation, that is to say, the resistance on the part of the father, on the part of the family, on the part of the therapist, or on the part of the institution.

Excluding the father from a diagnostic evaluation on a seemingly reasonable basis could, in fact, turn out to be disastrous, as this next example points out.

EXAMPLE 3:

A second-year resident in child psychiatry was assigned an 11-year-old sixth grade boy and his family for potential psychotherapy. Despite the resident's request that both mother and father appear for the initial evaluation, only mother and child came to the clinic. Mother explained that father's work schedule prevented his accompanying them to a 3:00 P.M. appointment.

Tommy, the identified patient, was a management problem at school. His teacher had noted the youngster's impulsive tendency to talk out in class. Tommy's verbal blurtings and fidgety tendencies made his class and teacher antsy, thoroughly impeding the class's group learning. Mother said that the problem had existed for several years, but the school had recently "run out of patience with the behavior." Tommy's problems extended into the home, although not as seriously. Although, according to his mother, Tommy's problem had been going on "for years," it had become worse in the last three months since father's mother had died. Tommy's alleged close relationship with his father had become significantly disrupted by the father's grief and ongoing depression. Moreover, Tommy's mother had begun to lose patience with her son during the same time frame, resulting in many fights between the two of them. The mother denied any significant medical or family history.

Physical and mental status examination confirmed the behavioral overactivity, poor attention span, distractability, and impulsivity. In addition, however, Tommy spoke about his problems with his father reluctantly, preferring to be angry with his mother over her berating of him. Once, with significant emotional lability, he began to cry about his father's "disappearance" into sadness. It was only a brief cry; when it occurred, the child's motor irritability calmed but did not abate.

The resident was confused about the relative impact of what appeared to be attention deficit problems and neurotic conflict on the child's behavior. But he felt that the differential diagnosis was clear, and he intended to begin treating this youngster with psychostimulant medication. He deferred the initiation of drug treatment only because it was his supervisor's policy that both parents be seen, whenever possible, in the clinic intake procedure. Besides, the supervisor also thought that family therapy might be a useful treatment modality.

The resident had more or less planned his subsequent inquiry, but when the father walked into the clinic office, this trainee became genuinely, and correctly, preoccupied with the man's appearance. The father, a 27-year-old plumber, periodically lifted his left eyebrow, occasionally with significant force and frequency. When this eyebrow lift was most apparent, the father would faintly grunt and then rapidly clear his throat, as if trying to conceal the minor vocalization. The resident's questioning yielded a compelling history. At age 14 the father developed a habit spasm with his left eyebrow, after watching a "Popeye" cartoon that showed that children's hero making the same facial gesture. The father, finding the cartoon character's expression "funny," began to imitate it. Soon the imitation ran out of control. The father would feel compelled to lift his eyebrow; when he tried to inhibit the movement he would feel an intense mental "pressure" that would not relent until the gesture took place, then in an explosive way. The father finally gave in to this pseudocompulsion. Three years later he began to grunt when the eyebrow "pressure" was most severe, becoming able, as the resident suspected, to cover that symptom with throat clearing. No one in the family, including the father, paid any overt attention to this peculiarity, hence its denial by mother in her recounting of the family history.

The resident made the provisional diagnosis of Gilles de la Tourette's syndrome in the father, subsequently confirmed by a consulting neurologist. Having seen the father, the resident then scrutinized the youngster in a careful physical examination. In all of the youngster's periodic fidgiting, the resident noted Tommy's consistent rubbing of his thumb against his middle finger on one hand. Noting a tic in the boy as well, the resident sent Tommy to a specialty clinic in a nearby city for a more exhaustive evaluation of possible Gilles de la Tourette's syndrome.

In this situation, the resident and supervisor both agreed that, had it not been for the father's participation in the evaluation, the diagnosis of Gilles de la Tourette's syndrome would not have been considered at all. In addition, the child would likely have had psychostimulant medication prescribed as an adjunct to family therapy, to ease what would have been labeled attention deficit disorder with hyperactivity. Such medication could have exacted miserable effects on a youngster with tics and with a first-degree relative with Gilles de la Tourette's syndrome. In similar circumstances, Youngerman and Canino (1983) have pointed out how diagnostic inclusion of the sometimes absent father of "violent" or overly aggressive children can turn up a paternal history of bipolar affective disorder. The children may then have a salutary response to lithium treatment, when the symptoms have proven refractory to other therapies.

The Treatment Sphere

The father's involvement in family therapy is generally indicated and desirable. But this is not an inevitable phenomenon, because father involvement cannot be forced, as the next example illustrates.

EXAMPLE 4:

The therapist was contacted by Ruth, a woman in her 40s, divorced several years from Dick. Despite the long period of divorce, she insisted that she wanted to bind a hurt relationship between Dick and the youngest of their three children. The therapist wanted to know which of the family members would participate in the treatment. Ruth indicated that she, Dick, and the two younger children could commit to the process. The eldest daughter would not attend, since she was currently hospitalized on a local psychiatric service and could not tolerate additional family stress.

In the first session Dick, in his late 40s and an insurance claims investigator, appeared quite paranoid but did not fully decompensate. All of the family members present agreed that there was constant chaos within the family. The youngest child, Mary, said that she couldn't get along with her father. Dick said that he felt "no respect" coming from Mary. "I'm simply hit up for support." Invectives were then hurled between daughter and father. Mary broke into tears, at which point Dick turned to Ruth and began an irrational fulminating at her lawyer for a history of unreasonable financial demands. Tom, the only son, came to the session late. He added that he had extraordinary difficulties in the family as well. He claimed that he was at the mercy of his mother's fragile self-esteem and very labile moods. Mother, experiencing one or another pressure (and not always generated by Dick), would usually ask Tom to rectify the problem. As Tom was describing his position in the middle of the family's dysfunction, Dick renewed his need for respect from his younger daughter and financial justice from his exwife. Bitterly he accused Mary of visiting him only with resentment. She agreed. Mother saw this as the family's main problem. Tom, who did not want to get involved, suggested that his mother, with her lability, was as much a disruptive force in the family's misery as was his father.

At the second appointment, a few weeks later, Dick continued his pained sputtering at Ruth and her lawyer, resentful of the legal agreement concerning financial support. Despite Dick's near decompensation, Ruth remained quietly firm: "I'm out of this," she claimed. "I just want to make it better between you and Mary. I lead my own life, and I want the two of you to get along." The therapist tried to focus the family on the different ways that members viewed the family's problems. Dick responded by continuing to yell about the lawyer. The therapist interrupted, noting that the support payment was not an issue that could be resolved in a treatment with the children present. Ruth reported that she had no wish to change things and that the financial settlement was already legally determined. The therapist ventured that it might make more sense for the two children to come to treatment in order for him to gain some understanding of their family, since neither parent was interested in moving from the current tactical position.

Ruth phoned the next week and asked if the therapist would see the father individually to help resolve Dick's obvious difficulties. The therapist refused, saying that he could remain available to the family, and especially to any part of the family that wanted to focus on problems. He would, if Dick phoned, refer him to another therapist. Ruth sounded pained and asked why the therapist had taken this determined stand. The therapist explained that he could be most helpful, under the circumstances, by working with the children alone and not by siding with one parent against the other. Ruth pleaded that the therapist reconsider. The therapist replied that he could not collaborate with her in her wish to see the family's difficulties as generated solely by Dick. The therapist repeated the offer to see the children alone, until such time as the parents were willing to do more than blame each other for the family's difficulties.

In this situation, both of the ex-spouses experienced severe and disorganizing psychopathology. While the request for help sounded reasonable on the surface, neither parent could accept introspection as a part of the therapeutic process. The request for therapy quickly unfolded as a veiled attempt to deny the reality of circumstances that disappointed each of the ex-spouses. Treatment was seasoned by an intermittent demand for justice by each of the parents. Spousal reactivity abounded despite the children's needs. The therapist refused to collude with either parent's fantasies, but rather explained the attempts at self-exculpation as projection of the problem onto the the ex-spouse. The offer to see the children alone was made to enable the younger generation, hungering for an explanation, to gain some objectivity about the continuing interparental bickering.

We believe father should not be arbitrarily excluded from family therapy as a matter of convenience. Frequently, the father's absence or avoidance is not discussed in the treatment because of a pervasive but unspoken fear or hostility. For example, the father may intimidate the other family members, and occasionally, the therapist, into believing that his presence will sacrifice the well-being of the treatment situation.

EXAMPLE 5:

> Stuart, the middle of three college-age brothers, was seen initially while hospitalized. He had repeatedly stolen money from his family to support a rapidly expanding cocaine habit, and he had entered the hospital on account of his addiction. His father, an Ivy League law school graduate, was an attorney active in charitable community service. Two brothers, older and younger, were attending the father's alma mater. Mother worked as a receptionist in the father's office.

> Stuart was a vexation and disappointment to each of these achievement-oriented family members. He stole. He was kicked out of school. He failed at jobs. The other men in the family were all academic stars. The men were hard working, selfless, and indefatigable, and mother initially presented herself as dedicated to all of them. But as the therapy unfolded, she emerged as depressed and brittle, a "no-self" who smothered Stuart, putting everyone else's needs ahead of her own. Stuart was the identified scapegoat for the family's more pervasive difficulties.

> During the ensuing months, the same therapist saw Stuart individually and the family conjointly. The three successful men remained manifestly oblivious to mother's needs. As she began to express her feelings of emptiness, it became clear that Stuart's dysfunctional behavior was directly related to mother's neediness. He would act irresponsibly and then get caught. He served as a carrier for the "bad parts" of mother that were not allowed to breathe in an achievement-oriented atmosphere.

Mother could not easily acknowledge her neediness and her frustrated spiteful and hostile fantasies. She buried these under the facade of diligent receptionist, devoted wife, and caring mother.

As mother's sensitivities were progressively verbalized, father's work demands increased. He excused himself from the therapy sessions to meet professional demands that could not be scheduled at any other time. The therapist stressed the importance of father's attendance. While father agreed to make therapy his first priority, he usually managed to find professionally sanctioned reasons for his irregular attendance. The therapist, not fully understanding the father's resistance, did not investigate the behavior further.

Instead, the treatment was continued without the father's regular participation. Two trends began to emerge. Mother became more comfortable talking about her upset and despair. As she did so, Stuart stayed out of trouble. He became more conscious of the requirement that he act dysfunctionally in order to take the pressure off his mother. As Stuart and mother became more convinced of the value of the family work, the other two boys and father began to take a more rigidly critical stance toward Stuart to protect themselves from the family's impending reequilibration. The two boys joined their father in the pressures of outside involvements, canceling attendance and requesting unusual appointment times. Father and sons decided that therapy should be terminated because Stuart's behavior was allegedly impossible (when in fact he was drug free, in school, and working hard). In the face of the loss of his treatment, Stuart stole money, bought drugs, and got caught. The family system returned to its original dysfunctional pattern.

Involvement with Children

The father's involvement with his children in everyday life must be distinguished from the father's participation in the assessment process or in the therapy. It is to be expected that the father's participation in treatment will, in some fashion, mirror his activity as parent and spouse. This assumption is, in fact, the basis for the heavy emphasis on transference and resistance in psychoanalytically oriented treatment of any kind. A steady state exists in the emotional climate between relationships in treatment and those outside of treatment. Resolution of difficulties in the treatment situation—especially difficulties based on unacknowledged conflicts or unrecognized anxieties—is regularly seen to affect relationships outside the treatment. The emotional climate in the family in therapy asserts itself predictably enough in the treatment setting to assert that, when difficulties have been identified—and especially if the transferential components of these difficulties are worked through in treatment—there is marked improvement in the quality of a father's involvement in his children's lives. Conversely, treatment failure, when it is reflected on and understood, often occurs because of the same familial difficulties that impede the father's harmonious involvement with his children in everyday life, for example, loyalty conflicts (Examples 1 and 2), ongoing parental battles (Example 4), or chronic paternal preoccupation as a defense (Example 5).

PROBLEMS WITH FATHER INVOLVEMENT

As we have discussed, father involvement is effected in three discrete spheres: in the assessment of the child or family's dysfunction, in the treatment, and in everyday life. Obstacles to the father's participation in any or all of these areas can be scrutinized from the perspectives of transference and resistance. We will consider such obstacles as they are generated by the father and family members, and we will identify their corollary counterforces, countertransference and counterresistance, as they exist in the therapist and in the mental health profession as an institution.

The reactions of the mental health profession, often based on *institutional and individual countertransference,* frequently limit the father's participation in assessment and treatment. Historically, the profession has tended to conceptualize a child's psychological birth as either the product of a maturational unfolding of biogenetic competencies or as a developmental phenomenon emanating from mother-child interactions. Until recently, developmental psychologists saw mothers as the exclusive source of most of their young children's meaningful psychological experiences. Fathers were relegated to an occasional pivotal role (Freud, 1921) or to the periphery of experience entirely (Pine, 1982). The father's function as protector and supporter of the mother-child unit (Gurwitt & Ferholt, 1982) did not automatically include him in the mainstream of early childhood experience. In the last decade, however, we have seen emerging scientific interest in the father's capacity to be nurturing and generative with his young children (Lamb, 1976, 1981; Cath, Gurwitt, & Ross, 1982), a capacity that retrospective common sense tells us has existed all along, but which we, as a profession, have only recently rediscovered.

The derivatives of this institutional reaction can be seen in a variety of ways: in the fact that few clinical services that direct themselves to the mental health of children offer evening appointments to accommodate working fathers (or mothers); in the fact that fewer men (than women) are employed to deliver such services; in the fact that few clinics supply reading material in their waiting rooms that are appropriate to a male clientele; and in the fact that most intake procedures, forms, and rating scales are directed more toward the mother than the father of child patients (Ferholt & Gurwitt, 1982). The institutional forces at work in the debate between Cohen (1979) and Gurwitt and Ferholt (1984, personal communication) noted previously, are a further example, in our opinion, of such countertransferential influences.

Fathers as a group must also deal with shared stereotypes, often based on socially mediated transferences. These collectively sanctioned transferences tend to keep fathers away from the psychotherapeutic situation. As an early way station on the road to paternal identity (Ross 1975), little boys identify with their mother's nurturance and generativity. Such capacities become, epigenetically, part and parcel of good fathering, although they may remain relatively repressed. Shared social values surrounding masculinity can generate conflicts around a man's more "feminized" past, rendering a father anxious and/or hostile toward a treatment situation that he sees as passive, or as inflicting passivity or powerlessness, or as dominated by women or by "affected, pantywaisted men." The mental health system then becomes the inheritor, through projection, of shared inner conflicts surrounding masculinity and femininity, activity and passivity, and power and weakness. It is around these issues that, because we are all human, the institutional countertransference of the profession, the unique countertransference of individual mental health professionals, and the socially mediated transferences begin to mesh. This is illustrated in the following example.

EXAMPLE 6:

A children's mental health clinic in a large metropolitan area was run by a female psychiatrist in her mid-70s. This physician was a much sought-after teacher, as her infectious intelligence and wit were amplified by years of experience with hundreds of children in emotional distress. She had attended medical school at a time when few women did, and the institutional gossip mills suggested that she had come to psychiatry through pediatrics, after she had been actively discouraged from a career in surgery.

This therapist was conducting a demonstration interview through a one-way screen. A 7-year-old markedly depressed boy had been brought to the clinic. His mother, a beautiful woman, had made it clear how she at one and the same time cherished her husband's success in business but resented the overwhelming amount of time that he devoted to it. The father was a pleasant man and a natty dresser, infatuated with the strength of his success. At the midpoint in the midday interview, the father began to look at his watch repeatedly. Each time he did so, the youngster would look longingly at his father, as if to wish that the man would give him more than the time of day.

Toward the end of the interview, the senior psychiatrist asked the family to return the following week at 11:00 A.M. The father, rather decisively, said that he could not interrupt his business in the middle of the day. The therapist, having already correctly assessed that this self-employed man was highly manipulative, countered sternly but with kindness: "You'll have to make a decision between your business and your family." When he left the interview room, the father was overheard muttering to his wife: "What a controlling bitch I can't stand being in the same room with her! I'm going to stay away from her!"

A seasoned psychotherapist, not under the sway of countertransference reactivity, might already predict that the roots of the father's problem, his narcissistic vulnerability, were evident in his parting shot. While that may be true, and while the interview had in fact been conducted with dignity and extraordinary finesse, the transference and countertransference issues that we have thus far outlined lurked not too far in the background.

Obstacles generated by fathers themselves extend, of course, beyond these socially, culturally, or institutionally mediated phenomena. One obstacle to his participation surrounds his reaction to ongoing familial warfare and loyalty conflicts, as illustrated in Example 2. Fathers who appear emotionally intact may exhibit narcissistic defenses, such as pathologic preoccupation (Lansky, 1985) and find themselves unable to become involved with assessment, treatment, or the child's life. Internal anxieties, including those surrounding fear, shame, and guilt, may keep fathers from participation. Such avoidance should be seen as protection from the threatened uncovering of deeper conflictual issues. The next example illustrates an interesting manifestation of a father's transference to his son which, if unrecognized, would have prematurely terminated a treatment and compromised the child's well-being.

EXAMPLE 7:

The Goldbergs sought treatment for themselves and their 10-year-old son Adam. Adam had had periosteal sarcoma the year before and had lost his left leg below the knee. At the time the Goldbergs came for consultation, Adam had begun to master the use of a new prosthesis.

Mr. Goldberg explained that he had initiated the consultation because Adam's mother was "overprotecting him" since the discovery of the illness. Mr. Goldberg had asked his son to go camping with him, and when father made the offer at the dinner table, mother gasped, cried, and begged Adam not to go "lest he get hurt." Adam, confused, refused his father's offer. Father, furious, called him a "sissy" and chided his wife for her "smothering." He screamed at his wife that she and he had not spent a night away together since Adam's illness. The following day, father, exceedingly guilty about his "wild" outburst, made arrangements for family therapy.

The therapist contracted with the family for six sessions, with the manifest focus on Mrs. Goldberg's difficulties "letting go" of her son and "realigning" with her husband. Toward the end of the second session, the therapist thought that he noted an increased agitation in this otherwise overcontrolled father. Mrs. Goldberg had just claimed that she, in fact, begged her husband to spend time with Adam since the illness, but that he had refused. Father, controlled and calm, countered: "How can I spend time? You're always in the middle of things!" At that Mrs. Goldberg shrugged and cried. Then father began to fidgit. The therapist asked the father about it, but drew no response. The therapist couldn't immediately fathom the father's reaction, as the treatment was proceeding in fine form. The next morning the father, his composure perfect, telephoned to thank the therapist for the two treatment sessions, but indicated that the family would not return. When questioned, the father indicated that the family had agreed that it had gotten what it had come for and that there was no need to continue. The therapist reminded the father of his agitation the prior evening and asked if there was anything bothering the man. Father replied: "No, I guess so . . . I mean no . . . not." Sensitive to the slip, the therapist invited the father to return that afternoon for an individual session. The father hesitatingly agreed.

After several minutes apologizing for having "bothered" the therapist, the father began slowly to unravel his story. It seems that the camping invitation to Adam had been "staged" by the father. His wife, the night before, had begged him to spend more time with their ill child. Mrs. Goldberg feared that the child would die without a good memory of his father in the last part of his life. Father, certain that mother would, in her overprotective way, balk at a manifestly appropriate but latently agitating suggestion that the father and son go camping, had bet on a process that would guarantee his distance from his son but make mother look like the perpetrator.

At that point, father looked at the therapist, guiltily tearful. He explained his difficulty with Adam's illness. Their only child, their only son, Adam was the father's wonderful prize, his firstborn, his heir. Father was miserable at the thought that he would outlive his son. He had such hopes, wishes, aspirations for the child, and he was in the financial position to offer him "the world." But he couldn't promise the child his life. Father confronted a powerlessness, a threat to masculinity, that he feared in an uncanny way. The man, a partner in a famous law firm, had scrambled his way up the ladder of success to mitigate his fear of his own father's business failures. His guilt about his own successes, it seemed, visited themselves on the back, or more correctly, the leg of his prized boy.

Following several assessment sessions, the father agreed to continue in individual treatment.

Easily analyzable manifestations of transference can often be extremely valuable therapeutically. The following example highlights Freud's (1924) observation that, early in its appearance, transference and resistance are inseparable. It illustrates the therapeutic traction that evolves from a simple clarification.

EXAMPLE 8:

The Westins—Joe, a 30-year-old account executive, Marge, 29 years old and at home with Little Joe, 18 months old—had come for a family evaluation because the marriage had "gone on the rocks" shortly after the child was born. Sex had virtually ended between the couple, although Marge made advances and Joe continually rebuffed her. After an initial evaluation, in which the therapist found Joe somewhat depressed but Marge and the baby without apparent psychiatric dysfunction, the family agreed to return the following week.

In the interim, Marge called to cancel the next appointment. She explained that the therapist had made Joe "real nervous." She couldn't elaborate further, claiming only that Joe asserted: "He (the therapist) didn't treat me well."

Reflecting on the allegation and coming up baffled, the therapist decided to call Joe at work. The man was initially quite combative on the telephone, loudly asserting that the therapist had been "partial" to Marge, maybe even "flirtatious" during the evaluation. When the therapist, still dumbfounded, asked Joe for examples, the man replied: "It's just a feeling I got." The therapist told Joe that he took the objections seriously, and if Joe would return to the office by himself, the therapist would try to make a good referral based on Joe's needs. He agreed.

In his individual session, Joe admitted that his feelings didn't seem terribly sensible but kept insisting that there was something about the therapist that was troubling. The therapist asked what thoughts came to mind, and Joe picked at a couple of straws before he hit paydirt: "A mannerism, a gesture?" He looked at the therapist: "No, the glasses." The therapist, a man in his late 30s, wore wirerimmed eyeglasses.

Then the story began to emerge. Joe was named for his mother's brother, an Army lieutenant who was killed in the last days of World War II. The loss, grievous in the family, was made worse because the mother treasured and admired this brother, while Joe's father was disparaged, one reason being the fact that he had been exempted from military service for medical reasons. The glasses were very evident in the soldier's picture that mother kept on the nightstand between her bed and Joe's father's.

When the transference implications were clarified at an elementary level, Joe could accept his nervousness as irrational. He and the therapist could also agree that an individual psychoanalysis seemed to be the treatment of choice in this particular situation.

In the analysis, mother's exclusion of the father became more and more apparent, with the dead brother and his namesake taking father's place as her incestuous partners in fantasy. Joe's guilt about his father was unremitting. At first, his abandonment of Marge appeared as his wish, in identifying with his father, to punish his mother for her betrayal. As time went on, however, it became clear that another manifestation of Joe's aggression was really at stake. He delighted in the historical gratification in his relationship with his mother. Anytime that his father, or his uncle in fantasy, would seem to take mother away from him, he would be furious. Fantasies of "getting rid" of father, of smashing the treasured picture, began to emerge. Sexually avoiding Marge allowed Joe to enact his guilt and his rage: When the baby was born, he guiltily abandoned his wife to a new Little Joe, to pay in kind for his previous incestuous sins. At the same time he, guiltily identifying with his own father, wanted to "do in" this valued baby and get "mother" back only for himself. In the analytic transference, it became obvious that the initial trepidation and fear of the therapist masked the wish to kill him—and that irrational, unconscious phenomenon made it difficult for Joe to return in the first days of treatment. Resolution of Joe's difficulties helped him greatly in the paternal role.

An interesting, and perhaps unique, perspective on transference is provided in the family therapy setting. Because all members of the family are present, the therapist can view not only the transferences to the analyst, but also transferences operating between individual family members. The professional can more easily appreciate transferential elements, in children especially, to persons outside the family. These intrafamilial transferences frequently operate in complementary and collusive, albeit very costly, ways. From the children's perspective, obstructions to father involvement may occur because of their participation in loyalty conflicts. They may feel that they have driven father away. Although such collusion is often conscious (Examples 1 and 2), the unconscious roots in protectiveness or fear must also be appreciated. The child may side with the parent who is perceived as either stronger (Example 1) or more vulnerable (Example 2), identifying with the point of view of this parent while extruding the other parent from the family. Such splitting (used here in its systems sense, but ultimately resulting in split attitudes toward each parent) often forces coalitions that are tantamount to oedipal conspiracies (Example 2), where mother is seen as both castrating to the father and seductive to the child. Father, in the same situation, may be seen as powerful, punishing, or vindictive—squashing mother and driving her crazy—or as annihilating or castrating to the child. Father can intimidate from a distance, either by escalating loyalty conflicts in the children or by creating the sense that the treatment or the family will be jeopardized if threatening issues surface in the therapy.

The therapist must, of course, consider his or her own contribution to the father's poor participation in assessment and treatment. Often obstacles that appear to belong to the psychic makeup of father are really the results of unrecognized and unacknowledged (countertransference) coalitions between the therapist and one parent. A male therapist may appear as the rescuer to mother and give the father the impression that a conspiracy is under way. A female therapist may be a competitive force with mother for the father's attention.

If we adhere to a fundamental sense of unique individuality in the human psyche, then the problems inherent to father involvement in assessment, treatment, and family life cannot be solved by simple rules of thumb. While we have outlined some of the frequently occurring obstacles to this sort of involvement, our work merely serves a heuristic purpose, as a prescription for further investigation and elaboration. Those of us who have studied father involvement in everyday living understand that even a relative absence of father is normative and expected (Atkins, 1981, 1982, 1984). As long as there is coparental accord on the role of the father in the child's life, and as long is there is a sense of justice, fair play, and collaboration among those who service the mental well-being of families, there is a wide range of father involvement that can be considered normal.

REFERENCES

Abelin, E. (1971). The role of the father in the separation-individuation process. In J. B. McDevitt & C. F. Settlage (Eds.), *Separation-individuation.* New York: International Universities Press.

Abelin, E. (1975). Some further observations and comments on the earliest role of the father. *International Journal of Psychoanalysis, 56,* 293–302.

Atkins, R. N. (1981), Finding one's father: The mother's contribution to early father representations. *Journal of the American Academy of Psychoanalysis, 9,* 539–559.

Atkins, R. N. (1982). Discovering daddy: The mother's role. In S. Cath, A. Gurwitt, & J. M. Ross (Eds.), *Father and child: Developmental and clinical perspectives.* Boston: Little Brown.

Atkins, R. N. (1984). Transitive vitalization and its impact on father-representation. *Contemporary Psychoanalysis, 20,* 663–676.

Berg, B., and Rosenblum, N. (1977). Fathers in family therapy: A survey of family therapists. *Journal of Marriage and Family Counseling, 3,* 85–91.

Blotcky, A. D., Tittler, B. I., Freidman, S., & DeCarlo, T. J. (1980). An exploration of change in parent-child relationships during the course of a family-oriented treatment program. *Family Therapy, 7,* 139–145.

Cath, S., Gurwitt, A., & Ross, J. M. (Eds.) (1982). *Father and child: Developmental and clinical perspectives.* Boston: Little Brown.

Cohen, R. (1979). The approach to assessment. In J. Noshpitz (Ed.), *Basic handbook of child psychiatry* (Vol. 1). New York: Basic.

Ferholt, J. B., & Gurwitt, A. R. (1982). Involving fathers in treatment. In S. Cath, A. Gurwitt, & J. M. Ross (Eds.), *Father and child: Developmental and clinical perspectives.* Boston: Little Brown.

Freud, S. (1921). *Group psychology and the analysis of the ego.* Vol. 18, Std. ed. London: Hogarth.

Freud, S. (1924). *Collected papers.* London: Hogarth.

Gurwitt, A. R., & Ferholt, J. M. (1984). Correspondence with R. Cohen.

Lamb, M. E. (Ed.) (1976). *The role of the father in child development.* New York: Wiley.

Lamb, M. E. (Ed.) (1981). *The role of the father in child development.* 2nd ed. New York: Wiley.

Lansky, M. R. (1984). The psychiatrically hospitalized father. *International Journal of Family Psychiatry, 5,* 135–152.

Lansky, M. R. (in press). Preoccupation as a mode of pathological distance regulation. *International Journal of Psychoanalytic Psychotherapy.*

Martin, B. (1977). Brief family intervention: Effectiveness and the importance of including the father. *Journal of Consulting and Clinical Psychology, 45,* 1002–1010.

Minuchin, S. (1974). *Families and family therapy.* Boston: Harvard University Press.

Pine, F. (1985). *Clinical Theory and Developmental Process.* New Haven: Yale.

Ross, J. M. (1975). The development of paternal identity: A critical review of the literature on nurturance and generativity in boys and men. *Journal of the American Psychoanalytic Association, 23,* 783–817.

Ross, J. M. (1977). The epigenesis of paternal identity during a boy's first decade, *International Review of Psychoanalysis, 4,* 327–348.

Ross, J. M. (1979). Fathering. *International Journal of Psychoanalysis, 60,* 317–327.

Shapiro, R. J., & Budman, S. H. (1973). Separation, termination, and continuation in family and individual therapy. *Family Process, 12,* 55–67.

Slipp, S., Ellis, S., & Kressel, K. (1974). Factors associated with engagement in family therapy. *Family Process, 13,* 413–427.

Wylder, J. (1982). Including the divorced father in family therapy. *Social Work, 37,* 479–482.

Youngerman, J. K., & Canino, I. A. (1983). Violent kids, violent parents: Family pharmacotherapy. *American Journal of Orthopsychiatry, 53,* 152–156.

CHAPTER 7

Father Involvement and Responsibility in Family Therapy

BERND HEUBECK, JOHANNA WATSON, AND GRAEME RUSSELL
Macquarie University

Researchers have increasingly recognized over the past decade that fathers play a significant role in their children's development from birth onwards (Kotelchuck, 1976; Lamb, 1976; Parke & Sawin, 1976). The father's masculinity, nurturance, limit setting, power, and participation in family decision making have all been found to be important factors in his son's sex-role development (Biller, 1981a). Paternal nurturance also appears to be closely associated with cognitive competence in boys (Radin, 1981). In addition, there has been a strong emphasis in research studies on the detrimental effects of paternal absence, be it physical or psychological (see Biller, 1981a, 1981b; Hetherington, Cox & Cox, 1978). The review by Lynn (1974) also attests to the importance of the father for his child's mental health, as do many results from family interaction studies that have compared disturbed versus "normal" families (for reviews see Hetherington & Martin, 1979; Jacob, 1975).

Although interest in fathers is on the upsurge, there is little evidence that family theory, policies, or practices presume that mothers and fathers have equal responsibility for children (see Chapter 2). Rather, it is still commonly assumed, either explicitly or implicitly, that mothers are the primary parent, that they have the ultimate responsibility for children, and that they should take the blame if something goes wrong. It is becoming increasingly common for researchers to argue that family problems are associated with a lack of involvement by fathers and with their failure to share equally in responsibilities for domestic work and family nurturance (Baumrind, 1980; Patterson, 1982).

This research emphasis on the relationship between family problems and the lack of responsibility taken by men for children is consistent with

191

recent developments in the treatment of these problems. Although fathers have mostly been characterized as uninvolved, resistant, and absent from child and family treatment, recent clinical writings make evident that there is growing acceptance of the need for father involvement and a greater sensitivity to the problems of engaging fathers in the helping process. Family therapists stress the necessity of directly observing interactions among all family members in order to decrease an exclusive reliance on mothers' reports. The presence of the father in the session is seen as particularly necessary to enable the therapist to deal with any resistance on the father's part to the treatment of his family. In conjoint sessions the therapist can help parents achieve vital consensus on how to handle their child's problem behavior. Further, Gurman and Kniskern (1981, p. 750) concluded from the (meager) evidence available that "the father's presence clearly improves the odds of good outcomes. . . ." Finally, involving fathers in treatment seems to be advisable in the light of research on generalization (e.g., Forehand & Atkeson, 1977) that shows that the important members of a child's environment need to be programmed to help and maintain any gains made during treatment. Thus there is no shortage of arguments for the inclusion of the father in assessment and treatment.

Recent research and clinical writings are consistent, therefore, in their arguments for involving fathers, and there appears to be a general feeling of optimism that if this is achieved, positive outcomes will follow. Such a view, however, needs to be tempered with the recognition that under some circumstances (e.g., in cases of violence and sexual abuse), the process of involving fathers might be very different from other situations, and that it might be slow and delicate.

This chapter is based on ideas about shared-parenting responsibilities and equity between mothers and fathers (in line with the arguments presented in Chapter 2). It is divided into three sections. The first presents a brief outline of the major approaches to family therapy, with an emphasis on systems theory. This part also includes consideration of the recent feminist critique of family therapy, which denounces such therapy's narrow focus on the immediate family system and its ignoring of the broader social context and patriarchal structure of society. The next section presents a comprehensive review of findings regarding the engagement of fathers in family therapy. This is followed by a review of findings that link father involvement to the outcome of family therapy, examining the question of whether involving fathers necessarily makes a difference. It is noted that the lack of precision in family therapy theory and research makes it very difficult to evaluate critically the position of fathers within this context. The final section of the chapter summarizes the findings and discusses implications for research and the practice of family therapy.

FAMILY THERAPY AND ASSUMPTIONS ABOUT THE ROLE OF FATHERS

The term "family therapy" has been applied to any approach that has as its major focus the treatment of family relationships rather than individual pathology. Thus the *Handbook of Family Therapy* (Gurman & Kniskern, 1981) includes chapters on marital therapy as well as behavioral parent training, because these approaches aim at changing one or some relationships within families. At least four major theoretical approaches or schools of family therapy have been differentiated (see Green & Kolevzon, 1982; Hare-Mustin, 1983): Psychoanalytic (which focuses on historical and unconscious sources of family conflict), behavioral (which stresses social exchange and cognitive processes), communicative (which emphasizes the ways in which family members send and interpret verbal or nonverbal messages), and systems approaches. In practice therapists commonly combine two or more approaches and think more or less systemically.

It is clearly systems theory that has come to be identified most closely with family therapy. A basic tenet is that the family as a group produces results that cannot be predicted by knowing family members separately. In particular, psychological problems or symptoms are seen not as residing in individuals, but rather as the outcome of difficulties arising from the interactions and structures characteristic of the entire family system. Individual diagnostic labels are eschewed as being unable to represent these interactional complexities. Treatment aims at minimizing blame and guilt and tries to encourage all family members to contribute to the solution of a problem.

However, these general beliefs held by systemic therapists need to be explicated further to specify the role of fathers in family therapy. Are fathers viewed as having the same status and responsibility as mothers? In which family interactions and structures do fathers play a crucial part? Is minimizing blame and guilt the best strategy to involve fathers? What kind of contributions toward the solution of family problems do therapists expect from fathers? A comprehensive theory of father involvement in family treatment must address all these questions to become useful to the practitioner. Different therapy schools have addressed different aspects of father involvement, and therefore only fragments of a comprehensive theory exist in the literature. As a first step toward an integration, some nonanalytic approaches to family therapy and their assumptions regarding shared parenting are considered.

Behavioral Approach

While behavioral conceptions have often been criticized as being only dyadic in scope, Patterson's (1982) theory is clearly systemic, representing the most sophisticated formulation of coercive family processes in the empirical literature. Mothers, who carry the main responsibility for child management, are found to become the "unacknowledged victims" (Patterson, 1980) of a coercive system that erodes their mood and increases their irritability and feelings of depression. Patterson (1982) finds that fathers are usually only slightly affected by family stresses, and speculates this is so because they do not see family management as a significant feature of their responsibility. Fathers are observed to take the role of a somewhat playful spectator, leaving the major child-management tasks to the mother. As coercive families progress toward "anarchy," fathers are observed to remain the least involved.

One of Patterson's (1982) main hypotheses states that disruptions in the parental alliance place the caretaker at risk in "her" skillful performance of family management practices, which ultimately leads to increased antisocial child behavior. However, Patterson (1982, p. 284) believed "that the father makes his primary contribution to family management by providing a support system." This would involve reinforcing the caretaker for "her" child-management skills, bringing friends over, or arranging pleasant weekend activities. Also, "most fathers can and do carry out *some* adjunct child management activities" (p. 285, our emphasis) and back up their partner's discipline when at home. Patterson realized that in few families are roles shared and was aware of Chodorow's (1978) call for "equal parenting," but seemed to take the attitude that at least one person should be committed to the role of caretaker. As a result we can assume that in behavioral family therapy, most fathers will be trained as "helpers" to their wives.

From clinical experience Patterson (1976) judged that for about a third of families, simple training in child management is sufficient to solve their problems. Another third of cases, however, he saw as requiring much more, "the teaching of negotiation skills and the partial resolution of marital conflicts and depression being the most common" (p. 306). In this context the use of the Spouse Observation Checklist (Weiss, Hops, & Patterson, 1973) allows couples to express very specific likes and dislikes with the daily behavior of their partner in areas such as child care/parenting, household management, employment/education, communication, and independence. Such an assessment would seem to provide a solid basis from which to negotiate new role arrangements. The resulting solutions, however, have come under fire from feminists for being sexist, because behavior therapists often do not seem to examine the underlying inequalities of many contingency contracts that they have partners sign (e.g., Hare-Mustin, 1983).

Problem-Centered Systems Therapy

Another program that explicitly addresses the issue of father involvement is Epstein and Bishop's (1981) problem-centered systems therapy. Early research had indicated that a balance of division of labor in the family along with a sharing of some roles by the parents was associated with children's emotional health (Westley & Epstein, 1969). Epstein and colleagues' McMaster model of family functioning consequently included the role dimension as well as problem solving, communication, affective responsiveness, affective involvement, and behavior control. In the assessment interview, the therapist routinely explores whether the family has reached a working consensus on the allocation of roles and whether all necessary family functions are being fulfilled. Roles should be allocated to suitable family members, and the system needs to be sufficiently flexible to allow for the reallocation of roles if individuals are overloaded. A healthy family is seen as collaborating and making sure that jobs get done, that is, that members are accountable.

Bishop (1985, personal communication) has described how this assessment transfers into the therapeutic stage: "If a family does not allocate roles in an open and explicit manner, we might set a specific task to have them discuss the jobs around the house and who they thought should do each. Then they would return for a session when we would finalize the allocations." This approach seems capable of encouraging shared-parenting arrangements and meeting feminist criticisms regarding role overload. At the same time, fairly traditional arrangements might go unchallenged because the evaluation rules are still quite abstract.

In the development of the Family Assessment Device (Epstein, Baldwin, & Bishop, 1983), a lot of the specifics of the interview assessment unfortunately have been lost. While the role subscale is shown to discriminate between clinical and nonclinical groups, items like "We have trouble paying our bills" do not tell us anything about the role distribution between mothers and fathers. Sending the family home to renegotiate responsibilities could also be criticized as disadvantaging a family member with less bargaining power. The activity of the therapist in "finalizing" role allocations needs further clarification as well.

Structural Family Therapy

Structural family therapy (Minuchin, 1974; Minuchin & Fishman, 1981) focuses on concepts like boundaries, alignments, and power in family systems. The term "boundaries" refers to the rules defining who participates in a subsystem and how. An example from Minuchin (1974, p. 61) is probably best able to convey the "flavor" of this approach: "A father and mother, stressed at work, may come home and criticize each other but then detour their conflict by attacking a child. This reduces the danger to the subsystem, but stresses the child. Or the husband may criticize the wife, who then seeks a coalition with the child against the father. The boundary around the spouse system thereby becomes diffuse. An inappropriately rigid cross-generational subsystem of mother and son versus father appears, and the boundary around this coalition of mother and son excludes the father." While there is no specific discussion of the father's role, the ability of a family to function well is seen as depending on "the degree to which the family structure is well defined, elaborated, flexible and cohesive" (Aponte & VanDeusen, 1981, p. 315).

Consequently, structural family therapists would want to engage fathers more with their children if they appeared excluded from the interaction, and would try at the same time to bring the spouses together to execute parental authority jointly. Therapeutic goals seem restricted, though, to those interaction patterns that structurally support symptomatic behavior. Enmeshment or disengagement is not necessarily seen as dysfunctional in itself, as it may vary over time and also has to be judged in relation to the family's societal context (Aponte & VanDeusen, 1981, p. 312). However, elaboration is lacking on what the current social context of Western society implies for the involvement of fathers in work and family life.

Strategic Family Therapy

Strategic family therapists share many concepts (and some techniques) with those who have a structural orientation (see Stanton, 1981). Marital problems, for example, are seen as the outcome of unsatisfactory hierarchical arrangements. When partners fail to negotiate a satisfactory relationship, one of the spouses may develop a symptom in an attempt to balance the division of power in the dyad. "This power refers to the possibility not only of dominating the other but also of comforting, reforming, taking care of, and taking responsibility for the other spouse" (Madanes, 1981, p. 29). Sometimes a child may develop a symptom instead, focusing the parents' concern on him or her and thus helping them to avoid their own difficulties. Most child problems are thought to include a triangle consisting of an overinvolved parent-child dyad (a cross-generational coalition) and a peripheral parent (Stanton, 1981). Except for isolated case examples, though, one finds very few specific statements relating to the father role and division of responsibility for children. This impression was further confirmed by a detailed review of Haley's *Leaving Home* (1980).

Haley (1976) argued that at the first interview the therapist should make a strategic decision about whom to address and how. With a concerned mother and a peripheral father, "it is best to ask the father about the problem first because one wishes to define him as involved in the therapy and also to find out how much responsibility he will be willing to take when action is requested" (Haley, 1976, p. 23). At the same time, the therapist has to make sure that the mother is not made to feel inadequate. In other cases the therapist may decide to speak to the mother first and thus bolster her position. "But this decision should be made in relation to the presenting problem not to the therapist's idea about the proper status position of either sex, which is not the issue of therapy" (Haley, 1976, p. 22).

Further, Haley (1976) argued that ideally everyone should be included in the tasks that the therapist assigns to the family to carry out between sessions. The best task is seen as one that uses the presenting problem to change the family structure and introduces more complexity and choices. Strategic family therapy is meant to be done in stages, however, and Haley (1976, p. 141) warned not to "rush into the marriage" before there is improvement in the presenting problem. Advocating "courtesy therapy," he urged therapists to beware of ideal models of the family and to avoid crystallizing power struggles between family members. At times the therapist may paradoxically exaggerate the hierarchical contradictions in a marriage through directives that are "designed to provoke the spouses to reorganize in a more congruous hierarchy" (Madanes, 1981, p. 63). Hare-Mustin (1983), however, has seriously questioned this practice as potentially reinforcing stereotyped role expectations.

Functional Family Therapy

Barton and Alexander's (1981) functional family therapy combines behavioral and systemic thinking. They first identify regular occurrences of interactional sequences in families in order to then classify them according to their functional outcome as distance creating, intimacy creating, or regulating processes. "The functional family therapist does assume that these functions are such powerful purposive outcomes of behavior and process that therapeutic goals should not include changing them" (Barton & Alexander, 1981, p. 424). Only the *form* of the process that generates or controls them is meant to be changed. Barton and Alexander (1981) alluded to cultural practices that socialize males to become task-oriented problem solvers. "These males can be extraordinarily threatened by situations in which their task-oriented problem-solving attempts do not function to promote popularized or idealized forms of intimacy, but can in essence, produce distance" (p. 415). Unfortunately they did not clarify whether the goal of therapy would consequently be to achieve the "popularized" form of intimacy in another way.

Alexander and Parsons (1982) reported the case of an involved mother whom they asked to keep extensive daily charts for each child, thus encouraging her to maintain her "merging" function. She also had to hand over these charts to her husband at night for him to make decisions regarding allowances, curfews, etc. which the wife then carried out. "The plan allowed Father his separating function (he could read a chart rather than interact with the children directly), while at the same time allowing Mother her merging fuction (she could carry out decisions and thus ligitimize her mothering role)" (p. 68). This school does not believe that "both men and women must achieve a balance of distance and contact," but rather that "all people must have options available to them, and they must not be forced into developing one particular option" (Alexander, Warburton, Woldron, & Mas, 1985, p. 143). Only family members themselves have the right to determine their underlying functional structure, while the therapist can help them to achieve the same outcomes in a healthier way. "After the therapist has helped all family members maintain and express their functions in ways they all enjoy, then family members may initiate a developmental process of changing functions, *if they so choose*" (p. 143). This latter process is seen as taking "a long period of time" (p. 143).

From a feminist point of view Functional Family Therapists have been charged with denying options to families by not exploring alternative functions with them. For the example given above Avis (1985, p. 148) asserts that "maintaining existing functions blatently reinforces traditional roles, leaving the mother with primary responsibility for parenting and depriving the children of a relationship with their father." She also criticizes the suggestion that families following traditional patterns have freely chosen their roles as ignoring the coercive influence of tradition, socialization, and societal expectations. This of course is a central theme in the general feminist critique of family therapy.

Feminist Perspectives

Several recent writers have taken a feminist perspective and criticized family therapy theory and practice at a quite fundamental level (e.g., Hare-Mustin, 1978, 1983; James & McIntyre, 1983; Taggart, 1985). They take systems theory to task for its definition of dysfunction in terms of factors internal to the family, while it ignores the contribution of the wider socio-political structure. James and McIntyre (1983, p. 123) accused family therapists of ignoring the fact that "contemporary society creates, even requires, a family form that actually produces the pattern of behavior that we judge 'dysfunctional'." These authors also argued that the emphasis on parameters of the system leads to the neglect of issues specifically associated with women and their position in the family, as they are influenced by broader social patterns. A strict adherence to systems theory would mean that therapists overlook the differences in power that exist in most families and that are reinforced and supported by cultural patterns. As Taggart (1985) has pointed out, systems theory has the potential to promote a view that members of the family system are co-responsible for violence, rape, and incest. As such, this approach may support current stereotyped models of women and reinforce traditional family patterns and power relationships.

Hare-Mustin (1978, 1983) was also concerned with how family therapists might uncritically accept traditional family patterns and actively or unwittingly reinforce them through their techniques and practices. More than James and McIntyre, she made some fairly specific criticisms of the actual practices adopted, the stereotyped assumptions behind them, and the ways in which they reinforce traditional sex-role behaviors. She argued for greater availability by fathers, a more equitable division of responsibilities at home, a greater participation by fathers in decision making about children, and a greater emotional contribution by men. At the same time, however, she offered several cautions about placing an exclusive emphasis on encouraging greater father involvement.

First Hare-Mustin argued that therapists "should not rush in to 'restore' the power in the family to the father" (1978, p. 186) by having him take a greater share of responsibility within the home. Any shift in this area, Hare-Mustin proposed, needs to take account of the fact that men often have power and status elsewhere, and that many women might resist a shift in power at home because it could lead to a reduction in their authority and self-esteem. A second caution is that greater involvement by fathers could help to perpetuate traditional sex roles. Here Hare-Mustin drew on research literature that shows that fathers interact preferentially with sons and place higher value on traditional sex roles. Third, Hare-Mustin argued that some of the techniques employed to help engage fathers (e.g., scheduling sessions for the father's convenience and initially focusing on him), could in fact help to reinforce the father's position of power within the family (1983, p. 195).

However, Hare-Mustin failed to recognize that the family responsibilities associated with paid work and the demands of employment, which are more likely to impinge on men, together with the "inability" of men to seek help and be emotionally expressive (see O'Neil, 1980) are all part of the same social and political structure that feminist authors argue should be taken into account for women. A balanced view of the problems associated with engaging all members in family treatment should take these factors into account when considering the position of men.

Summary

Overall, it appears that some non-analytic therapy approaches are quite sensitive to the stresses of the mother role (behavioral family therapy), the appropriate allocation of roles in the family (problem-centered systems therapy), and the structurally proper involvement of parents in the family hierarchy (structural/strategic family therapy). Functional family therapists, while very sensitive to distance/closeness issues in relationships, need to further clarify whether they are prepared to accept an uninvolved father as a fact of life. Unfortunately, none of these approaches has spelled out clearly enough their therapeutic goals with regard to the father role, but the range of possibilities seems to span equal sharing to traditional but supportive arrangements. With Libow, Raskin, and Caust (1982) we see enough common ground between feminist and family systems therapy to warrant an intensification of the dialogue between the two. But we also believe that to be productive this interchange has to include a full exploration of "the male restraints." Our own thinking emphasizes shared parenting responsibilities, taking into account the difficulties that both men and women experience in dividing up responsibilities for breadwinning as well as child care within current social and therapeutic contexts.

ENGAGEMENT OF FATHERS IN PARENT TRAINING AND FAMILY THERAPY

In examining participation rates and difficulties in getting fathers involved in family treatment, it should be remembered that reluctance to accept medical or psychological advice is a widespread problem that cannot simply be reduced to sex differences. According to Blackwell (1979), about half of outpatients and a quarter of inpatients fail to take their prescribed medication, and Becker and Mainman (1975) concluded that lack of compliance with medical recommendations is unrelated to sex or marital status. Between 20 and 57 percent of general psychiatric outpatients fail to return after a first visit (Baekeland & Lundwall, 1975). This latter review finds a tendency for women to drop out of outpatient treatment more often than men.

Attrition rates from family therapy similarly vary between 25 and 58 percent (Heubeck, 1983a). Engagement is usually defined in these studies as attendance of more than two, three, or four clinic appointments. While easily measurable, such an index obviously does not reflect qualitative differences in fathers' therapy involvement. With these limitations in mind, this review first examines how many fathers participate in family therapy and how often they attend. The second part focuses on factors that determine whether fathers attend or not. The effect their participation has on the engagement of the whole family is examined in the third section.

Excluded from this review are the closely linked areas of male sex-role socialization (see O'Neil, 1980) and engagement studies that have focused on men as individual clients (e.g., Vaillant, 1972) or families in general (e.g., Sager et al., 1967). While numerous interesting hypotheses could be derived from linking these literatures, the main purpose here is to examine the engagement of fathers in family therapy. From a scientific point of view this field is highly exploratory and has only just reached the stage where hypotheses are being developed to test in methodologically adequate studies.

Participation Rates of Fathers

Rice (1978, p. 64) echoed a common lament when he wrote: "A major problem faced by the marital and family therapist is in getting the male spouse to actually come to therapy." Sixty family therapists returned questionnaires for Berg and Rosenblum's (1977) U. S. study. The father was reported to be much less likely than the mother to call the clinic and ask for help, and he was clearly seen as the most resistant family member. Not only was he reported to be the person most frequently absent from sessions, but he was also most often held responsible if the entire family canceled an appointment. Berg and Rosenblum also found a tendency ($p < .10$) for fathers to refuse the family format of treatment more often than mothers did. These findings have been replicated in a pilot study of 25 Sydney therapists with an average of seven years' experience in marital/family counseling (Heubeck, 1983b). Interestingly, in both surveys mothers and fathers were equally often seen as responsible for the premature termination of family therapy. Another U. S. survey, of 18 clinical programs that offered behavioral parent training during the preceding year, indicated that eight of them required father involvement. While in 70 percent of families the father was seen as participating to some degree, 76 percent of therapists rated father's involvement to be less extensive than that of mothers. Nobody rated fathers as more involved than mothers (Budd & O'Brien, 1982).

Very few data have been published to back up these general perceptions by therapists. A simple useful statistic would report the proportion of families in which a father joins other family members at any stage during a treatment program. A recent review (Budd & O'Brien, 1982) suggested that over the 12-year period from 1970 to 1981, fathers were involved in only 13 percent of families who took part in studies of behavioral parent training. However, this figure is not necessarily representative of nonresearch settings. A program that put a lot of effort into involving both parents of heroin addicts was able to recruit 71 percent of fathers to come to the initial family evaluation session (Stanton & Todd, 1982). Therapists in Berg and Rosenblum's study (1977) estimated that 30 percent of their families turned up for the first interview without the father, while Gaines and Stedman (1981, p. 50) reported "that fathers typically fail to come for evaluation appointments."

A more useful statistic to judge the father's participation would detail his actual session-by-session attendance. Stanton, Steier, and Todd (1982) not only gave a clear description of the selection of families in treatment, but also reported that fathers attended 54 percent of (unpaid) family therapy sessions in which they were expected (mothers, 56 percent). In other studies, however, the considerable latitude given to the use of the term "family therapy" seems to have served to blur completely the simplest and most reliable information family therapy researchers could report. The theoretical orientation of the therapist is usually regarded as more defining of this approach than who is actually seen in the consultation room (e.g., Gurman & Kniskern, 1978a; Szapocznik, Kurtines, Foote, Perez-Vidal, & Hervis, 1983); thus editors have not insisted on this vital information being provided as part of research reports in the area of family therapy.

Factors Determining Whether Fathers Attend Family Treatment

The reasons why some fathers attend family treatment while others do not are likely to be complex, and the current status of research findings does not allow definitive statements about them. Findings can be classified according to their emphasis on one of four factors: personality, family role, work role, and the clinic.

Personality.   The father has often been described as passive, inadequate, authoritarian, and resistant. Slipp, Ellis, and Kressel (1974) attributed the difficulty in engaging families from the lowest socioeconomic group at least partly to the authoritarian attitude of the fathers. Families with a severely disturbed member had a high dropout rate, but if both spouses were low in authoritarianism on the California F scale, the engagement rate was 100 percent. Firestone and Witt (1982, p. 219), however, found fathers completing a behavioral parent-training program to be "more rigid and defensive but otherwise indistinguishable from drop-outs" on the MMPI (Minnesota Multiphasic Personality Inventory). When clinicians rated a father favorably on a semantic differential after the initial session, the family was less likely to drop out of treatment in Gaines and Stedman's (1981) investigation. Finally, in a retrospective telephone study by Shapiro and Budman (1973), families who had dropped out of treatment later perceived their father to have been the least enthusiastic about continuing treatment. Those families who had stayed in treatment most often named him as the most enthusiastic of all family members. This result led these researchers to hypothesize that fathers play a pivotal role in the engagement of families.

Family Role. Kressel and Slipp (1975) developed a Family Roles and Attitudes Inventory that husbands and wives answered separately after the initial interview. They found few statistically reliable differences, but a family was more likely to remain in treatment when the husband held a relatively positive view of family life, especially with regard to perceived ease of communication. There was also some evidence to suggest that if he saw himself as sharing in domestic activities, or nominated his wife as the family leader, the family was more likely to stay in treatment. Wives who continued in therapy, however, were more dissatisfied with matters in the family than either their husbands or wives who terminated therapy. They disagreed with their spouse that domestic chores were shared and that communication was easy. They seemed to have more power in the relationship with their husbands than did terminating wives, that is, they more often felt in charge of family affairs or felt that decision making was shared, and they were more likely to contribute to family income. What emerges is a portrait of the couple that continues therapy which seems consistent with research on shared parenting and clinical experience. These authors speculated that in "drop-out families," women married to men with authoritarian attitudes would run into a wall if they tried to challenge rigid role relations. Therefore they may have given up on expecting help and friendship from their spouse.

Work Role. "Pathogenic role rigidity in fathers" was posed by L'Abate (1975) as a central concept from which dysfunctional family patterns as well as paternal resistance to involvement in family therapy can be delineated. Although not an empirical investigation, this clinical and theoretical analysis is mentioned here because it links the work and family sphere with the clinic. Men who cannot shift from a professional to a fatherly role are said to maintain the one-way communication at home that they practice at work as engineers, doctors, or army officers. The emphasis is on objectivity, achievement, and avoidance of feelings. They "know what is best" for their families and have only one problem: they don't understand why the family does not follow their instructions. L'Abate (p. 73) saw this as a "failure on the father's part to assume responsibility for himself and to consider critically his role vis-a-vis his wife and his child." For these men, the primary commitment to their occupational role often serves as a reality factor to excuse them from treatment.

Seventy-six percent of the therapists in Berg and Rosenblum's (1977) study indicated that the father's work schedule was the reason most frequently cited by him for not attending sessions. Heubeck (1983b) also found this to be the case with 64 percent of therapists naming the father's work schedule. We do not know how mothers use their spouse's work involvement to give a "message" to therapists, but "my spouse won't attend" was clearly seen as the reason most frequently cited by mothers for not coming to a family session (Berg & Rosenblum, 1977; Heubeck, 1983b). While in some families the father's work schedule may be nothing but a convenient excuse, in others the employer might put pressure on the father, and he would lose his pay for following an invitation that does not make sense to the employer in the context of expectations about role divisions between family and work. In partial contradiction, however, is a study in which engaged families tended to have fathers and mothers with high occupational prestige and fathers who worked many hours (Blechman, et al., 1981).

The Clinic.   How the clinic invites the father or responds to his queries is the third important factor determining his attendance. Berg and Rosenblum (1977) reported that the percentage of families successfully engaged was significantly correlated (.39, $p < .01$) with the lateness of the hour at which the family was seen. In this same study, 68 percent of therapists also indicated that they would see the family for the scheduled period of time if the family arrived for the first interview without the father (which occurred in about 30 percent of families). When these families return home, fathers can easily be confirmed in their attitude that they are peripheral to the problems and not really needed at the clinic. It then becomes less likely that they will attend future sessions and, as we conclude below, their absence will lower the chances of their children receiving the full course of treatment. In the Sydney survey, however, 14 of 24 therapists indicated that they would adjust their practice in this situation by seeing the family for a shorter time, and four were even prepared to not see them at all (Heubeck, 1983b).

When the father is contacted or begins to attend sessions at the clinic, the full richness of direct interaction with the therapist comes into play. Stanton and Todd's clinical examples (1982) illustrate the complexities involved when family therapists try to actively engage fathers of heroin addicts. There are indications (Beck & Jones, 1973) that male therapists are more successful than females in getting husbands involved and keeping them in treatment. Warburton, Alexander, and Barton (1980) similarly found that mothers strongly coalesce with female therapists, while fathers form stronger coalitions with male therapists in the first session of family therapy. The therapist's gender may thus exert a considerable influence in the early phases of intervention, and male and female therapists face very different family behavior patterns solely as a function of gender.

Families are also more likely to stay in treatment when their therapist likes them and gives them a good prognosis (e.g., Shapiro, 1974). Fathers who perceived their therapist's negative evaluation in Gaines and Stedman's (1981) study may well have discouraged their families from further attendance, which is one possible explanation for the correlation found between therapist ratings of fathers and family dropout. Shapiro and Budman (1973) found that more active family therapists had fewer dropouts than those who provided little structure and guidance in early treatment sessions. For husbands/fathers in particular, a favorable outcome seemed to be associated with active restructuring operations on the part of the therapist (Russell et al., 1984). Removal of a child from being used in spouse conflicts (triangulation) and diffusion of cross-generational coalitions (such as parent-child against other parent) and thus the establishment of more appropriate system boundaries (see Minuchin, 1974) were associated with an increase in husbands' reports of marital and life happiness. The authors speculated that these restructuring interventions were often directed toward engaging the husband/father more actively in marital and parental subsystems. Having found a "way back into the family," husbands may have "a more positive evaluation of their marriages and their lives in general" (Russell et al., 1984, p. 249).

From these studies it becomes apparent that it is the interaction between therapist and father that creates the father's role in family treatment. However, it is not the intention of this chapter to go deeper into these complex issues of therapeutic processes as they unfold from session to session. Rather we wish to examine the beginning (engagement) and end points (outcome) of treatment in order to arrive at conclusions about the feasibility of fathers' involvement in family therapy.

Effects of Father Participation on Engagement

Very few studies have been done on the effects that father participation has on the engagement of families in therapy. Studies are consistent, however, in showing a positive relationship. Slipp, Ellis, and Kressel (1974) reported that if either spouse alone sought treatment for the child, one third of families dropped out, whereas engagement was nearly perfect (93.4 percent) when spouses initiated the contact together. La Barbera and Lewis (1980) reported that 72 percent of families in which the father came to the intake session ended up continuing their child's treatment beyond this point. By contrast, significantly fewer families (47 percent) followed through with the recommended treatment when the father did not attend. These figures are strikingly similar to those of Le Fave (1980), where 69 percent of families continued treatment when the father had attended the first interview compared with only 43.9 percent when he had not attended the initial session.

Notwithstanding numerous methodological problems and the possibility that the more highly involved fathers came to the first interview, these studies indicate that the dropout rate can be reduced 25 percent if one can get fathers to attend the initial interview. Whether having fathers attend and having families follow through with the recommended treatment influence outcome is of course another question. This is examined in the next section.

FATHER INVOLVEMENT IN CHILD AND FAMILY TREATMENT AND THERAPY OUTCOME

So far we have argued that father participation in the treatment of his children is desirable on social, theoretical, and ideological grounds. It also seems to improve the chances of family attendance at treatment sessions. We still do not know, however, what the *ultimate benefits* of father involvement are in terms of treatment outcome. Nor do we know what *kind of father participation* affects therapeutic changes in child and family relationships.

The Hypothesis

In a major review of family therapy outcome studies, Gurman and Kniskern (1978a) concluded that (1) the involvement of both partners in marital counseling greatly enhances the probability of a good outcome for the couple, and (2) the father's participation in treatment has a "very strong" influence on improvement in the family. As evidence for the latter hypothesis, they cited Love, Kaswan, and Bugental's (1972) study in which a significant correlation ($r = .55$, $p < .01$) was reported between the number of father appointments and the child's improvement in school grades three semesters after an information feedback treatment devised by the main author. However, a single correlation does not make a summer, especially as improved school grades were also correlated ($r = .60$, $p < .05$) with the mother's attendance in the parent counseling condition. The second study mentioned by Gurman and Kniskern (1978a) also lends little weight to their argument. In the good-outcome group of this process study, therapists directed their speech most often to fathers, while in the poor-outcome group the mothers were spoken to most (Postner et al., 1971). The researchers themselves questioned the reliability of their findings in light of the large number of variables examined and with only 11 Jewish families under study the results would seem to have little generalizability anyway.

However, in 1981 Gurman and Kniskern reiterated their hypothesis (without presenting new evidence): "Which family members are involved in treatment seems to exert a powerful effect, especially regarding the involvement of the father in family therapies. . . . The father's presence clearly improves the odds of good outcomes in many situations" (p. 750). Unfortunately, this assertion seems to reflect widespread clinical experience and belief more than empirical research evidence. It is possible that the poverty of research rather than misguided impression may account for this inconsistency. In the first part of the following review we play devil's advocate and question Gurman and Kniskern's hypothesis in the light of a number of empirical reports. However, noting the restrictions in these studies we will then turn to develop an argument in support of a modified hypothesis regarding beneficial effects of father involvement in child and family treatment.

"One Parent Is Enough to Do the Job"

If families really function like abstract systems and the behavior of members is as interdependent as concepts like homeostasis lead us to believe, it should be possible to change a child and family by changing a part of the system (see Freeman, 1977). Leading figures like Erikson, Rabkin or the therapists of the Mental Research Institute may work only with the complainant, e.g., the wife or parents of the IP, since "it is held that (a) this person . . . is concerned enough to do something different, and (b) effective intervention can be made through any member of the system. . . ." (Stanton, 1981a, p. 369).

Support for this notion is found in the recent study by Szapocznik and colleagues (1983) comparing the effectiveness of conjoint treatment with what they called "one-person family therapy," which was also conducted in a structural-strategic framework. Both treatments proved to be equally effective on well-chosen measures in bringing about symptom reduction in the adolescent drug users and improvement in family functioning. In fact, a slight advantage of family therapy conducted through one person was noted in terms of continued symptom reduction in the referred person 6 to 12 months later. Unfortunately, the authors did not report which person was actually seen.

"In almost all reports, mothers are the primary recipients of parent training, with fathers being involved in only a few cases" (Gordon and Davidson 1981, p. 531), but hundreds of reports now demonstrate the successful use of behavioral parent training with a wide variety of children, especially for discrete well-specified behavior problems (Berkowitz & Graziano, 1972; Graziano, 1977; Johnson & Katz, 1973; O'Dell, 1974). Not only can mothers achieve symptom reduction in the identified patient, but they can also be taught to improve communication among family members. In Reiter and Kilmann's (1975) study, this led to an increase in perceived family integration for mothers and fathers on Van der Veen's (1965) Family Concept Q Sort. Moreover, a case study by Adubato, Adams, and Budd (1981) demonstrated that a mother could independently teach her husband to implement successfully the same child-management techniques she learned to use with her mentally handicapped son at an outpatient clinic.

When fathers were directly included in behavioral parent training, only minimal benefits seemed to accrue. Martin (1977) compared a waiting-list control group with a mother-training group ($N = 14$) and a group in which 14 couples took part in training together. While the training was effective, the changes in child problems for the father-included group were almost identical to those for the mother-only group at termination of training and at follow-up. Using a similar design, Firestone, Kelly, and Fike (1980) found that only the two-parent group reported significantly less conduct problems at termination compared with the waiting-list control group. However, at follow-up both treatment groups had improved significantly compared with pretest behavior and were indistinguishable from each other. Adesso and Lipson (1981) expanded this design to include a group for fathers only. Training of parents in all three groups was found to be effective in reducing mild child behavior problems in nine weeks, with gains being maintained after three months. Although no significant differences were found between the training groups at follow-up, the results of the mother- and father-only groups did not hold as well as those of the couples group.

Even the belief held by many family therapists that the marital relationship is crucial to treatment outcome has been challenged. Oltmanns, Broderick, and O'Leary (1977) found the pretreatment level of marital discord to not be related to the degree of positive change in the child at termination of behavior therapy or at five-month follow-up. (Not surprisingly, the treatment that was focused on the child did not produce changes in marital adjustment.)

Taken together, these studies call into question the globality of Gurman and Kniskern's hypothesis. For many situations, active involvement in treatment of only one adult seems sufficient, especially with mildly disturbed volunteer families. The involved adult has mostly been the mother, but can also be the father (see Adesso & Lipson, 1981).

Behavioral (as well as nonbehavioral) family therapy also produces negative effects. Gurman and Kniskern (1978b) found that 5 to 10 percent of patient or family relationships worsened as a result of family therapy, which is quite consistent with frequencies of deterioration reported for other treatment modalities (see Bergin, 1971). Adding this fact to our discussion, we might conclude that involvement of fathers in treatment neither helps nor harms child and family relationships.

The studies discussed have, however, a number of limitations. Most cases dealt with in these studies would have to be classed as mild to moderately difficult. We suspect, though, that the type and severity of the presenting problems may be correlated with the importance of father participation, for example, the more severe the problem the more needed the father may be to help rectify it. With the few exceptions noted, the outcome measurement was usually restricted to the child's problem behavior. It is conceivable that father participation has a stronger impact on other dimensions, such as closeness to his child or depression in the mother. Further, it seems necessary to consider qualitative differences in father involvement as predictors of outcome.

The final point concerns the lack of theoretical conceptualization in the studies discussed. It is our belief that a theory of responsibility would best be able to represent the most relevant social and psychological dimensions of father involvement. Therefore we have begun to develop a model that eventually is meant to cover the distribution of responsibility within families as well as between families and helping agencies. A fundamental distinction in this model concerns the attribution of responsibility for the cause of a problem versus the responsibility to do something about it or even solve it (Brickman et al., 1982). Therefore, in presenting the evidence for specific positive effects that father participation can have on treatment, the question of blame and self-held responsibility are considered first. Subsequently we will examine which specific contributions fathers can make toward solving child and family problems.

Specific Kinds of Father Involvement and Treatment Outcome

Responsibility for Cause.   One investigator (Watson, 1985) examined maternal and paternal self-held responsibility for the cause of children's disturbed behavior and its relationship to family therapy outcome. The mothers and fathers of 70 children aged between 7 and 15 years, who had been consecutively referred for psychiatric treatment, were interviewed separately before the initial clinic assessment. Families that attended at least three sessions were followed up two months after discharge and interviewed in their home. Families that attended less than three sessions were contacted by telephone. Standardized consensual measures (Child Behavior Checklist [CBCL], Achenbach & Edelbrock, 1983) were completed before and after therapy by the child's parents (separately) and the child's teacher. The therapist was also asked to rate the child's level of disturbance. Children could be classified as severely disturbed not only by their referral status to a backup psychiatric service but also by their mean ranking at the ninety-ninth percentile of the Total Behavior Problem Scale of the CBCL. Four male and four female therapists offered systems-oriented family therapy lasting six to eight sessions.

Therapists were unaware of the research emphasis on parental responsibility, and techniques were not aimed specifically at increasing paternal responsibility. Parents were asked open-ended questions relating to their feelings of responsibility for the child's disturbed behavior. Content analyses of responses indicated that parents could be categorized into one of three groups: (1) those who felt actively responsible for their children—they referred to their own behavior in a specific situation or accepted that parents have global responsibility for the child; (2) those who felt passively responsible—they were vaguely aware that they may have contributed to the child's behavior but could not be any more specific (e.g., "I might be, but I wouldn't know how") or referred to some vague genetic link (e.g., "He might have got it from me, apparently I was a bugger of a kid"); or (3) those who felt no responsibility whatsoever—they usually replied with a blunt "no," although a few added justifications such as that the other children in the family had "turned out OK."

As had been expected in this disturbed sample, few fathers took active responsibility for their children's behavior problems. Eighty-six percent of fathers took little or no responsibility for their child's failure to conform. Only 14 percent took active responsibility, compared with 32 percent of mothers (chi square [dF 2] = 8.30, $p < 0.02$).

Most families with actively responsible fathers mutually agreed with the therapist on when to terminate therapy. When mutual termination was used as the criterion for "treatment," the pretherapy degree of paternal self-held responsibility did predict successful outcome, but was not as good a predictor as the mothers' degree of self-held responsibility. The lower predictive value of the fathers' responsibility when compared with the mothers' may be due to the small numbers of fathers who took responsibility in the first place. The best pretherapy predictor of outcome was that at least one parent took active responsibility. This finding retained its predictive value even when all possible demographic variables were taken into account.

If the low levels of paternal responsibility in part contributed to the fact that the children were severely disturbed, any increase in responsibility might be expected to be accompanied by a decrease in the level of disturbance. This question was also examined. While mothers' responsibility polarized with therapy such that the shift was a bilateral one away from vague responsibility, fathers significantly increased their feelings of responsibility: thirty-six percent felt actively responsible after therapy for the causes of their children's behavior. This represented a significant shift away from passive responsibility or denial of responsibility toward greater active responsibility (chi square [df 2] = 7.76, $p < 0.01$). An increase in the father's degree of self-held responsibility was predictive of a positive outcome, not only on global measures such as the parents' subjective opinion and therapist and coder ratings of outcome, but also on standardized measures like the CBCL. This finding retained its predictive value even when all demographic variables were taken into account. For mothers, the bilateral shift related only to global measures, but less strongly than for fathers. Finally, in contrast to pretherapy levels of responsibility, the paternal and not the maternal level of posttherapy responsibility is most strongly associated with a positive outcome.

Thus both parents are important. From the current findings, the most plausible explanation is that the mother's pretherapy level of responsibility predicts outcome success. However the acceptance of greater responsibility for the child's problems by the father has the most significant impact on outcome.

Responsibility for Solution. While responsibility for the origin of a problem involves the question of blame for past omissions or commissions, responsibility for the solution of a problem involves an assessment of who might be able to control events in the future (Brickman et al., 1982, p. 369). In his clinical practice the main author (B.H.) has often experienced that with difficult families the blame question has to be resolved before a family can "get down to business" and successfully assign responsibilities for solutions. No study to date has directly investigated this question in relation to fathers in family therapy. However, we believe this dimension to be of great importance, and we review here some relevant studies to examine what types of contributions fathers can make toward family therapy outcome.

Retrospectively, fathers certainly felt that they had made a contribution to a successful outcome in Watson's (1985) study, which was described previously. Only 3 percent of fathers who saw things as having changed felt that they were not responsible for that change (compared with 14 percent of mothers). Whether this reflects a greater self-serving bias on the part of fathers or a greater change in their involvement can partially be answered from the findings on the Kvebaek family sculpture technique (Cromwell, Fournier, & Kvebaek, 1980), which was used as a pretreatment and post-treatment measure of family relationships in the same study. From the child's point of view, the relationship with his or her father was the most distant before treatment and became the closest after treatment. This improvement in the father-identified-patient relationship was seen by all family members as the most significant of all changes. The fact that this was so obvious to every family member suggests that it was not confined to a passive "feeling" of greater understanding and closeness on the part of the father, but was actively reflected in the father's everyday interactions with his child.

Blotcky and colleagues (1980) also found the father-child dyad to be the most amenable to change of all family relationships, with significantly less "double bind" communication and more interpersonal closeness after a family-oriented treatment program. These results appear consistent with those of Stanton and coworkers (1979), who found support for the notion of an active coalition between mothers and sons in families with a heroin addict, while fathers initially were disengaged; significant changes were noted in the father-identified-patient relationship after treatment. While fathers participated more often than before, mothers were able to take a less central role in family communications.

Taplin and Reid (1977) observed greater sharing of the difficult task of controlling an aggressive and/or hyperactive child in 17 families after a social learning intervention. While fathers provided significantly fewer positive consequences for deviant child behavior and increased their punishment of it, mothers were able to reduce significantly their overall aversiveness to deviant and prosocial child behavior. "The mother's reduction in punitiveness was in turn accompanied by profound shifts in her perception both of the problem child and of herself" (Patterson & Fleischman 1979). Fathers also perceived significantly fewer problems, and 80 percent of mothers (Patterson & Reid, 1973) saw the entire family as functioning better.

Taken together, these treatment studies indicate that a change in the father-identified patient relationship is possible and beneficial. Findings reported in Stanton and colleagues (1979) and in Taplin and Reid (1977) also demonstrate that greater involvement by the father allows the mother to play a less strained role in family interactions from which presumably further benefits can follow.

A case study by Kelly, Embry, and Baer (1979), however, highlights another important interactional pattern that therapists have to take into account when assigning responsibilities for change to fathers. A couple was taught the use of differential attention and time-out in order to improve their 5-year-old son's noncompliant behavior. While the mother learned to ignore some child behaviors effectively, she found it difficult to increase her attention to his appropriate behavior when the father was present. "She reported that the father's attention appeared to have a greater reinforcement value than her own, and this was more actively sought by the child" (p. 391), making her feel like an unwanted participant in the interaction. The parents also still disagreed on rules for the child to follow and complained about a lack of support for each other as well as a lack of shared triadic activities. In response to this situation, another training phase was introduced focusing on spouse support and family interaction. This resulted in immediate increases in shared activities and positive statements among family members. While in the initial training the mother had increased her average attention rate to the child's positive behavior from 16 percent to only 21 percent, she was able to increase her rate. to 53 percent with the father's support. This training phase also produced a 40 percent increase in one parent's attention to child compliance with the other parent's instructions. Improvements in child behavior were maintained over at least six months and some positive generalization to areas of marital disagreement was noted.

Thus it would seem that there are a variety of ways in which therapists can use fathers as family change agents. Depending on the circumstances, the therapist may ask the father to take more responsibility for disciplining a child, improve his communication with the identified patient, or concentrate on supporting his spouse in her parenting, all of which can contribute to successful child and family outcomes.

SUMMARY AND IMPLICATIONS

Overview of Research Findings

Despite the paucity of research, the findings reviewed in this chapter allow us to draw the following conclusions about the involvement of fathers in family therapy:

1. Having the father attend the first interview appears to increase the chances of the family remaining in family therapy.
2. For many situations it seems sufficient for a successful outcome to actively involve only one adult in treatment, especially in the case

of mildly disturbed, volunteer families. This adult has often been the mother, but can equally well be the father.

3. While deterioration rates in family therapy are no worse than in other treatment approaches, no study to date has shown detrimental effects of father involvement in family treatment.

4. Studies are not consistent in showing across-the-board beneficial outcome effects of father participation. Rather, specific measures of father involvement have been found to have specific effects on outcome.

5. Positive outcomes have been associated with the degree to which fathers take responsibility for the causes as well as the solutions of family problems.

6. Family therapy has been associated with positive changes in the quality of the father-child relationship and with mothers being relieved from the strain of carrying the sole responsibility for child problems.

The present review, therefore, gives support to the proposal that practitioners be encouraged to include fathers in treatment. Nevertheless, findings reviewed here also suggest that there is a need for much more caution than shown by Gurman and Kniskern (1981). Research still has a long way to go before we can confidently state what kind of father involvement "improves the odds of good outcomes," to what degree, in which type of family, and with what type of problems (see Kiesler, 1966).

Implications for Future Research

A point frequently made throughout this review has been that there is a general lack of research into father participation and family therapy. Moreover, there is a critical absence of methodologically adequate research into the specific effects that father participation has on family therapy outcome. The following lines of investigation should prove especially fruitful:

1. Investigations of the processes surrounding the support parents give to each other in daily child-rearing situations. This seems to be a more promising area of research for illuminating paternal effects than is simply using general marital adjustment scales.

2. The responsibility dimension in particular deserves more attention, especially following the model proposed by Brickman and coworkers (1982), which focuses on responsibility both for the causes and the solutions of problems.

3. Investigation of the meaning that participation in therapy has for fathers, and whether treatment leads to changes in their self-concepts and motivations.
4. Research into family therapy to focus on the relationship between *specific* changes in father-involvement and outcome. To find specific contributions, researchers need to measure the kinds of father involvement in treatment (independent variables) as well as a range of possible outcomes (dependent variables). Single case designs could also be used and phases in which the father manages a child be alternated with phases when the mother has this responsibility.

Hypotheses for research into father participation and family therapy might also be obtained from findings of recent research into the impact that increased paternal participation has on child development outcomes. One study (Zelazo, Kotelchuck, Barber, & David, 1977) has reported that increased father involvement in play can lead to a positive change in the quality of the father-child relationship. Other studies have suggested that children raised in families in which the father is highly participant perform better on some cognitive tests and are less stereotyped in their attitudes to adult sex roles (see Radin & Russell, 1983 for a review of this literature). This latter finding, it should be noted, does not support Hare-Mustin's (1983) speculation that if therapists increase paternal participation, the emphasis will be even greater on traditional sex roles.

Overall, however, little research has been done on the impact of specific changes in the quantity and quality of father involvement; as was concluded in Chapter 2, it is not possible at this stage of research to be confident about cause and effect. Further, effects might vary according to whether fathers choose to become more involved or are coerced into taking more responsibility. Finally, if family therapists are to focus on issues concerned with increased paternal participation, more emphasis will need to be given to research that specifically addresses this issue, rather than arguments being based solely on findings from research into traditional families.

Gender Issues

Questions associated with father involvement and the relative power position of men and women are issues that family therapists will need to continue to grapple with, given the current social emphasis on changing sex roles. The recent flourishing feminist literature makes an important contribution in this regard.

However, when adopting a feminist perspective therapists should avoid the tendency to stereotype fathers and family relationships. The prevailing images of the oppressed housewife/mother and distant, authoritarian father certainly do not encourage a differentiated exploration of male socialization, personality, relationships, and support systems. There is also a danger of feminist treatment being one-sided and hazardous to families, as O'Leary, Curley, Rosenbaum, & Clarke (1985) point out using the example of assertion training for abused wives. Instead we recommend a much more differentiated and questioning approach to family treatment which involves at least the following four considerations:

1.   When a child presents a problem, gender issues need not be directly relevant for therapeutic practice. In many cases the family can be treated as a consumer who asks for *advice with simple child problems.* If the therapist provides exactly that, for example, in the form of a short behavioral parent training program, and the problems are resolved, the matter can rest there.

2.   *When child problems are woven into family patterns that are oppressive,* the issue becomes the assessment of the level at which the structure is oppressive. Is it the individual level, the structure of family responsibilities, sex-role socialization, or conditions impinging from outside the family (e.g., unemployment)? Therapists and families have to clarify to which factors they want to attribute the blame for the presenting problems, as these attributions will often direct the choice of therapeutic intervention.

It is not necessary to assume that all problems are associated with gender and power, as some feminist writings tend to argue. If therapists want to introduce power and gender issues when clients do not present their problems in these terms, a renegotiation of the therapeutic contract between therapist and client is necessary. If family members agree that these are important issues on which to work, the issues should be included in the goals of therapy. The therapist has to recognize, though, that these goals need to be achievable and that individual families cannot necessarily be burdened with the job of vicariously solving society's ills. Ethical questions also need to be considered here, especially with reference to the possibility that families might deteriorate (Gurman & Kniskern, 1978b). At the same time, this seems to be the very situation in which family therapists can make their greatest contribution not only in terms of individual gains but also in terms of improved communication and greater sharing within families.

3.   *The therapist's own gender and sex-role attitudes* may exert considerable influence and create or prevent certain expressions and interactions in the families seen. Therapists therefore will need to learn to understand these processes as they affect their assessment of families, their choice of

interventions and the ability of family members to make use of the guidance offered. (A male therapist, for instance, may have to work much harder to gain the trust of a twice divorced mother who is currently being abused by her third husband.)

4. As was noted in the introduction to this chapter, the approach to father involvement should be different when *domestic violence and sexual abuse* are involved. Cook and Frantz-Cook (1984), for example, have advocated the use of a seven-stage therapy process for wife-battering, with the first three stages involving separate sessions with same-sex therapists. The argument is also made for a change (at least initially) in the basic theory of intervention, from an emphasis on systemic-interactional and "therapeutic" considerations to a legal-protective framework. Hall and Ryan (1984) also stressed that it is necessary at all times to hold the man responsible for the violence he perpetuates and never accept the excuse that such violence is provoked. Indeed, the man's acceptance of responsibility for his violent behavior is seen as the *sine qua non* of successful therapy with him. There are other indications that this emphasis may facilitate change: Men who were ordered by a court to attend a program were more likely to say that they felt responsible for incest than those who attended voluntarily (Sagatun, 1982). Unfortunately there is a general lack of controlled research with abusive fathers, and Sagatun's 1982 one-short survey cannot inform us on the "attributional effects of therapy with incestuous families" either.

A consistent theme in recent writings has been the relationship between incest and domestic violence and the *lack of responsibility* taken by men for family work and nurturance (Herman, 1981; Russell, 1984; Schecter, 1983; Scutt, 1983). Scutt (1983) emphasized the need to focus on shared responsibility rather than "helping out," and argued that if a shift in responsibilities did occur, then:

Beating will not erupt out of disagreements over responsibilities for child care and child rearing; mother and father will recognize that caring for children is a responsibility and privilege for men and women equally, and the theory will become practice. (Scutt, 1983, p. 282)

Involving Fathers More in Therapy

It was argued earlier in the chapter that special attention needs to be given to the difficulties that fathers experience either in attending therapy sessions in the first place, in becoming active participants in the process of treatment, or in taking more responsibility for child management. The findings presented in this chapter indicate three areas which need to be addressed to facilitate father involvement: (1) work, (2) family, and (3) clinic. Issues relevant to the difficulties involved in the first two of these areas, work and family, are discussed more fully in Chapter 2, while the main emphasis here is on the therapist and clinic.

As a first step, the general orientation of clinics may need to be changed to adopt a *presumption of shared responsibility,* to presume from the very beginning that fathers will be involved and to take account of the difficulties associated with male socialization and societal expectations about male work and family roles. The question then would not be, "Should the father be involved?" but, "Why shouldn't the father be involved?" The adoption of such a presumption requires that a critical evaluation be made of clinical practice and employment policies. Some of the specific issues that need to be addressed are as follows:

1.   Conditions need to be established in the clinic that will allow families to be seen after hours (this, of course, is just as much an issue for employed mothers). This will necessarily involve attention being given to the employment conditions of therapists, for example, introducing flexible hours of employment. Employment conditions might also be looked at from the point of view of presuming that therapists themselves could have shared responsibility for children.

2.   Special attention should be directed at the issue of training therapists, with more emphasis being given to recent research findings on highly participant fathers and the difficulties couples experience when they attempt to change family responsibilities, to writings concerning the changing nature of relationships between males and females, and to feminist writings on the family. Therapists in training need to be introduced to a systemic-interactional approach to involving fathers in family therapy. They should avoid using personality-type labels like resistant, authoritarian, and so on and to not focus too narrowly on the nuclear family. Instead they need to gain a thorough understanding of the family-work-clinic triangle in which fathers have to make decisions about their involvement.

3.   Therapists need to develop *particular strategies and skills* which help to overcome initial hurdles and engage fathers in family therapy. Often, however, the therapist's first contact is with the mother. She needs to get a clear indication of whom the therapist expects to attend assessment and treatment sessions. This decision should not be left to any one member of the family. Reluctance on the mother's part to involve the father should be carefully explored. Any fears a mother expresses in this context need to be acknowledged and worked through. In some situations her reluctance can be relabeled as a protective maneuver, which allows the therapist to side with the mother. However, in order to avoid "triangulation" (Minuchin & Fishman, 1981) and maintain maneuverability, the

therapist must obtain permission in every case to speak to the husband and father directly.

We conclude this chapter by presenting a selective list of strategies to be used when contact is made with fathers. These draw on the ideas of L'Abate (1975), Stanton and Todd (1982), and Tonti (1982), and all have been successfully employed by one of us (B.H.) in clinical work with families.

a. Whenever possible, personally invite the father to the initial session and give a rationale for why he is needed there: "So that I can hear your point of view and get the full picture," thus demonstrating a need for information as well as impartiality.

b. Clarify the referral process and demonstrate openness: "How much do you know about the referral? This is what I know. . . ."

c. Invite the father to express his wishes: "What would you like to see happen about your child's problems?" Acknowledge that his goals for treatment may be different from those of other family members.

d. Introduce the idea that he has something to gain by coming to the clinic.

e. Utilize the presenting symptom as proof of the family's need for the father's participation.

f. Keep the focus on the presenting problem, and emphasize the father's responsibility to contribute. If necessary remind him that change may depend on his participation.

g. Treat the invitation of the father as a crisis-inducing event that shifts responsibility for the problem at least partially to the father. Therefore, be nonjudgmental and avoid confrontations and expressions of blame.

h. Reassure the father of his importance. If necessary, reframe a father's negative concept of his value and role in the family. "Maybe you are too good a provider" is an example of a possible response to a father's resigned comment, "I am not there anyway . . ."

i. Acknowledge that there are good reasons why he finds it hard to come in. Be accepting of a busy work schedule as a valuable contribution to the family. You many, however, elaborate a dilemma of priorities in a benevolent and concerned way, for example, around the themes of family happiness versus more material goods, without showing a personal preference.

j. If possible, give choices. You may, for example, offer several appointment options, thus demonstrating that you are trying to fit in with the father's timetable.

k. If at this stage you still have not gained his cooperation you might warn the father that changes could take place which he does not like.

l. You can further consider to exert pressure by contacting the referring court, school, or welfare agency.

m. You may ask the father to come for one assessment session only or to come as an observer.

n. As a minimal contract you can offer to keep the father informed about the treatment. Try to arrange a specific time when you are going to ring him and give him the option of joining sessions later without losing face.

REFERENCES

Achenbach, T., & Edelbrock, C. (1983). *Manual for the Child Behavior Checklist and Revised Child Behavior Profile.* Burlington, VT: University of Vermont Department of Psychiatry.

Adesso, V. J., & Lipson, J. W. (1981). Group training of parents as therapists for their children. *Behavior Therapy, 12,* 625–633.

Adubato, S. A., Adams, M. K., & Budd, K. S. (1981). Teaching a parent to train a spouse in child management techniques. *Journal of Applied Behavior Analysis, 14,* 193–205.

Alexander, J. F., Warburton, J., Waldron, H., & Mas, C. H. (1985). The misuse of functional family therapy: A non-sexist rejoinder. *Journal of Marital and Family Therapy, 11,* 139–144.

Aponte, H. J., & VanDeusen, J. M. (1981). Structural family therapy. In A. S. Gurman & D. P. Kniskern (Eds.), *Handbook of family therapy.* New York: Brunner/Mazel.

Avis, J. M. (1985). Through a different lens: A reply to Alexander, Waldron and Mas. *Journal of Marital and Family Therapy, 11,* 145–148.

Baekeland, F., & Lundwall, L. (1975). Dropping out of treatment: A critical review. *Psychological Bulletin, 82,* 738–783.

Barton, C., & Alexander, J. F. (1981). Functional family therapy. In A. S. Gurman & D. P. Kniskern (Eds.), *Handbook of family therapy.* New York: Brunner/Mazel.

Baumrind, D. (1980). New directions in socialization research. *American Psychologist, 35,* 639–652.

Beck, D. F. & Jones, M. A. (1973). *Progression family problems: A nationwide study of clients and counselors' views on family agency services.* New York: Family Service Association of America.

Becker, M. H., & Mainman, L. A. (1975). Social behavioural determinants of compliance with health and medical care recommendations. *Journal of Medical Care, 13,* 10–24.

Berg, B., & Rosenblum, N. (1977). Fathers in family therapy: A survey of family therapists. *Journal of Marriage and Family Counseling, 3*, 85–91.

Bergin, A. E. (1971). The evaluation of therapeutic outcomes. In A. E. Bergin & S. L. Garfield (Eds.), *Handbook of psychotherapy and behavior change.* New York: Wiley.

Berkowitz, B. P., & Graziano, A. M. (1972). Training parents as behavior therapists: A review. *Behavior Research and Therapy, 10,* 297–317.

Biller, H. B. (1981a). The father and sex role development. In M. E. Lamb (Ed.), *The role of the father in child development.* New York: Wiley.

Biller, H. B. (1981b). Father absence, divorce, and personality development. In M. E. Lamb (Ed.), *The role of the father in child development.* 2nd ed. New York: Wiley.

Blackwell, B. (1979). Treatment adherence: A contemporary overview. *Psychosomatics, 20*, 27–35.

Blechman, E. A., Budd, K. S., Christophersen, E. R., Szykula, S., Wahler, R., Embry, L. H., Kogan, K., O'Leary, K. D., & Riner, L. S. (1981). Engagement in behavioral family therapy: A multisite investigation. *Behavior Therapy, 12,* 461–472.

Blotcky, A. D., Tittler, B. I., Friedman, S., & DeCarlo, T. J. (1980). An exploration of change in parent-child relationships during the course of a family-oriented treatment program. *Family Therapy, 7,* 139–145.

Brickman, P., Rabinowitz, V. C., Karuza, J., Coates, D., Cohn, E., & Kidder L. (1982). Models of helping and coping. *American Psychologist, 37,* 368–384.

Budd, K. S., & O'Brien, T. P.(1982). Father involvement in behavioral parent training: An area in need of research. *Journal of the American Behavior Modification Association, 5*, 85–89.

Chodorow, N. (1978). *The reproduction of mothering: Psychoanalysis and the sociology of gender.* Berkeley: University of California Press.

Cook, D. R., & Frantz-Cook, A. (1984). A systemic treatment approach to wife battering. *Journal of Marital and Family Therapy, 10,* 83–93.

Cromwell, R., Fournier, D., & Kvebaek, D. (1980). *The Kvebaek family sculpture technique.* Jonesboro, TN: Pilgrimage.

Epstein, N. B., Baldwin, L. M., & Bishop, D. S. (1983). The McMaster family assessment device. *Journal of Marital and Family Therapy, 9*, 171–180.

Epstein, N. B., & Bishop, D. S. (1981). Problem-centered systems therapy of the family. In A. S. Gurman & D. P. Kniskern (Eds.), *Handbook of family therapy.* New York: Brunner/Mazel.

Firestone, P., Kelly, M. J. & Fike, S. (1980). Are fathers necessary in parent training groups? *Journal of Clinical Child Psychology, 9* , 44–47.

Firestone, P., & Witt, J. E. (1982). Characteristics of families completing and prematurely discontinuing a behavioral parent-training program. *Journal of Pediatric Psychology, 7*, 209–222.

Forehand, R., & Atkeson, B. M. (1977). Generality of treatment effects with parents as therapists: A review of assessment and implementation procedures. *Behavior Therapy, 8,* 575–593.

Freeman, D. S. (1977). The family systems practice model: Underlying assumptions. *Family Therapy, 4*, 57–65.

Gaines, T. J. R., & Stedman, J. M. (1981). Factors associated with dropping out of child and family treatment. *The American Journal of Family Therapy, 9*, 45–51.

Gordon, S. B., & Davidson, N. (1981). Behavioral parent training. In A. S. Gurman & D. P. Kniskern (Eds.), *Handbook of family therapy.* New York: Brunner/ Mazel.

Graziano, A. M. (1977). Parents as behavior therapists. In M. Hersen, R. M. Eisler, P. M. Miller (Eds.), *Progress in behavior modification.* New York: Academic Press.

Green, R. G., & Kolevzon, M. S. (1982). Three approaches to family therapy: A study of convergence and divergence. *Journal of Marital and Family Therapy, 8*, 39–50.

Gurman, A. S., & Kniskern, D. P. (1978a). Research on marital and family therapy: Progress, perspective, and prospect. In S. L. Garfield & A. E. Bergin (Eds.), *Handbook of psychotherapy and behavior change,* 2nd ed. New York: Wiley.

Gurman, A. S., & Kniskern, D. P. (1978b). Deterioration in marital and family therapy: Empirical, clinical, and conceptual issues. *Family Process, 17*, 3–20.

Gurman, A. S., & Kniskern, D. P. (1981). Family therapy outcome research: Knowns and unknowns. In A. S. Gurman & D. P. Kniskern (Eds.), *Handbook of family therapy.* New York: Brunner/Mazel.

Haley, J. (1976). *Problem solving therapy.* San Francisco: Jossey-Bass.

Haley, J. (1980). *Leaving home: The therapy of disturbed young people.* New York: McGraw-Hill.

Hall, R., & Ryan, L. (1984). Therapy with men who are violent to their spouses. *The Australian and New Zealand Journal of Family Therapy, 5*, 281–282.

Hare-Mustin, R. T. (1978). A feminist approach to family therapy. *Family Process, 17*, 181–194.

Hare-Mustin, R. T. (1983). Psychology: A feminist perspective on family therapy. In B. Haber (Ed.), *The women's annual: 1982–83.* Boston: Hall.

Herman, J. (1981). *Father-daughter incest.* Cambridge MA: Harvard University Press.

Hetherington, E. M., Cox, M., & Cox, R. (1978). The aftermath of divorce. In J. H. Stevens & M. Matthews (Eds.), *Mother/child father/child relationships.* Washington DC: National Association for the Education of Young Children.

Hetherington, E. M., & Martin, B. (1979). Family interaction. In C. Quay & J. S. Werry (Eds.), *Psychopathological disorders of childhood.* New York: Wiley.

Heubeck, B. (1983a) *Dropping out of family therapy.* Paper presented at Macquarie University, North Ryde, Australia.

Heubeck, B., (1983b). *Fathers' participation in family therapy: A survey of 25 Sydney therapists.* Unpublished data.

Jacob, T. (1975). Family interaction in disturbed and normal families: A methodological and substantive review. *Psychological Bulletin, 82*, 33–65.

James, K., & McIntyre, D. (1983). The reproduction of families: The social role of family therapy. *Journal of Marital and Family Therapy, 9,* 119–129.

Johnson, C. A., & Katz, C. (1973). Using parents as change agents for their children: A review. *Journal of Child Psychology and Psychiatry, 14,* 131–200.

Kelly, M. L., Embry, L. H., & Baer, D. M. (1979). Skills for child management and family support, training parents for maintenance. *Behavior Modification, 3*, 373–396.

Kiesler, D. J. (1966). Some myths of psychotherapy research and the search for a paradigm. *Psychological Bulletin, 65,* 110–136.

Kotelchuck, M. (1976). The infant's relationship to the father: Experimental evidence. In M. E. Lamb (Ed.), *The role of the father in child development.* New York: Wiley.

Kressel, K., & Slipp, S. (1975). Perceptions of marriage related to engagement in conjoint therapy. *Journal of Marriage and Family Counseling, 1,* 367–377.

La Barbera, J. D., & Lewis, S. (1980). Fathers who undermine children's treatment: A challenge for the clinician. *Journal of Clinical Child Psychology, 9,* 204–206.

L'Abate, L. (1975). Pathogenic role rigidity in fathers: Some observations. *Journal of Marriage and Family Counseling,* 69–79.

Lamb, M. E. (1976). Interactions between 8-month-old children and their fathers and mothers. In M. E. Lamb (Ed.), *The role of the father in child development.* New York: Wiley.

Le Fave, M. K. (1980). Correlates of engagement in family therapy. *Journal of Marital and Family Therapy, 6,* 75–81.

Libow, J. A., Raskin, P. A., & Caust, B. L. (1982). Feminist and family systems therapy: Are they irreconcilable? *The American Journal of Family Therapy, 10,* 3–12.

Love, L. R., Kaswan, J., & Bugental, D. E. (1972). Differential effectiveness of three clinical interventions for different socioeconomic groupings. *Journal of Consulting and Clinical Psychology, 39*, 347–360.

Lynn, D. B. (1974). *The father: His role in child development.* Monterey, CA: Brooks/Cole.

Madanes, C. (1981). *Strategic family therapy.* San Francisco: Jossey-Bass.

Martin, B. (1977). Brief family intervention: Effectiveness and the importance of including the father. *Journal of Consulting and Clinical Psychology, 45*, 1002–1010.

Minuchin, S. (1974). *Families and family therapy.* Cambridge, MA: Harvard University Press.

Minuchin, S., & Fishman, C. (1981). *Family therapy techniques.* Cambridge, MA: Harvard University Press.

O'Dell, S. (1974). Training parents in behavior modification: A review. *Psychological Bulletin, 81,* 418–433.

Oltmanns, T. F., Broderick, J. E., & O'Leary, K. D. (1977). Marital adjustment and the efficacy of behavior therapy with children. *Journal of Consulting and Clinical Psychology, 45*, 724–729.

O'Leary, K. D., Curley, A., Rosenbaum, A., & Clarke, C. (1985). Assertion training for abused wives: A potentially hazardous treatment. *Journal of Marital and Family Therapy, 11,* 319–322.

O'Neil, J. M. (1980). Male sex role conflicts, sexism, and masculinity: Psychological implications for men, women, and the counseling psychologist. *The Counseling Psychologist, 9,* 61–80.

Parke, R. D., & Sawin, D. (1976). The father's role in infancy: A re-evaluation. *The Family Coordinator, 25*, 365–371.

Patterson, G. R. (1976). The aggressive child: Victim and architect of a coercive system. In L. A. Hamerlynck, L. C. Handy, & E. J. Mash (Eds.), *Behaviour modification and families: Theory and research* (Vol. 1). New York: Brunner/ Mazel.

Patterson, G. R. (1980). Mothers: The unacknowledged victims. *Monograph of the Society for Research in Child Development, 45,* 1–64.

Patterson, G. (1982). *A social learning approach (Vol. 3): Coercive family process.* Eugene, OR: Castalia.

Patterson, G. R., & Fleischman, M. J. (1979). Maintenance of treatment effects: Some considerations concerning family systems and follow-up data. *Behavior Therapy, 10,* 168–185.

Patterson, G. R., & Reid, J. B. (1973). Intervention for families of aggressive boys: A replication study. *Behaviour Research and Therapy, 11,* 383–394.

Postner, R. S., Guttman, H. A., Sigal, J. J., Epstein, N. B., & Rakoff, V. M. (1971). Process and outcome in conjoint family therapy. *Family Process, 10*, 451–473.

Radin, N. (1981). The role of the father in cognitive, academic, and intellectual development. In M. E. Lamb (Ed.), *The role of the father in child development.* New York: Wiley.

Radin, N., & Russell, G. (1983). Increased father participation and child development outcomes. In M. E. Lamb & A. Sagi (Eds.), *Fatherhood and family policy.* Hillsdale, NJ: Erlbaum.

Reiter, G. F., & Kilmann, P. R. (1975). Mothers as family change agents. *Journal of Counseling Psychology, 22*, 61–65.

Rice, D. G. (1978). The male spouse in marital and family therapy. *The Counseling Psychologist, 7*, 64–67.

Russell, C. S., Atilano, R. B., Anderson, S. A., Jurich, A. P., & Bergen, L. P. (1984). Intervention strategies: Predicting family therapy outcome. *Journal of Marital and Family Therapy, 10,* 241–251.

Russell, D. E. H. (1984). The prevalence and seriousness of incestuous abuse; Stepfathers vs. biological fathers. *Child Abuse and Neglect, 8,* 15–22.

Sagatun, I. J. (1982). Attributional effects of therapy with incestuous families. *Journal of Marital and Family Therapy, 8,* 99–104.

Sager, C. J., Masters, Y. J., Ronall, R. E., & Normand, W. C. (1967). Selection and engagement of patients in family therapy. *American Journal of Orthopsychiatry, 37,* 715–723.

Schecter, S. (1983). *Women and male violence.* New York: South End Press.

Scutt, J. (1983). *Even in the best of homes.* Melbourne: Penguin.

Shapiro, R. J. (1974). Therapist attitudes and premature termination in family and individual therapy. *The Journal of Nervous and Mental Diseases, 159,* 101–107.

Shapiro, R. J., & Budman, S. H. (1973). Defection, termination, and continuation in family and individual therapy. *Family Process, 12,* 55–67.

Slipp, S., Ellis, S., & Kressel, K. (1974). Factors associated with engagement in family therapy. *Family Process, 13,* 413–427.

Stanton, M. D. (1981). Strategic approaches to family therapy. In A. S. Gurman & D. P. Kniskern (Eds.), *Handbook of family therapy.* New York: Brunner/Mazel.

Stanton, M. D., Steier, F., & Todd, T. C. (1982). Paying families for attending sessions: Counteracting the dropout problem. *Journal of Marital and Family Therapy, 8,* 371–373.

Stanton, M., Todd, T. C., et al. (1982). *The family therapy of drug abuse and addiction.* New York: Guilford.

Stanton, M. D., Todd, T., Steier, F., Van Deusen, J., Marder, L., Rosoff, R., Seaman, S., & Skibinski, E. (1979). *Family characteristics and family therapy of heroin addicts: Final report, 1974–1978.* Philadelphia: Philadelphia Child Guidance Clinic.

Stedman, J. M., Gaines, T., & Costello, R. (1983). Prediction of outcome in family-oriented therapy from family characteristics. *Family Therapy, 10,* 211–218.

Szapocznik, J., Kurtines, W. M., Foote, F. H., Perez-Vidal, A., & Hervis, O. (1983). Conjoint versus one-person family therapy: Some evidence for the effectiveness of conducting family therapy through one person. *Journal of Consulting and Clinical Psychology, 51,* 889–899.

Taggart, M. (1985). The feminist critique in epistemological perspective: Questions of context in family therapy. *Journal of Marital and Family Therapy, 11,* 113–126.

Taplin, P. S., & Reid, J. B. (1977). Changes in parent consequences as a function of family intervention. *Journal of Consulting and Clinical Psychology, 45,* 973–981.

Tonti, M. (1982). Two steps in the integration of the husband-father in dysfunctional families. *Social Casework, 12,* 176–179.

Vaillant, G. E. (1972). Why men seek psychotherapy: I: Results of a survey of college graduates. *American Journal of Psychiatry, 129,* 645–651.

Van der Veen, F., (1965). The parent's concept of the family unit and child adjustment. *Journal of Counseling Psychology, 12,* 196–200.

Wahler, R. G. (1980). The insular mother: Her problems in parent-child treatment. *Journal of Applied Behavior Analysis, 13*(2), 207–219.

Warburton, J., Alexander, J. F., Barton, C. (1980). Sex of client and sex of therapist: Variables in a family process study. Paper presented at the Annual Convention of the American Psychological Association, Montreal.

Watson, J. M. (1985) Parental explanations of emotional disturbance and their relationship to the outcome of therapy. Unpublished doctoral dissertation, Macquarie University, Sydney, Australia.

Weiss, R. L., Hops, H., & Patterson, G. R. (1973). A framework for conceptualising marital conflict, a technology for altering it, some data for evaluating it. In L. A. Hamerlynck, L. C. Handy & E. J. Mash (Eds.), *Behavior change: Methodology, concepts and practice.* Champaign, IL: Research Press.

Wells, R. A., & Dezen, A. E. (1978). The results of family therapy revisited: The nonbehavioral methods. *Family Process, 17,* 251–274.

Westley, W. A., & Epstein, N. B. (1969). *The silent majority.* San Francisco: Jossey-Bass.

Zelazo, P. R., Kotelchuck, M., Barber, L., & David, J. (1977). Fathers and sons: An experimental facilitation of attachment behaviors. Paper presented to Society for Research in Child Development, New Orleans.

CHAPTER 8

Fathers of Children with Mental Handicaps

DONALD J. MEYER
University of Washington

My son, Jay, is 16 and moderately mentally retarded. I think the most important question is *not*, "What *is* mental retardation?" It is "What does mental retardation *mean*? What does it do to us?"

Turnbull, Brotherson, Summers, and Turnbull, in press

For fathers, attempting to interpret the meaning of a child's disability can be a lonely exercise. Relatively little is known about the experiences of fathers of children with handicaps, compared with what is known about mothers of disabled children or what has been learned about fathers of nonhandicapped children in recent years. Few programs exist to help fathers explore what it means to be the parent of a disabled child, even though there is growing recognition among parents (Gallagher, Cross, & Scharfman, 1981) and among professionals serving handicapped children and their families (Cummings, 1976; Meyer, Vadasy, Fewell, & Schell, 1982) that fathers wish increased involvement with their disabled children and have unique concerns that have been largely unaddressed by practitioners.

This chapter reviews the research literature on the impact of a child's disability on the father and the implications this has for those working with families. Following this is an overview of the handful of programs that specifically focus on the father of the child with special needs.

Portions of this chapter are based on material in Meyer, D. J., Fathers of Children With Handicaps: Developmental Trends in Fathers' Experiences Over the Family Life Cycle. In R. R. Fewell and P. F. Vadasy (Eds.), *Families of Handicapped Children: Needs and Supports Across the Lifespan.* Austin, TX: Pro-Ed (1986).

Amid the explosion of research on fathers in the last 10 years, fathers of children with special needs have been relatively ignored. The traditional focus of research on parents of children with special needs has been the mother. In a review of 24 studies of parents' adjustment to a child's disability, Blacker (1984) found that fathers were rarely assessed. This failure to include fathers in research has led to overreliance on maternal information and a subsequent assumption that what is valid for mothers is also valid for fathers (Wolfensberger, 1967). What Parke and Sawin (1977) suggested about research with families appears to apply to research with exceptional families: It is time to stop talking of dyads (mother/child) and begin talking in terms of triads.

Studies that are available on fathers are often subject to several limitations. The first is that most focus on a father's reaction to the child's diagnosis and on the father's initial adaptation. Far fewer studies examine the effects of the disability on the father as the child grows into adulthood, although Wikler (1981) and Olshansky (1962) reported that parents experience continued, though changing, stresses throughout their child's life.

Second, with rare exceptions (such as Delaney, 1979; Stoneman, Brody, & Abbott, 1983), there has been a dearth of observational or experimental studies of fathers interacting with their handicapped child (Lamb 1983; McConachie 1982). Hetherington made an observation about research on fathers that appears especially true when applied to fathers of handicapped children: "A major reason fathers were ignored (by psychologists) was that fathers were inaccessible. To observe fathers you have to work at night and on weekends, and not many researchers like to do that" (Collins 1979, p. 49). Findings on fathers are more often based on clinical impressions, ratings of parent attitudes, or even interviews with mothers about fathers' involvement and experiences.

Finally, the vast majority of studies focus on parents' reactions to organically caused mental retardation in a child, as opposed to other "special needs" such as chronic illness, physical disability, sensory impairment, or even mild retardation due to sociocultural factors. Necessarily, this chapter focuses primarily on fathers of children who are mentally retarded.

Still, the reader is cautioned in making inferences from the research presented: Even within the disability of mental retardation there are variables that will result in a wide range of experiences for fathers. For instance, parents of children with autism (children who are almost always mentally retarded as well) have reported more overall stress than parents of children with Down syndrome (Holroyd & McArthur, 1976). Intervening variables such as the child's age, sex, behavioral characteristics, level of retardation, and physical incapacitation, as well as mediating factors such as the father's support and belief systems, allow for a wide range of experiences for fathers of children with special needs. Both intervening variables and mediating factors are discussed in context throughout this chapter.

THE IMPACT OF DISABILITY ON THE FATHER

The Initial Diagnosis

All day yesterday there were tears beneath my eyes, waiting to stream through the facade of workaday reality. On the train into the city I wanted to cry. But of course I couldn't. And I didn't know what good crying would do. Finally everything surfaced when I got home. Foumi and I got into a senseless argument as to whether hereditary factors were the cause of Noah's possible—indeed very likely—retardation or autism. (Greenfeld, 1972, p. 52)

Adapting to the role of a father can be a profound and sometimes unsettling experience. Numerous researchers have found that fathers—as well as mothers—often experience depression and mild stress following the birth of a baby. These feelings may result from fatigue, economic worries, changes in routine, and role adjustments. For most men, becoming a father is a happy, though occasionally difficult, transition.

Throughout the mother's pregnancy, the expectant father has addressed what Duvall (1962) has referred to as his "developmental tasks": He has planned for the child's arrival, attempted to learn what it means to be a father, and supported his wife through the pregnancy and childbirth.

Given the anticipation a father experiences prior to a child's birth and the father's readiness to attach to his child (Greenberg & Morris, 1974; Parke, 1981), the impact of the diagnosis of a disability on the father is not difficult to imagine. Because many fathers today play a larger role in their child's life than did fathers of previous generations, there is reason to suspect that fathers today will experience their child's handicap more immediately.

The early literature on parental reactions and adaptation to the disability suggested that parents, when confronted by the "novelty shock" of the child's diagnosis, proceed through predictable stages leading to a final resolution (American Medical Association, 1964; Menolascino, 1977). In a review of 24 articles and books attempting to describe a family's reaction to a child's handicap, Blacher (1984) noted that most authors observed similar stages. The stages were, for the most part, not empirically derived but were based on clinical observations of small samples and occasionally on interviews of mothers. (Fathers, according to Blacher, were rarely assessed.) Typical of the stages described by these authors are disintegration, characterized by shock, denial, and emotional disorganization; adjustment, when parents partly accept and partly deny the existence of the handicap, and may look for someone or something to blame for the child's defects; and reintegration, or mature adaptation, when parents begin to function more effectively and realistically. Following reintegration parents apparently are assumed to settle into a life that, while not entirely normal, is not unduly stressful.

An emerging view of parental adaptation to a child's disability proposes that while parents regain equilibrium following the initial shock of the diagnosis, their adjustment may be temporary. Parents, this view holds, are subject to chronic, stressful reminders of the tragedy of the child's disability throughout the child's life (Olshansky, 1962; Wikler, 1981).

Wikler (1981) contended that these stressful crises occur "when a discrepancy emerges between what parents expect of a child's development and of parenting as opposed to what actually takes place when rearing a mentally retarded child" (pp. 283–284). Some of these crises, she noted, are related to the characteristic hardships of mental retardation, such as stigmatized social interactions and prolonged burden of care. Others are typical parental responses to retardation, such as confusion concerning child care, lack of appropriate information, and periodic grieving. Wikler's concept of recurring crises and stress, especially as they pertain to fathers, are further discussed in context in the remainder of this chapter.

A family crisis has been defined as an event that creates unusual difficulties for the family (Kirkpatrick, 1955). An event that is permanent and involuntary (such as a child's handicap) creates a greater crisis (Price-Bonham & Addison, 1978) than an event that is discrete or short term. According to Wikler (1981), the impact of the child's diagnosis will be the most disturbing crisis parents will face during the handicapped child's life. However, as we shall see, it will not be the last crisis.

When parents receive their child's diagnosis, their dreams for their fantasized ideal child are abruptly crushed. Insensitivity by professionals at the time of diagnosis may exacerbate parental grief. Some of the fathers of children with Down syndrome with whom Erickson (1974) met reported difficulty obtaining information from the doctors, and others only learned about the disability after their wife had been informed. Roos (1978), a clinical psychologist as well as a father of a daughter with mental retardation, complained about an attitude of "professional hopelessness" toward mental retardation from the medical community. Besides generating self-fulfilling prophecies, this attitude can influence parents to "either develop similar expectations or resent those who adopt such a negative approach toward their child" (Roos 1978, p. 15).

Following the diagnosis, parents may grieve the loss of the hoped for child. During this time parents may, in their anger and frustration, seek to hold someone—themselves, each other, the doctors, or God—responsible for their child's handicap. When the evidence is slow to emerge, as is not the case with Down syndrome, parents may alternately accept and deny the existence of the handicap.

Husbands and wives may adapt in different styles and at different paces to their child's handicap. A father of a boy with Down syndrome wrote about his wife's reaction to the diagnosis:

My God, I thought, Polly where is your head? . . . I'd known Polly for two years now and I'd never seen her duck an issue. The only thing she couldn't tolerate was not hearing the truth. But here she was . . . telling us that the doctors were flat out wrong, that nothing was the matter with Wayne. . . . At the time of diagnosis, we all nodded our agreement, not because it was pleasant, but because it seemed to square with the facts. But not Polly! (MacDonald & Oden, 1978, p. 15)

These differences in adaptation can place added stress on the marriage (Price-Bonham & Addison, 1978). Opportunities to support one another effectively may be diminished if, for instance, one parent is grieving and the other is worried about the burden of care presented by the child's special needs (Wikler, 1981).

The impact that the child's handicap has on the father has been investigated by several authors and researchers. Cummings (1976) noted that because fathers currently play a larger role with their children, "there is increasing likelihood of fathers experiencing the handicaps more immediately and sentiently than did fathers only two generations ago" (p. 247). His survey of fathers with mentally retarded children revealed that fathers were often depressed and preoccupied with their child's special needs; many felt inferior as fathers, and many were dissatisfied with their children and spouse.

Fathers have also been found to perceive their handicapped child as a threat to their self-concept. Fathers who view their handicapped child as an extension of their egos are apt to become more isolated, to reduce or withdraw from social interactions (Call, 1958; Illingworth, 1967).

At this stage, one intervening variable that may influence the effect of the handicap on the father is the child's sex. Various authors (Farber, Jenné, & Toigo, 1960; Tallman, 1965) have reported that a mentally retarded son appears to have a greater initial emotional impact than does a daughter. Similarly, Grossman (1972) reported that fathers are more accepting of mentally retarded daughters than they are of sons with this handicap.

The difficulties fathers experience may have second-order effects on other family members. When a father reacts to the disability by decreasing his involvement, he increases the mother's burden, exacerbating the adverse effects the disability will have on the family (Lamb, 1983). Several authors have suggested that the father's attitude about the handicap may set the pattern for the attitudes of other family members (Peck & Stephens, 1960; Price-Bonham & Addison, 1978). Farber's (1962) finding that parents of a retarded boy show a lower degree of marital integration than do parents of a retarded girl supports this notion. The greater impact on the father of a retarded son will affect the couple's marital integration.

Disproportionately high desertion rates by fathers of handicapped children have been reported (Reed & Reed, 1965), as have high divorce rates in families with handicapped children. However, some researchers (Schufeit & Wurster, 1976) have claimed that, when matched for social class, the divorce rate for families with mentally retarded children does *not* differ significantly from the rate for families with nonhandicapped children. Turnbull and colleagues (in press) have attempted to resolve the mixed research results by suggesting that for many marriages, the impact of a child's handicap can be the "straw that breaks the camel's back."

Conversely, many families claim that a child's handicap has strengthened their marriage and brought the family closer together. Gath's (1977) study showed that while negative measures were higher for the family of a child with Down syndrome, this group also had higher positive measures when compared with families with nonhandicapped children. Almost half of the parents of the handicapped children felt that their marriage was strengthened after the birth of the handicapped child.

Other variables that may influence the impact of the diagnosis on the father are parental characteristics and access to resources. Farber (1960), Grossman (1972), Moore and coworkers (1982), and Rosenberg (1977) found that class, education, and income are inversely related to stress in parents of children with special needs.

Interpersonal supportive resources available to fathers of children with special needs have been examined by Gallagher, Cross, and Scharfman (1981). Their data suggest that a major source of strength is the quality of the husband-wife relationship. Fathers reported that support from their wife and friends was very important, while support from neighbors was less important.

Preschool Years

Even though I had been exposed to all this information (about Down syndrome), none of it prepared us for living with Moose. . . . No one told us that we would wash more diapers for Moose than for any of the other children or that he'd need them for a year and a half longer. No one told us we'd have to learn more patience when talking to Moose because it took him longer to understand verbalizations. (MacDonald & Oden, 1978, p. 46)

Developmental milestones that nonhandicapped preschoolers achieve with relative ease may require an extraordinary investment of time and energy from the handicapped child's teachers and parents. Normally trying periods, such as the so-called "terrible twos" may extend for several years. Consequently, the child's delayed development will have an impact on the parents during the preschool years. Because the intense nurturing that parents normally provide during a child's infancy and preschool years must be sustained over a longer period for a developmentally disabled child, the need for one parent—usually the mother—to be home and available is also extended (Wikler 1981).

It is also during the preschool years that the disability will often become more obvious. When the child does not attain normal developmental milestones, parents are at risk for increased stress. Two of the five predictable crises that result from a discrepancy between parents' expectations and the child's development (Wikler, 1981) occur during the preschool years, and these are when the child should have been walking (12 to 15 months of age) and talking (24 to 30 months). These poignant reminders of their child's disability may reawaken the parents' grief for the loss of their idealized normal child.

Further, Wikler contended that as the disability becomes more apparent, parents experience stressful stigmatized social interactions. Fathers, more so than mothers, are affected by the physical aspects of a child's disability. Additionally, because fathers are more sensitive than mothers to the child's effect on the family's social and community image, the behavioral attributes of the child's disability can add to the father's stress. (Price-Bonham & Addison, 1978).

During these early years the child's disability can deeply change the parents' relationship. A mother may expend much time attending to the child's needs, and the father may "view the retarded child as interfering with his previously companionate relationship with his wife" (Farber & Ryckman, 1965, p. 1). Couples may spend years without socializing outside of the home (Illingworth, 1967). Many may give up activities they previously enjoyed together, according to Lonsdale (1978), who also found that both fathers (41.7 percent) and mothers (50 percent) alter their social life.

The disability also influences the child's relationship with his or her parents. In one of the few observational studies of handicapped children and their fathers, Stoneman, Brody, and Abbott (1983) found that fathers and mothers of 16 children with Down syndrome aged 4 to 7 years structured their interactions with their children by assuming dominant manager, teacher, and helper roles during play situations more often than did parents of nonhandicapped children. Further, mothers of children with Down syndrome (who were observed to be less contingently responsive to both parents compared with their nonhandicapped peers) assumed the teacher role more than twice as frequently as fathers. When observed in a triadic family grouping, however, both groups of children more often failed to respond to the teaching attempts of their mother than those of their father, possibly, the authors suggested, because children regarded the father in the teaching role as more novel and hence more interesting than the mother. A final finding was that, when observed in a triadic grouping, fathers of both groups of children assumed the manager role less than mothers and spent more time in solitary activity during the triadic family grouping, suggesting that the parental role differences that exist for nonhandicapped children exist also for parents of children with Down syndrome.

Similarly, a study by Mitchell (1979) involving a group of eight children and their families suggested that fathers of children with Down syndrome were very similar to fathers of nonhandicapped children in their interactions with their child. Shannon's (1978) observations of 29 father-child dyads revealed that fathers of handicapped preschoolers did not interact or participate in nurturing or caregiving activities more or less often than did fathers of nonhandicapped preschoolers. These data, however, contrast with a study by Gallagher, Cross, and Scharfman (1981) of fathers of moderately to severely handicapped children. While their research re-family roles resembling those of effective families of nonhandicapped children, the authors concluded that "the traditional father roles of physical playmate and model for the male child are largely diminished or not present at all with the moderate to severely handicapped child" (p. 13).

Several authors have noted that fathers express more concern than mothers over future problems, such as economic and social dependence and legal and educational matters (Hersh, 1970; Love, 1973; Meyer, et al., 1982). Liversidge and Grana (1973) reported that at a meeting, fathers of deaf preschoolers wondered aloud "Will she be happy?," "Will he have normal children of his own?" and "Will he be able to earn a living?"

Fathers' orientation toward the child's future is a function of traditional parental roles that may be intensified when a handicapped child is present. Fathers, according to Gumz and Gubrium (1972), have a tendency to perceive their mentally retarded children in terms of an instrumental crisis, meaning they are especially concerned about the cost of providing for the child. They question whether the child will be successful, whether the child will be self-supporting in the future. Conversely, mothers have a tendency to experience the diagnosis of retardation as an expressive crisis, that is, mothers are especially concerned with the emotional strain of caring for the retarded child. They want the child to get along well with others and be happy, regardless of academic achievement or job success.

While traditional parental roles and concerns appear to be somewhat more defined in families with handicapped children, they are by no means exclusive. Gumz and Gubrium (1972) found that a high percentage of mothers were concerned about the high cost of raising a retarded child, and fathers were also concerned with the day-to-day concerns of raising a child with special needs.

School Years

When Wayne was born, I had wondered what we'd done to deserve the tragedy of his handicap. That feeling faded as we began to think of Wayne as a person and not a diagnosis. As Wayne grew, I began to wonder what he had done wrong to deserve *me*. Sometimes I couldn't believe my own incompetence at fathering. (MacDonald & Oden, 1978, p. 33)

Throughout a child's school years, families encourage the child's independence, growth, and acquisition of basic academic, physical, and social skills. A handicap deeply affects what is expected of and obtained by a child at this stage.

Parents are at risk for stress at the very beginning of a child's school years. Wikler (1981) contended that the beginning of public school—when the handicapped child enters a special education program instead of kindergarten or first grade—is a stressful period for the parents. They are reminded of the child's delay in a new way and are stigmatized by the child's placement, which labels the family as different. Even parents whose child is "mainstreamed" with nonhandicapped children may experience stress when they are reminded frequently of the discrepancy between their child and the nonhandicapped peers (Gallagher, Beckman, & Cross, 1983). According to a review by Turnbull and Blacher-Dixon (1980), other aspects of mainstreaming that can be stressful are sharing the handicapped child's stigma, feeling a lack of common interests with other parents, worrying about their child's social adjustments, and providing the support services necessary for their child in the nonhandicapped school setting.

As the discrepancy grows between the child's size and his or her developmental capabilities, stressful public encounters increase for the parents (Wikler, 1981). Chronic problems, such as a lack of eating or ambulatory skills, become more burdensome as the child grows older and larger.

Cummings (1976) studied 60 fathers of school-age children with mental retardation. Using four self-administered tests, Cummings sought to assess the fathers' prevailing mood (especially as it was influenced by the mentally retarded child); their self-esteem (both generally and in terms of their evaluation of their worth as a father); their interpersonal satisfactions with family workers and others; and their attitudes toward child rearing.

When compared with an equal number of fathers of nonhandicapped children, Cummings found that fathers of mentally retarded children showed significant differences on three of the four variables. On the variable of prevailing mood, fathers of mentally retarded children were depressed and preoccupied with their child's special needs. The interpersonal satisfaction variables revealed a significant decrease in the fathers' enjoyment of the index child and in their evaluation of their wife and other children. In self-esteem variables, these fathers scored lower on expressed self-acceptance and sense of paternal competence. On the basis of his findings, Cummings suggested that these fathers may feel relatively inferior in their role as father and also in their male role.

When he examined age differences, Cummings found that fathers of older handicapped children (9 to 13 years) showed slightly lower psychological stress levels than did fathers of younger (4 to 8 years) handicapped children. Older fathers also had slightly lower ratings on depression and higher ratings on both enjoyment of child and evaluation of wife.

These data, however, are inconsistent with studies reviewed by Gallagher, Cross, and Scharfman (1981), which suggest that stress increases with the child's increasing age, owing to the increasing difficulty of managing the handicapped child and the visibility of the handicap.

Adolescence

We consider ourselves lucky that Moose has lived into adolescence and is still healthy. But beyond that, we really haven't known what to expect. A lot of horrors we had anticipated haven't occurred. But what should we look forward to? Will he learn to cook? Will he ever have a hobby? What sorts of skills will he be able to develop? Will he have lasting friends? (MacDonald & Oden, 1978, p. 130)

The teen years are a period usually characterized by adolescents' attempts to establish their own identity and differentiate themselves from their parents. For the adolescent who is handicapped, teenage experiences are disturbingly different from those of nonhandicapped peers, causing special concern for parents. Cognitive handicaps may limit the child's appreciation of pubertal changes. Developmental delay may become increasingly apparent as the child's body becomes that of an adult while his or her abilities remain those of a much younger child, which increases the difficulty of peers in accepting the handicap.

Although handicapped adolescents may, like their nonhandicapped peers, begin to prepare for a future occupation, prospects for economic independence are usually dim. A mentally retarded son's lack of vocational opportunity can be a serious worry for the father. Not only do fathers fear the long-term financial support that might be necessary (Hersh, 1970), but they may feel deprived of the satisfactions of the son's achievements. The handicapped adolescent's emerging sexuality may be especially troubling when he or she lacks the cognitive skills to be a capable, nurturing parent.

The onset of puberty, the beginning of menstruation for girls, and concern over the child's sexuality all cause stress for parents of handicapped adolescents (Wikler, 1981). This stress is stimulated by the discrepancy between the adolescent's physical appearance and his or her mental and social abilities. Compounding this stress are parents' fears that their child will be sexually exploited.

Although this stage poses troubling problems for handicapped teenagers and their families, the picture is not totally bleak. Parents of handicapped children who successfully weather these crises often experience great personal growth. Rudd Turnbull, a lawyer specializing in disability law and the father of a moderately retarded teenage son, demonstrates a father's potential for personal growth in this period:

Jay forces me to deal with paradoxes: about how the exceptional in life (mental retardation) becomes unexceptional by reason of its familiarity, about how a person's disability (Jay's) contributes to another's ability (mine) by stimulating growth, and about how the mysteries of life (why me?) are answered, bit by bit, ever so certainly. (Turnbull, et al. in press)

Adulthood

After Moose finished school, we had to do a lot of thinking about his development as an adult. Moose had learned to fix himself simple meals (and do) his own laundry. . . . But we had to wonder how far his development as an independent adult would go. What were his limits? What could we realistically expect of him and where should we draw the line? . . . Is it reasonable to expect him to be able to take work in a "sheltered" workshop? How realistic is it to consider that he might be able to work at a real job? . . . Would he understand things like rent payments? Moose was used to having a large family around. Wouldn't he be lonely? (MacDonald & Oden, 1978, pp. 187, 188, 196)

Following a child's teen years, the family typically enters a stage wherein it functions as a "launching center" for the child (Duvall, 1962).

This stage usually begins when a family's first child leaves home as a young adult and ends when the last child leaves home, leaving the parents with an "empty nest."

For families with a handicapped child, the launching stage may occur either earlier or much later than usual. It may take place much earlier than usual if the family institutionalizes the handicapped child, or it may extend for the life of the child if the child continues to live with the parents as an adult.

Fathers of children with handicaps may anticipate this stage for years before it actually occurs. Vadasy, Fewell, Meyer, and Schell, (1984) found that the father of a very young handicapped child is already concerned about the child's future well-being as an adult. Whereas the father of a nonhandicapped child can look forward to a time when the child is independent and child-related expenses are reduced, the father of a handicapped child may be required to continue emotional and financial support after the child becomes an adult (Price-Bonham & Addison, 1978). This support throughout the child's adulthood will crystallize the relationship at a parent-child status (Birenbaum, 1971), rather than the relationship developing into a more mature form.

Wikler (1981) noted that as the handicapped child approaches adulthood, parents can face three significant crises: the child's twenty-first birthday; the question of placement of the child outside the home; and the question of guardianship and care of the handicapped adult child.

The handicapped young adult's twenty-first birthday can be an especially troubling milestone for families. For the families Wikler studied, this birthday was the second most stressful crisis for parents, the first being the initial diagnosis. The twenty-first birthday can be a double crisis: While it normally symbolizes a child's independence, it reminds parents of a child with special needs of the many barriers to the child's independence. Further, this birthday signals a transitional crisis: Schools cease to provide services after this year, and adult services are often inadequate. Parents of older children with mental retardation often feel more isolated, less supported, and more in need of services than parents of young children who are retarded (Suelzle & Keenan, 1981). Even when services are available, parents need to resume many of the responsibilities that school staff had assumed, to ensure the child's well-being.

DeBoor's (1975) portrait of a father with a mildly retarded 21-year-old daughter finds him facing situations that other fathers may never face: bills from various agencies and doctors; his daughter's promiscuity, immaturity, and inability to hold a job; and bureaucracies that are now seen as adversaries rather than allies. The father is no more certain of what will become of his daughter at age 21 than he was when she was 7. DeBoor's study supports Wikler's contention that for many parents, the responsibilities and burden of care increase instead of decrease as the child ages.

Families, according to Duvall (1962), go through "middle years" that begin when the last child leaves home and end with the retirement of the principal breadwinner or the death of one of the spouses. This phase of family life may abruptly end at a spouse's premature death or, conversely, may be delayed indefinitely by the presence of a dependent child who continues to live with the parents.

The latter is often the case for families with a handicapped child. Parents of older handicapped children cannot anticipate enjoying many of the activities available to parents of nonhandicapped children of adult age (Birenbaum 1971). Unless they have other children, they cannot look forward to the special joys of becoming grandparents. They will not be able to enjoy the freedom normally available when children reach adulthood. Bob Helsel (Helsel & Helsel, 1978), a father of a 30-year-old man with cerebral palsy and mental retardation, stated:

It seems to me as I approach retirement age and would like lots of personal freedoms, (my son) will present a problem limiting my ability to go where I want when I want. I don't know whether a solution will be found to give me the freedom that I would like to have or whether we'll just continue to be somewhat limited because of Robin. (p. 107)

During a family's final years, a handicapped adult child may post special problems that other aging parents do not have to face. With the prospect of death looming larger in their lives, parents worry about their child's care after they die. Also during these final years, aging parents often rely on their adult children to care for them when the parents become too old or sick to care for themselves. Parents cannot rely on a handicapped child for such care and support.

IMPLICATIONS FOR INTERVENTION

Among parents and professionals working with families of persons with developmental disabilities, recognition is growing that more needs to be done to address the concerns of fathers. Further, these concerns need to be addressed more systematically (Cummings, 1976; Lamb, 1983) and throughout the child's life (Meyer, 1986). This section suggests implications for intervention for fathers throughout the child's life span, and recommends systematic approaches to addressing fathers' concerns.

At the time of diagnosis, often at the very beginning of a handicapped

child's life, the profound shock felt by parents can be aggravated by professional insensitivity. Price-Bonham and Addison (1978) noted seven major
errors professionals made relative to informing parents of a child's disability: (1) delay in defining the problem, (2) false encouragement of parents, (3)
too much advice on matters such as institutionalization, (4) abruptness, (5)
being hurried, (6) lack of interest, and (7) hesitancy to communicate.

Fathers, it appears, often experience additional stress when treated as
second-class parents at the time of their child's diagnosis. Many of the
fathers of children with Down syndrome that Erikson (1974) met with
reported difficulty in obtaining information from the doctors, and others
only learned about the disability after their wife had been informed. These
fathers recommended that professionals wait to inform the parents of the
diagnosis until both parents are together, and that they provide parents
with a supportive and knowledgeable person to talk to during this time. As
one father said: "There is no optimal time to be told your child has Down
syndrome but there is an optimal way in which parents can be informed"
(Erickson, 1974, p. 23).

As the child grows and begins to participate (usually with the mother) in
early intervention programs, fathers "characteristically have fewer opportunities to do something directly helpful for their handicapped child,
something which provides concrete evidence of their loving, caring, and
benevolent concern" (Cummings, 1976, p. 253). Because organizations for
parents and handicapped children offer fewer services for fathers than
mothers and request and obtain less participation from them, fathers have
fewer opportunities to share their concerns and reduce their stress, Cummings added.

Clearly, many fathers desire to do something that will ameliorate their
child's disability. However, many fathers and also mothers are uncertain of
what the father's role should be. In a study of parents of young handicapped children, Gallagher, Cross, and Scharfman (1981) found that

Across all groups there was general agreement that there should be more father
involvement with the handicapped child. The fact that this does *not* happen or *has
not* happened is an area in need of investigation, but there is no doubt that it *should*
happen. (p. 12)

Interventionists working with handicapped children and their families
also recognize the importance of father involvement. Markowitz's (1983)
interviews with early childhood special education program representatives
revealed that, when asked how a father's involvement affects family functions, two thirds of the representatives observed one or several of the
following positive trends: improved family communication, reduced stress

and tension, more sharing of burdens and responsibilities, enhanced family support system, increased acceptance of the child, more consistent discipline, and more harmonious family functioning.

One way to address the desire for increased father involvement and fathers' need for support and information is to try to increase fathers' typically low attendance at programs for parents of children with special needs. Many so-called parent programs, however, are functionally "mother programs," because they are often held at times inconvenient for fathers and they tend to reflect mothers' concerns (Meyer, et al. 1982). Encouraging increased father attendance at meetings primarily attended by mothers, however, may not be beneficial for either parent. When Markowitz (1983) asked representatives of early childhood special education programs how mothers behave when both mothers and fathers participate in programs, almost half described mothers as quieter, "taking a back seat," being intimidated or self-conscious, compared with their behavior when fathers do not participate. Only 13 percent of the interviewers reported a positive reaction, such as increased maternal comfort, to the father's presence. According to almost half of the program representatives, fathers who *do* attend activities or meetings are quieter and do not share feelings, information, or experiences as readily as mothers. It appears that in the interest of providing an opportunity for parents to express their feelings openly and to obtain information addressing their often different concerns, fathers and mothers may be served better in separate programs.

Programs for Fathers of Children with Handicaps

A few programs specifically designed for fathers of children with handicaps now exist and, according to preliminary reports, appear to benefit the participants and their families.

UCLA Intervention Program's Fathers Group. One Los Angeles program, the Father's Group, is currently open to any father whose child attends the University of California at Los Angeles Intervention Program. Begun in 1979, the Fathers Group presently offers fathers two options for involvement: meetings that include the child with special needs on Saturday mornings, and weekday evening meetings without the child. The monthly Saturday morning meetings presently attract a core group of seven fathers and their children. On the basis of the fathers' desires, the meeting approximates the child's weekday intervention program; fathers and children participate together in play, table, and outdoor activities to give the father an increased understanding of the child's educational program. Occasionally the fathers and children will make a field trip to a zoo, a restaurant, or the beach. During the last hour of the program, a "rap" group, led by a male social worker, is available for interested fathers.

One Wednesday a month, an evening group is held for fathers who cannot attend the Saturday morning play group or do not feel comfortable in a play-group setting. These meetings serve primarily as a source of information for fathers, with guest speakers on topics identified by fathers, such as therapies, family stresses, or preparing a will for a child with special needs. The group leaders report that mothers, on occasion, attend these meetings with their husband.

Families involved in the Fathers Group are generally middle- to upper-income intact families. Children range in age from 20 months to 3 years, with handicaps ranging from mild to severe mental retardation or cerebral palsy. The leaders for both Saturday and evening groups are an early childhood special educator at the Intervention Program and her husband, a clinical psychologist.

The goals of the UCLA Intervention Program Fathers Group are to enable fathers to feel more confident and competent with their child with special needs, and to increase mothers' sense of support. Although no evaluation data are available, leaders report mothers' mentioning feeling supported because fathers "care enough to attend the program." Further, leaders report that "graduate" fathers occasionally return to the program to obtain support and to provide information and support to fathers of younger children.

The Fathers Group at St. Joseph School for the Deaf.   Although some of the children are also developmentally delayed, the primary handicap of children of the fathers in this group in New York's South Bronx is profound deafness.

The weeknight meetings at St. Joseph's attract lower- to middle-income fathers of deaf children from infancy to six years of age from intact families, representing diverse ethnic backgrounds (hispanic, black, caucasian, and immigrant East Indian and Italian).

The Fathers Group seeks to expand participants' knowledge of deafness and child development and to promote sharing of concerns about the child and fathers' comfort in a school setting. Another goal is to teach fathers signing skills, especially important since fathers of children who are deaf often never learn to communicate with their children by use of a formal sign language.

According to the facilitators, each meeting offers sign language instruction and instruction on topics identified by fathers, such as cognitive, speech, and language development or reading readiness. Discussions of emotional concerns were avoided during the first year, because the fathers were perceived as "not ready" for personal sharing. In subsequent years, however, leaders report that fathers discussed personal concerns such as the child's future. On occasion, leaders may engage the fathers in role playing to explore, for example, how they would respond when their child is called "deaf and dumb," or how they should introduce and interpret for their child at a work-related party. Except for occasional socials with the children and the mothers, the meetings are primarily intended for fathers only.

Although no data were presented in an article on the program by its leaders (Crowley, Keane, & Needham, 1982), the authors reported that fathers found the program helped them understand and deal with their deaf child. They found that fathers, after one year of involvement in the program, were more objective in observing their child's behavior; were more willing to participate fully in all aspects of their child's development; solicited advice from group leaders and other fathers for ways of dealing with behavior problems; and were less apt to compare their deaf child negatively with siblings or hearing peers than the year before. In a telephone interview, one leader shared the information that some mothers initially felt threatened by the program and resented the father's time away from the home. Later, mothers reported enjoying the father's increased involvement with the deaf child, and the father's desire to learn more about the disability and its implications.

Fathers of Disabled Children Program. Begun in 1983 by two Milwaukee fathers who attended a workshop for fathers at a Down Syndrome Congress National Meeting, the Fathers of Disabled Children Program meets twice a month on Saturday morning. One meeting a month is a play group with the children with special needs in attendance. The meeting is held at a Milwaukee early intervention center, where fathers engage their child in art projects, preschool activities, or swimming.

The other monthly meeting takes place at Milwaukee County Association for Retarded Citizens (the program's sponsor) and is for fathers only. Facilitated by the fathers themselves, the meetings have as their goal the working through of surface feelings and discussion of the anxiety, anger, frustrations, and also joys that fathers of handicapped children often feel, in order to provide mutual support. Informational topics and guest speakers are rarely on the meeting agenda because they are seen as taking valuable time away from discussions of personal concerns.

Although no evaluation data have been collected on participants, one father-facilitator felt the program benefits a father by providing him camaraderie, support, and an opportunity to share feelings with other fathers who can accurately empathize with his experiences. Mothers, it was reported, look forward to Saturday mornings when the fathers take the child with special needs to the meetings.

SEFAM's Fathers Program.   A program for fathers and their handicapped preschoolers that is examining the benefits of participation for parents is the Supporting Extended Family Members (SEFAM) Program at the University of Washington in Seattle. SEFAM, a Handicapped Children's Early Education Demonstration Program from 1981 to 1984 (funded by the Department of Education) is an outgrowth of a pilot Fathers Program offered at the University's Experimental Education Unit since 1978 (Delaney, Meyer, & Ward, 1980). On the basis of the pilot effort and a review of the research, SEFAM staff developed program activities that encourage a father to (Meyer et al. 1982):

Learn to read his child's cues and interpret his child's behavior.

Develop an awareness of activities, materials, and experiences suitable to the child's current stage of development.

Practice his skill as the child's primary caregiver.

Learn more about the nature of the child's handicap.

Discuss his concerns with other fathers in a similar situation.

Develop an awareness that he, as a parent, will be his child's primary educator and advocate.

Explore the changing role of the father in today's society.

Examine the impact of the child's handicap on the entire family structure.

SEFAM Fathers Program activities are built around three major components: support (father to father), involvement (father and child), and education (the father learning more about the implications of his child's disability). At biweekly Saturday morning meetings cofacilitated by a father of a handicapped child and a special education teacher, fathers share concerns, joys, and information during a "fathers' forum"; learn and enjoy activities with their children; and obtain information from guest speakers that reflect participants' concerns. As a demonstration program, SEFAM staff have prepared a detailed curriculum for implementing programs for fathers of children with special needs, and have provided demonstration, training, or technical assistance to programs wishing to involve fathers, including two of the programs mentioned previously (Fathers and Disabled Children Program, UCLA Fathers Group).

Delaney (1979) studied the pilot Fathers Program in one of the few observational studies conducted with fathers of children with special needs, observing the fathers' playing, nurturance, visual surveillance, and ignoring behaviors. Delaney's research revealed that participants showed a significant decline in ignoring behavior (both in terms of frequency and duration) across seven sessions and a concurrent increase in combined playing, visual surveillance, and nurturing behaviors. He concluded that increasing the father's awareness of his child's development significantly reduced the amount of the father's ignoring behavior toward the child with special needs.

Vadasy, Fewell, Meyer, and Greenberg (1985) compared fathers who were newly enrolled in SEFAM's Fathers Program with fathers who had participated in the program for at least one year, to determine whether a father's social supports, stress, or self-esteem might change over the course of his involvement in the program. In addition to this treatment–no treatment comparison, they retested 11 participants one year later to obtain a pretest–posttest measure. They further hypothesized that fathers' participation in the program might have second-order effects on their wives, who would experience increased support in their role. Both mothers and fathers were therefore asked to participate in the evaluation. Fathers Program families are largely middle-class and intact.

Fathers who had participated in the program reported less sadness ($p < .001$), less fatigue ($p < .05$), more satisfaction ($p < .05$), less pessimism over future concerns ($p < .05$), greater success versus failure as a person ($p < .05$), less guilt ($p = .01$), less stress due to the child's incapacitation ($p = .05$), fewer total problems ($p = .01$), and better decision-making ability ($p < .05$) than did newly enrolled fathers. Program fathers also reported greater satisfaction than new fathers with their level of religious involvement ($p < .05$), neighborhood involvement ($p = .06$), and people with whom they could share their most private feelings ($p < .05$).

Wives of men who had been enrolled in the pilot program reported fewer feelings of failure ($p = .05$), more positive feelings of attractiveness ($p < .10$), less stress due to the child's characteristics ($p = .08$), and more satisfaction with the time they had to themselves ($p < .08$) than did wives of newly enrolled fathers. While Vadasy and coworkers' (1985) findings should be regarded as preliminary, they support parents' and professionals' opinion that more needs to be done to address fathers' concerns.

Increasing Fathers' Involvement

Increasing paternal involvement in schools and parent programs is seen as desirable. But what factors influence a father's involvement? Also what can schools and programs do to encourage increased father involvement?

Markowitz's (1983) exploratory study reported several factors determining fathers' participation. Interviewing directors of preschool programs for young handicapped children, Markowitz found that of the directors she interviewed:

> Fifty percent reported that fathers who had a traditional concept of parents' roles were less likely to become involved in their child's education.
>
> Forty percent mentioned that fathers were more likely to become involved if the child had a special meaning to the father, such as firstborn, namesake, or first son.
>
> Two thirds noted that the fathers' work schedule influenced their level of involvement. They reported that fathers who did shift work, were unemployed, or had flexible schedules were often more involved than fathers who had traditional work schedules.
>
> Over 50 percent also noted that fathers were more likely to be involved if the child had a severe or specific handicap (such as cerebral palsy or Down syndrome) than if the child had a mild or unspecified developmental delay. This suggested to Markowitz that fathers may need or want more evidence of the child's disability than do mothers, to convince them that their participation is important.

Markowitz concluded that fathers who do participate are usually in their mid 20s to early 30s in age and are generally more educated than those who do not participate.

Markowitz (1983), Meyer and colleagues (1982), and Turnbull and coworkers (in press) have made recommendations for programs that seek to further involve fathers. The following points made by these authors are worthy of review.

Staff Attitude Toward Fathers.   The field of education, like those of psychology, medicine, and the social sciences, has for too long ignored the "other parent." Of the attention that psychologists have given to fathers, Parke (1981) wrote: "We didn't just forget fathers by accident; we ignored them because of our assumption that they were less important than mothers in influencing the developing child" (p. 4). Unless staff members believe that fathers are important, expect them to be involved, and treat them as equal partners, programs will not be successful in increasing father participation (Markowitz, 1983). Effective means of acknowledging fathers include addressing program correspondence to both parents, not just mothers; adapting program advertisements, brochures, and newsletters to appeal to fathers as well as mothers; and recruiting male staff members to facilitate fathers' comfort (Markowitz, 1983).

Flexible Scheduling. Evidence of a program's attitude toward fathers is reflected in its staff's willingness to maintain a flexible schedule in order to accommodate fathers, as a father's work schedule may interfere with his participation in a weekday parent program. According to a 1985 survey I conducted of 16 U.S. Handicapped Children's Early Education Program (HCEEP) demonstration sites, the time of day a parent program was offered correlated with the level of father participation. When asked to estimate the number of fathers per 10 mothers attending parent programs, those programs that held day meetings ($n = 4$) attracted no fathers. Those programs that held day *and* evening meetings ($n = 3$) attracted an average of 2.6 fathers per 10 mothers, while programs offering evening meetings ($n = 9$) attracted an average of 5.3 fathers per 10 mothers.

Of the previously mentioned programs specifically for fathers, all reported meeting either in the evening or on Saturday mornings. Of the latter, all reported that meeting times of 10 A.M. until noon were optimal. These hours do not require a father to rise as early as he might on a weekday, and free him to spend the rest of the day with his family.

Further, all programs reported an "open door" policy toward fathers. Instead of requiring attendance, this policy gives fathers permission to *not* attend when the program schedule conflicts with important family responsibilities or functions, and allows a father to attend when he feels it will benefit himself and his family. Required attendance is seen as an additional demand on a family that may already be facing too many demands because of the child's special needs. Further, this policy supports the growing notion that parent involvement must tolerate a range of parent involvement choices and be flexible enough to provide parents the option to *not* be involved, if that is their desire (Kaiser & Hayden, 1984; Turnbull & Turnbull, 1982).

Programs for Fathers. As mentioned previously, fathers wish to be involved with their special child yet are often unsure how to show their love and concern for their child (Cummings, 1976; Gallagher, Cross, & Scharfman, 1981). Fathers also have fewer opportunities than mothers to share their experience and special problems related to the special child (Cummings, 1976). However, as Markowitz's (1983) findings suggest, increasing fathers' attendance at so-called parents meetings (which are, in effect, mothers' meetings) may benefit neither fathers nor mothers. According to Kaiser and Hayden (1984) "Most failures to 'get fathers involved' seem to have been attempts to transfer methods developed for a different population (mothers)" (p. 280). This suggests the need for models that are designed for and reflect the interests of fathers and that complement programs for mothers and the child's education program.

While it is unrealistic to presume that any one model will meet all fathers' needs, fathers' programs have the potential to benefit many fathers and also mothers. Due to the relative novelty of the concept, the ideal model for involving fathers has yet to be determined. SEFAM's Fathers Program, which has developed and field tested a handbook for implementing programs for fathers of handicapped children (Meyer, Vadasy, Fewell, & Schell, 1985) shows promise, especially in urban and middle-class communities. It has yet to be adapted for rural areas, or for low-income or minority populations.

Regardless of the particular model developed, programs that wish to address fathers' needs will help fathers if they provide fathers with opportunities for:

Support.   By providing fathers an opportunity to discuss their concerns with other fathers in a similar situation, programs can help decrease fathers' sense of isolation and increase the social supports available to them. Through discussion, fathers can examine the impact the child's handicap has had on themselves, their wife, and their entire family. Fathers who share their family's experiences with other fathers can increase their understanding of relatives' needs and how to help their family members cope with individual stresses.

Fathers of handicapped children, like many fathers, are exploring the new roles and options available to men. Because most men lack models for the role of male caregiver, fathers interested in being nurturing parents need a supportive environment in which to gather information, ask questions, and share their thoughts about child development, discipline, eating habits, and other typical child-related concerns. In this respect, a fathers' program is a men's group—supporting its members in roles that differ from traditional male sex roles—and also a parents' group. To provide fathers with a positive model, as well as to ensure fathers' comfort, these programs should be led by a male staff member, by a "model" father, or preferably be cofacilitated by both.

Involvement.   Programs that actively involve the father with the handicapped child can expand a father's knowledge of activities and experiences that are enjoyable for both father and child. Involvement in activities in the program can foster increased father-child involvement outside the program. Given the father's importance as the child's play partner (Clarke-Stewart, 1980), increased father-child involvement may contribute to the child's cognitive and social development, as well as foster attachment.

Programs for fathers and children provide fathers with an opportunity to practice caregiving skills. As research suggests (Kotelchuck, 1976; Ross, Kagan, Zelazo, & Kotelchuck, 1975), increasing caregiving has implications for increasing father-child attachment, as well as increasing the respite that is available to mothers. When programs involve children along with fathers, the mother has respite during the hours that the father and child are in the program and, as the father becomes increasingly comfortable in providing care for the special child, the mother's chances for additional respite increase.

Education.   Studies by Hersh (1970) and Love (1973) have shown that fathers, more so than mothers, are concerned with their handicapped child's future problems, such as educational, vocational, legal, and economic matters. Fathers of handicapped infants and preschoolers need information on how to answer questions from relatives and strangers, encourage their child's development, and obtain additional information on the disability itself (Meyer et al., 1982). Programs for fathers can provide information that addresses these and other paternal concerns. Information may be written, presented by facilitators or guest speakers, or shared by father participants.

McConachie's (1982) study of fathers of young handicapped children suggests that the beginning of single-word speech, which allows a father to understand his child more easily, may encourage the father to spend more time in concentrated interaction. Consequently, programs that provide opportunities for a father to learn to better read his special child's cues and behavior (which may be less clear than those of a nonhandicapped child) may help promote a child's socioemotional development. As Lamb (1983) has noted: "The security of attachment relationships depends on the meshing of the parent's and infant's behavior, usually expressed in terms of the adult's sensitive responsiveness to the infant's signals and needs" (p. 128).

An educational component complements facilitators' efforts to provide fathers with support and involvement. Studies comparing the relative superiority of parent groups that are primarily supportive with those that are primarily educational are inconclusive. However, a program that combines educational and supportive approaches seems to offer the most to parents of handicapped children (Seligman & Meyerson, 1982; Tavormina, Hampson, & Luscomb, 1976).

CONCLUSION

Gallagher, Cross, and Scharfman (1981) cautioned against automatically assuming that fathers of handicapped children are under debilitating stress. Indeed, in the research reviewed, the behavior of fathers of handicapped children resembles in many ways that of fathers of nonhandicapped children. Yet as Turnbull and Turnbull (1978) pointed out, parents have a lifelong requirement to adjust continually to their child's mental retardation or other handicap. Wikler, Wasow, and Hatfield's (1981) findings that social workers overestimate parents' early stresses and underestimate stresses that occur later in the family life cycle are indicative of the perceptions of those working with exceptional children and their families. Unfortunately, the small body of literature concerning older families does not yet provide empirical support for these clinical and professional impressions of family experiences.

Not only do families require opportunities for support throughout the child's life, but fathers also require a choice of programs in which their participation is more than tokenism. Fathers' fuller involvement will result when programs and other services directly and immediately reflect the concerns of fathers. By providing fathers with options, professionals who serve families will not only address fathers' concerns and need for support, but also may offer the special child's mother needed respite and support in her efforts. Finally, an involved father helps assure that the special child will have two active, informed, and available parents to meet the child's many physical, emotional, and intellectual needs.

REFERENCES

American Medical Association (1964). *Mental Retardation: A Handbook for the Primary Physician.* New York: American Medical Association.

Birenbaum, A. (1971). The mentally retarded child in the home and family cycle. *Journal of Health and Social Behavior, 12,* 55–65.

Blacher, J. (1984). Sequential stages of parental adjustment to the birth of a child with handicaps: Fact or artifact? *Mental Retardation, 22,* 55–68.

Call, J. (1958). Psychological problems of the cerebral palsied child, his parents and siblings as revealed by dynamically oriented small group discussion with parents. *Cerebral Palsy Review, 10,* 3–15.

Clark-Stewart, K. A. (1980). The father's contribution to children's cognitive and social development in early childhood. In F. A. Pederson (Ed.), *The father-infant relationship: Observational studies in the family setting.* New York: Praeger.

Collins, G. (1979). A new look at life with father. *New York Times Magazine,* June 17, pp. 31, 49–52, 65–66.

Crowley, M., Keane, K., & Needham, C. (1982). Fathers: The forgotten parents. *American Annals of the Deaf, 127,* 38–40.

Cummings, S. T. (1976). The impact of the child's deficiency on the father: A study of mentally retarded and chronically ill children. *American Journal of Orthopsychiatry, 462,* 246–255.

DeBoor, M. (1975). What is to become of Katherine? *Exceptional Children, 418,* 517–518.

Delaney, S. W. (1979). Facilitating attachment between fathers and their handicapped infants. Unpublished doctoral dissertation, University of Washington, Seattle (University Microfilms No. 79-27, 768).

Delaney, S. W., Meyer, D. J., & Ward, M. J. (1980). Fathers and infants class: A model for facilitating attachment between fathers and infants. Unpublished manuscript, Experimental Education Unit, University of Washington, Seattle.

Duvall, E. M. (1962). *Family development.* Philadelphia: Lippincott.

Erickson, M. (1974). Talking with fathers of young children with Down syndrome. *Children Today, 3,* 22–25.

Farber, B. (1960). Family organization and crisis: Maintenance of integration in families with a severely mentally retarded child. *Monographs of the Society for Research in Child Development,25*(1) (serial no. 75).

Farber, B. (1962). Effects of a severely mentally retarded child on family. In E. P. Trapp (Ed.), *Readings on the exceptional child.* New York: Appleton-Century-Crofts, pp. 225–245.

Farber, B., Jenné, W., & Toigo, R. (1960). Family crisis and the decision to institutionalize the retarded child. NEA Research Monograph Series, no. A-1. Washington, DC: Council for Exceptional Children.

Farber, B., & Ryckman, D. B. (1965). Effects of severely mentally retarded children on family relationships. *Mental Retardation Abstracts, 11,* 1–17.

Gallagher, J. J., Beckman, P., & Cross, A. H. (1983). Families of handicapped children: Sources of stress and its amelioration. *Exceptional Children, 50,* 10–19.

Gallagher, J., Cross, A., & Scharfman, W. (1981). Parental adaptation to a young handicapped child: The father's role. *Journal of the Division for Early Childhood, 3,* 3–14.

Gath, A. (1977). The impact of an abnormal child upon the parents. *British Journal of Psychiatry, 130,* 405–410.

Greenberg, M., & Morris, N. (1974). Engrossment: The newborn's impact upon the father. *American Journal of Orthopsychiatry, 44,* 520–531.

Greenfield, J. (1972). *A child called Noah.* New York: Holt, Rinehart and Winston.

Grossman, F. K. (1972). *Brothers and sisters of retarded children: An exploratory study.* Syracuse, NY: Syracuse University Press.

Gumz, E. J., & Gubrium, J. F. (1972). Comparative parental perceptions of a mentally retarded child. *American Journal of Mental Deficiency, 77,* 75–180.

Helsel, E., Helsel, B., & Helsel, M. (1978). The Helsel's story of Robin. In A. Turnbull & R. Turnbull (Eds.), *Parents speak out.* Columbus, OH: Charles E. Merrill.

Hersh, A. (1970). Changes in family functioning following placement of a retarded child. *Social Work, 15,* 93–102.

Holroyd, J., & McArthur, D. (1976). Mental retardation and stress on parents: A contrast between Down syndrome and childhood autism. *American Journal of Mental Deficiency, 80,* 431–436.

Illingworth, R. S. (1967). Counseling the parents of the mentally handicapped child. *Clinical Pediatrics, 6,* 340–348.

Kaiser, C., & Hayden, A. (1984). Clinical research and policy issues in parenting severely handicapped infants. In J. Blacher (Ed.), *Severely handicapped young children and their families: Research in review.* Orlando, FL: Academic.

Kirkpatrick, C. (1955). *The family as process and institution.* New York: Ronald.

Kotelchuck, M. (1976). The infant's relationship to the father: Experimental evidence. In M. E. Lamb (Ed.), *The role of the father in child development.* New York: Wiley.

Lamb, M. E. (1983). Fathers of exceptional children. In M. Seligman (Ed.), *The family with a handicapped child: Understanding and treatment.* New York: Grune and Stratton.

Lonsdale, G. (1978). Family life with a handicapped child: The parents speak. *Child: Care, Health and Development, 4,* 99–120.

Love, H. (1973). *The mentally retarded child and his family.* Springfield, IL: Charles C. Thomas.

Liversidge, E., & Grana, G. (1973). A hearing impaired child in the family: The parent's perspective. *Volta Review, 75,* 174–184.

MacDonald, W. S., & Oden, C. W. (1978). *Moose: A very special person.* Minneapolis: Winston.

Markowitz, J. (1983). Participation of fathers in early childhood special education programs: An exploratory study of factors and issues. Unpublished manuscript, George Washington University, Washington, DC.

McConachie, H. (1982). Fathers of mentally handicapped children. In N. Beail & J. McGuire (Eds.), *Fathers: Psychological perspective.* London: Junction.

Menolascino, F. J. (1977). *Challenges in mental retardation: Progressive ideology and services.* New York: Human Sciences.

Meyer, D. (1986). Fathers of children with handicaps: Developmental trends in fathers' experiences over the family life cycle. In R. R. Fewell & P. F. Vadasy (Eds.), *Families of handicapped children: Needs and supports across the lifespan.* Austin, TX: Pro-Ed.

Meyer, D., Vadasy, P., Fewell, R., & Schell, G. (1982). Involving fathers of handicapped infants: Translating research into program goals. *Journal of the Division for Early Childhood, 5,* 64–72.

Meyer, D., Vadasy, P., Fewell, R., & Schell, G. (1985). *A handbook for implementing programs for fathers of handicapped children.* Seattle: University of Washington Press.

Mitchell, W. M., Jr. (1979). Fathers of Children with Down syndrome. Harvard University, available from University of Michigan, PO Box 1346, Ann Arbor, MI, 48106. Order no. 8010535.

Moore, J. A., Hamerlynck, L. A., Barsh, E. T., Spieker, S., & Jones, R. R. (1982). *Extending family resources.* Children's Clinic and Preschool, Seattle.

Olshansky, S. (1962). Chronic sorrow: A response to having a mentally defective child. *Social Casework, 43,* 190–193.

Parke, R. D. (1981). *Fathers.* Cambridge, MA: Harvard University Press.

Parke, R. D., & Sawin, D. E. (1977). The family in early infancy: Social interaction attitudinal analyses. Paper presented at Biennial Meeting of Society for Research in Child Development, New Orleans (ERIC Document Reproduction Service No. ED 162 742).

Peck, J. R., & Stephens, W. B. (1960). A study of the relationship between the attitudes and behavior of parents and that of their mentally defective child. *American Journal of Mental Deficiency, 64,* 839–844.

Price-Bonham, S., & Addison, S. (1978). Families and mentally retarded children: Emphasis on the father. *The Family Coordinator, 3,* 221–230.

Reed, E. W., & Reed, S. C. (1965). *Mental retardation: A family study.* Philadelphia: Saunders.

Ross, G., Kagan, J., Zelazo, P., & Kotelchuck, M. (1975). Separation protests in infants in home and laboratory. *Developmental Psychology, 11,* 256–257.

Roos, P. (1978). Parents of mentally retarded children—misunderstood and mistreated. In A. Turnbull & H. R. Turnbull (Eds.), *Parents speak out.* Columbus, OH: Charles E. Merrill.

Rosenberg, S. A. (1977). Family and parent variables affecting outcomes of a parent-mediated intervention. Unpublished doctoral dissertation, George Peabody College for Teachers, Nashville, TN.

Schufeit, L. J., & Wurster, S. R. (1976). Frequency of divorce among parents of handicapped children. *Resources in Education, 11,* 71–78.

Seligman, M., & Meyerson, R. (1982). Group approaches for parents of exceptional children. In M. Seligman (Ed.), *Group psychotherapy and counseling with special populations.* Baltimore: University Park Press.

Shannon, L. B. (1978). Interactions of fathers with their handicapped preschoolers. University of Kentucky, available from University of Michigan, PO Box 1346, Ann Arbor, MI 48106. Order no. 7918117.

Stoneman, Z., Brody, G., & Abbott, D. (1983). In-home observations of young Down syndrome children with their mothers and fathers. *American Journal of Mental Deficiency, 87,* 591–600.

Suelzle, M., & Keenan, V. (1981). Changes in family support networks over the life cycle of mentally retarded persons. *American Journal of Mental Deficiency, 86,* 267–274.

Tallman, I. (1965). Spousal role differentiation and the socialization of severely retarded children. *Journal of Marriage and the Family, 27,* 37–42.

Tavormina, J., Hampson, R., & Luscomb, R. (1976). Participant evaluations of the effectiveness of their parent counseling groups. *Mental Retardation, 14,* 8–9.

Turnbull, A. P., & Blacher-Dixon, J. (1980). Preschool mainstreaming: Impact on parents. In J. Gallagher (Ed.), *New directions for exceptional children* (Vol. 1). San Francisco: Jossey-Bass.

Turnbull, A. P., Brotherson, M. J., Summers, J. A., & Turnbull, H. R. (in press). Fathers of disabled children. In B. Robinson & R. Baret (Eds.), *Fatherhood.* Austin: Pro-Ed.

Turnbull, A. P., & Turnbull, H. R. (1978). *Parents speak out: Views from the other side of the two-way mirror.* Columbus, OH: Charles E. Merrill.

Turnbull, A. P., Turnbull, H. R. (1982). Parent involvement in the education of handicapped children: A critique. *Mental Retardation, 20,* 115–122.

Vadasy, P. F., Fewell, R. R., Meyer, D. J., & Greenberg, M. T. (1985). Supporting fathers of handicapped young children: Preliminary findings of program effects. *Analysis and Intervention in Developmental Disabilities, 5,* 151–163.

Vadasy, P. F., Fewell, R. R., Meyer, D. J., Schell, G., & Greenberg, M. T. (1984). Involved parents: Characteristics and resources of fathers and mothers of young handicapped children. *Journal for the Division of Early Childhood, 8*(1), 13–25.

Wikler, L. (1981). Chronic stresses of families of mentally retarded children. *Family Relations, 30,* 281–288.

Wikler, L., Wasow, M., & Hatfield, E. (1981). Chronic sorrow revisited: Attitudes of parents and professionals about adjustment to mental retardation. *American Journal of Orthopsychiatry, 51,* 63–70.

Wolfensberger, W. (1967). Counseling the parents of the retarded. In A. A. Baumeister (Ed.), *Mental retardation, appraisal, education, and rehabilitation.* Chicago: Aldine.

CHAPTER 9

The Abusing Father

ANN H. TYLER
Family Support Center, Salt Lake City, Utah

The importance of fathers and their role in child care and family life has been discussed by many writers. Little, however, has been published about the father who mistreats his child sexually or physically. With many more fathers assuming or sharing the role of the primary caretaker of a child, there is increased opportunity for dysfunctional relationships between father and child to surface. The significant increase in divorce, remarriage, and other alternative family living arrangements would indicate that many of today's children are exposed to more stepfathers and mothers' boyfriends or lovers than were children previously. According to the literature, one of the strongest correlates of abuse victimization is the factor of a girl having a stepfather (Finkelhor, 1979; Russell, 1980). Therefore, if more children are parented by a nonbiological male, are they more vulnerable to being abused? Most parents, natural and step, agree that simply by virtue of being parents, adults have the potential to exploit or abuse a child. Why is one parent, however, able to cope with considerable stress and adversity while continuing to provide nurturance for the child, while another parent strikes out and hurts the child? In certain family relationships, abusive behavior may be as typical as is love (Straus & Hoteling, 1981). In this chapter we basically ask about the abusing father's ability to parent effectively in the future. Do we know enough about these fathers to design successful treatment interventions?

Child specialists and researchers generally agree that most child abuse is complex and multidetermined; that the consequences are myriad, depending on the nature of the abuse; and that the various forms of abuse do not represent one phenomenon. To begin this inquiry, then, it is necessary to examine what we know and do not know about the dynamics of child abuse when perpetrated by a father.

REVIEW OF THE LITERATURE

Incidence

Tragically, in the United States more children under the age of 5 die of child abuse than die of disease (American Humane Association, 1981). Because child abuse reporting laws are implemented differently in each of the 50 states, the exact figures on the numbers of families and children involved in all forms of child abuse are not known. However, the most recent statistics indicate that in both the injury and fatality reports of child physical and child sexual abuse, the victim/child relationship to the care-taker was parental (80 percent) (American Humane Association, 1981). The incidence varies according to the age of the child and the nature of the abuse (Gil, 1970; Jason, Burton, Williams, & Rochat, 1982; Kempe & Helfer, 1968; Kempe & Kempe, 1976). Some states have more carefully documented child abuse registries than others, but most clinicians agree that the reported incidence represents only the tip of the iceberg (Tyler, 1978). Very likely, the actual number of children abused and neglected annually in the United States is at least one million (Straus & Hoteling, 1981). Although physical abuse accounts for approximately 80 percent of the recent child abuse referrals, it is speculated that the public may be more willing to report physical abuse than to report intrafamilial sexual abuse (Giarretto, 1982). Thus incest victims may belong to the most unre-ported group of child abuse victims. The number of sexual abuse cases reported to the American Humane Association increased from 1975 in 1976 to 22,918 in 1982 (Finkelhor, 1984). Recent random-sample surveys (Kercher, 1980; Russell, 1983) and other surveys of nonclinical popula-tions (Finkelhor, 1979) indicate that 12 to 38 percent of girls and 3 to 9 percent of boys have experienced some form of unwanted sexual contact before the age of 18 years. Since these data have been gathered retrospec-tively, caution must be used in making generalizations with regard to today's children; however, application of even very conservative sexual abuse estimates to America's children under 18 years of age results in approximately 210,000 new sexual abuse cases yearly.

Etiology of Abuse

Child abuse is multifaceted and multidetermined. Fathers can be involved in abuse not only as perpetrators but also as passive witnesses and as partners whose unsupportiveness may contribute to maltreatment by a partner. A combination of individual and social/cultural factors is proba-bly responsible for the abusive behavior of parents.

Psychiatric Approach. There have been several theoretical perspectives for understanding the etiology of child abuse. The psychiatric approach focused on the parents and their personality traits as the principal cause. Child abuse was assumed to be a manifestation of mental illness. Estimates indicate, however, that less than 10 percent of abusing parents can be classified as psychotic (Kempe & Helfer, 1972; Spinetta & Rigler, 1972; Mrazek & Kempe, 1981). The psychiatric model, which emphasizes the psychopathology of offenders, has created some controversy. Critics of the theory are quick to point out that the population studied consists of already reported sex offenders; because of the large number of suspected unreported cases, other social/cultural forces must be at work.

Social/Cultural Model. A second approach is a social/cultural model in which the social values and the cultural organization are viewed as important in the etiology of abuse. There is some suggestion that the level of violence in a family is reflective of the level of violence in the community (Bellack & Antell, 1974). Because of the widespread existence of child abuse, it is possible that certain socialization patterns promote abuse. Belief in the value of physical punishment to establish appropriate social conduct (Burgess & Holmstrom, 1975; Garbarino, 1977a) is used to legitimize use of force. Although victims of intrafamilial sexual abuse or incest are seldom hurt by extreme force or violence, they are as exploited and as vulnerable as physically abused victims because of their subordinate position and their conditioning to comply with caretaker authority.

Social/Situational Model. A third approach to understanding the etiology of child abuse is the social/situational perspective, where the social situation in which a parent lives and the family interaction patterns combine to give clues about the cause and nature of the abuse. Child abuse may occur as a result of several factors: culture and family justification of physical punishment to establish appropriate social conduct; parents' selective forgetting of the consequences (Bandura, 1973); role reversal, in which the child is viewed as the "responsible" party; and lack of parental empathy, in which the abuser is insensitive to the victim's emotional feelings and/or physical pain. The reciprocal nature of child abuse is an important feature in this approach. The child may actually elicit his or her own abuse by being perceived as different and/or by developing a set of interaction behaviors that trigger abuse (Bell, 1971; Bell, 1977; Martin, 1976).

A patriarchal social structure is often blamed for the sexual exploitation of children. In our culture, men are typically socialized differently than women. Because a male's self-esteem appears to be more closely correlated with his heterosexual success, a man may be more likely than a woman to use sex as a method of getting basic emotional needs met. Men have, until recently, experienced fewer opportunities to nurture their children, and thus may not be as sensitized to offering affection without a sexual component. A summary of findings from a recent study of two clinical populations of abusing and nonabusing males by Parker and Parker (personal communication, 3 May 1985) suggested that "the reason stepfathering has been linked to sexual abuse . . . is because stepfathers are less likely to be in the home during the early socialization period of their children. It is their absence, rather than their lack of paternal involvement or genetic investment, that is responsible for their usual high representation among abusive fathers." Thus according to Parker and Parker's study, when stepfathers are present in the home during a child's first three years of life, their "involvement" and risk of abusing do not differ from the biological fathers' involvement and risk of abusing. However, results also indicated that the abusers perceived having received significantly poorer treatment by their fathers than did the control group. This finding apparently contributed a factor independent of the involvement variable. Since both groups of men in this study were from clinical populations and matched only by agency, results must be interpreted with caution. Whether the factors contributing to lowering the inhibition to abuse are situational or related to personality factors, both have been correlated with deviant parental behavior.

Characteristics of Physically Abusing and Sexually Abusing Fathers: Similarities and Differences.

Historically, child physical and child sexual abuse have been characterized and analyzed as one phenomenon, in spite of suspected differences. An epidemiologic study by Jason and colleagues (1982) comparing population-based data on sexual and physical child abuse was able to differentiate the two types of abuse. Ninety-one percent of children confirmed as sexually abused were girls, compared with 50 percent girls confirmed as physically abused. The age of the sexually abused child was not correlated with rural or urban demography. While most abused children lived with their natural mother, this was more frequent with sexual abuse than with physical abuse ($p < .001$). Males were the identified offenders in 98 percent of the documented sexual abuse cases and in 56 percent of the physical abuse reports. In Finkelhor and Hoteling's (1983) study, sexual abuse by a stepfather was five times greater than such abuse by a natural father.

A study by Tyler (1983) investigated the marital adjustment, life stress, social support, history, and demographic variables of 20 sexually abusing, 20 physically abusing, and 20 nonclinic fathers. An extensive review of the literature had indicated that these may be important variables in the determination of child abuse (Finkelhor, 1979; Mayer, 1983). Extensive clinical experience with this population also supported the judgment that these variables may be correlated with the occurrence of abuse. Results of the study must, of course, be interpreted with care, because the sample was based on subjects' availability and consequently was nonrandom. Certainly more normative data are needed from a variety of populations; however, this study was one of perhaps a few existing studies that have included a comparison group and attempted to match for socioeconomic status.

Interestingly, the reported sexual abuse cases referred for treatment in Utah represented a broad socioeconomic spectrum, whereas the median income for sexual abuse families in the United States in 1979 was only $9285—a figure approximately $10,000 less than the United States median income (Finkelhor, 1984). One can only speculate about the reasons for this. Perhaps Utah's increased implementation of the strict child abuse reporting laws and the severe penalties invoked for noncompliance are responsible for the wider socioeconomic range of reported cases. The difference could also be an artifact of the Utah population. The clinical sample was predominantly caucasian and middle-class, with a Mormon religious orientation.

Father's History. Indeed, history is often the best predictor of what will occur in the future. Several researchers have found childhood victimization in the background of sexual abusers (Finkelhor, 1979; Groth & Burgess, 1979; Tyler, 1983) and in the background of physical abusers (Justice & Justice, 1976; Lenoski, 1974).

In Tyler's (1983) study, even though the groups were matched in educational level, occupation, social status, and family size, there were important differences in their histories that must have influenced the respondent's attitudes and behaviors (Table 9.1). Inspection of a correlation matrix (Table 9.2) suggested relationships between a subject's condition and a history of having been sexually abused or physically abused, current sexual dysfunction, alcohol abuse, spouse abuse, and the father's age.

Alcohol may play a significant role in the abuse of children (Finkelhor, 1984; Mayer, 1983), some studies showing as many as 25 percent of offenders using alcohol excessively (Swanson, 1968). Our clinical experience suggests that alcohol use does not in and of itself cause the abuse, but that the offender drinks to facilitate an already existing desire to sexually abuse. In other words, the offender does not drink and then unwittingly abuse. He drinks so that he can abuse. Whereas alcohol use may have something to do with loss of impulse control in child and spouse physical abuse, it seems to serve a different function in child sexual abuse.

TABLE 9.1.   Demographic Descriptions of Sexually Abusing, Physically Abusing, and Nonabusing Fathers[a]

Descriptor	Sexual Abuser	Physical Abuser	Nonclinic
Father's mean age	34.7	28.5	29.7
Child's mean age	7.1	3.5	2.9
Mean number of children in family	3.7	2.8	2.6
Mean social class score[b]	2.9	3.0	3.2
Race			
Caucasian	16	18	17
Black	1	1	0
Spanish American	2	1	1
Other	1	0	3
Abuse received as child			
None	1	2	17
Physical	11	15	2
Sexual	15	2	1
Both	7	1	0
Abuse of spouse			
Not at all	14	13	20
Occasionally	5	2	0
Often	1	5	0
Alcohol abuse			
Not at all	10	9	17
Occasionally	2	5	3
Often	8	6	0

Source: Tyler, A. H. (1983). Child-abusing and nonabusing fathers. Doctoral dissertation, University of Utah, Salt Lake City.

[a]$N = 60$.

[b]As measured by Hollingshead, Four Factor Index of Social Status, in which Class 1 denotes higher executive or professional employment, Class 4 denotes clerical work, and Class 7 denotes unskilled labor.

The sexually abusing fathers in Tyler's study also reported significant sexual dysfunction, which was defined as an inability to achieve sexual satisfaction in an adult relationship, although the professed sexual preference was for an adult female partner. It is possible that (1) these men did not have the interpersonal skills necessary to sustain a mature sexual relationship and/or (2) because of the sample's predominantly patriarchal and religious culture, these men somehow rationalized that sex within a

TABLE 9.2. Correlation Matrix of Dependent and Demographic Variables Among Sexually or Physically Abusing Fathers

	AVI	ADI	AVA	ADA	DAS	ISSI	SRRS	SXAB	SXD	AGE	ALCH	SPOA	RELKID	DRUGS
AVI	1.00	.30	.49**	.29	.48**	.70**	-.32*	-.01	-.41**	.06	-.18	-.36*	-.14	-.16
ADI	.30	1.00	.31*	.56**	.26	.68**	-.37*	-.02	-.31*	.28	-.38*	-.12	-.06	-.27
AVA	.49**	.31*	1.00	.67**	.73**	.78**	-.33*	-.27	-.49**	-.07	-.16	-.30	-.13	.00
ADA	.29	.56**	.67**	1.00	.59**	.79**	-.35*	-.32*	-.39*	.03	-.21	-.28	-.20	-.05
DAS	.48**	.26	.73**	.59**	1.00	.63**	-.33*	-.35*	-.52**	-.15	-.11	-.34*	-.11	-.01
ISSI	.70**	.68**	.78**	.79**	.63**	1.00	-.46**	-.20	-.53**	.07	-.32*	-.32*	-.13	-.13
SRRS	-.32*	-.37*	-.33*	-.35*	-.33*	-.46**	1.00	.26	.45**	-.17	.22	.29	.13	.16
SXAB	-.01	-.02	-.27	-.32*	-.35*	-.20	.26	1.00	.27	.26	.21	.10	.27	.07
SXD	-.41**	-.31*	-.49**	-.39*	-.52**	-.53**	.45**	.27	1.00	.02	.26	.42**	.07	.17
AGE	.06	.28	-.07	.03	-.15	.05	-.17	.26	.02	1.00	-.01	-.11	-.11	-.14
ALCH	-.18	-.38*	-.16	-.21	-.11	-.32*	.22	.21	.26	-.01	1.00	.15	-.06	.42**
SPOA	-.36*	-.12	-.30	-.28	-.34*	-.32*	.29	.10	.42**	-.11	.15	1.00	.43**	.25
RELKID	-.14	-.06	-.13	-.20	-.11	-.13	.13	.27	.06	-.11	-.06	.43**	1.00	-.07
DRUGS	-.16	-.27	.00	-.05	-.01	-.13	.16	.07	.17	-.14	.42**	.15	-.07	1.00
PAB	-.36*	-.19	-.19	-.34*	-.25	-.41**	.24	.03	.36*	-.16	.27	.18	.03	.13

Source: Tyler, A. H. (1983). Child-abusing and nonabusing fathers. Doctoral dissertation, University of Utah, Salt Lake City.

AVI = Availability of integration
ADI = Adequacy of integration
AVA = Availability of attachment
ADA = Adequacy of attachment
DAS = Marital adjustment
ISSI = Interview Schedule of Social Interaction total score
    (combined AVI, ADI, AVA, ADA)
SRRS = Stress

SXAB = History of sexual abuse
SXD = Sexual dysfunction
AGE = Age of father
ALCH = History of alcohol abuse
SPOA = History of spouse abuse
RELKID = Relationship to child (stepfather or natural father)
DRUGS = History of drug abuse
PAB = History of physical abuse

* Significant LE = .01.
** Significant LE = .001.

261

family system—even though with a child—was preferable to sex outside the family.

The nonclinic fathers and the physically abusing fathers and their children were five to six years younger than the sexually abusing fathers and their children. However, more recent referral data from our clinics show the median age of the sexually abused victim is now 5 instead of 7 years. With the increase in prevention programs in preschool and day-care centers, perhaps the younger child is reporting inappropriate sexual contact sooner. The history of the father's having experienced some form of maltreatment as a child was significant in this study's population.

It would appear that the eliciting phase of abuse stresses the parents' own abusive rearing as an important factor in predisposing them to be physically or sexually abusive in disciplining their children or in meeting their own emotional needs.

The social learning theory has often been used in an attempt to explain this phenomenon. Perhaps sexual arousal is a form of conditioned response, so that a man imprinted or conditioned with early sexual experiences finds children sexually arousing later in life. It is also possible that the important factor here is not the conditioning but having had a model who physically abused or found children sexually stimulating. Interestingly, when a multiple discriminant function analysis was performed, the most important predictor variable was the history of having been abused as a child (see Figure 9.1).

Marital Relationship.   Abuse may also be triggered by poor husband/wife interaction. Previous research has indicated that there is no statistically significant difference in marital adjustment of physically abusive versus nonabusive parents (Butler & Crane, 1979) as measured by three self-report questionnaires. In Tyler's (1983) study, however, the total score on the Dyadic Adjustment Scale (Spanier, 1976), which measures marital consensus, satisfaction, cohesion, and affection, discriminated between the two abusive groups and the nonclinic group. The dyadic consensus subscale, which is a measure of how much agreement exists between partners, correlated with the group condition. To negotiate agreement requires that a couple have some communication skills; thus it is suggested that sexually abusing families do not have these skills sufficient so that individual needs are expressed and stresses are worked through in a functional manner. When the marital relationship breaks down, the father may turn to his daughter because (1) he is in a position of power and can control the relationship, (2) he is too inhibited because of low self-esteem or moral values to find sexual gratification outside the family, or (3) this enmeshment serves to keep the family together, if for no other reason than to protect the secret of incest.

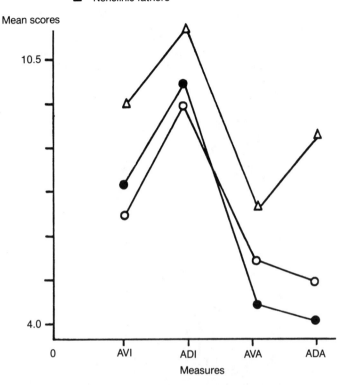

● Sexually abusing fathers
○ Physically abusing fathers
△ Nonclinic fathers

Figure 9.1.   Mean scores on the Interview Schedule of Social Interaction (ISSI) as a function of group membership. AVI, availability of integration; ADI, adequacy of integration; AVA, availability of attachment; ADA, adequacy of attachment.

The physically abusing group also reported less marital satisfaction than the nonclinic group. Justice and Justice (1976) described the marital dyad in physically abusing families as "symbiotic" in nature. The relationship is a passive-dependent one where neither partner believes that he or she is capable of surviving alone. Coexistent with this belief is that only one person in a relationship can have his or her needs met, and it appears that most of the energy in this system is tied up with the marital dyad, each person seeking to meet or have met his or her emotional needs. Perhaps the child's needs serve to impede the marital dyad and, consequently, when a passive marital partner cannot directly express aggression toward the spouse, the child may become the target for abuse. The marital relationships appear quite different and thus require different kinds of interventions (see Figure 9.2).

Social Isolation.   Whether social isolation is an established familial pattern over generations or occurs as a result of economic or social events

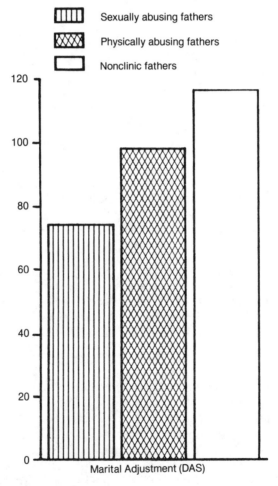

Figure 9.2.   Mean criteria scores on the Dyadic Adjustment Scale (DAS) as a function of group membership.

alienating the family system from the community, there is evidence that isolation from strong support systems contributes to the incidence of child physical and child sexual abuse (Garbarino, 1977a, 1977b). A social support system is crucial as situational stresses increase. A potent support system provides individuals with relationships that may be necessary for feedback opportunities and enduring personal attachments (Garbarino & Sherman, 1980; Weiss, 1973; Weiss, 1974). However, abusive and neglectful families often fail to use social supports. Lenoski (1974) reported that 81 percent of the abusive families studied preferred to resolve their crisis alone. Young (1964) concluded that 95 percent of the abusive families had no lasting relationships outside the family, and 85 percent of these families did not have membership in a social group.

To determine what, if any, differences existed between the social support systems of physically abusing fathers, sexually abusing fathers, and nonabusing gathers, Tyler (1983) examined the three groups' responses on the Interview Schedule of Social Interaction (Henderson et al., 1980), which yields four dimensions of a social support system. This questionnaire was designed to obtain information on the availability and adequacy of social integration and attachment, and the results demonstrated significant differences among the three groups (see Figure 9.1). Interestingly, the nonclinic and the sexually abusing fathers reported more available, broad social networks than did the physically abusing fathers, while the nonclinic and physically abusing fathers reported more available and adequate close attachments than did the sexually abusing fathers.

Some of the sexual abusers reported no attachment figure, and those who did often reported that the one person they were closest to, fondest of, and so on, was a child or a friend. The physical abusers reported available attachment figures but indicated that they wanted more from those figures—again the strong symbiotic relationship (Justice & Justice, 1976). The sexual abusers reported wanting a more adequate attachment, an appropriate response in view of their extreme emotional isolation. The nonclinic fathers were satisfied with both the availability and the adequacy of their primary relationships.

Incest is described in terms of a marital dyad dysfunction where the parents' primary closeness is with the child rather than with the spouse. Roles are confused and intergenerational boundaries are crossed (Giarretto, 1982) in an attempt to meet emotional needs. The dyad fails itself and the children in the primary functions of emotional support and supervision, and caring becomes sexualized (Giarretto, 1982; Mrazek & Kempe, 1981). The sexually abusing fathers who reported healthy marital relationships may have been denying the truth *or* their perceptions of what a relationship can provide may be very different from those of the other fathers.

The availability of social integration, which represents the number of available acquaintances in a broad social network, discriminated between physical abusers and nonclinic fathers better than between sexual abusers and nonclinic fathers. The physical abusers had significantly fewer people available to them; thus they appear more socially isolated than the other fathers. The nonsignificant effect of adequacy of integration suggests that the fathers' *perception* of the effectiveness of their social network is not significantly different, even though the availability of the network is quite different between the groups. Physical abusers seem satisfied with few friends, while sexual abusers report loneliness and a desire for more friends.

Stress.   Stress has been linked to child abuse whenever research has been designed to identify it; however, it is not the occurrence of stress but rather its unmanageability that is related to child abuse (Garbarino, 1977a; Mayer, 1983). Clinically, both the physical and the sexual abuser demonstrate poor impulse control and low frustration tolerance, with acting-out behaviors physically, sexually, and in other areas of their lives. The combination of stress, poor impulse control, and low frustration tolerance is viewed as contributing to both forms of child abuse.

Tyler's (1983) study used the Social Readjustment Rating Scale (Holmes & Rahe, 1967) to measure life stress of the abusing and nonabusing fathers. Both groups of abusers reported more stressful life events than did the nonclinic group; however, the sexual abusers' mean score (439) was significantly higher than the physical abusers' (316) or the nonclinic fathers' (284) (see Figure 9.3). Interestingly, the nonclinic fathers in the study reported stress scores that were higher than those of physical abusers in a 1975 study by Justice and Duncan (1975). Perhaps the social support system of the nonabusing father serves to act as a buffer against stressful experiences. When comparing Justice and Duncan's (1975) study with Tyler's (1983) study, although the reported 1983 stress scores of the abusing groups were much higher, the pattern of differences between abusing and nonabusing was similar. The abusing parent had significantly higher reported frequencies in "change in financial state," "trouble with in-laws," "sex difficulties," and "change in living conditions."

In the study by Justice and Duncan (1975), it was also concluded that the symbiosis (which was described as "the attachment that one individual establishes with another in an effort to be taken care of" (p. 31) of physically abusing parents makes the individual more "vulnerable to life changes, which in turn produce stress" (p. 115). It seems just as likely that high levels of stress can result in an individual turning to a support system that may enhance this symbiotic relationship with spouse, child, or the

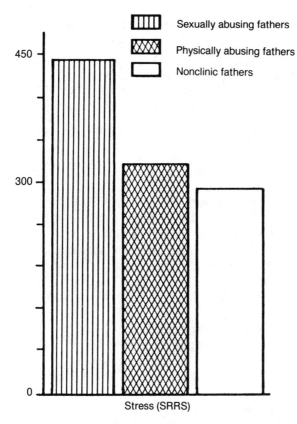

Figure 9.3. Mean criteria scores on the Social Readjustment Rating Scale (SRRS) as a function of group membership.

broader social network. Stress may exacerbate the need for support, or a viable support system may buffer the effects of stress. It appears evident that U. S. society of the 1980s, with its fast pace of living, unpredictable economic conditions, and high rate of geographic mobility, is experiencing more stress, as measured by the Social Readjustment Rating Scale.

Summary of Abusing Father's Profile.   It is evident that there are similarities, yet perhaps important differences, in the profiles of sexually abusing and physically abusing fathers. The literature suggests that social isolation, poor marital adjustment, stress, lack of empathy, low self-esteem, role reversal, and the history of having been abused are important components of child abuse. Few studies have attempted to differentiate between the physical abuser and the sexual abuser in these dimensions. Certainly more normative data from a variety of populations are needed, and results of the studies must be interpreted with care. It appears, however, that there is an overall difference between physical abusers, sexual abusers, and nonabusing fathers (Finkelhor & Hoteling, 1983; Jason et al., 1982; Tyler, 1983). Implications for treatment, intervention strategies, and prevention are considered next.

TREATMENT

The most important predictor variable in any form of child abuse may be the history of the perpetrator having experienced some form of childhood abuse. The implications of this are far reaching. If indeed the child is father of the man, then treatment of both the father *and* the child assumes great importance. If the behavior is learned through imprinting, modeling, or some kind of reinforcement, then perhaps educational and support therapy that impacts the entire family system can mitigate the generational effects of child abuse.

The importance of obtaining childhood history data during the initial clinical interview of any abusive father cannot be emphasized too strongly. Our experience is that access to this information is limited only by the clinician's unwillingness to ask the necessary questions:

1. How were you parented?
2. Were you ever physically or sexually abused? By whom? At what age?

It is evident, then, that physically and sexually abusing fathers are very often victims themselves of poor childhood experiences; however, their age, their support systems, their marriage, and their parent-child interaction patterns appear to be different. Thus our discussion on treatment separates the two groups.

Physically Abusing Fathers

For the father to provide adequate parenting for his child, improvements in two separate areas must take place. There must be both individual psychological improvement and family interaction improvement—both husband/wife and parent/child.

Social Isolation.   In Tyler's (1983) study using the Interview Schedule of Social Interaction, physically abusing fathers reported significantly fewer people available to them in their social network, yet they also reported this as being satisfactory. Although excellent support groups are available for these men, they have to want to increase their network before they will commit to attendance. Clinicians want to see these fathers become more involved outside the nuclear family, learning to use alternative lifelines, such as friends, outside family members, a crisis nursery, or other social service agency. Many of these fathers have difficulty using such resources because they have not learned to trust other adults and feel that asking for help only confirms their "badness" and increases their low self-esteem. Because of this, individualized therapy may need to precede any group work; however, a major goal here is to increase quantitatively and qualitatively the individual's social network as quickly as possible.

Parent-education classes are important in teaching child development, age-appropriate expectations, and the child's goals of misbehavior, in addition to providing feedback from other parents. The insularity of abusive families may serve to hide the father's behavior at home from peers and extended family; thus these fathers are less likely to have contact with normal models of child rearing than do fathers in other families. A heterogeneous parenting group in which abusing and nonabusing fathers participate together might alleviate distorted perceptions of appropriate social behavior.

Self-help groups, such as the nationally organized Parents Anonymous chapters, are available to parents who have experienced problems with physical abuse. For some reason we have experienced less success with these groups than with the self-help groups for sexual abusers. Perhaps use of the adjective "anonymous" attributes something negative to the state of being a parent, or perhaps this group of parents does not want the broad social network that the sexual abusers seem to almost demand.

Another implication of the limited social contacts that abusing fathers report concerns the kind of network they can provide for their children. Without appropriate feedback and reinforcement, children in these families may perpetuate the same deviant behavioral patterns as their father. Children activity groups for both victims and siblings could provide feedback opportunities.

Marital Adjustment. Physically abusing fathers commonly report wanting a more satisfactory marital relationship, although more satisfactory may indeed mean more pathological. As previously stated, typically the marital dyad in a physically abusing family is symbiotic and passive-dependent in nature (Justice & Justice, 1976); most of the energy in the system is tied up by the parents who seek to meet, or have met, their own emotional needs. The child's needs may impede the marital dyad and, consequently, the child becomes a target for abuse. When a father can view his child as an age-appropriate individual (not a need-satisfying object), and when he can tolerate the child's negative behaviors, his ability to parent effectively is dramatically enhanced.

Stress. A study by Justice and Duncan (1975) concluded that, on the basis of results from another questionnaire, the symbiosis of physically abusing parents makes the individuals more "vulnerable to life changes, which in turn produce stress" (p. 115). It seems just as likely that high levels of stress result in an individual turning to his support system, which, in this case, is his spouse. Again, helping the father utilize other resources to resolve or adapt to his stresses will serve to remove the child as a target for the parent's frustration. Anger control and stress management are important components of therapy for the physical abuser.

Sexually Abusing Fathers

Many view most child abuse as a symptom of family dysfunction, and principal function of intrafamilial sexual abuse (incest) seems to be to ward off family disintegration. From a treatment perspective, however, it is important to emphasize that the father is factually and morally responsible for the sexual abuse. Contrary to physical abuse, in which the child may be viewed as actually eliciting his or her own abuse by being perceived as different and/or by developing a set of interaction behaviors that trigger abuse (Bell, 1971, 1977; Martin, 1976), in sexual abuse the child has no role in eliciting the abuse. (Of course, when a father's attention has become sexualized and the child has become eroticized, the child may develop behaviors that appear quite seductive.) The father's acknowledgment of responsibility for the incest is not enough. The dysfunctional behavior must be stopped immediately, and family treatment needs must be recognized and addressed.

Social Isolation. Sexually abusing fathers often report extreme emotional isolation. In Tyler's (1983) study, some reported no attachment figure whatever, and those fathers who did often reported that the one person they were closest to, fondest of, and so on was a child or friend. These fathers also reported that, although their social network was greater than that of the physically abusing fathers, it was not adequate for them. Though less socially isolated, they desired more friends. The success of groups, such as Parents United for Sexual Abusers (Giarretto, 1982), certainly confirms this finding. If the sexually abusing fathers' perception of the inadequacy of their support systems is accurate, their ability to benefit from the group for both peer support and confrontation is very helpful in

addressing issues of appropriate use of power, resolution of authority conflicts, decreasing use of denial and regression to manage stress, and setting
and maintaining of appropriate boundaries. Group therapy is one of several modalities generally employed simultaneously with other forms of
therapy.

Marital Adjustment.   Marital discord and a poor sexual relationship
are significant correlates of intrafamilial sexual abuse. Extremely poor
communication between husband and wife does not allow for individual
expression and negotiation of needs. Contrary to the physically abusing
father who appears to be enmeshed in the marital relationship, the incest
father appears to be almost disengaged from the relationship. The goal in
therapy would be to facilitate either reengagement of the couple, helping
them to learn appropriate ways of meeting each other's emotional needs,
or separation, so that the father can seek appropriate adult relationships
outside the family.

Stress.   The typical incest offender is described as a father whose sexual preference is generally an adult female and who resorts (regresses) to
involvement with children only when under stress. Successful therapy with
the incestuous father depends on his self-awareness and his capacity for
insight. Since situational and personal stress plays an important part in the
motivation of the incest father, the therapeutic process concentrates on
client education and rehearsal of coping behaviors. The approach is cognitive, and emphasizes alteration of thought patterns and activities.

Typically, our clinical assessment reveals a father who reacts to crisis
situations by reexperiencing early abuse trauma and the resultant emotional feelings of anger, rejection, fear, and so. It may be that the traumatic
experience facilitated an imprinting or a conditioning process of arousal,
so that the man finds children arousing later in life. Teaching the person
methods to control and reduce stress, relabeling the stress and the reactions, and providing alternatives to the abuse are integral components of
this cognitive restructuring. Since complete elimination of stress is not
possible, the learning of new coping skills is imperative.

Summary

Appropriate treatment for the abusing father depends on the nature and
extent of the abuse, the offender's marital relationship, the extent to which
he accepts responsibility for the abuse, has capacity for insight and self-
awareness, and is willing to utilize community resource and support systems. Individual, couple, and family therapy are all important therapy
modalities for this population. Because the history of childhood trauma is

prevalent in many of the fathers' own backgrounds, individual therapy may need to precede any couple or family treatment. In our experience, court-ordered treatment for the offender is preferred by both the client and the therapist. A threat of parole revocation often helps to ensure client participation in long-term treatment. Participation in self-help groups, such as Parents Anonymous and Parents United, is encouraged. The recidivism rate of offenders in the Parents United Program in Santa Clara, California, was reported by Giarretto (1982) to be less than 2 percent.

A great deal of caution must be used when interpreting any of these data, because this is still a very new field. Research needs to focus on evaluation of the different treatment modalities and programs. In addition, highly specialized training programs for clinicians need to be developed.

SUMMARY AND CONCLUSIONS

This chapter discussed the role of the father in child abuse and implications for treatment. Several theoretical approaches to understanding child abuse were discussed; despite different emphases on individual and social/cultural factors, it is generally agreed that abuse is multidetermined. Although they have similarities, child physical abuse and child sexual abuse also have differences in characteristics that are important considerations in planning treatment and interventions.

Clinical history, marital adjustment, stress factors, and social isolation are important influences on a father's parenting ability. The socialization of males, which places little emphasis on acquisition of nurturing skills or sensitivity to emotional needs, may play some role in the incidence of sexual abuse, specifically incest. Perhaps increased and supported participation of fathers in child rearing would result in a change in a father's understanding of his children and his own sense of being worthwhile. Increased empathy and self-esteem might enhance marital adjustment and willingness to participate in a group.

As divorce rates increase, so too do the number of marriages and stepfathers. The high incidence of sexual abuse by stepfathers suggests the need for early marital and family therapy in remarriage situations. Certainly, the quality of a child's relationship to the father, whether stepfather or natural father, helps to determine the child's vulnerability to abuse, and it may be that increased father participation in child rearing, rather than decreased contact, will serve to enhance the quality of the father-child relationship.

It is suggested that boys be exposed to child-care experiences quite early in their lives, starting with doll play and supervised babysitting in the family setting. Required high school classes that grant community service credit to boys who work in day-care centers would guarantee some exposure to child-care experiences. To facilitate bonding, fathers can be included in the birthing process of their child; be encouraged to hold, feed, and diaper their infant; and be granted paternity leave if desired. Finally, the whole concept of job sharing and flex time for fathers needs to be explored and supported. Quality parenting takes time and a great deal of effort.

REFERENCES

American Humane Association (1981, November). *National analysis of official child neglect and abuse reporting*. Denver, CO: U. S. Department of Health and Human Services, Office of Human Development Services (DHHS Publication No. [HDS] 81-30232).

Bandura, A. (1973). *Aggression: A social learning analysis*. Englewood, Cliffs, NJ: Prentice-Hall.

Bell, R. Q. (1971). Stimulus control of parent or caretaker behavior by offspring. *Developmental Psychology, 4,* 63–74.

Bell, R. Q. (1977). *Child effects on adults*. Hillsdale, NJ: Erlbaum.

Bellack, L., & Antell, M. (1974). An intercultural study of aggressive behavior on children's playgrounds. *American Journal of Orthopsychiatry, 44,* 503–511.

Burgess, A. W., & Holmstrom, L. L. (1975). Sexual trauma of children and adolescents. *Nursing Clinics of North America, 10,* 551–563.

Butler, J. F., & Crane, D. R. (1979). Self-report schedules for use in assessing the marital adjustment of abusive and nonabusive parents. *The American Journal of Family Therapy, 5,* 80–128.

Finkelhor, D. (1979). *Sexually victimized children*. New York: Free Press.

Finkelhor, D., & Hoteling, G. (1983). *Sexual abuse in the national incidence study of child abuse and neglect*. Report to National Center for Child Abuse and Neglect.

Finkelhor, D. (1984). *Child sexual abuse: New theory and research*. New York: Free Press.

Garbarino, J. (1977a). The human ecology of child maltreatment: A conceptual model for research. *Journal of Marriage and the Family, 39,* 721–736.

Garbarino, J. (1977b). The price of privacy in the social dynamics of child abuse. *Child Welfare, 56,* 565–575.

Garbarino, J., & Sherman, D. (1980). High-risk neighborhoods and high-risk families: The human ecology of child maltreatment. *Child Development, 51,* 188–198.

Giarretto, H. (1982). *Integrated treatment of child sexual abuse*. Los Angeles: Science and Behavior Books.

Gil, D. G. (1970). *Violence against children: Physical child abuse in the United States.* Cambridge, MA: Harvard University Press.

Groth, N. A., & Burgess, A. W. (1979). Sexual trauma in the life histories of rapists and child molesters. *Victimology, 4,* 253–264.

Henderson, S., Duncan-Jones, P., Byrne, D. G., & Scott, R. (1980). Measuring social relationships: The interview schedule for social interaction. *Psychological Medicine, 10,* 723–734.

Holmes, T. H., & Rahe, R. H. (1967). The social readjustment rating scale. *Journal of Psychcosomatic Reasearch, 2,* 213–218.

Jason, J., Burton, A., Williams, S., & Rochat, R. (1982). Epidemiologic differences between sexual and physical child abuse. *Journal of American Medical Association, 247,* 344–348.

Justice, B., & Duncan, D. F. (1975). Physical abuse of children as a public health problem. *Public Health Reviews, 4,* 183–200.

Justice, B., & Justice, R. (1976). *Abusing family.* New York: Human Sciences Press.

Kempe, C. H., & Helfer, R. E. (Eds.). (1968). *The battered child.* Chicago: University of Chicago Press.

Kempe, D., & Helfer, R. (Eds.). (1972). *Helping the battered child and his family.* Philadelphia: Lippincott.

Kempe, R. S., & Kempe, C. H. (1976). Assessing family pathology. In R. E. Helfer & C. H. Kempe (Eds.), *Child abuse and neglect: The family and the community.* Cambridge, MA: Ballinger.

Kercher, G. (1980). *Responding to child sexual abuse.* Huntsville, Tx: Sam Houston State University, Criminal Justice Center.

Kercher, G., & McShane, M. (1983). *The prevalence of child sexual abuse victimization in an adult sample of Texas residents.* Huntsville, TX: Sam Houston State University.

Lenoski, E. F. (1974). *Translating injury data into preventive and health-care services: Physical child abuse.* Master's thesis, University of Southern California School of Medicine, Los Angeles.

Lustig, N., Dresser, J. W., Spellman, S. W., & Murray, T. B. (1966). Incest. *Archives of General Psychology, 14,* 31–40.

Martin, H. (1976). *The abused child: A multidisciplinary approach to developmental issues and treatment.* Cambridge, MA: Ballinger.

Mayer, A. (1983). *Incest: A treatment manual for therapy with victims, spouses, and offenders.* Tampa, FL: Learning Publications.

Mrazek, P. B., & Kempe, C. H. (1981). *Sexually abused children and their families.* New York: Pergamon Press.

Russell, D. (1980). *The prevalence and impact of marital rape in San Francisco.* Paper presented to American Sociological Association, New York.

Russell, D. (1983). Incidence and prevalence of intrafamilial and extrafamilial sexual abuse of female children. *Child Abuse and Neglect, 7,* 133–146.

Spanier, G. B. (1976). Assessing the quality of marriages and similar dyads. *Journal of Marriage and the Family, 38,* 14–28.

Spinetta, J., & Rigler, D. (1972). The child-abusing parent: A psychological review. *Psychological Bulletin, 77,* 296–304.

Straus, M., & Hoteling, G. T. (Eds.). (1981). *The social causes of husband-wife violence.* Minneapolis: University of Minnesota Press.

Swanson, D. W. (1968).; Adult sexual abuse of children (the man and circumstances). *Diseases of the Nervous System, 29,* 677–683.

Tyler, A. (1978). *Conceptualization and development of a model crisis nursery.* Master's thesis, University of Utah, Salt Lake City.

Tyler, A. H. (1983). *Child-abusing and nonabusing fathers.* Doctoral dissertation, University of Utah, Salt Lake City.

Weiss, R. S. (1973). *Loneliness: The experience of emotional and social isolation.* Cambridge, MA: MIT Press.

Weiss, R. S. (1974). The provision of social relationship. In L. Rubin (Ed.), *Doing unto others.* Englewood Cliffs, NJ: Prentice-Hall.

Young, L. (1964). *Wednesday's children: A study of child abuse and neglect.* New York: McGraw-Hill.

CHAPTER 10

Overseas Fathers: Vulnerabilities and Treatment Strategies

GORDON K. FARLEY AND SIDNEY WERKMAN
University of Colorado School of Medicine

Although working for a period of time overseas is an increasingly common option for fathers, overseas family life is largely an unstudied event. This chapter reviews what is known about the effects of overseas life on families, with particular attention to fathers. The motivations for moving overseas are described, as are the special demands of overseas life, specifically the highly visible public role assumed by fathers who are representatives of their country. The considerable vulnerabilities of life in such a role are examined. Alterations in patterns of interaction in the family and particular views that children and wives have of their father and spouse who works in a foreign country are considered. The particular characteristics and problems of fathers serving in the military overseas are highlighted. Vignettes from clinical cases illustrate important points regarding overseas families. Finally, common mental health problems of overseas fathers are discussed and useful therapeutic techniques offered for mental health professionals who work with such problems.

MOTIVATIONS FOR WORKING OVERSEAS

Any father who chooses to work overseas makes a statement about his life priorities. Career heads the list of these priorities, and this choice, in turn, complicates fatherhood and mental health treatment of overseas fathers. While consciously a man may think he simply chose at random to work overseas, in fact he has made a fateful career decision that often involves difficult or dangerous situations, separation from relatives, and loss of access to the recreational and social activities of the United States. Because of the unusual financial and career satisfaction enticements, a father who makes an overseas work commitment tends to be goal directed, ambitious, competitive, hard working, and demanding. These very qualities often add to the difficulty in raising children and adapting to the competing demands of career, spouse, and family. In the tensions among these various demands, career typically comes first.

The motivations for a father to choose a profession with overseas options or obligations are many. Some fathers see an overseas move as an opportunity to advance a stagnated career. Others value the opportunity to regulate the intimacy of their relationships both within and outside the family through geographic distance and mobility. The latter motivation is largely unconscious. Obviously, many variations are to be found in the motivations of fathers who work overseas.

SCOPE OF THE PROBLEM

In a survey done in 1976 (Luebke, 1976), approximately 1,375,000 military personnel, 236,000 people engaged in private sector activities, and 110,000 civilian government employees were living overseas. Each family and each situation is unique. However, we describe and develop here typical patterns of adaptation that have emerged from clinical study and research findings with this unusually varied population.

In a situation in which all goals are directed toward career rather than family, little time, effort, or interest may be left over for noncareer concerns. Free time is used for golf, spending time with a spouse, socialization, and other adult activities. Fatherhood may seem an imposition. The father feels married to his job rather than to his family. One harried, overseas executive described it this way to one of the authors:

You can't relax. It's a pressurized 24-hour-a day job. When you're over here and there's something to be done you have to do it because there are so few people available. You are on the scene; you live on the post. So they call you. We are always understaffed. There is always tension and you never feel you have completed a job. Your family suffers because of this, and you just count your days until you can get back to the United States. It gets to my wife and children when I just can't be with them, especially when they had become accustomed to my coming home at night, getting out the barbeque grill, and spending the evening with them back in the States.

A father caught up in an overseas organization feels he must respond to demands put on him. There is no one else, no backup structure to call on, and jobs are either done by the person on the spot or are not done at all. When errors and losses occur, it seems particularly clear whose responsibility they are, whereas in a large corporation in the United States responsibility and blame are often diffused.

ADDITIONAL DEMANDS OF OVERSEAS LIFE

Along with great pressure is the unavoidable element of living a *representational role*. The American man overseas is highly visible because of his language, dress, and habits. Frequently such a man is the representative of a well-known company, the government, or the military. He is observed both during his working hours and his recreational time in the overseas community. His role can be very pleasing, although at times difficult.

Difficulties in Living a Representational Role

The father's living a representational role can result in his *idealization* by the child. A father who wears medals, makes speeches, rides in a chauffeur-driven car, and leaves home frequently on mysterious emergency missions might seem more like a television character than a dad to a child. The child then does not know an actual father, but only an adult who is deferred to and feared, like a school principal. At the same time that the father's work appears important and glamorous, the child may know little of the actual mechanics and day-to-day details of what the father does. The child thinks that the father knows all the answers to problems and, indeed, is perfect. The mother, in an effort to present her children with a favorable view of their father who spends little time at home, may unconsciously strengthen this idealization. The child may feel that it is impossible to live up to the father's expectations, and demoralization may result. Alternatively, the child may rebel against the father to express a sense of independence and separation from the great demand for conformity and effectiveness. The father in a representational role must be alert to the problem this role implies and be ready to demythologize himself to his children with fact and experiences. He needs to tell his children about what he actually does, to describe the positives and negatives of his work, and to point out that he makes mistakes. The father needs to emphasize that it is not necessary to be perfect, that he is well aware that he is not perfect, and that perfection is, in fact, not a very desirable quality.

When a father forgets to demythologize himself, he may carry his representational role into family involvements and demand unrealistic subservience and dependence from his wife and children.

Transience

Three years is the median time for an overseas assignment. At the end of this time it is possible to close the desk on mistakes and move on to another post without having to live with the consequences of actions or to learn from them. Frequently an overseas job is a stepping stone to another better job, rather than a destination, and a sense of never being fully committed results. This feeling of transience is not helpful when the complex developmental issues that may arise in family life need to be worked out (Werkman, 1972). For example, a child with a physical handicap or learning disability needs many years of dedicated concern. To become proficient in the activities of daily living, the handicapped child needs concentrated attention over a long period of time. Overseas fathers have great difficulty recognizing this, because they live in another time scale, that of short-term goals and lesser importance assigned to distant consequences. Even physically healthy children need an attentive father, one who is available for the many hours needed in piano lessons, dancing, dramatics, or basketball.

Lack of Supports

A father may become confused and uncertain about child rearing and need the advice and ideas of other men who have been through similar situations with their children. He needs a validator, an observer or commentator, who can offer useful suggestions. Intimates who are willing to offer honest, candid, wise appraisals about delinquent acts or sexual problems in children are difficult to find when short-term relationships with people of different backgrounds or nationalities are the rule.

Isolation

Overseas fathers get out of step with U. S. standards of child rearing, and the children, when the family returns home, have had unusual backgrounds and experiences that are difficult to share with their age mates. Such children are at risk for experiencing alienation, distorted sexual practices, and troubling separation events (Werkman, 1972). Particularly in the present, when child rearing is radically changing in the United States, it is important for fathers to follow these trends. For example, fathers in the United States now participate more in the feeding, clothing, and nurturing of their children (Lamb, 1982). This pattern is still an unusual one for the father overseas.

Families of Origin

An overseas father cannot check with a brother or sister about child care. He loses touch with the aging, physical illness, alcoholism, and financial problems of relatives left at home. He cannot take part in the family business, help to resolve a family estate, or be involved in U. S. community activities. Overseas life offers a temporary reprieve from extended family stresses but it also extracts a cost. The temporary aspect of overseas life makes difficult the investment in any long-term interests, and the overseas family may live out a "heritage of transience" (Werkman, 1978) that emphasizes instant intimacy, risk taking, and distorted idealization of many aspects of experience.

In addition to the disadvantages of overseas life to the father, there are many benefits. In the United States, a very common source of domestic dispute is the division of labor in the household. Mothers and fathers are very likely to argue about who does certain tasks such as cooking, cleaning, laundry, and chauffeuring. In a foreign country in which low-priced labor may be available, these arguments are likely to arise less often.

FATHERS IN THE UNIFORMED SERVICES

Obviously there is no single type of "military father," and any discussion of a generalized kind of military fathering experience does violence to the uniqueness and variety of people in the armed services. However, we often seem to see, perhaps particularly in the exaggeration and distortions of what are considered "military" characteristics, some recurring themes that show through the many variations in style of life between commissioned and noncommissioned officers, the different military services, and posting to various parts of the world. The armed services all tend to program the lives of their personnel and to focus on issues of discipline, conformity, submerging of personal goals, and mission-directed activity in similar ways. Such qualities often get transferred from the field situation to the home, as described very well by J. A. Kenny, an Air Force mental health professional (Kenny, 1967):

First, the father with his command and obey military background is more apt to be strict. *Obedience* is a military virtue, self-expression is not. The father may translate the military manner into the discipline of the children. A second factor which lessens acting out among children is the total authoritarian impact of the military community. The father is in a duty status twenty-four hours a day, seven days a week. He is responsible for the behavior of his dependents. For example, if a child misbehaves on the school bus, and the father does not take appropriate corrective action, the case may be reported to the father's commanding officer.

In such situations children are at risk for the development of somewhat rigid, authoritarian character structures themselves and for the whole range of passive-aggressive, rebellious, and delinquent acts that occur so often in similar father-child interaction patterns. The important issue for the father, and for the therapist working with such a father, is to make this pitfall, the "command and obey" ethic, known and conscious so that the father and the family have a choice about how to mold their behavior.

For example, it takes a strong father to support children in the normal range of adolescent self-expression, imperfections, and experimentation when such activities may be misinterpreted. The father can be helped to encourage the child in his or her own unique and individual developmental possibilities while still remaining aware of the reasonable limits of behavior. In more serious cases in which actual delinquency by a child has occurred, it is important for a father to be able to stand up and support the child—as he would a child who has epilepsy or diabetes—while still paying attention to the significance of the delinquent act. Too often such situations degenerate into a shouting match in which the father says, "You are destroying my career," rather than looking for a rational, negotiated, and therapeutically effective solution.

Separation from Family and Changes in Individual Roles

Many military tours demand months of "detached duty" in foreign countries, a considerable time at sea, or alert watches during emergencies. At such periods the lacuna left by the father's absence means that the mother loses a crucial support; she either feels pained and helpless at the loss or she takes on a new authority role. Family structure alters radically, often in ways that a father may not comprehend (Frank, Shanfield, & Evans, 1983). The mother may experience a sense of growth that then complicates her relationship with a returned husband and certainly makes his reentry one that demands considerable forethought.

Problems of the Father Reentering the Family

Though a wife and children may feel deserted during the husband's detached duty, they also will take on new responsibilities and authority. The wife's growth may complicate relationships with her military husband. One mother in the military described with considerable sensitivity the subtle shifts in power that may occur when a father has been away for an extended time:

Many women get a big charge from being overseas because they are forced to become independent when their husbands are away. They change from being the "little wife" and find that they become effective, independent human beings.

Husbands have to watch out, though, because when they do come home they find that their wives took over many of the jobs and prerogatives in the home.

Children in such cases find themselves caught between an absent father and a mother who has changed from being a "little wife" into a self-reliant, assertive, confident person with many new competencies. Naturally they look to the mother for directions and answers. When the father returns from detached duty, he may find that his children have changed or become alienated in baffling ways, as described by the following service wife and mother:

You find a great deal of over-mothering because the only place women are really needed is with their children. So wives overcompensate when husbands are gone by requiring their kids to stay home a lot more. They overfeed them and overprotect them. A son may be put in a husband's role, and all kinds of trouble develop.

It takes a sensitive husband, and an even more sensitive therapist when such a situation comes to professional attention, to figure out what has happened. The overt symptom simply is that the child rejects, criticizes, or ignores the returning father. The father may then find himself turning back to the techniques and formulas used with troops, as described by this officer:

Giving and obeying orders are so much a part of overseas life, and rank is so built into the military situation, that many fathers never think to have discussions with the children at home. Fathers think teenagers follow their lead, but their children are not in the Army with them. A 13-old girl is not going to worry about the Army's mission when she wants to smoke pot.

Under the stress of return, uncertainty, and irritation at not being obeyed, the military father only too often relies on his field experience, and this reliance immensely complicates relationships with his family. Just such a situation was recalled by an experienced military wife:

Fathers try to run their home like they do their companies. Some men never take off their uniforms even when they are at home! They give demerits and chew out their children in foul, barracks language. Let's say a sergeant has had a hard day. He comes home, looks at the duty roster, and finds that his teenage son has not taken out the garbage in three days. He calls the kid before him for inspection, reads him the riot act, and then tells him he will do his work or get so many demerits. Then the punishment he gives out is unbelievably disproportionate to the crime.

EVALUATION, DIAGNOSIS, AND
TREATMENT TECHNIQUES

The work of diagnosis and treatment is to unravel the many threads of family structure, career-family tensions, adult-child differences, developmental needs, and the legitimate requirements of an overseas career situation. We now consider the technical diagnostic and therapeutic work that can help resolve these complex, demanding situations.

The core conflicts of overseas life that result in psychological symptoms include (1) parent-child tension, (2) mid-career issues, (3) loss of perspective about the meaningfulness of a job or a relationship to a boss, (4) children who express their disturbance through drug use, school difficulties, or sexual problems, and (5) role confusion.

A child expelled from school or in trouble in the community can potentially ruin a father's overseas career. It is not unusual for a child to need to be sent back to the United States, and if so at least one parent must accompany the child. Wives complain that fathers do not take enough time with the children, and husbands level a similar accusation at their wives. Each tends to complain that the other is not involved enough.

Symptom Patterns

Another way of looking at diagnostic issues is to note symptoms. The primary symptoms seen in fathers are anxiety and inability to function at work. Depressive symptoms, sleep disturbance, and rare manic episodes may also be seen. Very often the ticket of admission for treatment is a complaint about being overworked, worn out, and/or disturbed about a child or a spouse. Some overseas fathers have well-defined psychiatric disorders and can benefit from careful medical and psychiatric evaluation and consideration of the use of psychopharmacological treatment.

Little psychotic behavior and few schizophrenic episodes are seen, as people with such disorders show problems before they are given responsible, adult, overseas jobs. However, short-term drug-induced psychotic behaviors do occur.

Facilities for Treatment

The first line of defense consists of ministers, counselors, and physicians in the overseas post. In addition, competent American-trained mental health professionals now practice in most of the large cities of the world. When a post does not contain facilities for accurate diagnosis, referral of a patient or client to a community that does have such facilities is a consideration. Most overseas communities now publish resource directories that list mental health professionals. The situation is different from that in the United States, however, in that there are not nearly the number of specialized facilities for dealing with problems. For example, there is a dearth of the inpatient treatment facilities needed for short-term evaluation and treatment of drug-related problems and depression.

The diagnostician and therapist will typically hear a patient present a mix of psychophysiologic symptoms, including headaches, fatigue, hypochondriasis, jitteriness, difficulty in eating, and irritability of the gastrointestinal tract, before he goes on to discuss family problems. Many of these problems may seriously compromise the ability to function adequately in the work place, and they may go undiagnosed and untreated for many years. As a result, the patient may not be consciously aware that irritability or demandingness is a symptom of depression or that complaints about children or spouse may, similarly, be aspects of depression.

Specialized Mental Health Counselors in the United States

A number of facilities on both U.S. coasts have developed short-term, focused diagnostic procedures for overseas personnel who return with psychological and psychiatric problems. These facilities specialize in working on the immediate issues presented by the patient, and they formulate structured, cognitive treatments that can be helpful in a short period of time.

Whether the person is overseas or in the United States, most issues can be diagnosed and effectively resolved in a few months of careful treatment. When a patient must be returned to the United States, the therapist should prepare thoroughly for that return by making a referral to a good therapist in the town where the patient is going and doing everything possible to protect the patient's present and future career while therapy is taking place.

Confidentiality

The assurance of confidentiality is a critical issue in treatment of people overseas. The therapist must have clear guidelines about what is to be reported to the patient's superior. If a report is necessary, it should be discussed openly with the patient. Writing the report together and reviewing the final form of the report can help in building a working alliance. Often a therapist can be a helpful advocate for a patient who is not functioning well but whose problem can predictably be worked on effectively in a short time.

The Stigma of Mental Health Problems

A therapist can also be an advocate in regard to the stigma of mental health problems. A father's representational role may encourage him not only to deny personal problems but to exaggerate the consequences of problems being known to superiors and others in his organization. Therapists must discuss these issues, learn the reality of the situation, and defuse the concern that any therapeutic problem will be a "black mark" on a person's record. Sometimes this work must go on over months and through much political work within the patient's organization.

Many fathers hope to defer or cover up problems while they are overseas. The overseas post becomes a lighted fuse or a time bomb, and the major wish is to get home before an explosion occurs. The following is how one father expressed it:

Here in India we all watch each other too closely. We call it a fishbowl syndrome. People won't admit they have problems with drinking or with their children or when they feel their jobs are on the line. Most people want to hide their problems, and in a way they are right. There is just no place to talk about the things that bother you, much less the little things that make you feel good. You always have the sense that somebody is going to judge you, somebody who doesn't know you very well. People just want to get through the year or through their tour and get out. It's a feeling that they just don't want anyone else to know what their problems are.

As a result, problems simmer for a long time only to explode in divorce, major mental health disturbance, or abandonment or abuse of children or spouse on return to the United States (Werkman, 1980). A great deal of conflict, grieving, and disappointment are deferred in overseas life, though it would be much better if it were worked through at the time it occurs.

The VIP Syndrome

Therapists often treat Very Important Persons differently than they would a more usual patient. This special treatment is often to the detriment of the therapeutic work.

Many patients in need of mental health services overseas are in a highly visible position at the top of their own community hierarchy. They have implicit or even explicit control over the therapist's life, through the referral of patients or sharing of social and official activities. It is important that the therapist define clearly a sense of independence and autonomy to forestall the development of what can be nasty, even paranoid, power struggles with commanding officers and heads of corporations over such issues as alcoholism, sexual dysfunction, or aggressive acts.

CASE HISTORY

This case history illustrates a number of the issues that have to do with overseas life such as the VIP syndrome, changing family relationships, military personnel, and fathers in a representational role.

A 41-year-old man, who was an Air Force colonel overseas, complained that he was at his wit's end about his 16-year-old son who was expelled from a Department of Defense school for smoking pot. The man was an articulate, serious, direct person who was exceedingly tentative about all issues and blamed himself for his son's difficulties.

His son stole money from his mother, stole several rings from relatives, and refused to work in school. The adolescent said, "I know I'm a turkey and deep down I know there's nothing good about me."

Mother and father quarreled about handling their son. Both believed the other should be tougher and more reliable. The father began to drink excessively and work late or attend meetings at night, trying to avoid the difficulties with his family, and had difficulty sleeping. (These responses became apparent only through questioning, as the man was overtly an extremely effective person who did not volunteer information of a conflicted nature.)

Colonel F. said: "All parents' feelings about their children must be measured, and mine are hardly an exception. In my darkest thoughts I sometimes think his behavior is unconsciously designed to destroy us, to retaliate for the spankings I gave him when he was a small child. I think he is frightened of me physically. At the same time he is very much like me. I was fat as a child, stole, cut up, didn't do well in school. But then my parents read me the riot act and I shaped up."

We see here the beginning of a problem that includes generational repetition of symptoms, a very concerned father who uses self-defeating tactics but then becomes irritated at and critical of his son. He is either overly measured and thoughtful or impulsive and harsh. There is no middle ground. Colonel F. is aware of this problem and it is this that preys on him and increases his sense of depression.

This case illustrates the need for several interventions: family diagnosis, thorough diagnosis of depressive potential in Colonel F., and careful attention to the 16-year-old's problems.

SUGGESTIONS FOR THE THERAPIST

Support Network

It is often helpful for the therapist to connect a father with other fathers, people who can discuss problems with children, bosses, future jobs. This helps to combat the feeling of isolation experienced by many patients. Father support groups or men's groups that deal with these issues have been organized in some overseas stations. In this group setting, fathers who have gained some mastery over the difficulties of overseas life can help those who are struggling with the new challenges.

Adult-Child Conflicts and Differentiations

The therapist can help the father who wants to treat the child with too much rationality, negotiation, and discussion to understand the difference between healthily autonomous adult behavior of father and mother overseas in regard to children's hours, drinking, and sexuality and the need to set definite limits on children's acceptable behavior. The unambivalent setting of reasonable limits is particularly important.

Spending Ordinary Time

The therapist can help the father learn or relearn what are legitimate children's pleasures and activities—rock video, fashions, Little League baseball, hiking, and so on (Werkman et al., 1981). One of the most powerful things a therapist can teach a father is to spend much time with a child in ordinary activities, such as throwing a baseball or having an ice cream cone together after the child's ballet class. This is "spending ordinary time." Many fathers understand the dramatic, brilliant activities, such as a weekend in Rome, but have no conception of the importance of moment-by-moment, day-by-day involvement with children.

At times the therapist can be most helpful by recognizing that father-child problems are, indeed, family problems and that family diagnosis and therapy can be the most useful approach to solving the problems.

Changing Relationships

Children's relationships with their fathers may be quite altered by the fact of life overseas (David & Elkind, 1966). In the first place, children usually have no voice in the decision to live overseas. Fathers may expect the child to be excited about the prospect of a new and challenging adventure, whereas the child may be angry and resentful about leaving behind familiarity, friends, and comfort. The child's mother may actively although unconsciously support the child's expression of resentment through a variety of means. The decision to move overseas may represent a pseudoconcensus much more than a true concensus of opinion in the family, children and the spouse feeling that they have no choice in the matter.

Father-Child Competitiveness

Issues of competitiveness between fathers and, particularly, sons tend to be overemphasized in an overseas setting. Removed from the modulating and attenuating influences of their peer groups both fathers and sons tend to focus rivalrous feelings on each other.

Problems involved in competition with children yield very well to family therapy in which a father might discover, for example, that he devaluates children or is resentful of the amount of time a child takes. The family might then begin to develop family priorities as well as career priorities and individual ones.

Nurturing

Because their job demands achievement, success, and competition, many overseas fathers have had little experience in simple aspects of intimacy and nurturing role modeling, which includes many hours of effort, ingenuity, and faith. It is clear that children learn best by modeling the behavior of important adult figures. They can only learn what it is to be a father through their father's behavior (Popplewell & Sheikh, 1979; Easterbrooks & Goldberg, 1984; Carlson, 1984; Miller & Roll, 1977). They can only learn that fathers nurture by having a father figure who is nurturing toward them.

Children reared overseas with the mother as the center of the family (a frequent situation) do not know what it is to have a male identification figure. They may develop fantasy father figures, but these are inevitably out of focus—too good, too demanding, too perfectionistic, too lax. A father who works hard overseas—a natural tendency in achievement-oriented people on short-term tours, who have the best of intentions and the wish to give their family "a better life"—may deprive the child of the experience needed most—fathering. This experience is very difficult to replace later on. The therapist can help patients by pointing out examples of good fathering and offering opportunities for activities such as hikes, and then discussing the effects of such activities.

Treatment of this kind is useful not only for the children but for the father, who can reconnect himself to his own childhood and his own feelings about fatherhood from a generation past.

Type A Fathers

The most prevalent type of person seen overseas is the somewhat demanding, somewhat perfectionistic, self-blaming, highly energetic person. Overseas work selects for this type. In addition, a sense of uncertainty and insecurity about personal worth seems to go with the overseas territory. The therapist can help patients examine these defenses so that they might relax and allow a more nurturing, accepting, loving person to emerge, one in whom the issues are not good and bad, right and wrong, but rather acceptance, play, sharing, involvement, commitment. Many fathers need to be taught that family activities are not competitive games in which self-respect is won or lost, but pleasurable involvements that, in a sense, have no end point other than that of family pleasure and solidarity. Rigid overseas patients often complain that if they give up their driving, demanding ways they will have nothing left. It is important to point out, however, that many issues in life are not either/or issues but rather are shaded, and there is no one correct way to behave or deal with others.

The therapist can help the father identify a mentor for himself, someone who knows what it is to be a good father and who has a disinterested yet effective concern about a father in trouble.

Return to the United States

The most difficult challenge in the cycle of international life is that of readapting to life in the United States. Most families report that it is far less stressful to move from one foreign country to another than it is to experience the jolt of coming back home (Werkman, 1975, 1980). As one 20-year-old recalled: "I hated everyone and everything I saw here and had to tell myself over and over again: 'Whoa, this is your country; it is what you are a part of.'"

Returnees to the United States leave important elements of themselves behind—languages gained, friends, customs, cultural events—when they give up a foreign way of life. They must change from being observers and guests, perpetual sightseers, to being active participants in a culture without the *International Herald Tribune* and the omnipresence of the American Embassy. This involves a heavy, often painful dose of living in the reality of the present rather than the fantasy and idealization of the past; the constant, even support of the father in the family is needed to make the transition successfully.

SUMMARY

Fathers who work overseas tend to place unusual emphasis on the importance of a career. This fact inevitably complicates relationships with children and spouse. The family's life becomes dominated by the work situation, particularly when, as is often the case, the father works in a highly visible international business organization or in the U.S. government. Such representational roles frequently result in an exaggeration and idealization of the importance of the job and the father, to the detriment of family relationships.

Transience becomes a central issue for overseas fathers and their families. Frequent moves from country to country can become crystallized into a style of life in which important developmental needs and relationships are ignored. Lack of intimate, supportive friends in the brittle overseas environment makes it difficult to address interpersonal issues and the complexity of relationships. Fathers, wives, and children may all lose touch with in-laws, parents, and other important relatives, and they cannot participate in political, civic, and recreational activities that enhance a sense of community, commitment, and roots.

Military fathers and their families must grapple with distinctive nuances of discipline, vulnerability to censure, and exposure to overt danger. In such families, the "command and obey" attitude may be transferred into the home. Children are particularly at risk when they find that their behavior reflects on father's advancement and career.

Treatment issues revolve around an accurate assessment and diagnosis of the specific types of problems encountered in overseas fathers and their families; careful attention to defining useful treatment facilities throughout the world; and the use of time-limited, focal treatment plans for this transient population. Of particular concern are issues of confidentiality and the potential stigma of mental health problems for the overseas father.

REFERENCES

Carlson, B. E. (1984). The father's contribution to child care: Effects on children's perceptions of parental roles. *American Journal of Orthopsychiatry, 54,* 123–136.

David, H. P., & Elkind, D. (1966). Family adaptation overseas: Some mental health considerations. *Journal of Mental Hygiene, 50,* 92–99.

Easterbrooks, M. A., & Goldberg, W. A. (1984). Toddler development in the family: Impact of father involvement and parenting characteristics. *Child Development, 55,* 740–752.

Frank, M., Shanfield, S. B., & Evans, H. E. (1983). The in and out parent: Strategies for managing reentry stress. *Military Medicine, 196,* 846–849.

Kenny, J. A. (1967). The child in the military community. *Journal of the American Academy of Child Psychiatry, 6,* 51–63.

Lamb, M. E. (1982). Paternal influences on early social-emotional development. *Journal of Child Psychology and Psychiatry, 23,* 185–190.

Luebke, P. T. (1976). *American elementary and secondary community schools abroad.* Washington, DC: American Association of School Administration.

Miller, L., & Roll, R. (1977). Relationships between son's feelings of being understood by their fathers and measures of son's psychological functioning. *Journal of Genetic Psychology, 130,* 19–25.

Popplewell, J. F., & Sheikh, A. A. (1979). The role of the father in child development: Review of the literature. *International Journal of Social Psychiatry, 25,* 267–284.

Werkman, S. (1972). Hazards of rearing children in foreign countries. *American Journal of Psychiatry, 128,* 992–997.

Werkman, S. (1975). Over here and over there: American adolescents overseas. *Foreign Service Journal, 52,* 13–16.

Werkman, S. (1977). *Bringing up children overseas.* New York: Basic Books.

Werkman, S. (1978). A heritage of transience. In E. J. Anthony & C. Chiland (Eds.), *The child in his family: Children and their parents in a changing world.* New York: Wiley.

Werkman, S. (1980). Coming home: Adjustment of Americans to the United States after living abroad. In G. V. Coelho & P. J. Ahmed (Eds.), *Uprooting and development: Dilemmas of coping with modernization.* New York: Plenum.

Werkman, S., Farley, G. K., Butler, C., & Quayhagen, M. (1981). The psychological effects of moving and living overseas. *Journal of the American Academy of Child Psychiatry, 20,* 645–657.

CHAPTER 11

Hospital-Based Intervention for Fathers

ROSS D. PARKE AND ASHLEY BEITEL

University of Illinois

Ideas about the father's role in the family have been undergoing a shift in the past decade. Fathers are now recognized as playing important direct and indirect roles in their infant's development. Fathers have a direct impact on the infant's social and cognitive development through caretaking and play. The father can also *indirectly* affect the infant's development, however, by his mediating impact on the mother and the mother-infant interaction (Parke, Power, & Gottman, 1979; Lewis & Feiring, 1981).

At the same time that the father is being recognized as an important contributor to infant development, cultural trends are increasing the opportunities for and pressure on fathers to assume a more active role in early infant care and development. This is evidenced in several ways. First, an increasing number of mothers work full-time outside the home, either for economic or other reasons (Hoffman, 1984). This often results in the father assuming a greater proportion of the responsibility for infant caretaking (Russell & Radin, 1983). A second emerging phenomenon that results in a larger role for the father in child rearing is the greater frequency with which fathers are assuming custody for children as a result of divorce or other legal action (Orthner, Brown, & Ferguson, 1976). In most of these custody cases, fathers are required to provide for all the physical and psychological child-care needs that had previously been at least partly the responsibility of the mother. Third, physicians are permitting shorter postpartum hospital stays for mothers and newborn infants. Mothers may arrive home not yet fully recovered from childbirth, a situation that places increased demands on the father in terms of housekeeping and infant caregiving. Fourth, recent research has shown that fathers participate more in early child care in the case of infants born prematurely (Yogman,

293

1982) and of a cesarean section delivery (Vietze et al., 1980). In the first case, the increased demands placed on the family by the preterm infant promoted heightened father involvement, while in the second situation the reduced capacity of the mother may have stimulated greater paternal participation (Parke & Tinsley, 1985). Fifth, mothers are returning to work much sooner after birth than in previous years (Bronfenbrenner, 1974). Therefore fathers must increase their involvement in child care or alternative care must be found. Finally, the father has become the main supportive "other" in families, owing to greater mobility of U. S. families and the resulting reduction in the probability that the extended family can function as a primary support system. The shift from the extended family support network to a self-contained nuclear family is increasing (Masnick & Bane, 1980).

In view of the role that fathers can play in early infant development and in the maintenance of marital and family stability through support of their wife (Belsky, 1981, 1984), it is important to examine the supportive services that are available to aid fathers in the execution of their parental role. Also important is careful evaluation of the impact of supportive programs for fathers, not only on the men themselves but also on infants and mothers. This chapter examines specifically hospital-based interventions designed to increase and enhance paternal involvement.

DO FATHERS NEED SUPPORT?

In spite of the accumulating evidence that fathers can execute caregiving and stimulatory activities for infants, such as feeding, diapering, bathing, and playing, with skill and competence (Lamb, 1977; Parke & O'Leary, 1976; Parke & Sawin, 1980; Power & Parke, 1982), there is also evidence that fathers often need support to reach their full potential in these roles, for several reasons. First, the paternal role, in comparison with the maternal role, is less well defined and articulated in terms of its expectations and duties. This is particularly true in an era of changing definitions of the paternal role in light of the societal changes just noted (Parke & Tinsley, 1984). Second, in contrast to girls, boys receive little preparatory socialization during childhood geared toward training for the parental role, especially the child-care and nurturant aspects of the role.

Third, direct evidence indicates that fathers may be more dependent on spousal support to perform competently in the parenting role than are mothers. In a recent study of 4- to 8-month-old infants and their parents, Dickie and Matheson (1984) examined the relationship between maternal and paternal competence and spousal support. Parental competence was judged on the basis of home observations of mother-infant and father-infant interaction and involved a variety of components including emotional consistency, contingent responding, and warmth and pleasure in parenting. Two measures of spousal support were generated: (1) emotional support—a measure of affection, respect, and satisfaction in the husband-wife relationship, and (2) cognitive support—an index of husband-wife agreement in child care. These investigators found that spousal support is a stronger correlate of competence in fathers than in mothers. The level of emotional and cognitive support successfully discriminated high- and low-competence fathers but failed to discriminate high- and low-competence mothers. Others (Belsky, Gilstrap, & Rovine, 1984; Lamb & Elster, 1985) have obtained similar results, namely, that the quality of father-infant interaction is significantly correlated with measures of the mother-father relationship, whereas mother-infant interaction is relatively unrelated to the spousal relationship. Although spousal support is implicated in this research, other forms of supportive intervention may possibly achieve the same goal of increasing paternal competence. Fathers do require support, and in the next section some of the ways in which this support is implemented are examined.

MODELS OF INTERVENTION: UNDERLYING ASSUMPTIONS

Each model or program of intervention for parents, fathers as well as mothers, makes certain assumptions about the capacities of parents and the nature of the transition to parenthood. It is important that these often implicit assumptions be made explicit, since the types of programs developed may be very different in terms of timing, duration, form, and target.

One type of model is the *deficit model.* According to this model, fathers have a deficit in some aspect such as parenting skills, information about infants, or beliefs about their own role or capabilities. Under the information-deficit rubric would fall the hospital-based Brazelton exam demonstration programs, which assume inadequate information about the infant's capacities. Other programs assume that parents are skill deficient in areas such as social interaction and caregiving, and the goal of these programs is to improve these skills. Still others assume that belief systems are deficient. For example, fathers may believe either that they are unimportant in early infant development or that involvement with infants is inconsistent with the male role. Alternatively, the belief deficiency may lie in the mother, who believes that the father's role in infant care and/or stimulation is a minor one.

A second type of model can be termed the *optimization model.* In contrast to the deficit model, no assumption about skill, information, or belief deficits on the part of fathers is made. Instead, this model implicitly assumes that the prenatal and postnatal environments are not maximally geared to permit parental behavior to develop properly. It further assumes that after appropriate reorganization of the environment, parenting behavior will be performed optimally. The early-contact model falls into this category, with its assumption that physical contact between newborn and father will elicit optimal paternal parenting behavior.

A complex variant of this approach is one that assumes that the transition to parenthood is a natural but stressful period. It recognizes that fathers, mothers, and couples undergo a period of disequilibrium as a result of the stress, changes, and reorganization necessitated by the birth of a child. However, it makes no assumption about specific parental deficits that require remediation. Intervention, in this case, takes the form of provision of a supportive forum for exploring and dealing with the ongoing changes. Implicit in this model is the assumption that most couples under the transition satisfactorily; support is aimed at facilitating a natural process of disequilibration and reorganization of family roles on the part of both mother and father. In previous eras, the extended family and clear role expectations made supportive intervention of this type unnecessary. In this model no skills are explicitly taught, and no specific environmental arrangements are organized; instead the goal is to facilitate the reestablishment of a new set of rules and roles associated with the transition. The work by Cowan and Cowan (1985) involving a couple's support groups from pregnancy to the early postpartum period exemplifies this approach to facilitating the negotiation of a natural life transition. Examples and evaluation of each of these approaches are given here.

MEDICAL SITES AS INTERVENTION SETTINGS FOR FATHERS

A variety of sites are available for intervention and the choice will, in part, depend on the target, type, and purpose of the intervention. The goal of this chapter is to explore the advantages and disadvantages of utilization of medical settings as intervention sites. Medical facilities, including hospitals, clinics, and physicians' offices, are popular intervention sites especially for expectant or new parents. Several features of these settings make them particularly useful and effective as intervention sites. First, parents are accessible, since they may be coming to the setting for medical reasons already. Second, the status and authoritativeness of the setting may enhance both the attention paid to an intervention and the persuasive impact of the intervention. Third, motivation may already be high during the periods in which contact is made in these settings, namely, pregnancy and the early postpartum period. The first two days postpartum is an optimal time for intervention. Motivation and interest are usually high. Parents are not only accessible but easily monitored. Once they go home with the baby, the demands of child care may limit their availability. In addition, intervention during the period in which family relationships are being established, before the dynamics of the family system become resistant to modification and change, may be advantageous. On the negative side, fathers, in contrast to mothers, often are excluded from participation in many supportive activities offered by medical facilities, usually because of scheduling of activities such as postpartum infant-care demonstrations at times when fathers cannot attend. Further, fathers have often been excluded from participation in labor and delivery and have not been provided opportunities for contact and interaction with their infant in the early postpartum period. These issues are explored more fully in the following section.

Intervention in medical settings can assume a variety of forms, in part depending on the timing of the intervention program. The concept includes both policies that control father access to the activities in the setting and explicit intervention programs.

Intervention During Preparenthood

Parent education often begins well before individuals require parenting skills. As Klinman discusses in Chapter 15, this instruction can begin as early as the elementary or high-school years. In light of the relationships that have been demonstrated among fathers' sex-role orientation (Russell, 1978, 1982a, 1982b, 1982c), their relationship with and modeling of their own father (Sagi, 1982), and their anticipatory socialization (Steffensmeier, 1982), intervention can profitably begin prior to pregnancy. Although early primary preventive intervention has only recently been recognized as important by hospitals and medical personnel, the specialty of family medicine has as its basic philosophy involvement with the whole family and explicit planning for major life transitions, such as the onset of parenthood. Family physicians are in a unique position to develop attitudes and beliefs concerning the importance of paternal involvement in parenting. However, most medically based interventions begin in pregnancy.

Intervention During Pregnancy

During pregnancy two principal forms of medical-setting-based interventions are common. First, husbands may accompany their pregnant wife during obstetrician visits. This gives the physician the chance to share with the father detailed information concerning the progress of the developing fetus. With unexpected cesarean section deliveries, a frequent reason given for paternal dissatisfaction is the lack of communication between the obstetrician and the father (May & Sollid, 1984). Prenatal visits are the optimal time for the physician to develop a good "working" relationship that would prevent this problem. Given the limits of the obstetrician's time, involvement of nursing staff may be a cost-effective way to educate fathers about the progress of fetal development. In light of the evidence that the onset of quickening may be associated with heightened paternal involvement and interest, in combination with the suggestion that parental attachment may begin in pregnancy, opportunities to monitor fetal progress closely may be an important antecedent of later paternal involvement with the infant. As early as 12 weeks into a pregnancy, a father could listen to the fetal heartbeat, and at 18 weeks he could view the infant on a sonogram. Involvement of fathers in these commonly used monitoring procedures would add little time or expense.

Childbirth Classes.   Childbirth classes are becoming a standard part of the services of most hospitals, and fathers as well as mothers are participating in these preparatory groups. Future parents attend prenatal classes to learn about the physiologic processes of pregnancy and birth. Under the guidance of an instructor, the expectant mother learns and practices breathing exercises appropriate for the different stages of labor. These exercises help the mother to relax and thereby reduce the pain that accompanies the contractions. The father plays a role in this process by timing contractions and providing support and encouragement for the wife during labor and delivery. Self-selection may often operate in prenatal preparation classes which makes evaluation of their effects difficult. Unfortunately, experimental studies have not been carried out with fathers as the primary targets. However, studies that have involved fathers who self-selected to participate in childbirth classes show little evidence that this type of preparation affects the father's interaction with his infant (Parke, O'Leary, & West, 1972) or the father's postpartum adjustment to his fatherhood role (Wente & Crockenberg, 1976). In assessing the impact of Lamaze childbirth classes, the latter investigators stated, "Many men said they were pleased with their training for childbirth but felt totally unprepared for what comes after" (p. 356). In part this is due to the fact that preparation classes do not usually focus on postpartum caretaking skills. This, combined with the fact that only a small percentage of fathers participate in prenatal classes, makes it clear that pregnancy cannot be an isolated period of intervention. Research to date has failed to separate out the self-selection bias introduced by the contrast of highly motivated men in prepregnancy classes with nonparticipants. The factor carrying the variance in the self-selected sample may be the men's belief in the value of their involvement, demonstrated by their participation, rather than the added knowledge or confidence gained from the classes. Therefore, the impact of childbirth classes on a father's subsequent interaction with his infant and/or his spouse is not known. It is highly likely, however, that a husband's attendance at childbirth classes will increase the likelihood of his being present during labor and delivery. Next we examine the impact of the father's presence during labor and delivery on both mother and infant as well as on father's subsequent performance of his paternal role.

Attendance During Labor and Delivery

Paternal participation in labor and delivery has increased over the last 15 years. Even as late as 1972, fathers were permitted in the delivery room in only 27 percent of American hospitals; not until 1974 did the American College of Obstetricians and Gynecologists endorse the father's presence during labor. By 1980, fathers were admitted to delivery rooms in approximately 80 percent of American hospitals. A growing body of research suggests that the presence of the husband during labor and delivery has a variety of positive outcomes for both mother and infant. Moreover, evidence suggests that the behavior of fathers during labor is different from that of other types of support figures (Klein, Gist, Nicholson, & Standley, 1981). Fathers were five times more likely to touch their wives than nurses were to touch their patients, and according to mothers' postpartum reports, the husbands' presence was rated as most helpful. Some evidence indicates that women whose husbands participated in both labor and delivery reported less pain, received less medication, and felt more positive about the birth experience than women whose husbands were present only during the first stage of labor (Henneborn & Cogan, 1975). Fathers may be indirectly affected by the reduction in maternal medication: Earlier research (Parke, O'Leary, & West, 1972) found that fathers interact less with heavily medicated infants and more with an active, alert infant. Other evidence indicates that the presence of a supportive companion—although not necessarily a father—results in a significantly lower incidence of problems of labor and birth (cesarean birth, meconium staining, fetal distress) (Sosa, Kennell, Klaus, Robertson, & Urrutia, 1980).

Moreover, the father's presence during the second stage of labor and delivery increased the mother's emotional experience at the birth; mothers reported the birth as a "peak" experience more often if the father was present. Similarly, the father's emotional reaction to the birth was heightened by being present at the delivery (Entwisle & Doering, 1981). In another study, Petersen, Mehl, and Leiderman (1979) followed couples from the sixth month of pregnancy until six months after the birth. Using both observations and interviews of father, they found that a positive birth experience for the father was associated with enhanced attachment to the infant. These investigators also found that longer labor at home, in contrast to hospital delivery, was associated with greater paternal attachment. Finally, they noted that birth-related events were stronger predictors of attachment than were data from the pregnancy period, thus arguing that self-selection factors were not as important as the birth experience itself to subsequent involvement with the baby. Recently, Palkovitz (1985) has argued that this conclusion concerning the relative importance of the birth experience and prenatal attitudes and predispositions may be unwarranted in view of the limited range of attitudes examined by Petersen and colleagues.

In another study of the impact of birth attendance, (Bowen & Miller, 1980), three groups of fathers were compared: (1) prepared birth attenders, (2) unprepared birth attenders, and (3) unprepared nonbirth attenders. From in-hospital observations Bowen and Miller found that fathers who were present at delivery exhibited more distal attachment behavior (e.g., inspection, verbalization, and smiling) but not more proximal behaviors (e.g., touching and holding). Preparation did not relate to paternal attachment. Self-selection of the fathers into the groups seriously undermines any conclusions from this study. Nevertheless, the evidence tentatively suggests that the presence of the father has positive benefits for both the mother and the father. Finally, in light of the data demonstrating that maternal medication during labor and delivery can have a depressive and disorganizing effect on the infant and on the mother (Conway & Brackbill, 1970; Murray et al., 1981), the father's presence may indirectly benefit the infant as well.

Little is known about the effect of the father's presence during a cesarean delivery. In one small sample study, 13 fathers who were present during their infant's C-section delivery were compared with 10 fathers who were not present for the cesarean delivery (Cain, Pedersen, Zazlow, & Kramer, 1984). In interviews conducted three to four months later, the fathers who were present described more positive feelings, greater involvement in decisions related to labor and delivery, and less delay in handling their baby than fathers who were not present during the surgery. Observations of parent-infant behaviors indicated no differences between the present and absent fathers, with the exception that the absent fathers showed more intense affect toward the infant. In view of the sample size and the number of measures, a conservation interpretation of no long-term impact on parent-child interaction would be warranted.

Opportunities for Early Postpartum Contact with the Infant

In light of the widespread but not well-substantiated belief that a critical period for bonding exists and therefore opportunities for extended mother-infant contact during the postpartum period will positively influence maternal-infant attachment, interest in father-infant contact has emerged. The assumption accompanying this interest is that there might be a critical bonding period for fathers as well. Father contact is of interest not only as a form of potential intervention for fathers, but also as a strategy for determining the types of mechanisms that may be involved in mediating any observed effects. As Goldberg (1983) noted, "to the extent that fathers and mothers are similarly affected by early contact with the infant, psychological rather than physiological mechanisms would seem to be implicated" (p. 1377).

What is the impact of extended father-infant contact during the newborn period on the subsequent father-infant relationship? Some early studies of this issue were nonexperimental examinations of the effects of early contact on father-infant interaction. Jones (1981) found that fathers who *chose* to hold their infants in the first hour after delivery demonstrated more nonverbal behavior (touching, holding) toward their infant during observation at one month than those who did not have this early contact. However, fathers self-selected themselves to have early contact, and this methodological problem severely limits any conclusion. Perhaps the fathers would have been more involved regardless of the early contact. In this case, early contact could be viewed as an index of father interest rather than a factor that altered later father-infant interaction patterns. Palkovitz (1982) suggested that the timing and duration of contact may affect subsequent father involvement with his infant. Fathers who spent more time with their infants in the hospital demonstrated greater overall involvement and more social play with their infants when observed alone with their infant in the home at five months. Moreover, the length of time the father spent with the infant at the occasion of the initial contact was significantly related to the amount of father-infant social play, face-to-face orientation, and expressions of pleasure during triadic interaction (mother-father-infant) at five months. An intriguing finding concerned the timing of initial contact. The longer after delivery before fathers held their newborn, the longer the father contacted the infant at the first encounter and the more he engaged in caregiving during father-infant observations at five months. This provides little support for the early contact hypothesis (Klaus & Kennell, 1981) and suggests that the total amount of time may be more important than the timing of first contact in the hospital. This issue merits closer experimental scrutiny. Unfortunately, interpretation of this study is difficult for a number of reasons. First, the information concerning timing and duration of first contact in the hospital was based on interviews five months postpartum. This reliance on retrospective self-report seriously limits the value of this study. Second, self-selective factors were operative and no attempt was made to experimentally control who received the different contact experiences.

Experimental studies permit a more adequate evaluation of this issue. In the first experimental study of this type, Rödholm (1981) compared play behavior of two groups of Swedish fathers whose infants had been delivered by cesarean section. Fathers in one group were permitted to handle the infant for a 10-minute period 15 minutes after the delivery, while fathers in a comparison group were allowed only a brief look at the baby after the delivery. When the infants were 3 months old, the fathers in the contact group were found to engage in more face-to-face play and affectionate touching than those in the control group. In a United States investigation, Keller, Hildebrand, and Richards (1981) compared fathers who had extended contact alone with their infant (approximately four hours in total) with fathers who followed a traditional schedule of only visiting their wife and baby together during the postpartum period. Behavioral assessments at six weeks postpartum indicated that extended-contact fathers engaged in significantly greater "en face" behavior and more vocalizing during feeding than did traditional contact fathers. Moreover, the extended-contact fathers had a more positive attitude toward baby care, were responsible for a greater percentage of baby care, viewed their infant as more attractive, and reported playing with their baby longer each day than did traditional contact fathers. However, others have failed to find any effects of early contact on fathering behavior. Toney (1983) compared fathers who held their infant for 10 minutes during the first hour after delivery with fathers who first held their infant 8 to 12 hours after delivery. Between 12 and 36 hours after delivery, fathers were observed changing the infant's shirt and diaper. No differences between the hold and no-hold groups of fathers were found. Nor did Pannabecker, Emde, and Austin (1982) find any effects of early contact on father-infant interaction, although their study included a Brazelton exam demonstration in addition to increased contact. In view of these negative results as well as of failures to replicate earlier findings on extended maternal contact (Goldberg, 1983; Lamb & Hwang, 1982; Svejda, Campos, & Emde, 1980) no firm conclusions concerning the benefits of early father contact on father-infant interaction are warranted.

In view of the gradual reduction of average length of maternal hospitalization following childbirth, it may be that opportunities for father-infant contact in the hospital are becoming less critical. At the same time, a reduced lying-in period may increase the importance of father participation in the period after the mother and infant leave the hospital. The availability of paternity leaves may provide fathers with greater opportunity to participate in the early care of the infant.

Information and Skill-Training Programs for Fathers

A variety of explicit hospital-based intervention programs have been designed for fathers in recent years.

Demonstration of Newborn Capacities.   One approach is to demonstrate the sensory, perceptual, and social capacities of the infant to parents. This approach is consistent with a cognitive mediational model of parent-infant interaction, which assumes that parental interaction is, in part, determined by the assumptions that parents make about the infant's capabilities (Parke, 1978). By increasing or correcting parents' perceptions about infant abilities, interaction patterns will be modified.

Impact on Mothers.   Work with teenage mothers and their preterm infants has shown that a combination of exposure of the mother to a demonstration of the Brazelton Neonatal Assessment Scale (BNAS) and her regular use of an adaptation of the exam with her infant at birth and at one-week intervals during the first month yielded positive outcomes in a number of domains (Widmayer & Field, 1980). At one and four months, parent-infant interaction in both structured feeding and face-to-face situations was rated as more optimal than these measures with other teenage mothers, and the infant control scored higher on the Bayley mental index at 12 months than did the infants of the control mothers. However, there were few differences between the Brazelton exposure group and a second intervention group in which the mothers administered the modified form of the Brazelton exam to their infant for the first month but did not see a demonstration of the exam, which suggests that the opportunity to actively administer the exam may be more important than mere passive exposure to its administration.

In a subsequent study, Worobey and Belsky (1982) compared passive exposure to the Brazelton exam (in which mothers only observed administration of the exam), active exposure to the exam (in which mothers elicited responses themselves), and verbal exposure only (in which mothers simply heard a summary of their infant's performance). Observations at one month indicated that only *active exposure* enhanced the responsive, stimulating nature of maternal care. Other evidence suggests that passive visual or verbal exposure is ineffective (McLaughlin et al., 1983), while active exposure is successful in influencing confidence with and knowledge of infants.

Impact on Fathers.   This intervention strategy has been extended to include fathers in a number of recent investigations. Myers (1982) taught mothers or fathers to perform the Brazelton exam on their own infants, with attention being drawn to the infant's most positive interactive and physical abilities. In comparison with control parents, both mothers and fathers in the treatment condition had more knowledge of infant development at both the newborn period and at a four-week follow-up. Moreover, the treatment fathers reported being more involved in caretaking with their infant at four weeks than were control fathers. However, there were no differences in parent-infant interaction during a structured 10-minute observation session.

Similarly, another recent investigation has found positive effects on fathers of exposure to a Brazelton exam demonstration during the early postnatal period in the hospital. Beal (1984) gave first-time fathers a Brazelton demonstration on their 2- to 3-day-old infant. A control group of fathers received no intervention. To assess the impact of this brief intervention, Beal observed father-infant interaction at eight weeks postpartum. During a two-minute father-infant interaction session, the interaction pattern among the intervention group was characterized by a higher degree of father-infant mutuality. In addition, the fathers who received the Brazelton Neonatal Assessment Scale demonstration perceived their infant as less difficult than did fathers in the control group. These findings suggest that both father-infant interaction patterns and paternal perceptions can be modified by this short intervention. Since all of the exposed fathers also attended prenatal classes, labor, and delivery, it would be interesting to assess whether this type of intervention would be effective for less interested and involved fathers.

Finally, other researchers (e.g., Pannabecker, Emde, & Austin, 1982) have failed to find any impact of active Brazelton exposure on father-infant interaction during a one-month pediatric visit. In view of the inconsistency across studies, as well as the methodologic limitations of these studies (see the following), no firm conclusions are warranted.

Impact on Mothers and Fathers as a Unit.   In response to conceptual calls to treat the family system rather than merely mother-infant or father-infant alone (Belsky, 1981; Pedersen, Anderson, & Cain, 1977; Parke, 1979, 1981), two recent studies have examined the impact of exposure to a Brazelton demonstration on mother and father together. The assumption is that mothers and fathers indirectly as well as directly influence their infant, and the influence is often mediated through the mother-father unit. In an Australian intervention study, Dolby, English, and Warren (1982) found that active exposure of mother and father together to the Brazelton exam positively affected both maternal and paternal involvement as indexed by home observations and interviews when the infant was 6 months old.

In an American-based exploration of this issue, Belsky (1985) improved on Dolby and colleague's design. In his study, Belsky targeted either mothers or mothers and fathers together. Families were assigned to either an active exposure (i.e., parent(s) actively elicited responses from the newborn) or a passive exposure (i.e., parent(s) were given a verbal description of the infant's performance of the exam) to the Brazelton exam. Assessments of mother-infant interaction in the dyad and mother-infant, father-infant, and husband-wife interaction in the triad revealed no effects of experimental intervention across the groups at one, three, and nine months. However, there were modest positive effects on both the paternal and marital measures for a subsample of fathers and mothers who rated the demonstration as interesting and enjoyable and who established rapport with the facilitator. These analyses can only be viewed as suggestive but do indicate that more attention needs to be paid to motivational factors as a possible qualifier of the utility of this type of intervention.

Possibly even more important are the methodologic implications of the Belsky study for interpreting previous work. The results of the Belsky study, in which active and passive exposure groups were compared rather than comparison being made of an exposure group with a no-treatment control group, raises questions about earlier studies that used only no-treatment controls (e.g., Beal, 1984; Dolby, English, & Warren, 1982; Myers, 1982). The success of these earlier studies may have been due to a Hawthorne effect rather than to exposure to the Brazelton demonstration per se. However, the use of different types of assessment situations (e.g., structured versus naturalistic) makes direct comparisons difficult. In any case, the inconsistent pattern of results suggests that no definite conclusions can be drawn concerning the effectiveness of this type of hospital-centered intervention. Researchers need to determine whether it is the knowledge imparted, the attention drawn to the parent(s), or the altering of self- or spouse perceptions that serves as the active ingredient. Perhaps only then can we understand why results have been equivocal. It may be that for certain subsamples of fathers, this intervention is useful.

Direct Teaching of Parenting Skills.   A more direct approach involves the direct teaching of fathering skills. The medium used can vary and can include face-to-face demonstrations, provision of written information, or use of film or videotape. In view of the long history of successful modification of a variety of behaviors through observational learning (Bandura, 1977), a film intervention was developed by Parke and his colleagues (Parke et al., 1980).

The project involved an assessment of the effect of exposure to a specially designed intervention during the postpartum hospital period on the attitudes and behavior of fathers. Briefly, one group of fathers saw a 15-minute videotape, *Fathers and Infants,* while a control group of fathers followed the usual hospital routine and saw no videotape presentation. To assess the impact of the intervention, a variety of attitudinal and observational measures of father-infant interaction were secured in the hospital in the early postpartum period and in the home at three weeks and three months for both intervention and control groups. At three months, the typical level of father participation in routine caretaking activities in the home was assessed. The purpose of the project was to assess the effectiveness of this limited intervention on paternal attitudes, interaction patterns, and levels of participation in infant care.

During the mother's postpartum hospitalization, 16 fathers were shown the videotape and 16 fathers were not. In the videotape, three different fathers successfully played with, fed, and diapered their baby. In addition, a narrator emphasized the wide range of newborn cognitive and social capacities as well as the active role that fathers can assume in early care and stimulation of infants. The videotape was designed to serve four purposes: (1) to modify the father's sex-role attitudes concerning the appropriateness of infant caretaking for adult males, (2) to provide specific demonstrations of feeding and diapering, (3) to provide information concerning a newborn's perceptual and cognitive capabilities, and (4) to demonstrate a number of ways fathers can play with babies, emphasizing contingent responses to infant cues.

Fathers were shown the videotape in a room on the maternity floor one or two days after the birth of their infant. Fathers in both film and control conditions followed a similar schedule of assessments. Briefly, the fathers filled out an attitude questionnaire and were observed during a 20-minute period with their infant in the hospital, and again at three weeks and three months in the home. At three months, a parental diary of caretaking activity was completed. All assessments for the film group were completed after viewing the film.

Results showed that the film increased fathers' knowledge about infant perceptual abilities and that fathers who saw the film believed more strongly that infants need stimulation than did fathers who did not see it. In addition, for fathers of boys, viewing of the film modified their sex-role attitudes concerning the appropriateness of their participation in caretaking activities. On the basis of diary reports of caretaking activities in the home, fathers of boys who saw the film were more likely to diaper and feed at three months than were fathers in the no-film control group. For fathers of girls, exposure to the film did not produce any changes in the amount of either diapering or feeding in the home at three months.

Observational data revealed that the film modified father behavior in a variety of ways. The film was effective in increasing the amount of caretaking behavior exhibited during feeding, both in the hospital and at three months. The film significantly increased the stimulatory behavior of fathers of first-born boys in the hospital period, but not at later time periods. Examination of father-infant behavior sequences showed that as the "film" fathers decreased their total amount of stimulation over the three time points, the probability of these behaviors being contingent on infant cues concurrently increased. Thus as the infant's behavioral repertoire expanded over the first three months, "film" fathers changed their interaction style, from being a highly stimulating one to one that was highly contingent on infant behavior.

A similar pattern emerged for affectionate behavior. There were no film effects in the hospital or at three weeks, but at three months "film" fathers displayed more affection than control fathers during feeding. However, control fathers were more affectionate than "film" fathers during play. Once again, examination of sequences revealed that this decrease in overall amount of affection was coupled with an increase in responsiveness. In spite of the lower amount of affection that "film" fathers displayed during play, the manner in which the affection was displayed was more closely linked to infant signals for these fathers than it was for control fathers.

In summary, the film intervention significantly modified selected aspects of father behavior and attitudes both in the hospital and through the first three months of their infant's life. Of particular interest is the finding that the level of father participation in feeding and diapering increased as a result of this very limited intervention even after a three-month period, at least in the case of boys. The heightened impact of the film for fathers of boys merits comment. The most plausible explanation for this finding is a predispositional one. Since fathers are already differentially predisposed to interact more with male infants than with female infants, the film served to strengthen these already existing tendencies. As discussed elsewhere, there is a substantial body of literature in support of the claim that fathers both expect to and do show higher involvement with male than female infants (see Parke, 1979; Pedersen, 1980). Similarly, previous social-influence literature suggests that it is easier to produce further change in a direction that is already favored than in a nonfavored direction (McGuire, 1968).

Further evidence of the effectiveness of film intervention during the postpartum period comes from a recent study by Arbuckle (1983). In this project Arbuckle used a film intervention developed by Parke and colleagues (1980). Entitled *Becoming a Family,* the film demonstrated the same behavior, such as feeding and diapering, playing, and recognizing infant capabilities, as were included in Parke and colleague's (1980) film intervention. In contrast to the earlier film, this film depicted *both* mothers and fathers actively engaged in caregiving and game playing. Assessment of the impact of the film four to six weeks later indicated that first-time fathers who saw the film, in comparison with a no-film control group of fathers, had greater knowledge of infant sensory and cognitive capabilities and were higher in their perception of the importance of providing affection and stimulation. Moreover, the experimental fathers reported higher levels of involvement in the daily caregiving of their babies four to six weeks after the intervention. No sex-of-infant differences were reported. In spite of the limitation of this study by the reliance on self-report measures, the similarity of findings across these two film intervention studies underscores the potential value of this approach for modifying paternal behavior. Further work is clearly justified. Particularly important are studies that isolate the effective components of these film intervention programs. Film interventions should also be compared with other types of interventions such as medical staff instruction, discussion groups, or informational booklets. By addressing the relative effectiveness of different approaches, the most optimal and most cost-effective procedures for different groups will become evident.

Another set of studies illustrates the potential role that health-care providers such as pediatricians can play in supporting parents of young children. Although these studies have focused on mothers, the interventions could be useful in promoting father parenting competence as well. In a study by Chamberlain (1979), mothers who participated in an educational program concerning child development during pediatric well-baby visits increased their knowledge of child development and their perceptions of being supported in the caregiving role. A related study (Whitt & Casey, 1982) showed that mothers who were provided with an office-based pediatric intervention program emphasizing physical and preventive child care, developmental norms, and information on infant communication abilities during well-baby exams demonstrated more positive relationships with their infant than did mothers who received no such program. The potential of this type of intervention for fathers depends, in part, on changes in work schedules that would permit fathers to participate more regularly in follow-up visits to the pediatrician. Alternatively, intervention programs could be offered on a more flexible basis, such as evenings and weekends, to accommodate fathers.

Although the full potential of hospital and other health-care facilities as settings for providing supportive programs for fathers is not yet realized, the studies reviewed here illustrate the value of these settings for modifying the parenting behavior of fathers as well as mothers.

Interventions Beyond the Postpartum Period

To conceptualize hospital-based programs as limited to postpartum interventions excludes a wide range of hospital- and clinic-based activities. First, medical settings are useful sites for monitoring and evaluating the impact of earlier hospital-based programs. At the time of well-baby checkups, brief evaluation can be made of a program's effectiveness. Second, interventions in the postpartum period may often have short-term effects; this suggests the need for continuing interventions that focus on the progress and needs of developing infants. Fathers who have limited knowledge of newborn capacities, abilities, and needs may need information about the capabilities and needs of older infants and children as well. Similarly, fathers who needed supportive intervention to increase their involvement in parenting tasks may need continued support to sustain this involvement as their infant develops. Both medical sites and medical personnel can play a central role in these kinds of continuing intervention efforts. Badger, Burns, and Vietze (1981), who worked with adolescent mothers, and Minde and colleagues (1980), who worked with parents of preterm infants, have successfully conducted hospital-based follow-through programs over the first year of infancy.

Two recent experimental studies designed to increase the level of paternal competence and involvement also illustrate the value of intervention beyond the postpartum period for fathers. In one study, Dickie and Carnahan (1980) provided training to mothers and fathers of 4- to 12-month-old infants in order to increase the parents' competence. Utilizing Goldberg's notion of competence as parental ability to assess, predict, elicit, and provide contingent response experiences for their infants, these investigators gave eight two-hour weekly training sessions. The training emphasized individual infant variation, knowledge of the infant's temperament and cues, provision of contingent experiences, and awareness of the infant's effect on the parents. Fathers who participated in the training sessions, in contrast to fathers who did not participate, increased their interactions with their infant; specifically, they talked, touched, held, and attended more to the infant and gave more contingent responses to infant smiles and vocalizations. The infants of the trained fathers sought interaction more than infants of fathers in the control group. However, mothers in the trained group decreased their interactions. In view of the fact that training increased the wives' judgments of their spouses' competence, it is possible that the wives encouraged their competent husbands to assume a greater share of the infant care and interactional responsibilities. Interestingly, this finding underlines the reciprocal nature of the mother-father relationship and provides further support for viewing the family as a social system in which the activities of one member have an impact on the behavior of other family members. Finally, these data are consistent with findings in nonhuman primates that father-infant involvement varies inversely with the degree of maternal restrictiveness (see Redican & Taub, 1981; Parke & Suomi, 1981, for reviews).

As a number of recent studies suggest, efforts to modify father-infant interaction need not be restricted to fathers of very young infants. Zelazo, Kotelchuck, and David (1977) selected 20 very-low-interacting fathers and their 12-month-old firstborn sons for an intervention study. These fathers did little caretaking or playing and were present only occasionally when their child was awake. Twelve fathers received an intervention involving play with their infants for one half hour per day for four weeks in the home. To facilitate the play interaction, a schedule of games and toys was provided for the father. Using a social learning strategy (see Bandura, 1977), the experimenters both demonstrated the games, toys, and styles of interaction and coached the fathers in these activities prior to the intervention period. A control group of eight low-interacting fathers received no intervention. To assess the impact of the intervention on the infant's behavior, a lab-based parent-infant interaction session was held before and after the training period. This consisted of a 20-minute free-play period, with both parents in the room reading, followed by a series of maternal and paternal departures. In comparison to the infants in the control group, infants in the experimental group increased their interaction with their father in the free-play session; these infant boys looked more at their father and initiated more interaction with him. Separation protest was not affected by the experimental intervention. This was surprising in view of earlier reports that as father involvement increased, separation upset in the presence of a stranger lessened (Kotelchuck, 1972; Spelke et al., 1973). Although the Zelazo study was a pioneering one, it had a number of limitations. First, the fathers were instructed to initiate interactions in the preintervention lab session, and so it is unclear whether there were increases in father behaviors directed to their infant. Second, the investigators did not monitor the amount of interaction between father and infant in the home as a follow-up to their intervention program. In spite of these limitations, the investigation further underlines the modifiability of the father-infant relationship. It also serves as a reminder that modification of early social interaction patterns is not necessarily limited to a particular period. As both Zelazo and colleagues and many earlier investigators (e.g., Rheingold, 1956; Skeels, 1966) have demonstrated, infant responsiveness to adults can be modified at a variety of age levels.

MAXIMIZING INTERVENTION EFFECTIVENESS: MATCHING FATHERS AND STRATEGIES

Fathers are not homogeneous, although fathers as intervention targets are often assumed to possess similar skills, needs, beliefs, and values. As pointed out by Lamb in Chapter 1, fathers vary in terms of their role concept and their beliefs about the value of paternal involvement. They differ in their actual ability or skills to perform parenting tasks, in their perception of their skills, and in their degree of self-confidence. The family context in which fathers are embedded varies in terms of the degree of spousal support available to the father, the level of family stress, and the distribution of mother and father responsibilities. Each of these variants, in turn, affects father performance and involvement as a parent. Fathers also vary in terms of their accessibility for intervention. This articulation of possible variations in fathers suggests that assessments should be made prior to the selection of an intervention strategy. In addition to the usual conceptualization of the early postpartum hospital period as an opportunity for intervention, this period can be usefully viewed as an opportunity for assessment of family needs, which in turn will guide the selection of intervention strategies. Families could be organized along these dimensions of knowledge, skill, and value of paternal involvement as well as by the degree of intrafamilial and extrafamilial support for fathers as a means of more effectively choosing an appropriate intervention program.

Fathers with clearly determined deficits in skill or information are good candidates for short-term interventions, such as Brazelton demonstrations or instructional programs involving infant care techniques. In contrast, such programs may be unnecessary for fathers who are already well informed and/or experienced with infants.

Motivation and role dimensions merit consideration as well. Fathers who are highly motivated and express a desire to acquire skills and information are obviously better candidates for intervention. Paternal role definition has been shown to be a more potent predictor of father involvement than attendance at delivery, early infant contact, or childbirth preparation classes (Palkovitz, 1982). Therefore fathers who define their major role as breadwinner and view infant and child care as a woman's responsibility are poor candidates for skill-oriented interventions. Instead, in this type of traditional family, efforts may be better directed at educating the father about maternal needs for support. Problem solving about informal and formal social support for the wife may be time better spent, since short-term interventions are unlikely to change belief systems. Intervention should be designed to enhance capacities in the direction determined by the couple's beliefs.

During assessment for the form of intervention required, the full family unit including the mother should be taken into account. Mothers often play a gatekeeper function in relation to caregiving activities, by which they control the access that fathers have to caregiving opportunities. To maximize the impact of an intervention aimed at enhancing a father's skill and confidence, a complementary intervention must be aimed at modifying the mother's perceptions and beliefs about the father's capability to contribute to infant care. No lasting change in role definitions in the family can be achieved if maternal beliefs concerning the legitimacy and desirability of father's contribution are not modified as well. In addition, this type of program could involve educating mothers not only about the father's need for spousal support but about the benefits of paternal involvement for both her children and herself.

Accessibility of fathers is another dimension that merits consideration. Some fathers, due to either low interest or scheduling conflicts, are not available during the prenatal period but are available during the postpartum hospital period. Although the first 48 hours does not appear to be critical for bonding, it may be a period of high motivation on the part of parents. It may be the first time the father recognizes the reality of the situation, now that there is a baby he can see and hold. In turn he may be highly motivated to acquire information and skills to aid him in his new role.

THE IMPACT OF FATHER INTERVENTION PROGRAMS ON CHILDREN AND PARENTS

What are the effects of father interventions on children and parents? Few studies have addressed the issue of whether hospital-based interventions aimed at modifying father-infant interaction do, in turn, affect infant development. Evidence is accumulating, however, that the quality of father involvement can affect children's social and cognitive development (Lamb, 1981; Parke, 1981; Radin, 1982). If interventions can affect father-infant interaction, then longitudinal studies are required that examine the impact of intervention-induced changes in father-infant relationships on infant social and cognitive development. However, there is little evidence that the types of short-term interventions that have been implemented produce any lasting impact on either father-infant interaction or infant outcome.

While it is attractive to assume that evidence of the impact of existing variations in fathering on children's development can form the basis for understanding future variations, it is misleading to assume that continuing increases in father participation will produce orderly linear modifications in children's development (see also Chapter 1). First, there may be a threshold for father effects beyond which no greater effect of involvement will be found, which would suggest that increases in father participation may not significantly alter children's development. Therefore, child outcomes may not be what we should examine, but rather spousal satisfaction. A child may develop well regardless of which parent provides the care, but the mother may be affected greatly, and therefore also the family, if mother's satisfaction with her roles and responsibilities is affected by the level of father participation in child care. As was found with maternal employment, it is not whether mother works outside the home that is crucial to child outcome, but rather whether mother is satisfied with such work or with staying at home—whether she *chose* to do what she is doing (Hoffman, 1984).

Second, it is unlikely that all areas of development would be equally affected by interventions to modify father (and mother) family roles. Rather than searching for global outcomes in either the social or cognitive domain for evidence of the impact of interventions to modify fathering, specific aspects of children's development, those most likely to yield effects, should be addressed. In view of the father's role as play partner and the importance of play activity for subsequent peer relations (MacDonald & Parke, 1984; Parke, MacDonald, Beitel, & Bhavnagri, 1986), a focus on social competence with peers might be justified in a search for the effects of intervention.

Third, many of the variations in family organization may have relevance for children only at later points in the life cycle, such as the advent of their own parenting career. This suggests that the stage of the child's development needs to be taken into account when an intervention is designed, since the needs and the impact will vary with the developmental level of the child.

These changes may have at least as much and possibly a greater impact on fathers themselves. A number of areas may be affected, including the father-child relationship, the father's self-perception of his own sex role, and his attitude toward women's roles. In addition, the marital relationship may be affected, as will the father's attitude toward and involvement in his outside occupation.

Some evidence (e.g., Russell, 1982a,b,c) indicates that both fathers' relationships with their children and their satisfaction with the father role improve as a result of increased involvement. Moreover, self-perceptions of sex roles may shift as a result of assuming the caregiving role (Feldman, Birigen, & Nash, 1981). As a result of increased involvement with their own children, fathers may develop increased empathy and sensitivity to a wider range of social cues. This hypothesis awaits empirical evaluation.

Fathers may become less involved in work as a result of their increased family involvement. Alternatively, men who try to maintain a high work commitment while increasing their family involvement may experience heightened role strain, such as resentment of work or family demands, and possibly increased marital conflict. As in the case of children, the effects on fathers will depend on a variety of factors including the age of the father, his career position, and the age of the child at the time of evaluation. The reason for the increase in father participation merits consideration, since forced and voluntary increases may yield different effects. Fathers who assumed shared or primary caretaker roles in Russell's (1982a, 1982b, 1982c) Australian sample seemed to continue in that role when the decision had been based on belief in the value of paternal involvement rather than on economic necessity for the family.

Another result of these changes is the shifting expectation that all fathers should engage in increased caregiving. Fathers who participate may come to be considered the norm, and relatively uninvolved fathers may be viewed as nonnormative. The role of shifting expectations in promoting further change in fathering merits investigation.

Finally, it is important to recognize that the assumption of a causal link between shifts in fathering and changes in fathers themselves needs to be validated, in order to eliminate the alternative possibility that fathers who become more involved already differ in these dimensions. The two hypotheses may not be mutually exclusive. A father's developmental history is important to his sex-role identity and the probability of his valuing paternal involvement. On the other hand, assumption of responsibility for a child has a profound effect on a man's beliefs and behaviors.

Since changes in the paternal role potentially modify maternal behavior, it is important to evaluate the impact of change on mothers. Again, changes in a variety of spheres merit examination, such as changes in the mother's relationship with her children and her spouse, and changes in her occupational sphere. While it is assumed that some positive effects may flow from shifts toward more egalitarian family roles, such as reduced strain between family and work roles for women, new strains may arise as couples attempt to fashion new forms of relationships without clear and well-articulated guidelines. As noted previously, the possibility that some women may resent the intrusion of fathers into the child-rearing domain merits investigation.

IS INTERVENTION ALWAYS JUSTIFIED?

Considerable care must be taken with implementation of support systems. The important issue of parents' rights needs to be considered. An implicit model of many intervention programs for fathers is the egalitarian rather than the more traditional family organization. However, the goal should not be to shift all families toward an egalitarian family arrangement, but rather to provide the quality and quantity of support that will enable family members to enact their roles competently within their own ideological framework. For some families this may mean minimal father participation, while in other families it may mean shared responsibility between spouses. Too often "more" is equated with "improvement"; in many families, however, increased father participation may cause conflict and disruption as a result of the threat to well-established and satisfying role definitions. Intervention, therefore, should be sensitively geared to the needs of individual families and the dynamics and ideology of the couple should be given primary recognition. (See Chapter 1 for further discussion of this issue.)

SOME REMAINING ISSUES

A variety of issues remain unresolved in this relatively new area of inquiry. The relative effectiveness of different types of intervention programs needs to be examined. Evaluation should address the issue of cost effectiveness as well, in light of an eventual goal of widespread dissemination.

More attention needs to be given to the goals of the intervention. Some programs focus on teaching specific caregiving skills, while others focus on increasing father knowledge about infant capabilities. Few explicit efforts have been made to modify fathers' beliefs concerning their abilities and their roles. In light of the fact that individuals select activities that they perceive themselves competent to perform, interventions aimed at modifying fathers' beliefs in their abilities would be worthwhile (Bandura, 1977). The relative value of focusing on one or more of these goals needs to be evaluated in future studies, as does the value of going beyond the limits of the perinatal period or the hospital setting.

Moreover, only a small amount of work has been devoted to the issue of the target of intervention. While father alone or the father-infant dyad has received the most attention, the mother-father unit as the intervention target is beginning to receive some attention. As noted earlier, complementary programs aimed at both fathers *and* mothers may be an effective strategy for promoting long-term change in family organization.

Another target of intervention is the physician. Assessment and modification of physician attitudes and beliefs about the importance of the father's role in family development have received little attention. Traditionally, fathers have not participated in routine visits to the obstetrician during pregnancy. Although the obstetrician-expectant mother relationship has been the standard, redefinition of the standard to include the husband in a triadic wife-husband-physician relationship may increase father involvement. Inclusion of fathers may yield a number of benefits, such as higher physician acceptance of the father's presence during delivery and potentially greater satisfaction with the birth and less dissatisfaction with unplanned events, such as C-section deliveries.

Finally, intervention at the level of the hospital itself merits consideration. Hospital policies that permit fathers more access to labor and delivery settings are only a first step. Hospitals and health maintenance organizations (HMOs) can begin to include in their prenatal and delivery packages provision for involving and educating fathers. Moreover, these programs need to be scheduled at times when fathers can participate. The traditional 10 A.M. postpartum feeding and diapering demonstration may not be enough. Other institutional changes involve policies that permit fathers as well as mothers to room in with a hospitalized child (Lamb, Russell, & Sagi, 1983). The goal is to develop a hospital policy that recognizes fathers legitimate and equal participants in infant and child care.

The identity of the intervention agent—in spite of a long history of sociopsychological research on this issue—has received no systematic attention. Presumably, males would be more effective in modifying paternal behavior and beliefs than would female intervention agents. Although hospitals have allowed fathers to spend more time with their wife and infant, most hospitals continue to perpetuate sex-role differences. If hospitals seek to increase paternal involvement, they should begin to model such behavior. Child-care demonstrations could be performed by male medical personnel instead of by female nurses, who are the traditional transmitters of such information.

The timing issue merits more systematic attention, particularly the issue of the interplay between timing and type of intervention. Perhaps no single time period is more or less appropriate. Instead, fathers have different needs and goals during the wife's pregnancy, at delivery, and in the later postpartum period. Interventions that are sensitively gauged to meet these changing needs and goals are likely to be most successful in producing lasting change. This argues for a multitime intervention strategy, rather than intervention at an optimal time point.

To date, most evidence of the effectiveness of different intervention strategies indicates only short-term effects. There is no consistent evidence that early hospital-based interventions for fathers produce long-term changes in either fathers' behavior or in children's or mothers' behavior. It is clearly possible that more effective strategies will yield long-term effects, although such strategies are likely to be more costly. It is unlikely, however, that relatively brief one-time interventions will produce long-term changes. Stable and lasting changes are likely to come about either by a shift in belief systems and values of the family concerning the necessity and/or desirability of father participation or by a program that builds in explicit strategies for periodic interventions, which serve to maintain the earlier modifications. Organismic and systems-oriented theorists would argue for the former, while behaviorally inclined interventionists would favor the latter strategy. It is important to underscore that these approaches to long-term change are not incompatible or mutually exclusive.

In spite of the limitations of many of the intervention studies reviewed in this chapter, their theoretical value should not be dismissed. Even short-term changes that are produced by an experimental intervention can make valuable theoretical contributions. Much of our knowledge of fathers' role in the family right after a child is born is based on correlational evidence. In most cases there is no firm basis for assuming a causal relationship among variables or any clear indication of the direction of the effect. In light of our theoretical assumptions concerning bidirectionality and mutual influence among members of the family system, methods to better specify directionality are helpful. Through experimental intervention studies, causal relationships between a change in some aspect of father involvement, such as increased caregiving, and a shift in either mother's behavior or in some aspect of infant development can be determined. While these strategies alone are insufficient for building an ecologically valid account of the father's role in infancy, their value as part of the repertoire of methodologic strategies available to researchers of early social relationships is often underestimated. Finally, just as these experimental strategies can be useful for theory testing, theory, in turn, can serve as a guide for building more effective intervention strategies. Greater utilization of theory would probably increase the value of many intervention efforts in this area.

In closing this chapter, a life-span perspective on these issues serves to remind us that the impact of intervention strategies may vary as a function of both cohort and time of testing. As noted earlier, not only is there more necessity for intervention programs than in the past, but it is also likely that the impact of intervention programs will affect fathers in different ways than in earlier eras. In a more traditional era characterized by more rigid gender roles for mothers and fathers, the difficulty of recruitment of fathers into an intervention program may have been more significant, and the stability of change produced by such a program may have been more limited, owing to the lack of societal support to sustain patterns of increased father involvement.

Fathers do need support in the parenting role, but the best means of providing that support using the hospital as an intervention context remains an unresolved issue.

REFERENCES

Arbuckle, M. B. (1983). The effects of educational intervention on fathers' relationships with their infants. Unpublished doctoral dissertation, University of North Carolina, Greensboro.

Badger, E., Burns, D., & Vietze, P. (1981). Maternal risk factors as predictors of developmental outcome in early childhood. *Infant Mental Health Journal, 2,* 33–43.

Bandura, A. (1977). *Social learning theory.* Englewood Cliffs, NJ: Prentice-Hall.

Beal, J. A. (1984, April) The effect of demonstration of the Brazelton Neonatal Assessment Scale on the father-infant relationship. Paper presented at International Conference of Infant Studies, New York.

Belsky, J. (1981). Early human experience: A family perspective. *Developmental Psychology, 17,* 3–23.

Belsky, J. (1984). A family perspective on the transition to parenthood. Paper presented at conference on Transition to Fatherhood, Washington, DC.

Belsky, J. (1985). Experimenting with the family in the newborn period. *Child Development, 56,* 407–414.

Belsky, J., Gilstrap, B., & Rovine, M. (1984). The Pennsylvania Infant and Family Development Project, I: Stability and change in mother-infant and father-infant interaction in a family setting at one, three and nine months. *Child Development, 55,* 692–705.

Bowen, S. M., & Miller, B. C. (1980). Paternal attachment behavior as related to presence at delivery and preparenthood classes: A pilot study. *Nursing Research, 29,* 307–311.

Bronfenbrenner, U. (1974). Developmental research, public policy and the ecology of childhood. *Child Development, 45,* 1–5.

Cain, R. L., Pedersen, F. A., Zaslow, M. J., & Kramer, E. (1984). Effects of father presence or absence during a Caesarean delivery. *Birth, 11,* 10–15.

Cairns, R. B. (1977). Beyond social attachment: The dynamics of interactional development. In T. A. Alloway, P. Pliner, & L. Krames (Eds.), *Attachment Behavior.* New York: Plenum.

Chamberlain, R. W. (1979). Effects of educating mothers about child development in physicians' offices on mother and child functioning over time. Paper presented at American Psychological Association meeting, New York.

Conway, E., & Brackbill, Y. (1970). Delivery medication and infant outcome: An empirical study. *Monographs of the Society for Research in Child Development, 35,* 24–34.

Cowan, C., & Cowan, P. A. (1983). Individual and couple satisfaction during family formation: A longitudinal study. Paper presented at annual meeting of American Psychological Association, Anaheim, CA.

Cowan, P. A., & Cowan, C. P. (1985). Becoming a family: Couple relationships during family formation. In P. Berman & F. Pedersen (Eds.), *Transition to fatherhood.* New York: Academic.

Dickie, J., & Carnahan, S. (1980). Training in social competence: The effect on mothers, fathers and infants. *Child Development, 51,* 1248–1251.

Dickie, J., and Matheson, P. (1984). Mother-father-infant: Who needs support? Paper presented at annual meeting of American Psychological Association, Toronto.

Dolby, R., English, B., & Warren, B. (1982, March). Brazelton demonstrations for mothers and fathers: Impact on the developing parent-infant relationship. Paper presented at International Conference on Infant Studies, Austin, TX.

Entwisle, D. R., & Doering, S. G. (1981). *The first birth.* Baltimore, MD: Johns Hopkins Press.

Feldman, S. S., Birigen, Z. C., & Nash, S. C. (1981). Fluctuations of sex-rated self-attributions as a function of stage of family life cycle. *Developmental Psychology, 17,* 24–35.

Goldberg, S. (1983). Parent-infant bonding: Another look. *Child Development, 54,* 1355–1382.

Henneborn, W. J., & Cogan, R. (1975). The effects of husband participation on reported pain and the probability of medication during labor and birth. *Journal of Psychosomatic Research, 19,* 215–222.

Hoffman, L. (1984). Work, family, and socialization of the child. In R. D. Parke (Ed.), *Review of child development research* (Vol. 7): *The family.* Chicago: University of Chicago Press.

Jones, C. (1981). Father to infant attachment: Effects of early contact and characteristics of the infant. *Research in Nursing and Health, 4,* 193–200.

Keller, W. D., Hildebrand, K. A., & Richards, M. E. (1981, April). Effects of extended father-infant contact during the newborn period. Paper presented at meeting of Society for Research in Child Development, Boston.

Klaus, M. H., & Kennell, J. H. (1976). *Maternal-infant bonding.* St. Louis: Mosby.

Klaus, M. H., & Kennell, J. H. (1981). *Parent-infant bonding.* St. Louis: Mosby.

Klein, R. P., Gist, N. F., Nicholson, J., & Standley, K. (1981). A study of father and nurse support during labor. *Birth and the Family Journal, 8,* 161–164.

Kotelchuck, M. (1972). The nature of the child's tie to his father. Unpublished doctoral dissertation, Harvard University, Cambridge, MA.

Lamb, M. E. (1977). Father-infant and mother-infant interaction in the first year of life. *Child Development, 48,* 167–181.

Lamb, M. E. (Ed.) (1981). *The role of the father in child development.* 2nd ed. New York: Wiley.

Lamb, M. E., & Elster, A. B. (1985). Adolescent mother-infant-father relationships. *Developmental Psychology, 21,* 768–773.

Lamb, M. E., & Hwang, C.-P. (1982). Maternal attachment and mother-infant bonding: A critical review. In M. E. Lamb & A. L. Brown (Eds.), *Advances in Developmental Psychology* (Vol. 2). Hillsdale, NJ: Erlbaum.

Lamb, M. E., Russell, G., & Sagi, A. (1983). Social policy implications. In M. E. Lamb & A. Sagi (Eds.), *Fatherhood and family policy.* Hillsdale, NJ: Erlbaum.

Lewis, M., & Feiring, C. (1981). Direct and indirect interactions in social relationships. In L. P. Lipsitt (Ed.), *Advances in infancy research* (Vol. 1). New York: Ablex.

MacDonald, K., & Parke, R. D. (1984). Bridging the gap: Parent-child play interaction and peer interactive competence. *Child Development, 55,* 1265–1277.

Masnick, G., & Bane, M. J. (1980). *The nation's families: 1960-1990.* Boston: Auburn House.

May, K. A., & Sollid, D. T. (1984). Unanticipated Cesarean birth from the father's perspective. *Birth, 11,* 87–95.

McGuire, W. J. (1968). The nature of attitudes and attitude change. In G. Lindzey & E. Aronson (Eds.). *Handbook of social psychology* (Vol 3). Reading, PA: Addison-Wesley.

McLaughlin, F., Drake, D., Deni, R., & Constantini, F. (April 1983). Sequential analysis of maternal behavior recorded after passive exposure to Brazelton Neonatal Assessment procedures. Paper presented at biennial meeting of Society for Research in Child Development, Detroit.

Minde, K., Shosenberg, N. E., Marton, P., Thompson, J., Ripley, J., & Burns, S. (1980). Self-help groups in a premature nursery—a controlled evaluation. *Journal of Pediatrics, 96,* 933–940.

Murray, A. D., Dolby, R. M., Nation, R. L., & Thomas, D. B. (1981). Effects of epidural anesthesia on newborns and their mothers. *Child Development, 52,* 71–82.

Myers, B. J. (1982). Early intervention using Brazelton training with middle-class mothers and fathers of newborns. *Child Development, 53,* 162–171.

Orthner, D., Brown, T., & Ferguson, D. (1976). Single-parent fatherhood: An emerging life style. *Family Coordinator, 15,* 429–438.

Palkovitz, R. (1982). Fathers' birth attendance, early extended contact, and father-infant interaction at five months postpartum. *Birth, 9,* 173–177.

Palkovitz, R. (1984). Parental attitudes and fathers' interactions with their 5-month-old infants. *Developmental Psychology, 20,* 1054–1060.

Palkovitz, R. (1985). Father's birth attendance, early contact, and extended contact with their newborns: A critical review. *Child Development, 56,* 392–406.

Pannabecker, B. J., Emde, R. N., & Austin, B. C. (1982). The effects of early extended contact on father-newborn interaction. *Journal of Genetic Psychology, 141,* 7–17.

Parke, R. D. (1978). Parent-infant interaction: Progress, paradigms and problems. In G. P. Sackett (Ed.), *Observing behavior* (Vol. 1): *Theory and applications in mental retardation.* Baltimore: University Park Press.

Parke, R. D. (1979). Perspectives on father-infant interaction. In J. Osofsky (Ed.), *The handbook of infant development.* New York: Wiley.

Parke, R. D. (1981). *Fathers.* Cambridge, MA: Harvard University Press.

Parke, R. D., Hymel, S., Power, T. G., & Tinsley, B. R. (1980). Fathers and risk: A hospital based model of intervention. In D. B. Sawin, R. C. Hawkins, L. O.

Walker, & J. H. Penticuff (Eds.), *Psychosocial risks in infant-environment transactions.* New York:Bruner/Mazel.

Parke, R. D., MacDonald, K., Beitel, A., & Bhavnagri, N. (in press). The interrelationships among families, fathers and peers. In R. Peters (Ed.), *New approaches to family research.* New York: Bruner/Mazel.

Parke, R. D., & O'Leary, S. E. (1976). Family interaction in the newborn period: Some findings, some observations, and some unresolved issues. In K. Riegel & J. Meacham (Eds.), *The developing individual in a changing world* (Vol. 2): *Social and environmental issues.* The Hague: Mouton.

Parke, R. D., O'Leary, S. E., & West, S. (1972). Mother-father-newborn interaction: Effects of maternal medication, labor and sex of infant. *Proceedings of the American Psychological Association,* 85–86.

Parke, R. D., Power, T. G., & Gottman, J. M. (1979). Conceptualizing and quantifying influence patterns in the family triad. In M. E. Lamb, S. J. Suomi, & G. R. Stephenson (Eds.), *The study of social interaction: Methodological issues.* Madison, WI: University of Wisconsin Press.

Parke, R. D., & Sawin, D. B. (1980). The family in early infancy: Social, interactional, attitudinal analyses. In F. Pedersen (Ed.), *The father-infant relationship: Observational studies in a family context.* New York: Praeger.

Parke, R. D., & Suomi, S. J. (1981). Adult male-infant relationships: Human and nonhuman primate evidence. In K. Immelmann, G. W. Barlow, L. Petrinovich, & M. Main (Eds.), *Behavioral development: The Bielefeld Interdisciplinary Project.* New York: Cambridge University Press.

Parke, R. D., & Tinsley, B. R. (1984). Historical and contemporary perspectives on fathering. In K. A. McCluskey & H. W. Reese (Eds.), *Life-span development psychology: Historical and generational effects in life-span human development.* New York: Academic.

Parke, R. D., & Tinsley, B. R. (in press). Fathers as agents and recipients of support in the postnatal period. In Z. Boukydis (Ed.), *Support for parents in the postnatal period.* New York: Ablex.

Pedersen, F. A. (Ed.) (1980). *The father-infant relationship: Observational studies in the family setting.* New York: Praeger.

Pedersen, F. A., Anderson, B. J., & Cain, R. L. (1977, March). An approach to understanding linkages between the parent-infant and spouse relationships. Paper presented at Biennial Meeting of Society for Research in Child Development, New Orleans.

Petersen, G. H., Mehl, L. E., & Leiderman, P. H. (1979). The role of some birth-related variables in father attachment. *American Journal of Orthopsychiatry,* 49, 330–338.

Power, T. G., & Parke, R. D. (1982). Play as a context for early learning: Lab and home analyses. In I. E. Sigel and L. M. Laosa (Eds.), *The family as a learning environment.* New York: Plenum.

Radin, N. (1982). Primary caregiving and role-sharing fathers. In M. E. Lamb (Ed.), *Nontraditional families.* Hillsdale, NJ: Erlbaum.

Redican, W. K., & Taub, D. M. (1981). Male paternal care in monkeys and apes. In M. E. Lamb (Ed.), *The role of the father in child development.* 2nd ed. New York: Wiley.

Rheingold, H. L. (1956). The modification of social responsiveness in institutional babies. *Monographs of the Society for Research in Child Development, 21,* 63.

Rödholm, M. (1981). Effects of father-infant post-partum contact on their interaction 3 months after birth. *Early Human Development, 5,* 79–85.

Russell, G. (1978). The father role and its relation to masculinity, femininity and androgyny. *Child Development, 49,* 1174–1181.

Russell, G. (1982a). *The changing role of fathers?* St. Lucia, Queensland: University of Queensland Press.

Russell, C. (1982b) Shared-caregiving families: An Australian study. In M. E. Lamb (Ed.), *Nontraditional families: Parenting and child development.* Hillsdale, NJ: Erlbaum.

Russell, G. (1982c). Highly participant Australian fathers: Some preliminary findings. *Merrill Palmer Quarterly, 28,* 137–156.

Russell, G., & Radin, N. (1983). Increased paternal participation: The father's perspective. In M. E. Lamb & A. Sagi (Eds.), *Fatherhood and family policy.* Hillsdale, NJ: Erlbaum.

Sagi, A. (1982) Antecedents and consequences of various degrees of parental involvement in childrearing: The Israeli project. In M. E. Lamb (Ed.), *Nontraditional families.* Hillsdale, NJ: Erlbaum.

Skeels, H. (1966). Adult status of children with contrasting early life experiences. *Monographs of the Society for Research in Child Development, 31,* 3.

Sosa, R., Kennell, J. H., Klaus, M. H., Robertson, S., & Urrutia, J. (1980). The effect of a supportive companion on perinatal problems, length of labor and mother-infant interaction. *New England Journal of Medicine, 303,* 597–600.

Spelke, E., Zelazo, P., Kagan, J., & Kotelchuck, M. (1973). Father interaction and separation protest. *Developmental Psychology, 9,* 83–90.

Steffensmeier, R. H. (May 1982). A role model of the transition to parenthood. *Journal of Marriage and the Family, 44,* 319–334.

Svejda, M. J., Campos, J. J., & Emde, R. N. (1980). Mother-infant "bonding": Failure to generalize. *Child Development, 51,* 775–779.

Toney, L. (1983). The effects of holding the newborn at delivery on paternal bonding. *Nursing Research, 32,* 16–19.

Vietze, P. M., MacTurk, R. H., McCarthy, M. E., Klein, R. P., & Yarrow, L. J. (1980, April). Impact of mode of delivery on father- and mother-infant interaction at 6 and 12 months. Paper presented at International Conference on Infant Studies, New Haven, CT.

Wente, A. S., & Crockenberg, S. B. (1976). Transition to parenthood: Lamaze preparation, adjustment difficulty, and the husband-wife relationship. *Family Coordinator, 25,* 351–357.

Whitt, J. K., & Casey, P. H. (1982). The mother-infant relationship and infant development: The effect of pediatric intervention. *Child Development, 53,* 948–956.

Widmayer, S. M., & Field, T. M. (1980). Effects of Brazelton demonstration on early interactions of preterm infants and their teenage mothers. *Infant Behavior and Development, 3,* 79–89.

Worobey, J., & Belsky, J. (1982). Employing the Brazelton scale to influence mothering: An experimental comparison of three strategies. *Developmental Psychology, 18,* 736–743.

Yogman, M. W. (1982). Development of the father-infant relationship. In H. E. Fitzgerald, B. M. Lester, & M. W. Yogman (Eds.), *Theory and research in behavioral pediatrics* (Vol. 1). New York: Plenum.

Zelazo, P. R., Kotelchuck, M., Barber, L., & David, J. (1977, March). Fathers and sons: An experimental facilitation of attachment behaviors. Paper presented at meeting of Society for Research in Child Development, New Orleans.

CHAPTER 12

Adolescent Fathers from a Clinical Perspective

ARTHUR B. ELSTER
University of Utah Medical Center

Over 500,000 infants are born each year in the United States to women under 20 years of age (National Center for Health Statistics, 1984). An increasing number of publications during the past several years attest to the interest that researchers and clinicians now have in the fathers of these infants. Reasons for the increasing interest derive from concern for the developmental and physical welfare of children born to young parents, realization that involvement of partners could improve the effectiveness of health-care delivery to pregnant adolescents and young mothers, concern for the problems experienced by young fathers, and general concern for the societal costs of supporting pregnant adolescents and young families.

As the number of special programs dealing with adolescents increased during the late 1970s, it was inevitable that the attention directed at adolescent pregnancy would be broadened to include the male partner. It was in the entertainment media, however, that some of the issues surrounding young fathers received the most notoriety. Especially poignant was the short film entitled, *Teenage Fathers* (Children's Aid Society of California), which won an Oscar in 1978. In this film, a teenager becomes pregnant. While the girl decides she wants to keep the baby rather than allow it to be adopted, the boy struggles with his ambivalent feelings of wanting to be socially responsible for his actions but not yet wanting to assume the role of parent. The question the film raises is what ethical rights does or should a male partner have in deciding the outcome of pregnancy during adolescence. For example, if the boy advocates adoption but the girl decides against this option, should he be financially responsible for child support?

Equally moving was the segment in the film *Saturday Night Fever* during which one of John Travolta's friends was involved in an out-of-wedlock pregnancy. He was depressed over the situation, became frustrated when none of the gang would talk with him about his feelings, and eventually killed himself by jumping off a bridge. Television shows, including segments from *The White Shadow* and *The Phil Donahue Show,* have also addressed the issue of adolescent fathers. As our society has come to accept pregnant adolescents and young mothers, so has it come to more openly face the issues surrounding adolescent fathers.

The Teen Mother and Child Program (TMCP) at the University of Utah School of Medicine has had a father's outreach component since the program's inception. A special counselor has the assigned role of identifying, assessing, and providing supportive services to the partner of the teens in the program. Much of what is presented in this chapter comes from our clinical and research experience with fathers in the TMCP. While fathers in Utah may come from different cultural and religious backgrounds than do fathers in other regions of the country, it is our impression from reviewing research done elsewhere and discussing teenage fathers with other clinicians and researchers that there are considerably more similarities than differences among fathers from different subcultures.

To better serve this special group of fathers, it is important to know who these youths are, the rationale for providing them services, and the ways they themselves are affected by pregnancy and parenthood. The chapter concludes with a discussion of clinical approaches to working with young fathers. Unless otherwise noted, the terms "adolescent" and "teenage" are used interchangeably. While these refer to overlapping but different groups (i.e., teenage refers to anyone 13 to 19 years old, while adolescent refers to a developmental process that has a less clearly defined age range), from a clinical perspective they denote similar populations.

CHARACTERISTICS OF ADOLESCENT FATHERS

While the literature commonly refers to partners of pregnant adolescents as "adolescent fathers," this is not always accurate. As can be seen in Table 12.1, from national birth certificate data only 30 percent of adolescent mothers have partners who are themselves adolescent (National Center for Health Statistics, 1984). There are substantial social differences in that black adolescents appear more likely than whites to have an adolescent partner. Conversely, of the 125,305 fathers who were under age 20 in 1982, 82.5 percent had teenage partners. Interestingly, 21,814 (17.5 percent) young fathers had older partners.

For a variety of reasons that will be discussed later, parenthood occurring during the school-age years is potentially more devastating to young

TABLE 12.1.   Percent of Infants Born in the United States During 1982 Who Had Fathers Under 20 Years of Age, by Age and Race of Mother[a]

Mother's Age (Years)	Total	Race of Mother	
		White	Black
< 20	30%	28.6%	37%
20–24	2%	2.0%	2%
25–29	0.1%	0.1%	0.2%

[a] Data from National Center for Health Statistics (1984).

fathers than if it occurs after graduation. Narrowing the concept of adolescent pregnancy to school-age pregnancy, therefore, probably has more relevance when discussing the adverse affects of role transition to parenthood. Unfortunately, since birth certificate data lump fathers' ages into five-year intervals, it is impossible to analyze the number of school-age fathers nationally.

In our TMCP we serve only adolescents who are 17 or younger at the time of entry into the program. During the past several years, 45 percent of male partners were under age 20 and 30 percent were still school-age (under age 19) at the time of delivery. In general, therefore, in up to one third of couples both partners are probably of school-age.

A primary question to ask when discussing the characteristics of adolescent fathers is whether these youth differ psychosocially from other youth not involved in pregnancy and parenthood. It is tempting to imply that the study of factors that relate to adolescent sexual behavior or contraceptive use might contribute to our understanding of differences between adolescent fathers and nonfathers. This represents a conceptual "leap-of-faith" that may have some validity, but because of the many diverse factors affecting sexuality and fertility, probably adds relatively little to our understanding of the question posed earlier. Few studies have investigated differences in characteristics between adolescent fathers and nonfathers.

Pauker (1971) reported a study in which the Minnesota Multiphasic Personality Inventory (MMPI) was administered to a large group of ninth-grade students. Ninety-four of the boys subsequently were involved in a pregnancy during adolescence. A control group of nonadolescent fathers, matched by age, school attended, and socioeconomic background, was identified and MMPI scores between the groups were compared. On only 3 of 13 subscales were significant differences found. Pauker concluded that since the two groups had such a great degree of premorbid similarity, psychological dysfunction contributed little to out-of-wedlock conception among boys.

Supporting Pauker's conclusion are the results of a study by Williams-McCoy and Tyler (1985), in which psychosocial characteristics were compared between a group of 24 unwed black adolescent fathers and a group of 27 nonfathers. All subjects were between 15 and 19 years of age and came from similar family backgrounds. The groups did not differ in a measure of locus of control, in interpersonal trust, or in coping style. Some differences were found, however, in that the fathers were older and more likely themselves to have been born out of wedlock. The notion that adolescent fathers are more likely to have parents or siblings who had a school-age or premarital pregnancy is supported by findings from multiple studies (Card & Steel, 1981; Rivara, Sweeney, & Henderson, 1985; Robbins & Lynn, 1973; Williams-McCoy & Tyler, 1985). It appears as if role modeling for adolescent pregnancy is just as strong for young fathers as it is for young mothers.

Data from our TMCP suggest that a substantial proportion of adolescent fathers may have significant psychosocial developmental difficulties prior to the pregnancy. As shown in Table 12.2, at the time of their entry into the program, half of the male partners were neither in school nor graduated, 52 percent of partners 20 years old or older had not graduated from high school, and 17 percent were reported to have either an attention deficit disorder (i.e., hyperactivity) or a learning disability. Fifty percent of

TABLE 12.2. Markers of Psychosocial Adjustment of Male Partners of Primagravida Teens (n = 291) Participating In the Teen Mother and Child Program at the University of Utah School of Medicine

Psychosocial Variable	Percent of Fathers (at entry)
Educational status	
Enrolled in school	23%
Not enrolled in school	49%
Graduated or in college	28%
Highest grade completed[a]	
Ninth	8.5%
Tenth–eleventh	43.5%
Twelfth	48%
Learning problems (attention deficit disorder or learning disability)	17%[b]
Conduct problems	
Behavior problems (e.g., truancy, running away)	60%[b]
Judicial involvement	50%[b]

[a] For partners ≥ 20 years of age ($n = 119$).
[b] Based on 58 subjects.

fathers had some involvement with the judicial system. Recognizing that one of the main developmental tasks of adolescence is to obtain an education that allows for vocational advancement and financial independence, these data imply that some young fathers, even before the additional stresses and economic burdens of parenthood, are having adjustment problems. It may be that adolescents who become fathers do not have severe psychopathology and therefore test reasonably well on measures such as the MMPI. They may, however, have experienced significant "failures," as measured by academic difficulties and judicial involvement, and be susceptible to a variety of adverse social behaviors, such as pregnancy, substance abuse, delinquency, or suicide. Perhaps the path that these youth take is, then, to some degree determined by role models in their environment.

Another question to be asked when discussing the characteristics of the partners of adolescent mothers is whether adolescent fathers differ from older fathers. Again, the answer may have significance in determining health care services.

Nakashima and Camp (1984) reported on comparisons among three groups of fathers: 20 adolescent fathers, 15 older fathers with adolescent partners, and 16 older fathers with older partners. Assessments were made of marital conflict, parental attitudes, ego development, vocabulary, and abstract thinking. Older fathers with older partners were found to have better vocabularies, to be better educated, and to have a higher level of ego development than fathers in the other two groups. Marital conflict was perceived as less for the older father-adolescent partner group. In general, the two groups with adolescent partners had few differences.

Supporting these results, Lamb and Elster (1985) also found few differences among groups of fathers differentiated by age. In their study, 51 adolescent mother-infant-father triads were studied in a naturalistic home setting when the child was approximately 6 months of age. Both parents independently completed several questionnaires, including Spanier's (1976) Dyadic Adjustment Scale, which assessed the quality of the partners' relationship, and a version of the Life Experience Questionnaire (Sarason, Johnson, & Siegel, 1978), which assessed the occurrence and stressfulness of recent life events. The fathers were placed into three groups, those less than 19.5 years old ($n = 18$), those 19.6 to 22 years of age ($n = 17$), and those 22.1 to 29.9 years of age ($n = 16$). Most couples were married or living together (81 percent), caucasian, and from middle- to lower middle-class socioeconomic backgrounds. While younger fathers tended more frequently to be in school, age was not related to the likelihood of being employed. No group differences were found for any of the four subscales of the Dyadic Adjustment Scale as reported by either father or mother. The younger fathers, compared with the two older groups, experienced a greater degree of both positive and negative life events during the preceding six months. Overall, the father's age differentiated little regarding mother-infant, father-infant, or mother-father interactions.

In summary, only recently have we begun to know more about the characteristics of adolescent fathers. Data currently available suggest that some of these youth, while not having serious psychopathology, may nevertheless have difficulty with psychosocial adjustment. Other differences between adolescent fathers and nonfathers are unclear and need to be studied. Fathers of infants of adolescent mothers are not a homogeneous group; age and prepregnancy psychosocial adjustment are only two of the markers that could be used to study individual differences. How such differences affect issues such as level of commitment to partner and child, ultimate educational-vocational achievement, and parental behavior are critical areas in which research is needed.

WORKING WITH ADOLESCENT FATHERS

Irrespective of the current level of knowledge about the characteristics of adolescent fathers, clinicians have a social responsibility to develop some degree of services for these youth. What follows is a discussion of why adolescent fathers should be involved in clinical services, the sorts of problems experienced by adolescent fathers, and some clinical approaches for working with this population.

Rationale for Providing Services to Adolescent Fathers

Services should be provided to adolescent fathers to promote better parental behaviors; to assist the communication between partners, thus helping them to make more enlightened decisions about the future; and to provide psychosocial guidance, thus helping fathers to adjust better to their situation.

Fathers affect child development both directly, through their own behaviors, and indirectly, through their effect on the mother and consequently her parental behaviors (Parke, Power, & Fisher, 1980). From empirical and clinical data, many adolescent fathers, at least many of those who stay involved in the relationship, report that they are ready for parenthood (Hendricks & Montgomery, 1983) and want to learn more about pregnancy and their child (Elster & Panzarine, 1983). In contrast to the past concept that young fathers were not interested in remaining involved with the mother and their infant, it now appears that more adolescent fathers are maintaining an ongoing relationship. Fathers, like their adolescent partner, could benefit from assistance in learning how to provide quality parental behavior.

Adolescent males who remain involved with their partner's pregnancy frequently appear to have a committed relationship (Furstenberg, 1976; Hendricks & Montgomery, 1983). The very nature of the crisis related with premarital conception implies, however, that there are long-term relationship issues that have not been discussed or resolved. Involving fathers in clinical services can help couples to contemplate more clearly future decisions, such as school, work, marriage, or contraception. This type of discussion may also lead to young fathers being more financially involved and accepting of their child, even if the couple's social relationship dissolves.

Finally, teenage fathers have problems of their own for which they may need help. These may include a wide range of emotional, educational, or legal problems. Assisting these prospective or new fathers with such issues could have wide impact on mother, child and society as well as the father himself.

Problems Experienced by Adolescent Fathers

From a conceptual viewpoint, the experience of adolescent pregnancy and parenthood may affect young fathers differently than older fathers because these events represent a premature role transition, adolescent couples are generally engaged in a relatively unstable relationship, and there are opposing social forces affecting adolescents' level of involvement.

Premature transition to parent and/or spouse affects fathers socially, developmentally, and vocationally. Society prescribes the assumption of social roles in the following order: completion of formal education, obtaining a skill for financial independence, marriage, and then parenthood. The completion of each step sequentially is socially rewarded, and established support mechanisms exit. For example, completion of high school or college is associated with an emotionally intense graduation process; starting a job is associated with the social rewards of the esteem of moving away from home and being a "swinging single"; marriage connotes entry into the more adult world associated with a greater level of social maturity; and parenthood gives fathers the esteemed roles of provider and progenitor. When the steps do not occur as expected, however, problems can arise. Even though he is more accepted today than in the past, the male partner of an adolescent mother is still viewed somewhat negatively: "Why did he get his girl pregnant?" "He should have been more careful." "He is irresponsible." In addition to being socially castigated, young fathers who remain involved with their partner and child may find themselves isolated from their normal peer group network. Work, parenthood responsibilities, and having a monogamous relationship may remove them from usual peer group activities. Young fathers and couples may find that they have less and less in common with their old friends. This social isolation adversely affects the ability of these parents to cope with the diverse set of social stresses that many of them inevitably experience. In addition, since peer groups are important mechanisms for psychosocial development, adolescent fathers may not have the opportunity for the social interaction necessary for them to understand themselves as completely as possible. This may lead to premature closure on issues such as appropriate sex-role behavior, views on parenthood and parenting, and personal ethics and morals. Finally, premature transition to parenthood affects adolescents by limiting the amount of formal education they receive and consequently their vocational opportunities (Card & Wise 1978; Kerckhoff & Parrow, 1979; Marsiglio, in press). Even when youth were matched on several educational variables prior to pregnancy, Card and Wise (1978) found that age of parenthood was inversely related to ultimate educational attainment. Young fathers achieved less educationally, and never caught up, when compared with men who postponed parenthood.

Interesting new analyses of data from the National Longitudinal Survey of Work Experience of Youth (Marsiglio, in press) further emphasize the educational problems of young fathers. Cross tabulations between age at fatherhood and completion of high school revealed that the probability of dropping out of school for teenage fathers was .44, compared with .22 for older fathers and .12 for nonfathers. Data such as those presented here (Card & Wise, 1978; Kerckhoff & Parrow, 1979; Marsiglio, in press;), however, do not answer the question whether pregnancy and parenthood disrupt the psychosocial development of adolescence or, as data from the TMCP presented earlier regarding educational status suggest, that young fathers have psychosocial difficulties prior to pregnancy and parenthood.

A second unique aspect of pregnancy and parenthood in adolescence is that the partners are frequently involved in a relatively unstable relationship as compared with adults. Adolescent couples involved in a pregnancy usually have dated for at least 6 to 12 months and consider themselves "engaged" (Gispert & Falk, 1976; Kinch, Wearing, Love, & McMahon, 1969). While these relationships are not fleeting "one-night stands," they still are not built on the concept of permanence. Developmentally, adolescents are experimenting with their sexuality. Relationships, while meaningful at the time, are more important in the broader context of social experimentation whereby appropriate sex roles, attitudes, and behaviors are defined. When a pregnancy occurs, therefore, it most often is not associated with a relationship that was intended to be enduring. The consequence of adolescent couples maintaining their relationship, at least in marriage, is unfortunately predictable. Results of multiple studies demonstrate that couples who marry during adolescence have a much higher divorce rate than do couples who marry at later ages (Burchinal, 1965; Inselberg, 1962; McCarthy & Menken, 1979).

The third unique aspect of parenthood for adolescent fathers is that they are faced with opposing social and emotional pressures affecting their decision regarding how involved to become or to remain with their partner and child. Forces influencing increased commitment include the affiliation they might have for their partner, their desire to be a father, their sense of social responsibility, and the legal pressures for financial support. Forces opposing a continued commitment include being socially ostracized by the girl's parents and possibly not being allowed to continue the relationship, not being ready for parenthood and recognizing that it will impede education and vocational advancement, and not being willing to make a long-lasting emotional commitment to the relationship. Both sets of forces are powerful. Whereas in the mid-nineteenth century the prohibitions against extramarital pregnancies and out-of-wedlock births were strong (Vinovskis, in press), in today's society the social sanctions prohibiting extramarital conceptions and births have lessened dramatically. Young fathers, like young mothers, now have a choice about whether to continue the relationship.

In summary, adolescent fathers may experience a series of emotional and social problems that occur in part because of the premature nature of their role transition and in part because of difficulties they had prior to pregnancy and parenthood. These problems may be acute in nature, such as negative changes in relationships with parents, friends, or partners, or long-term, such as truncated education, limited vocational achievement, and divorce. It should not be forgotten, however, that pregnancy and parenthood may provide some teenage fathers with substantial emotional benefits. While researchers and clinicians tend to view teenage pregnancy in negative terms, this view is clearly not always correct. Some teenage couples do remarkably well with school, family life, and parenting. What differentiates these teens from other youth who do not perform as well? The answer to this question, on an empirical basis, would be the degree of prepregnancy psychosocial adjustment and the presence of a social support network. Research data are needed to corroborate this speculation.

CLINICAL APPROACHES FOR WORKING WITH ADOLESCENT FATHERS

Several basic principles should be followed by those who work with adolescent fathers. While each of these may not be relevant or even possible for each agency or provider, they nevertheless provide guidelines based on empirical and research data.

1. *Choose a specific type of outreach approach.* Most adolescent pregnancy programs that work with fathers do case identification and contact with the permission and cooperation of the pregnant adolescent. This approach has the advantages of convenience and a relatively good likelihood of success if the teen is in agreement with the idea of involving her partner. An alternative approach is to identify, out of a group of adolescent males, those who have been involved in a pregnancy. The advantages here are that a greater number of fathers can probably be identified, fathers not still involved with their partner can be identified, and anticipatory guidance can be provided to young men whether or not they have been involved with a pregnancy.

2. *Ensure that a clear, consistent message is provided by the entire staff that prospective and new fathers are welcomed.* Subtle verbal and nonverbal messages from anyone associated with the program implying blame or legal recourse may be enough to scare away a frightened young father. It is important that clinical, nursing, and administrative staff all be committed to the concept that pregnancy and parenthood is a family affair.

3. *Obtain information from the young father as well as the teen mother.* Hearing one side of a compelling story by a pregnant teenager may serve to reinforce preconceived notions about adolescent fathers, but the story may misrepresent the truth. Clinicians should withhold judgment until both partners can be interviewed. We have had several situations where the girl and her mother did not want her partner involved, regardless of his feelings. It is important that data be obtained from each party if a comprehensive plan is to be developed.

4. *Provide fathers with concrete assistance.* In our experience most of the couples in the TMCP consider that they have no major problems with their relationship. Issues more important for these people center around financial problems, living situation, social isolation, etc. Providing information on vocational training, job opportunities, parenting, and child development may have more relevance to young fathers than emotional issues.

5. *Involve fathers in all aspects of care.* Unless one of the partners declines, fathers should be encouraged not only to attend clinic visits, but also to go with their partner and/or child into the examination room. Not only does this provide emotional support for the mother, it also educates the father and allows him to reinforce the instructions provided. This is especially important in regards to contraceptive services.

While working with adolescent fathers can be frustrating because of poor compliance, lack of interest by the fathers, or lack of program human and financial resources, viewing pregnancy and parenthood from a holistic approach can have real benefits. Past approaches directed narrowly at just the pregnant teenager neglected others who also affect her pregnancy and are themselves affected by the pregnancy.

Adolescent fathers can be a major source of social support to young mothers; the converse is true also.

REFERENCES

Burchinal, L. G. (1965). Trends and prospects for young marriages in the United States. *Journal of Marriage and the Family, 27*, 243–254.

Card, J. J., & Wise, L. L. (1978). Teenage mothers and teenage fathers: The impact of early childbearing on the parents' personal and professional lives. *Family Planning Perspectives, 10*, 199–205.

Card, J. J., & Steel, L. (1981). Special tabulations from Project Talent, American Institutes for Research in the Behavioral Sciences. Data presented in *Teenage pregnancy: The problem that hasn't gone away* ———. New York: Alan Guttmacher Institute, p. 35.

Elster, A., & Panzarine, S. (1983). Adolescent fathers: Stresses during gestation and early parenthood. *Clinical Pediatrics, 22*, 700–703.

Furstenberg, F. F. (1976). The social consequences of teenage parenthood. *Family Planning Perspectives, 8*, 148–164.

Gispert, M., & Falk, R. (1976). Sexual experimentation and pregnancy in young black adolescents. *American Journal of Obstetrics and Gynecology, 126*, 459–466.

Hendricks, L. E., & Montgomery, T. (1983). A limited population of unmarried adolescent fathers: A preliminary report of their views on fatherhood and the relationship with the mothers of their children. *Adolescence, 1*, 116–120.

Inselberg, P. M. (1962). Marital problems and satisfaction in high school marriages. *Marriage and Family Living*, February, 74–77.

Kerckhoff, A. C., & Parrow, A. A. (1979). The effect of early marriage on the educational attainment of young men. *Journal of Marriage and the Family, 41*, 97–107.

Kinch, R. A. H., Wearing, M. P., Love, E. J., & McMahon, D. (1969). Some aspects of pediatric illegitimacy. *American Journal of Obstetrics and Gynecology, 105*, 20–31.

Lamb, M. E., & Elster, A. B. (1985). Adolescent mother-infant-father relationships. *Developmental Psychology, 21*, 768–773.

Marsiglio, W. (1986). Teenage fatherhood: High school accreditation and educational attainment. In A. Elster & M. E. Lamb (Eds.), *Adolescent fatherhood.* Hillsdale, NJ: Erlbaum.

McCarthy, J., & Menken, J. (1979). Marriage, remarriage, marital disruption and age at first birth. *Family Planning Perspectives, 11*, 21–30.

Nakashima, I. I., & Camp, B. W. (1984). Fathers of infants born to adolescent mothers: A study of paternal characteristics. *American Journal of Diseases of Childhood, 138*, 452–454.

National Center for Health Statistics (1984, September). *Monthly Vital Statistics Report. Advanced Report of Final Natality Statistics, 1982*. Washington, DC: U. S. Government Printing Office, Vol. 33 (6) (Supplement).

Parke, R. D., Power, T. G., & Fisher, T. (1980). The adolescent father's impact on the mother and child. *Journal of Social Issues, 36*, 88–106.

Pauker, J. D. (1971). Fathers of children conceived out of wedlock: Pre-pregnancy, high school, psychological test results. *Developmental Psychology, 4*, 215–218.

Rivara, F. P., Sweeney, P. J., & Henderson, B. F. (1985). A study of low socioeconomic status, black teenaged fathers and their non-father peers. *Pediatrics, 75*, 648–656.

Robbins, M. B., & Lynn, D. B. (1973). The unwed fathers: Generation recidivism and attitudes about intercourse in California youth authority wards. *The Journal of Sex Research, 9*, 334–341.

Sarason, I. G., Johnson, J. H., & Siegel, J. M. (1978). Assessing the impact of life changes: Development of the life experience survey. *Journal of Consulting and Clinical Psychology, 46*, 932–946.

Spanier, G. B. (1976). Measuring dyadic adjustment: New scales for assessing the quality of marriage and similar dyads. *Journal of Marriage and the Family, 38*, 15–32.

Williams-McCoy, J. E., & Tyler, F. B. (1985). Selected psychosocial characteristics of black unwed adolescent fathers. *Journal of Adolescent Health Care, 6*, 12–16.

Vinovskis, M. (1985). Adolescent sexuality, pregnancy, and childbearing in early America: Some preliminary speculations. In J. Lancaster and B. Hamburg (Eds.), *School-age pregnancy and parenthood: Biosocial dimensions*. Hawthorn, NY: Aldine.

FOUR

Programs and Policies

CHAPTER 13

Fathers in Hard Times: The Impact of Unemployment and Poverty on Paternal and Marital Relations

SHIRLEY AISHA RAY AND VONNIE C. McLOYD
University of Michigan

In the 1980s the number of poor and unemployed Americans increased dramatically. For the first time the poverty rate equalled rates from the 1960s, and unemployment figures duplicated those of the Great Depression of the 1930s. The official definition of poverty has remained basically unchanged for a generation. A person is defined as living in poverty if his or her cash income from all sources is less than three times the cost of an adequate diet as defined by the government (Harrington, 1984). In 1983 the official government poverty line for a family was $10,000, about 33 percent of the median income of American families in 1982.

Currently one person in seven, or 14 percent of the American population, is officially poor. One of every five American children under age 18 lives in poverty (Children's Defense Fund, 1984). Thirty-eight percent of all the poor today are children, giving America the dubious distinction of being the only industrialized nation in the world in which children are the largest age group living in poverty (Williams, 1985). There are more poor children in the United States today than at any time since 1965, before the Great Society programs began. Indeed, of the 13.4 million poor children, 3.3 million joined the ranks of the poor after 1981. Data indicate that 13 percent of America's poor children live in intact or male-headed households, while 55

The authors gratefully acknowledge the generous assistance of Mary Dugas, Alexis Kennedy, Margot Michael, Denise Person, and Linda Shultes in the preparation of this manuscript.

339

percent live in female-headed households (Children's Defense Fund, 1984). Close to 2.5 million of the nation's poor children live in families in which at least one person has a full-time job, a figure that belies the prevalent view that a full-time job throughout the year necessarily exempts one from poverty (Williams, 1985). The trend toward an increasingly young poverty population is not abating and is expected to continue into the next decade (Wilson & Neckerman, 1984).

The figures for unemployment reflect an equally grim reality for children and their families. The nation reacted with disbelief when the unemployment rate reached 10 percent in September 1982, its highest level in 42 years. In 1985, three years after the low point of the most recent recession, unemployment in several regions and among certain groups remained as high or higher than it was in late 1980, the last prerecession period (Children's Defense Fund, 1985). Unemployment has not been under 7 percent since 1980, well above the 4 percent regarded by government officials as "natural" or acceptable in the 1960s, and it is projected that it will continue in the 7 to 8 percent range through the 1980s (Williams, 1985). Especially hard hit are midwestern and eastern states where the economic decline of major industrial centers continues to prompt the closing of primary industrial facilities. Perhaps even more ominous than the present bulge in unemployment is the longer-term upward creep in the figures. Data indicate that at the end of each recession of the last two decades or so, unemployment fell, but did not drop to its previous low (Arenson, 1982).

The costs of unemployment are borne not only by individual workers but by their families as well. As of March 1984, 5.7 million American children, or roughly 10.6 percent of the 60.5 million American children under 18 years of age, had at least one officially unemployed parent (Children's Defense Fund, 1985). Indeed, owing in part to the fact that they are younger and often lack job seniority and competitive job skills, workers with children are more likely to be unemployed than workers without children (Liem & Rayman, 1982). It is estimated that children are more likely to experience parental unemployment than the death of a parent, divorce, or even major illness (Siev, 1983).

A vastly disproportionate share of the burden of poverty and unemployment in America is borne by African-Americans, women, and their children, though we know least how these groups experience and cope with job loss (Buss & Redburn, 1983a, Liem & Rayman, 1982). Two-parent African-American families and female-headed African-American families are twice as likely as comparable European-American families to live in poverty. African-American children are almost three times as likely as European-American children to be poor. In 1983, close to half (46 percent) of all African-American children lived in poverty, compared with 17 percent of

European-American children (Children's Defense Fund, 1985). Contributing to this discrepancy is the relatively high number of African-American children who live in female-headed families. In 1979, 42 percent of African-American children, compared with 12 percent of European-American children, lived in such families (Children's Defense Fund, 1980). Currently, 46 percent of all female-headed families are African-American, while 15 percent are European-American (Children's Defense Fund, 1984).

The figures for unemployment tell a similar story. In November 1984, 15 percent of African-American workers (nearly 2 million) were unemployed, compared with a national average of 7.1 percent (Children's Defense Fund, 1985). Generally, African-American women have the highest rate of unemployment, followed by African-American men, European-American women, and European-American men, respectively (Children's Defense Fund, 1985). African-American children are about twice as likely as European-American children to have at least one parent currently unemployed and about three times as likely to have no parent currently employed (Children's Defense Fund, 1980).

These alarming facts have focused the concern of social scientists on the long-range effects of economic adversity on human growth and development. In addition, the growing interest in the contribution of fathers to the development of their children has raised questions about the effects of job loss, prolonged unemployment, and reduced income on the functioning of families and of men in the paternal role.

The current precarious position of unemployed and poor fathers has evolved over the last half century, during which time critical changes in the demographic characteristics of the work force and in the industrial base of capitalism, coupled with continued racial discrimination in the labor market, has affected the way economic deprivation is experienced by fathers and families. Historical changes in the labor market participation of women have had a profound effect on the ability of families to respond to the job loss and/or low income of fathers. During the 1930s, most mothers neither worked outside the home nor contributed earned income to the family. When their husband became unemployed, wives and their adolescent children represented a reserve labor force that, if employed, could help to make up the husband's lost income. In 1980, 56 percent of mothers with children under 18 years of age, compared with 8.6 percent of mothers in 1940, were in the labor force (Hoffman, 1984). Women work, in part, because their income is necessary to meet regular family expenses in a period of rising inflation. The large number of married women wage earners in the labor force in the 1980s and extremely high rates of adolescent unemployment have robbed families of a potential buffer against the male wage earner's income loss (Moen, Kain, & Elder, 1983; Rosen, 1983).

Dramatic and disturbing changes in the industrial base of the United States are having a profound effect on fathers and families. Basic industries characterized by high wages, productivity, and skilled labor, such as steel and automobile production, are declining. The impact of this decline is reflected in the relatively higher unemployment figures in the northeastern United States, which historically has been the most heavily industrialized region of the country, and in the increased demand in this region by families experiencing unemployment for social services such as welfare, food stamps, and emergency shelter (Citizens' Commission on Hunger in New England, 1984). The total number of plant closings and the number of workers affected during the past two decades is not known. But a 1970 census of manufacturing corporations representing 40 percent of the total United States manufacturing work force showed that 1000 plant closings eliminated 280,000 jobs (Buss & Redburn, 1983b). Between January 1979 and January 1984, 11.5 million workers aged 20 and over lost jobs due to plant relocation, slack work, or the elimination of a job position (Children's Defense Fund, 1985). In addition, the increase in service sector jobs and reduction in manufacturing jobs have implications for the future skill preparation and training of workers. Generally, service sector jobs require a less skilled and lower paid work force than manufacturing jobs (Grubb & Brody, 1985). "Economic hotspots," regions of the country where the unemployment rate hovers around 20 percent, may portend a trend that will continue through the end of this century (Garbarino, 1983, p. 1). It has been suggested that because poverty and unemployment in the 1980s are "so much more systemic and structural" than they were in the 1960s, they are also more persistent and pernicious (Harrington, 1984, p. 12). These changes indicate that fathers caught in these economic trends risk at the least a period of unemployment or long periods of chronic unemployment with an increased probability of poverty.

An additional factor that has contributed to the position of economic disadvantage of working- and lower-class families has been discrimination against workers of color in hiring, firing, promotions, and wages. This is a particularly important factor in explaining poverty and joblessness among African-American fathers. A vicious cycle of discrimination begun in childhood threatens the health, development, and well-being of young African-American males, limits their educational attainment (e.g., completion of high school), increases the likelihood that they will be involved with the criminal justice system, and limits the preparation for employment in a highly competitive and increasingly technologically based labor market.

The labor force participation rates (the percentage of individuals working or looking for work) of African-American males underscore the economic problems of African-American fathers. Because of the increase of women in the labor market, the labor force participation of all males has dropped in the last 20 years; for European-American males the decrease between 1960 and 1982 was 86 percent to 79.2 percent, but for African-American males during the same period the decrease was 83 percent to 74.7 percent (these figures represent African Americans and other non-white races). Between 1972 and 1982, the labor force participation rates for adult African-American men fell from 79 percent to 75 percent, meaning that 425,000 men between 20 and 64 years of age left or never entered the labor force. At special risk are African-American males between 16 and 19 years of age. During 1972 and 1982, many young men in this age group (potential fathers for their generation) never entered the labor force. Their participation rates dropped from 46 percent to 40 percent, virtually assuring that they will be in a disadvantaged position in competing for future employment (McGhee, 1984).

For African Americans, labor market discrimination accounts for one half to three quarters of the difference between their earnings and the earnings of European Americans (Grubb & Lazerson, 1982). Over the last 15 years, researchers have preferred to explain the deteriorating state of African-American family functioning by focusing on welfare dependence. More recent analysis suggests that it is the inability of African-American men to secure stable employment through which they can support their families that explains the rise in poverty, particularly of poor African-American female-headed households (Wilson & Neckerman, 1984). Together, racial discrimination and structural changes in the economy, such as the shift of manufacturing employment from central cities to outlying urban areas, and the shift from manufacturing to service employment, have exacerbated the employment problems of lower-class African-American males (Wilson, 1980).

Discrimination against working- and lower-class *women* in the labor market also affects fathers and children because the woman's income often is necessary to assure the family a relative degree of economic stability. In 1980, working wives contributed 26 percent of the total family income. When one considers that the income of working women is 60 percent that of men (U. S. Department of Labor, 1981), it is clear that the elimination of sex discrimination in the labor market would raise the income of women and thereby the economic resources available to their husband and children.

Because work is a central aspect of adult life that helps to define an individual's worth in society and relationship to family and community, sudden job loss, particularly if such loss is prolonged, can seriously threaten physical health, psychological well being, and family relationships (Brenner, 1973). In a class-conscious and affluent nation such as the

United States (Hess, 1970; Rubin, 1976; Sennett & Cobb, 1973), how does a poverty- or near-poverty-level income and the daily struggle to procure essential goods and services influence the person's overall development? How does the father experience his job loss or poverty? How do other factors such as quality of marital relations prior to job loss, age, and social class influence the father's response to poverty or loss of work? How does economic hardship affect the father's response to his children?

In the sections that follow we review the research literature that details the effects of unemployment and poverty on the mental and physical health of fathers, marital relations, and father-child relationships. We discuss child outcomes only as they relate to father-child relationships and give only minor attention to documented effects of paternal unemployment and poverty on the later development of offspring (adolescence and adulthood). Our discussion concludes with an examination of some of the social policy implications of research on the relationship between economic adversity and marital and paternal relationships.

ORGANIZATION OF RESEARCH ON ECONOMIC ADVERSITY

Society's interest in the relationship between family functioning and macroeconomic factors has a long history. Concern with the social impact of economic phenomena tends to increase during recessions and depressions, when the victims of hard times are more visible and in greater need of available social supports. Generally, social science researchers have concentrated on poverty and job loss as two critical conditions that may increase family stress and impair family relationships and individual development. Case studies of unemployed families completed during the 1930s and 1940s (e.g., Angell, 1936; Bakke, 1940) and quantitative studies conducted since the 1970s have characterized the unemployment research. Research on poor families, which peaked during the 1960s and 1970s, has been primarily descriptive and qualitative. In contrast to research on unemployment, which focuses primarily on the job loss of the male rather than the female worker, poverty research has concentrated on women with children. Poor fathers are generally represented in this literature (if they are mentioned at all) as absent, a condition that is blamed for contributing to the poverty of their families. This very different treatment of fathers is reflected in this literature review. The scholarly work on unemployment offers a richer set of findings regarding paternal role and economic change than does the research on poverty.

Anthropological and sociological research completed in the 1960s and early 1970s (e.g., Hannerz, 1969; Ladner, 1971; Stack, 1974; Young, 1970) provides descriptive data on children and families of distinct cultural groups, such as African Americans. An important question raised in many of these studies is the extent to which racial oppression affected the development of children. To a degree, these studies could be included in poverty or unemployment literature, but because the intention of the authors appears to have been to examine other microsocial and macrosocial dimensions (e.g., racism), which albeit may have economic ramifications, we have chosen to consider this literature as a separate category.

POVERTY AND UNEMPLOYMENT COMPARED

In reviewing the research on economic deprivation and the paternal role, it becomes clear that poverty and unemployment are distinct economic phenomena that have both similar and different effects on individuals and families. While both phenomena are a result of specific economic policies (Grubb & Brody, 1985), the impact of each on the individual and family depends on a variety of factors. Four conditions of economic deprivation can be identified: (1) unemployment of long duration that leads to poverty, (2) unemployment that does not lead to poverty, and (3) short-term and (4) chronic poverty caused primarily by the exploitation of workers whose wages are kept low through class, racial, and sexual discrimination in the labor market.

Unemployment is not simply an experience of deprivation, and it need not lead to poverty (Hyman, 1979). Though the probability that a family will be poor quintuples if the family head is unemployed (Grubb & Lazerson, 1982), rarely have the dynamics of this shift in economic status been documented. Caplovitz (1979) stressed the need to differentiate between the objective experience of income loss and the subjective feeling of being poor. Also few researchers have studied the dynamic pattern of spells of unemployment and employment and their impact on fathers and family functioning. Because of the sudden nature of unemployment, many workers may be psychologically and financially unprepared for job loss. On the other hand, workers whose jobs are characterized by seasonal layoffs may be relatively undaunted by initial job loss.

Ferman and Gardner (1979) have noted that many workers (especially African Americans and low-skilled workers) may experience a process they label as downward "skidding and bumping," in which workers take a series of jobs that are low paying and less stable than those held previously. They may finally come to rest in a poorly paying job with few benefits and no security, and may have to rely periodically on public income support programs to supplement earned income. In addition, the process of searching for a job may rob the unemployed father of a sense of dignity, usefulness, and purpose.

Poverty is generally not experienced as a sudden life event; rather individuals appear to slip in and out of poverty, a significant number experiencing long spells of poverty at any given time (Bane & Ellwood, 1983). The primary causes of adult poverty are exploitation of workers through low wages (Hyman, 1979) and long-term severe unemployment. Over the years, scholars and public policy analysts have debated the objective and subjective aspects of poverty. Some critics argue that the official poverty statistics are unnecessarily gloomy because many noncash benefits such as food stamps and public housing are not counted as income. Conversely, others point out that the official poverty line does not reflect the amount of income actually needed to buy the most basic necessities of life, resulting in a gross undercount of the poverty population (Grubb & Brody, 1985; Harrington, 1984).

The subjective impact of poverty also has been the subject of much debate. While the condition of being poor clearly affects developmental outcomes (Coles, 1970, 1971; Grubb & Brody, 1985; Hurley, 1969; Looff, 1971), researchers have questioned the long-term psychological impact of poverty, particularly the transmission of a set of attitudes and behaviors across generations (Corcoran, Duncan, & Gurin, 1983; Hill & Ponza, 1983; Lewis, 1966; Valentine, 1968). But poverty is a relative concept, not an absolute value. As Galbraith stated, "People are poverty stricken when their income, even if adequate for survival, falls markedly behind that of the community . . . they are degraded, for in the literal sense, they live outside the grades or categories which the community regards as acceptable" (Galbraith, cited in Miller & Rein, 1966).

Social science research on poverty has attempted to explain why certain groups (e.g., African Americans, Hispanic Americans, women with children) are disproportionately poor. Family structure, particularly father absence and matriarchy, has been a popular explanation for a host of perceived problems and inadequacies in African-American families (Moynihan, 1965). Dysfunctional psychological characteristics of the poor transmitted across generations also have been regarded as primary factors that keep the poor impoverished (Lewis, 1965, 1969). Much of this research has been severely criticized for the cultural and class biases of the researchers, the tendency to stress perceived deviance prior to the establishment of group norms, the muting of distinctions between class and culture, and the emphasis on measuring the behavior of distinct groups against European-American middle-class norms (Billingsley, 1968; Rainwater & Yancey, 1967; Valentine, 1968). Scholars have argued persuasively that African-American families provide a nurturant haven for children in a racist and hostile world. In the attempt to emphasize the considerable adaptive capacity of African-American families, the sometimes devastating impact of racism often has been given short shrift as a factor that retains these families in the ranks of the poor and the unemployed.

Existing research has not adequately differentiated the categories of "the poor." The most common terms used to describe the poor are blue-collar poor, working class, lower-working class, lower-lower class, underclass, permanent poor, and chronic poor. But the distinct and shared features of these subgroups are not always carefully documented by researchers, perhaps because of the tendency to view the poor as a homogeneous group (Lewis, 1966). Furthermore, dramatic economic and public policy changes have created new categories of the poor. For example, until recently stable working-class individuals were not considered members of the poor (Lewis and Herzog, 1971). But high unemployment due to plant closings and reduction in eligibility for workers' compensation have drawn some members of the stable working class into the ranks of the "near poor" and the "new poor" (Children's Defense Fund, 1984; Citizens Commission on Hunger in New England, 1984).

The distinctions between culture and class need to be further clarified; specifically, how is the behavior of poor fathers toward their children influenced by class and by culture? In addition, further study and elaboration are needed on the degree to which economic changes and features of the labor market, (e.g., unemployment, high inflation, class, and racial discrimination) affect paternal roles and interaction patterns. Social class differences in child rearing that can have profound influences on individual development have been documented (Bronfenbrenner, 1958; Deutsch, 1973; Hess, 1970). But while the distinctions between classes are important, the within-class variations also need to be identified and their developmental significance recognized. Typologies of within-class variations offered by some scholars identify two to four types of value/behavioral clusters (e.g., "hard-living" and "settled-living" families) which characterize familial styles and roles among the poor (Hannerz, 1969; Howell, 1973; Lewis, 1966; Liebow, 1967; Rubin, 1976; Schulz, 1968, 1969). These typologies, although limited, offer a model for continuing work in this area.

In this chapter the terms "blue collar" and "working class" refer to workers in skilled and unskilled labor markets who are more likely to have stable jobs, higher salaries, and better benefit packages and to be unionized than workers labeled "lower class." The term "lower class" is used to distinguish those workers who are more marginal, less stable, less skilled, and more vulnerable.

THE EFFECTS OF UNEMPLOYMENT

Mental and Physical Health of Unemployed Fathers

Research on the effects of unemployment on the mental and physical health of adult males is extensive (see Dooley & Catalano, 1980, and Eisenberg & Lazarsfeld, 1938 for reviews). A reason frequently given by researchers for their tendency to focus on men rather than on women in the study of the effects of unemployment is that men are more likely to be the main source of support for their household (Schlozman & Verba, 1978). In view of this logic and the fact that those in the household who rely on the adult male for support are more likely to be children than adults, it is indeed puzzling that so few researchers have singled out for study men with dependent children (as opposed to husbands or adult males) or examined how fatherhood mediates the effects of unemployment. This trend is evident in both individual studies in which the individual is the unit of analysis (e.g., relationship between employment status of an individual and his or her mental and physical health) and aggregate studies in which the units of analysis are geographically defined communities (e.g., relationship between local unemployment rates or size of work force and admissions to psychiatric hospitals). This relative paucity of information about fathers is compounded by the fact that in several prominent studies, the proportion of men in the sample who had dependent children is unspecified (e.g., Cohn, 1978; Goodchilds & Smith, 1963; Gore, 1978). This renders impossible any isolated judgment regarding whether the findings would hold in a sample of fathers with dependent children. However, the patterns of effect reported for unemployed fathers in the few existing studies generally parallel those for research subjects described only as unemployed heads of household or unemployed men.

Studies suggest that unemployment may pose a threat to the mental and physical health of at least some fathers. Indeed, fatherhood itself may exacerbate vulnerability. Unemployed heads of household (undifferentiated by sex) with dependent children express more life dissatisfaction than do unemployed wage earners without dependent children (Schlozman & Verba, 1978). In addition to their anxiety about meeting financial responsibilities and the possibility of losing social status, unemployed heads of household feel less positively about their children (Sheldon & Fox, 1983), are more pessimistic about their children's future (Ginsburg, 1942), and worry that the children will sense the parents' own apprehensive feelings about finances and the future (Rayman & Bluestone, cited in Cunningham, 1983; Sheldon & Fox, 1983). In recent studies of samples comprised exclusively or predominantly of men with dependent children, unemployment has been found to be associated with increased depression, anxiety, hostility, alcohol consumption, eating and sleeping problems, somatic complaints (Buss & Redburn, 1983a; Kasl & Cobb, 1979; Liem, 1981; Marsden, 1975), diminished self-satisfaction and self-esteem (Kasl & Cobb, 1979), and increased rates of neurosis, psychoticism, suicide, and nonsuicidal death (Liem, 1981; Theorell, Lind, & Floderus, 1975).

A study conducted by Liem and Liem (cited in Liem & Rayman, 1982) is especially noteworthy because of its clarification of the causal relationship between unemployment and stress symptoms. These researchers intensively interviewed 40 blue-collar and 40 white-collar fathers (all had at least one child under the age of 18 living in the home) during the 12-month period following their involuntary loss of job. Relative to employed fathers, unemployed fathers showed greater psychiatric symptomatology (e.g., depression, anxiety, hostility, psychoticism) at one and four months after loss of job. Unemployed fathers who became reemployed by the fourth month initially had symptom levels comparable to those of continuously unemployed men, but following their return to work they had symptom levels even lower than the continuously employed controls. On the basis of this finding, Liem and Liem concluded that emotional distress is a result rather than a cause of unemployment. Case studies, many of which were conducted during the Depression, generally concur with recent empirical findings (Angell, 1936; Bakke, 1940; Ginsburg, 1942; Jahoda, Lazarsfeld, & Zeisel, 1971; Komarovsky, 1940).

Among the factors that ameliorate physical and mental stress symptoms in unemployed workers are shorter periods of unemployment (Kasl & Cobb, 1979; Schlozman & Verba, 1978), high social support (Gore, 1978; Kasl & Cobb, 1979), and increased financial resources (Bakke, 1940; Little, 1976; Moen, 1983). Economic conditions attendant to job loss also may buffer potentially negative effects of unemployment. Unemployed workers living in areas of low unemployment have been found to experience significantly more dissatisfaction with self than unemployed workers living in areas of high unemployment (Cohn, 1978). Apparently, high local unemployment or massive job loss due to plant closings makes it more likely that the unemployed worker will attribute his unemployment status to macroeconomic conditions rather than to personal failure. However, when the unemployment rate is low and job loss is an isolated occurrence, the external attribution of cause is not possible, making it more likely that the individual will blame himself and suffer negative self-evaluation (Buss & Redburn, 1983b; Cohn, 1978; Moen, 1983).

Social class and race also are major mediators of the effects of unemployment on mental and physical health. Generally, effects are less severe and persistent in white-collar workers than in blue-collar workers (Buss &

Redburn, 1983a; Cohn, 1978; Liem & Rayman, 1982; Moen, 1983; Schlozman & Verba, 1978). The mental health of white-collar workers is less vulnerable to the threat of unemployment, it is believed, because white-collar unemployed workers are more likely than blue-collar unemployed workers to have components of self-concept that are positively evaluated but not directly related to their work (e.g., being well read) (Schlozman & Verba, 1978), to retain a sense of professional identity even in the face of unemployment, and in many cases, to have opportunities to practice their profession in some attenuated fashion (Cohn, 1978; Schlozman & Verba, 1978).Also white-collar workers tend to be less reluctant to migrate in search of jobs and therefore are less apprehensive about job loss. They typically have greater financial resources which, in turn, increases their ability to cope with extended periods of joblessness (Buss & Redburn, 1983a). In his study of unemployed middle-class professional men, Little (1976) found that fully 48 percent of the men agreed or strongly agreed that losing their job "might not have been such a bad break after all." They viewed unemployment positively because it represented an opportunity to reorient their career (34 percent) and expand their interests (13 percent), did not really pose a threat to their future (24 percent), offered relief from the stressful demands of work (13 percent), and provided a needed stimulus or challenge (7 percent).

Blue-collar workers, while less likely than white-collar workers to derive a sense of self-esteem from their profession per se, are thought to be more likely to gain a sense of worth from their ability to hold a steady job and provide for their dependents. Bereft of the opportunity to be a responsible breadwinner, the blue-collar father in particular (compared with the mother) often has no other positive identity to assume. Further support for this general line of argument is evidence that both high educational attainment (among white-collar workers) and availability of an alternative role (e.g., mother) buffer potentially negative effects of unemployment on self-attitudes. It has also been suggested that while lower-status workers generally have more firsthand experience with economic hardship than do middle-class families, certain conceptions of reality that arise out of a life checkered with economic crises (e.g., feelings of distrust, external locus of control) may actually reduce the value of prior hardship in promoting adaptive responses to economic stress (Elder, 1974).

There is at least tentative evidence that African-American men suffer more acute and prolonged stress from sudden job loss than do nonminority men and men from other minority groups. Buss and Redburn (1983a) found that at both one year (first wave) and two years (second wave) after they were terminated from their blue-collar job when a steel mill closed, African-Americans and European ethnic minorities (including Eastern and Southern Europeans and Spanish-speaking minorities) were significantly more likely than nonminorities who lost their job to report feelings of weakness, victimization, helplessness, and depression. Somatic problems also were more prevalent among African-Americans than nonminorities. Four years (third wave) after the shutdown, family and somatic problems and feelings of victimization were more frequent among African-Americans than European ethnic minorities. (Nonminorities were not interviewed in the third wave).

The heightened sense of victimization that persisted among African-American workers may have been the result of job discrimination practices that operated to reduce the likelihood of finding a new job, let alone one that was stable and personally satisfying. The Buss and Redburn findings do not support the speculation of some scholars that minorities cope with unemployment better than white workers because they have had more experience with unemployment and economic setbacks and as a result have developed more social support networks (Fisher, 1983).

To summarize, in the face of unemployment, workers who are middle-class, nonminority, experience shorter periods of unemployment, lose their job in the context of massive unemployment, and have increased financial resources, high social support, and no dependent children experience comparatively fewer mental stress symptoms. Since unemployed fathers compared with employed fathers are more likely to be depressed, anxious, hostile, and dissatisfied with themselves (Buss & Redburn, 1983a; Liem, 1981; Marsden, 1975), they may have little of the energy and patience necessary to support and nurture the child adequately. The child may react with increased anxiety and other mental stress symptoms, and the father-child relationship may become less satisfying and harmonious.

Marital Relations of Unemployed Men

In their treatment of marital relations, researchers typically have sought to determine first how income and job loss affect power and affective relations between husband and wife, and second the ways in which preunemployment marital relations mediate the effects of income and job loss. Severe economic loss may produce a crisis in family resources and maintenance that undermines the instrumental base of the husband's prestige and power in the family.

Elder (1974) analyzed longitudinal archival data collected on 167 children and their families from 1932 to 1939. Among his many findings was that adults who as children were members of economically deprived families during the Depression (families that lost more than 34 percent of their 1929 income by 1933, the year during the Depression when economic indicators reached their lowest point) were more likely than adults who as children were members of nondeprived families (families that lost less than 34 percent of their 1929 income by 1933) to report that mother, rather than father or both parents, decided major issues affecting the family. In deprived families, mother dominance was more prevalent than either father dominance or egalitarian marital relations. The most extreme cases of unilateral dominance by mothers occurred in deprived families with unemployed fathers. The relationship between economic deprivation and maternal dominance held in both social classes (working class and middle-class) and was not accounted for by pre-Depression characteristics such as higher educational attainment by mother. There is recent evidence that family problems attendant to job loss may be more persistent among African-Americans than among other ethnic minorities (Buss & Redburn, 1983a).

During the Depression, Komarovsky (1940) studied 59 families (with at least one dependent child over the age of 10) in which the husband, the sole provider of the family prior to job loss, had been unemployed for at least one year. She found three patterns of breakdown among couples in which unemployment undermined the power and prestige of the husband (21 percent): Unemployment served to disclose a hitherto concealed lack of respect for the husband, to weaken previous coercive control of the wife by the husband, or to lower the status of the husband, who was loved and respected but was the victim of new marital conflicts created by the job crisis. The decline in the husband's status appeared to be due to two unemployment-related outcomes, namely, loss of earning power and increased presence in the home. Loss of earning power made it more difficult for the husband to control the wife by withholding or granting money, material goods, and services. Second, it became less possible to satisfy conflicting interests, the result being new and difficult financial choices and tests of the husband's authority.

With the role changes and difficult choices about the expenditure of inadequate sums of money often attendant to job and income loss, the stage is set for criticism, quarrels, and conflict between husband and wife. A circular process may be set in motion in which conflict diminishes expressions of love and respect which in turn lessens joint problem solving, leading to more conflict (Elder, 1974). Common to most marital arguments in economically deprived families are disagreements over expenditures, criticism of the husband's faults as a provider, and attempts by the more powerful spouse to impose his or her will (Elder, 1974). Most husbands react to their loss of status with renewed and ever more strident demands for respect, increased involvement in activities outside the home, and increased stubbornness, especially in response to their wife's request for help with housework (Komarovsky, 1940). At least during the Depression era, few husbands or wives were satisfied with the realignment of power that often followed job loss.

One common outcome of unemployment or income loss, namely, the increased presence of the husband in the home, provides fertile conditions for marital alienation and disagreements (Caplovitz, 1979; Komarovsky, 1940; Liem, 1983; Marsden, 1975). The wife may become more acutely aware of her husband's weaknesses and faults and experience disillusionment with him as a result. In addition, long-standing and newly discovered disagreements and attitudinal differences between husband and wife (e.g., methods of housekeeping, child-rearing practices, division of household duties) may escalate into open conflict because of increased interaction (Komarovsky, 1940; Liem, 1983). A prevalent irritant centers around the husband's share of household duties. Even after he is no longer actively looking for a job, the husband often expects his wife to continue to do all household work, much to the chagrin of the wife (Komarovsky, 1940; Powell & Driscoll, 1973). This problem intensifies when the wife begins to search for a job (Powell & Driscoll, 1973). Even when the husband assumes household duties, his ineptness, mistakes, or idiosyncratic approach may instigate conflict with his wife. The wife, in turn, may decide to do the work herself, yet harbor resentment against her husband for his inability or unwillingness to meet her standards (Bakke, 1940).

Evidence from a relatively large corpus of studies indicates that marital dissolution is more likely in families in which the husband is unemployed (Bishop, 1977; Furstenberg, 1981). Especially noteworthy are findings from two large nationally representative longitudinal data sets. On the basis of measures taken over a seven-year period, Hoffman and Holmes (1976) found that husbands in the Panel Study of Income Dynamics who experienced unemployment or high job turnover were more likely to experience marital dissolution than were husbands working full-time. In line with these findings are those of Cherlin (cited in Bishop, 1977), who studied marital separations of 30- to 44-year old women in the National Longitudinal Survey. He found that marriages were more stable when the husband worked throughout the year and/or had a high income.

However, if economic adversity can act as a disruptive force in marital relations, it also can serve as a unifying force, drawing the couple closer in mutual support (Moen, Kain, & Elder, 1983). Thomas, McCabe, and Berry (1980) studied middle-aged (35–54 years old) men who had held professional or managerial positions prior to unemployment, which ranged in duration from one month to over a year. Fifteen percent reported that relations with their wife had actually improved since they lost their job, whereas one third (37 percent) indicated that relations with their wife had deteriorated. Almost half (48 percent) reported no change in marital relations following job loss. The degree of income loss was unrelated to the quality of marital relations. In keeping with this finding, Brinkerhoff and White (1978) found no relationship between marital satisfaction and unemployment in their study of couples in which the husband relied on seasonal industries for employment.

Even more surprising are the findings of a study conducted by Root and Mayland (cited in Thomas, McCabe, & Berry, 1980) of blue-collar unemployed men and their wives. Unemployment ranged from less than one month to over a year, and most suffered substantial income loss. The number of respondents who stated that unemployment had a positive effect on their family (40 percent) actually was greater than the number who said it had a negative effect (30 percent). Twenty-seven percent reported that unemployment had both positive and negative effects or no effect at all. Furthermore, only four (6 percent) workers and their spouses indicated that the husband had lost respect in the eyes of family members since becoming unemployed. Length of unemployment was not associated with reported effects on families or the husband's status within the family. Caplovitz's (1979) study of the impact of recession and inflation on families also indicated that financial pressures are more likely to have a favorable impact on marriages (e.g., increased closeness and understanding) than an unfavorable impact (28 percent versus 14 percent).

Whether unemployment has positive, negative, or no effects on conjugal relations greatly depends on the state of preexisting conjugal relations. The essential effect of economic adversity appears to be one of accentuation or exaggeration of preexisting marital states (Moen, Kain, & Elder, 1983). Weak, unsatisfying marriages tend to disintegrate under the pressures created by economic loss, while stable marriages gain renewed commitment and resilience under the same circumstances. For example, the strains and tensions generated by the husband's unaccustomed presence in the home are greater in couples that did not voluntarily spend a considerable amount of time together before unemployment (Marsden, 1975). If the couple had spent less time together than they desired prior to unemployment, the husband's increased presence in the home might ameliorate previous feelings of neglect by the wife (Jahoda, Lazarsfeld, & Zeisel, 1971). Though economic crisis generally increases the frequency of marital quarrels (Caplovitz, 1979; Elder, 1974; Ginsburg, 1942; Jahoda, Lazarsfeld, & Zeisel, 1971; Komarovsky, 1940), quarrels are most frequent and acrimonious in previously unsatisfying marriages (Fineman, 1983; Jahoda, Lazarsfeld, & Zeisel, 1971; Marsden, 1975).

The precrisis attitude of the spouse toward her unemployed husband also has consequences for the husband's prestige and status following job loss. If the wife's acceptance of her husband's authority stems from utilitarian interests or fear rather than from love, admiration, or tradition, the husband's status and the family's stability are more likely to deteriorate in the face of unemployment (Komarovsky, 1940).

Preexisting family relations are strong predictors of successful family adjustment to job or income loss. A longitudinal study by Cavan and Ranck (1938) is especially noteworthy because of extensive pre-Depression information about target families. These researchers found that in the long run, previously well-organized families characterized by a high degree of unity and reciprocal functioning among their members adjusted to paternal job and income loss more successfully than previously disorganized families, which tended to suffer increased disorganization and disintegration. Angell (1936) interviewed college students during the Depression about their family life (and in a few instances the family life of college friends) before and after a sudden and ostensibly permanent decrease of at least 25 percent of family income. The response of families depended on the degree of integration and adaptability of the family unit prior to income loss and whether the husband retained or was supplanted in his role as primary breadwinner.

Besides high marital and family integration, family and sex-role flexibility foster successful family adaptation and recovery following income and job loss. Cavan and Ranck (1938) found prolonged family disorganization when family members resisted making necessary role changes (e.g., submission of an unemployed father to a son who is employed). Angell (1936) reported that families limited in their adaptability were least resilient, owing in part to an entrenched materialistic philosophy and rigid conventional conjugal roles. There also is recent evidence that rigid sex roles impede successful adjustment to the husband's unemployment (Powell & Driscoll, 1973).

To summarize, unemployment appears to accentuate preexisting marital states, fomenting marital discord and dissolution in previously unsatisfying marriages but drawing the partners of previously happy marriages closer in mutual support. Families characterized by flexible sex roles and high marital and family integration are comparatively more resilient in the face of job loss. As we shall see in the next section, the quality of marital relations has far-reaching implications for the unemployed father's relationship with his child.

Father-Child Relations of Unemployed Men

Unemployment or income loss may set the stage for acute father-child conflict, in part because income loss often results in disruptive role changes and undermines strategies customarily used to discipline and socialize children. If older children replace or share with the mother the father's original role of breadwinner, they may grow increasingly resentful of the authority of the father, who usually responds by becoming even more arbitrary and controlling (Bakke, 1940). Because less money is available, parents have less recourse to material goods and costly activities to reward, punish, or otherwise control their children's behavior (Bakke, 1940; Caplovitz, 1979; Komarovsky, 1940). An unemployed father is not in a good position to "bribe" his children into following his orders or wishes with tangible goods, to withhold goods and activities as a means of punishment, or to offer desirable substitutes for undesirable activities. In fact, he may relinquish customary restrictions, albeit begrudgingly (e.g., curfew), in compensation for general privations (Komarovsky, 1940). Not surprisingly, when asked about child-rearing problems, unemployed fathers and their spouse are more likely than employed parents to describe child-rearing problems created by the lack of money or by stress in one or both spouses and less likely to focus on normal developmental or age-related difficulties or things happening outside the home (Liem, 1983).

Father-child conflict is compounded by the fact that both parents in an unemployed family are experiencing considerable stress and thus have fewer psychological resources with which to resolve conflict amiably (Bakke, 1940). Adolescent children apparently are not oblivious to the behavioral stress symptoms in their unemployed father. Elder (1974) found that adolescent children whose father was economically deprived were more likely than children of nondeprived fathers to wish that "father were happier." Though children were less likely to make such a wish for father than mother, perhaps because of greater contact with mother, fully 90 percent of those who did were from economically deprived families. This effect was unrelated to sex or social class (working-class versus middle-class).

Economic hardship may enhance the affective status of mother relative to father; reduce the attractiveness of father to children, especially boys, as a role model, companion, and confidant; and increase the tendency to identify with and seek the companionship of nonfamilial adults (Elder, 1974). Elder found that boys in economically deprived families lost more affection for their father and gained less warmth toward their mother than did girls (Elder, 1974). With increasing economic hardship, mother was more likely than father to be regarded by the child as both a companion and someone to rely on in times of need. One result of the mother's emotional significance in deprived families was an increased tendency for children from these families to align themselves with mother in mother-father feuds. These effects were unrelated to social class.

Numerous studies have established a link between unemployment and child abuse (Gelles & Straus, 1982; Gil, 1970; Justice & Justice, 1976; Light, 1973; Steinberg, Catalano, & Dooley, 1981; Young, 1964), though these studies tend to leave unspecified whether the abuser and the person unemployed is the father, mother, or other household member. Paternal unemployment may trigger child abuse for several reasons: (1) Abuse by the father may be a consequence of increased contact and conflict with the child that result from the unemployed father's increased presence in the home (Belsky, 1980). (2) Relatedly, the father may assume a more central role as disciplinarian (Parke & Collmer, 1975). (3) If the unemployment has resulted in a real or perceived loss of status in the home, the father may attempt to reestablish his status and self-esteem by exercising physical force against his children (Belsky, 1980; Parke & Collmer, 1975). (4) Unemployment may be accompanied by other frustrating circumstances such as lack of monetary resources (Parke & Collmer, 1975). (5) Child abuse may be an outcome of increased marital dispute provoked by unemployment. A feuding spouse may redirect his or her anger and hostility onto the child because the child is the subject of the disagreement (e.g., opposing views about child-rearing), interferes with the feuding parents (Herrenkohl, Herrenkohl, & Egolf, 1983), or aligns himself or herself with one of the parents. It will be recalled that one of the results of the increased emotional significance of mother in economically deprived families is an increased tendency among children to align themselves with mother in conjugal conflict (Elder, 1974).

It is important to emphasize, however, that unemployment does not have uniformly negative effects of father-child relations. Indeed, unemployment not only may fail to undermine father-child relations, it may actually improve them, in part because of increased contact between father and child. Also more honest and open communication with the child by both father and mother may result from the need of the parents to gain the child's cooperation in reducing expenditures (Caplovitz, 1979) and to ensure that deprivations are understood to be the result of financial pressures rather than parental disapproval of the child (Liem, 1983). Among the 7- to 11-year-olds studied by Komarovsky (1940), improvement in father-child relations was actually a more frequent outcome of paternal job loss than was deterioration. In Thomas and colleague's (1980) study of middle-aged fathers who had held professional or managerial positions prior to unemployment, 11 percent of these fathers reported that unemployment had improved their relations with their children. Only 17 percent indicated that unemployment had adverse effects, while over half (53 percent) stated that job loss had no effect. Similarly, in Rayman and Bluestone's study (cited in Cunningham, 1983) of persons who lost their job in the aircraft industry, improvement (15 percent) of parent-child relations was as likely to occur as was deterioration (15 percent).

Among the mediators of the effects of unemployment on father-child relations are preexisting father-child relations, the marital relationship, the age of the child, and the social class of the family involved. In Komarovsky's (1940) study, a positive father-child relationship prior to unemployment characterized all cases in which the fathers of young children *gained* status following job loss and all cases in which the fathers of children 15 years old or older *maintained* their parental authority (none of the latter fathers gained status). The actual quality of these father-child relations varied, ranging from authoritative and interested fathers who were admired by their children to lenient, noninterfering fathers who evoked more affection than admiration from their children. Among those fathers whose authority deteriorated subsequent to job loss, two dominant types of preunemployment father-child relations were evident, namely, coercive, disinterested fathers who were feared by their children and rigid, interfering fathers who commanded no respect but sought to impose on their children antiquated standards of decorum (Komarovsky, 1940).

Marital relations, particularly the attitude of the wife toward her husband, have critical implications for the father's relationship with his children following unemployment and income loss. Both Komarovsky (1940) and Bakke (1940) found that the husband's loss of power and authority in marital relations was associated with a loss of authority in his role as father. As Komarovsky (1940) explained, "To keep his authority with the children the man has to maintain it with his wife. Apparently the father does not rule alone. His prestige needs the mother's endorsement" (p. 114).

The mother's prominence in the child's life makes it possible for her first to shape the child's understanding of the economic crisis and the father's ensuing behavior through her interpretation (Elder, 1974) and second to foster desirable or undesirable father-directed behavior by the child. For example, Ginsburg (1942) observed numerous attempts by wives of unemployed men to reinforce "dad" as the authority in the household, such as encouraging children to take their homework to father for help or directing the children to father for approval of special privileges. If the mother has lost respect for her husband, holds him in contempt, and blames him for the disruption in their lives, an outcome more likely when the wife's precrisis acceptance of her husband's authority is based on utilitarian interests, she is unlikely either to present a sympathetic interpretation of the father's unemployment to the child or to encourage child behaviors that acknowledge the authority of the father.

Further evidence of the mediating effects of marital relations on parental relations comes from Elder's (1979) study. He found that if marital integration was high (spouses were sexually well adjusted, close, friendly, and highly compatible) prior to income loss, economic deprivation fostered warm, close feelings toward the parents in 8- to 10-year-old boys. However, in the context of marital discord, income loss occasioned increased hostility toward the father by the children, especially boys, an effect no doubt related to the fact that these fathers tended to be inconsistent in discipline, hostile, punitive, or indifferent toward their sons and less capable of performing family roles effectively than fathers who had harmonious relations with their wife. It is not surprising, then, that boys under conditions of marital strain, compared with those whose parents enjoyed relatively harmonious relations prior to income and job loss, were less well adjusted during adolescence (e.g., diminished ambition, goal directedness, and sense of family security; increased passivity, withdrawal, depression) and adulthood (e.g., high consumption of alcohol, depression, increased incidence of broken marriages). Girls appear to have been more insulated from the psychic costs of marital discord in the context of economic deprivation by their close relationship with their mother (Elder, 1979).

Paternal unemployment, marital relations, and the father-child relation are interrelated in yet another way. Specifically, paternal unemployment may affect the child's relationship with father indirectly by virtue of the situation's ferment of marital instability, as noted earlier. When marriages end, whether through divorce, separation, or desertion, the child usually spends some time living in a single-parent household, most often (90 percent) headed by his or her mother (Blechman, 1982). Data on the nature of father-child relations when the mother and father are divorced or separated are quite sparse, but it seems likely that these relations might differ in both positive and negative ways from the relationships children have with a father who is married to the child's mother.

The fact that employment status influences the decision of parents to marry subsequent to the conception of a child, as well as the timing of marriage, also may have implications for the child's development and the frequency and quality of father-child relations. In his six-year study of adolescent mothers, Furstenberg (1981) found that marriage was much more likely to occur during the prenatal period if the father held a full-time job than if he was unemployed. The marriage rate began to rise sharply as the young mothers reached their late teens and the fathers began to find steady employment. Women who married prior to delivery were much more likely to marry the father of the child than those who deferred marriage. Children whose mother married their biological father, compared with children whose mother married another man, showed superior cognitive development and social adjustment. Furstenberg (1976) speculated that marriage between the biological parents proved to have a salutary effect on the child's development because of the continuity of the relationship between the child and the father.

The participation in child rearing of fathers who did not live with the mother was generally higher when the father had been married to the mother. If the mother married a man who was not the father of the child, the child did not see his or her biological father on a regular basis and often did not have even occasional contact. Apparently, restricting contact between the child and his or her biological father was a strategy used by mothers to reduce the risk of rivalry between the two men and to secure the husband's loyalty and obligation to his stepchild (Furstenberg, 1976).

The age of the child may determine whether paternal unemployment spawns an increase or a decrease in the willingness of the child to accept father's control. Komarovsky (1940) found no cases of postemployment improvement of the father's authority among children 15 years old or older and an increased tendency among these children, compared with younger children, to lose respect for the father. Young children are less likely than adolescent children to challenge the father's authority subsequent to his job loss, contended Komarovsky, because they tend to accept the father's authority uncritically, are likely to regard the father's growing irritability as an act of nature about which they can do nothing, and while aware of the family's loss of social prestige, tend to be less sensitive to it. In the Komarovsky study, when loss of respect for the father occurred in young children and unemployed adolescents, it was primarily due to adverse changes in the father's behavior toward the child, whereas for gainfully employed adolescents it derived from the father's loss of money and the interchange of economic roles.

An economy so acutely depressed that jobs are available neither for fathers nor adolescent children may actually serve to mitigate the father's potential loss of authority with adolescent children. Jahoda, Lazarsfeld, and Zeisel (1971) concluded that paternal unemployment had no effect on paternal authority in families living in a small one-factory community in Austria during the Depression. Perhaps the fact that everyone in this community suffered unemployment when the factory closed permanently, including adolescent children who might otherwise have become wage earners, lessened the possibility of a decline in the father's authority.

Though existing research findings are suggestive, at best, social class (lower versus middle) may moderate the effects of paternal unemployment on father-child relations, at least in African-American families. While paternal unemployment appears to have no effect on the lower-class child's attitude toward the father, in middle-class children it appears to undermine esteem for the father (Heiss, 1975). Perhaps unemployed fathers are more likely to be taken for granted in lower-status groups, the father neither gaining nor losing admiration or control as a result of employment because of the comparatively high incidence of paternal unemployment among African Americans, especially in the lower socioeconomic strata (Moen, 1983), and because family members recognize that unemployment is due to race and class discrimination rather than to enduring personal inadequacies (Heiss, 1975; Schwartz & Henderson, 1964).

In summary, because it tends to undermine the mental health functioning of fathers and thus their parenting skills, and because it restricts the father's ability to provide for the needs of his family, paternal unemployment may reduce the attractiveness of the father to the child and lead to a deterioration of the relationship between the two. However, this outcome appears less likely if the precrisis father-child relationship was positive, if marital relations are relatively harmonious, if the child is a preadolescent, and if the family is from a working-class or lower-status background. In some families unemployment actually is followed by an improvement in father-child relations, perhaps because of the increased time available for father-child interaction. Improvement appears unlikely, however, if the precrisis relationship between father and child was distant or contentious.

THE EFFECTS OF POVERTY

Mental Health of Poor Fathers

A substantial body of research reports a link between behavioral disorder and poverty but scholars do not agree on the causal direction of the association (Dooley & Catalano, 1980). Poor working-class and lower-class men need to think of themselves as good fathers and breadwinners, but they are repeatedly confronted with their inability to perform the expected marital and parental role of provider (Liebow, 1967; Rainwater, 1974) and the failure they feel as workers becomes generalized to their performance as fathers, husbands, and friends. Low self-esteem, a sense of having little control of one's life, and a sense that the future holds little promise of advancement or improvement characterizes the psychology of lower-class men (Liebow, 1967). These men perceive the world as unstable and unpredictable and themselves as inadequately prepared to cope with its vicissitudes (Rainwater, 1974).

Some working-class men may adopt rebellious and antisocial behavior (e.g., heavy drinking, violence, erratic employment patterns, unstable family relationships) as a way of asserting their manhood. Even more stable settled men report feeling the pressure of economic uncertainty, although they are less likely to express their frustrations in antisocial ways. Many working-class men respond to family responsibilities and economic pressure by withdrawing psychologically and emotionally through involvement in projects that permit them to feel a sense of competence (Rubin, 1976). Economically strapped men often use their peer group as a refuge from home, family, and work pressures, but these friendships are not necessarily deep, intimate, or of long duration (Liebow, 1967).

The dearth of literature on the psychological impact of poverty on fathers does not permit firm conclusions. The literature that is available does suggest that many working-class fathers, be they in the upper or lower working class, experience some stress, reduced sense of self-esteem, and alienation which may negatively influence their capacity to perform expected paternal and marital role tasks.

Attitudes toward work and toward the type of job one performs are completely intertwined with the family's economic position (Bloom-Feshbach, Feshbach, & Heller, 1982). While the poor father's experience is unrewarding and undervalued and may induce negative feelings about himself, his work, and his future, it is not clear that it negatively affects his attitude toward his children and spouse. For example, it is not certain that poor fathers feel less affection for their children than do more affluent fathers, but it seems reasonable to conclude that a father's poverty may influence the range of options available to him for demonstrating his affection (e.g., purchasing gifts may be an option infrequently chosen by poor fathers). Poverty also appears to be related to the psychological withdrawal of some poor fathers, but the effect of this withdrawal on the family may be mediated by a range of factors including the duration of economic adversity, the quality of marital and father-child relations prior to the withdrawal, and the ages and sex of the children.

Research on the mental health of poor fathers raises far more questions than it answers. To more clearly identify the effects of economic adversity on the father's mental health and his capacity to perform paternal and marital role tasks, future research needs to identify those factors that may mediate the negative effect of low income and job loss on fathers and husbands.

Marital Relations of Poor Fathers

As noted earlier, working-class men derive a sense of respect, self-esteem, and status from the ability to provide for children and spouse. The father's relationship with the mother of his children can be adversely affected by his inability to provide adequately for his family (Furstenberg, 1976; Hannerz, 1969; Lewis, 1966; Liebow, 1967; Rubin, 1976). Characteristics of low-income and working-class men, namely poor education, poor job skills, erratic employment history, and in some cases race, because of its association with job discrimination, combine to limit their employment options and diminish their ability to perform paternal role tasks consistently (Hannerz, 1969; Liebow, 1967). In addition, a reserve of unskilled workers allows employers to keep wages low and to offer no or few fringe benefits and little job security. Menial jobs, generally without a career ladder, do not permit workers to anticipate advancement to better paying, more interesting and secure employment. Researchers report that working-class and lower-class men experience high job dissatisfaction. The lack of an improved job future may lead to a cavalier attitude toward work. The undervaluing (i.e., low wages) of the husband's labor affects the worker's sense of self and has repercussions on his personal and family relationships (Liebow, 1967; Rubin, 1976).

The combination of economic and emotional problems associated with job insecurity, early marriage, and early childbirth places incredible role strain on individuals who have to adopt both new marital and parental roles often within the first year of marriage (Furstenberg, 1976; Rubin, 1967). The arrival of children does not permit couples sufficient time to gain a substantial financial base, in part because the wife may leave the work force during childbearing years. Economic hardship can become a dominant marital theme permeating every aspect of family life and adjustment to marriage. Children may not only increase financial strain but also can be the source of emotional stress to young couples who report feeling trapped by circumstances, the consequences of which they did not anticipate. Young fathers often experience the child's arrival as an intrusion into their relationship with their wife. The wife's attention to the infant may make the husband feel jealous and threatened. These feelings may have consequences for long-term marital and parental relationships. Exacerbating these tensions are economic constraints (e.g., the cost of child care) that limit the capacity of the young couple to share adult time away from children (Rubin, 1976).

Ambivalence and suspicion seem to characterize male-female relationships in poor families. In a study of depression in working-class women, Zur and Longfellow (1980) found that marital relations were very strongly influenced by economic factors, particularly by the husband's capacity to be the provider. Husbands were characterized by wives as economic providers, child caregivers, providers of emotional support, and occasional assistants in household tasks. The degree to which the husband assisted his wife in any of these tasks corresponded to reported stress reduction in the wife, specifically a lessening of depression and anxiety, a decrease in concern about money, and a more positive outlook on life. Father's economic problems, especially unemployment, tended to increase the mother's sense of stress. In fact, women participants frequently cited men as contributing to stressful problems. This apparent contradiction, that is, that the husband is both a source of anxiety and of relief from anxiety, captures some of the complexity of marital relations in economically stressed families. The economically disadvantaged husband's ability to provide economic support reduced the wife's stress, but both spouses were aware of the unstable nature of jobs available to him.

In African-American communities, economic deprivation may contribute to a lack of trust, an increased sense of suspicion toward members of the opposite sex, and a tendency to view members of the opposite sex as exploitative. Marriage as a lifelong commitment to one woman is seen by men to be a difficult achievement because of the perceived loss of independence, the suspicion that the wife will exploit the husband, and the recognition that earning enough money to support a family is extremely difficult (Liebow, 1967; Schulz, 1969).

Marital infidelity, desire for independence, and alcohol abuse, among other personal problems, contribute to separation and marital dissolution in poor families. But these explanations may camouflage a more subtle and complex issue, namely, the wife's expectations that her spouse provide for her and their dependents. His inability to meet her expectations, which he accepts as reasonable, "are a standing reminder of his failure as husband and father" (Liebow, 1967, p. 129). To both the husband and wife, his ability to provide income to his family has both a basic labor market value and a symbolic value, the latter associated with the provision of support (Liebow, 1967; Rubin, 1976).

A small number of researchers have differentiated among economically strapped families subgroups that manifest distinct marital behaviors, in African-American working- and lower-class communities (Hannerz, 1969; Schulz, 1968, 1969) and in working-class European-American communities (Howell, 1973; Rubin, 1976). According to these researchers, one group of families, "mainstream families" (Hannerz, 1969), although economically deprived, share many values with middle-class American families. Husbands in mainstream families spend more time with spouse and children than with peers, are often involved in work around the house, and are perceived by wife and children to be the authority figure in the home, although younger husbands are more likely to share authority with their wife (Hannerz, 1969; Schulz, 1968, 1969). These fathers/husbands share a commitment to their family, assume the role of primary provider, and value positive marital relations. The father's inability to be a steady provider does not appear to diminish his authority position within the family regardless of the age or sex of his children (Hannerz, 1969; Lewis, 1966; Schulz, 1968, 1969; Silverstein & Krate, 1975). The wife and children appear to recognize that the father's earnings are not due to personal inadequacies but rather to race and class discrimination. Some researchers have found that the husband's age seems to contribute to his ability to lead a more mainstream life in which he is more involved with family roles and obligations (Rubin, 1976).

Scholars also have described subgroups of poor males who as husbands are much more likely to be engaged in illicit means of earning a living, may openly engage in extramarital relations involving the birth of children, may spend a greater amount of time with peers than with their family (Hannerz, 1969; Schulz, 1968, 1969), and may be involved in heavy alcohol abuse and violence (Howell, 1973; Rubin, 1976). These fathers often lose the respect of their wife and have a strife-filled household (Schulz, 1968).

The limited amount of literature on marital relationships in economically disadvantaged families provides a mixed set of findings. Economic factors such as low wages, menial jobs, and labor market discrimination can clearly limit the husband's capacity to support his family. His age and race can contribute additionally to his earning problems and adjustment to marriage and fatherhood. If the husband's employment problems are viewed by his wife as externally caused, his capacity to retain authority and harmony within their relationship is undiminished (Hannerz, 1969; Liebow, 1967; Schulz, 1969; Silverstein & Krate, 1975). But if the husband is unable to perform other important relational tasks (e.g., remain monogamous), his marital relationship is jeopardized (Liebow, 1967; Schulz, 1969).

While there appear to be cultural differences in the way couples respond to economic adversity, there are also interesting commonalities across cultures which suggest the shared experience of class. For example, in both Rubin's and Liebow's studies, wives reported feeling that their expectations had been betrayed by their low-wage-earning husband. One must be careful in drawing conclusions about working-class marital relations from this literature. In future research cultures and class effects need to be separated, and within each of those categories subgroup behaviors must be distinguished. Economic hardship can adversely affect marital relationships but the degree to which it does so appears to depend on a wide variety of factors.

Father-Child Relations of Poor Men

Researchers generally acknowledge that the poor father's economic status can influence his contact and involvement with his children. However, drawing conclusions regarding economic factors and the father-child dyad from an observation at only one point in time may give an inaccurate picture of this relationship (Furstenberg, 1976; Liebow, 1967). Father-child interaction has its own life course, which is affected by the ages and maturity of the father and child, the father's economic security, his commitment to performing paternal role tasks, the quality of his relationship with the mother, the degree to which he feels he has voluntarily assumed the father role, his peer group, and physical proximity that makes regular contact possible (Liebow, 1967). Poor fathers' emotional closeness to their children may vary from no contact at all with children to residing and interacting with children on a daily basis, sharing intimate thoughts, play, and chores (Furstenberg, 1976; Liebow, 1967; Young, 1970).

Employment at wages too low to support a family or an erratic work history that does not permit the maintenance of a regular income often forces impoverished fathers to reside permanently or intermittently away from their children (Lewis, 1966; Liebow, 1967), but this residential pattern does not necessarily adversely affect the father's involvement with and stated commitment to provide for his offspring (Liebow, 1967; Silverstein & Krate, 1975; Zur & Longfellow, 1980). Poor residential fathers, however, are more likely than poor nonresidential fathers to report playing with their children on a daily basis. On the other hand, poor nonresidential biological fathers appear to express more affection toward their children than do residential biological fathers. This behavior is much like the phenomenon of the doting grandparent who is not responsible for daily child-care tasks and can afford to be indulgent and attentive (Liebow, 1967). Poor nonresidential fathers are more likely to see their children and have authority over them if they contribute to the child's support (Furstenberg, 1976).

For some families, social welfare policies, specifically eligibility requirements for Aid to Families with Dependent Children (AFDC), directly contribute to the father's absence from his children's home, although he often remains in contact with the children (Young, 1970). The dissonance between the father's need to assert his masculinity through having children and his repeated failures at providing for them often leads to desertion of his family (Schulz, 1969). The impact of father absence on the child's development, which has been a much debated issue in poverty research (Herzog & Sudia, 1970, 1973), may be mediated by a variety of factors, including the continuous or discontinuous pattern of absence (Furstenberg, 1976), the quality of the father-child relationship, and the child's access to other significant caring adult males. Indeed, mothers' boyfriends and stepfathers appear to play critical, supportive, and paternal roles in the lives of the children of the women with whom they are involved (Liebow, 1967; Silverstein & Krate, 1975; Zur & Longfellow, 1980), as do males in kin networks (e.g., grandfathers and uncles) (Martin & Martin, 1978; Stack, 1974; Young, 1970). When these paternal figures are unavailable or unappealing to children, especially to boys, the children may seek male models outside the home (Silverstein & Krate, 1975).

Poor fathers generally express a high degree of interest in their children's education, welfare, and health and a willingness to sacrifice for their children (Lewis, 1966). They enjoy their children's companionship (Liebow, 1967) and personal characteristics, such as pleasant dispositions, intelligence, and cooperativeness though they tend to dislike stubbornness, disobedience, and noisiness (Zur & Longfellow, 1980). They also dislike the added financial burden, loss of freedom, and children's impingement on adult relationships (Liebow, 1967; Rubin, 1976) and the requirement that they be a protector and stern disciplinarian (Zur & Longfellow, 1980). They often express fear about their children's future, which they see as uncertain and problematic, and concern that they will not be able to provide those things (e.g., education, material goods) that would help transport their children out of poverty (Rubin, 1976).

The child's age and the cultural background of the poor father appear to influence the father's response to the child. Impoverished Appalachian fathers are invested in and indulgent with their infants but may be uninvolved with older children (Looff, 1971). Poor southern urban African-American fathers have been found to be very involved with and affectionate toward children regardless of the child's age (Coles, 1971), but are especially indulgent and playful with babies and toddlers. In addition, they encourage and expect older boys to adopt caring and loving behaviors toward very young children (Young, 1970). It is not clear why fathers prefer certain developmental periods, or whether these performances are in any way related to economic factors such as the cost of providing for infants in contrast to adolescents.

Schulz (1968, 1969), describing father-child interaction in poor intact families, identified three types of fathers: (1) those who are monogamous, consider home and family matters a priority, support their family through legitimate means, and value good parent-child relationships, (2) those who value the paternal role, have good relationships with their wife and children, and may support their family through illegitimate activities, which does not lose them the respect of their children, and (3) those who are not fully committed to their wife and children, may be openly involved in extramarital relationships, and only intermittently support their family. Children of the first two father types respect their father, express affection for him, and accept his authority; any difficulties he may have in providing for them are not seen as caused by his behavior. Fathers of the third type have trouble exerting authority and control over their children, who perceive them as weak. Adolescent sons may attempt to create confrontations with the father and will take their mother's side against the father. Adolescent daughters of the third paternal type tend to see men as exploiters of women, but publicly try to minimize the importance of their father's indiscretions (Schulz, 1968).

The research reviewed in this section shows that the relationships of poor fathers and their children must be understood as a life-span phenomenon that includes the developmental maturity of individuals within the dyad, their permanent characteristics (e.g., sex), the cultural meaning applied to their roles, and the relational aspects of their roles. It appears that the father's absence from the child's home at a given time does not necessarily signify that his absence is permanent or that he is uninvolved with his child. The father's absence in some cases may be a survival tactic that helps to make his wife and children eligible for income transfer programs.

Research on within-culture variability in fathering styles needs further elaboration. Different paternal styles were identified in research conducted in the late 1960s and early 1970s in poor African-American communities. Do these paternal styles exist in poor African-American communities in the 1980s, or have they been replaced by new fathering styles that reflect the changing economic conditions of the last two decades? How do children in poor households respond to different paternal styles? Are these fathering styles different from those that appear in other ethnic and socioeconomic groups? On balance, we know far less about the relationship poor men have with their daughters than their relationship with sons. Future research might address the following questions: Are there other attitudinal and behavioral differences between sons and daughters in relation to poor fathers? How does the poor father's relationship to sons versus daughters vary over time? To what extent do the changing fortunes of economically disadvantaged fathers influence their interaction with sons versus daughters?

While poor fathers appear to be invested in their children, their paternal lives are characterized by a sense of frustration at being unable to fulfill prescribed role tasks. How is this frustration dealt with by the father and experienced by his children? The research suggests that desertion of the family and emotional withdrawal may be two responses available to economically stressed fathers that may have dire consequences for the father-child relationship. Are there other less devastating and more beneficial responses to stress and frustration that poor fathers utilize? Is the poor father's perception that his children's future is uncertain conveyed to them? What are the consequences of the father's vision on the child's attitude about the future? Finally, how does observation of the father's psychological and economic struggles affect the child's attitudes toward work, education, marriage, and family? Does the child perceive his or her life chances to be better than, the same as, or worse than the father's?

Research studies reviewed in this chapter have linked paternal unemployment and poverty to a variety of undesirable outcomes. Unemployment compromises the mental health functioning of fathers and is associated with a variety of physical maladies in both fathers and their children (Margolis, 1982). It may increase marital discord, undermine the parenting skills of the father, reduce the admiration the child feels for the father, and lead to a general deterioration of the father-child relationship. Families characterized by preexisting marital and father-child relations that are essentially positive tend to weather the storm of unemployment without major damage to family relations, and in some cases increased understanding and communication result. Even in such fortuitous instances, however, unemployment often exacts a costly toll on the economic well being of the family in the form of lost wages, assets (e.g., the home), job seniority, and medical insurance.

Men who live in poverty appear to suffer increased mental stress and alienation and reduced self-esteem. These feelings seem to negatively influence their capacity to perform expected paternal and marital role tasks, effects that are attenuated if the wife and children attribute the man's employment and income problems to external causes. The extent to which poor nonresidential fathers see their children and have authority over them depends to a large extent on their ability to contribute to the children's support. What implications do these findings have for the development of social policies that ameliorate the adverse effects of paternal job loss and poverty? In the section that follows, we briefly review some of the key public income transfer programs that are designed to reduce the hardship of economically strapped families and discuss some of the issues that must be considered in the development of more effective social policies.

THE SOCIAL POLICY IMPLICATIONS ON CHILDREN AND FAMILIES OF RESEARCH ON PATERNAL POVERTY AND UNEMPLOYMENT

Because unemployment is shaped by broad social, economic, and political forces, it cannot be eliminated by individual or family efforts alone (Moen, 1979, 1983). Implementation of fiscal and monetary policies at the macro level to discourage or remedy a sluggish labor market and the provision of social supports in the form of job training, job creation, and unemployment insurance are the two major strategies that have been used to deal with economic change in the United States (Moen, 1983). The first strategy is based on the assumption that a vigorous economy provides the best kind of job insurance to workers, but as Moen (1983) pointed out, even in periods of "full employment" a substantial segment of the labor force (usually set at 4 percent) is jobless. Furthermore, during the lag between implementation of government policies and economic response, millions of workers and their families suffer.

The second strategy, which seeks to help those who remain unemployed despite the implementation of macroeconomic policies, has achieved only modest success. Unemployed workers and their families rarely escape financial hardship. Unemployment compensation, regarded as the main support program for middle- and working-class unemployed individuals, has been an important mechanism for easing financial hardship, but only for some workers and only to a moderate degree. Indeed, the majority of unemployed Americans do not collect unemployment benefits. In the summer of 1982, 10.4 million people were officially counted as unemployed, but only 42 percent received unemployment benefits, which were on the average only 46 percent of earned income before taxes (Harrington, 1984).

Many of the unemployed poor do not receive benefits because (1) they do not meet state eligibility requirements (typically defined by a specific amount of employment), (2) they work in occupations not covered by unemployment insurance (e.g., domestic work), or (3) they have exhausted their benefits before securing new employment (Moen, 1983). The duration of unemployment benefits varies by state, but in 1981, 26 weeks was the modal maximum period of time workers were eligible to receive unemployment payments, and very few states offered extended benefits programs when unemployment reached extremely high levels (Margolis, 1982). A substantial proportion of unemployed workers (30 percent in 1980) exhaust their benefits before gaining new employment.

Even for those who receive unemployment compensation, a substantial drop in income and attendant financial hardships are virtually unavoidable. In 1975, the maximum benefit was 50 percent of former wages in 31 states and 30 to 60 percent in the remaining 21 states (this includes all states plus the District of Columbia and Puerto Rico). As of July 1979, only 12 states provided additional compensation based on the number of individuals dependent on the wage earner (Margolis, 1982).

Aid to Families with Dependent Children-Unemployed Parent (AFDC-U) is another income transfer program targeted to unemployed workers in 27 states (Margolis, 1982). In addition to having an unemployed parent, the family must divest itself of a major portion of its accumulated assets in order to be eligible for this program. This latter stipulation severely restricts the number of persons served by AFDC-U. In a recent study of unemployment insurance *exhaustees,* only 11.5 percent were eligible for AFDC-U, and only 1.6 percent of those studied would have been better off financially if they had received AFDC-U payments rather than unemployment compensation benefits. In 1980 only 10.6 percent of families experiencing unemployment were receiving AFDC-U payments (Margolis, 1982). Thus this program provides assistance to few families hit by unemployment.

Some scholars have suggested that the impact of unemployment on families is less severe in the 1980s than it was during the Great Depression (Thomas, McCabe, & Berry, 1980). Several economic and social factors are thought to mitigate the negative impact of unemployment in recent years compared with the 1930s, particularly a relatively more substantial and robust income transfer and social support system for the unemployed including unemployment compensation, severance pay, food stamps, Medicare, and welfare as well as employment opportunities for spouses (LeGrande, 1983; Thomas, McCabe, & Berry, 1980). It is clear that economically vulnerable families in the 1980s who make use of public welfare programs are objectively better off than families in the 1930s that had no such programs available (Moen, 1982). But it is not certain that their relative advantage over families in the 1930s persists during periods of high inflation or if the worker's unemployment becomes chronic and benefits are terminated or expire (Buss & Redburn, 1983b). In addition, any discussion regarding the use of family support programs by economically disadvantaged families in the 1980s must consider the public antipathy directed toward individuals and families who must rely on these programs (Grubb & Lazerson, 1982) and the small percentage of the economically disadvantaged who are eligible for these benefits.

The limited effectiveness of extant policies and programs in eliminating unemployment and in cushioning the financial blow of unemployment dictates that alternative or supplementary policies be implemented to counteract recessionary setbacks and high unemployment rates. One alternative proposed by several scholars involves a redistribution of the impact of unemployment such that a more equitable sharing of the burden results (Margolis, 1982; Moen, 1979). As we have seen, certain individuals (e.g., young parents, blue-collar workers, African-Americans) are more likely to be affected adversely during periods of economic recession. Work-sharing, one example of a redistribution policy, has been used to manage unemployment in Europe and Japan for many years (Margolis, 1982). Experimentation with work-sharing in the United States has been extremely limited. (In 1979, 1.8 percent of the work force was on involuntarily shortened schedules [Margolis, 1982].) Under this program, when companies must reduce their total work hours, perhaps because of a slump in demand, the hours of all workers are cut back (e.g., 30 percent) instead of certain individuals being laid off (e.g., 30 percent of the work force). Unemployment insurance then compensates the workers for some proportion of the wages lost due to the reduced hours (Margolis, 1982; Moen, 1979).

Work-sharing offers many advantages. It enables the worker to continue in his or her role as provider, it avoids the loss of status that may accompany unemployment, and according to some estimates it is less expensive than worker layoff when the amount of money spent for unemployment compensation of these workers is considered (Margolis, 1982). These advantages appear to outweigh potential drawbacks of work-sharing (e.g., the inflationary impact, drop in productivity) (see Margolis, 1982 for a detailed discussion of this issue).

Obviously fiscal and monetary policies need to be directed toward preventing or shortening periods of recession (Moen, 1979). Failing major success of such policies in preventing joblessness (failure that is virtually guaranteed given the free movement of capital permitted by capitalism, policy needs to be directed toward reducing the duration of unemployment. The longer the period of unemployment, the more likely families are to suffer serious financial hardship. Current policies appear at odds with this goal, given that programs to limit the duration of unemployment, such as the Comprehensive Employment and Training Act (CETA), recently have been dismantled or merged with more modest job-training programs (Moen, 1983). Also needed are public policies that facilitate the employment of women (e.g., flexible work hours, day care, nondiscriminatory hiring and wage structure). The availability of a second wage earner in two-parent families, and the availability of unemployment compensation, especially to single-parent women who work in jobs covered by unemployment insurance, buffer in substantial ways the impact of unemployment (Moen, 1983).

Because of the "cut and run" tactic used by some companies to shut down plants, stringent federal legislation has been proposed in Congress to discourage relocation and ameliorate its effects. Among the proposed requirements are the following: (1) at least one year's prenotification of the plant closing, (2) additional compensation and severance payments to displaced workers, usually a maximum of a worker's salary, (3) filing of an economic and social impact statement, (4) continued health and welfare benefits coverage for at least one year, (5) guaranteeing workers the right to transfer to other facilities owned by the corporation, and (6) continued payment of tax revenues to the community for at least one year (Buss & Redburn, 1983b). In light of the human cost of unemployment, these proposals warrant serious study.

Existing public policies generally have ignored the plight of poor men as wage earners and fathers. Since the 1970s, legislators have increasingly drawn a distinction between the "deserving poor," those unable to work such as the disabled and the elderly, and the "undeserving poor," those who should work but often do not or who work sporadically, such as poor female household heads and marginally employable males (Harrington, 1984; Jencks, 1985). The latter men, some whose unemployment benefits have run out and some who were never eligible for these benefits because of the nature of their former employment, may be eligible for "general assistance" grants. But general assistance grants are insufficient for even one individual to live on, much less a family. For example, in Illinois, a relatively generous state in terms of welfare benefits, the average monthly general assistance payment in 1983 was $144 (Bogira, 1983).

Income transfer programs for the poor were originally designed to provide temporary relief to widowed women and their children; they have evolved into the Aid to Families With Dependent Children (AFDC) program for poor mothers and children. Historically, fathers have been excluded from welfare support regardless of how long they have been unemployed or how desperate their poverty. Their exclusion has been intentional. Since 1935, an objective of state legislatures has been to ensure that the provision of welfare aid does not disrupt local market requirements for labor. Exclusion of lower-class fathers from welfare, for which their wives and children may be eligible, has the effect of maintaining a surplus labor pool and of contributing to the absence of fathers from poor households (Piven & Cloward, 1971).

The overall impact on *child* poverty of income transfer programs channeled through either parent (AFDC, AFDC-U) has been weak (Grubb & Lazerson, 1982; Harrington, 1984). In 1984 an average family eligible for available government assistance received $0.45 per person per meal in food stamps and $24.32 per week in AFDC payments (Children's Defense Fund, 1984). The ineffectiveness of income transfer programs to move large numbers of individuals out of poverty is in part a reflection of the failure of the United States to develop a comprehensive national family policy and to commit substantial resources to the elimination of poverty, inequality, and unemployment. Compared with all other industrialized nations, the United States provides the fewest benefits and income supports for economically disadvantaged families (Kamerman & Kahn, 1983). In addition, states vary in their commitment to assist economically troubled families (Grubb & Lazerson, 1982; Piven & Cloward, 1971) and generally have been unable or unwilling to replace lost federal revenue (Grubb & Brody, 1985). The present national administration appears to be retreating even further from assisting vulnerable families. By instituting an economic policy that fights inflation by increasing unemployment while simultaneously reducing (and dismantling) support programs for poor and unemployed families, the Reagan administration has contributed to the suffering of fathers and their families (Amidei, 1985; Children's Defense Fund, 1984; Citizen's Commission on Hunger in New England, 1984; Grubb & Brody, 1985).

Three general policy initiatives would help to reduce the suffering of fathers and their families. First, substantial reductions in social welfare programs that serve poor families, begun with the Omnibus Budget Reconciliation Act of 1981 (OBRA), must be reversed and these programs funded at levels that will support poor families and children in the mid 1980s. (See Children's Defense Fund, 1985, pp. 71–80, for a specific proposal for reducing child and family poverty.) While programs such as AFDC-U and the Women, Infants, and Children (WIC) program (a nutritional program for pregnant and nursing mothers and their infants) have been unpopular, they have been impressively effective in providing *some* buffer against economic hardship. Nutritional programs have been shown to have a direct positive effect on the health of children, the poorest children benefiting the most (Grubb & Brody, 1985). But overall, income transfer programs as presently conceived cannot eliminate poverty because they do not provide poor families with an income above the poverty level, because they are not indexed to reflect changes in the cost of living, because they are based on an antiquated notion of who constitutes the poor, and because many poor families simply do not receive AFDC benefits. For example, in 1976, a peak year for welfare enrollment, less than half of the 25 million Americans officially defined as poor received AFDC benefits (Harrington, 1984).

Second, changes in eligibility requirements for income transfer programs must be expanded so that poor fathers who cannot find work or earn enough to support their family do not have to choose between leaving home so their family is eligible for AFDC or residing with the family, thereby making the family ineligible for welfare. The extension to all 50 states of AFDC-U, Cost-of-Living Adjustment (COLA), indexing, and expansion of eligibility requirements would be immediately helpful to currently unemployed fathers and their family. In addition, unemployment compensation programs should be expanded to cover all workers who need it. Third, support programs to help workers and their family cope with potentially stressful events such as plant closings, layoffs, and job loss must be developed. These efforts should include help in retraining, job search, and financial support for relocation of families.

While it is not within our scope here to propose a comprehensive solution to the problem of paternal unemployment and poverty, we can suggest three long-range objectives that would help to alleviate the suffering of economically stressed families, minimize developmental risk to children living in economically disadvantaged households, and strengthen the provider role of fathers. These policy recommendations are made with the recognition that their implementation requires a reordering of national goals and a redistribution of national resources. Current Congressional debates over the federal budget make plain that the tide of federal dollars is flowing toward the Pentagon and away from poor families and children; witness the recent votes for the MX missile and against continuation of unemployment benefits for unemployed workers (*New York Times*, 4 April 1985). Assuming that this trend will continue, it is estimated that between 1980 and 1990 we will witness an increase of 86 percent in the national defense budget and a decrease of 18.7 percent in federal funds earmarked for poor families and children (Children's Defense Fund, 1985).

First, a national discussion and evaluation of the political economy of families under capitalism is needed, with the goal of making the economic, political, and social environment in which families function equitable and humane. Second, a comprehensive national family policy is needed that will lift all vulnerable families out of poverty and unemployment. Third, there must be a national commitment of the resources necessary to assist troubled and vulnerable families through economic hard times.

The first task involves the evaluation of the impact of the present economic system on poor families and the elimination of negative effects of the marketplace on family functioning. This debate should include a discussion of the development of programs that (1) eliminate poverty by doing more than transferring income through tax and welfare programs, (2) broaden our conceptualization of public work programs that rebuild the infrastructure of the country and train workers in needed skills, (3) create a national economic plan that projects a future direction and goals for economic growth and development and includes an expansion of public ownership of corporations and industries, and (4) abolish inequality in the workplace by elimination of discrimination based on race and sex.

One possible outcome of this debate might be to limit and restrict corporate control of activities such as plant closings. It appears that we cannot rely solely or even primarily on private enterprise to act on behalf of workers, families, and children. The assumptions of free-market thinkers that changes in the economy are inevitable and ultimately beneficial to society as a whole are not borne out by the data on the impact of economic dislocation and deprivation on families (Grubb & Lazerson, 1982). Decisions regarding economic growth must be made with the interests and input of poor and working-class fathers, mothers, and children.

Government must play the leading role in bridging the contradiction between family and individual needs and corporate responsibility. Some Americans yearn for a model of the family mired in America's rural past and mourn changes considered antithetical to optimal family functioning, for example, maternal employment and day care (Grubb & Lazerson, 1982). But these individuals must not fail or refuse to recognize that the problems of American families, particularly poor and working-class families, are rooted in the economic reality of America in the twentieth century, and it is in this historical period that the solutions must be sought.

The second and third tasks, the development of a comprehensive national family policy and funding to support proposed programs, are essential to help poor families and children in the future. It appears that because of structural changes and current economic policies, some sectors of the current poor and unemployed population will be economically disadvantaged for some time to come (Grubb & Brody, 1985; Wilson, 1980) and will be joined by new victims of economic change. The need for a comprehensive family policy is apparent (Kamerman & Kahn, 1983), in part because welfare benefits are so inadequate and are not indexed, but more importantly because the suffering of poor families and children is immoral in a nation with the enormous resources of the United States. This family policy should create institutional and programmatic structures that assist families with children (e.g., a national licensed and regulated day-care system that serves working parents) and should support intrafamily efforts to care for children (e.g., income support to unemployed fathers).

We recognize that the development of such a policy is not an easy task, but there are powerful moral and social reasons to commit time, energy, and resources to its creation. As Grubb and Lazerson (1982) have so carefully outlined, the search for a national family policy has been prompted in part by the need to standardize and coordinate the large and diverse family support programs provided by the states. These programs constitute a de facto family policy, albeit inconsistent, contradictory, biased, and poorly financed. Finally, we recognize that the development of a comprehensive family policy will only truly benefit fathers and their families if it follows on the heels of substantive changes in the degree to which macroeconomic factors, racism, class division, poverty, unemployment, and sexism affect family functioning and parental and marital relationships. A family policy that leaves, for example, racial and sexual discrimination untouched and does not question or curb the behavior of corporations vis-a-vis family interests will fail to address the fundamental contradictions of American social, political, and economic life.

REFERENCES

Amidei, N. (1985). Poor children and American social policy: Are we meeting our responsibilities? In J. Boulet, A. M. DeBritto, & S. A. Ray (Eds.), *Understanding the economic crisis: The impact of poverty and unemployment on children and families.* Ann Arbor: University of Michigan Bush Program in Child Development and Social Policy.

Angell, R. C. (1936). *The family encounters the Depression.* New York: Scribner's.

Arenson, K. W. (1982). Shadow of joblessness darkens more of nation. *New York Times,* January 10.

Aschenbrenner, J. (1975). *Lifelines: Black families in Chicago.* New York: Holt, Rinehart and Winston.

Bakke, E. (1940). *Citizens without work.* New Haven, CT: Yale University Press.

Bane, M., & Ellwood, D. T. (1983). *Slipping into and out of poverty: The dynamics of spells.* National Bureau of Economics Research Working Paper No. 1199.

Belsky, J. (1980). Child maltreatment: An ecological integration. *American Psychologist, 35,* 320–335.

Billingsley, A. (1968). *Black families in white America.* Englewood Cliffs, NJ: Prentice-Hall.

Bishop, J. (1977). *Jobs, cash transfers, and marital instability: A review of the evidence.* Madison: University of Wisconsin Institute for Research on Poverty.

Blechman, E. (1982). Are children with one parent at psychological risk? A methodological review. *Journal of Marriage and the Family, 44,* 179–196.

Bloom-Feshbach, S., Feshbach, J., & Heller, K. A. (1982). Work, family, and children's perceptions of the world. In S. Kamerman & C. D. Hayes (Eds.), *Families that work: Children in a changing world.* Washington, DC: National Academy Press.

Bogira, S. (1983). Life in the safety net: $144 a month. *The Reader,* 24 June.

Brenner, H. M. (1973). *Mental illness and the economy.* Cambridge, MA: Harvard University Press.

Brinkerhoff, D. B., & White, L. K. (1978). Marital satisfaction in an economically marginal population. *Journal of Marriage and the Family, 40,* 259–267.

Bronfenbrenner, U. (1958). Socialization and social class through time and space. In E. Maccoby, T. Newcomb, & R. Hartley (Eds.), *Readings in social psychology.* New York: Holt, Rinehart and Winston.

Buss, T. F., & Redburn, F. S. (1983a). *Mass unemployment: Plant closings and community mental health.* Beverly Hills, CA: Sage.

Buss, T. F., & Redburn, F. S. (1983b). *Shutdown at Youngstown: Public policy for mass unemployment.* Albany: State University of New York Press.

Caplovitz, D. (1979). *Making ends meet: How families cope with inflation and recession.* Beverly Hills, CA: Sage.

Cavan, R. S., & Ranck, K. H. (1938). *The family and the Depression.* Chicago: University of Chicago Press.

Children's Defense Fund (1980). *Portrait of inequality: Black and white children in America.* Washington, DC: Children's Defense Fund.

Children's Defense Fund (1984). *American children in poverty.* Washington, DC: Children's Defense Fund.

Children's Defense Fund (1985). *A children's defense budget: An analysis of the President's FY 1986 budget and children.* Washington, DC: Children's Defense Fund.

Citizens' Commission on Hunger in New England (1984). *American hunger crisis: Poverty and health in New England.* Cambridge, MA: Harvard University School of Public Health.

Cohn, R. M. (1978). The effect of unemployment status change on self-attitudes. *Social Psychology, 41,* 81–93.

Coles, R. (1970). *Uprooted children: The early life of migrant farm workers.* Pittsburgh, PA: University of Pittsburgh Press.

Coles, R. (1971). *The south goes north.* Boston, MA: Little, Brown.

Corcoran, M., Duncan, G. J., & Gurin, P. (1983). *Psychological and demographic aspects of the underclass.* Paper presented at Annual Meeting of Population Association of America, Pittsburgh.

Cunningham, S. (1983). Shock of layoff felt deep inside family circle. *American Psychological Association Monitor,* January, *14.*

Deutsch, C. P. (1973). Social class and child development. In B. M. Caldwell & H. N. Ricciuti (Eds.), *Review of child development research* (Vol. 3). Chicago: University of Chicago Press.

Dooley, D., & Catalano, R. (1980). Economic change as a cause of behavioral disorder. *Psychological Bulletin, 87,* 450–468.

Eisenberg, P., & Lazarsfeld, P. F. (1938). The psychological effects of unemployment. *Psychological Bulletin, 35,* 358–390.

Elder, G. (1974). *Children of the Great Depression.* Chicago: University of Chicago Press.

Elder, G. (1979). Historical change in life patterns and personality. In P. Baltes & O. Brim (Eds.), *Life span development and behavior* (Vol. 2). New York: Academic.

Ferman, L. A., & Gardner, J. (1979). Economic deprivation, social mobility, and mental health. In L. A. Ferman & J. P. Gordus (Eds.), *Mental health and the economy.* Kalamazoo, MI: W. E. Upjohn Institute for Employment Research.

Fineman, S. (1983). *White collar unemployment: Impact and stress.* New York: Wiley.

Fisher, K. (1983). Economic cold spree freezes "outsiders." *American Psychological Association Monitor,* January, *14.*

Furstenberg, F. (1976). *Unplanned parenthood: The social consequences of teenage childbearing.* New York: Free Press.

Furstenberg, F. (1981). The social consequences of teenage parenthood. In F. Furstenberg, R. Lincoln, & J. Menken (Eds.), *Teenage sexuality, pregnancy, and childbearing.* Philadelphia: University of Pennsylvania Press.

Garbarino, J. (1983). *Child welfare and the economic crisis.* Unpublished manuscript, College of Human Development, Pennsylvania State University, University Park.

Gelles, R. J., & Straus, M. (1982). Violence in the American family. In J. P. Rosenfeld (Ed.), *Relationships: The marriage and family reader.* Glenview, IL: Scott, Foresman.

Gil, D. (1970). *Violence against children: Physical child abuse in the United States.* Cambridge, MA: Harvard University Press.

Ginsburg, S. W. (1942). What unemployment does to people. *American Journal of Psychiatry, 99,* 439–446.

Goodchilds, J. D., & Smith, E. E. (1963). The effects of unemployment as mediated by social status. *Sociometry, 26,* 287–293.

Gore, S. (1978). The effect of social support in moderating the health consequences of unemployment. *Journal of Health and Social Behavior, 19,* 157–165.

Grubb, W. N., & Brody, J. G. (1985). Ketchup and other vegetables: The plight of children under Ronald Reagan. In J. Boulet, A. M. DeBritto, & S. A. Ray (Eds.), *Understanding the economic crisis: The impact of poverty and unemployment on children and families.* Ann Arbor: University of Michigan Bush Program in Child Development and Social Policy.

Grubb, W. N., & Lazerson, M. (1982). *Broken promises: How Americans fail their children.* New York: Basic.

Hannerz, U. (1969). *Soulside: Inquiries into ghetto culture and community.* New York: Columbia University Press.

Harrington, M. (1984). *The new American poverty.* New York: Holt, Rinehart and Winston.

Heiss, J. (1975). *The case of the black family: A sociological inquiry.* New York: Columbia University Press.

Herrenkohl, R., Herrenkohl, E., & Egolf, B. (1983). Circumstances surrounding the occurrence of child maltreatment. *Journal of Consulting and Clinical Psychology, 51,* 424–431.

Herzog, E., & Sudia, C. (1970). *Boys in fatherless families.* Washington, DC: U. S. Government Printing Office.

Herzog, E., & Sudia, C. (1973). Children in fatherless families. In B. Caldwell & H. Ricciuti (Eds.), *Child development and social policy.* Chicago: University of Chicago Press.

Hess, R. D. (1970). Social class and ethnic influences on socialization. In P. H. Mussen (Ed.), *Carmichael's manual of child psychology* (Vol. 3). 3rd ed. New York: Wiley.

Hill, M., & Ponza, M. (1983). *Poverty across generations: Is welfare dependency a pathology passed from one generation to the next?* Unpublished manuscript. Ann Arbor, MI: Institute for Social Research.

Hoffman, L. W. (1984). Work, family, and the socialization of the child. In R. D. Parke (Ed.), *The family: An interdisciplinary perspective; Review of child development research* (Vol. 7). Chicago: University of Chicago Press.

Hoffman, S., & Holmes, J. (1976). Husbands, wives, and divorce. In J. Morgan (Ed.), *Five thousand American families: Patterns of economic progress* (Vol. 4). Ann Arbor: University of Michigan.

Howell, J. T. (1973). *Hard living on Clay Street: Portrait of blue collar families.* Garden City, NY: Anchor.

Hurley, R. L. (1969). *Poverty and mental retardation: A causal relationship.* New York: Vintage.

Hyman, H. H. (1979). The effects of unemployment: A neglected problem in modern social research. In R. K. Merton, J. S. Coleman, & P. H. Rossi (Eds.), *Qualitative and quantitative social research.* New York: Free Press.

Jahoda, M., Lazarsfeld, P., & Zeisel, H. (1971). *Marienthal: The sociography of an unemployed community.* Chicago: Aldine-Atherton.

Jencks, C. (1985). How poor are the poor. *New York Review of Books.* (Vol. 32), 41–49.

Justice, B., & Justice, R. (1976). *The abusing family.* New York: Human Sciences.

Kamerman, S. B., & Kahn, A. J. (1983). Income transfers and mother-only families in eight countries. *Social Service Review, 57,* 448–464.

Kasl, S. V., & Cobb, S. (1979). Some mental health consequences of plant closing and job loss. In L. A. Ferman & J. P. Gordus (Eds.), *Mental health and the economy.* Kalamazoo, MI: W. E. Upjohn Institute for Employment Research.

Komarovsky, M. (1940). *The unemployed man and his family.* New York: Dryden.

Ladner, J. A. (1971). *Tomorrow's tomorrow: The black woman.* Garden City, NJ: Anchor.

LeGrande, L. (1983). Unemployment during the Great Depression and the current recession. Washington, DC: Library of Congress Congressional Research Service, Report #83-15-E.

Lewis, H. (1966). Child rearing among low-income families. In L. A. Ferman, J. L. Kornbluh & A. Haber (Eds.), *Poverty in America.* Ann Arbor, MI: University of Michigan Press.

Lewis, H., & Herzog, E. (1971). The family: Resources for change. In J. H. Bracey, Jr., A. Meier, & E. Rudwick (Eds.), *Black matriarchy: Myth or reality?* Belmont, CA.: Wadsworth.

Lewis, O. (1965). *La Vida: A Puerto Rican family in the culture of poverty.* New York: Vintage.

Lewis, O. (1969). The culture of poverty. In D. Moynihan (Ed.), *On understanding poverty.* New York: Basic.

Liebow, E. (1967). *Tally's corner: A study of Negro streetcorner men.* Boston: Little, Brown.

Liem, R. (1981). Unemployment and mental health implications for human service policy. *Policy Study Journal, 10,* 354–364.

Liem, R. (1983). *Unemployment: Personal and family effects.* Unpublished manuscript, Department of Psychology, Boston College, Boston, MA.

Liem, R., & Rayman, P. (1982). Health and social costs of unemployment. *American Psychologist, 37,* 1116–1123.

Light, R. (1973). Abused and neglected children in America: A study of alternative policies. *Harvard Educational Review, 43,* 556–598.

Little, C. B. (1976). Technical-professional unemployment: Middle-class adaptability to personal crisis. *Sociological Quarterly, 17,* 262–274.

Looff, D. H. (1971). *Appalachia's children: The challenge of mental health.* Lexington: University Press of Kentucky.

Margolis, L. (1982). *Helping the families of unemployed workers.* Chapel Hill: University of North Carolina Bush Institute for Child and Family Policy.

Marsden, D. (1975). *Workless: Some unemployed men and their families.* Baltimore, MD: Penguin.

Martin, E. P., & Martin, J. M. (1978). *The black extended family.* Chicago: University of Chicago Press.

McGhee, J. D. (1984). *Running the gauntlet: Black men in America.* Washington, DC: National Urban League.

Miller, S. M., & Rein, M. (1966). Poverty and social change. In L. A. Ferman, J. L. Kornbluh, & A. Haber (Eds.), *Poverty in America.* Ann Arbor: University of Michigan Press.

Moen, P. (1983). Unemployment, public policy, and families: Forecasts for the 1980s. *Journal of Marriage and the Family, 45,* 751–760.

Moen, P., Kain, E., & Elder, G. (1983). Economic conditions and family life: Contemporary and historical perspectives. In R. R. Nelson & F. Skidmore (Eds.), *American families and the economy: The high costs of living.* Washington, DC: National Academy Press.

Moynihan, D. P. (1965). *The Negro family: The case for national action.* Washington, DC: U.S. Government Printing Office.

Parke, R., & Collmer, C. (1975). Child abuse: An interdisciplinary review. In E. M. Hetherington (Ed.), *Review of child development research* (Vol. 5). Chicago: University of Chicago Press.

Piven, F. F., & Cloward, R. A. (1971). *Regulating the poor.* New York: Pantheon Books.

Powell, D. H., & Driscoll, P. F. (1973). Middle-class professionals face unemployment. *Society, 10,* 18–26.

Rainwater, L. (1974). *And the poor get children.* New York: New Viewpoints.

Rainwater, L., & Yancey, W. (1967). *The Moynihan report and the politics of controversy.* Cambridge, MA: MIT Press.

Rosen, E. I. (1983). *Laid off: Displaced blue collar women in New England.* Paper presented at annual meeting of Society for Study of Social Problems, Detroit.

Rubin, L. B. (1976). *Worlds of pain: Life in the working-class family.* New York: Basic.

Schlozman, K. L., and Verba, S. (1978). The new unemployment: Does it hurt? *Public Policy, 26,* 333–358.

Schulz, D. A. (1968). Variations in the father role in complete families of the Negro lower class. *Social Science Quarterly, 49,* 651–659.

Schulz, D. A. (1969). *Coming up black: Patterns of ghetto socialization.* Englewood Cliffs, NJ: Prentice-Hall.

Schwartz, M., & Henderson, G. (1964). The culture of unemployment: Some notes on Negro children. In A. B. Shostak & W. Gomberg (Eds.), *Blue-collar world: Studies of the American worker.* Englewood Cliffs, NJ: Prentice Hall.

Senate approves end to extended job loss benefits. (1985). New York *Times,* 4 April.

Sennett, R., & Cobb, J. (1973). *The hidden injuries of class.* New York: Vintage.

Sheldon, A., & Fox, G. L. (1983). *The impact of economic uncertainty on children's roles within the family.* Paper presented at meeting of Society for Study of Social Problems, Detroit, MI.

Siev, D. (1983). Unemployment's children: They're growing up old. *Democracy in Education, 2.*

Silverstein, B., & Krate, R. (1975). *Children of the dark ghetto.* New York: Praeger.

Stack, C. B. (1974). *All our kin: Strategies for survival in a black community.* New York: Harper and Row.

Staples, R. (1970). Educating the black male at various class levels for marital roles. *The Family Coordinator, 20,* 164–167.

Staples, R. (1971). The myth of the black matriarchy. In R. Staples (Ed.), *The black family.* Belmont, CA: Wadsworth.

Steinberg, L. D., Catalano, R., & Dooley, D. (1981). Economic antecedents of child abuse and neglect. *Child Development, 52,* 975–985.

Theorell, T., Lind, E., & Floderus, B. (1975). The relationship of disturbing life-changes and emotions to the early development of myocardial infarction and other serious illnesses. *International Journal of Epidemiology, 4,* 281–293.

Thomas, L. E., McCabe, E., & Berry, J. (1980). Unemployment and family stress: A reassessment. *Family Relations, 29,* 517–524.

U.S. Department of Labor (1981). New income levels defining poverty. *News,* 25 March, 81–156.

Valentine, C. A. (1968). *Culture and poverty.* Chicago: University of Chicago Press.

Williams, J. (1985). Hungry children. *Ann Arbor News,* 16 June, B4.

Wilson, W. J. (1980). *The declining significance of race.* Chicago: University of Chicago Press.

Wilson, W. J., & Neckerman, K. M. (1984). *Poverty and family structure: The widening gap between evidence and public policy issues.* Paper presented at conference Poverty and Policy: Retrospect and Prospects, sponsored by Institute for Research on Poverty (University of Wisconsin) and U. S. Department of Health and Human Services, Williamsburg, VA, 6–8 December.

Young, L. (1964). *Wednesday's children: A study of child neglect and abuse.* New York: McGraw-Hill.

Young, V. (1970). Family and childhood in a southern Negro community. *American Anthropologist, 72,* 269–288.

Zur, S., & Longfellow, C. (1980). The fathers. In D. Belle (Ed.), *Lives in stress: A context for depression.* Cambridge, MA: Harvard School of Education, Stress and Families Project.

CHAPTER 14

Employment and Fatherhood: Issues and Innovative Policies

JOSEPH H. PLECK

Wellesley College Center for Research on Women

This chapter considers how fathers' employment affects or sets a context for their role and behavior as fathers. It first considers general theoretical and empirical issues concerning the influence of men's paid work on their family roles. It then provides an overview of current experience in three social policy areas in which innovative practices that directly or indirectly support fathers are being implemented: alternative work schedules, parental leave for fathers ("paternity leave"), and work place-based parent education and support programs.

THEORETICAL AND EMPIRICAL ISSUES

Stimulated by the pioneering work of Rapoport and Rapoport (1965) and Kanter (1977), the observation is becoming commonplace that paid work on their family roles are interconnected, mutually influencing each other. While many aspects of the work-family relationship have received considerable attention (for a bibliography see Baden, 1981), this review focuses on three issues: the impact of fathers' amount of time spent at work on their time spent in child care, the effect of men's work schedules on their child care, and the degree to which fathers experience conflict between their work and family roles.

Some of the work reported here was conducted as part of the Fatherhood Project, supported by the Ford, Levi Strauss, Ittelson, and Rockefeller Family Foundations. Earlier versions of material in this chapter have benefited from comments by Urie Bronfenbrenner, Dana Friedman, Sheila Kamerman, Michael Lamb, James Levine, and Stanley Nollen.

As context, the average number of hours worked by married men in the United States has been edging downward in recent years, from 45.5 to 45.1 hours per week between 1968 and 1979 for those on full-time schedules, and from 44.5 to 43.8 hours per week for those on all schedules (Hedges & Taylor, 1980). At the same time, the proportion of workers holding a second job ("moonlighting") is steadily increasing, from 9.5 percent in 1969 to 11 percent in 1973 to 14.3 percent in 1977 (Quinn & Staines, 1979, p. 79).

According to an International Labor Organization study, the United States has less demanding job schedules and a shorter average workweek than most other countries in the world. The countries with the longest workweek are Egypt and South Korea (*Wall Street Journal,* 1981). In Poland in 1979, one of the principal workers' demands fueling the development of Solidarity was the demand for a five-day week. Male workers, especially fathers, complained that their current six-day workweek did not give them enough time with their family.

As defined by the Bureau of Labor Statistics (BLS), a job is classified as having a shift schedule if half the hours fall between 4 P.M. and midnight (evening shift) or between midnight and 8 A.M. (night shift). About 16 percent of all full-time nonfarm wage and salaried workers in 1978 worked on one or the other shift (Hedges & Sekcenski, 1979). Regarding part-time work, 12.5 percent of men and 33.0 percent of women worked less than 35 hours a week in 1977. Another dimension of part-time work is working part-*year* (defined by the BLS as less than 48 weeks per year); 28.2 percent of men and 43.6 percent of women report this pattern (Young, 1979). Unfortunately, breakdowns by parental status are not routinely reported.

It seems intuitively self-evident that the more time men spend in paid work, the less time they spend in the family. This basic relationship is worth detailed consideration from both a theoretical and an empirical viewpoint. It was axiomatic in mainstream family sociology during the 1960s that men's employment role accounted for their low participation in housework and child care. According to Blood and Wolfe's (1960) classic "resource theory," husbands perform less housework than wives because husbands have relatively less of the resource of time, due to their being employed. In Scanzoni's (1970) formulation of an exchange theory of marriage, husbands opt out of both child care and housework by exchanging their successful performance as breadwinners for their wife's performance of these domestic tasks.

While these formulations might be seen as justifying or rationalizing husbands' low family role performance, the negative time correlation between work and family can be interpreted in a more critical way. Grønseth (1971, 1972), for example, has portrayed men as being caught in a "breadwinner trap." In his analysis, all societies must structure who will hold the economic responsibility for the support of children. Western societies have created the "husband economic provider role" for this purpose. But, argued Grønseth, filling this role prevents men from relating to their children emotionally. This kind of argument is also one of the most basic and frequently expressed ideas in writings on "men's liberation" (Farrell, 1974; Goldberg, 1975).

Some might argue that neither the resource/exchange theory nor Grønseth's theory is correct. In their view, the work role is not a major reason for low family involvement, because men actually have considerable choice over the extent and intensity of their participation in paid work. The size of men's work role may simply reflect that men do not want to be more involved as fathers than they are. These different perspectives each interpret the negative work-family time correlation in a different way.

Empirically, the relationship between paid work and specifically child-care time is actually rather weak in magnitude. While several studies have reported a negative relationship between work and family roles (Blood & Wolfe, 1960; Robinson, 1977; Walker & Woods, 1976), their results concerning housework and child care combined, or housework alone, usually receive most attention. Further, these studies do not in all cases critically examine the actual magnitude of the relationship or use significance tests or multivariate analysis.

Pleck (1985) explored this relationship in more detail in analyses of two national surveys conducted in the mid 1970s, one administering time *diary* measures of time use (the 1975–76 Study of Time Use), and the other using respondents' summary *estimates* as the time-use measure (the 1977 Quality of Employment Survey). The particular format of the estimate measure was: "On the average, on days when you're working (and not working), about how much time do you spend taking care of or doing things with your children?" The estimates were multiplied by the appropriate number of days to yield a weekly estimate. Diary figures for fathers' child care tap only the most direct, explicit, narrowly defined forms of child care. The respondent estimate measure, however, appears to assess a broader range of activities, probably close to the total time respondents perceive themselves as available to their children.

In regression analyses controlling for family life-cycle stage, education, and sex-role attitudes, the metric regression coefficients for the effect of paid work on child care among husbands were weak in absolute terms: $-.008$ (nonsignificant) in the time diary survey and $-.164$ ($p < .01$) in the time estimate survey. The latter coefficient means concretely that a variation of one hour in paid work time is, on the average, associated with a 9.8-minute (.164 hours) change in child-care time.

The relationship between paid work and child care is also weaker than the relationship between paid work and housework (– .289 and – .221, both p's < .01, in the two surveys). The relatively weaker predictive effects on child care may reflect in part that fathers' mean time in child care is also lower than their mean reported housework time. Statistically, the strength of the negative correlation between two parts of a whole (in this case the 24-hour day) tends to be lower as the average size of either part is lower. In the relatively low range within which fathers' child-care time currently varies, fathers' time in paid work appears to have significant effects on child care in most surveys, but these effects are small in absolute magnitude even when they occur.

A further analysis explicitly compared the amount of unique variance in child-care time accounted for by paid work time and gender in the two surveys. While paid work accounted for some variance in child care in the combined sample in each survey, nearly as much or more variance remained to be accounted for by gender. Put another way, men's paid work time accounts for some variation in men's child care, but this variation occurs around a baseline that is not accounted for by men's jobs. A large father-mother differential in levels of child care remains even when work hours are controlled for.

Research has also focused on the effects on family life of other aspects of men's work schedules besides the number of hours worked. In analyses of husbands and wives in two-earner couples in the 1977 Quality of Employment Survey, Pleck and Staines (1983, 1985) found that contrary to expectation, characteristics of husbands' schedules had as many significant effects on a group of husbands' family role variables as wives' schedule variables did on wives'. But the pattern of effects varied by sex. Husbands' family role behavior appeared more responsive to job shift and the pattern of days worked (i.e., whether it included weekend days or was irregular), while wives' family experience was more responsive to number of hours worked. Specifically for child care, however, the combined group of schedule variables accounted for over 10 percent of the variance in employed mothers' child-care time, but almost no variance in employed fathers'. Husbands' job schedules appeared to influence other aspects of their family experience (including housework) more than child care.

A third area of relevant research concerns the extent to which fathers experience conflict between their work and family roles. Pleck, Staines, and Lang (1978, 1980) found in the 1977 Quality of Employment Survey that nearly equal proportions of employed men and women with families reported that their "job and [their] family life interfere with each other" either "a lot" (about 10 percent in each sex) or "somewhat" (about 25 percent). In both sexes, high interference was correlated with both number of hours worked per week and amount of child-care time. Later regression analyses (Staines & Pleck, 1983) suggested that the apparent sex equality in levels of work-family conflict occurred in spite of the fact that the regression coefficients for the effects of stressful schedule characteristics on conflict were greater for women than for men because men had higher average levels of these stressful conditions.

In summary, the existence of an empirical relationship between fathers' work schedules and their time in child care is theoretically insufficient to establish that fathers' work roles constrain their involvement as parents. In any event, the empirical relationship is rather weak. Nonetheless, other data indicate that fathers do experience their work and family roles as generating conflict, exacerbated when fathers spend more time at work.

Employment in the Context of Other Factors: A Model

In reviewing the theoretical issues and empirical results just discussed, two analytic questions need to be carefully distinguished: (1) Do fathers' work roles completely account for why fathers are substantially less involved than mothers with their children, and (2) do variations in fathers' work roles have effects on their fathering role? The first question must be answered negatively. However, fathers' work roles do exert some influence, though the effects are neither strong nor consistent.

The four-factor model of the facilitators of father involvement proposed by the Fatherhood Project (Lamb et al., 1985, in press; Pleck, Lamb, & Levine, 1985) provides a way of understanding how fathers' job characteristics affect their paternal involvement. The four factors specified by this model are motivation, skills, social supports, and the absence of institutional barriers.

Motivation becomes present in a variety of ways, such as modeling after or compensating against one's own father, a wife's employment, midlife self-reassessment, cultural images of the "new father," and the like. Skills develop as a function of motivation and opportunities to learn. Social supports refer to emotional support and validation as well as to the provision of concrete resources or help. Schedule and leave policies at the work place are the two most important institutional barriers, but also significant are the patterning of career demands in early adulthood and the average husband-wife wage ratio. Institutional barriers can also occur in legal, educational, health, and social service systems.

In this model, all four factors have to be present for father involvement to be maintained or increased. Thus the effect of any one factor on involvement is indirect rather than direct. Specifically, institutional barriers such as the amount and schedule of men's work hours will have an impact primarily on those who already have motivation, skills, and social supports that favor father involvement. For other fathers, a one-hour reduction in the work week is likely to lead to an hour of increased leisure, not child care. In analyzing how work place factors and innovations influence father involvement, one must be aware that these strategies will affect most strongly only a subgroup of fathers.

Since this motivated, skilled, and socially supported group does not appear to be a majority of U. S. fathers at the present time, it is understandable that even so basic a relationship as the effect of amount of paid work time on the amount of time spent in child care is relatively weak and sometimes negligible. Insofar as fathers' motivations, skills, and social supports for their fathering role may be increasing, however, it is likely that in the future the effect of work place-based constraints on fathers' involvement with their children will become statistically stronger and socially more apparent.

ALTERNATIVE WORK SCHEDULES

The term "alternative work schedules" refers primarily to three specific patterns for job schedules introduced in Europe and the United States during the last two decades: flexitime, the compressed workweek, and job-sharing/work-sharing. (As the term is usually defined, it excludes two other nonstandard job schedules long established in the labor market, shift work and ordinary part-time work, included in earlier discussion). This section focuses on the availability, utilization, and consequences of these three kinds of alternative work schedules for fathers. For more detailed analysis of the issues involved in implementing alternative work schedules, see Nollen (1982).

Alternative work schedules began to receive concerted attention from U. S. employers in the 1970s. The family was not initially seen as benefiting from workers having greater schedule flexibility. For example, the National Council for Alternative Work Patterns (1977) stated:

Recent innovations in working schedules are one aspect of the tremendous social and economic changes which are taking place in industrialized nations. While industry is facing pressure to increase productivity in order to compete in world markets, changing attitudes toward work, leisure, and education are occurring. The concept of alternative work patterns is intricately linked with achieving a balance between these three elements of life.

More recently, however, working parents and families are increasingly identified as significant potential beneficiaries of alternative work schedules (Bohen & Viveros-Long, 1981).

Flexitime

The concept of flexitime (the apparently alternate term "flextime" is actually a trademark for a particular company's time accumulator device) was first proposed in 1965 by Christel Kamerer, a German labor economist, as a strategy that might allow women with young children to enter the labor force while still taking the primary responsibility for housework and child rearing, and thus relieve West Germany's labor shortage. Nonetheless, at the outset employers usually adopted flexitime to combat other work place problems, such as absenteeism and tardiness, and to reduce urban commuting congestion (Bohen & Viveros-Long, 1981, pp. 62–63).

Flexitime means that workers have some choice about when to begin and end their work day. Each work place sets up its own system, but usually there are flexible bands in the morning and afternoon within which workers can determine their hours, and a "core" time (usually midmorning to midafternoon) when everyone must be present.

In 1978, following several years of hearings, Congress passed the Federal Employees Flexible and Compressed Work Schedules Act, mandating that for a three-year period federal agencies establish experimental programs in flexible hours. While this legislation directly affected only the federal civil service, it was important, since the federal government is the nation's largest employer and the personnel policies it establishes often become models for those in the private sector.

According to a report from the Bureau of Labor Statistics (BLS) (Hedges & Mellor, 1981), 7.6 million workers in 1980 (12 percent of all full time workers, excluding self-employed and farm workers) were on flexitime or other schedules that permitted them to vary the time their workday began and ended. Another 2.7 million part-time workers (working less than 35 hours a week) also reported they had freedom to depart from fixed schedules. Reflecting the encouragement provided by the 1978 Federal Employees Flexible and Compressed Work Schedules Act, one in five workers in federal public administration reported they were on a flexible schedule. The availability of flexible schedules varied somewhat by occupation and industry; rates were highest, for example, among sales workers, managers and administrators, professional and technical workers, and transport equipment operatives.

Companies do not, of course, introduce flexitime specifically because of an explicit concern to support men in their role as fathers. Nonetheless, flexitime can have an impact on men. Analyzing this impact entails consideration of three questions:

1. How available is flexitime to fathers?

2. When flexitime is available, to what extent do fathers actually change their schedules?
3. If fathers modify their schedules, do fathers become more involved with their children?

Flexitime is slightly more common for fathers (14 percent) than for mothers (10 percent) (Hedges & Mellor, 1981). Evidence on the extent to which fathers actually modify their schedule when flexitime is introduced or available appears to be limited to a single study. Winett and Neale (1980) interviewed parents of children under age 13 working in the Washington, DC headquarters of two different federal agencies before and after flexitime was introduced. The researchers found that 16 of 34 fathers (47 percent), compared with 18 of 37 mothers (49 percent), changed their schedule. In most cases, workers chose to start work earlier so that they could leave work earlier. Thus according to limited data, flexitime is available to fathers as frequently as it is to mothers, and when it is available, fathers actually change their starting and ending times about as frequently as mothers do.

The third and most important question about flexitime and fatherhood is the extent to which fathers on flexitime choose to use their schedule flexibility so that they increase their time with their children, or to exercise more child-care responsibility. In the first of the two federal agencies studied by Winett and Neale (1980), those who changed their schedule when flexitime became available (both fathers and mothers) increased their time with their spouse and children by an hour a day, while those who did not change their schedule showed no change. (While Winett and Neale did not report detailed analyses for fathers and mothers separately, they indicated that the two sexes showed the same patterns.) In the second agency, those changing schedule increased their family time by 37 minutes a day, compared with a 5-minute increase in the nonchangers.

Workers in this second agency were interviewed at several further points in time after the change. The difference between the schedule-changing and nonchanging groups dissipated by a year after flexitime was introduced. This can be interpreted as showing simply that flexitime caused no long-run increase in paternal involvement. Alternatively, this result may suggest that a single institutional policy change can have a short-term effect, but in the absence of other supportive factors the effect will not be maintained. This study supports the conclusion that when flexitime is made available, a substantial subgroup of fathers will use it to spend more time with their children, at least in the short run.

Data from this study illustrate the earlier analysis of how institutional barriers interact with other factors in determining a father's level of paternal involvement. Simply reducing an institutional barrier, such as by introducing flexitime, does not by itself increase involvement among all fathers exposed to the change. In Winett and Neale's (1980) study, only about half the fathers changed their schedule at all in response to flexitime. Those who had the motivation and other resources needed for greater involvement, and whose prior schedule in some way limited their involvement, were in turn a subgroup within those changing their schedule. This subgroup within the schedule changers probably accounted for the increased family time among the changers as a group. These employed fathers were limited in their involvement as parents to at least some degree by their particular work schedule; the introduction of flexitime appeared to lessen this barrier and enable them to increase their involvement.[*]

The "Compressed" Workweek

For the two other alternative work schedules—the compressed workweek and job-sharing/work-sharing—fewer data are available. The compressed workweek means a schedule in which a worker works full-time (i.e., 35 or more hours for the week) in fewer than five days. Four 10-hour days is a frequent example. Proponents of the compressed week argue that it increases workers' useful discretionary time because it reduces time spent commuting and concentrates free time together.

The 1978 federal legislation mandating greater availability of flexitime in federal employment also applied to the compressed workweek. About 1.9 million workers, 2.7 percent of the full-time adult work force, had a compressed schedule in 1980 (Hedges & Mellor, 1981), with little difference between the rates in men and women. Also the proportion of workers on compressed workweeks had risen from 1.7 percent in 1973. As with flexitime, the compressed workweek is not introduced by employers explicitly in response to men's needs as fathers.

[*] On behalf of the Family Impact Seminar, Bohen and Viveros-Long (1981) conducted a study of two federal agencies, one on flexitime for one year at the time of the study and the other on standard time, with no plans to introduce flexitime. Fathers in the flexitime agency did not report spending significantly more time in child care than did fathers in the standard time agency, though they did report spending two more hours a week in housework. This study is methodologically weaker than Winett and Neale's, since data were available only after flexitime was introduced and because the study is not able to distinguish between those who did and did not change their schedules when flexitime was introduced. In light of our model, the findings of this study are not really inconsistent with Winett and Neale's results. Since not all fathers change their schedule when flexitime becomes available, and not all who change their schedule have the motivation and other personal resources necessary for involvement, there is little reason to expect that, as a group, fathers in a firm that offers flexitime will spend more time with their children than fathers working for a firm not offering flexitime.

Maklan (1977a, 1977b) has conducted the single available study examining the effects of the four-day compressed workweek on men's family life. Drawing blue-collar male subjects from 12 industrial firms in Michigan and Minnesota, Maklan compared 91 workers on a four-day schedule with 46 workers on a five-day schedule. He found that four-day workers spent a great deal more time with their children than did five-day workers, 122 minutes per week compared with 23. (Some of this difference was due to one four-day father having a sick child whom he visited frequently.) More robust evidence is that four-day workers were twice as likely to have spent any time with their children on a given day, a finding holding true for both nonworkdays and also, surprisingly, workdays. This study contributes another piece of evidence that alteration of men's work schedules can potentiate greater paternal involvement.

Job-Sharing/Work-Sharing

Part-time work is, of course, nothing new in itself. Job-sharing is a new form of part-time work, designed to overcome the disadvantages that such work has traditionally had for both employees and employers. These disincentives for the employee have included few or no benefits, little or no opportunity for advancement, and often a low hourly wage rate. For the employer, the problem is lack of coordination between workers occupying different parts of a full-time schedule (for example, morning and afternoon telephone receptionists not having information from the other shift). Job-sharing means two people share the reponsibilities of one full-time job, taking on the additional burden of coordination with each other in return for greater fringe benefits and career opportunity.

In statistical terms, job-sharing is relatively rare. It occurs most frequently in teaching, especially at the elementary level. Major job-sharing demonstration and evaluation programs have been conducted in Wisconsin state employment (Project JOIN—Job Options and Innovations), in the Part Time Employment Program in the California State Department of Motor Vehicles, and in a union-initiated project among employees of California's Santa Clara County. When federal legislation concerning flexitime and compressed schedules passed in 1978, the Federal Employees Part-Time Career Employment Act was also passed. It was designed to ensure that part-time career employment existed as an employment option in the federal government, by mandating that each agency and department establish a comprehensive plan to evaluate its part-time hiring record and set its own goals and timetables for increasing the number of part-time workers at all grade levels.

In a national sample of 238 job sharers in a mail survey conducted by

New Ways to Work, an organization advocating alternative work patterns, only 13 percent of the sample were men (Meier, 1979). There is no evidence concerning the family behavior of men under formal job-sharing programs. However, Grønseth (1978) reported a study of a small number of Norwegian families in which both husband and wife decided to work part-time. Since their reason for doing so was to spend more time with their children, it is not surprising that Gronseth found that the fathers (and the mothers) spent considerably more time with their children than when they worked full-time.

"Work-sharing" is a somewhat broader term than job-sharing and includes all innovative approaches that involve both the reduction of work hours and the preservation of jobs and/or provision of additional job opportunities (McCarthy & Rosenberg, 1981). Besides job-sharing, other forms of work-sharing are simple reduction of hours, extended holiday and vacation, rotation layoff, and flexible retirement. Public and private employers are increasingly adopting programs such as reduced hours, rotational layoff, and extended vacation and holidays as a way of responding to a decreasing need for labor without laying off employees. For example, rather than fire one worker, a program is created in which five workers each reduce their hours by 20 percent. Although some workers welcome the possibility of reducing their hours, many do not, and for them hour reductions are involuntary. As a result, there has been experimentation with a number of plans to provide Shared Work Unemployment Compensation (SWUC), unemployment compensation to workers whose hours have been partially reduced. Workers are ordinarily eligible for unemployment compensation only if they are completely laid off.

Nollen (1980, p. 20) has written perceptively about an underlying difficulty with part-time work for men.

Masculine values block part-time employment. Full-time work is masculine and part-time work is feminine. . . . A masculine identity requires success, conquest, and singleness of purpose. Men stretch the limits. Herolike, they compete harder and win bigger. Do you know of any part-time heroes? . . . The fact is a man cannot succeed—read "be masculine"—unless he is totally dedicated to his (full-time) work.

While not usually thought of in relation to the family, job-sharing and work-sharing should be considered alongside flexitime and the compressed workweek when analyzing the impact of innovations in job schedules on the family. There appear to be no studies of the effects of the former policies on fathers' behavior in the family.

Overview and Future Prospects

All three forms of alternative work schedules are currently available to only a minority, but each is becoming more prevalent. Since studies indicate that these alternative schedules, especially flexitime, are associated with increased productivity (Nollen, 1979; Winett & Neale, 1980), the major barrier to their more widespread adoption by employers does not seem to be their cost. Rather, the difficulty is administrative conservatism and inertia, combined with specific technical problems. For example, according to older federal and state labor regulations, work occurring before or after certain times of day, and work of more than eight hours a day, are defined as overtime requiring extra pay. Both flexitime and the compressed workweek can lead to regular work being classified as overtime. These laws have now been changed.

For job-sharing and part-time work, benefits can be a problem. Simply prorating benefits according to hours worked means that these jobs have substantially fewer benefits than do full-time jobs, making these jobs potentially exploitative and decreasing workers' incentives to use them. But giving full benefits to less than full-time employees increases the total cost to employers, creating disincentives to making these kinds of jobs more available.

Some employers find that the benefits problem can be surmounted. For example, a Boston-area hospital offering job-sharing for the last several years reported that it had not yet had a case where both job-sharing employees in a pair needed health benefits. Almost all job sharers were women, many with a spouse with a family health benefit. Thus the hospital was able to assign a full-time health benefit to the worker who needed it, in trade for one of the other benefits going to the other member of the pair.

As already noted, only a subgroup of fathers utilize these alternative schedules when they are available. Studies of the effects of flexitime and the compressed workweek suggest that at least a substantial subgroup of fathers who take advantage of these schedules use them to increase their involvement with their children, at least in the short run. Although not consciously conceptualized as a strategy for increasing father involvement, alternative work schedules, if available, can among at least a subgroup of fathers make a difference.

PARENTAL LEAVE FOR FATHERS

Only a few years ago "paternity leave" was largely a rhetorical demand, advanced by small group of fatherhood activists. Today some forms of parental leave are actually available to U. S. fathers to a significant degree. Further, as part of a broader campaign to upgrade parental leave in general, both the federal government and individual states are considering mandating employers to provide at least some form of paternal leave, and mainstream unions are advocating for the wider extension of all forms of paternal leave. Policy analysts are explicitly including fathers in more general discussions of parental leave (Catalyst, 1981, 1983a, 1985; Kamerman, Kahn, & Kingston, 1983; Zigler & Muenchow, 1983). As Kamerman (1985) put it: "Parental leave is a children's issue, a family issue, a women's issue, and a social issue—but it is also a men's issue."

The term "paternity leave" has already acquired strong connotations, both positive and negative. To some it is the key to future change in sex roles and highly desirable; to others it is frivolous and irrelevant. Although paternity leave is the popular term, "parental leave for fathers" is perhaps preferable because it does not yet have such mixed associations. Also the conceptual rubric under which U. S. policies do now or in the future will give fathers the right to take leave is part of a policy for child-care leave for both parents, not a leave specifically targeted to fathers.

Legal and Administrative Context

A basic distinction needs to be made at the outset. Parental leave can be conceptually divided into two components: leave for the temporary medical disability associated with pregnancy and birth (as part of a more general policy for temporary medical disability), and leave for purposes of child care. Only women are theoretically eligible for the part of parental leave that is conceptualized as temporary medical disability (men may have claims for other kinds of temporary medical disabilities). But both sexes are theoretically eligible for the part of parental leave that is conceptualized as for child care.

In Kamerman, Kahn, and Kingston's (1983) analysis, legal policies concerning parental leave in the United States have focused primarily on the disability aspect of leave and been rooted primarily in laws regarding sex discrimination in employment. The basic law concerning this discrimination is Title VII of the Civil Rights Act of 1964, amended in 1972 and 1978. In 1966 the Equal Employment Opportunity Commission (EEOC) ruled that an employer could exclude maternity from medical disability insurance coverage without violating the law against sex discrimination. In 1972 the EEOC reversed itself. But in 1976 the Supreme Court held in *Gilbert vs. General Electric* that the exclusion of pregnancy-related disabilities from disability insurance programs did not constitute sex discrimination.

In response to the uproar about this decision, Congress passed the Pregnancy Disability Act of 1978 (technically an amendment to Title VII), which required pregnancy to be covered if other medical disabilities were covered (Kamerman, Kahn, & Kingston, 1983). The law did not mandate disability coverage where it did not presently exist, but only that pregnancy disability not be differentially treated. In March 1985, in *California Federal Savings vs. Guerra* (the *Garland* case), a federal court struck down on grounds of sex discrimination a California statute requiring employers to provide an unpaid pregnancy disability leave with the guarantee of return to the same or comparable job; California law did not specify a similar job guarantee at the end of unpaid leaves for other types of temporary medical disabilities. At this writing, the case is under appellate review.

Some might object to describing the situation of new mothers as a temporary medical disability, on the grounds that this classification reinforces our society's overly medicalized perception of birth and views women's parenting in only biological terms. There is perhaps some merit in this concern. At the same time, however, it is clear that the only legal or administrative grounds for many women currently receiving parental leave benefits is considering the time surrounding birth as a period of temporary medical disability. Further, if one is pragmatically interested in increasing the percentage of employed mothers who receive any parental leave benefit, politically it may be more feasible to do so by extending disability leave than by advancing the claim that women and men have the right to take a leave from work solely by virtue of being parents.

For many people, the only frame of reference for parental leave is medical disability leave for mothers. Because these individuals do not understand or accept the concept of child-care leave, they are unable to respond to a request from a father for "paternity leave." An extreme example is an employer quoted in the press about his first such employee: "Gynecology is not my field. . . . I don't know if this man has had a sex change operation or what."

Current advocacy efforts for the improvement of parental leave policies can be classified as concerning disability leave, child-care leave, or both. Policy initiatives concerning either child-care leave only or both disability and child-care leave are directly relevant to men as fathers. An example of an initiative focusing only on child-care leave is a bill considered in the Massachusetts legislature in 1985 (H.R. 3121) mandating employers to offer up to 16 weeks of unpaid child-care leave to parents of both sexes.

An initiative that targets both kinds of leaves is the Parental and Disability Leave Act of 1985 (H.R. 2020), developed and introduced by the Congressional Women's Caucus. This statute mandates employers to offer all employees 26 weeks of unpaid disability leave (this explicitly includes pregnancy; however, pregnancy-related temporary disability is usually medically certified for a maximum of 8 weeks), and 16 weeks of unpaid parental leave. Both leaves are job guaranteed. If passed, such bills would in effect mandate employers to offer unpaid paternity leave to fathers.

Comparative Data on Parental Leave for Mothers

Before examining current patterns and trends in the availability and utilization of parental leave by fathers, it is useful to examine the parental leave policies available to employed mothers. Kamerman, Kahn, and Kingston (1983) conducted an employer survey, and located other survey data, in order to describe the adequacy of employed women's parental leave benefits in terms of three criteria: (1) insurance—health insurance for the medical costs of the delivery for the mother, (2) job-protection— the right to take a leave of absence from the job, with the right to return to the same or a comparable job at the end of the leave, and with the maintenance of benefits and seniority, and (3) wage replacement—receiving the equivalent of full or partial salary while on the job-protected leave. The first of these applies only to disability leave, but the issues of job protection and wage replacement theoretically apply to both forms of leave.

Of the 250 firms responding to the Kamerman survey of 1000 companies with a net worth of at least $500,000, 95 percent stated they provided health insurance benefits to their female employees, though only 84 percent offered full coverage. The rate of this benefit was lower in the smaller firms in the sample, and women are far more likely than men to work in smaller firms. The 1977 Quality of Employment Survey (Quinn & Staines, 1979) found that 75 percent of married women employed 20 or more hours a week (the minimum employment necessary to be included in the survey) had some kind of employer-sponsored health insurance. Both the extent to which this insurance included maternity benefits and the coverage available through a husband's medical insurance are not known. Kamerman, Kahn, and Kingston (1983) estimated that 10 percent of all employed women in the child-bearing years lack any insurance coverage from any source.

Of the married women in the 1977 Quality of Employment Survey, 75 percent said they were entitled to some job-protected leave, a 12-percent increase since 1969. A Conference Board survey of large employers in 1978 found higher rates of such leave, but large firms are more likely to have better job leave policies, so that these findings overestimate their prevalence. The Kamerman survey found that 88 percent of employers provided this leave, but only 72 percent stated that they formally guaranteed employees on maternity leave the same or a comparable job and assured them protection of seniority. Kamerman, Kahn, and Kingston (1983) believed there was an informal job-guarantee policy in the other firms providing a leave. A leave of two or three months was the most common policy; three months or less was the rule in 61 percent of the firms. There was also variation in the length of prior employment required for the employee to be eligible and the extent to which benefit coverage was maintained by the employer during the leave. Most companies with a leave policy instituted it in the 1970s. The right to a job-protected leave at the time of childbirth has been largely but far from universally won by female workers.

Twenty-nine percent of the Quality of Employment Survey's female respondents in 1977 stated they were eligible for a maternity leave with pay, twice the proportion eligible in 1969. Like the other components of maternity policies, the availability of paid leave varies considerably. In the Quality of Employment Survey, nearly half of the employees in firms with 500 or more employees had this benefit, compared with less than 10 percent in firms with fewer than 10 employees. In Kamerman's survey, disability insurance (i.e., replacement of lost income during disability, not payment of medical costs) was available in somewhat less than half of large firms, and under prevailing conventions provided six weeks of insurance payments. Five states (New York, New Jersey, Rhode Island, California, and Hawaii) mandate employers to provide temporary disability insurance (TDI) to employees, explicitly including pregnancy; these programs are funded through a small payroll tax, usually contributed by employees. Thus except in these five states, only a minority of employed women— generally those in large companies—are entitled to paid maternity leave.

Types of Parental Leave for Fathers

Parental leave for fathers can take several different forms. The major categories are (1) long-term paid, (2) short-term paid, (3) long-term unpaid, and (4) other. The following discussion summarizes current data, from the United States and Sweden, on the availability and utilization of each form of paternal leave.

Long-Term Paid Leave at Time of Birth. When the term "paternity leave" is mentioned, the image usually evoked is long-term, paid, birth leave. When a length of time is specified, it is often six months. A tiny handful of organizations offer a substantial paid parental leave for which fathers are eligible, such as the Ford Foundation and Bank Street College. The Bank Street College of Education's Family (Maternity/Paternity) Leave Policy offers three full months of paid coverage. Both biological and adoptive parents are eligible, and for the latter, the child may be up to 36 months of age.

The Ford Foundation provides a paid "child care leave" of eight weeks, and an additional unpaid leave of 18 weeks, totaling 26 weeks in all. The policy applies to adoptive parents of children up to age 5, and the leave may begin up to four weeks before the expected birth or date of adoption. It must be taken within the first six months after the employee becomes a parent; the paid and unpaid portions of the leave do not have to be taken consecutively, however. Employees taking this leave (including the unpaid portion) are guaranteed a comparable position when they return, and the same job if at all possible. All benefits continue during the paid leave; during the unpaid part, all benefits except contribution to retirement and saving plans and the accumulation of sick and vacation days continue. If both parents work for the Ford Foundation, they receive the equivalent of one leave between them, but they can split it any way they wish. Although no systematic data are available, the number of fathers in either of these organizations who use the leave is quite low.

Sweden's Parental Insurance Plan gives fathers the same right to parental leave as mothers have (for detailed analysis, see Lamb & Levine, 1983). Finland and Norway also give the father some right to a portion of the overall parental leave, and several other European countries are debating the extension of parental leave to include fathers. Sweden's policies provide for several different categories of leave.

The basic leave provided ("parental leave in connection with the birth of a child") is a six-month leave available during the first nine months after the birth, which parents can divide between themselves. In 1978, about 10 percent of eligible fathers took one day or more of leave, and 5 percent took one month or more. The average number of days used by fathers taking a leave was 42. Among fathers in couples in which both spouses were employed full-time, 14 percent took one day or more. Although utilization rates have increased since the policy was first introduced in 1974, they now appear to have stabilized at the current level (Erler, 1982; Erler, Jaeckel, & Sass, 1982; Lamb, 1982; Lamb & Levine, 1983).

There are two possible explanations for this relatively low level of utilization: simple lack of interest by fathers in taking parental leave or a variety of social factors. It is no doubt likely that many Swedish fathers would not take a parental leave under any circumstances. But for other fathers, utilization may be significantly affected by several structural barriers. The first and most obvious is employers' attitudes toward fathers who take parental leaves. In a survey of 50 fathers who took one month or more of parental leave in 1980 and a survey of a small sample of employers, both surveys done in Goteborg, Sweden, Hwang (1982) found that a substantial proportion of both fathers and employers reported that employers do in fact view leave-taking fathers negatively and may penalize them in various ways. This result occurred in spite of explicit legal prohibitions of negative sanctions by employers against fathers who take leave.

In addition, fathers' utilization of the basic leave seems to be directly influenced by economic factors. For example, fathers employed in the private sector receive 90 percent of their regular salary while on leave, up to a set maximum level. Fathers with higher salaries give up more if they take a leave, perhaps explaining why they are somewhat less likely to do so. Fathers in public sector jobs receive 100 percent of their salary, with no maximum, and thus give up less when taking a leave than do private sector fathers. Correspondingly, fathers in the public sector take leaves somewhat more often (Lamb & Levine, 1983; Kamerman, 1980). Further, the higher the mother's earnings, the more likely is the father to take at least some leave (Kamerman, 1980). Families have more to lose economically if a high-earning parent of either sex in the private sector takes a leave.

Another important but often overlooked aspect of the leave policy itself also needs to be considered. Sweden's basic leave policy is unquestionably the most generous to fathers of any in the world. At the same time, it has an important limit: If both parents are employed, they must divide a fixed amount of leave between them. (This is also a feature of most U. S. leave policies when husband and wife have the same employer.) In this context, when a father does not take any paid leave, it is not clear to what extent this represents the father's desire to take no leave, the mother's desire to take all six months, or both. Hwang's (1982) survey of Swedish fathers who took parental leave found a few who had not wanted it themselves, but took it because their wife felt she could not leave her job for some or all of the leave to which she was entitled. While the father's own motivations are undoubtedly the strongest determinant of whether he will take a parental leave, other social factors contribute as well.

Short-Term Paid Leave at Time of Birth.   The second major category of parental leave used by fathers is short-term paid leave. Two of the 250 firms in Kamerman, Kahn, and Kingston's (1983) survey provided several paid leave days explicitly designated for fathers for purposes of parenting. However, about a quarter of the firms reported they permitted fathers to take a few days off with pay at the time of the birth of a child by using other paid leave, usually sick leave. Three or four days appeared to be an upper limit. The proportion of firms in which fathers were actually able to use sick days for this purpose was probably somewhat higher. No data are available on the extent to which fathers took advantage of these policies.

If one assumes that most workers have relative freedom to take sick days at will, the ability to use sick days for parental leave may seem a trivial matter. However, many workers are required to provide medical certification when they claim paid sick days. Some unions report that companies discourage workers from using their full entitlement of paid sick days. Thus even when sick days are formally available, there may be disincentives to their use for parenting purposes.

The real frontier of paid parental leave for fathers is not six-month paid leave, but rather the right to use sick days for paternity child care, or the right to a small number of paid leave days explicitly designated for use by fathers. One northeastern industrial union local, for example, negotiated for a single day off with pay for fathers on the day of the birth (Dudzic, 1983). After prolonged struggle, the company agreed, but only with the stipulation that the birth had to occur during the worker's actual shift on that day!

Swedish parental leave policies provide, in addition to the better-known long-term paid leave discussed earlier, a short-term paid leave for fathers. Under a provision of the "parental allowance for the temporary care of children," fathers are eligible to take 10 days of paid leave at the time of the birth of a second or subsequent child, a time when the mother is presumably unable to care for the other children. In 1976, 64 percent of eligible fathers used this benefit, for an average of 7.5 days; 40 percent of those eligible took all 10 days (Kamerman, 1980, p. 44). Thus Swedish fathers take advantage of this short-term leave far more frequently than they do the long-term leave.

Some might object that a leave as short as a few days is too brief to make much difference. Certainly, whatever it is that a paternity leave provides for the father, child, or family, a longer leave does more of it than a shorter one does. However, even a leave as limited as three or four days may be worthwhile to reduce stress in the new mother and family at a critical point and to facilitate later father involvement.

Unpaid Leave at Time of Birth.   The typical case reported in the media of a father fighting for paternity leave is a father in an organization in which women are routinely granted unpaid leave, but in which he has been denied one (and he is the first father ever to ask). This form of leave is becoming common in union contracts for state and municipal employees, including teachers. In the Catalyst (1985) survey of 384 companies responding to a mailing to the Fortune 1000 largest industrial and 500 largest financial and service companies, about a third (119 companies) said they offered unpaid leave to fathers; 35 percent of these leaves could be four months or longer. However, only 12 (about 10 percent) of these companies reported that a father had ever actually taken a leave.

Clearly, because of the income loss for the family, only a minority of fathers will take an unpaid leave for any significant duration. Media accounts of fathers struggling to receive an unpaid parental leave suggest that among those fathers who do want them, the desire for them is very strong. In addition to the desire to be actively involved with the newborn, other reasons include the mother being unable to take a leave from her job or the mother having postnatal medical complications.

Other Leave. Two other innovative patterns of paternity leave are beginning to appear that are not specifically birth related: reduced work time (the right to work part-time for a defined period when the worker's children are young), and personal or child-care days (the right to take a defined number of days off from work when a child needs care). These policies are available to fathers in only a few U. S. firms.

Both are available to all fathers in Sweden. Like the 10-day birth leave just discussed, these components of Swedish leave policy are far less well known than that country's long-term paid leave designated for birth. First, Sweden provides a "special parental leave" of 12 weeks to each parent, which can be taken any time during the first eight years and can be used in a variety of ways (taken all at once, used to reduce the parent's workday from eight to six hours over a longer period, assigned to the other parent). Although fathers use smaller amounts of it than do mothers, about one third of fathers use at least some of this leave (Erler, Jaeckel, & Sass, 1982). Fathers' utilization of this special leave is higher than their use of basic leave, even though the former is reimbursed at a lower rate than the latter (Erler, Jaeckel, & Sass, 1982; Lamb & Levine, 1983).

Sweden also provides 60 days per year of paid leave to the parents combined to take care of a sick child or to take care of children when the regular caretaker is unable to do so, until the children are 8 years old ("parental allowance for the temporary care of children"). About 40 percent of fathers take at least some of this leave, though they use less than 40 percent of all the days taken (Hwang, 1982). (The 10-day leave available to fathers at the time of the birth of a second or later child, discussed in the preceding section, is a special benefit under this program.)

Summary. To summarize the availability and utilization of these four types of paternal leave in the United States on the basis of the limited extant data, long-term paid birth leave is only rarely available to fathers, and rarely used when it is available. Short-term paid leave is available to fathers, primarily through use of sick days, in at least a quarter of large firms; no data exist concerning what proportion of fathers use it. Long-term unpaid leave is available to fathers in about one third of large firms, and frequently in public employment; fathers' utilization is low. No formal data indicate the prevalence or utilization of paternal leave for fathers of older children.

Effects of Paternal Leave

Little is known from formal research about the consequences of fathers' taking of parental leave. Investigation of the effects of parental leave is limited to two studies. In Hwang's (1982) survey of 50 Goteborg (Sweden) fathers who took a month or more of paid parental leave in 1980, most men were positive when asked to give an overall assessment of their parental leave experience. About 30 percent described it as a wonderful experience, a time of personal growth in which they were able to observe the child's development closely and consolidate a close relationship with the child. Another 40 percent felt that the experience was mostly positive, although their reasons for taking leave were not so much because they valued the experience intrinsically, but because they believed in equal parental responsibilities and opportunities.

The remaining 30 percent were more negative. Twenty-five percent felt that it was a difficult time for them, although they still felt that men should take some parental leave. The major positive element reported was the break from work. Five percent described the period at home as very strenuous, and something they would never do again. Many of these men had taken parental leave because their wife's employment situation made it imperative, rather than because they wanted to do so.

Lamb and colleagues (1982) compared 17 fathers taking leave of one month or more in Goteborg, Sweden, with 35 fathers who did not. For the 17, the average amount of time away from work was about three months, usually starting when the infant was 5 or 6 months old. The leave-taking fathers were in fact the primary caretaker while on leave. This study examined the hypothesis that fathers who are primary caretakers (while on leave) would show more of interactive styles with their infant that are typical of mothers (smiling, talking, kissing, hugging, touching). Significant differences remained between mothers' and fathers' behaviors. The samples in these two studies were small, and there is no evidence on the topic of perhaps most interest: on the long-run effects of leave on fathers' degree of involvement.

Overview and Future Prospects

The length, compensation, and timing of parental leave appear to make a considerable difference in the degree that fathers use it. In the Swedish data, short-term leaves were used more frequently than long-term ones.

Taking a few days of sick leave at a time may be less disruptive to a father's job than taking a long leave at the time of birth. Lamb (1982) suggested that higher proportions of fathers may take advantage of Sweden's short-term leave policies than of the long-term leave policy because the child is older and has been weaned.

An important reason, perhaps the major reason, for fathers' low utilization rate is their lack of motivation and their feeling that parental leave is inappropriate for them. But among those potentially interested in taking such a leave, there are other important barriers. At childbirth, probably only a small minority of even the motivated fathers take a leave longer than a few days or weeks, whether paid or unpaid. Fathers' rate of utilization of an unpaid leave longer than a few days is low largely because of the economic cost. Even when the leave is paid, utilization of long-term leave is low because of the potential negative career consequences such a leave has and because some policies are structured so that the father taking leave time reduces the amount of leave time available to the mother.

There is evidence that higher proportions of fathers will take advantage of leave policies that are explicitly short term or limited in other ways, particularly if they have considerable flexibility as to how to schedule the leave time. One reason more fathers use short-term leaves is that these are less disruptive than a long-term leave to the father's job prospects or career track, a disincentive to taking a leave even when loss of income is not an issue. Clearly, the duration, timing, financial implications, and context of parental leave make a big difference in whether fathers use it.

Long-term paid paternity leave is extremely unlikely to be accepted by U. S. employers on a wide scale. In Sweden and in the few U. S. firms in which long-term paid leave is available, fathers utilize it at low rates, which undermines support for this kind of leave. Simultaneously, this form of leave appears expensive to employers. The three other more limited kinds of paternity leave, however, should and realistically can be extended. The cost of these is far smaller, and the demand for them, as shown by rates of utilization, is far higher. The "packaging" of a leave affects the proportion of fathers likely to use it and how realistic it is that employers can be persuaded to offer it.

WORK-PLACE-BASED PARENT EDUCATION
AND SUPPORT

This third kind of work place initiative facilitating father involvement can be discussed briefly. Educational and support programs for parents, including fathers, based at the work place exist at over 100 companies, according to an estimate by Friedman (personal communication, 1983). In a typical case, the company has hired an outside parent-education organization or firm to provide an on-site program for employees, once a week for 10 weeks during the lunch hour. There is a fee for employees choosing to attend, but the program is also subsidized by the company. Other formats and schedules are available. One of the 10 sessions may focus specifically on fathers, but discussions of fathering may come up in other sessions. The program is publicized through the company's personnel or human resources office or through public affairs or community affairs offices.

One of the first examples, a seminar program entitled "Family and the company: Working at both so both will work," was developed by the Texas Institute for Families, under contract from the state's Department of Human Resources. It consists of sessions held at the work site dealing with conflicts that arise between job and family responsibilities, stress management, community resources, communications, and problem solving.

According to the program's developer (Oser, personal interview, 1982), the program was started because of the realization that the audience most absent in parent-education program is fathers. "We discovered that the way to reach most men in the labor force is to reach them through their jobs. So, we designed a program that takes men where they are, particularly white-collar managerial types where the priorities for 9 out of 10 of them are going to be their jobs. We designed a series of programs that would acknowledge their career orientation and at the same time try to establish that it's O.K. to have equal weight in the parenting role."

Of the several thousand parents that have participated in the program over the last several years in a variety of companies, fathers have made up less than 10 percent of all participants. Oser described the effect of the program for the typical male as "that they get more in touch that it's O.K. to have personal goals and that you don't need to sacrifice yourself; the tradeoff isn't me or my kid, it's possible to have both. . . . For most of the male participants there's a much greater understanding of what's required in taking care of children at different age levels, and what their role in that process is."

Unions are also getting involved in parent education and support. Local 8-149 of the Oil, Chemical, and Atomic Workers Union obtained a grant from the New York Council on the Humanities to sponsor a "study circle" for union members on "Family Values and Work Values." According to Dudzic (1983), chairperson of the political action and education committee of the Local, the objective is "to explore why the family sphere and the work sphere are so alien from each other, and what can be done about it. We hope to get our members to articulate some of these conflicts and build a core of people in the local who are committed to taking up the struggle for parenting needs."

Dudzic also noted that the Local wants to address the internal conflicts brought about by workers' involvement in parenting, especially male workers. "They are embarrassed to admit that they can't work overtime because they have to go home and cook supper for the kids. They don't like to talk about the fact that their wife has to work, and they feel uncomfortable about discussing bedtime stories or what kind of birthday party they should have for their kids. All these things go against the image that they were taught to have of themselves as providers, rather than as nurturers."

Catalyst (1983b) provides detailed information to employers who are considering offering a parent-education and support program, with a thoughtful analysis of many administrative and practical issues. Davis (1983) evaluated a work place-based fatherhood education workshop, comparing the 13 fathers attending the workshop with a control group of 14 in terms of two attitudinal measures about child rearing and fathering, and finding positive differences. Levant (in press) explicates the psychoeducational perspective on fatherhood education underlying the programs he develops in the work place.

Such work place-based parent-education and support programs will certainly never become common or reach more than a handful of fathers. But they probably will become more frequent in the coming years, and are an inexpensive way for the company to demonstrate a concern for the family and children of its employees.

OVERVIEW

To interpret the long-run limits on men's fathering role caused by the work place, and the extent to which meaningful change is possible or in the offing, one must consider the three specific work place innovations discussed so far in this chapter. Both the blocks to employers changing their policies and the factors hindering fathers from taking advantage of father-leave policies need to be recognized.

With use of the four-part model of the factors facilitating paternal involvement discussed at the outset of this chapter, alternative work schedules and parental leave can be viewed as examples of changes at the work place that reduce the structural barriers to paternal involvement that some fathers experience. Work place-based parent-education and support programs help provide some fathers with the skills and social supports they need for greater involvement.

The evidence does not suggest that greater provision of these work place innovations will, by itself, dramatically increase fathers' average level of involvement. But reduction of the structural barriers against father involvement presented by inflexible schedules and parental leave policies does seem to facilitate greater involvement among a subgroup of fathers. According to the model, this subgroup consists of fathers already motivated to be involved and in possession of skills and self-confidence as fathers. Likewise, when education and support programs for parents are offered at the work place, those fathers who are already highly motivated for involvement appear to make use of them.

Though the size of the subgroup of fathers that each policy or program affects is not the same, each policy makes a difference for at least some. There is no question, of course, that women currently have more to gain from policy changes in these three areas than do men. Nonetheless, it is important to recognize that such policies can and do have an impact on fathers. For those concerned to increase fathers' options to be actively involved with their children, promotion of good policies in these three areas should be a high priority. Fatherhood activists should devote increased attention and advocacy to alternative work schedules, the more limited kinds of parental leave for fathers, and parenthood education at the work place (for resources see Klinman, Kohl, & The Fatherhood Project, 1984).

Progressive work place policies that support employed fathers clearly occur less frequently than parallel policies for employed mothers. The working mother has been well established as a social issue; as yet, the working father has not. There has, of course, been considerable resistance by employers and society at large to the notion that employers should design policies to support employed mothers, and that it might be in an employer's self-interest to do so. However, there is far greater resistance to a similar view of employers' responsibility to employed fathers. This resistance derives from the real or imagined cost of implementing these policies, as well as from the deep-seated social belief that a father's fundamental obligation is breadwinning, not direct involvement with his children.

REFERENCES

Baden, C. (1981). *Work and family: An annotated bibliography, 1978-1980.* Boston: Wheelock College Center for Parenting Studies.

Blood, R. O., & Wolfe, D. M. (1960). *Husbands and wives.* New York: Free Press.

Bohen, H., & Viveros-Long, A. (1981). *Balancing jobs and family life: Do flexible work schedules help?* Philadelphia: Temple University Press.

Catalyst (1981). *Corporations and two-career families: Directions for the future.* New York: Catalyst (14 E. 60th St., New York, NY 10022).

Catalyst (1983a). *Maternity and parental leaves of absence.* New York: Catalyst.

Catalyst (1983b). *Work and family seminars.* New York: Catalyst.

Catalyst (1985). *Preliminary report on a nationwide survey of maternity/parental leave.* New York: Catalyst.

Davis, S. J. (1983). *Fatherhood education in the workplace.* Unpublished doctoral dissertation, School of Education, University of Florida, Gainesville, FL.

Dudzic, M. (1983). *Remarks at the "Changing the workplace" session of the Fatherhood Forum.* Unpublished.

Erler, G. (1982). Maternity and parental leaves in Europe. *Work Times, 1,* 1–5

Erler, G., Jaeckel, M., & Sass, J. (1982). *Results of the European study concerning maternity leave/parental leave/home care support measures in Finland, Sweden, Hungary, Austria, and German Federal Republic—summary.* Munich: Deutsches Jugendinstitut.

Farrell, W. (1974). *The liberated man.* New York: Random House.

Goldberg, H. (1975). *The hazards of being male.* New York: Nash.

Gronseth, E. (1971). The husband-provider role: A critical appraisal. In A. Michel (Ed.), *Family issues of employed women in Europe and America.* Leiden, The Netherlands: Brill, pp. 11–31.

Gronseth, E. (1972). The breadwinner trap. In L. K. Howe (Ed.), *The Future of the Family.* New York: Simon and Schuster, pp. 175–191.

Gronseth, E. (1978). Work sharing: A Norwegian example. In R. Rapoport & R. Rapoport (Eds.), *Working couples.* New York: Harper and Row, pp. 108–121.

Hedges, J. N., & Mellor, E. (1981). *10 Million Americans work flexible schedules, 2 million work full time in 3 to 4-1/2 days* (press release). Washington, DC: Office of Information, U. S. Department of Labor (issued February 24).

Hedges, J. N., & Sekcenski, E. (1979). Workers on late shifts in a changing economy. *Monthly Labor Review,* September, 14–22.

Hedges, J. N., & Taylor, D. E. (1980). Recent trends in worktime: Hours edge downward. *Monthly Labor Review,* March, 3–11.

Hwang, C. P. (1982). Presentation to Bank Street College Research Colloquium, New York, unpublished.

Kamerman, S. B. (1980). *Maternity and parental benefits and leaves: An international review.* New York: Columbia University Center for the Social Sciences.

Kamerman, S. B. (1985). Introductory address to the Association of Junior Leagues' Parental Leave Conference, Arden House, New York, March 7.

Kamerman, S. B., Kahn, A. J., & Kingston, P. W. (1983). *Maternity policies and working women.* New York: Columbia University Press.

Kanter, R. M. (1977). *Work and family life in the United States: A critical review and agenda for research and policy.* New York: Russell Sage Foundation.

Klinman, D., Kohl, R., & The Fatherhood Project (1984). *Fatherhood USA: The first national guide to programs, services, and resources for fathers.* New York: Garland.

Lamb, M. E. (1982). Why Swedish fathers aren't liberated. *Psychology Today,* October, 75–77.

Lamb, M. E., Frodi, A. M., Hwang, C., & Frodi, M. (1982). Varying degrees of paternal involvement in infant care: Attitudinal and behavioral correlates. In M. E. Lamb and A. Sagi (Eds.), *Nontraditional families: Parenting and child development.* Hillsdale, NJ: Erlbaum.

Lamb, M. E. & Levine, J. A. (1983). The Swedish parental insurance policy: An experiment in social engineering. In M. E. Lamb & A. Sagi (Eds.), *Fatherhood and family policy.* Hillsdale, NJ: Erlbaum.

Lamb, M. E., Pleck, J. H., Charnov, E. L., & Levine, J. A. (1985). Paternal behavior in humans. *American Zoologist, 25,* 883–894.

Lamb, M. E., Pleck, J. H., Charnov, E. L., & Levine, J. A. (in press). A biosocial perspective on paternal behavior and involvement. In J. B. Lancaster, J. Altman, & A. Ross (Eds.), *Parenting across the lifespan: Biosocial perspectives.* New York: Academic.

Levant, R. (in press). Client-centered skills training for families. In R. Levant (Ed.), *Psychoeducational approaches to family therapy.* New York: Springer.

Maklan, D. M. (1977a). *The four-day workweek.* New York: Praeger.

Maklan, D. M. (1977b). How blue-collar workers on 4-day workweeks use their time. *Monthly Labor Review,* August, 18–26.

McCarthy, M. E., & Rosenberg, G. S. (1981). *Work sharing case studies.* Kalamazoo, MI: W. E. Upjohn Institute for Employment Research.

Meier, G. S. (1979). *Job sharing: A new pattern for quality of work and life.* Kalamazoo, MI: W. E. Upjohn Institute for Employment Research.

National Council for Alternative Work Patterns (1977). *Resource packet for the National Conference on Alternative Work Schedules.* Washington, DC: National Council for Alternative Work Patterns.

Nollen, S. D. (1979). Does flexitime improve productivity? *Harvard Business Review, 57*(5), 4–8.

Nollen, S. D. (1980). What is happening to flexitime, flexitour, gliding time, the variable day? And permanent part-time employment? And the four day week? *Across the Board,* April, 6–21.

Nollen, S. D. (1982). *New work schedules in practice: Managing time in a changing society.* New York: Van Nostrand Reinhold.

Pleck, J. H. (1983). Husbands' paid work and family roles: Current research issues. In H. Z. Lopata & J. H. Pleck (Eds.), *Research in the interweave of social roles,* (Vol. 2): *Families and jobs.* Greenwich, CT: JAI Press.

Pleck, J. H. (1985). *Working wives, working husbands.* Beverly Hills, CA: Sage.

Pleck, J. H., Lamb, M. E., & Levine, J. A. (1985). Facilitating future change in men's family roles. In R. A. Lewis & M. Sussman (Eds.), *Men's changing roles in the family.* New York: Haworth.

Pleck, J. H., & Staines, G. L. (1983). Work schedules and work-family conflict in two-earner couples. In J. Aldous (Ed.), *Two paychecks: Life in dual-earner couples.* Beverly Hills, CA: Sage.

Pleck, J. H., & Staines, G. L. (1985). Work schedules and family life in two-earner couples. *Journal of Family Issues, 6,* 61–82.

Pleck, J. H., Staines, G. L., & Lang, L. (1978). *Work and family life: First reports on work-family interference and workers' formal childcare arrangements, from the 1977 Quality of Employment Survey.* Wellesley, MA: Wellesley College Center for Research on Women.

Pleck, J. H., Staines, G. L., & Lang, L. (1980). Conflict between work and family life. *Monthly Labor Review,* March, 29–32.

Quinn, R. P., & Staines, G. L. (1979). *The 1977 Quality of Employment Survey.* Ann Arbor, MI: Institute for Social Research.

Rapoport, R., & Rapoport, R. (1965). Work and family in contemporary society. *American Sociological Review, 30,* 381–394.

Robinson, J. P. (1977). *How Americans use time: A social-psychological analysis.* New York: Praeger.

Scanzoni, J. (1970). *Opportunity and the family.* New York: Free Press.

Staines, G. L., & Pleck, J. H. (1983). *The impact of work schedules on the family.* Ann Arbor, MI: Institute for Social Research.

Walker, K., & Woods, M. (1976). *Time use: A measure of the household production of goods and services.* Washington, DC: American Home Economics Association.

Wall Street Journal (1981). Workweek is shortest in U. S., survey finds. February 20, 32.

Winett, R. A., & Neale, M. S. (1980). Results of experimental study on flexitime and family life. *Monthly Labor Review,* November, 29–32.

Young, A. (1979). Work experience of the population. *Monthly Labor Review,* March, 53–57.

Zigler, E., & Muenchow, S. (1984). Infant day care and infant-care leaves: A policy vacuum. *American Psychologist, 38,* 91–94.

CHAPTER 15

Fathers and the Educational System

DEBRA G. KLINMAN
Bank Street College of Education

The educational system is one of the most pervasive social institutions surrounding family life in America, and its impact on the socialization process is considerable. A fundamental goal of the educational system is to ensure the transmission of the larger culture's values and beliefs—including an array of messages about what it means to be male or female in this society. The content of these messages was once taken for granted; however, during the last three decades the role of the educational system in socializing males and females has been repeatedly called into question.

Today, education that conveys options beyond the boundaries of traditional sex roles is increasingly available to at least some young women. Such is not the case for the great majority of males. Whether entering preschool, completing college, or confronting the responsibilities of first-time fatherhood, males receive little instruction in the "feminine" domain of nurturance. The idea that fatherhood is an important social role, or that males of any age might have an interest in learning how to care for young children, remains an alien concept in most schools. Similarly, most schools remain alien territory to the majority of fathers.

Nonetheless, there are some nascent signs of change. In The Fatherhood

---

The Fatherhood Project, a national research and demonstration project designed to encourage wider options for male involvement in child rearing, began in September 1981 with funding from The Ford Foundation, Levi Strauss Foundation, Ittleson Foundation, and Rockefeller Family Fund. Information describing the specific educational settings referred to in this chapter was obtained from self-report responses to The Fatherhood Project Questionnaire.

Project at Bank Street College in New York City, the ways in which educational programs and practices are beginning to encourage boys and men to take an expanded view of their own potential for nurturing the young—as babysitters, child-care professionals, and eventually as fathers—have been investigated.

The project has identified interesting signs of change in three arenas within the educational system. First, there is renewed interest in getting more adult males into the classroom, especially during the preschool and early childhood years, so they can serve as role models of nurturant manhood. Second, there are attempts to structure the kinds of "hands-on" educational experiences that encourage boys and young men to try out the behaviors and feelings associated with caring for children. Finally, there is an increasing awareness of fathers as potential consumers of parent-education classes, whether in formal settings like public schools and colleges or more informal settings within the community.

This chapter discusses each of the arenas in which change is percolating, and answers a variety of questions: What are the sources of impetus behind these changes? Where are there examples of successful change strategies already in place? What are the resistances and costs that limit the potential for more rapid and broad-based change? The chapter begins with an historical overview of how the educational system has been expected to socialize boys and men, thereby placing recent trends into longer-term perspective.

EDUCATION AND THE MALE ROLE

Historically, educational institutions (and the society they mirror) have held fairly clear expectations for masculine and feminine life scripts. When girls and young women went to school, it was to prepare for caregiving roles, usually within the family. Boys and young men, on the other hand, prepared to enter the world of work, eventually supporting their families financially and instrumentally. That schooling should differentiate between the sexes was a basic premise of the educational system. One eighteenth century educational treatise put it this way: "The respective employments of the male and female sex being different, a different mode of education is consequently required" (cited in Sexton, 1976, p. 33).

It was not until the middle of the twentieth century that the transmission of sex roles by educational institutions generated controversy. Interestingly—although often forgotten—the first wave of professional interest in altering what the schools were conveying about sex roles focused exclusively on a campaign to rescue young males from the feminizing influence exerted by the American classroom. In an abrupt shift, the next wave of reform focused on females and their right to educational equity in preparation for more equitable employment options as adults. Finally, and most recently, educators have begun to examine the limits that traditional sex roles impose on students of *both* genders. A variety of changing social forces and cultural attitudes preceded these recent waves of concern; we will examine their history briefly before returning to a more detailed look at the last three decades.

Throughout the eighteenth and much of the nineteenth centuries, much like the English educational system after which early American schools were modeled, education was largely an all-male domain: Boys were students, men their teachers. It was not until the mid-nineteenth century, when the movement toward free, compulsory public education captured the American imagination, that girls began to gain admission to schools in large numbers. Very quickly, this movement doubled the size of the school-going population, creating an enormous demand for qualified teachers. In response, normal schools were established as centers for teacher training. There were fewer than 15 normal schools prior to the Civil War, but well over 100 a mere decade later (Sexton, 1976).

Meanwhile, thousands of men who might have entered the teaching profession "went off to war, often never to teach again" (Lee, 1973). This scarcity of males opened the way for the admission of women into American normal schools. This was a momentous occurrence, marking women's first legitimate access to the possibility of professional training, and in time it would profoundly change the American educational system. Slowly, inexorably, the ratio of women to men within the teaching profession began to shift.

The balance was tipped by the Victorian social climate that prevailed in this country during the late nineteenth and early twentieth centuries. The reigning view of human nature asserted that, for young children to learn, their "hearts must be cultivated before their heads" (Sugg, 1978). Women— potential mothers all, with their "natural" capacity to reach a child's heart—were considered better able to influence the young mind. In addition, women of the era "were assumed to have better moral character than men, thus having a more uplifting influence during the impressionable years of early childhood" (Lee, 1973). Thus a number of social forces and public attitudes converged, and increasing numbers of women entered the teaching profession.

By the 1940s, teaching young children had become so thoroughly a female vocation that "only about one elementary school teacher in 14 was a man" (National Center for Education Statistics, 1979). With the end of World War II, the country turned its attention to the return of "our boys" to socially acceptable roles. The transition was not easily accomplished.

Men who had experienced the rigors of active duty chafed against the demands of "civilian conformity" (Ehrenreich, 1983). Furthermore, women who had taken on men's jobs during the war years were asked to abandon such work and return, without protest, to hearth and home. As the theme of reasserting masculine dominance and autonomy pervaded society, schools mirrored the larger culture. There arose a hue and cry about rescuing boys from the "feminized" environment of the American classroom. Perhaps the strongest voice in the chorus belonged to Patricia Sexton, who wrote:

Schools prepare boys for . . . emasculating white-collar jobs by confining them to deodorized hothouses, rewarding the best desk-sitters . . . converting restless males to the clerical way of life.

. . . [M]any boys are misfits in schools, as out of place as puppies around the good china. They are the school's chief troublemakers and the source of massive apathy and passive resistance to academic learning. We are forced to ask whether it is the boy or the school that is more maladjusted? (1965, p. 57)

Educational research seemed to provide support for the contention that boys were misfits in the classroom—expected by society to develop assertiveness and autonomy, then foiled by female teachers who rewarded passive conformity instead. Teachers were found to prefer dependence, neatness, and compliance in their students; they also directed the lion's share of their criticism and disapproval toward the classroom behavior of boys (Feshbach, 1969; Jackson & Lahaderne, 1967; Lippitt & Gold, 1959; Meyer & Thompson, 1956; Waetzen, 1962).

Several solutions were proposed to rescue boys from these unhappy circumstances. One of the most popular was the establishment of sex-segregated classrooms (Kernkamp & Price, 1972; Lyles, 1966; Tagatz, 1966). Educators took pains to design prototypical all-male environments that would be better attuned to the needs of young boys. Innovations included more physical activity, less seat work, less of a demand for quiet, more science equipment, and bringing such novelties as typewriters and live animals into the classroom. Not surprisingly, when such plans were implemented boys were reported to greatly prefer their lively new classroom regimens.

Another popular solution for saving boys from the detrimental effects of feminized schooling was to encourage more men to enter the teaching profession. In a later review of male and female teaching styles and their effects on students of both sexes, Gold and Reis (1982) characterized the impetus behind this apparently simple strategy: "Presumably, having more male teachers . . . would alter either the psychological environment of the schools or boys' concepts of their sex roles so as to create greater congruity between the two." Although these assumptions went untested, enthusiasm mounted for augmenting the ranks of male teachers. Over time, an almost limitless array of positive outcomes were predicted for those boys lucky enough to be taught by men, even though such claims had little or no empirical support. One catalog of benefits included:

> . . . the prevention of juvenile delinquency . . . ; the improvement of school performance . . . ; the circumvention of family disintegration problems . . . ; the augmentation of sex typing or reinforcing children with a masculine image . . . ; and the change in image of working with young children to a more "masculine" one. (Robinson, 1979, pp. 553-554)

As a group, girls were largely ignored throughout this era of concern over the failure of the educational system to produce sufficiently masculine boys. Signs of dissatisfaction with this neglect coincided with the gathering force of the women's movement during the late 1960s and early 1970s: "The women's liberation movement has caused increased awareness and indignation at unequal treatment of females in all institutions of society, and as one of these institutions, attention is focused on the school" (Frazier & Sadker, 1973, p. 94). Now, in a radical shift of focus, it was the link between girls and sex roles that came to the forefront within the educational system; concerns about the appropriate way to socialize boys lost currency.

The issue that generated the greatest fervor during the next several years was how to structure educational equity for girls in order to promote occupational equity for women. Title IX of the Education Amendments of 1972, enacted to prohibit sex discrimination in federally supported school programs, prompted massive reexamination of gender-linked inequalities, but it was not able to provide the direct programmatic support needed to put new ideas into practice. Then in 1974, Congress enacted the Women's Educational Equity Act Program (WEEAP, reauthorized in 1978), thereby appropriating the first funds ever earmarked for the support of programs to achieve educational equity for girls and women.

A total of 365 WEEAP grants were awarded between 1976 and 1980; all were targeted toward "developmental, demonstration, and dissemination projects of national, statewide, or general significance" (U. S. Department of Education, 1980). Many practical materials were published, including guidebooks, manuals for program replication, audiovisual training materials, and so forth. A review of these materials shows that several projects took the view that sex bias in the schools places limits not only on girls and women, but on boys and men as well. Just as girls were being excluded from "male" options in the work place, boys were being prevented from learning about the "female" domain of nurturance. Signs of movement toward a more inclusive look at the relationship between schools and sex roles became increasingly explicit by the end of the 1970s when the Women's Program Staff funded the development of a curriculum called "Being a Man" (Sadker, 1977) for classroom use with boys and young men. Its author contended:

One of the results of the feminist movement . . . has been to encourage men to pause and think about . . . the effects that sex role stereotyping has had on them. . . . [They] have discovered that sexism is a two-edged sword, and our society is cut deep with sexist restrictions imposed on males as well as females. (Sadker, 1977, p. 1)

A similar curriculum, "As Boys Become Men: Learning New Male Roles," appeared soon after (Thompson, 1980), and was more explicit in its intention to teach boys about developing their capacity for caring. For example, one chapter in the curriculum is called "Fathers and Children"; another is about "Emotions, Relationships, and Beyond." Again, this curriculum focused on the need to take a more balanced view of sex roles in the schools:

It has been too often assumed that sex equity is not a male issue. [I]t is time to challenge that assumption and look carefully at the experience of the male student in today's society. While boys need to understand and accept a more realistic view of the female role based on gender equality, they also need to be freed from the restrictions of the male role stereotype. That stereotype is alive and well in our schools. (Thompson, 1980, p. iii)

The educational pendulum was beginning to swing again, though this time the curve of the arc was to be substantially more gentle. In a relatively short period of time, the educational system had taken several turns, beginning with an emphasis on reinforcing traditional definitions of masculinity. Educators next focused on removing educational barriers to job equity for women, and eventually broadened their concern to include the different—though equally powerful—role restrictions confronted by children of both sexes. Overcoming these restrictions within an educational context meant that girls could receive encouragement to enter careers beyond motherhood and boys could be helped to accept fuller participation in the world beyond paid employment.

Unfortunately, very few practical tools are available to help educators encourage the nurturant capacity of boys and young men. Rather, what exists are a range of undocumented classroom practices—ideas that seem to work but which rarely have been subjected to empirical evaluation. As we turn now to a consideration of some of these ideas, it is important to remember that, in almost every case, we need more information about program effectiveness.

MEN AS ROLE MODELS OF NURTURANT MANHOOD

As we have already seen, enthusiasm for bringing more men into early childhood and elementary school classrooms is not new. Earlier efforts were motivated by the desire to create a more masculine environment in which young boys would perform better. Now a similar strategy is being used in a different way: to provide young children of both sexes with ample exposure to nurturant, caregiving adult men. In some cases this translates into familiar efforts to recruit more male teachers. More typically it means innovative ways of bringing fathers and other caring adult men into the classroom environment, not to teach but to demonstrate by example that men are interested in the experience of schooling. This approach seems particularly promising. Not only are fathers, grandfathers, uncles, and brothers a plentiful resource, but research suggests that, by itself, the strategy of increasing the ranks of male teachers is unlikely to be the panacea it was once assumed to be.

Repeated investigations have shown that when men and women assume the role of classroom teacher, they become considerably more alike than unalike in their styles of teaching (see, for example, Brophy & Good, 1974). In addition, the assumption that boys will perform better when taught by men has received only cautious and limited support. (For a thorough review of this topic, see Gold & Reis, 1982.) In a few studies, boys taught by men in nursery and kindergarten classes have shown greater masculine sex identification, better aptitude for math and spatial relations, and better school attitudes and behavior. However, none of these effects has been widely replicated, and most researchers have found considerably fewer positive effects than they hypothesized. Almost without exception, studies conducted during grades one through three have failed to find any student outcome differences that can be attributed to the sex of the teacher. The results in the upper elementary grades have been mixed: Some studies report gains for boys taught by men, others indicate better school performance and attitudes for children of both sexes when they are taught by women.

Not only is the research evidence equivocal, but there seem to be a variety of social, personal, and professional resistances that limit the rate at which men are willing to enter early childhood and elementary school teaching. These include the distrust of parents, the skepticism of female colleagues, the profession's relatively low wage scale, and the sense of having somehow violated society's expectations for gender-appropriate employment (Milgram & Sciarra, 1974; Seifert, 1973; and others).

Of course, in spite of these barriers it is important that men have the option of choosing a teaching career, and over the last three decades more and more men have been making such a choice. Remember that during the postwar years only 1 elementary school teacher in 14 was a man. Now the figure is closer to one in five (National Center for Education Statistics, 1979). Still, the trend is a slow one, and a practical alternative is to involve more fathers and other caregiving men in the day-to-day life of the classroom, whether or not these men have had any formal training as child-care workers or teachers.

This alternative strategy is being applied in a variety of settings, including a Quaker-run child-care center in Washington, DC; a public elementary school in rural Orient, Iowa; a parent cooperative outside of New York City; a Head Start center in Detroit; and in public school districts scattered across the state of Minnesota (Klinman, Kohl, & The Fatherhood Project, 1984). These different settings have, quite independently, adopted some strikingly similar strategies for involving fathers in the educational system.

First, they schedule special fathers' visitation events at times that allow for the work commitments of most men. Weekday evenings and Saturday mornings are popular times; so are regular classroom hours if fathers are given enough advance notice to rearrange their work schedule. (An interesting by-product of such flexible scheduling has been its appeal to working mothers as well.) When fathers do visit their young child's school, special efforts are made to involve them in classroom activities assumed to be of special interest to men (for example, carpentry or math skills). Frequently there are presentations by teachers, counselors, and principals (again, these focus on issues considered especially relevant to men) followed by informal discussion sessions.

These kinds of special events that bring fathers into the classroom once or twice a year are exciting to children, but they do little to change the ongoing learning context and its messages about gender-appropriate behavior. In fact, by rearranging the classroom schedule and treating male visitors as out of the ordinary, these programs may be subtly perpetuating the very stereotypes they seek to change. Extending the presence of caring adult males in the classroom can be accomplished through simple alterations in the daily curriculum: introducing children to storybooks about male caregivers, or encouraging children to write and talk about the men in their lives. Of course, it is important to note that all of these strategies need to be used with particular sensitivity to the needs and experiences of the many children who grow up in father-absent homes. These children should be encouraged to share their school experiences with other adult men in their lives: grandfathers, uncles, brothers, neighbors, friends, and so forth.

For the most part, then, these early childhood classroom innovations represent relatively minor low-cost alterations in schedule, activity focus, or curriculum. They tend to be initiated by individual educators—most frequently, male teachers or principals who report relatively little institutional support for their efforts. While they seem to be effective in bringing more male visitors into the classroom context, they generally fall short of achieving much ongoing classroom participation by fathers.

One further example differs in several ways. The Minnesota Council on Quality Education, initiated by that state's legislature during the early 1970s, provides funds for about 30 Early Childhood and Family Education (ECFE) programs, all of which are designed to enhance the relationship between parents and young children. While fathers are routinely invited to take advantage of all program components—discussion groups and family social events are typical—in about half a dozen cases specific father-child programs have been operating quite successfully for a number of years: for example, "Daddy and Me" at the Bloomington Family Center in Bloomington, and the "Dad's Group" at the Powderhorn Parent Project in Minneapolis (Klinman, Kohl, & The Fatherhood Project, 1984).

These programs meet weekly over the course of the school year, providing fathers and their children with "special" time to be together in settings that capitalize on the material and human resources of the public school system. These programs achieve unusually high and sustained levels of father involvement in the schools; other program effects have not been evaluated, although the need for more information is being highlighted by increasing competition for available state funds.

'HANDS-ON' CHILD-CARE EXPERIENCE FOR MALES

By the time children reach the age of about 10 years, school-based efforts to develop the nurturing potential of boys shift from the strategy of learning from role models to learning by doing. That is, some educators try to structure the kinds of "hands-on" educational experiences that encourage boys to try out the behaviors and feelings associated with caring for children. In most cases this involves some opportunity for boys to spend time taking care of infants or toddlers, often through the cooperation of a nearby child-care center.

When designed for preadolescents, these programs are usually billed as "babysitter training," and they are attractive to their young participants because of the promise of eventual paid work. Most of these efforts are initiated, developed, and run by women; in addition, unless there is considerable thought and attention devoted to strategies for attracting boys, they tend to be overwhelmingly female in their patterns of attendance. Unfortunately, the number of settings where boys are actively encouraged to participate in child-care activities is quite small, and the involvement of the public schools in such efforts is virtually nonexistent. This may reflect, in some measure, the expense involved in developing, staffing, and equipping this kind of innovation.

There are at least two interesting and stable examples of programs designed to provide preadolescent boys with direct opportunities to take care of young children (Klinman, Kohl, & The Fatherhood Project, 1984). One, which has been ongoing for nearly 10 years, operates at the Collegiate School, a private all-boys' school in New York City. It is structured as an after-school elective and involves a 10-week series of skill-based instruction in the basics of infant care. This program has gained a certain amount of celebrity thanks to the publication of a picture-storybook that describes its approach (Herzig & Mali, 1980) and the more recent production of an NBC after-school television special for children. The second program is one designed to teach the basics of preparenthood education to boys as well as girls from an early age; it operates at Germantown Friends School, a private coeducational Quaker school in Philadelphia. This program combines didactic instruction in a formal child-development curriculum with hands-on child-care experience throughout the school year. Additional examples of school-based child-care programs for preadolescents do, of course, exist, but they usually have difficulty both in attracting male participants and in maintaining their funding base over time. Again, they tend to operate in privately funded settings, and little is known about their effectiveness.

During the junior and senior high school years, opportunities for hands-on child-care experience are frequently included as components of preparenthood education classes within the public school system. Traditionally, such classes have been part of the home economics curriculum, long the domain of females both as teachers and as students. As recently as the last decade, "about 95% of the students in courses related to parenthood were young women" (Bartz, 1980). More recently there have been signs of progress in attempts to achieve federally mandated sex equity by balancing the ratio of male to female students in such programs. Interestingly, even small gains are sometimes highly touted, perhaps because they provide tangible evidence of success in overcoming the still powerful resistances which operate to exclude most young men from child-care experiences.

Unfortunately, even when young men do enroll in relevant classes, they have little opportunity to gain hands-on child-care experience, even though experiential programs that work well with young women of the same age cohort, and which could be adapted for use with young men, are common. One well-known example is the result of the "Education for Parenthood" initiative, launched in 1972 as a cooperative venture of the U. S. Office of Education, the Office of Child Development, and the National Institute of Mental Health. This initiative had two major components: to develop a high school classroom curriculum combining formal instruction in child development with direct experience in caring for young children, and to develop a similar curriculum for use by national voluntary youth-serving organizations (e.g., Boy Scouts, Girl Scouts, 4-H clubs).

Of the two, the school component had the benefit of more sustained financial support. The curriculum it produced, "Exploring Childhood" (Education Development Center, 1975), is a year-long, coeducational program for use in grades 7 through 12. By the end of the 1970s, this curriculum was being implemented in more than 2600 schools, 450 colleges and universities, and about 800 community agencies throughout the country (National Institute of Mental Health, 1978).

This curriculum is unusual not only for its widespread dissemination but also because it has been empirically evaluated in schools throughout North Dakota, South Dakota, and Minnesota (Mokros, 1982). Overall, the findings of this study suggest that exposure to the "Exploring Childhood" curriculum can have positive effects on the knowledge, attitudes, and actual parenting skills of participating students, and that young men may benefit most of all.

As in other evaluations, the current study demonstrated that girls are not only more likely to elect parenting and child development courses, but they also enter these courses with more knowledge about children, greater confidence in their childcare skills, and a more developed ability to analyze childrearing situations.

Yet, the small number of boys who enrolled in these courses clearly benefited from them. The study suggests the intriguing possibility that students who have little previous experience with children—*especially boys*—stand to benefit the most from parenting courses with field work components. Educators need to find ways to convince boys that parent education is an equal opportunity enterprise. (Mokros, 1982, p. 9)

But to convince young men of this, educators need to overcome a variety of barriers: peer pressure, parental attitudes, the lack of male involvement as teachers of home economics courses. In addition, for most adolescent males the eventuality of fatherhood is considerably less pressing than the imminent realities of finishing school and preparing to enter the labor market or college, so that their motivation to participate in child-care classes may be minimal. Of course, there are several hundred thousand teenage males who actually become fathers every year. Although these young men could benefit greatly from the opportunity to receive hands-on child-care training, they can find practical assistance in only a handful of educational settings anywhere in the country. One multisite attempt to remedy this situation is the Teen Father Collaboration, which now operates programs for young fathers in eight cites around the country (Klinman et al., 1986).

FATHERS AS CONSUMERS OF PARENT EDUCATION

The general neglect of adolescent fathers is not so surprising, given that parent-education programs for fathers of any age are relatively new, even though this country has a long tradition of providing formal and informal instruction in the art of motherhood (Brim, 1959). Parent education takes many forms: books and articles on child rearing, professional consultation, lectures and presentations, structured programs, and many combinations of these components. While it is difficult to estimate how many participants enroll in parent-education programs every year, the relative lack of participation by fathers is clear.

The overwhelming majority of parent education participants are women and have been throughout the history of the endeavor. A great many programs, of course, are specifically targeted at women. Others, such as printed materials, theoretically are available equally to both sexes; however, a recent study by Clarke-Stewart (1977) showed that mothers are more likely to read printed matter on parenthood. . . . Articles on child rearing are almost exclusively the domain of magazines and journals aimed at a female readership (Wolfe, 1977) and have always been geared to mothers rather than fathers. In organized parent education courses women also dominate. . . .

The notion, deeply embedded in Western culture, that mothers bear the primary responsibility for child rearing is clearly manifest in participation patterns of programs aimed at assisting parents in the performance of their roles. (Harman & Brim, 1980, pp. 105–106)

Because parent education programs have multiple goals and are broadly defined, they are somewhat more likely to occur under the aegis of various nonschool institutions–community mental health centers, social service agencies, recreational facilities, churches, hospitals–than within formal educational settings. Community-based parent-education programs specifically targeted to fathers are becoming increasingly available all around the country, often as extensions of the literally thousands of programs that already exist to serve mothers. Programs designed just for fathers and sponsored by educational institutions are far less common, but are more prevalent than school-based programs for young boys or adolescent males. Regardless of setting, the majority of parent-education programs tend to focus on certain stages of child development to the exclusion of others: infancy, the years between age 1 and 3, and adolescence seem to be the times when parents seek the most assistance and information (Harman & Brim, 1980).

Instances of parent education programs targeted to male audiences that exist within formal educational settings include fathering classes at Los Medanos College, Santa Barbara College, and Napa Valley College, all in California; and at Boston University, the University of Akron (Ohio), and the University of North Dakota (Klinman, Kohl, and The Fatherhood Project, 1984). One additional example is particularly interesting, since its approach has spread to several colleges in the state of Washington and to other communities throughout the country as well. In 1971, Seattle Community College launched a new concept in parent education: The program, called "Living and Learning with Baby," was based on the premise of experiential learning. Young mothers brought their infant with them when they attended classes on child care and child development, and learned by doing. An immediate success, this model attracted the attention of Seattle's fathers, who lobbied for a class of their own. When the community college established a Saturday morning father-child program in September 1975, it was the first of its kind anywhere in the country. Still in operation, this weekly program (which offers full college credit to fathers who complete its requirements) has three major components: experiential learning, mutual support, and the leadership of male early-childhood specialists, often fathers themselves. These components form the basis for similar programs at Washington State University in Pullman and Clark College in Vancouver. In addition, this experiential model underlies a program developed by the University of Washington in Seattle for fathers of young handicapped children—a critically underserved population of men throughout the country.

SUMMARY AND RECOMMENDATIONS

The American educational system, reflecting a long history of social change, now provides education beyond the boundaries of traditional sex roles to at least some young women. However, this is still not the case for the great majority of males. While some innovations do exist to encourage the nurturant potential of boys and men and greater involvement by fathers in the schools, they are largely undocumented, untested, and little known.

Nevertheless, there are interesting signs of change in three arenas of the educational system: attempts to bring more fathers into preschool and early childhood settings to serve as role models of male involvement, opportunities for boys and young men to learn about child care through first-hand experience, and increasing numbers of parent-education classes targeted to an all-male audience.

Efforts to bring fathers and other caring men into the early childhood classroom have had moderate success but have generally failed to achieve sustained father involvement in the schools, perhaps because they begin with the assumption that father involvement is "special" or "unusual." Fathers who are concerned about their child's experience of schooling should be matter of factly informed about and included in as many school-related events as possible, while the classroom itself should provide opportunities for children of both sexes to learn about and practice role flexibility.

School-based programs that provide hands-on child-care experience for young boys are costly, and only anecdotal evidence suggests that such early experiences have lasting effects on eventual styles of fathering. On the other hand, experiential child-care classes may help young boys become more open to caring experiences throughout childhood and adolescence. During the teenage years, it would be relatively inexpensive to increase male enrollment in parenting programs that already exist, although educators must make a concerted effort to overcome the resistances that still operate to exclude most young men from such experiences. In particular, the schools need to focus on a currently underserved population of males by targeting their parent-education programs to the hundreds of thousands of adolescents who actually become fathers every year in this country.

As for parenting-education programs for fathers, again it seems that experiential models hold the most promise for involving increasing numbers of men. In general, men who have already become fathers are more receptive to parenting education than are preparenting males, and community-based settings—perhaps because of their flexibility and informality—seem more successful than traditional school settings in attracting men as program participants. Certain populations of men are largely neglected, including fathers of school-aged children older than toddlers and younger than teenagers and fathers whose children have special educational needs because of handicapping conditions.

All in all, the strategies discussed in this chapter present promising evidence that the American educational system is beginning to recognize the importance of encouraging boys and men to take an expanded view of their potential for nurturing the young. While much work remains to be done, innovative educators throughout the country have already laid the groundwork for important kinds of change at every level of the educational system.

REFERENCES

Bartz, K. (1980). Parenting education for youth. In M. Fine (Ed.), *Handbook on parent education.* New York: Academic.

Brim, O. (1959). *Education for child rearing.* New York: Russell Sage Foundation.

Brophy, J., & Good, T. (1974). *Teacher-student relationships: Causes and consequences.* New York: Holt, Rinehart and Winston.

Clarke-Stewart, A. (1977). Parameters of parent education in the United States. In Final Report, *seminar in the care of the child.* Chicago: University of Chicago.

Education Development Center (1975). *Exploring childhood.* Newton, MA: Education Development Center.

Ehrenreich, B. (1983). *The hearts of men: American dreams and the flight from commitment.* Garden City, NY: Anchor/Doubleday.

Feshbach, N. (1969). Student teacher preference for elementary school pupils varying in personality characteristics. *Journal of Educational Psychology, 60,* 126–132.

Frazier, N., & Sadker, M. (1973). *Sexism in school and society.* New York: Harper and Row.

Gold, D., & Reis, M. (1982). Male teacher effects on young children: A theoretical and empirical consideration. *Sex Roles: A Journal of Research, 8* (5), 493–513.

Harman, D., & Brim, O. (1980). *Learning to be parents: Principles, programs, and methods.* Beverly Hills, CA: Sage.

Herzig, A. & Mali, A. (1980). *Oh, boy! Babies!.* Boston: Little, Brown.

Jackson, P., & Lahaderne, H. (1967). Inequalities of teacher-pupil contacts. *Psychology in the Schools, 4,* 204–211.

Kernkamp, E., & Price, E. (1972). Co-education may be a 'no-no' for the 6-year-old boy. *Phi Delta Kappa* (Bloomington, IN), *53,* 662–663.

Klinman, D., Kohl, R., & The Fatherhood Project (1984). *Fatherhood U.S.A.: The first national guide to programs, services, and resources for and about fathers.* New York: Garland.

Klinman, D., Sander, J., Rosen, J., & Longo, K. (1986). The teen father collaboration: A demonstration and research model. In M. Lamb & A. Elster (Eds.), *Adolescent fatherhood.* Hillsdale, NJ: Erlbaum.

Lee, P. (1973). Male and female teachers in elementary school: An ecological analysis. *Teachers College Record* (New York), *75*(1).

Lippitt, R., & Gold, M. (1959). Classroom social structure as a mental health problem. *Journal of Social Issues*, *15*, 40–49.

Lyles, T. (1966). Grouping by sex. *The National Elementary School Principal*, *46*, 38–41.

Meyer, W., & Thompson, G. (1956). Sex differences in the distribution of teacher approval and disapproval among sixth-grade children. *Journal of Educational Psychology*, *47*, 385–396.

Milgram, J., & Sciarra, D. (1974). Male preschool teacher: The realities of acceptance. *The Educational Forum*, 245–247.

Mokros, J. (1982). *Evaluating the effectiveness of parent education courses for adolescents* (Report). Newton, MA: Education Development Center.

National Center for Education Statistics (1979). *Digest of education statistics.* Washington, DC: U.S. Department of Health, Education and Welfare.

National Institute of Mental Health (1978). *Directory of child rearing programs suitable for school-age parents*. Rockville, MD: National Institute of Mental Health.

Robinson, B. (1979). Men caring for the young: An androgynous perspective. *The Family Coordinator*, 553–560.

Sadker, D. (1977). *Being a man: A unit of instructional activities on male role stereotyping.* Washington, DC: U.S. Department of Health, Education and Welfare.

Seifert, K. (1973). Some problems of men in child care center work. *Child Welfare*, *52*(3), 167–171.

Sexton, P. (1965). Are schools emasculating our boys? *Saturday Review*, *48*, 57.

Sexton, P. (1976). *Women in education.* Bloomington, IN: Phi Delta Kappa.

Sugg, R. (1978). The feminization of American education. In *Motherteacher.* Charlottesville: University Press of Virginia.

Tagatz, G. (1966). Grouping by sex at the first and second grade. *Journal of Educational Research*, *59*, 415–418.

Thompson, D. (1980). *As boys become men: Learning new male roles.* Denver: University of Colorado Institute for Equality in Education.

U. S. Department of Education (1980). *Women's Educational Equity Act Program annual report.* Washington, DC: U. S. Department of Education.

Waetzen, W. (1962). Is learning sexless? *Education Digest*, *28*, 12–14.

Wolfe, A. (1977). Parent education in popular literature. In *Final report, seminar on the care of the child*. Chicago: University of Chicago Press.

CHAPTER 16

Today's Father and the Social Services Delivery System: A False Promise

FRANK G. BOLTON, JR.

Arizona Department of Economic Security

The twentieth century social service professional is asked to deliver services with a nineteenth century perspective on the family. Under the burden of this antiquated view of families, and in the absence of a uniform family policy responsive to changes in family structure and function, social services continue to approach family problems differentially by family members' role. To avoid tedious historical explanation at this point, it may be easiest to describe this pattern of differential responsiveness as one built on gradations of responsibility within the family unit.

Within this system of graduated responsibility, the more responsible a person *should be* for the family, and the more responsible that person *may be* for the problems the family faces, the less help the person will receive from social services. Thus children are the most protected, mothers are ambivalently protected, and fathers are essentially ignored or even condemned. While much attention has been focused previously on service delivery problems of mothers and children, this chapter describes how the not-so-subtle paternal exclusion became a feature of the social services delivery system.

By way of introduction, consider the fundamental mismatch between fathers and social services. First, the concept of father-in-need is an oxymoron in social services. In the social services' definition of "family," a father who is present is a father who is (or should be) a provider. Almost any departure from this belief is uncomfortable. The resultant antipathy toward fathers-in-need borders on "blaming-the-victim" (Ryan, 1970). Second, alterations in paternal roles have gone virtually unrecognized by social services planners (Sagi & Sharon, 1984). Finally, fathers as a group have not advocated well for themselves (Klinman, Kohl, and The Fatherhood Project, 1984). Each of these points are elaborated on here.

While the aforementioned obstacles to service acquisition have been fundamental elements of social services for decades, changing paternal roles have elevated their importance. The failure to serve fathers is no longer simply an irritant to families. Rather it is becoming an increasingly destructive and even lethal reality that impacts a growing number of American families, families more dependent on fathers for a wider variety of roles than ever before. America can no longer afford a social services system that systematically separates some fathers from their family as a consequence of stereotypically defined perceptions of his role(s). One mechanism for altering this course is an expansion of that stereotypical view.

"WHERE'S POPPA?" THE "FAMILY" IN SOCIAL SERVICES

There is no uniform family policy in the United States (Steiner, 1981), no operational definition that guides service delivery. Apparently the definition of "family" is thought to be obvious. Services that are founded on "obvious" and intractable beliefs soon become artifacts, dinosaurs of an earlier age unable to respond to today's requirements. Some of this intractability can be found in the social services response to fathers. Fathers are not treated as the heterogeneous group of individuals they are. Rather they are treated as stereotypes who are either playing the role of paternal provider (the good guys) or not (the bad guys). In this way the family defines the father, rather than the reverse.

Through strict adherence to tradition and the ignoring of societal change, social services programming continues to embrace a view of families that finds fathers performing executive tasks (e.g., wage earning) and mothers performing nurturing tasks (e.g., homemaking and child rearing). The fact that only 16 percent of American families are currently operating with distinct sex roles of this type (Ross & Sawhill, 1975) fails to sweep this treasured belief from the bureaucratic mind. In defense of today's social services planners, however, it is not difficult to understand how such thinking became entrenched.

When rhetoric is stripped away, social services exist to keep social roles in balance. Defining family as a set of gender-related roles enables "the system" to step into a role when the individual ordinarily responsible falls down on the job. The result is a system that offers executive services (e.g., unemployment insurance) should the father fail and survival services (e.g., Aid to Families with Dependent Children) should the mother be thrown into an executive role through the father's absence (e.g., going to work). The implied expectation is that, if the father were there to perform his executive functions, this dependence would not occur. This introduces another subtlety of the social services' view of the father-in-need—blame.

DEFINING THE VICTIM: WHO'S AT FAULT?

There will always be more persons in need of social services than there are resources to serve them. Those most in need must be selected in some manner. Strategies for selection have their roots in earlier eras, for example, the British Poor Laws.

Within the "Poor Law" system, individuals were among the "worthy poor" if their dependence was not of their own making (e.g., a mother whose husband had died or abandoned her). Mothers and children were seen as victims, while fathers were seen as victimizers. Eligibility selection based on causation (self or others) persists, although not as obviously as in times past. The father-in-need is a victim of this legacy. In the absence of catastrophic events, fathers are not to become dependent or ask for help. To do so not only violates definitions of "family" but belies expected "father" behavior.

There exists an unreasonable stereotype of the American father. This stereotypical father is fiercely independent and will struggle against anything that might interfere with his self-sufficiency (e.g., welfare dependence). He provides a more abundant and successful life for his children than he has known. He is able to motivate the family to elevate itself, by its own bootstraps if necessary. In short, a "real father" reaches continuously toward independence and self-sufficiency, lives up to social expectations, and places his family outside the need for social altruism. This is a positive stereotype which is extremely destructive.

Fathers are measured against this positive stereotype. That father who fails to struggle against dependence, who must helplessly accept a one-down social position for himself and his family, and who is genuinely dependent on social altruism generates a destructive question: "What kind of a man would let that happen to his family?" The destructiveness of this question is that it is answered through oversimplified negative stereotyping.

NEGATIVE PATERNAL STEREOTYPING IN SOCIAL SERVICES DELIVERY

What has gone before in this chapter suggests the following hypothesis: If a father does not present himself to the social services system as having tried to play traditional father roles and failed through no fault of his own, he will be considered an aberration. This is secondary victimization by a system that assumes the father who does not fit the popular stereotype will fit a negative stereotype. These stereotypes are inaccurate and destructive, and they rob the father of his opportunity to be assessed and treated as a unique individual.

There are several reasons why negative paternal stereotypes continue to exist within the social services system. First, although the public is unfamiliar with the father-in-need, its general impression is a negative one. This is an extension of the "What kind of man . . . ?" question. Second, the level of public financing of social services is only sufficient to prevent outright chaos. Yet the public expectation is that social services will enable independent functioning. When this does not happen, the search for a person at fault usually ends with the father. After all, if it weren't for his inadequacy the family would not be in this condition. Third, both the public and professionals have difficulty connecting events in individual's lives to the repressive social realities that dictate the occurrence of these events (especially if the public and professionals are a part of the event). Finally, the father-in-need is a reminder to both the public and professionals of their own dependence on their job and the pressures of survival (Duncan, 1984). Their need to see themselves as different from the father-in-need is great. As a result, the stereotypical denigration of this father serves as a mechanism for distancing, security, and self-elevation.

In sum, an overloaded system, professionals who are frustrated in their efforts, a public that supports one level of service and expects another, and professionals who face complex family problems with few clear mechanisms for intervention provide a ripe medium for the generation of negative stereotypes. A stereotype is an answer, even if it is a wrong answer. Whether or not the stereotype provides a wall to separate the social services professional from someone he or she dislikes, fears, or identifies with too closely, the stereotype is real. Stereotypes of "bad fathers" can be separated into the following categories:

1. *The deserter.* This is the most commonly held negative paternal stereotype. The deserting father has been overexposed through academic reports (Moynihan, 1965), official statistics (Moles, 1979), and the popular press (*Newsweek*, 1965). The stereotype can be accurate, such as the father who refuses to pay child support.

The tragedy of this stereotype is that a father who does leave the family may simply be an unemployed father who is forced to leave to allow his family to be eligible for social services (Steiner, 1981). Steiner estimated that 18 percent of fathers absent from families receiving income supplements are absent for this reason. This may be an iatrogenic problem in social services policy.

2. *The manipulator.*   Approximately 80 percent of a social services agency's resources are concentrated on 20 percent of the families (Bolton, 1983). The repetitive contact and the chaotic disorganization these families present give the appearance of the families' manipulating the system through their apparent failure to benefit from services. The term in social services for such a family, and for the father within it, is "agency-wise."

The manipulator has become a public villian. He or she is believed to have discovered the secret to living well at taxpayer expense. As anyone familiar with the social services system knows, the person who can live well through the level of support provided by public assistance should not be known as "manipulator" but as "magician."

3. *The sire.*   The "brood sow" theory posits that welfare-dependent mothers seek to become pregnant in order to receive increased welfare benefits (Placek & Hendershot, 1974). The paternal counterpart to this has been empirically disproven (Furstenberg, Lincoln, & Menken, 1981).

Parents on public assistance are too wise to play this "zero-sum" game. Proportional benefits per child decrease as the absolute number of children increases and net income decreases. Parents on public assistance know this. It is much more likely that multiple parenthood is a product of carelessness in or ignorance of contraceptive precautions.

4. *The putative father.*   Although this term is slowly disappearing, it continues to be used as a description for the adolescent father. This use highlights the frequent paternal absence that characterizes the adolescent pregnancy. It is used without consideration of the reasons why the adolescent father is not available. Consequently it becomes destructive through its propensity to discourage searching for and working with such fathers (Elster & Lamb, 1986).

5. *The malingerer.*   Fathers who fail to "bring home the bacon" are suspect. The father with a condition that prevents self-sufficiency, especially if the condition is not immediately observable, is not confirmed by physical medicine, or has an unappealing etiology, may have difficulty receiving benefits. Acquiring full benefits can be much harder than finding employment. As a result, malingering can become contagious—the whole family may suffer.

6. *The perpetrator*. In many situations the father is guilty before proven innocent. This is true in aggressive events (child abuse) as well as passive events (inability to locate employment). Both are the father's "fault." In response, services are focused on mother and child. In the best case, token services are provided the father. In the worse case, social services agencies abandon him entirely.

Whether it is evidenced through definition or through services that will be provided if he is in need, the social services' view of fathers is too narrow and homogeneous. The father is expected to find a way to meet his familial responsibilities. If he does not, and his dependence on the system does not have demonstrable external causality, he is placed among the "unworthy poor" and services are delivered reluctantly if at all. This reluctance to serve begins with the initial construction of the system itself.

A FALSE START: THE SEARCH FOR A FATHER'S SOCIAL SERVICES SYSTEM

The first element thought to isolate fathers from social services is the fact that a "needy father" does not fit acceptable definitions. The second is an antipathy or ambivalence toward fathers-in-need, which grew out of the father's suspicious departure from accepted paternal roles. A third element would be the record of what has not been accomplished for fathers, which is longer than the record of what has been accomplished. A clinician might well describe this as a "passive-aggressive" attitude toward fathers.

From the early 1900s to the mid 1970s, social services all but ignored the father. For example, Aid to Families with Dependent Children (AFDC), more honestly entitled "mother's aid," initially targeted mothers and children abandoned by fathers, perhaps the genesis of the deserting-father stereotype. Only very slowly did the recognition arrive that families may struggle to survive even with a healthy father in the home. The federal response to this uncomfortable awareness (i.e., "Why doesn't he want to work?") was the AFDC-U program, which gives states the option of including special income to families in which an unemployed father is living in the home. Few states have sought to match the federal contribution making this possible.

Even in his limited role of "biological necessity" (Parke, 1981, p. 1), the father was denied recognition and identity. Maternal and child health defined medical programs; paternal health went largely unconsidered. Paternal roles in the family planning, pregnancy, labor, and delivery were unrecognized. The father's eventual participation in this critical part of his child's life was largely the result of pressure from the women's movement and medical care marketing. Left to their own devices, it is questionable whether public human services systems would have recognized the father's potential contributions. After all, labor and delivery are not "executive functions."

It is through "executive functions" that social services has recognized fathers. In fact, it is argued that fathers are better supported (at least economically) by unemployment, disability, and social security benefits than mothers are by any of the maternally directed programs (e.g., AFDC). Although arguable, this point ignores the reality that only those fathers who present with a need that matches narrow program eligibility are served. If the father in need is (1) a father who is unemployed but wishes to remain with his family, (2) a father who, by choice, is a single-father head of household who prefers a nurturant role, or (3) a father isolated from his children and their mother involuntarily (e.g., the adolescent or incarcerated father), there is little hope that social services can serve him effectively. Such contingencies have not been anticipated in our antiquated system.

Two examples from current practice may bring this point home. The first, an individual who plays nothing more than a biological role in his "families," finds a responsive system. The second, an individual who seeks to play a nurturant role in his family, finds the system elusive.

SELECTIVE RESPONSIVENESS: A TALE OF TWO FATHERS

The first father is known as "Pops." This "street name" grows out of the fact that he has fathered an unknown number of children by an unknown number of women in the government housing project in which he lives. At least five young mothers have delivered children reportedly fathered by this man. These mothers and their children have received public medical care since conception. They receive supplemental income. Although unemployed, they are eligible for job training, G.E.D. classes, homemaker services, emergency assistance, and crisis intervention services. Periodically they place their children in voluntary foster care or in a crisis nursery reimbursed through governmental monies. When the children were newborns, a nurse-social worker team assessed mother and child in the hospital and conducted follow-up visits in their home for up to one full year. This team remains only a telephone call away.

In contrast, consider Jerry. Jerry is an adolescent who fathered a child with a young woman with whom he had been "going steady" for about a year. They would like to be a "family," but income and parental attitudes interfere. Jerry elected to drop out of school to work in a fast-food restaurant in order to supplement the public assistance that the mother receives through their child's eligibility. She lives with her parents who are antagonistic toward Jerry. He does not see her, or their child, on a regular basis, but does contribute what money he can. Jerry does not see his old friends as a result of his lack of free time and because they do not understand the responsibilities he takes so seriously. His parents are angry, and all relationships within his family have taken a turn for the worse. He wants to be a real father, but recognizes that his chances are slight.

"Pops" and "Jerry," although oversimplified here, are reasonably representative of fathers in social services caseloads today. They are "fathers" of today; fathers who do not fit tight definitions and for whom there are no preexisting services. No one would suggest that the mothers and children described here should have their services reduced in any way. However, it is clear that definitional narrowness, pervasive antipathy, and inadequate program design have led to a service gap. Fathers who wish to play nurturant roles (roles completely acceptable within paternal behavior today) are not supported. Perhaps worse than not supporting these fathers because they do not fit eligibility criteria, the system is also inhibiting today's lower-income fathers from striving to become more involved in the nonexecutive functions of their family. It is at this point that a fourth causal factor in the lack of services to fathers—lack of recognition of new paternal roles—comes into play.

BUREAUCRATIC BLINDERS: THE INVISIBILITY OF CHANGING PATERNAL ROLES

According to Parke, "We didn't just forget fathers by accident; we ignored them on purpose because of our assumption that they were less important than mothers in influencing the developing child" (1981, p.4). Somehow, social services decision making has failed to recognize the social, economic, and political context of today's paternal roles. With regard to fatherhood, social services appear to accept Parke's thesis and are thus fixated in a different historical era than is modern social and behavioral research.

A constantly growing body of evidence points to the father's being more critical to all family roles than was previously recognized. Executive functions that serve as the building blocks of social services definitions and program design describe only one possible role. In addition, such elements as the cognitive capacity of the child, school performance, the child's general happiness, the paternal partner's ability to discipline effectively, the child's security and self-esteem and overall progress toward normal physical, social, and emotional development are all described as responsive to paternal presence and interaction (Kotelchuck, 1976; Lamb, 1978, Lamb, 1981; Lewis & Feiring, 1978; Parke, 1981; Sullivan & McDonald, 1979). And these are influences that continue to be critical even after family separation or divorce (Wallerstein & Kelly, 1982).

Paternal presence, quality of interaction, perceived competence, strength, self-confidence, and cognitive style are all known to influence relationships in the family (Radin, 1981). Both parents must be seen as contributors, especially to adequate psychological development of children (Lamb, 1981). The absence of a father is certain to influence overall family development and operation (Belsky, 1981). The question remains, When will social services programming begin to respond to this knowledge?

Social services' view of the family and the delivery system designed to match is described by a bilateral task system (mother versus father) that not only never meets but rarely even crosses. To consider (and programmatically prepare for) the possibility that one parent might play a role ordinarily identified with the other becomes an impossible task. Social services steps in when one of the role players is absent or failing through no fault of his or her own. If this occurs, the remaining parent is supposed to continue playing the role assigned to it by gender tradition. If the parent does otherwise, social services will in some cases withdraw support.

Taken to an extreme, failure of social services to recognize the possibility of interchangeable parental roles destroys families. If the father must leave to have his family supported, a family has been destroyed through no fault of its own. If a mother is forced to use child support and enforcement agents to squeeze an inadequate support payment out of a father who cannot afford it, the father may hide and withdraw all contact from his children. If an adolescent father is unable to receive support for his family until he finishes school, he may terminate his education and place his family at risk for ongoing poverty. If the single custodial father must place his children in the hands of other caretakers in order to work, he exposes those children to unknown risk. The list could go on, but the point is clear: To social services the lowest common denominator of "family" is mother and child. They survive quite well as a unit without "him." This is a clear case of the punishment offered to the unworthy poor (i.e., the father-in-need).

This chapter has described flawed and antiquated definitions for fathers, which result in underserved paternal populations; negative paternal stereotypes offered by a system that cannot understand how a man can play his role in any manner except one; a system that is built without programs for fathers and is surprised by the father who presents with a need; and finally a system that fails to recognize that the social responsibility demanded of the father is far greater than the narrow corner previously held for him in the family unit. The true tragedy, however, is that a system that exists to serve in reality punishes.

The father-in-need meets with a flat or negative response from the social services system because he is being punished—punished for not being who we once, unreasonably, expected him to be in every case. Ironically, those who pay the largest price in this punishment are the very mothers and children that the social services system considers to be innocent victims, worthy poor, and the focus of service. This represents the secondary victimization that characterizes participation in the social services system. The social services solution, to the poor, all too often means being victimized by the system that seeks to help but does not understand. The system, in this way, is self-perpetuating, but it is also destructive to the family it seeks to save, a curious paradox. However, until very recently fathers themselves contributed little time and energy to changing this reality.

STAND UP AND ACT LIKE A MAN!: ADVOCACY BY FATHERS

Mothers are a group; persons have little difficulty describing them as a group through their common roles. Fathers have very few common group identities, and those available seem either esoteric (custodial fathers) or negative (incarcerated fathers) and subject to social stigma. Who then represents the paternal interests of men who have no identified problem? No one.

A small group of social and behavioral science researchers is championing new paternal roles, but its voice is small, scientifically cautious (appropriately), and apolitical. An even smaller group of educated fathers makes news through such actions as suing employers for paternity leave, but it is seen as an oddity. The implication is clear, that until fathers begin to advocate for themselves, as a group in the political arena, change will not be forthcoming. The further implication is that it is time for the social services system to become more responsive to fathers.

NO PLACE TO HIDE: SEEKING CHANGE IN "THE SYSTEM"

Social services professionals know that what they are doing is not working. They are not serving families as they would wish, and they are seeing the same families with the same problems over and over again. It may be that they are not focusing on the problem, are treating the signs and symptoms of the pathology rather than the pathology itself, and are losing perspective on prevention in their frantic effort to undertake rehabilitation. It is likely that the father is more critical in these failures than is realized.

It is time that persons in social services take a studied look at what is believed to be the fathers' roles in the family. The purpose and range of these roles seem to have changed in today's world. It is time to review stereotypical perceptions of fathers from an empirical perspective. It is likely that on empirical examination, the "bad guys" (who take on a larger-than-life appearance when found in a caseload) will prove to be small in number given the vast number of families seeking help. It is time to enumerate the roles in a "family" from a nonsexist perspective. Only through this more comprehensive view will the system be able to count the father among its allies in keeping the family unit together.

It is time to stop wasting energy trying to create families that match our outmoded stereotypes. Resources should be used to enable families of varying descriptions to provide safe, secure, and productive homes for the children within them. We must recognize that need is not gender related. How long can we support gender-related service strategies in social services and still honestly claim to aid family units? The historical gap that exists between roles in the family today and our stubborn view of how things should be must be closed. "How things should be" is described by safe, happy, secure, and capable family units that can contribute to society as well as to the growth of children. Any "shoulds" beyond that are also beyond our right to comment.

Social services professionals today are being given a rare opportunity to stand at the forefront of change, rather than being behind and trying to catch up as in the past. Social services programs in the past have responded with understanding to such socially stigmatized situations as juvenile delinquency, domestic violence, and even sex crimes, but they cannot seem to hurdle the need to recognize new paternal roles.

If social services professionals do not present new options for fathers, it is doubtful that any other major societal representatives will, at least in an organized fashion. The lower socioeconomic status families that these professionals advocate for will not have the opportunity to benefit from the new importance given to the father's role in the family. If strengthening of all family units is to be honestly sought, then this advocacy must be undertaken. The time has come to embark on nontraditional programs within social services that serve fathers, all fathers. The Fatherhood Project of the Bank Street College, through its cataloging of innovative father programs (Klinman, Kohl, & The Fatherhood Project, 1984), has shown us it can be done. Now is the time to reach beyond these initial steps.

In summary, the time has come to redefine the social realities that dictate social services design and practice. Family policy and practice must be reviewed to determine their efficacy in today's world. Social services must change their focus from the dishonest one of mother and child (disguised as "family") to a full view of all of the actors. A realistic inventory of resources and their targets must be taken and a willingness to alter programs be offered. Stereotypes must be eliminated, policy appropriately widened, resources redirected, and priorities more equitably set. This process will be painful, to be certain. But a realistic appraisal of the pain that social services programs have caused fathers and families in the past through antiquated thinking and responses suggests that it is a small price to pay.

REFERENCES

Belsky, J. (1981). Early human experience: A family perspective. *Developmental Psychology, 17*(1), 3–23.

Bolton, F. G., Jr. (1983). *When bonding fails: Clinical assessment of the high risk family.* Beverly Hills, CA: Sage.

Duncan, G. J. (1984). *Years of poverty, years of plenty: The change of economic fortunes of American workers and families.* Ann Arbor: University of Michigan Institute for Social Research.

Elster, A. B., & Lamb M. E. (Eds.), (1986). *Adolescent fatherhood.* Hillsdale, NJ: Erlbaum.

Furstenberg, F. F., Jr., Lincoln, R., & Menken, J. (1981). *Teenage sexuality, pregnancy, and childbearing.* Philadelphia: University of Pennsylvania Press.

Klinman, D. G., Kohl, R., & The Fatherhood Project (1984). *Fatherhood USA.* New York: Bank Street College.

Kotelchuck, M. (1976). The infant's relationship to the father: Experimental evidence. In M. E. Lamb (Ed.), *The role of the father in child development.* New York: Wiley.

Lamb, M. E. (1978). The father's role in the infant's social world. In J. H. Stevens and M. Mathews (Eds.), *Mother/child, father/child relationships.* Washington, DC: National Association for the Education of Young Children.

Lamb, M. E. (Ed.) (1981). *The role of the father in child development.* Rev. Ed. New York: Wiley.

Lamb, M. E., & Sagi, A. (Eds.) (1983). *Fatherhood and family policy.* Hillsdale, NJ: Erlbaum.

Lewis, M., & Feiring, C. (1978). The child's social world. In R. M. Lerner & G. D. Spanier (Eds.), *Child influences on marital and family interaction: A life-span perspective.* New York: Academic.

Moles, D. C. (1979). Public welfare payments and marital dissolution: A review of recent studies. In G. Levinger & D. C. Moles (Eds.), *Divorce and separation: Context, causes, and consequences.* New York: Basic.

Moynihan, D. P. (1965). *The Negro family: The case for national action.* Washington, DC: U. S. Department of Labor, U. S. Government Printing Office.

Newsweek (1965). New Crisis: The Negro family. August 8, pp. 32–35.

Parke, R. D. (1981). *Fathers.* Cambridge, MA: Harvard University Press.

Placek, P. S., & Hendershot, G. E. (1974). Public welfare and family planning: An empirical study of the "brood sow" myth. *Social Problems, 21,* 658–673.

Radin, N. (1981). The role of the father in cognitive, academic, and intellectual development. In M. E. Lamb (Ed.), *The role of the father in child development.* 2nd ed. New York: Wiley.

Ross, H. D., and Sawhill, I. V. (1975). *Time of transition: The growth of families headed by women.* Washington, DC: Urban Institute.

Ryan, W. (1970). *Blaming the victim.* New York: Vintage.

Sagi, A., & Sharon, N. (1984). The role of the father in the family: Toward a gender-neutral family policy. *Children and Youth Services Review, 6,* 83–99.

Steiner, G. Y. (1981). *The futility of family policy.* Washington, DC: Brookings Institute.

Sullivan, J., & McDonald, D. (1979). Newborn oriented paternal behavior: Implications for concepts of parenting. In J. G. Howells (Ed.), *Modern perspectives in the psychiatry of infancy.* New York: Brunner-Mazel.

Wallerstein, J. S., & Kelly, J. B. (1982). The father-child relationship: Changes after divorce. In S. H. Cath, A. R. Gurwitt, & J. M. Ross (Eds.), *Father and child: Developmental and clinical perspectives.* Boston: Little, Brown.

Author Index

Page numbers in *italics* indicate pages on which full references appear.

Abarbanel, A., 90, 91, *94*
Abbott, D., 228, 233, *253*
Abelin, E., 167, *189*
Abrahams, B., 36, *54*
Achenbach, T., 210, *220*
Adams, B., 117, *131*
Adams, M.K., 208, *220*
Adams, P.L., 12, 15, *24*
Adamson, L., *102*
Addison, S., 230–233, 238, 240, *253*
Adeso, V.J., 208, 209, *220*
Adubato, S.A., 208, *220*
Ahrons, C.R., 90, *94*
Albrecht, S.L., 106, 107, 110, 113, *129*
Alexander, J., 89, *97*
Alexander, J.F., 197, 198, 205, *220, 226*
Alexander, J.W., 35, *55*
Als, H., *102*
Ambert, A.M., 120, *129*
Amidei, N., 374, *377*
Anderson, B.J., 78, *99,* 304, *321*
Anderson, E.A., 107, *133*
Anderson, S.A., *224*
Angell, R.C., 344, 349, 355, *377*
Anker, J., 121, *133*
Antell, M., 257, *273*
Anthony, E.J., *129*
Aponte, H.J., 196, *220*
Arbuckle, M.B., 307, *318*
Arenson, K.W., 340, *377*
Aschenbrenner, B.G., 32, 35, *55, 377*
Asher, S.J., 111, *129, 134*
Atilano, R.B., *224*
Atkeson, B.M., 192, *221*
Atkins, R.N., 167, 188, *189*
Austin, B.C., 302, 304, *320*
Avis, J.M., 198, *220*

Babchuk, W.A., 69, *94*
Baden, C., 385, *409*
Badger, E., 309, *318*
Baekeland, F., 200, *220*
Baer, D.M., 213, *223*
Bahm, R., 148, *160*
Bahr, H.M., 106, 107, *129*
Bakke, E., 344, 349, 353, 356, 358, *377*
Baldwin, L.M., 195, *221*
Ballentine, C., 121, *131* ᵥ
Ban, P.L., 70, 71, *95*
Bandura, A., 257, *273,* 305, 310, 315, *318*
Bane, M., 294, *320,* 346, *377*
Barber, L., 215, *226, 323*
Barnett, R.C., 13, *24,* 32, 35, 38, 52, 53, *55*
Barsh, E.T., *253*
Barton, C., 197, 205, *220, 226*
Bartz, K., 82, *95, 422, 427*
Baruch, G.K., 13, *24,* 32, 35, 38, 52, 53, *55*
Baumrind, D., 40, *55, 159, 191, 220*
Beal, J.A., 304, 305, *318*
Beck, D.F., 205, *220*
Becker, M.H., 200, *220*
Beckman, P., 235, *251*
Beitel, A., 23, 313, *321*
Bell, R.Q., 257, 270, *273*
Bellack, L., 257, *273*
Belsky, J., 71–73, *95,* 294, 295, 303, 304,
  318, 357, *377, 437, 440*
Benson, L., 4, 6, *24*
Berg, B., 168, *189,* 201, 202, 204, *221*
Bergen, L.P., *224*
Bergin, A.E., 209, *221*
Berkowitz, B.P., 208, *221*
Berman, P.W., 69–71, *95*
Berman, W.H., 112, *129*
Bernard, J., 105, *129*

443

Berry, J., 252, 254, 371, *382*
Bhavnagri, N., 313, *321*
Biller, H.B., 13–15, *24,* 73, *95,* 148, *159, 160,* 191, *221*
Billingsley, A., 346, *377*
Birenbaum, A., 238, 239, *250*
Birigen, Z.C., 313, *319*
Bishop, D.S., 195, *221*
Bishop, J., 353, *377*
Blacher, J., 228, 229, *250*
Blacher-Dixon, J., 235, *254*
Blackwell, B., 200, *221*
Blechman, A.E., 204, *221*
Blechman, E., 359, *377*
Block, J., 73, *95*
Block, J.H., 73, *95*
Blood, R.O., 386, 387, *409*
Bloom, B.J., 111, *129*
Bloom, B.L., 111, 112, *129*
Bloom-Feshbach, S., 362, *377*
Blotcky, A.D., 169, *189,* 212, *221*
Bodenheimer, B.M., 107, *129*
Bogira, S., 373, *377*
Bohen, H., 390, 391, 393, *409*
Bolton, F.G., Jr., 23, 433, *440*
Bowen, S.M., 300, *318*
Bowlby, J., 4, *25,* 69, *95*
Brackbill, Y., 300, *318*
Brandwein, R.A., 110, *129,* 144, *160*
Brazelton, T.B., *102*
Brenner, H.M., 343, *377*
Brickman, P., 209, 211, 214, *221*
Brim, O., 424, 425, *427*
Brinkerhoff, B.B., 354, *377*
Broberg, A., *25*
Broderick, J.E., 209, *224*
Brody, G., 228, 233, *253*
Brody, J.G., 342, 345, 346, 373, 374, 376, *379*
Bronfenbrenner, U., 294, *318,* 347, *377,* 385
Brophy, J., 419, *427*
Brotherson, M.J., *254*
Brown, C.A., 110, *129,* 144, *160*
Brown, P., 112–114, *129*
Brown, T., 82, *99,* 113, 118, 120, *132,* 138, 140, *161,* 293, *320*
Bryson, L., 49, *55*
Budd, K.S., 201, 202, 208, *220, 221*
Budman, S.H., 168, *190,* 203, *225*
Bugental, D.E., 207, *223*

Burchinal, L.G., 333, *335*
Burgess, A.W., 257, 259, *273, 274*
Burns, D., 309, *318, 320*
Burton, A., 256, *275*
Buss, T.F., 340, 342, 349–352, 371, *377*
Butler, C., *292*
Butler, J.F., 262, *273*
Byrne, D.G., *274*

Cain, A.C., 86, *96*
Cain, R.L., 78, *99,* 300, 304, *318, 321*
Cairns, R.B., *318*
Caldwell, R.A., 112, *129*
Call, J., 231, *251*
Camara, K.A., 16, *25,* 86, 91, *96,* 139, 142, 143, 146–149, *160, 161*
Camara, L.A., 116, 117, *131*
Camp, B.W., 329, *336*
Campbell, A., 106, *129*
Campos, J.J., 72, *95,* 302, *322*
Canino, I.A., 178, *190*
Cantor, N.L., 73, *95*
Caplovitz, D., 345, 353, 354, 356, 357, *377*
Card, J.J., 328, 332, *335*
Cardea, J.M., 143, *160*
Carlson, B.E., 289, *291*
Carnahan, S., 309, *319*
Casey, P.H., 308, *323*
Casto, R.F., 112, *133*
Catalano, R., 348, 357, 361, *378, 382*
Cath, S., 167, 182, *189*
Caust, B.L., 200, *223*
Cavan, R.S., 355, *378*
Cazenave, N.A., 6, *25*
Cease, L., 90, *95*
Chamberlin, R.W., 308, *318*
Chambers, D.L., 64, 65, *67*
Chang, P., 82, *95,* 118, *129*
Charnov, E.L., 7, 8, *26,* 52, *56, 411*
Chase-Lansdale, L., 74, *98*
Cheriboga, D.A., 110, 112, 113, *129*
Cherlin, A., 103, *129,* 138, *160*
Chess, S., 148, *160*
Chodorow, N., 194, *221*
Christophersen, E.R., *221*
Clark, T.L., 139, 142, 143, 146, 147, *162*
Clarke, C., 216, *224*
Clarke-Stewart, A., 424, *427*
Clarke-Stewart, K.A., 71, 72, 74, *95,* 248, *250*

Cleminshaw, H.K., 117, *131,* 148, *161*
Cline, D.W., 114, *134*
Clingempeel, W.G., 91, *95,* 121, *130,* 154, *160*
Cloward, R.A., 373, *381*
Coates, D., *221*
Cobb, J., 344, *383*
Cobb, S., 349, *380*
Cogan, R., 299, *319*
Cohen, L.J., 72, *95*
Cohen, R., 175, 183, *189*
Cohn, E., *221*
Cohn, R.M., 348–350, *378*
Coho, A., 113, *129*
Coleman, C., 105, *132*
Coleman, M., 86, *96*
Coles, R., 346, 367, *378*
Collins, G., 228, *250*
Collmer, C., 357, *381*
Constantatos, M., 143, 144, *160*
Constantini, F., *320*
Converse, P.E., 71, *101,* 106, *129*
Conway, E., 300, *318*
Cook, D.R., 217, *221*
Corcoran, M., 346, *378*
Costeloo, R., *225*
Cowan, C., 38, 54, *55,* 296, *318*
Cowan, P.A., 38, 54, *55,* 296, *318*
Cox, M., 16, *25,* 83, 85, 90, *95–97,* 105–117, 119–121, 123, *131,* 141–144, 148, 149, *161,* 191, *222*
Cox, R., 16, *25,* 83, 85, *96, 97,* 105–117, 119–121, 123, *131,* 141–144, 148, 149, *161,* 191, *222*
Coysh, W.S., 36, 38, *55*
Crane, D.R., 26, *273*
Crockenberg, S.B., 298, *322*
Cromwell, R., 212, *221*
Cross, A., 73, *99,* 227, 232, 234–236, 240, 247, 249, *251*
Crowley, M., 243, *250*
Cummings, S.T., 227, 231, 236, 239, 240, 247, *250*
Cunningham, S., 348, 357, *378*
Curley, A., 216, *224*
Cutler, L., *129*
Cutrona, C., *96*

David, H.P., 288, *291*
David, J., 214, *226,* 310, *323*

Davidson, N., 208, *222*
Davis, S.J., 408, *410*
DeBoor, M., 238, *251*
DeCarlo, T.J., 169, *189, 221*
De Frain, J., 30, 34–37, *55,* 143, *160*
Deinard, A.S., 82, *95,* 118, *129*
Delaney, S.W., 228, 244, *251*
Demos, J., 5, *25*
Deni, R., *320*
Derdeyn, A.P., 62, 63, 88, 89, *95, 96,* 124, *130*
Deutsch, C.P., 347, *378*
Dezen, A.E., *226*
Dickie, J., 294, 309, *319*
DiLalla, L., 107, 124, 127, *130*
Dixon, R.B., 66, *102,* 108, *134*
Dixon, S., *102*
Doering, S.G., 300, *319*
Dolby, R., 304, 305, *319, 320*
Dominic, K.T., 110, 115, 116, *130*
Dooley, D., 348, 357, 361, *378, 382*
Downs, A.C., 73, *98*
Dozier, C., *101*
Drake, D., *320*
Dresser, J.W., *274*
Driscoll, P.F., 353, 355, *381*
Dudzic, M., 403, 407, 408, *410*
Dugas, M., 339
Duncan, D.F., 266, 270, *274*
Duncan, G.J., 119, *130,* 346, *378,* 432, *440*
Duncan-Jones, P., *274*
Duvall, E.M., 229, 237, 239, *251*

Easterbrooks, M.A., 289, *291*
Edelbrock, C., 210, *220*
Egolf, B., 357, *379*
Ehrenreich, B., 6, *25,* 416, *427*
Eiduson, B.T., 35, *55*
Eirick, R., 143, *160*
Eisenberg, P., 348, *378*
Elder, G., 341, 350–354, 356–359, *378, 381*
Elkind, D., 288, *291*
Elliot, G.L., 84, *101,* 139, 141, 143, 146, 147, 149, *162*
Ellis, S., 168, *190,* 202, 206, *225*
Ellwood, D.T., 346, *377*
Elster, A.B., 23, *25,* 295, *319,* 329, 330, *335,* 433, *440*
Embry, L.H., 213, *221, 223*
Emde, R.N., 302, 304, *320, 322*

Emery, R.E., 107, 114, 124, 127, *130,* 148, *160*
English, B., 304, 305, *319*
English, D., 6, *25*
Ennis, D., 65, *96*
Entwisle, D.R., 300, *319*
Epstein, N.B., 195, *221, 226*
Erickson, M., 230, 240, *251*
Erikson, E.H., 69, *96,* 207
Erler, G., 401, 404, *410*
Espenshade, T.J., 119, *130,* 144, *160*
Evans, H.E., 282, *292*

Falk, R., 332, *335*
Farber, B., 231–233, *251*
Farley, G.K., *292*
Farrell, W., 387, *410*
Fast, I., 86, *96*
Feiring, C., 437, *440*
Feldheim, P., 71, *101*
Feldman, S.S., 32, 35, 36, *54, 55,* 70, 71, 87, *96, 99,* 313, *319*
Felton, B.J., 112–114, *129*
Fenster, C.A., 68, *99*
Ferguson, D., 82, *99,* 113, 118, 120, *132,* 138, 140, *161,* 293, *320*
Ferholt, J.B., 175, 182, 183, *189*
Ferman, L.A., 345, *378*
Ferri, E., 82, *96*
Feshbach, J., 362, *377*
Feshbach, N., 416, *427*
Fewell, R., 227, 238, 245, 248, *252, 254*
Fike, S., 208, *221*
Field, T., 30, *55,* 80, *96,* 303, *323*
Fiering, C., 293, *320*
Fineman, S., 354, *378*
Finkelhor, D., 255–259, 268, *273*
Firestone, P., 203, *221*
Fischer, J.L., 143, *160*
Fisher, K., 351, *378*
Fisher, T., 330, *336*
Fishman, C., 196, 218, *223*
Fleischman, M.J., 212, *224*
Floderus, B., 349, *382*
Folberg, H.J., 124, *130*
Foote, F.H., 202, *225*
Forehand, R., 192, *221*
Fournier, D., 212, *221*
Fox, E.M., 110, *129,* 144, *160*
Frank, M., 282, *292*

Frantz-Cook, A., 217, *221*
Frazier, N., 417, *427*
Freeman, D.S., 307, *222*
Freud, A., 68, 90, *96*
Freud, S., 63, 69, *96,* 136, *160,* 182, 186, *189*
Friedman, D., 385
Friedman, S., 169, *189, 221*
Frodi, A.M., 34, *55,* 80, 81, *99, 411*
Frodi, M., *25,* 34, *55,* 80, 81, *99, 411*
Fulton, J.A., 114, 116, 117, 120, *130*
Furstenberg, F., 104, 106–108, 110, 113, 116, *130,* 137, 143, *160,* 331, *335,* 353, 359, 360, 362, 363, 366, *379,* 433, *440*

Gaines, T.J.R., 202, 203, 205, *222, 225*
Gallagher, J., 227, 232, 234–236, 240, 247, 249, *251*
Galper, M., 90, *96*
Ganong, L.H., 86, *96*
Garbarino, J., 257, 265, 266, *273,* 342, *379*
Gardner, J., 345, *378*
Gasser, R., 82, *96,* 113, 118–120, *130,* 138, *160*
Gath, A., 232, *251*
Gelfand, D.M., 73, *95*
Gelles, R.J., 357, *379*
George, V., 82, *96,* 138, *160*
Gerber, G.L., 68, *98*
Gerhardt, V., 105, *130*
Gersick, K., 118, 119, *130,* 138, 140, *160*
Giarretto, H., 256, 265, 270, 272, *273*
Gil, D., 256, *274,* 357, *379*
Gilligan, D., 112, *130*
Gilstrap, B., 245, *318*
Ginsburg, S.W., 348, 349, 354, 358, *379*
Gispert, M., 332, *335*
Gist, N.F., 299, *319*
Glenn, N.D., 106, *130*
Glick, P.C., 16, *25,* 106, 108, 118, *130, 131, 133*
Gold, D., 416, 419, *427*
Gold, M., 416, *428*
Goldberg, H., 387, *410*
Goldberg, S., 301, 302, *319*
Goldberg, W.A., 289, *291*
Goldman, J.D.G., 11, *25*
Goldman, R.J., 11, *25*
Goldstein, J., 68, 90, *96*
Goldsmith, R., 22, *27*
Good, T., 419, *427*

Goodchilds, J.D., 348, *379*
Goode, W.J., 105, 113, *131*
Goodman, R.L., 106, 107, *128*
Gordon, S.B., 208, *222*
Gore, S., 348, 349, *379*
Gottman, J., 7, *26,* 105, *131,* 293, *321*
Graham, M., 124, *130*
Grana, G., 234, *252*
Graziano, A.M., 208, *221, 222*
Green, R.G., 193, *222*
Greenberg, M., 229, 245, *251, 254*
Greenfield, J., 229, *251*
Gregory, I., 146, 147, *160*
Greif, J.B., 82, 90, *96,* 115, 128, *131*
Gronseth, E., 30, 43, 45, *55,* 386, 395, *410*
Grossman, F.K., 231, 232, *251*
Grote, D.F., 90, *96*
Groth, N.A., 259, *274*
Grubb, W.N., 342, 343, 345, 346, 371, 373–376, *379*
Gubrium, J.F., 234, 235, *251*
Guidubaldi, J., 117, *131,* 148, *161*
Gumz, E.J., 234, 235, *251*
Gurin, P., 346, *378*
Gurman, A.S., 192, 193, 202, 206, 207, 209, 214, 216, *222*
Gurwitt, A.R., 167, 175, 182, 183, *189*
Gutmann, D., 70, *96*

Haddad, W., 90, *100*
Haley, J., 197, *222*
Hall, R., 217, *222*
Hamerlynck, L.A., *253*
Hames, R.B., 69, *94*
Hampe, G.D., 113, *133*
Hampson, R., 249, *254*
Hannerz, U., 345, 347, 362–365, *379*
Hare-Mustin, R.T., 193, 195, 197, 198, 199, 215, *222*
Harman, D., 424, 425, *427*
Harper, J., 30, 49, *55*
Harrington, D.M., 73, *95*
Harrington, M., 339, 342, 346, 370, 373, 374, *379*
Hatfield, E., 250, *254*
Hayden, A., 247, *252*
Hedges, J.N., 386, 391–393, *410*
Hriss, J., 360, 361, *379*
Helfer, R., 256, 257, *274*
Heller, K.A., 362, *377*

Helsel, B., 239, *251*
Helsel, E., 239, *251*
Helsel, M., *251*
Hendershot, G.E., 433, *441*
Henderson, B.F., 328, *336*
Henderson, G., 361, *382*
Henderson, S., 265, *274*
Hendricks, L.W., 330, 331, *335*
Hennenborn, W.J., 299, *319*
Herman, J., 217, *222*
Herrenkohl, E., 357, *379*
Herrenkohl, R., 357, *379*
Hersh, A., 234, 237, *249*
Hervis, O., 202, *225*
Herzog, E., 347, 366, 379, *380*
Herzog, R., 15, *25*
Hess, R., 142, 148, 149, *161*
Hess, R.D., 16, *25,* 116, 117, *131,* 344, 347, *379*
Hess, R.K., 89, 91, *96*
Hetherington, E.M., 16, *25,* 82, 85, *97, 98,* 105–117, 119–121, 123, 124, 127, *130, 131,* 141–144, 146, 148, 149, 152, *161,* 191, *222*
Heubeck, B., 201, 204, 205, *222*
Hildebrand, K.A., 302, *319*
Hill, C.T., 112, *133*
Hill, M., 346, *380*
Hingst, A., 116, *131*
Hipgrave, T., 12, *25,* 82, 83, *97*
Hodges, W.F., 121, *131*
Hoffman, L., 49, *55,* 293, 313, *319,* 341, *380*
Hoffman, M.L., 74, *97*
Hoffman, S., 353, *380*
Holmes, J., 353, *380*
Holmes, T.H., 266, *274*
Holmstrom, L.L., 257, *273*
Holroyd, J., 228, *252*
Hops, H., 194, *226*
Hoteling, G., 255, 256, 258, 268, *273, 275*
Howell, J.T., 347, 364, 365, *380*
Hulth, G., *25*
Hurley, R.L., 346, *380*
Huston, T.L., 32, 36, 38, *56*
Hwang, C.P., 23, *25,* 34, *55,* 80, 81, *98,* 302, *319,* 401, 402, 404, 405, *410, 411*
Hyman, H.H., 345, 346, *380*
Hymel, S., *56, 320*
Hynes, W.J., 114, *131*

Ihinger-Tallman, M., 105, *132*
Ilfeld, F., 89, *97*
Ilfeld, H., 89, *97*
Illingworth, R.S., 231, 233, *252*
Inselberg, P.M., 333, *335*

Jacklin, C.N., 69, *99*
Jackson, B., 54, *55*
Jackson, P., 416, *427*
Jacob, T., 191, *223*
Jacobs, J.W., 114, 115, *131*
Jacobson, D., 89, *97, 117, 132, 148, 161*
Jaeckel, M., 401, 404, *410*
Jahoda, M., 349, 354, 360, *380*
James, K., 198, 199, *223*
Jason, J., 256, 258, 268, *274*
Johnson, C.A., 208, *223*
Johnson, J.H., 329, *336*
Jones, C., 301, *319*
Jones, M.A., 205, *220*
Jones, R.R., *253*
Jencks, C., 373, *380*
Jenné, W., 231, *251*
Jurich, A.P., *224*
Juster, F.T., 10, 18, *25*
Justice, B., 259, 263, 265, 266, 269, 270, *274,* 357, *380*
Justice, R., 259, 263, 265, 269, *274,* 357, *380*

Kagan, J., 248, *253*
Kahn, A.J., 373, 376, *380,* 397–400, 402, *410*
Kain, E., 341, 353, 354, *381*
Kaiser, C., 247, *252*
Kamemer, C., 391
Kamerman, S.B., 373, 376, *380,* 385, 397–400, 402, 403, *410*
Kanter, R.M., 385, *410*
Karuza, J., *221*
Kasl, S.V., 349, *380*
Kaswan, J., 207, *223*
Katz, A.J., 82, *97*
Katz, C., 208, *223*
Keane, K., 243, *250*
Keenan, V., 238, *253*
Keller, W.D., 302, *319*
Kelly, J., 76, 77, 83, 85, 87, 91, *97, 101, 102,* 111, 112, 114, 115, 117, 120, 121, *134,* 139, 141–145, 148, 149, 154, 156, 157, *161, 163,* 437, *441*

Kelly, M.L., 208, 213, *223*
Kempe, C.H., 256, 257, 265, *274*
Kempe, D., 257, *274*
Kempe, R.S., 256, *274*
Kennedy, A., 339
Kennell, J.H., 299, 301, *319, 322*
Kenny, J.A., 281, *292*
Kercher, G., 256, *274*
Kerckhoff, A.C., 332, *335*
Kernkamp, E., 416, *427*
Keshet, H.F., 82, 83, 90, *97, 100,* 107, 110, 116, 119, 121, 123, *132, 133*
Kidder, L., *221*
Kiesler, D.J., 214, *223*
Kilmann, P.R., 208, *224*
Kimbal, G., 32, 34–37, *55*
Kinch, R.A.H., 332, *335*
Kingston, P.W., 397–400, 402, *410*
Kirkpatrick, C., 230, *252*
Kitson, G.C., 103, 105, 106, 110–114, 116, *132*
Klaus, M.H., 299, 301, *319, 322*
Klein, R.P., 299, *319, 322*
Klinman, D., 23, 54, *55,* 297, 409, *410,* 420–422, 424, 425, *427,* 430, 439, *440*
Kniskern, D.P., 192, 193, 202, 206, 207, 209, 214, 216, *222*
Kogan, K., *221*
Kohl, R., 54, *55,* 409, *410,* 420–422, *427,* 430, 439, *440*
Kolevzon, M.S., 193, *222*
Komarovsky, M., 349, 352–358, 360, *380*
Kompara, D.R., 86, *97*
Koopman, E.J., 83, *98*
Kornhauser, L., 65, *99, 107, 132*
Kotelchuck, M., 53, *55,* 70–73, *97,* 191, 215, *223, 226,* 248, *252, 253,* 310, 319, *323,* 437, *440*
Kramer, D.A., 114, *134*
Kramer, E., 300, *318*
Krate, R., 364, 365, 366, 367, *382*
Kraus, S., 110, *132*
Kressel, K., 168, *190,* 202, 203, 206, *223, 225*
Kurtines, W.M., 202, *225*
Kvebaek, D., 212, *221*

La Barbera, J.D., 206, *223*
L'Abate, L., 203, 204, 219, *223*
Ladner, J.A., 345, *380*

Lahaderne, H., 416, *427*

Lamb, M.E., 3, 4, 7–18, 20, 21, *25, 26,* 30, 34, 36, 38, 41, 42, 45, 46, 52, *55, 56,* 69, 71–74, 77, 80, 81, *97, 98,* 154, *161,* 182, *189,* 191, *223,* 228, 232, 239, *252,* 280, *292,* 294, 295, 302, 312, 316, *319,* 329, *335,* 385,, 389, 401, 402, 404–406, *411,* 433, 437, *440*

Lang, L., 70, 78, *100,* 388, *412*

Langlois, J.H., 73, *98*

Lansky, M.R., 168, 184, *189*

Lazarsfeld, P., 348, 349, 354, 360, *378, 380*

Lazerson, M., 343, 345, 371, 373, 375, 376, *379*

Lee, P., 415, *427*

Le Fave, M.K., 206, *223*

LeGrande, L., 371, *380*

Leiderman, P.H., 300, *321*

Lein, L., 45, *56*

LeMasters, E.E., 135, *161*

Lenghi, E.F., 259, 265, *274*

Levant, R., 408, *411*

Levin, H., 13, *27*

Levine, J.A., 4, 7, 8, 12, 20, *25, 26,* 30, 42, 52, *56,* 385, 389, 401, 402, 404, *411*

Levinger, G., 119, *132*

Levy, D.M., 6, *26*

Lewis, H., 347, 362, 364, 366, 367, *380*

Lewis, K., 140, *162*

Lewis, M., 70, 71, *95,* 293, *320,* 437, *440*

Lewis, O., 346, 347, *380*

Lewis, S., 206, *223*

Libbee, K.M., 119, *133*

Libow, J.A., 200, *223*

Liebow, E., 347, 361–367, *381*

Liem, R., 340, 349–351, 353, 356, 357, *381*

Light, R., 357, *381*

Lincoln, R., 433, *440*

Lind, E., 349, *382*

Lippitt, R., 416, *428*

Lipson, J.W., 208, 209, *220*

Little, C.B., 349, *381*

Litwack, T.R., 65, 68, *96, 98*

Liversidge, E., 234, *252*

Longfellow, C., 363, 366, 367, *383*

Longo, K., *427*

Lonsdale, G., 233, *252*

Loof, D.H., 346, 367, *381*

Lou, M., 63, 64, 66, 67, *102*

Love, E.J., 332, *335*

Love, H., 234, 249, *252*

Love, L.R., 207, *223*

Lowenstein, J.S., 83, *98*

Lowery, C.R., *161*

Luebke, P.T., 278, *292*

Luepnitz, D.A., 82, 83, 90, 91, *98,* 109, 119, 121–124, *132,* 139, 142–145, 148–151, *161*

Lundwall, L., 200, *220*

Luscomb, R., 249, *254*

Lustig, N., *274*

Lyles, T., 416, *428*

Lynn, D., 3, *26*

Lynn, D.B., 191, *223,* 328, *336*

Lynn, D.R., 73, *98*

Maccoby, E.E., 69, *99, 161*

MacDonald, K., 313, *320, 321*

MacDonald, W.S., 231, 233, 235–237, *252*

MacTurk, R.H., *322*

Madanes, C., 196, 197, *223*

Mainman, L.A., 200, *220*

Maklan, D.M., 394, *411*

Manuda, R., 112, 114, *129*

Marder, L., *225*

Margolis, L., 369–372, *381*

Markowitz, J., 240, 241, 245–247, *252*

Marsden, D., 349, 351, 353, 354, *381*

Marsiglio, W., 332, *335*

Martin, B., 169, *189,* 191, 208, 222, *223*

Martin, E.P., 367, *381*

Martin, H., 257, 270, *274*

Martin, J.A., *161*

Martin, J.M., 367, *381*

Marton, P., *320*

Mas, C.H., 198, *220*

Masnick, G., 294, *320*

Mason, P.R., 113, *132*

Matheson, P., 294, *319*

May, K.A., 298, *320*

Mayer, A., 259, 266, *274*

McArthur, D., 228, *252*

McCabe, E., 353, 354, 371, *382*

McCarthy, J., 103, *129,* 333, *336*

McCarthy, M.E., *322,* 395, *411*

McCloughlin, C.S., 117, *131*

McConachie, H., 228, 249, *252*

McDermott, J., 148, *161*

McDonald, D., 437, *441*

McGhee, J.D., 343, *381*

McGuire, W.J., 307, *320*
McHale, S.M., 32, 36, 38, *56*
McIntyre, D., 198, 199, *223*
McLaughlin, F., 303, *320*
McLoyd, V.C., 23
McMahon, D., 332, *335*
McShane, M., *274*
Mehl, L.E., 300, *321*
Meier, G.S., 395, *411*
Mellor, E., 391–393, *410*
Melton, G.B., 65, *99*
Mendes, H., 82, *99,* 118, 120, *132,* 138, 140, 141, *161*
Menolascino, F.J., 229, *252*
Menken, J., 333, *336,* 433, *441*
Meredith, D., 150, *161*
Messinger, L., 86, *99*
Meyer, D., 227, 234, 238, 249, 241, 244–246, 248, 249, *251, 252, 254*
Meyer, W., 416, *428*
Meyerson, R., 249, *253*
Michael, M., 339
Milgram, J., 420, *428*
Miller, B.C., 300, *318*
Miller, L., 289, *292*
Miller, S.M., 346, *381*
Milner, J.R., 12, 15, *24*
Minde, K., 309, *320*
Minuchin, S., 173, *189,* 196, 205, 218, *223*
Mitchell, W.M., Jr., 234, *253*
Moln, P., 341, 349, 350, 353, 354, 361, 369–372, *381*
Moir, R.N., 113, *132*
Mokros, J., 423, *428*
Moles, D.C., 432, *441*
Moles, O.C., 119, *132*
Montgomery, T., 330, 331, *335*
Moore, J.A., 232, *253*
Morgan, J.N., 119, *130*
Morgan, R., 139, 142, 143, 146, 147, *162*
Morgenbesser, M., 90, *99,* 121, *132*
Morris, N., 229, *251*
Moynihan, D.P., 346, *381,* 432, *441*
Mnookin, R.H., 63–68, *99,* 107, *132*
Mrazek, P.B., 257, 265, *274*
Muenchow, S., 397, *412*
Murch, M., 119, *132*
Murray, A.D., 300, *320*
Murray, T.B., *274*

Mussen, P.H., 13, *26*
Myers, B.J., 304, 305, *320*

Nakashima, I.I., 329, *336*
Nash, S.C., 32, 35, 36, *54, 55,* 70, 71, 87, *96, 99,* 313, *319*
Nastasi, B.K., 117, *131*
Nation, R.L., *320*
Neale, M.S., *412*
Neckerman, K.M., 340, 343, *383*
Needham, C., 243, *250*
Nehlo, N., 121, *132*
Nehls, N., 90, *99*
Nelson, G., 117, *132*
Nichols, R.C., 111, *134*
Nicholson, J., 299, *319*
Nollen, S.D., 385, 390, 392, 393, 395, 396, *411*
Nord, C.W., *130,* 143, *160*
Norton, A.J., 16, *25,* 103, 118, *131, 132*

O'Brien, T.P., 201, 202, *221*
O'Dell, S., 208, *223*
Oden, C.W., 231, 233, 235–237, *252*
Okpaku, S.R., 65, 67, 68, *99*
O'Leary, K.D., 148, *160, 162,* 209, 216, *221, 224*
O'Leary, S.E., 70, 73, *99,* 294, 298, 299, *321*
Olshansky, S., 228, 230, *253*
Oltmanns, T.F., 209, *224*
O'Neil, J.M., 200, 201, *224*
Orthner, D., 82, *99,* 113, 118, 120, *132,* 138, 140, 161, *162,* 293, *321*
Owen, M.T., 74, *98*

Palkovitz, R., 300, 301, 311, *320*
Palmer, S., 116, *132*
Pannabecher, B.J., 302, 304, *320*
Panzorine, S., 330, *335*
Parke, R.D., 7, 23, *26,* 35, *56,* 70, 71, 73, *99–101,* 154, *162,* 191, *224,* 228, 229, 246, *253,* 293, 294, 298, 299, 303–305, 307, 308, 310, 312, 313, *320, 321,* 330, *336,* 357, *381,* 434, 435, 437, *441*
Parrow, A.A., 332, *335*
Pasley, K., 105, *132*
Patterson, G.R., 191, 194, 212, *224, 226*
Pauker, J.D., 327, *336*
Payne, D.E., 13, *26*
Peck, J.R., 232, *253*

Pedersen, F.A., 70, 78, 79, *99, 100,* 300, 304, 307, *318, 321*
Peplau, L., 112, *133*
Perez-Vidal, A., 202, *225*
Perry, J.D., 117, *131,* 148, *161*
Person, D., 339
Petersen, G.H., 300, *321*
Peterson, J.L., 117, *132*
Peterson, J.S., 143, *160*
Pine, F., 182, *190*
Piven, F.F., 373, *381*
Plecek, P.S., 433, *441*
Pleck, E., 5, *26*
Pleck, J.H., 4–10, 12, 14, 21–23, *26,* 37, 42, 49, 52, *56,* 70, 78, *100,* 137, *162,* 387–389, *411, 412*
Polatnick, M., 21, *26*
Ponza, M., 346, *380*
Popplewell, J.F., 289, *292*
Porter, B., *162*
Postner, R.S., 207, *224*
Powell, D.H., 353, 355, *381*
Power, T.G., 7, *26, 56,* 71, *100,* 293, 294, *320, 321,* 330, *336*
Price, E., 416, *427*
Price-Bonham, S., 230–233, 238, 240, *253*
Pruett, K.D., 17, *27,* 80, *100*
Putney, R.S., 112, *132*

Quayhagen, M., *292*
Quinn, R.P., 386, 399, *412*

Rabinowitz, V.C., *221*
Radholm, M., 302, *322*
Radin, N., 13, 14, 16, 17, 22, *27,* 30–32, 34–39, 41–44, 46, 52, *56, 57,* 74, 80, *100,* 191, 215, *224,* 293, 312, *321, 322,* 437, *441*
Rahe, R.H., 266, *274*
Rainwater, L., 346, 361, *381*
Ranck, K.H., 355, *378*
Rapoport, R., 385, *412*
Raschke, H.J., 103, 112, *132,* 148, *162*
Raschke, V., 148, *162*
Raskin, P.A., 200, *223*
Ray, S.A., 23
Rayman, P., 340, 348–350, *381*
Redburn, F.S., 340, 342, 349–352, 371, 372, *377*
Redican, W.K., 310, *322*
Reed, E.W., 232, *253*

Reed, S.C., 232, *253*
Reid, J.B., 212, *224, 225*
Rein, M., 346, *380*
Reis, M., 416, 419, *427*
Reiter, G.F., 208, *224*
Reppucci, N.D., 91, *95,* 121, *130,* 154, *160*
Rheingold, H.L., 310, *322*
Rholes, W.S., 139, 142, 143, 146, 147, *162*
Rice, D.G., 201, *224*
Richards, M.E., 302, *319*
Rigler, D., 257, *275*
Riner, L.S., *221*
Ripley, J., *320*
Rivara, F.P., 328, *336*
Robbins, M.B., 328, *336*
Roberts, J., 110, 112, 113, *129*
Robertson, S., 299, *322*
Robinson, B., 417, *428*
Robinson, J.P., 71, 78, *100,* 387, *412*
Robson, K.S., 70, *100*
Rochat, R., 256, *274*
Rodgers, W.L., 106, *129*
Roll, R., 289, *292*
Roman, M., 90, *100*
Roos, P., 230, *253*
Rosen, E.I., 341, *382*
Rosen, J., *427*
Rosen, R., 139, 142–144, 148, 149, *162*
Rosenbaum, A., 216, *224*
Rosenberg, G.S., 395, *412*
Rosenberg, S.A., 232, *253*
Rosenblum, N., 168, *189,* 201, 202, 204, *221*
Rosenthal, K.M., 82, 83, 90, *97, 100,* 107, 110, 116, 119, 121, 123, *132, 133*
Rosoff, R., *225*
Ross, G., 248, *253*
Ross, H.D., 430, *441*
Ross, J.M., 167, 182, 183, *190*
Rossi, A.S., 69, *100*
Roth, A., 62, 66, *100*
Rothberg, B., 121–123, *133*
Rovine, M., 295, *318*
Rubin, L.B., 344, 347, 362–365, 367, *382*
Rubin, Z., 112, *133*
Russell, C., 205, *224,* 297, 313, 314, *322*
Russell, D., 217, *224,* 255, 256, *274*
Russell, G., 12, 16, 17, 22, *27,* 30–38, 40–50, 52, 53, *56, 57,* 74, 79, 80, *100,* 110, *133,* 215, *224,* 293, 297, 313, 314, 316, *321, 322*
Rustad, M., 71, *100,* 137, *162*

Rutherford, E., 13, *26*
Rutter, M., 7, 16, *27*
Rutter, R., 148, *162*
Ryan, L., 217, *222*
Ryan, W., 429, *441*
Ryckman, D.B., 233, *251*

Sadker, D., 418, *428*
Sadker, M., 417, *427*
Sagatun, I.J., 217, *225*
Sager, C.J., 210, *225*
Sagi, A., 13, 17, *27,* 30, 35, 41, 42, 45, *57,* 80,
   100, 101, 297, 316, *319, 322*
Sagi, S., 430, *441*
Sales, B., 63, 64, 66, 67, *102*
Sander, J., *427*
Santrock, J.W., 84, *101, 102,* 117, 120, *133,*
   139, 141–150, *162, 163*
Sarason, I.G., 329, *336*
Sass, J., 401, 404, *410*
Sawhill, I.V., 430, *441*
Sawin, D., 191, *224*
Sawin, D.B., 70, *99, 101,* 154, *162,* 294, *321*
Sawin, D.E., 228, *253*
Scanzoni, J., 386, *412*
Scharfman, W., 227, 232, 234, 236, 240, 247,
   249, *251*
Schecter, S., 217, *225*
Schell, G., 227, 238, 248, *252, 254*
Scherman, A., 119, *133*
Schench, E.K., 71, *101*
Schlesinger, B., 82, *101,* 110, 115, 116, 119,
   130, 133, 138, *163*
Schlozman, K.L., 348–350, *382*
Schrepf, N.A., 12, 15, *24*
Schufeit, L.J., 232, *253*
Schulz, D.A., 347, 364–368, *382*
Schwartz, M., 361, *382*
Sciarra, D., 420, *428*
Scott, E., 89, *96*
Scott, R., *274*
Scutt, J., 217, *225*
Seagull, A.A., 115, 116, *133*
Seagull, A.W., 115, 116, *133*
Seaman, S., *225*
Sears, R.R., 13, *27*
Seifert, K., 420, *428*
Sekcenski, E., 386, *410*
Seligman, M., 249, *253*
Sennett, R., 344, *382*

Sexton, P., 414, 415, *428*
Shanfield, S.B., 282, *292*
Shannon, L.B., 234, *253*
Shapiro, R.J., 168, *190,* 203, 205, *225*
Sharon, N., 430, *441*
Sheikh, A.A., 289, *292*
Sheldon, A., 348, *382*
Shelley, P., 136
Sherman, D., 265, *273*
Shorter, E., 63, *101*
Shosenberg, N.E., *320*
Shultes, L., 339
Siegel, J.M., 329, *336*
Siev, D., 340, *382*
Silverstein, B., 364–367, *382*
Sitterle, K.A., *101*
Skeels, H., 310, *322*
Skihinski, E., *225*
Slipp, S., 168, *190,* 202, 203, 206, *223, 225*
Smith, C.W., 82, *101*
Smith, E.E., 348, *379*
Smith, R.M., 82, *101*
Sollid, D.T., 298, *320*
Solnit, A.J., 68, 90, *96*
Sosa, R., 299, *322*
Spanier, G.B., 47, *57,* 104–108, 110–114,
   116, 119, *130, 133,* 262, *275,* 329, *336*
Spelke, E., 310, *322*
Spellman, S.W., *274*
Spicer, J.W., 113, *133*
Spieker, S., *253*
Spinetta, J., 257, *275*
Springer, C., 142, 155, *162*
Stack, C.B., 345, 367, *382*
Staines, G.L., 18, 21, *27,* 386, 388, 389, *412*
Standley, K., 299, *319*
Stanton, M.D., 195, 197, 202, 205, 207, 212,
   219, *225*
Staples, R., *382*
Stedman, J.M., 202, 203, 205, *222, 225*
Steel, L., 328, *335*
Steffensmeier, R.H., 297, *322*
Steier, F., 202, *225*
Stein, J.A., 110, 112, 113, *129*
Steinberg, J., *55,* 80, *98*
Steinberg, L.D., 357, *382*
Steiner, G.Y., 430, 433, *441*
Steinman, S., 90, 91, *101*
Stephens, M., *101*
Stephens, W.B., 232, *253*

Stolberg, A.L., 121, *133*
Stone, P.J., 71, *101*
Stoneman, Z., 228, 233, *253*
Straus, M., 255, 256, *275,* 357, *379*
Strecker, E., 6, *27*
Sudia, C.E., 15, *25,* 366, *379*
Suelzle, M., 238, *253*
Sugg, R., 415, *428*
Sullivan, J., 437, *441*
Summers, J.A., 254
Suomi, S.J., 310, *321*
Sussman, M.B., 105, 106, 110, 111, 114, 116, *132*
Svejda, M.J., 302, *322*
Swanson, D.W., 259, *275*
Sweeney, P.J., 328, *336*
Szalai, A., 71, 78, *101,* 137, *162*
Szapocznik, J., 202, 207, *225*
Szykula, S., *221*

Tagatz, G., 416, *428*
Taggart, M., 198, 199, *225*
Tallman, I., 231, *254*
Taplin, P.S., 212, *225*
Taub, D.M., 310, *322*
Tauber, M.A., 73, *101*
Tavormina, J., 249, *254*
Taylor, C., 82, *96,* 113, 118–120, *130,* 138, *160*
Taylor, D.E., 380, *410*
Taylor, S.E., 105, *133*
Tedder, S.L., 119, *133*
Tepp, A.V., 115, 116, *133*
Theorell, T., 349, *382*
Thies, J.M., 86, *101*
Thomas, A., 148, *160*
Thomas, D.B., *320*
Thomas, L.E., 353, 354, 357, 371, *382*
Thompson, D., 418, *428*
Thompson, G., 416, *428*
Thompson, J., *320*
Thompson, L., 105–107, 110, 112–114, 116, 119, *133*
Thompson, R.A., 65, 69, *94, 99, 101,* 110, 124, *133,* 152, 153, *163*
Tinsley, B.R., *56,* 70, *99,* 294, *320, 321*
Titler, B.I., 169, *184*
Tittler, B.I., *221*
Todd, T.C., 202, 205, 219, *225*
Todres, R., 82, *101,* 138, *162*

Toigo, R., 231, *251*
Toney, L., 302, *322*
Tonti, M., 219, *225*
Travolta, J., 325
Tronick, E., *102*
Turk, D.C., 112, *129*
Turnbull, A.P., 235, 237, 246, 247, 249, *254*
Turnbull, H.R., 237, *254*
Tyler, A., 256, 258–262, 265, 266, 268, 270, *275*
Tyler, F.B., 328, *336*

Urrutia, J., 299, *322*

Vadasy, P.F., 227, 238, 245, 248, *252, 254*
Vaillant, G.E., 201, *225*
Valentine, C.A., 346, *382*
Van der Veen, F., *226*
VanDeusen, J.M., 196, *220, 225*
Venters, M., 105, *134*
Verba, S., 348–350, *382*
Vietze, P.M., 294, 309, *318, 322*
Vinovskis, M., 333, *336*
Visher, E.B., 86, 87, *101*
Visher, J.S., 86, 87, *101*
Viveros-Long, A., 390, 391, 393, *409*

Waetzen, W., 416, *428*
Wahler, R., 221, *226*
Waldron, H., 198, *220*
Walker, K., 71, 78, *101,* 137, *162,* 387, *412*
Wallerstein, J., 76, 77, 83, 85, 87, 91, *97, 101, 102,* 111–115, 117, 120, 121, *134,* 139, 141–144, 146, 148, 149, 155–157, *161–163,* 437, *441*
Warburton, J., 198, 205, *220, 226*
Ward, M.J., 244, *251*
Warren, B., 304, 305, *319*
Warshah, R.A., 84, *101, 102,* 117, 120, *133,* 139, 141–147, 149, 150, *162, 163*
Wasow, M., 250, *254*
Watson, J.M., 210, 212, *226*
Wearing, M.P., 332, *335*
Weaver, C.N., 106, *130*
Wechsler, R.C., 121, *131*
Weinstein, J.R., 90, *96*
Weiss, R., 140, 145, 152, *163*
Weiss, R.L., 194, *226*
Weiss, R.S., 111, 112, 115, *134,* 265, *275*
Weitzman, L.J., 66, *102,* 108, *134,* 144, *163*

Wells, R.A., *226*
Wente, A.S., 298, *322*
Werkman, S., 280, 281, 286, 288, 290, *292*
West, S., 298, 299, *321*
Westley, W.A., 195, *226*
Westman, J.C., 114, *134*
White, L.K., 354, *377*
White, S.W., 111, *129, 134*
Whiteman, V., 112, 114, *129*
Whitt, J.K., 308, *323*
Whobrey, L., 63, 64, 66, 67, *102*
Widmayer, S.M., 303, *323*
Wikler, L., 228, 230, 231, 233, 235, 237–239, 250, *254*
Wilding, P., 82, *96,* 138, *160*
Williams, J., 339, 340, *382*
Williams, S., 256, *274*
Williams-McCoy, J.E., 328, *336*
Wilson, W.J., 340, 343, 376, *382, 383*
Winett, R.A., 392, 393, 396, *412*
Wise, L.L., 332, *335*
Witcher, W.C., 92, *95*
Witt, J.E., 203, *221*
Wolfe, D.M., 386, 387, *409*

Wolfensberger, W., 228, *254*
Wood, D.D., 73, *95*
Woods, M., 71, 78, *101,* 137, *162,* 387, *412*
Worobey, J., 303, *323*
Wurster, S.R., 232, *253*
Wylder, J., 169, *190*

Yancey, W., 346, *381*
Yankelovich, D., 22, *27*
Yarrow, L.J., *322*
Yoder, J.D., 111, *134*
Yogman, M.W., 71, *102,* 293, *323*
Young, A., 386, *412*
Young, L., 265, *275,* 357, *383*
Young, V., 345, 366, 367, *383*
Youngerman, J.K., 178, *190*

Zaslow, M.J., 78, *99,* 300, *318*
Zeisel, H., 349, 354, 360, *380*
Zelazo, P.R., 215, *226,* 248, *253,* 310, *323*
Zigler, E., 397, *412*
Zill, N., 117, *130, 132,* 143, 148, *160, 163*
Zur, S., 363, 366, 367, *382*

Subject Index

Abusing fathers, 255–273
  characteristics of, 258–268
  treatment for, 268–272
  see also Child abuse; Sexual abuse
Academic achievement, 14–15, 42, 74
Adolescence, 236, 360, 368, 423, 425
Adolescent fathers, 325–335, 359–360, 435, 437
  characteristics of, 326–330
  numbers of, 326–327
  problems experienced by, 331
  therapy for, 330–335
Adolescent mothers, 303, 309, 359
Adolescent pregnancy, incidence, 325
Adolescent sexual behavior, 327
Adolescent unemployment, 341. *See also* Unemployment
Adult-child conflicts, 108, 288
African Americans, 340–343, 345–347, 350–351, 360, 364, 367–368, 371
Age of child differences, 11. *See also* Adolescence; Infancy; Junior high school; Preadolescence; Senior high school
Aid to Families with Dependent Children (AFDC), 336, 373–374, 431, 434–435
Aid to Families with Dependent Children-Unemployed Parent (AFDC-U), 370–371, 373–374, 434
Alcohol abuse, 254, 287, 364–365
Alternative work schedules, 390–396, 408. *See also* Flexitime; Work schedules
Anger control, 270
Antisocial behavior, 361. *See also* Delinquency
Assessment in therapy, father involvement, 175–178
Attachment, 76, 229, 248

Attitudes regarding father involvement, 50, 259, 306, 312. *See also* Social support
Attitudes toward women's roles, 313
Authoritarian character structures, 281–283
Authority of father, 199, 355–356, 358, 360, 364, 367, 369
Autism, 228

Babysitting, 421–422
Behavioral family therapy, 194–195, 209, 213
Behavioral styles of mothers and fathers, 11–12. *See also* Caregiving; Parent-child play
"Best interests of the child" doctrine, 61–94, 107, 125, 138, 159
Best interests standard, problems with, 64–68
Blue-collar parents, 354, 371. *See also* Working-class status
Bonding, 301
Brazelton Neonatal Assessment Scale (BNAS), 303, 304–305
Breadwinner trap, 387
Breadwinning roles, 6–7, 17, 22–23, 29–30, 33, 37, 45, 314, 348, 350, 352, 356, 361, 363–364, 386, 414, 418, 429–433. *See also* Family roles; Paternal roles

Career orientation, 291, 314, 329, 350, 357, 407
Caregiving, 11, 75, 94, 137, 293, 306–307, 312, 315, 414
Caregiving role, 72, 76, 81
Cerebral palsy, 239, 246
Cesarean-section deliveries, 294, 298, 300, 316

Changing fathers' roles, 3–24, 38–39, 109, 248. *See also* Primary caregivers
Child abuse, 255–273, 357, 434
  etiology of, 256–258
  incidence of, 256
Childbirth preparation classes, 80, 298–299
Childbirth, 293, 299–300
Childcare, 5, 385–389, 397, 421–424
Child-care experience for males, 421–424
Child-care leave, 398
Child development in father-custody homes, 141–151
Child-parent relations, 143–144. *See also* Attachment; Adult-child conflicts; Bonding
Child placement, 238
Children with mental handicaps, fathers of, 227–250
Child support, economic, 109, 113, 123–125, 127, 144
Child's social adjustments, 235
Clinical history, fathers, 272
Compensation hypothesis, 35, 389
Competence of the father as custodial parent, 140–141
Components of parental involvement, 8. *See also* Paternal accessibility; Paternal interaction; Paternal responsibility
Comprehensive Employment and Training Act (CETA), 372
Compressed workweek, 393–394. *See also* Alternative work schedules
Cost effectiveness, 315
Counterresistance, 175
Countertransference, 167–168, 174, 182, 184, 188
Couple support groups, 296
Cultural norms and expectations, 18, 38, 50, 413. *See also* Social support
Custodial fathers, 118–120. *See also* Custody; Father-custody families
Custody, 107, 108, 113, 125, 135–139, 293
Custody disputes, 61–94

Day care, 376
Deafness, child, 242–243
Deficit model, 295
Delinquency, 282, 284, 329
Depression, 287, 351, 363
Developmental milestones, 233

Diagnosis, fathers and, 284
Disabilities, children's, 227–250
Disability insurance, 400
Disciplinary roles, 291, 357, 437. *See also* Authority of father; Paternal roles
Discrimination, *see* Racial discrimination; Sex discrimination
Divorce, 16, 38, 47, 61, 77, 82, 92, 103–128, 135–159, 232, 255, 272, 293, 333, 340, 353, 359
  and coping, 150–151
  effects on fathers, 103–128
Divorced fathers, 103–128
  emotional and psychologic adjustment, 109–110
  social relations and support systems, 112–113
Divorced spouses, relationships between, 114
Divorce mediation, 156
Divorce negotiation, 65–66, 107
Divorce rate, 103–104, 137–138
Down syndrome, 230–231, 234, 240, 243–244, 246
Drug abuse, 287
Dual-career families, 78–79. *See also* Breadwinning roles; Maternal employment

Early contact, 301
Economic concerns, 39, 234, 237
Economic necessity, 50, 357
Economic stress, 16
Educational attainment, 332, 342, 350
Educational system, 249, 413–427
Empathy, 80
Employee benefits, 396, 401
Employers' attitudes, 401–402
Empty nest, 238
English common law, 62
Exclusion of fathers, 297
Expert testimony, 65
Exploitation of workers, 346

Factory relocation, 372. *See also* Job loss; Unemployment
Family conflict, 16, 270. *See also* Marital conflict

Family dynamics, 17, 22, 30, 47–50, 169, 173, 231, 240, 260, 262–263, 265, 269–271, 331, 351–355, 358–359, 369. *See also specific entries under Marital*
Family mobility, 280
Family policy, 347, 429–430
Family roles, 193–200, 313, 386–388. *See also* Breadwinning roles; Caregiving role; Paternal roles
Family structure, 148
Family therapy, 167–188, 191–220
   father involvement, 167–188, 191–220
   responsibility in, 9–10, 79, 210–212, 315
Father(s):
   adaptation to child disabilities, 229–239
   in American history, 4–7
   and education, 249
   as emotional support, 7
   groups, 241–245, 316
   history of abuse, 259
   masculinity, 13–15, 20. *See also* Masculinity
   as moral teachers, 5
   in nontraditional families, 77–87, 246. *See also* Changing fathers' roles
   outreach programs, 326
   programs, 247–248
   as single parents, 82–87. *See also* Father-custody families
   in traditional families, 68–77. *See also* Breadwinning roles; Family roles; Paternal involvement; Paternal roles
Father absence, 14–16, 84–85, 89, 120, 156, 191, 282–284, 340, 346, 359, 366, 373, 421, 432–433
   temporary, 282–284
Father-child:
   attachment, 13, 249, 370
   competitiveness, 289
   conflict, 355–356
   relationships, 39, 41, 43–44
Father custody, history of, 135–138
Father-custody families, 88, 107, 135–159. *See also* Single fathers
Fatherhood Project, 389
Father involvement in therapy, problems with, 182–188
Fathers of Disabled Children Program, 243–244

Fathers Group at St. Joseph School for the Deaf, 242–243
Female-headed families, 341. *See also* Father absence
Femininity, 18, 413, 416
Feminism, 418
Feminist perspectives in family therapy, 198–200, 215–217
Flexible retirement, 395
Flexible scheduling of therapy, 247
Flexible work schedules, 23, 39, 246, 391–393, 396. *See also* Alternative work schedules
Flexitime, 391–393, 396
Food stamps, 371
Full-time work, 386
Functional family therapy, 197–198

Gender-appropriate employment, 420
Gender roles, 106, 430, 439. *See also* Breadwinning roles; Caregiving role; Sex-role development
Gilles de la Tourette's syndrome, 177, 178
Great Depression, 351–352, 355, 371

Handicapped children, 425
High father involvement, 6, 16–17, 29–54, 81, 245–249, 313–314
   effects on children, 40–43, 50, 312
   effects on fathers, 43–46
   and family characteristics, 30–32, 34
   see also High paternal involvement
High paternal involvement:
   effects on couple relationships, 47–52
   effects on mothers, 46–47
   instability of, 38–39
Hispanic Americans, 346
History of maltreatment as a child, 262
Hospital-based interventions, 293–317
Hospital policies, 316
Housework, 386–388, 430

Identification hypothesis, 35
Income support programs, 345
Income transfer programs, 371, 373–375
Infancy, 425
Infant-father attachment, 41
Inflation, 374
Intervention, models of, 295–296, 333–335
Intervention for families with handicapped children, 239–249

Job creation, 369
Job flexibility, 34
Job-guarantee policy, 397–400
Job loss, 339–376
Job-sharing, 371–372, 393–396
Job training, 369, 375
Joint child custody, 83, 89–93, 104,
    120–124, 126, 154, 170
Judicial decision making, 61–94
Judicial discretion, 65–68
Junior high school, 422

Knowledge of child development, 304,
    308–309, 315

Labor force participation, 342–343
Labor market discrimination, 343. See also
    Discrimination
Legal custody, 90
Life stress, 266–267, 270–271, 329, 349,
    356, 363–364
Lower socioeconomic class, 360–361,
    363–364. See also Blue-collar
    parents; Working-class status

Male therapists, 246
Manufacturing work force, 342
Marital adjustment, 232, 262–264, 269,
    271–272
Marital attitudes, 48–50
Marital conflict, 48, 105–108, 116, 148–
    149, 314, 352, 354, 356, 369. See also
    Parental conflict
Marital counseling, 206
Marital dissolution, 353, 364. See also
    Divorce
Marital and family stability, 294
Marital infidelity, 364
Marital quality and father involvement,
    47–48
Marital relationships, 260, 262–265, 295,
    331, 333, 339–376
Marital satisfaction, 313
Masculinity, 18, 42, 45, 191, 366, 417–419
Maternal career aspirations, 50–51
Maternal employment, 11, 13, 15, 31, 35,
    39, 46–47, 49, 78–79, 136–137, 294–
    295, 313, 341, 343, 372, 376, 388–389,
    408
Maternal gatekeeping, 312

Maternal instinct, 37
Maternal preference in child custody, 62, 66
Maternal work schedules, 388
Maternity benefits, 399
Maternity leave, 23, 400
Medical disabilities, 397–398
Medicare, 371
Mental health, 362, 369
Mental illness, 257
Mental retardation, 227–250
Methodologic limitations, 40, 44, 47, 118, 148
Middle-class, 356, 360, 364, 370. See also
    Social class; White-collar parents
Military fathers, 277, 281–284, 287, 291
Modeling, 289, 328, 367, 389, 417, 419–
    421, 423
Monetary policies, 369, 372
Mother-child relationships, 46
Mothers' support for paternal involvement,
    21–22
Mothers' role overload, 47
Motivations for custody, 140

Noncustodial fathers, 108–118
Nonhuman primates, 310
Nontraditional sex roles, 109. See also
    Changing fathers' roles

Obedience, 281
Obstetricians, 298, 315
Optimization model, 296
Overseas fathers, 277–291
    numbers of, 278–279
Overseas work, motivations for, 277–278

Paid work, 385, 387–388, 390
Parental conflict, 114–115, 123–124, 142.
    See also Marital conflict
Parental leave, 408
    for fathers, 396–406
    for mothers, 397–400
Parental responsibilities, 8, 30–31, 52–53,
    117
Parental roles, 136, 424
Parental sensitivity, 71, 234
Parental sex role attitudes, 50–51, 45, 33,
    34–35
Parental teaching, 234
Parent-child play, 11, 41, 71–73, 78, 242,
    293, 302, 306–307, 313

Parent education, 269, 297–299, 406–409, 422, 424–425
Parenting opportunities, equality of, 53–54
Parenting skills, 120, 123
Parenting style, 149
Parent training, engagement of fathers, 200–206
Part time work, 394–395, 401, 404
Participation rates of fathers in family therapy, 201–202
Paternal accessibility, 8, 9, 312
Paternal attachment, 300
Paternal competence, 11–12, 21, 35–36, 49, 70, 83, 87, 117, 126, 140–141, 295, 309, 389–390, 408
   relation to paternal involvement, 20–21
Paternal desertion, 232
Paternal employment, 34, 385–409
Paternal engagement, 8, 9
Paternal influences, 7, 12–18, 73–75, 191, 293
Paternal interaction, 8–9, 11
Paternal involvement, 7–12, 16, 18, 31, 35, 71, 80–81, 117, 122–123, 143, 145, 154, 181–182, 195, 240–241, 244, 248, 284, 288, 293, 295, 302, 306, 309–311, 315–316, 333, 358, 365–367, 386–390, 392–395, 405, 408, 437
   changes over time, 10–11
   and couple support, 37–38
   determinants of, 18–23, 32–39, 228
   early, 71
   and institutional practices, 22–23, 389, 393
Paternal motivation, 14, 18–20, 40, 42–43, 69, 87, 137, 153, 191, 233, 245, 258, 272, 289–290, 297, 305, 389–390, 402, 406, 408, 414, 419–421, 436
Paternal nurturance, 6, 30, 413, 418, 423
Paternal participation in labor and delivery, 299–300, 316
Paternal responsibility, 44, 191
Paternal role definition, 311, 369
Paternal roles, 3–24, 38–39, 193–200, 203, 248, 317, 345, 353, 362, 366, 385, 408, 432, 434, 436–437, 439
Paternal self-confidence, 36, 45, 236, 346
   relation to paternal involvement, 20–21, 36
   see also Self-esteem

Paternal sensitivity, 21, 42, 69–70, 72, 75, 244, 307, 313
Paternal stereotyping, negative, 430–434, 439
Paternal stimulation, 307
Paternal unavailability, 167
Paternal work roles, 203–204
Paternity leave, 23, 303, 396–406
   in Sweden, 401–402
Pediatricians, 308
Peer acceptance, 237
Physical child custody, 90
Physical punishment, 257
Plant closings, 374
Poor fathers:
   marital relations of, 362–365
   mental health of, 361–369
Postpartum period, 309
Poverty, 339–376, 429–440
   effects of, 346, 361–369
Poverty rate, 339
Preadolescence, 421–422
Pregnancy leave, 398
Preparenthood intervention, 297
Preterm infants, 294, 309
Primary caregivers, 29–54, 88, 125, 136, 374, 405
Problem-centered systems therapy, 195–196
Psychiatric symptomatology, 349
Psychoanalytic perspectives, 167–188
Psychological dysfunction, 327
Psychoticism, 257, 284, 349
Public policy, 347, 429–430
Public work programs, 375

Race, 349, 361. See also African Americans; Hispanic Americans
Racial discrimination, 342, 345, 347, 361, 375
Remarriage, 85–87, 103, 111, 113, 142, 173, 255, 258, 272
Resistance, 174, 186. See also Counterresistance
Role concepts, 311, 315. See also Paternal roles
Role-sharing families, 29–54, 79–82, 192, 194

Schizophrenia, 284
School enrollment, 235

Schooling, 414–419
Self-concept, 76, 83, 231, 350
Self-esteem, 48, 51, 113, 171, 236, 245, 257, 262, 349–350, 357, 361–362, 437. *See also* Paternal self-confidence
Self-help groups, 269, 272
Senior high school, 422
Sensitivity, sex differences in, 69, 70
Separation or divorce, reasons for, 105–107
Separation protest, 310
Service sector jobs, 342
Severance pay, 371
Sex of child differences, 11, 73–74, 84–85, 88, 108, 116, 120, 126, 146–148, 151–152, 155–156, 158–159, 231, 356, 359, 368, 414–419
Sex discrimination, 343, 345, 375, 397, 418
Sex offenders, 257
Sex-role attitudes, 13–15, 18, 41–42, 45, 306, 387
Sex-role development, 16–17, 33, 39, 63, 151–152, 199, 313, 355, 413, 415–417, 425, 430
Sex-role ideology and paternal involvement, 36–37
Sex-role models, 5–6, 13, 15–16
Sex-role orientation, 80
Sex-role socialization, 201
Sex of teacher, 416–421
Sex of therapist, 206, 246, 316
Sexual abuse, 256, 258–268
Sexual dysfunction, 260, 287
Sexual exploitation of children, 257
Sexuality, 332
Sexually abusing fathers, treatment, 270–271
Shift schedules, 386
Sick leave, 402, 403
Single fathers, 93–94, 104, 435. *See also* Father-custody families
Single mothers, 16. *See also* Custody; Divorce; Father absence
Single-parent households, 359. *See also* Custody; Divorce; Father absence
Skill-training programs for fathers, 303–309
Sleep disturbances, 284
Social class, 259, 342, 346–347, 349, 356, 358. *See also* Middle class; Working-class status

Social competence, 42, 74, 313
Social isolation, 16, 264–272, 280–281, 332. *See also* Social support
Social learning theory, 262, 310
Social networks, *see* Social Support
Social policy, 369–376. *See also* Family policy
Social programming:
 advocacy, 429, 438
 eligibility, 430
 exclusion from, 430, 434
 paternal stereotypes, 429–434
Social services, 429–440
Social support, 50, 54, 128, 138, 149–150, 158, 194, 248, 264–271, 280, 294–296, 311, 314, 317, 335, 349, 351, 353, 366–367, 389–390, 408, 436
Somatic problems, 351
Splitting, 188
Staff attitude toward fathers, 246
Stepfamilies, 104
Stepfathering, 258
Stepparenting, 87
Stigma of mental health problems, 286
Strategic family therapy, 196–197
Stress, *see* Life stress; Economic concerns
Structural family therapy, 196
Suicide, 349
Supporting Extended Family Members (SEFAM) Program, University of Washington in Seattle, 244–245, 248

Teen Mother and Child Program (TMCP), University of Utah, 326–328, 332
Teen Father Collaboration, 424
Teenage fathers, *see* Adolescent fathers
Teenage mothers, *see* Adolescent mothers
Tender years doctrine, 63, 138, 159
Time use, 387
Traditional paternal attitudes, 77–87, 246
Transference, 174–175, 186–188. *See also* Countertransference
Transition to parenthood, 229, 296, 333, 363
Treatment sphere, father involvement in, 178–181
Treatment techniques, evaluation, diagnosis, 284, 287
Type A fathers, 290

UCLA Intervention Program's Fathers
Group, 241–242
Unemployed fathers, mental and physical
health, 348–351
Unemployed men:
father-child relations, 355–361
marital relations of, 351–355
Unemployment, 339–376, 429–440
Unemployment benefits, 369–370, 372,
373, 395
Uniform Marriage and Divorce Act, 64
Unpaid leave, 403, 404

Visitation, 110, 114, 116, 125, 142, 157
Vocational advancement, 329

Wage-ratio, husband-wife, 389
Welfare, 371, 374, 376, 435–437
White-collar parents, 350. *See also* Middle-
class; Social class
Women, Infants, and Children (WIC)
Program, 374
Women's attitudes regarding paternal
involvement, 21–22, 49
Working-class status, 347, 356, 363–365,
370, 375–376. *See also* Blue-collar par-
ents; Lower socioeconomic class
Work-family conflict, 388
Work role responsibilities, 277–279, 389
Work schedules, 204, 385, 388–396. *See
also* Alternative work schedules
Work-sharing, *see* Job-sharing

(*continued from front*)

Handbook for the Practice of Pediatric Psychology *edited by June M. Tuma*

Change Through Interaction: Social Psychological Processes of Counseling and Psychotherapy *by Stanley R. Strong and Charles D. Claiborn*

Drugs and Behavior (Second Edition) *by Fred Leavitt*

Handbook of Research Methods in Clinical Psychology *edited by Philip C. Kendall and James N. Butcher*

A Social Psychology of Developing Adults *by Thomas O. Blank*

Women in the Middle Years: Current Knowledge and Directions for Research and Policy *edited by Janet Zollinger Giele*

Loneliness: A Sourcebook of Current Theory, Research and Therapy *edited by Letitia Anne Peplau and Daniel Perlman*

Hyperactivity: Current Issues, Research, and Theory (Second Edition) *by Dorothea M. Ross and Sheila A. Ross*

Review of Human Development *edited by Tiffany M. Field, Aletha Huston, Herbert C. Quay, Lillian Troll, and Gordon E. Finley*

Agoraphobia: Multiple Perspectives on Theory and Treatment *edited by Dianne L. Chambless and Alan J. Goldstein*

The Rorschach: A Comprehensive System. Volume III: Assessment of Children and Adolescents *by John E. Exner, Jr. and Irving B. Weiner*

Handbook of Play Therapy *edited by Charles E. Schaefer and Kevin J. O'Connor*

Adolescent Sexuality in a Changing American Society: Social and Psychological Perspectives for the Human Service Professions (Second Edition) *by Catherine S. Chilman*

Failures in Behavior Therapy *edited by Edna B. Foa and Paul M.G. Emmelkamp*

The Psychological Assessment of Children (Second Edition) *by James O. Palmer*

Imagery: Current Theory, Research, and Application *edited by Aneés A. Sheikh*

Handbook of Clinical Child Psychology *edited by C. Eugene Walker and Michael C. Roberts*

The Measurement of Psychotherapy Outcome *edited by Michael J. Lambert, Edwin R. Christensen, and Steven S. DeJulio*

Clinical Methods in Psychology (Second Edition) *edited by Irving B. Weiner*

Excuses: Masquerades in Search of Grace *by C.R. Snyder, Raymond L. Higgins and Rita J. Stucky*

Diagnostic Understanding and Treatment Planning: The Elusive Connection *edited by Fred Shectman and William B. Smith*

Bender Gestalt Screening for Brain Dysfunction *by Patricia Lacks*

Adult Psychopathology and Diagnosis *edited by Samuel M. Turner and Michel Hersen*

Personality and the Behavioral Disorders (Second Edition) *edited by Norman S. Endler and J. McVicker Hunt*

Ecological Approaches to Clinical and Community Psychology *edited by William A. O'Connor and Bernard Lubin*

Rational-Emotive Therapy with Children and Adolescents: Theory, Treatment Strategies, Preventative Methods *by Michael E. Bernard and Marie R. Joyce*

The Unconscious Reconsidered *edited by Kenneth S. Bowers and Donald Meichenbaum*

Prevention of Problems in Childhood: Psychological Research and Application *edited by Michael C. Roberts and Lizette Peterson*

Resolving Resistances in Psychotherapy *by Herbert S. Strean*

Handbook of Social Skills Training and Research *edited by Luciano L'Abate and Michael A. Milan*

Institutional Settings in Children's Lives *by Leanne G. Rivlin and Maxine Wolfe*

Treating the Alcoholic: A Developmental Model of Recovery *by Stephanie Brown*